14-0551
14.95

THE
TEACHING
OF
CHRIST

3rd EDITION

THE TEACHING OF CHRIST

A CATHOLIC CATECHISM FOR ADULTS

Edited by
Ronald Lawler, O.F.M. Cap.   Bishop Donald W. Wuerl
Thomas Comerford Lawler

Our Sunday Visitor Publishing Division
Our Sunday Visitor, Inc.
Huntington, Indiana 46750

Nihil Obstat:
Rev. Joseph J. Kleppner
Censor Librorum

Imprimatur:
Most Rev. John B. McDowell, D.D., Ph.D.
Auxiliary Bishop—Vicar General of Pittsburgh
February 14, 1991

Our Sunday Visitor Publishing Division
Our Sunday Visitor, Inc.
200 Noll Plaza
Huntington, Indiana 46750

International Standard Book Number: 0-87973-850-2
Library of Congress Catalog Card Number: 75-34852

PRINTED IN THE UNITED STATES OF AMERICA

850

THE TEACHING OF CHRIST
A Catholic Catechism for Adults
by
LORENZO ALBACETE
ROMANO STEPHEN ALMAGNO, O.F.M.
JORDAN AUMANN
DONALD CONNOLLY *
JOHN FINNIS
GERMAIN GRISEZ
JOHN J. HUGO *
FREDERICK M. JELLY, O.P.
GEORGE F. KIRWIN, O.M.I.
MARY ELISE KRANTZ, S.N.D.
RONALD LAWLER, O.F.M.Cap.
THOMAS COMERFORD LAWLER
+DAVID M. MALONEY
JOSEPH MINDLING, O.F.M.Cap.
JOHANNES QUASTEN *
+JOHN F. WHEALON
+DONALD W. WUERL

* Deceased

ACKNOWLEDGMENTS

Scripture quotations are taken from the New Revised Standard Version Bible, © 1989 by the Division of Christian Education of the National Council of the Churches of Christ in the USA. Used by permission.

Quotations from the Constitutions, Decrees, and Declarations of the Second Vatican Council used in this book are from the translation, with some amendments, appearing in *The Documents of Vatican II*, Walter M. Abbott, S.J., General Editor. Reprinted with permission of AMERICA. All rights reserved. © 1966 by America Press, 106 W. 56th St., New York, NY 10019.

English translation of excerpts from the Roman Missal, Rite of Baptism of Children, Rite of Christian Initiation of Adults, Rite of Confirmation, Rite of Penance, Rite of Anointing and Pastoral Care of the Sick, Rite of Marriage and Rite of Ordination. Copyright © 1974, 1973, 1971, 1969, International Committee on English in the Liturgy, Inc. All rights reserved.

Table of Contents

Part Four
IN CHRIST: FULFILLMENT OF ALL

Appendixes

Indexes

Prefatory Note

In 1973, a group of bishops, priests, Religious and lay people involved in the work of catechesis began a project that culminated in the publication in 1976 of the First Edition of *The Teaching of Christ: A Catholic Catechism for Adults*. At the time of its publication, *Theological Studies* wrote that *The Teaching of Christ* is "undoubtedly the best manual to date for adult catechetical instructions...." *La Civiltà Cattolica* called it "one of the best catechisms to appear since the Council."

Since then, *The Teaching of Christ* has been translated into more than ten languages and has gone through two major revisions. The Third Edition represents the most recent effort to include clarifications and new citations reflecting recent statements of the magisterium in an effort to keep the text as current as possible. The continuing success and enduring usefulness of *The Teaching of Christ* rests, among other things, on its ability to present in a concise and yet readable manner a summary of the Catholic faith as it emerges from the words of Sacred Scripture, the teaching of councils and other magisterial documents, the living tradition of the Church and the writings of the fathers and doctors of the Church. *The Teaching of Christ* captures something of both the timelessness and the immediacy of our faith.

It is my hope that this edition will continue to be of assistance to all of those engaged in the catechetical effort as we strive to share with all as fully as possible our faith in and love of the Lord Jesus. Those members of the Church who assist in the work of catechesis are engaged in a sacred service that ensures that the Lord's teaching be handed on in its integrity from one generation to the next. May the Lord reward them.

Archbishop Pio Laghi
Pro-Prefect, Congregation for Seminaries and Institutes of Study

From the Second Edition, 1983

The Teaching of Christ is a very beautiful and authentically Catholic explanation of the faith of the Church. It speaks in an attractive and contemporary manner: in the language of Holy Scripture, in the sayings of the Fathers, in the words of the Second Vatican Council, and in the prayers of the Divine Liturgy, both ancient and new.

It is a positive, serene account of the hope that is in us who acknowledge Jesus as Lord and live His life in the Catholic Church. The chapter on ecumenism speaks confidently and hopefully of the mission of the Church in a divided world. Parents, teachers, and all who have the happy responsibility of sharing their faith with others will rejoice in this thoroughly up-to-date book.

It is my conviction that *The Teaching of Christ* will be of invaluable assistance in strengthening the faith of our people, besides being a beautiful introduction to the Risen Lord and His saving doctrine.

William Cardinal Baum
Prefect, Sacred Congregation for Catholic Education

From the First Edition, 1976

The Teaching of Christ seems attuned to the fulfillment of [the bishops'] hopes. It is based unmistakably and unashamedly on the *General Catechetical Directory.* . . . It starts and finishes with the conviction that the faith is not a conclusion from academic researches and human reflections but a "given," no static "deposit of the faith," but a dynamic *given* by God Himself through His Christ to the Church, to be lived not in a departmentalized fashion but *integrally,* with commitment of intellect, heart, will and total personality.

It is difficult to imagine a book concerned with the content of the faith that would be more comprehensive in the ground covered, the result of more widespread consultation of those who should be the witnesses to the faith than the work of the present editors. It is completely Christo-centric as all Catholic Christian catechesis should be. Its basic scheme is *through Christ, with Christ* and *in Christ.* In other words, it presents the vertical and horizontal Church, the Cross still at work in the world, the Crucified Christ our tie with one another. It presents the received message, creed and cult, faith and action, of the Total Christ as catechesis identifies each of us with Him and He identifies all of us with God and His people.

Its editors, contributors and consultants have kept the book nonpolemical in character except in so far as any witness to the full content of the faith inevitably provokes question or contradiction. The claims of Christianity concerning God, Christ and the means of identity with both are altogether too staggering not to excite reaction. Yet those claims are here set forth calmly, objectively and competently.

The method of procedure has been patient as well as comprehensive. The editors have prepared their book in action and reaction with fourteen other contributors and some seventy consultants from virtually every English-speaking part of the world. It has been the work of two full years of close study of the General Catechetical Directory in the light of the presumed direction of the National Catechetical Directories. . . .

This Christo-centric nature of the doctrinal and spiritual content of the book is outlined in the very table of contents; the development of the chapters confirms it fully. It seems somehow appropriate that *Our Sunday Visitor,* a family publication, should have welcomed its publication, since there is no member of the family, capable of study, for whom it is not designed. It is indispensable to Confraternity of Christian Doctrine teachers. It is bound to enrich the reading of parents about their religion. A better textbook for schools could scarcely be imagined at the moment, and its universality, orthodoxy, clarity and style should make it ideal for study groups in catechesis or religious education generally.

If it be said that this, that, or the other point could have been included, the criticism merely echoes the words of the Gospel:

"But there are also many other things which Jesus did; which, if they were written every one, the world itself, I think, would not be able to contain the books that should be written." — John 21.25

John Cardinal Wright
Prefect, Sacred Congregation for the Clergy

Vatican City, July 1975

Introduction

This is a Catholic catechism for adults. It is a catechism in the sense that it is a comprehensive summary of doctrine. It is Catholic in that the doctrine it presents is the teaching of the Catholic Church.

The title of the catechism has been chosen to echo the firm belief of the Church that Jesus Christ, who nearly two thousand years ago taught here on earth, continues to act in and through His Church. That which the Church teaches as the teaching of Christ is in very truth His teaching.

The Catholic Church believes and teaches that Jesus Christ is *the* Teacher of faith. He taught His followers visibly during His earthly life. He teaches in every teacher who proclaims the Gospel faithfully. By His Holy Spirit He has guarded the word entrusted to His Church at its beginning, and He has guided its development so that all the Catholic faith teaches decisively as His word is indeed His. Hearers of the word are able to believe Jesus Himself when His grace has enabled them to hear His voice in words others speak in His name.

Recent years have seen many developments in the Church's expression of its faith. A contemporary catechism must take into account the wealth of the teaching of Second Vatican Council, the renovation in the liturgy and concern for Scripture, the fresh emphases on ecumenism and the social requirements of the Gospel.

All this a catechism must integrate into a balanced account of the whole message of faith. For the whole of the good news of Christ must be spoken faithfully and appropriately to every age. The central mysteries of faith do not change. New circumstances may require new ways of communicating them effectively, but catechesis must always stress those truths of faith that are basic and central: the mystery of God, the Father, Son, and Holy Spirit, the Creator of all; the mystery of Christ and of His saving work; the mystery of the Holy Spirit, guiding the Church and calling it to holiness; and the mystery of the Church, in which the People of God are bound together in the Mystical Body of Christ and called to live a new life.

A catechism must present fully and in a carefully authenticated way the teaching of the Church itself. And it is only the teaching of Christ and of His Church that a catechism should present. A catechism is not the place for purely personal theological opinions or for taking sides in the debates of scholars on questions which have no decisive solution in the authentic teaching of the faith. Rather, a catechism should give that authentic teaching as fully and clearly as possible, primarily as a guide to the faith and life of those who have recognized the presence of Christ teaching, ruling, and sanctifying in His Church.

Because the faith is so rich, and because those to whom it is announced are so varied, there can never be a perfect catechism. The difficulties involved in writing an adequate catechism may seem greater than ever in times like our own marked by much spiritual confusion. But such times as these also need more urgently a full and balanced account of the faith, an account that is accurate, clear, comprehensive, up to date, and in language readily understandable in the world today.

This book is an effort to give such an account.

+

The first and second edition of this book went through a number of printings in the United States since its appearance in late 1976 and after its second edition in 1983.

Wherever it has appeared, *The Teaching of Christ* has been well received by the hierarchy and by Church leaders on every level. It came to critical acclaim by scholars in learned journals in all parts of the world. It is being used in many ways: in seminaries and in university courses; in the education of clerical leaders; in formation programs for religious; in secondary schools; in giving instructions to converts; in pastoral work of every kind.

A number of significant changes are made in this third edition. A new translation of Scripture has been used throughout. With this translation, the text of the catechism seeks to avoid whenever possible language that might seem to indicate a bias toward the masculine gender.

Moreover, in the past several years many important authoritative documents have been published by the Church in questions of faith, morality, worship, and discipline. Frequent references are made to these documents so that the catechism can keep its readers in contact with the living teaching of the Church.

The text of the book remains for the most part that of the previous edition. The principal overall guide followed in the preparation of this catechism was the *General Catechetical Directory*, published by the Holy See in 1971. That *Directory* gives norms and guidelines for teaching the faith and for the preparation of catechetical materials.

The *General Catechetical Directory* has since been supplemented by other very important documents. In 1974, the Third General Assembly of the Synod of Bishops was held in Rome to reflect on the nature and requirements of evangelization today. The Fourth General Assembly of the Synod of Bishops, held in Rome in 1977, centered its study on the problems and needs of contemporary catechesis, especially that meant for children and young people. Each of these synods asked the Holy Father to gather its teachings into a document addressed to the whole Church. In response, Pope Paul VI published an

Apostolic Exhortation, *Evangelii Nuntiandi*, in 1975, and Pope John Paul II issued an Apostolic Exhortation, *Catechesi Tradendae*, in 1979.

Meanwhile, national hierarchies have been preparing special catechetical directories, which are to supplement the universal guidelines published in 1971 with attention to the special needs of diverse areas. Thus the bishops of the United States, after extensive consultations and much study, published in 1979 a national catechetical directory, *Sharing the Light of Faith*.

+

All these documents concerning catechesis present the same vision. Catechesis is concerned first of all with handing on the word of God, the good news of Christ. It takes its starting point in the free gift of divine revelation, and the gift of faith by which God has enabled us to recognize His reality, His presence, and His word.

God has revealed Himself to men in many ways. In the early days of salvation history He revealed Himself through His prophets, though He did not communicate through them all that He wished us to know of Him and of His saving mercy. In every age and in every culture God has made it possible for men to know Him and to draw near to Him in faith; for He wills all men to be saved. But the partial revelations of God are by no means adequate substitute for the full revelation that He has given us in Christ.

Christ, in His being, in His deeds, and in His words, is the perfect revelation of the Father. In Him we have been taught most perfectly of the living and true God; through Him we have learned the ways of life most adequately. Christ willed that the full revelation He gave us should be preserved always for the salvation of all men in the Church that He founded on Peter and the other apostles, that is, in the Catholic Church, which He guards always by His own presence and the gift of His Spirit. The first task of catechesis is to hand on this fullness of divine revelation that has been given to us in Christ.

A catechism, then, should give a complete account of the Catholic faith. This does not mean that every saying of Scripture and every declaration of the Church is to be incorporated. Rather, it means that the faith is to be presented in a full and balanced way. God's revelation is concerned chiefly with leading us to know God Himself in such a way that we may become His friends. Hence it is concerned chiefly with the mystery of God Himself and of His plan for saving us in Christ. A catechism should present the message of Christ and His Church with a fullness that enables men in the circumstances of their time to grasp the faith in all its essential aspects, so that they may be able to respond to God's grace with an informed faith. A catechism should include everything that the Church in its teaching considers important for growth in faith.

A catechism should hand on the divine message faithfully, explaining its rich significance in accord with the understanding that the Church has always had, and continues to have, of its own teaching. To different times and cultures it is necessary to speak the word of God in varying ways. But great care must always be taken that new forms express faithfully and fully the message that God intended to communicate and that the Spirit of God has taught the Church to speak.

A catechism should make clear both the personal and the ecclesial nature of faith. The faith God gives us in Christ is intended both to unite each person in faith and love with God and to bind all believers in one family of faith. The gift of faith is given to the individual, but it enables each to recognize and love the word of God spoken to all through the Church. The inner gifts of God's grace enable one to recognize God speaking in those whom He has sent. If one's faith is mature, it will be one's personal faith, held with the most firm personal conviction, in knowledge that it is God's word that one believes. But it will also be the faith of the Church that one believes.

Authentic Catholic faith is never partial or selective. It is always global. We say yes to the whole mystery of faith, and to each of its elements, because of our personal faith in God. We believe the truth that God reveals because we believe God, and we have found that He is a God present to us, teaching in the midst of His Church. When Peter came to recognize that God was in Christ, he was prepared to believe any word of Christ, for it was clear to him that God is to be believed always. "You have the word of eternal life. We have come to believe and know that You are the Holy One of God" (John 6.68-69).

A catechism should not only state Catholic faith, but also gather the testimony of many "witnesses." In declaring the teaching of the Church, a catechism notes how the faith of the Church is rooted in the Scriptures; it points out how councils of the Church in times past have spoken this message. It calls forth as witnesses to the faith the Fathers of the Church, the saints, the popes. The liturgy and life of the Church in the past and the present are cited to show how these too bear testimony to what the Church believes and teaches.

This "witness" form of catechesis is most appropriate here, for a catechism is addressed first of all (though not exclusively) to those who have already found faith in Christ. Though their faith may yet be in need of instruction, they already know that Christ's word is entirely reliable. To them the Church speaks in the voices of those in whom Christ's followers have regularly recognized His voice, and have been led by His Spirit to love. In all the witnesses the Church appeals to, the faithful are invited to hear the voice of Christ and the Father in the light of the Spirit. St. Paul speaks of this mystery of faith in his First

Epistle to the Thessalonians; he rejoices that they were able to hear the human witness God had given them, recognize the real source of this teaching, and believe only God. "We also constantly give thanks to God for this, that when you received the word of God that you heard from us, you accepted it not as a human word but as what it really is, God's word, which is also at work in you believers" (1 Thess. 2.13).

+

Although a catechism is addressed primarily to those who have already fund faith in Christ, and have recognized His presence in the Church, it is addressed also to those who are weak in faith, or entirely without faith. To them it should speak of the ways that lead toward faith.

God calls men to faith in many ways. But there are certain common patterns. Love inclines people toward faith; intelligence and reflection give support; but faith itself is the free gift of God.

Love stimulates a desire for faith. Perfect love, the love of divine charity, presupposes faith; but there is also a preliminary love. It is the earnest desire to cling to what one begins to see as good. The prospect to finding faith is interesting and appealing only when one begins to grasp the goodness of a life of faith.

When Jesus led the apostles toward faith, He first invited them to friendship with Himself. As they came to know Him, they began to realize the richness of a kind of life they had not known before, and they wished to share in it fullness. A catechism should try to show something of the richness of the life to which Christ calls us in faith, and to show how effectively the new life of Christ fulfills the actual desires and longings of the human heart.

When Jesus invited men to faith, He clearly respected their intelligence. His words were accompanied by signs of their truth, in the wisdom of His teaching, in the goodness of His life, in the power of the deeds He performed.

People normally need good reasons to clear their way toward faith. Certainly there is no conflict between intelligence and faith. Human reasoning alone, however, is not sufficient to establish personal faith. No one can be driven to personal faith by dialectics, for faith involves believing God, not complex argumentation. But intelligence can stimulate the pursuit of personal faith.

A catechism does not give a full and systematic apologetics (that is, a rational defense of the faith), but it does present many of the evidences that have led thoughtful persons toward faith. The whole message of faith is itself a sign of its own truth; for when it is reflected on with care, it is grasped as an astonishingly profound response to the deepest questions people ask. A catechism speaks of course of that greatest of signs, the resurrection of Jesus, and the effects this has had on history and in the lives of countless millions. It speaks also of the most visible sign of faith, the Church itself, sealed with certain characteristic marks that make it unique in the world and arouse a wonder that can incline one toward faith.

Faith itself is a gift. The Gospels portray the progress of St. Peter toward faith. He had seen Christ's goodness, wisdom, and power. He had come gradually to have more firm views about Christ and who He was. But when the Lord's invitation led Peter from opinion to a ringing profession of faith, Christ told him that his new confident conviction was not the result of merely human insight. "Blessed are you, Simon son of Jonah! For flesh and blood has not revealed this to you, but My Father in heaven" (Matt. 16.17).

Scripture speaks in many ways of the gift of faith. Faith brings one to a new life with a new way of knowing (cf. John 1). It gives vision: faith opens the eyes of one born blind (cf. John 9). God Himself opens the eyes of the heart (cf. Eph. 1.18) and brings one into the freedom of faith. No one can come to faith unless the Father draws him (cf. John 6.44); but one who is drawn by God, and does not resist God's gift, comes to realize that it is God who calls.

For that reason, one who desires strength in personal faith must do more than examine the evidences for Christianity. When one begins to realize personally the reality of God, he begins to realize also that he must call upon the Lord for light. God surely is not pleased by pretense. But He is pleased by the prayers of those who, moved by divine signs and heartened by grace, cry out for a faith they do not have, or have but faintly. He Himself is the Light and source of light for which they long.

+

The general plan and overall outline of this catechism are readily shown by the table of contents.

The sources quoted or cited most frequently in this catechism are Sacred Scripture and the documents of the Second Vatican Council. The references for these are given in parentheses in the running text. The references for other sources, of which there are many, are given in footnotes, which are used in this catechism almost exclusively for source citations. Abbreviations used in the text and footnotes are listed immediately after this Introduction and are listed again at the end of the volume for easy reference.

Between the chapters and the indexes are six appendixes. The first four of these are on the Bible, the Popes of the Church, the General Councils of the Church, and on the Fathers and Doctors of the Church. The fifth contains, along with brief comments, the texts of a number of prayers loved and cherished in the Church. The sixth appendix is an annotated bibliography. This lists a number of basic reference tools, but also includes many other works recommended for additional reading and study on the subjects covered in the individual chapters of the catechism.

+

Many people assisted in the preparation of this book. We are especially grateful to the many members of the hierarchy in several countries who read a preparatory draft of this catechism. Their comments and suggestions have been invaluable.

We are grateful also for the assistance given by many members of the academic community. Among these we would like to mention especially His Eminence , William Cardinal Baum, J. Edward Coffey, S.J., William A. Hinnebusch, O.P., Joseph J. Kleppner, Robert Mc-Creary, O.F.M.Cap., William E. May, Philip F. Mulhern, O.P., James T. O'Connor, and Dominic J. Unger, O.F.M. Cap.

We would like to acknowledge also the special editorial assistance given us by Russell Shaw.

We express sincere thanks to Frank J. Schneider, whose assistance and encouragement sustained the work from its first beginnings.

Then we express our gratitude of His Eminence, John Cardinal Wright, Prefect of the Sacred Congregation for the Clergy, for many other kindnesses and especially for graciously writing a Prefatory Note for this book. *Requiescat in pace.*

We are grateful also to Archbishop Pio Laghi, Pro-Prefect of the Sacred Congregation for Seminaries and Institutes of Study, who has so kindly contributed a Prefatory Note to this edition.

THE EDITORS

List Of Abbreviations

Documents of the Second Vatican Council

AA	Decree on the Apostolate of the Laity (*Apostolicam Actuositatem*)
AG	Decree on the Missionary Activity of the Church (*Ad Gentes*)
CD	Decree on the Bishops' Pastoral Office in the Church (*Christus Dominus*)
DH	Declaration on Religious Freedom (*Dignitatis Humanae*)
DV	Dogmatic Constitution on Divine Revelation (*Dei Verbum*)
GE	Declaration on Christian Education (*Gravissimum Educationis*)
GS	Pastoral Constitution on the Church in the Modern World (*Gaudium et Spes*)
IM	Decree on the Instruments of Social Communication (*Inter Mirifica*)
LG	Dogmatic Constitution on the Church (*Lumen Gentium*)
NA	Declaration on the Relationship of the Church to Non-Christian Religions (*Nostra Aetate*)
OE	Decree on Eastern Catholic Churches (*Orientalium Ecclesiarum*)
OT	Decree on Priestly Formation (*Optatam Totius*)
PC	Decree on the Appropriate Renewal of Religious Life (*Perfectae Caritatis*)
PO	Decree on the Ministry and Life of Priests (*Presbyterorum Ordinis*)
SC	Constitution on the Sacred Liturgy (*Sacrosanctum Concilium*)
UR	Decree on Ecumenism (*Unitatis Redintegratio*)

Other abbreviations

AAS	Acta Apostolicae Sedis
ACW	Ancient Christian Writers
ASS	Acta Sanctae Sedis
DS	H. Denzinger-A. Schönmetzer, Enchiridion Symbolorum Definitionum et Declarationum de Rebus Fidei et Morum
EV	Enchiridion Vaticanum
MG	J. P. Migne, ed., Patrologiae cursus completus, series graeca
ML	J. P. Migne, ed., Patrologiae cursus completus, series latina

Part One

The Invitation To Faith

1

The Hope Of Our Calling

Christ is our Teacher. "You call Me Teacher and Lord — and you are right, for that is what I am" (John 13.13).

All that the Catholic faith teaches is Christ's answer to us in our search for the meaning of life and in our desire to lay hold of what the heart longs for. The message of Christ is a message of joy to a world in need of hope.

This chapter speaks of the goodness of the life to which Christ invites us. It shows how Christian hope is realized already in part in this world. Already Christ enables us to live a new life, a life supported by divine gifts, that we may care in love to make this world a presence of God's kingdom. It shows how the Christian life is essentially a life of hope, pointing confidently toward perfect fulfillment of the gifts God has already planted in our hearts. Finally, the chapter speaks of the central role of Christ in our hope and in our life.

The End Is the Beginning

Life is mysterious. It stirs rich hopes in our hearts even as it bears within itself profound tragedies. "Hope and joy, grief and anxiety" (GS 1) are strangely intermingled in the world, and we cannot help asking: Why do we exist? What is the meaning and purpose of our lives?

The "hope and joy" in life are very real. Though the world is wounded by sin, it remains the world God made and found "very good" (Gen. 1.31). The beautiful things He has made still mirror God in countless ways, and delight the human heart. In every kind of art and science and skill we can find enjoyment in our work (cf. Eccle. 2.24). Especially great gladness surges up wherever we give and experience friendship and the reality of unselfish love.

But the "grief and anxiety" in life are also real. Human history is in large part a record of wars and personal failures and tragedies. Human puzzlement over pain is recognized also in the Gospels. The apostles asked Christ why a certain man had been born blind (cf. John 9.2). They were moved by the calamities that strike so often, as when the tower of Siloam fell and brought death to eighteen (cf. Luke 13.4).

What is this life that promises so much and yet so frequently disappoints?

Already in childhood we learned that those we know and love are taken by death. We first saw sickness and became aware of pain. Others may have tried to explain to us why these things were so, but we were not really satisfied. For they knew, and we perhaps sensed their awareness, that their answers were not adequate. But the questions posed are far too important to remain completely unanswered. Why are we, and why do we live in a world like this?

Our Questions Answered in Christ

The answer to our persistent queries is Christ. In all that He was and did, Christ was providing the answer to our deepest questions. In all His life and teaching, Christ was responding to our concern about the meaning of life, and was showing how great is the hope that He brings.

He brought realistic hope to the real world. He, the Crucified, did nothing to gloss over the mystery of evil and pain. Because He understood and cared, He wept in the presence of human sorrow (cf. John 11.35); but He knew and taught that suffering is not unrelieved and meaningless evil. He, the Lord of all, tasted suffering, sanctified it, and made it redemptive. In His light we can learn that God does not love pain; in His life they can see Him make suffering itself a tool of redemption. He teaches us confident hope and intelligent joy even in a world far from its final perfection.

The mystery of life is complex and profound. So also is Christ's answer to it. Christ's answer is found in His entire life, and in the life He taught and made possible on this earth. His answer is more than words. It is also action, and He invites us to act with Him in the gift of the Spirit. "But above all, Jesus Himself at particularly solemn and highly significant moments calls Himself Teacher..., and He proclaims the singularity, the uniqueness of His character as Teacher: 'You have one Teacher' (Matt. 23.8), the Christ."[1] He came to give a new life which makes everything different. "I came that they may have life, and have it abundantly" (John 10.10).

The End within Time

Christ lived on this earth a perfect human life, and He invited us to adopt His way of life. In the Beatitudes (cf. Matt. 5.3-10) He teaches us to live now in a new spirit, and to find happiness in so living. He calls us out of shallow and meaningless forms of life to the gladness of sharing here and now in a priceless good. "The kingdom of heaven is like treasure hidden in a field, which someone found and hid; then in

---

[1]Pope John Paul II, Apostolic Exhortation, *Catechesi Tradendae* (October 16, 1979) n. 8 (EV 6.1777).

his joy he goes and sells all that he has and buys that field" (Matt. 13.44).

When Christ taught here on earth, men and women flocked to Him. Indeed, the world has always been drawn toward Christ. Over the centuries he has been loved by countless millions who have known Him only through faith. He has, it is true, been sharply rejected, too. Many reject Him at least partially in ignorance and misunderstanding, as St. Paul did before God's grace transformed him (cf. 1 Tim. 1.13; Acts 9.1-20). Others turn against Christ with deliberate hostility, for they have decided not to abandon the pride and selfishness of their lives, and great goodness embitters those who are enmeshed in sin (cf. John 3.19-20).

But those who, touched by grace, come to know Christ, and who wish to lay aside the burden of their sinful and empty lives, have drawn close to Him. For the life He actually lived on earth reveals a goodness so universal that it endlessly attracts the human heart. "He has done everything well" (Mark 7.37). Thus people spoke of Him, and they sought from Him the way to live.

The apostles Christ sent did not preach a miserable life, one to be endured solely in the hope of a future reward. They themselves endured many crosses, and they taught that we must be willing to endure suffering out of love. But their message, Christ's message, was one of joy. They have received from Christ the power to live in a better way, and they proclaimed Christ "so that you also may have fellowship with us" (1 John 1.3).

The Truly Human Life

Christ teaches how to live on earth in a genuinely human way. The Catholic faith does not make us less human, but more human. It urges us to be faithful to the deepest longings of the human spirit: to be bearers of peace, and to be themselves a blessing to others.

Christ teaches a good human life. But He is not a mere philosophical teacher of virtue, and His message is not merely a set of wise sayings. He showed what goodness is by the way He lived; and He gives those who approach Him the power to become good. "But to all who received Him, who believed in His name, He gave power to become children of God" (John 1.12).

He makes us more human by enabling us to draw on the resources of God. He who is the most loved of all is Himself the Son of God, and He lives the life of God as well as the life of man. So also He calls us to become fully human by becoming children of God. Thus we are called to share on earth in the life of God: by faith to share in the light of God's wisdom, and by hope and love to be drawn into the warmth of His life.

Those who have begun to live such a life of faith, hope, and love, sharing in the energy and joy of God's love, ought to share with others the blessing they have discovered. They should pass on to others the good news they have learned, and "spread abroad a living witness to Christ, especially by means of a life of faith and charity" (LG 12).

Task of This World

Christ Himself considered this world worth His care. He came into this world to reconcile it with the Father, and He sends those who love Him to continue this work among all the nations.

There are many creative tasks to be performed in this world. Generous hearts have often longed for the joy of being able to do much good. They desire the blessings asked for in the prayer often attributed to St. Francis of Assisi: "Lord, make me an instrument of your peace. Where there is hatred, let me sow love; where there is injury, pardon. . . ."

Christ teaches those who come to Him how to live lives which are fruitful, lives which make a difference in this world. There is a reign of God, a kingdom of truth and life, of justice, love, and peace, to be built on earth. There is suffering around us, and there is need to be healed and supported; the unstable world needs the anchor of hope. God offers to all who wish it the opportunity to be bearers of a healing that goes beyond all human expectation.[2]

Faith and Human Progress

Because one is called to share in divine life, it is a divine task to humanize the world. For this reason, faith has much to say of the sacred significance of one's constant effort to better the circumstances of life in this world. Today, especially with the help of science and technology, humankind "has extended its mastery over nearly the whole of nature, and continues to do so" (GS 33).

But the wisdom which faith and love bring is necessary to control technology itself. Technology can enslave us; technical progress does not guarantee happiness. Still, technology can enrich life in many ways, by making the necessities of life more plentiful, improving communication, and providing time for leisure and for concern for others. Indeed, science and technology are useful means in the task of making this world serve God's kingdom.

The Lord directs His disciples to care about the hungry and the weak. In a complex society, scientific and technological advances are tools by which persons can subdue the earth (cf. Gen. 1.28) for the

---

[2]Cf. Pope John Paul II, Encyclical, *Dives in Misericordia* (November 30, 1980) n. 2 (EV 7.861-866).

benefit of the whole human family and the glory of our Creator. Technical progress is so rich and varied today that it has become possible — and therefore obligatory — for more persons than ever before to be actively concerned with the material and social well-being of their fellow men and women. There is also a duty to be concerned about the political and economic structures of the world, for these too can be changed for the better. Followers of Christ should work for a just society.

The social teachings of Christ and His Church encourage a determination to make the world better. Since Christ is with us, peace and justice and mercy are not to be considered unattainable ideals. The fact that this world "will pass away" (Matt. 24.35) is no excuse for lack of concern about injustice and misery in it. For the rebuilding of our broken world glorifies God, and contributes to the coming of the better world of God's eternal kingdom.

Those who sincerely try to fulfill their earthly tasks can never entirely fail. At times their efforts may be frustrated and their immediate goals not achieved. But the presence in the world of persons who ceaselessly labor to reshape the world according to the mind of Christ is itself a healing of the earth. A world with a St. Francis of Assisi or a St. Vincent de Paul is already a better world.

The Final Goal of All

"For we know that if the earthly tent we live in is destroyed, we have a building from God, a house not made with hands, eternal in the heavens" (2 Cor. 5.1).

God willed that people should come to their perfect fulfillment in eternal life, but He willed that they come to that perfect life through their own willing cooperation. It was not God's will simply to create persons already in heaven's happiness; nor was it His will to create persons for a life of endless struggle. Rather, He made people on earth to know and to love and to serve Him, and one another in His name, and so became worthy to arrive at an eternal life which is the fulfillment of a divine life begun in time.

The Longing and Hopes of Time

The life God offers us here is both intensely real and intensely hopeful. But it is a life of faith that longs for vision, of hope that hungers for satisfaction, and of love that patiently bears a multitude of frustrations, for it is a life lived in knowledge that God has called us as a human family toward Himself and complete fulfillment.

The gifts God gives us now call out for fulfillment in eternal life. Clearly the saving of persons requires more than an eventual bringing about of a world situation in which an abundance of the good things of life will be enjoyed by all who are then living. For God loves and calls to Himself every person of every time and every place. No one is unimportant to Him. Moreover, people desire more than that which even a wonderfully developed earth could ever provide.

God plants divine hunger in human hearts. We long not only for peace and justice, and for a good share of material things, but for far more: to see God face to face, to understand far more clearly than we now can, and to love and to be loved in ways not possible in the conditions of time.

To Eternal Life through Time

Eternal life, then, is the fulfillment of longings already planted in us. By faith we now know God dimly, but we hunger for that which faith leaves obscure. We long for a quality of love and a joy of life that can be had only when one possesses in a new and radically richer way the life of the Lord.

Still, heavenly life is not the only precious life we know. It is a great good also to be able to serve God and one another in darkness and difficulties. St. Paul wrote of the tension he felt: "I am hard pressed between the two: my desire is to depart and be with Christ, for that is far better; but to remain in the flesh is more necessary for you" (Phil. 1.23-24). Thus it is possible for one to wish to remain in this world for the time that God allots, even when aware that the heavenly life we are called to is "far better."

For God did not make people simply for heaven, but for coming to heaven through generous and good acts that His grace enables us to perform here and now. God's gift was not to be only the blessed life of heaven, but the further gift of letting us gain blessedness as a merited reward.

"Worthy is the Lamb that was slaughtered to receive power and wealth and wisdom and might and honor and glory and blessing!" (Rev. 5.12). Thus even the glory of Jesus in heaven is presented as being infinitely richer because He came there in His humanity through what He did and what He suffered on earth.

So also the eternal life of those who serve God freely and gladly on earth; it is a life infinitely more blessed because of that service, because of the hardships gladly borne and the acts of mercy willingly done. Regarding those "who have come out of the great ordeal" (Rev. 7.14), Scripture says: "They will hunger no more, and thirst no more; the sun will not strike them, nor any scorching heat" (Rev. 7.16). Inexpressible in the gladness of those who have freely served God and one another and have merited life forever.

The Perfect Fulfillment

Heaven is perfect fulfillment, and it is in the light of it that our present life makes sense. When we come to the blessed vision of the Trinity, we shall know ourselves in a better way. For we were born of God, and created to share the life of the Father and the Son and the Holy Spirit. In the presence of Christ in His glorified humanity we will ourselves become more authentically human than we have ever been. When the body has risen to newness of life, the value of earthly things will be more deeply understood. All the sacramental signs and the symbols of faith, all the prophetic words, and all the precepts of life God has given, are fully understood only in the light of that fullness of life into which all grace is to blossom.

We live now a pilgrim life, among sacraments and symbols. But one who believes and hopes and loves possesses already the living seeds of that life which is beyond signs. It is our joy to have received the life God gives now, and freely to serve Him now, making His kingdom present even now on earth among men.

"Beloved, we are God's children now; what we will be has not yet been revealed. What we do know is this: when He is revealed, we will be like Him, for we will see Him as He is. And all who have this hope in Him purify themselves, just as He is pure" (1 John 3.2-3).

Jesus Christ: True God and Eternal Life in Time

Father. . . ,
in the wonder of the incarnation
your eternal Word has brought to the eyes of faith
a new and radiant vision of your glory.
In him we see our God made visible
and so are caught up in love of the God we can not see.[3]

Jesus Christ, our Savior, true man and true God, is the eternal Word. He is "the only Son of God, eternally begotten of the Father, God from God. . . , one in Being with the Father."[4] Remaining God, He came down from heaven and was made man, and lived among us, teaching us and showing us how to live. Our Redeemer, He suffered and died for us, and rose again in glory. In the Church which He founded He continues His saving acts even now, and in the fulfillment of time He will come again, in power and majesty.

---

[3]Roman Missal, Preface I for Christmas.
[4]Roman Missal, The Order of Mass, Profession of Faith. The creed used in the Mass is essentially the creed of the First Council of Constantinople, 381 (DS 150).

Center of Christian Life

The Christian way of life is the way of Christ. He is Himself the Way, the Truth, and the Life (cf. John 14.5). He revealed to us the Father, and He taught us by words and by example how to live our earthly lives. He draws us to holiness, He who is Himself "the divine Teacher and Model of all perfection" (LG 40). He is the center of God's entire plan of salvation.

"Man cannot live without love. He remains a being that is incomprehensible for himself, his life is senseless, if love is not revealed to him, if he does not encounter love, if he does not experience it and make it his own, if he does not participate intimately in it."[5]

The Beginning and the End

All creation is in, through, and for Christ. "In Him all things in heaven and on earth were created... all things have been created through Him and for Him." (Col. 1.16). He is the One who binds the universe together. He is why we are. Through Him we come to know the Father; with Him we come to new life; in Him we find eternal life. "I am the Alpha and the Omega, the first and the last, the beginning and the end" (Rev. 22.13).

The Church teaches only Christ. He is the "fullness of all revelation" (DV 2). "We must therefore say that in catechesis it is Christ, the Incarnate Word and Son of God, who is taught — everything else is taught with reference to Him — and it is Christ alone who teaches — anyone else teaches to the extent that he is Christ's spokesman, enabling Christ to teach with his lips."[6] To learn Christ is to learn the Father (cf. John 14.9); to know Him is to live in God's Holy Spirit. All that God reveals to us is Jesus, all that God wills for us shines forth in His life and in His words. This is the completion and goal of Catholic teaching; that those who believe "may have all the riches of assured understanding and have the knowledge of God's mystery, that is, Christ Himself, in whom are hidden all the treasures of wisdom and knowledge" (Col. 2.2-3).

To know Christ is sufficient. He is not only the Life and the Truth, but also the Way by which we come to these (cf. John 14.6). By words that speak truly of Him and of His Gospel, by sacraments that make His saving power present, by lives that do His work on earth, the Catholic Church teaches the whole message of Christ.

5Pope John Paul II, Encyclical, *Redemptor Hominis* (March 4, 1979) n. 10 (EV 6.1194).
6Pope John Paul II, Apostolic Exhortation, *Catechesi Tradendae*, (October 16, 1979) n. 6 (EV 6.1774).

Part Two

Through Christ:
Coming To Knowledge Of God

2

The Father
Of Our Lord Jesus Christ

God is. "Before the mountains were brought forth, or ever You had formed the earth and the world, from everlasting to everlasting You are God" (Ps. 90.2). All of creation gives testimony to God; all has reality only from Him.

"No one has ever seen God. It is God the only Son, who is close to the Father's heart, who has made Him known" (John 1.18; cf. Matt. 11.27). Christ reveals the Father in many ways Christ is the "image of the invisible God" (Col. 1.15), and He makes the Father known by what He Himself is. In His words Christ declares the mystery of God, and by His saving works He makes it possible for us to have a living faith.

In this chapter we speak of the mystery of God our Father, of God revealing Himself, and of the ways we come to know God. The chapter notes that human reason can come to a knowledge of the existence of God, and how faith supplies for the limitations of reason. It then discusses attributes of God, something of what the infinite and infinitely perfect God is like.

God Reveals Himself Personally

In the abundance of His love God wishes to be known by the creatures He has made. "In His goodness and wisdom, God chose to reveal Himself. . ." (DV 2).

God indeed dwells in "unapproachable light" (cf. 1 Tim. 6.16), but He enables us to know Him, so that He might give us true fullness of life. We are held down by the burden of our sins and our limitations, but God wishes us to be raised up into sharing His life. God wants us to know Him, and He "chose to reveal Himself and to make known the hidden purpose of His will (cf. Eph. 1.9) by which through Christ, the Word made flesh, man has access to the Father in the Holy Spirit and comes to share in the divine nature (cf. Eph. 2.18; 2 Peter 1.4)" (DV 2).

The Content of Revelation

God Himself is the principal reality which is revealed. He who knows us perfectly wishes us to know Him. All else that He reveals — of ourselves, of creation, of commandments and sacraments — is intended to lead us to Him who is our Life. To discover God by reason is the crown of intellectual life. But to know Him by faith is eternal life for us. "And this is eternal life, that they know You the only true God, and Jesus Christ whom You have sent" (John 17.3).

Faith is a response to God's revelation of Himself; it begins a personal friendship which leads toward the blessed "vision" of God, that is, a life of perfect intimacy with Him in eternity. All faith is rooted in God. The creeds of the Church begin with "I believe in God." When we say these words we are not only professing our belief that there is a God, but are acknowledging the testimony God gives about Himself. It is in the light that God gives that we believe in Him. To have saving faith is to believe God bearing witness to Himself.

Such belief in God is not the final conclusion of a long philosophical argument. It is true that God leads many to genuine faith through paths of philosophical reflection on the things that are. But to come to faith is to recognize and accept that it is God Himself who reveals Himself to humans. This recognition of God is the beginning of a new life.

Faith and Grace

Revelation and faith are personal gifts of a living God. God acts freely in this world and in the human heart. He causes the truth about Himself to be proclaimed, and He makes it possible for the hearer to recognize this truth: "It is the Lord!" (John 21.7). "For this faith to be shown, the grace of God and the interior help of the Holy Spirit must precede and assist, moving the heart and turning it to God, opening the eyes of the mind, and giving 'joy and ease to everyone in assenting to the truth and believing it' " (DV 5).[1]

By the gentle assistance of grace God makes it possible for us to have personal faith. He does not, however, force us to believe in Him. He makes Himself present in the world by His saving deeds and words, and in human hearts by His grace, and He invites us to recognize our Lord. One who comes to faith recognizes God in the light of God's own witnessing.

"The LORD is my light and my salvation" (Ps. 27.1). "For it is the God who said, 'Let light shine out of darkness,' who has shone in our hearts" (2 Cor. 4.6). God is Himself the light by which we believe, and

---

[1] The interior quotation is from the Second Council of Orange, 529, canon 7 (DS 377).

is the goal of all our knowing and striving. From God we learn what God is like, and we realize why He is to be believed before all else. "If we receive the human testimony, the testimony of God is greater" (1 John 5.9).

Coming to Know God

God is most real, and near to us in many ways (cf. Deut. 4.8). Even without the gift of faith it is possible to know with certainty that God exists.

Even many who do not yet know that God exists long for possession of truth and fullness of life, and for a wholeness of being that can in fact be found only in God. They seek a Reality of whose existence they are now unaware. One who finds God after such longing and search finds Him whom one has been seeking all along. In fact, our whole being was made in such a way that it needs the richness of God to fulfill it. "You have made us for Yourself, and our heart is restless until it rests in You."[2]

The Mystery of Unbelief

Although God has made Himself personally accessible to us in many ways, there yet remains in the world much unbelief (cf. Matt. 17.16). The Church is sensitive to the fact of atheism, and is aware there are many different reasons why people are alienated from their God (cf. GS 19-21).

Some reject faith in God because they consider it humiliating for anyone to admit the existence of One far superior to themselves. Others deny the reality of a good God to express "violent protest against the evil in the world" (GS 19), though not in the healing way in which Christ taught the saints to fight against evil. Others have in effect abandoned hope of knowing God, because their philosophical prejudices have convinced them that only the material things that science explores can be truly known, or because they simply deny all possibility of absolute truth. Many put their hearts elsewhere and never really consider the question of God; they are "choked by the cares and riches and pleasures of life, and their fruit does not mature" (Luke 8.14). Many are also pushed toward unbelief by the pressures of governments committed by policy to atheism and the depersonalization of the subjects, or by the unbelieving molders of cultures who in greed and lust have turned from God.

"Undoubtedly, those who willfully try to shut out God from their hearts and to avoid religious questions are not following the dictates

[2]St. Augustine, *Confessiones* 1.1.1 (ML 32.661).

of their consciences, and hence they are not free of fault" (GS 19).

But the extent of their willfulness is hard to assess. Those who do not know God are often victims of the sins of others as well and "believers themselves often bear some responsibility for this situation" (GS 19). Atheism can be a reaction to the unworthy ways in which some believers, in their words, attitudes, and behavior, give inadequate witness to God. "To the extent that they neglect their own training in the faith, or teach erroneous doctrine, or are deficient in their religious, moral, or social life, they must be said to conceal rather than reveal the authentic face of God and religion" (GS 19).

Human Reason and the Existence of God

The Church "holds and teaches that God, the beginning and end of all things, can by the natural light of human reasons be known with certainty from created things, 'for since the creation of the world the invisible things of Him are perceived, being understood through the things which have been made' (Rom. 1.20)."[3]

This solemn teaching of the Church reflects the teaching of Scripture concerning the natural ability of man to know the reality of his Maker. "For all people who were ignorant of God were foolish by nature; and they were unable from the good things that are seen to know the one who exists, nor did they recognize the artisan. . . . For from the greatness and beauty of created things comes a corresponding perception of their Creator" (Wisd. 13.1,5). Those who profess to be seeking God but fail to find Him because they are distracted by the things of creation that they do see, are not readily excusable. "For if they had the power to know so much that they could investigate the world, how did they fail to find sooner the Lord of these things?" (Wisd. 13.9).[4]

Reflection on the moral order of the universe can also lead to a natural knowledge of God. Aware of their human duties to be just and truthful and temperate, many come to realize that this insistent call to goodness, which they hear in their conscience, in fact manifests the reality of One who rightfully demands goodness of them. "When Gentiles, who do not possess the law, do instinctively what the law requires, these, though not having the law, are a law to themselves. They show that what the law requires is written on their hearts" (Rom. 2.14-

---

[3]First Vatican Council, Session 3, April 24, 1870, *Dogmatic Constitution on the Catholic Faith*, ch. 2 (DS 3004). Cf. DV 6.

[4]Many of the Fathers and Doctors of the Church developed orderly and forceful arguments to show how the human mind can find its way to knowledge of God's existence. An early example is in St. Augustine's *De Libero Arbitrio*, Book 2 (ML 32.1239-1270 = ACW 22.74-137). The celebrated "five ways" of St. Thomas Aquinas (*Summa Theologica* 1, 2, 3) present in outline a variety of methods by which a thoughtful person might come to know the existence of God.

15). Thus they recognize that there is One who is Lord and Judge of all.[5]

Experience and Limits of Natural Revelation

Over the course of centuries people of various nations and cultures have in fact come to a knowledge of God by reflection on the physical and moral orders God has created. The philosophers and sages of many nations have pointed out various paths by which people may come to know Him who is the source of all. People have indeed proved able to realize that this world, which bears clear marks of its own transiency and borrowed reality, must be caused to be by One who is the Author of time and all passing things.

There is no reason to suppose that God does not assist with His grace those who seek Him with sincere hearts but who do not have any clear voices to bring them the gift of supernatural revelation. Fathers of the Church often said that the Christ, the Logos, the Word, the source of all wisdom, gave this knowledge to men and women by giving them intelligence and quietly guiding it.[6]

It is certainly possible for a person to come to a knowledge of God by rational reflection on things that are. In everyday life, however, emotions, pleasures and problems, the demands of work, and so on, tend to obscure the way to God through finite things. In the actual circumstances of a given human life it might be very difficult to come to a certain knowledge of God in a deliberate, rational way. It could be especially difficult to do so in time to allow one's whole life to be illumined by the knowledge of God. Even more difficult would it be to gain a knowledge free of serious error. History tells of many philosophers and cultures that came to know that there is a God, but did not come to know Him well, and thought of Him in ways that discouraged efforts to serve Him with faithful love.

Hence it is only by the gift of God's revelation that even "those religious truths which are by their nature accessible to human reason can, even in the present state of the human race, be known by all men with ease, with solid certitude, and with no trace of error" (DV 6).[7] Reason and the world indeed bear witness to God, but the chief witness to God is God Himself.[8]

---

[5]The argument from conscience is articulated carefully in Cardinal Newman's *A Grammar of Assent*, ch. 5.

[6]Cf., e.g., St. Justin Martyr, *Apologia* 1.46 (MG 6.397).

[7]The Second Vatican Council is here quoting the First Vatican Council, Session 3, April 24, 1870, *Dogmatic Constitution on the Catholic Faith*, ch. 2 (DS 3005).

[8]Thus the word "revelation" is always to be used with care. Cf. United States Catholic Conference, *Sharing the Light of Faith — National Catechetical Directory for Catholics of the United States* (1979) n. 50: "The word 'revelation' is used in this document to refer to that divine public revelation which closed at the end of the Apostolic Age. The terms 'manifestation' and

God Manifests His Reality and Presence

God reveals Himself more clearly and directly than do His works which speak of Him. He Himself speaks. He personally seeks out the creatures He has made to give them saving knowledge of Himself. "For thus says the Lord GOD: I, I Myself will search for My sheep, and will seek them out. . . . I will seek the lost, and I will bring back the strayed, and I will bind up the injured, and I will strengthen the weak . . . I will feed them in justice" (Ezech. 34.11, 16).

To seek God is nothing more than to respond to one's Maker, the Creator who keeps us in being, who cares for us and pursues us. To seek God is really to allow oneself to be found, and to say yes in the light of a wisdom that is greater than all human thought.

God reveals Himself through the deeds of salvation history and through the words of the prophets. Most of all, He has spoken to us through His Son (cf. Heb. 1.2). But it is not only in external ways that God speaks. He who made our minds and hearts speaks also within us. He gives those whom He calls to know Him a light by which they can with certainty recognize that it is the Lord of all who calls them to life.

The Free Gift of Faith

The life of faith is built on God. It is His gift. The gift of faith is the beginning of a new life that God freely gives, a gift that only God can give. "For by grace you have been saved through faith, and this is not your own doing; it is the gift of God" (Eph. 2.8).

It was not merely words and visible signs that led Christ's disciples to the fullness of faith. When the apostles began to realize who Christ really was, they cried out in longing to the God they were aware of only obscurely: "Increase our faith!" (Luke 17.5). For faith is the living fruit of two freedoms, that of God who freely gives light, and that of a person who personally uses free will to respond to God with the power God's grace gives.

St. Peter could have logically argued that Jesus must be the Messiah, for the signs were so cogent. That, however, would not of itself have given him fullness of faith. Only when St. Peter's human thoughts had been transformed by the gift of God to the firmer faith he had longed for did Christ say to him: "Blessed are you, Simon son of Jonah! For flesh and blood has not revealed this to you, but My Father in heaven" (Matt. 16.17).

The path of coming to faith, then, is different from that of coming to merely natural knowledge of God. God initiates the series of acts, by causing in the world the presence of witnesses to Himself. In the

'communication' are used for the other modes by which God continues to make Himself known and share Himself with human beings through His presence in the Church and the world."

human heart He gives grace, and speaks, stimulating the hearer to see the reasonableness of belief and at the same time moving the hearer to prayer, to a burning desire for faith, and to an openness to God that changes everything. Then God causes that transforming recognition in which the hearer realizes, in the light of God's gift, that it is God Himself who is present and inviting to life. The hearer believes, because God has made it possible for the hearer to realize that it is God Himself who bears witness to Himself. Although human freedom is such that one is able to resist the grace of faith, it is indeed most intelligent and right for a creature, brought by God to recognize God, to assent to God's word willingly, joyfully, wholeheartedly.[9]

Faith and Salvation

"Faith is the beginning of human salvation, the foundation and root of all justification, 'without which it is impossible to please God' (Heb. 11.6)."[10]

Knowledge of God growing out of faith is far stronger and more secure than any other knowledge we have. It is based not merely on the strength of human insight and interpretation, but on God Himself. God gives the believer's faith not only a rich content, but also such firmness and certainty that the believer can build one's whole life on it. "Everyone then who hears these words of Mine and acts on them will be like a wise man who built his house on rock. The rain fell, the floods came, and the winds blew and beat on that house, but it did not fall, because it had been founded on rock" (Matt. 7.24-25).

Knowledge of God has been given to us chiefly through Jesus Christ, who revealed to us the Father (cf. John 1.18) and who is Himself "the fullness of all revelation" (DV 2). "He is the image of the invisible God" (Col. 1.15). "For in Him the whole fullness of deity dwells bodily" (Col. 2.9). In Him "the goodness and loving kindness of God our Savior appeared" (Titus 3.4).

The God of Revelation

God reveals Himself to us as a Lord whose greatness exceeds our understanding, but also as a Father who is near to us and truly loves us.

God reveals Himself as a saving God. Through events in the history of salvation, and through the divinely inspired words accompanying and clarifying those events, He makes Himself and His saving plan known (cf. DV 2).

---

[9]Cf. First Vatican Council, Session 3, April 24, 1870, *Dogmatic Constitution on the Catholic Faith*, ch. 3 (DS 3008-3011).

[10]Council of Trent, Session 4, January 13, 1547, *Decree on Justification*, ch. 8 (DS 1532).

God is very different from us and from all the things we experience. We come to be and we pass away; we exist only because He causes us to be. Reality is His by nature. He not only exists and lives, but He is the fountain and source of all being and life. Nothing exists without Him. Asked to make His name known when He spoke to Moses of His saving will, He proclaimed the richness of His being: "I AM WHO I AM. . . . Thus you shall say to the Israelites, 'I AM has sent me to you' " (Exod. 3.14).

We cannot fully grasp the transcendent mystery of God. He is eternal, perfect, and infinite.[11] We are temporal, flawed, and finite. He is the holy God before whom we stand in awe and sense our smallness. Yet His greatness is a majesty of goodness. In His splendor He is utterly beyond us, but in His bountiful mercy "God is with us" (Matt. 1.23; cf. Rev. 21.3). In His saving words and deeds He makes Himself truly near to us and known to us, so that we may have friendship with Him.

A Personal God

God makes clear the truth that He is a personal God by all the deeds He did for the Israelites. With forceful will and great mercy, the saving God brought them from slavery, gave them precepts of life, overcame their foes, and brought them to a promised land. He gave them not only external freedom, but He gave them the way to the greater and more personal freedom to know truth and to love what is enduringly good. By His saving work He taught them that "among you is the living God" (Jos. 3.10).

Thus He showed how He who sustains and rules all that is, is a Father who knows and cares. He reveals that it is He, a saving Person, who is the first principle of all that is. He shows that the world is not the product of some blind, uncaring power or force. Mightier than all the forces in nature is the Lord who gives being, the Lord who is our Father.

All-knowing

God's knowledge encompasses everyone and everything, all that is, was, and will be. He knows the sorrows of His people and He foresees how He will save them (cf. Exod. 3.19-22). The farthest regions of the universe are familiar to Him: "He determines the number of the stars; He gives to all of them their names" (Ps. 147.4). Not even the most trivial things escape Him: "And even the hairs of your

---

[11]A person can come to know certain attributes of God by rational reflection as well as by revelation. A classic discussion of God's attributes, incorporating rational arguments for them, is that of St. Thomas Aquinas, *Summa Theologica* I, 3-26.

head are all counted" (Matt. 10.30). The future and the most hidden secrets of our hearts are open to Him (cf. Matt. 24.36; Ps. 139.1-4).

God is, then, truly all-knowing, omniscient. " 'All things are bare and open to His eyes' (Heb. 4.13), even those things which are yet to be by the free action of creatures."[12]

Loving

To know God is to know One who loves His people and wishes to save them. "I have loved you with an everlasting love; therefore I have continued My faithfulness to you" (Jer. 31.3). Even in the earlier days of salvation history, before God had revealed how fully men and women of every nation and people belong to Him and are called to become His children in the eternal Son who became our brother, He made Himself known as our Father. He is One to be infinitely trusted; He will never fail us, "For You are our Father, though Abraham does not know us and Israel does not acknowledge us; You, O LORD, are our Father; our Redeemer from of old is Your name" (Isa. 63.16). "It is the LORD your God who goes with you; He will not fail you or forsake you" (Deut. 31.6).

The love of God is revealed in His mercy. "It is 'God, who is rich in mercy' (Eph. 2.4), whom Jesus Christ has revealed to us as Father: it is His very Son who, in Himself, has manifested Him and made Him known to us (cf. John 1.18; Heb. 1.11)."[13]

Almighty

God's power and majesty are limitless. In the creeds of the Church we profess our belief in "God the Father almighty." The Church proclaims the glory of God: "There is one true and living God, Creator and Lord of heaven and earth, almighty, eternal, immeasurable, incomprehensible, infinite in intellect, in will, and in every perfection. Since He is one unique spiritual substance, entirely simple and unchangeable, He must be declared really and essentially distinct from the world, most blessed in and of Himself, and inexpressibly exalted over all things that exist or can be conceived other than Himself."[14]

This definition of Catholic faith about God compresses into a few words much that the Father has revealed of Himself through the prophets and through Jesus His Son, and guarded and clarified through the Holy Spirit in the Church's prayer and reflection. Even those truths

---

[12]First Vatican Council, Session 3, April 24, 1870, *Dogmatic Constitution on the Catholic Faith*, ch. 1 (DS 3003).

[13]Pope John Paul II, Encyclical, *Dives in Misericordia* (November 30, 1980) n. 1 (EV 7.857).

[14]First Vatican Council, Session 3, April 24, 1870, *Dogmatic Constitution on the Catholic Faith*, ch. 1 (DS 3001).

about God that do not at first seem to be clearly related to faith and hope are in fact of religious importance. In knowing of God's power, His changeless strength, and in knowing that He is present everywhere, and that He transcends the world but is with all who dwell in the world, one grasps ever more richly the greatness of the Love who has shaped all things.

To say that God is almighty is to say that He can do all things. He is all-powerful, omnipotent. "For nothing will be impossible with God" (Luke 1.37). God never lacks the power to keep His promises; His will is never frustrated by those who seek to oppose Him. "For it is always in Your power to show great strength, and who can withstand the might of Your arm? Because the whole world before You is like a speck that tips the scales, and like a drop of morning dew that falls on the ground. But You are merciful to all, for You can do all things" (Wisd. 11.21-23).

Eternal and Changeless

In a restless and changing world, God reveals His own unchanging constancy. "For I the LORD do not change" (Mal. 3.6). In His very being, too, God is unchanging. The many elements in the changing world alter one another, and depend on one another, but the powerful and merciful God is utterly independent and suffers no alteration. "Lord, You have been our dwelling place in all generations. Before the mountains were brought forth, or ever You had formed the earth and the world, from everlasting to everlasting You are God. . . . For a thousand years in Your sight are like yesterday when it is past, or like a watch in the night" (Ps. 90.1-4).

We are swept by the currents of time, but God dwells in an eternity to which every moment of all time is always present, and He watches over all things with unchanging love. His eternal changelessness is not like that of a rock which cannot of itself change, but is that of the utter fullness of life and love that is always totally present to us who depend on Him that we may be.

Spirit and Present Everywhere

God is a spirit. This means that God is not a material body, restricted to this place or that, with the limitations that are inseparable from matter.

Human minds find it difficult to grasp the meaning of spiritual reality, to understand how something can be real without having spatial and temporal dimensions. Even St. Augustine experienced difficulty in grasping the meaning of God's spirituality.[15] Yet God's

---

[15]Cf. St. Augustine, *Confessiones* 5.10.19-20; 5.14.25 (ML 32.715-716, 718).

spiritual reality is no mere abstraction. It is a reality more intense and mighty than that of beings encountered in space and time.

God is present to all. Yet He is "not far from each one of us," for in Him "we live and move and have our being" (Acts 17.27-28). He is everywhere, omnipresent. "Where can I go from Your Spirit? Or where can I flee from Your presence? If I ascend to heaven, You are there; if I make my bed in Sheol, You are there. If I take the wings of the morning and settle at the farthest limits of the sea, even there Your hand shall lead me, and Your right hand shall hold me fast" (Ps. 139.7-10).

Although God is everywhere present, and His presence and power keep in being each thing that is, He is in special ways present to those who love Him. For God has many other gifts to give us, and He dwells in those who love Him (cf. John 14.23) in a presence of infinite personal concern.

Transcendent and Holy

While God is ever with us and always present to the world He made, He is utterly distinct from the world. Every kind of pantheism, every tendency to identify God with the world or to see Him as some dimension or aspect of the visible universe, fails utterly to grasp the greatness of God.

St. Augustine speaks clearly of the majesty of the God who out of His love has made lovable things. He asks: "What do I love when I love my God?" It is true that the beauty and goodness of creation can move one to love God, but it is no part of creation that one loves in loving God. "I asked the earth . . . I asked the sea, the depths . . . and they replied: 'We are not your God. Look above us.' . . .I asked the sky, the sun, the moon, the stars, and they said: 'Neither are we the God whom you seek.' And I said to all these things. . . : 'You have told me concerning my God that you are not He. Tell me something about Him.' With a loud voice they cried out: 'He made us.' My questioning was my looking upon them, and their reply was their beauty."[16]

All things bear witness to God, but He is other than them all. He is their Maker, radically different from the changing things He has made. "It is He that made us, and we are His" (Ps. 100.3). Their beauty is but a reflection of His, and an invitation to hunger for Him.

God is transcendent. He is exalted far above the universe, for it exists only at His bidding; before the universe and its time, He is; His changeless and eternal reality is in its perfection entirely distinct from the dependent reality of finite things. "Even heaven and the highest heaven cannot contain You" (2 Chron. 6.18). God is indicated by each thing that is, but all things together cannot begin to tell of the majesty of God.

[16]St. Augustine, *Confessiones* 10.6.9 (ML 32.783).

Scripture frequently expresses God's otherness by proclaiming that He is perfectly holy. He is "the Holy One" (Isa. 5.24; cf. Lev. 11.44-45; Jos. 24.19; Isa. 6.3; etc.) His holiness is far more than freedom from any touch of moral evil, for God cannot sin. References to His holiness also express more than His hostility to the moral evil that wounds and bruises creation and calls for punishment by Him (cf. Isa. 42.24-25; Ezech. 28.22). Primarily the references to God's holiness are to His absolute perfection. Because God is so far exalted above all finite things, the creature cannot personally be worthy even to gaze on or to speak of God; but this same perfection is also the root of that divine mercy which heals sinners and calls them to God (cf. Isa. 6.5-7).

The holiness of God attracts the human heart because of the goodness it implies, a goodness of such intensity that it touches the sinful heart with awe and reverential fear. The splendor and holiness of God must be taken seriously; He who is holy and requires holiness is the Lord and Judge of all. The fear of the Lord is the beginning of wisdom (cf. Prov. 1.7). Such fear is not terror; it is a sublime reverence intimately related to hope and love. "You who fear the Lord, wait for His mercy; do not stray, or else you may fall. You who fear the Lord, trust in Him, and your reward will not be lost. You who fear the Lord, hope for good things, for lasting joy and mercy. Consider the generations of old and see; has anyone trusted in the Lord and been disappointed? Or has anyone persevered in the fear of the Lord and been forsaken?" (Sir. 2.7-10).

The One God

There is only one God. In Him alone is our hope; and he who fears the Lord should fear no one else. "So acknowledge today, and take to heart that the LORD is God in heaven above and on the earth beneath; there is no other" (Deut. 4.39). His is the one mighty wisdom, the one infinite love, that shapes the world and governs all things; His is the one infinite goodness and beauty for which all hearts long. To Him we should entrust the love of our whole heart. "Hear, O Israel: The LORD is our God, the LORD alone. You shall love the LORD your God with all your heart, and with all your soul, and with all your might" (Deut. 6.4-5).

This one God is the blessedness that everyone longs for. " 'Come,' my heart says, 'seek His face!' Your face, LORD, do I seek. Do not hide Your face from me" (Ps. 27.8-9). Everything that is learned in the study of faith speaks of Him. For He is the last goal of every person, the final good that moves and stirs all the longings of all; He is the "Love that moves the sun and other stars."[17]

17Dante, *Divine Comedy*, Paradise, Canto 33.

3

God The Lord And Creator Of All

"O LORD, our Sovereign, how majestic is your name in all the earth!" (Ps. 8.1). Everything that God has made is a voice that speaks His glory and goodness. "The heavens are telling the glory of God; and the firmament proclaims His handiwork. Day to day pours forth speech, and night to night declares knowledge. There is no speech, nor are there words; their voice is not heard; yet their voice goes out through all the earth, and their words to the end of the world" (Ps. 19.1-4).

The Lord God who created all things created all of us. "Have we not all one Father? Has not one God created us?" (Mal. 2.10). "The rich and the poor have this in common: the LORD is the maker of them all" (Prov. 22.2).

In this chapter we speak of God the Creator. The chapter treats of the meaning of creation, and of the account of creation given us in Scripture; and it shows how there can be no real conflict between Christian faith and human reason, or between the truths of the faith and genuine scientific truth. It notes how the Creator God continues to sustain all things in being, and guides them by His providential care. Finally, the chapter speaks of God's invisible creation and of the reality of angels.

Creator of Heaven and Earth

God reveals Himself to us as our Creator. To know His grandeur and to know our dignity as persons made in the image of God (cf. Gen. 1.26-27) we must begin to grasp His creative power. "Thus says the LORD, the Holy One of Israel. . . . : 'Will you question Me about My children, or command Me concerning the work of My hands? I made the earth, and created humankind upon it; it was My hands that stretched out the heavens, and I commanded all their host' " (Isa. 45.11-12). To know God truly is to know that He is "Creator of heaven and earth."[1]

The philosophers of antiquity and the pagan nations knew something of God, but they did not know Him as the Creator of all. In their myths and philosophies they expressed the conviction to which the

[1]The Apostles' Creed (DS 30).

Lord in His mercy had led them, that is, that God is far above us in His wisdom and strength. But the relationship expressed by the word "Creator" they did not know. Even to His chosen people in the Old Testament era God revealed this aspect of His reality only gradually.

When God brought the Israelites out of the slavery of Egypt "with a mighty hand and an outstretched arm" (Deut. 5.15), they knew that He was a mighty God. When He won their battles, when He manifested Himself in the glory of Sinai (cf. Exod. 19.10-19), when He led them to the promised land, they knew that His power surpassed all their understanding. But it was only little by little that God led them to a full understanding of His limitless power over all that is. Finally, when His word led their prophetic teachers to understand that He is the Creator of all, they came to know that nothing whatever could in any way resist Him. For all things come to be and remain in existence only by His creative power. To know the creative might of the good God is to know that He "can do all things" (Job 42.2); it is to know that no one is ever in a position "to contend with Him" (Job 9.3). It is folly to turn against the creative Love who gives us being. "Shall the thing made say of its maker, 'He did not make me'?" (Isa. 29.16).

Doctrine of Creation

The Catholic faith speaks clearly of the many facets of the revealed doctrine of creation. "This one and only true God, of His own goodness and 'almighty power,' not in order to increase or to acquire His happiness, but in order to manifest His perfection through the blessings He bestows on His creatures, by a most free decision 'from the very beginning of time created out of nothing both the spiritual and the corporal creature, that is, the angelic and the earthly, and then the human creature, which is as it were common to both, being composed of spirit and body.' "[2]

"Out of Nothing"

To say that God made all things "out of nothing" is not, of course, to suggest that "nothing" is some kind of existing stuff out of which God fashioned the world, much as a carpenter makes a table out of wood. Rather, it means that all things "in their whole substance have been produced by God."[3] That is, all things other than God, and all the

---

[2]First Vatican Council, Session 3, April 24, 1870, *Dogmatic Constitution on the Catholic Faith*, ch. 1 (DS 3002). The inner quotation is from the Fourth Lateran Council, November 1215 (DS 800).

[3]First Vatican Council, Session 3, April 14, 1870, *Dogmatic Constitution on the Catholic Faith*, canon 5 on God the Creator of all things (DS 3025).

elements that enter into their constitution, have been made by Him and are utterly dependent on Him.

Only God has existed forever. There was a beginning to creation.[4] "In the beginning when God created the heavens and the earth. . ." (Gen. 1.1). Before the first moment of creation, there was no earth, no universe, no elements; there was not even time.

When did creation and time begin? We do not know. But God always is. Things came to be when God chose,[5] and it was from Him they received all their reality.

Created Freely

God is not the name of some impersonal force; He is not merely some dimension or depth of the universe. He is a personal God, a God of knowledge and love who is forever, entirely distinct from all He chose to make. He created freely, out of love.

God needed nothing. Nothing He made was made so that He might benefit from it. There was no poverty in Him calling for fulfillment. Nothing forced Him to create. But in the rich interpersonal love that is God the Blessed Trinity, God most freely chose to create.

In His generosity God freely willed that what had not been should be, to taste the blessing of existence. Some creatures He made to share even in the glory of being persons, of being free, and of being called to share the boundless richness of His own life. Creation was and is no struggle for God. "For He spoke, and it came to be; He commanded, and it stood firm" (Ps 33.9).

Creation in the Book of Genesis

The first two chapters of Genesis describe the creation of the world and of the first man and woman. They teach us truth about God's mercy, and they do this with great simplicity and poetic beauty, and with reverence and awe. Clearly, however, they are not chapters written in the manner of a scientific textbook; their concern is not with dates and physical processes, but with other truths. The myths of paganism are corrected in the Genesis creation accounts. For there are no evil forces or elements involved in the work of creation. There are no ancient evil powers independent of God. There is no aimless and inexplicable force of cosmic generation. The whole of visible creation and all that is in it is the work of a good and mighty God, and all that He created was good. "God saw everything that He had made, and indeed, it was very good" (Gen. 1.31).

A number of important religious truths are taught in the Genesis

---

[4]Cf. Pope Pius XII, Encyclical, *Humani Generis* (August 12, 1950) (DS 3890).
[5]Cf. Council of Florence, Bull, *Cantate Domino* (February 4, 1442) (DS 1333).

accounts of creation, but there is nothing in those accounts that rightly understood could ever justify fears of a conflict or confrontation between faith and science. The Bible, to be sure, does not teach evolution; neither does it say anything to oppose scientific theories about bodily evolution.[6] It simply is not concerned with the kinds of questions the scientist deals with. It would be a mistake to try to interpret Scripture in ways to make it say whatever scientific theory or experience concludes at a given time.

Interpreting the Genesis Account

Scripture always speaks the truth, but it sometimes uses poetic or figurative language, and like all great literature, it speaks the truth in a number of different ways (cf. DV 12). The Fathers of the Church interpreted the details of the Genesis narrative of creation in a rich variety of ways.

The sacred writer of the first creation account (cf. Gen. 1.1-2.4) portrays the work of creation as extending over a period of six "days," and says that on the seventh day God "rested from all the work that He had done in creation" (Gen. 2.3). This account is obviously not a technical report on the timing and mode of creation. As early Christian writers noted,[7] the six "days" of creation could hardly have been solar days such as we now know, for according to the account in Genesis the sun was not made until the fourth "day." Nonetheless, the structure and literary form of the creation narrative serve the memory and at the same time reinforce other sacred teachings. In presenting the creative task of God in the way it does, Genesis suggests the dignity of work and the sacredness of a Sabbath rest. God "blessed the seventh day and hallowed it" (Gen. 2.3). In the account of human origin the dignity of human labor is honored, and our right to and need for times of contemplative quiet are recalled.

St. Augustine sees here also another meaning: a promise of eternal rest. When Scripture says that God "rested" after His work of creation, this does not mean that God was "tired." Rather, God there promised rest to those who labor, "so that you may understand that you too will have rest after your good works, and will have rest without end."[8]

Important sacred truths are taught in the Genesis account. Some of these touch upon the foundations of Christian religion, such as, for example, the creation of all things by God at the beginning of time, the particular creation of man, the fact of original sin, and so on.

Revelation does not discuss the date of human beginnings or the

---

6Cf. Pope Pius XII, Encyclical, *Humani Generis* (August 12, 1950) (DS 3896).

7Cf., e.g., St. Augustine, *De Genesi ad Litteram* 1.10-12, 18-14 (ML 34.253-256 = ACW 41.24-26, 29-33).

8St. Augustine, *Sermo* 9.6 (ML 38.80).

precise pattern of God's creative acts; it does not discuss the physiology or psychology of the first human beings. But it does teach that each human person is of surpassing dignity, essentially different from every merely material being in this world. It does not teach that our first parents were sophisticated or enjoyed a rich culture; but it does teach that they were created in the full friendship of God.

Faith and Human Reason

Scientists and philosophers often inquire into matters on which revelation and faith shed a decisive light. For God's word is given to us as a response to deep human questions that God Himself has planted within us. These questions have given rise to the human sciences by which scholars carry out their responsibility to understand and to master the world. Philosophers and scholars of every culture have never ceased to wonder about the complex realities which faith also illumines, such as the origin of things, the nature of the sacred, and the meaning of human life. They have viewed the intricate reality of this world from many different viewpoints, and they have gained insights into many important truths. Many, however, have also fallen into error.

Impossibility of Real Conflict

We are called both to believe God and, as far as possible, to master the world through the use of our God-given intelligence. Faith and reason are of course fundamentally in harmony, for God is the one source of both. "Although faith is above reason, there can never be any real disagreement between faith and reason, since the same God who reveals mysteries and infuses faith has put the light of reason in the human mind, and God cannot deny Himself, nor can truth ever contradict truth."[9]

In the conflicts and disagreements which do in fact occur among people on these matters, it is never faith and human wisdom that are opposed. Differences develop rather among people who either have not grasped the true meaning of what the faith teaches or have gone astray in the human sciences. "The false appearance of such a contradiction arises for the most part because the dogmas of faith have not been understood and explained according to the mind of the Church, or because false conjectures are taken for verdicts of reason. Therefore, 'we define that every assertion contrary to a truth of enlightened faith is utterly false.' "[10]

---

[9]First Vatican Council, Session 3, April 24, 1870, *Dogmatic Constitution on the Catholic Faith*, ch. 4 (DS 3017).

[10]First Vatican Council, Session 3, April 24, 1870, *Dogmatic Constitution on the Catholic Faith*,

The Sureness of the Faith

It is important to understand what it is the Church teaches. One would be mistaken, for example, if one were to interpret the first chapters of Genesis in a slavishly literal way, viewing them as if they were intended to provide a factual description of the manner in which creation took place. On the other hand, one would be even more seriously mistaken if one were to abandon the literal truth of the doctrines which the Church has found in the Genesis account, or if one sought to give a radically different meaning to those doctrines because the philosophy or scientific theories fashionable at a given time might seem to be in conflict with the message of faith.

There is an enduring and meaningful content of faith.[11] One who has recognized a sacred truth as a part of divine revelation will have complete certainty of its truth. One will not let difficulties turn one aside from a message recognized as divine. "For the doctrine of faith which God has revealed has not been proposed, like a philosophical invention, as something to be perfected by human intelligence, but it has been handled over as a divine deposit to the Spouse of Christ, to be faithfully guarded and infallibly declared. Hence also that meaning of the sacred dogmas which Holy Mother Church has once declared is perpetually to be retained, and that meaning is never to be departed from under the pretense and pretext of a deeper comprehension of them."[12]

Doctrine can indeed be said to develop and to be more fully comprehended through the assistance of the Holy Spirit over the ages. But that which has been once proclaimed and recognized as the meaningful word of God is enduringly true. Its significance may come to be more fully realized, but what the Church has once infallibly proclaimed as the content of God's message will never be found to be false.

Pluralism

The message of faith can be expressed in more than one way. Even the Gospels speak the same truth in ways that are often distinctively different. Indeed, the same message may receive a variety of expressions suited to various cultures. But whatever the plurality of

ch. 4 (DS 3017). The internal quotation is from the Fifth Lateran Council, Session 8, December 19, 1513, Bull, *Apostolici Regiminis* (DS 1441).

[11]Pope Paul VI, Apostolic Exhortation, *Evangelii Nuntiandi* (December 8, 1975) n. 65 (EV 5.1680); Pope John Paul II, Apostolic Exhortation, *Catechesi Tradendae* (October 16, 1979) n. 26 (EV 6.1824).

[12]First Vatican Council, Session 3, April 24, 1870, *Dogmatic Constitution on the Catholic Faith*, ch. 4 (DS 3020). Cf. DV 8.

forms of expression, genuine Christian teaching always expresses the same enduring truth.

There is, then, a kind of "pluralism" acceptable in the expression of the Catholic faith, but there is never a pluralism in which different persons believe different doctrines. So also is there a legitimate and beneficial pluralism of theological research and thought, but the theological speculations and investigations of each must always be subordinate to and in harmony with the faith. The unity of the Catholic faith involves a common acceptance of the message of Christ. This acceptance is not merely of a set of words, but it means confessing the truth He teaches in the sense in which He proclaimed it and causes it to be proclaimed in His Church.[13]

The Church welcomes not only a certain pluralism of expression, but also a certain philosphical pluralism. A Catholic philosopher is by no means required to accept the methods and techniques of any particular philosophy. Indeed, the creative work of many philosophical schools has been found useful in understanding and serving the message of faith.

There is, however, a kind of "Christian philosophy" that has developed over the centuries. That is, there is a certain "philosophical heritage which is perennially valid" (OT 15), because it teaches a number of truths which have been divinely revealed but which are also accessible to the rational inquirer — such as the existence of God and certain truths about Him, the freedom and immortality of man, the validity of the natural law.[14] People have come to know and explore these truths in a great variety of methods, and the Church encourages the development of each. But every Christian philosophy will be in harmony with the truth of the principles of the faith, and will accept as central to their true meaning what is spoken of them by the message of faith itself.

Faith sometimes completes and heals human philosophies; it is never corrected or altered by them. Certain human philosophies are essentially dedicated to the articulation and defense of positions incompatible with Christian faith, positions purposely developed as alternatives to Christianity. Any philosophical theory which holds that God is finite, or impersonal, or incomplete and developing, or merely some "depth" in visible things, would of course be entirely unacceptable to one who has received the light of Christ. On the other hand, if a secular philosophy expresses vividly many truths precious and important to a given culture, and only incidentally teaches some points contrary to the faith, a Christian need not utterly reject it. Rather, the

---

[13]Cf. Pope Paul VI, Apostolic Exhortation, *Paterna Cum Benevolentia* ("On Reconciliation within the Church," December 8, 1974) (EV 5.815-848). Cf. also Congregation for the Doctrine of the Faith, *Instruction on the Ecclesial Vocation of the Theologian* (May 24, 1990).

[14]Cf. Pope Pius XII, Encyclical, *Humani Generis* (August 12, 1950) (DS 3892).

believer may seek, by valid methods proper to philosophy itself, to remedy its defects, and thus to allow this human wisdom also to serve the revealed wisdom of faith.

Science and Faith

Catholic teaching urges all to respect the dignity of human sciences.

It is true that there can be abuses in the pursuit of science. Some persons, for example, tend to put excessive confidence in the so-called "scientific method" and to consider as true, or perhaps even knowable, only that which can be empirically verified. "No doubt today's progress in the sciences and technology, which by virtue of their method cannot penetrate to the innermost meanings of things, can foster a certain phenomenalism and agnosticism, when the research method which those disciplines use is wrongly regarded as the supreme rule for discovering the whole truth" (GS 57). This abuse, however, flows from a philosophical error, not from the nature of science itself.

Cultivation of the sciences is part of our proper service to God as His creatures. Through the arts and sciences we can contribute to fulfillment of the common human duty to "elevate the human family to a more sublime understanding of the true, the good, and the beautiful" (GS 57). Indeed, study of the sciences can nourish reverence for many positive values: "strict fidelity toward truth in scientific research, the necessity of working together with others in technical groups, a sense of international solidarity, an ever clearer awareness of the responsibility of experts to aid men and even to protect them and to desire to make the conditions of life more favorable to all. . ." (GS 57).

Certainly each of the human arts and sciences is free in its sphere to use its own principles and its own method. Not only does the Church not forbid this, but it asserts its recognition of "this just liberty"[15] and indeed "affirms the legitimate autonomy of human culture and especially of the sciences" (GS 59).

God Sustains and Rules the World

God did not create the world and then abandon it. Created things not only have their origin in Him but could not continue to exist if He did not continue to keep them in being. "How would anything have endured if You had not willed it? Or how would anything not called forth by You have been preserved? You spare all things, for they are Yours, O Lord, who love the living" (Wisd. 11.25-26).

---

[15]First Vatican Council, Session 3, April 24, 1870, *Dogmatic Constitution on the Catholic Faith,* ch. 4 (DS 3019). The words are quoted by the Second Vatican Council in GS 59.

God cares for the world with great love, ever directing it towards the goal for the sake of which He made all things. All things have been created in Christ, through Christ, and for Christ (cf. Col. 1.16), and the divine plan is "to gather up all things in Him, things in heaven and things on earth" (Eph. 1.10). The Genesis account portrays man and woman as created last in God's visible creation (cf. Gen. 1.26-27), but the human person is the crown and purpose of the visible world (cf. Ps. 8.4-8). "For all things are yours. . . the world or life or death or the present or the future — all belong to you, and you belong to Christ, and Christ belongs to God" (1 Cor. 3.21-23).

God in His providence never ceases to care for the world. "By His providence God watches over and governs all things which He has made, 'reaching from end to end mightily, and ordering all things sweetly' (Wisd. 8.1)."[16] "He covers the heavens with clouds, prepares rain for the earth, makes grass grow on the hills. He gives to the animals their food, and to the young ravens when they cry" (Ps. 147.8-9).

God's providence extends to all His creatures, and in a special way to the persons He has made. "Look at the birds of the air; they neither sow nor reap nor gather into barns, and yet your heavenly Father feeds them. Are you not of more value than they?" (Matt. 6.26). And it is a saving providence: God "desires everyone to be saved and to come to the knowledge of the truth" (1 Tim. 2.4).

Predestination

The proper destiny of each of us is eternal life with God, for God calls and invites all to Himself and wills all to be saved (cf. 1 Tim. 2.4).

We are predestined in the sense that God's merciful gift precedes and makes possible every mercy, especially that of eternal salvation. Certainly there is no predestination in which God selects certain persons not to attain eternal life with Him and withholds from them the gift of salvation. At the same time, the predestination of which we speak does not mean that in the past God planned things that would mechanically occur in future time, that God is as it were sitting in heaven watching pages of history already written turn before Him. Rather, it is a predestination that fully respects the freedom that God Himself gives us.

The mystery of God's eternity transcends time; every moment of time is always present to Him, and it is His eternal mercy that guides us toward the salvation He wills for all. Yet history remains history, and we must each live our own life — an adventure in freedom.

---

[16]First Vatican Council, Session 3, April 24, 1870, *Dogmatic Constitution on the Catholic Faith*, ch. 1 (DS 3003).

For God does not force the creation that He guides with a gentle love.

We can do no saving deeds at all without the God who sustains us in being and who alone enables us to do good. But God also allows us to resist His grace, to refuse the life He offers, to do the things He forbids. For God made every person free and He wills that all come to Him freely.

God's respect for the freedom of persons does not reflect unconcern on His part. He continues to show immense love and care even when His own creatures turn away from Him. Judas is addressed as "friend" even as he is about to betray Christ (cf. Matt. 26.50). God's mercy and goodness are constantly stressed in Scripture. "Bless the LORD, O my soul, and do not forget all His benefits — who forgives all your iniquity, who heals all your diseases, who redeems your life from the Pit, who crowns you with steadfast love and mercy, who satisfies you with good. . ." (Ps. 103.2-5).

Forever He is offering life. " 'Come.' And let everyone who hears say, 'Come.' And let everyone who is thirsty come. Let anyone who wishes take the water of life as a gift" (Rev. 22.17).

Significance of Doctrine of Creation

God's revelation of Himself as Creator provides a radical foundation for the humility one should have before God, and also for the respect we should have for the dignity of created reality.

Our Creaturely Status

Clearly it is folly to resist the One who has made us and who keeps us in existence. "Shall the ax vaunt itself over the one who wields it, or the saw magnify itself against the one who handles it? As if a rod should raise the one who lifts it up, or as if a staff should lift the one who is not wood" (Isa. 10.15).

We should have a bracing fear of God, founded on the recognition of reality. The book of Daniel teaches us this from the story of Nebuchadnezzar. When his pride turned him from God, he lost also his intelligence, and he learned that his intelligence could endure from the beginning to the end of one blasphemous sentence only by God's favor (cf. Dan. 4.29-34). So there was nothing for him to do but "praise and extol and honor the King of heaven; for all His works are truth and His ways are justice; and he is able to bring low those who walk in pride" (Dan. 4.37).

Dignity of Creation

God has created a real world. Though He creates out of nothing, He brings into existence enduring realities; He calls to being, and to participation in a plan that has eternal significance. "I know that whatever God does endures forever; nothing can be added to it, nor anything taken from it" (Eccle. 3.14).

It is real life, not play-acting, that goes on in this real world. The world of creation is crowned by and is to be subdued by free persons, persons whose free choices in creation will have significance for all eternity.

Those who see the world as a product of forces blind and unfree also see the world and the life in it as without real meaning, and themselves as without real freedom and without real hope. It is a far greater vision of human dignity that comes from faith's recognition that the Source of our being is indeed infinitely greater than all the forces of space and time. Our duty to salute God as Creator is also the honor of recognizing the sublime dignity of creation, which is indeed the fruit of eternal love.

Angels

"Countless hosts of angels stand before you to do your will; they look upon your splendor and praise you, night and day."[17]

God's creation extends to more than the visible creation. Scripture speaks also of the angels as His creatures. The faith of the Church recognizes the words of Scripture about angels as far more than figurative speech about God's providential care, and it knows that there really are purely spiritual persons made by God who rejoice to know Him and to share His life.[18]

Angels have frequent roles in the history of salvation, in both the Old Testament and the New. Though the number of angels is clearly large, Scripture gives us the names of only three of them: Raphael, Gabriel, and Michael. Christ speaks of the angels and their care. "Take care that you do not despise one of these little ones; for, I tell you, in heaven their angels continually see the face of My Father in heaven" (Matt. 18.10). "Do you think that I cannot appeal to My Father, and He will at once send Me more than twelve legions of angels?" (Matt. 26.53). In another passage we read that "angels came and waited on Him" (Matt. 4.11).

The angels are powerful realities. They are not impersonal forces,

---

[17]Roman Missal, Eucharistic Prayer IV.

[18]Cf., e.g., Fourth Lateran Council, November 1215, *The Catholic Faith* (DS 800); First Vatican Council, Session 3, April 24, 1870, *Dogmatic Constitution on the Catholic Faith*, ch. 1 (DS 3002); Pope Paul VI, *Professio Fidei* ("The Credo of the People of God," June 30, 1968) (EV 3.537-566).

but persons, spiritual beings of surpassing intelligence. Though we in fact know but little about them, they are instruments of God's providence for us in mighty but hidden ways. Hence the liturgy of the Church celebrates them in feasts, and in the daily Eucharistic sacrifice joins its worship to that of the angels. The liturgical celebration of angels recalls the Catholic belief that angels of God watch with care over each human person as agents of God's love. For this reason Catholics are encouraged to invoke the intercession of angels as they do that of the saints (cf. LG 50).[19]

[19]Cf. St. Thomas Aquinas, *Summa Theologica* I, 50-74.

4

Man and Woman — The Glory Of God

"What are human beings that You are mindful of them, mortals that You care for them?" (Ps. 8.4). Life is of itself a great mystery. "He often exalts himself as the absolute measure of all things or debases himself to the point of despair" (GS 12). Through art and industry the human family has worked wonders that delight the imagination; at the same time, human history is also a record of sin and sorrow, a series of relentless waves eroding human self-respect. Grandeur and misery, holiness and sin, hopes and fears mark the mystery of our reality. But Catholic faith proclaims that "all things on earth should be related to man as their center and crown" (GS 12). Even more, human life is touched by the love of God Himself. "Yet You have made them a little lower than God, and crowned them with glory and honor. You have given them dominion over the works of Your hands; You have put all things under their feet" (Ps. 8.5-6).

In this chapter we speak of each human person as the image of God, wonderful in body and soul, and of God's design in creating and in giving profound unity to the whole human race. We also speak of social nature and personal dignity of each human being, of how Christ reveals the meaning of our being, and of the tasks to which we are called.

The Image of God

As the first account of the creation of the world reaches a climax in the first chapter of Genesis, God is portrayed as creating man and woman as the crown and glory of all that He had made. "Then God said: 'Let us make humankind in our image, according to our likeness; and let them have dominion' " (Gen. 1.26). Much of Scripture, from the first poetic pages of Genesis that speak so many essential truths about humanity, to the Gospels, in which we learn in Christ most fully the secret of what we are, is an elucidation of the meaning of the human person. Since each human person is the "image of God," what we are told of God helps reveal to us what we are; what we see of humanity, schooled and aided by faith, teaches us of God.

Both in our individual being and in our social reality we mirror the God who made us.

Physical and Spiritual

Intimately joined in each living human being are physical reality and spiritual reality.

Made of the "dust of the ground" (Gen. 2.7), of the same elements of which the earth is shaped, the human person is the spokesperson and priest of all material reality. "Through his bodily composition he gathers to himself the elements of the material world. Thus these elements reach their crown through him, and through him raise their voice in free praise of God" (GS 14). We are essentially bodily creatures, and no one should be "allowed to despise his bodily life" (cf. GS 14). As the body of Christ is most holy to Christians, so is there also a sacredness in the bodily dimension of every human life.

But a human person is God's image more in one's specifically human qualities. It is the spiritual principle of each that makes one the living flesh that one is. It is this spiritual principle, or soul, that makes us open to understanding and love of the infinite Love who called us to life.

A human person is not composed of body and soul as though these were distinct beings, for a human person is not simply a soul which "has" a body. Body and soul make a single living person. The soul is not alien to the body, but the living principle that causes the body to be the human flesh it is — the flesh that must be dear to one and is part of our being. Christianity has no hatred of matter. It is a religion of incarnation. Our soul is not material, but it is created to give human life to a body, the body that with it makes up the living person.

The soul of a person does not exist before the body. God immediately creates each individual soul[1] at the coming to be of the living person. Nor is it one's destiny to live forever as simply a soul when death dissolves the body. True, the soul continues to exist as a spiritual reality after a person's death; and God calls one to Himself and sustains their being and joy in Him even before the final resurrection (cf. Phil. 1.23). But the salvation of a person is not the salvation of a soul only, but of a whole person, and it will be fulfilled only in the resurrection of the body, and in the life of fully living persons gathered together in the joy of the Lord.

Human Intelligence and Freedom

We are like God especially in the capacities that we have as persons. We mirror God in our intelligence, our concern for good and evil, our freedom, and our immortal destiny (cf. GS 15-17).

In our intelligence we are God's image. By human arts and technological skills we have wonderfully transformed the material world

[1]Cf. Pope Pius XII, Encyclical, *Humani Generis* (August 12, 1950) (DS 3896).

which God made and committed to humankind as its master (cf. Gen. 1.26). But we should prize wisdom even more than technology. In fact, the greater our technological power becomes, the more we need wisdom. Wisdom implies the ability to grasp the meaning of things, and to understand what is truly valuable. God made us able to ask questions, to philosophize, and to catch important insights into creation and its purposes. However, it is chiefly through revelation that God illumines our minds with the wisdom needed to shape the world wisely (cf. GS 15).

Our consciences also make us godlike. Unlike other living things, human persons have a restless concern for what is truly good and evil, however often we waver in that concern. "For man has in his heart a law written by God" (GS 16; cf. Rom. 2.15).

Our freedom, too, makes us like God, who is supremely free. Human nature is not driven simply by blind forces or instincts. We have responsibility and freedom. "If you choose, you can keep the commandments, and to act faithfully is a matter of your own choice" (Sir. 15.15). Even in our fallen state we retain this freedom to make our own choices, to act or not to act, to do this or to do that.[2]

Human freedom is not full and perfect as God's is. The pressures of circumstances can limit greatly a person's freedom and responsibility. Yet as long as a person has the power to live in a human way, one retains a measure of this freedom.

In creating the first human persons God also gave them another freedom, one which is restored to us by Christ. This is the freedom to live in God's friendship, and by the aid of grace to do the good things that one's heart longs for, and to fulfill one's divinely implanted longings.

Death and Immortality

No living things made of matter have personal knowledge of God, and none have immortality, except human beings. Obviously we are mortal. We do die. But we do not totally die. "And just as it is appointed for mortals to die once, and after that the judgment, . . ." (Heb. 9.27). What we call death is not a complete ceasing to be. Rather, it is a transition to another state of living. "Lord, for your faithful people life is changed, not ended."[3]

One who loves Christ at death does not find death utterly terrible. To die for Christ is "to depart and be with Christ" (Phil. 1.23). Nevertheless, death is a great enemy that we naturally fear and hate. Though our soul survives death and can be with the Lord, it is not good for us

---

[2]Cf. Council of Trent, Session 6, January 13, 1547, *Decree on Justification*, ch. 1 (DS 1521). Cf. also St. Thomas Aquinas, *Summa Theologica* I-II, prologue.

[3]Roman Missal, Preface I used in Masses for the dead.

to lose that flesh which is part of what we are. Our immortality is not merely that of the soul, but also that of the body in eternal life in the resurrection, when "death has been swallowed up in victory" (1 Cor. 15.54).

Each of us is like God in being destined to live forever. This is one reason why every human person, however young or old, however useless or limited in terms of worldly possibilities, is to be treated with great reverence.[4]

"Saving One's Soul"

In much Catholic pastoral and devotional writing the expression "to save one's soul" is extremely common (cf. Matt. 16.26). In the Epistles of St. Paul the "flesh" is often opposed to the "spirit." We are not to live "according to the flesh," but by the spirit (cf. Rom. 8.13).

"Flesh" is used in Scripture in various senses. Sometimes it is spoken of as a principle to be opposed. In these cases and others it is more than a person's physical reality. It is a person as we know him or her, a person in one's sinful state. In other passages "flesh" stands simply for the whole of human nature, body and soul. Thus, the Word of God "became flesh" (John 1.14), that is, became human with a human body and a human soul.

"Saving one's soul" has the meaning of saving oneself entirely, saving one's total self for eternal life. Care for one's soul is not nurturing some inner part of oneself, but rather care for one's whole being by nurturing love of God and neighbor, and by responding to the graces that enable one to have that friendship in God that blossoms into eternal life. One reaches full salvation only when body and soul together are joined in the joy of the resurrection, when the family of God rejoices before Him in eternal life.

Our Social Nature

We are images of God not merely in our personal and individual being, but also in our social nature, and in the love which binds one to another. God is a Trinity of Persons bound in mutual love, and He did not make human persons to be solitary. "It is not good that the man should be alone" (Gen. 2.18). There is a "certain likeness between the

---

[4]Congregation for the Doctrine of the Faith, *Letter on Certain Questions concerning Eschatology*, (May 17, 1979) n. 3 (EV 6.1539): "The Church affirms that a spiritual element survives and subsists after death, an element endowed with consciousness and will, so that the 'human self' subsists. To designate this element, the Church uses the word 'soul,' the accepted term on the usage of Scripture and Tradition. Although not unaware that this term has various meanings in the Bible, the Church thinks that there is no valid reason for rejecting it; moreover, she considers that the use of some word as a vehicle is absolutely indispensable in order to support the faith of Christians."

union of the divine Persons and the union of God's sons in truth and charity" (GS 24).

What our human nature is, is revealed also in the inclination God has given us to enter into various communities, first the family, and then other forms of community.

Male and Female

The Genesis account of human origins, with much subsequent revelation, proclaims the divine origin and sacredness of human sexuality and its purposes, the divine institution of marriage, and the dignity and nobility of woman, who had been degraded in so many societies of fallen humankind.

Genesis, stressing the great unity of the human family, presents the image of Eve, the first woman, as being formed by God from the very flesh of Adam (cf. Gen. 2.21-22).

Scripture stresses the equality and complementarity of man and woman. They complete each other, relieving the loneliness of the human condition. They see each other as equals, so that in marriage they may become deeply one. Marriage ought to be monogamous: one man and one woman are to become one in it. Such is the vision of Genesis (cf. Gen. 2.23-24). Christ the Lord appeals to this when He declares that divorce is wrong, contrary to the will expressed by the Creator from the beginning (cf. Matt. 19.4-9).

Man and Woman in Society

To become more fully what we are, to develop our powers and our possibilities, we need to live in social friendship and cooperation with fellow humans. "Social life is not something added on to man. Hence, through his dealings with others, through reciprocal duties, and through fraternal dialogue he develops all his gifts and is able to rise to his destiny" (GS 25).

In social life and the pursuit of the common good, the dignity and worth of each person must always be remembered. Individuals must make sacrifices for the common welfare, but the personal dignity of no person may be assailed or violated for any social good whatever. For societies exist to ennoble and enrich persons; persons are not mere means by which societies reach desired ends (cf. GS 75).

Created in Harmony

Scripture tells us little about the condition of human beings in the springtime of their creation. The creation account in Genesis is not scientific anthropology, nor is it a record put down shortly after the events occurred. Scientific evidence indicates that men and women were on earth perhaps tens or hundreds of thousands of years before the story of creation was written.

The purpose of the Genesis account of creation is to tell us certain truths that help us to understand the essentials of the human condition. For example, the evils we experience, revelation instructs us, were not inevitable. Human misery is not to be explained by saying that an evolving world must have deep and mysterious pain. Nor was human misery part of God's original design for us. Rather, much of the discord and pain is the fruit of the first human sin and subsequent deliberate sin. This is not a pessimistic view. On the contrary, viewed in the light of redemption, it points toward vast hope.

Christ and Creation

We were not made to be only images of God, knowing and honoring Him indirectly, learning of Him through things He had made. From the very beginning it was God's plan that human persons should become His children by adoption and share the richness of the life of the Trinity.

Christ was already foreshadowed at the very beginning of human history. The first parents of our race were created in grace, so sharing in Christ's sonship that the Son "might be the firstborn within a large family" (Rom. 8.29). Christ, who was to gather together all God's human children into the unity of His Mystical Body, that is, the Church, is the "firstborn of all creation" (Col. 1.15), the first in rank in God's plan. It was because of what the world was to become that all things were made. Adam, as the first man, is in one sense a type and image of Christ; but Christ is absolutely first in the divine plan, in dignity, and in the richness of all that human beings can be.

"Christ, the final Adam, . . . fully reveals man to man himself and makes his supreme calling clear" (GS 22). By the perfection of the human life He lived, He reveals to us what a human person is and can be. In Him humanity is seen in its most perfect state. He as man is a model for every human life (cf. Matt. 11.29). In the gift of His Spirit calling us to divine life, Christ helps us to understand the greatness of the human vocation (cf. GS 22).

Created in Holiness

The first parents of mankind were created in that grace which made them share in the divine sonship. There is much about the first parents we do not know. They may have been very much underdeveloped in their natural human endowments. But the first parents were made in a certain universal harmony: grace and virtues bound them in peaceful friendship with God; their hearts were at peace, with no inner turmoil, which has been called concupiscence, thrusting them toward evil; they were at peace with the world and possessed special gifts of God that were appropriate to their grace and innocence.[5]

By nature, of course, they were as material creatures subject to the dissolution of death and to the pains and afflictions our state suggests. But they were friends of God, and God would have kept each of them "immune from bodily death had he not sinned" (GS 18).[6] In their innocence, prior to their sin, God guarded them also from the suffering and anxiety that are the fruit of sin. They had a peaceful self-possession that gave them a wisdom suited to their state.

These things are taught us to assure us that the sorrows of humanity are not what would have been had our first parents remained faithful to God, and that when Christ's redeeming work has brought forth all its fruit, sorrows will be no more. The tears of Christ at the tomb of Lazarus (cf. John 11.35) are signs of divine compassion for the sorrows that have come upon men and women as a result of human malice, not as part of the original will of their Maker.[7] However primitive and simple life may have been before sin, it was a life deeply at peace.

Creatures and the Creator

Human persons at peace and in friendship with God have both a grandeur and an awareness of their own status as creature. The first pages of Genesis speak of the nearness of man and woman to God, and of God's care for them, and also of the obedience God demanded of them. As Lord and Author of life, God gives them commands of life (cf. Gen. 2).

Nothing is more honorable for a person than to recognize the reality of God and the truth of the relationships one has to God. For God is the source of all he or she is and possesses. All the possibilities of life and friendship, all the limitless scope of what one can become, depend utterly upon God. But God is generous, and He invites us to the greatest of hopes. We are called to share the divine life, to inherit the fullness of everything that is.

Prideful refusal to acknowledge God does not exalt anyone. Such refusal requires one to distort truth, to deny the goodness which alone

---

[5]Cf. Council of Trent, Session 5, June 17, 1546, *Decree on Original Sin 1* (DS 1511) and 5 (DS 1515); Council of Orange, 529, canons 1 (DS 371) and 19 (DS 389); Pope Paul V, Bull, *Ex Omnibus Afflictionibus* (October 1, 1967) (DS 1926). Cf. also GS 13.

[6]Cf. also Council of Trent, Session 5, June 17, 1546, *Decree on Original Sin 1* (DS 1511).

[7]Cf. John Henry Cardinal Newman. "Tears of Christ at the Grave of Lazarus," in *Parochial and Plain Sermons* (San Francisco, Ignatius Press, 1987) p. 564.

gives hope. Nothing is more foolish than to resist God, to rebel against Him who is infinitely powerful and from whose might we have whatever strength and being we have. In the one who salutes God's glory and gives thanks for the splendor He has given and wills to give each one, there is a greatness of soul built on truth. The proud man or woman is not a noble rebel striking out against forces that would humiliate his or her spirit. Rather, such a person is a ridiculous and mean spirit. Against a Love who calls one to possess everything, one prefers the emptiness of a lie, a pretense that one whose whole reality is a fruit of Love and a call to Love could root oneself on something other than God, that is, on the nothingness one would be without the divine gift.

The Tasks of Creatures

We were created to "have dominion" over the earth and to "subdue it" (Gen. 1.26, 28). As it was not beneath God's dignity to create a material universe, so it is not beneath us to master it with the skills of our science and technology, with the beauty of our art and imagination. The whole work of technology, while it can become inhuman and cruel if not subjected to wisdom, is a part of the human mission, and has a value to be respected. The service it gives to human persons, the enrichment of life it makes possible, is something willed by God for wise use. Suffering and death are punishments for sin, but humankind was called to work even in the blessed state before the fall. Creative work gives us great dignity and those who have power to shape society should make all human labor as creative as possible.

All material reality and all human work are to serve the good of persons. Our task is even more to make human lives that are rich and good, human lives that mirror God on earth. We are made to serve God and to glorify Him on earth. This does not mean that we are to satisfy God's needs. God has no needs, and certainly we have no resources that would enrich Him. But we can glorify Him by allowing the abundance of His goodness to shine in us and in the life we build with our brothers and sisters. God seeks His glory, and wishes His glory to be sought on earth, not for His sake but for ours.[8] For this is His glory: that His children grow in love and in every precious gift before Him.

Our task is also to prepare ourselves to enter the blessed vision of God, that is, to live with God in the infinite riches of His life. We might sometimes wonder why God did not create us from the start in the blessedness of heaven. Why are there all the labors of time? Why the pain and tears that mar human history? We are overwhelmed by

8Cf. St. Thomas Aquinas, *Summa Theologica* II-II, 132, 1 ad 1.

the mystery of evil. Christian faith sheds much light on this mystery, as it speaks of sin, of Christ's cross, and of the meaning of love, but it does not dissolve the mystery.

Still, there is much that is understandable in God's will to make us first live in a life that is a time of trial and free service of Him. God loves freedom; and God loves to give people the glory of being causes of the good things that flow from His own mercy. In our lives He blesses us most of all with the ability to do and to act in ways that are holy and generous. The richest gift He gives His people is the gift to do freely what is good — to mirror Him in not merely being good but in causing good.

So God wishes us not merely to enjoy eternal life, but to do the deeds that, by His mercy, merit it. It is His will that when we rejoice before Him in the beatific vision we stand with Jesus in the glory of God's free sons who love Him and love one another because we have chosen to.

Thus part of our vocation is to take responsibility for this world and make it a presence of God's kingdom, and so to become worthy of dwelling with Him forever. Our vocation is to acknowledge our own status as creatures and our God-given glory.[9] It is to grow into the humility and magnanimity of Mary, the mother of Jesus, who realized so fully what she was: "My soul magnifies the Lord, and my spirit rejoices in God my Savior, for He has looked with favor on the lowliness of His servant. Surely, from now on all generations will call me blessed; for the Mighty One has done great things for me, and holy is His name" (Luke 1.47-49).

---

[9]Pope John Paul II, Encyclical, *Laborem Exercens* (September 14, 1981) nn. 1 and 25 (EV 7.1389-1392, 1498-1503).

5

Our Sin And The Faithfulness of God

"God saw everything that He had made, and indeed, it was very good" (Gen. 1.31). Revelation teaches that God made us rightly (cf. Eccle. 7.30), but that we brought upon ourselves a multitude of evils. Seeing so many of the evils that flow from our sinful condition, some have grown weary and bitter and have criticized God and complained of His ways, or have even denied Him (cf. GS 19).

In this chapter we speak first of the mystery of evil, and of how our personal sins and those of the fallen angels touch upon it. We then speak of how God promised a Redeemer, and of how in the old covenant God sustained the hopes for redemption, the redemption which Christ came to work. For it is "through Christ and in Christ" that "the riddle of sorrow and death is illumined" (GS 22).

The Mystery of Evil

Human history is heavily marked with suffering and grief. Much of Sacred Scripture itself is a record of human sorrow.[1] Though the books of Scripture recall the vast mercies of God and are the source of boundless hope and confidence in Him, they are also starkly realistic in noting the tragedies and afflictions the flesh is heir to.

But the Scriptures remind us that God does not love human suffering. The person of faith knows that God is infinitely good, that He wills and causes endless blessings for us, and that He does not will any evil at all as such or for its own sake. God does allow evil to be done, and does justly inflict punishments, but this is always in the service of a greater good.

When Scripture teaches us that "good things and bad, life and death, poverty and wealth, come from the Lord" (Sir. 11.14), it is reminding us that all things are subject to the providence of God. When Scripture tells us that "God did not make death, and He does not delight in the death of the living" (Wisd. 1.13), it is pointing out that the infinitely good God does not take pleasure in the sorrows that He is His wisdom and mercy permits. God may indeed cause punishments or other purely physical evils for the sake of the greater goods He wills

[1]Cf. John Henry Cardinal Newman, "Scripture a Record of Human Sorrow" in *Parochial and Plain Sermons* (San Francisco, Ignatius Press, 1987), vol. 1, pp. 206-212.

for us, and without His creative and sustaining powers no bad deed could be done; but never does He will or cause any moral evil or sin.[2]

Human Reactions

Sensitivity toward the pains and afflictions of others is commonly a sign of a generous heart. The saints have shared Christ's response to evil. Like Him they have had great compassion on persons who suffer (cf. Matt. 15.32) and have wept over the folly and sins of the human family (cf. Luke 19.41-44). They have been tireless in imitating Jesus, who in a world of many ills "went about doing good" (Acts 10.38). Those who thus share with deep feeling the sufferings and losses of so many are supported by their confident trust in Him who wishes us to care even in circumstances which may seem at times hopeless. For He will sustain those who care until the day when He will "wipe away every tear" (Rev. 7.17) from the eyes of those who have suffered but have yet continued to call out to Him.

Not all of us react to ills and sufferings the same way. More than a few persons have cited the presence of evil in this world as their reason for denying the very existence of God (cf. GS 19). Some indeed are so pressed by their sorrows that they feel tragically driven toward rebellion against their Lord. Others, however, use the pain they experience or observe as a facile pretext for unbelief. With specious logic they argue that if God were all-powerful He could remove the world's sorrows, and if He were infinitely good He would want to do this, but there is in fact an ocean of sorrows in the world, and therefore there cannot be an all-powerful, all-good God who is its Lord.

The Example of Job

The problem of evil is deeply explored in the Old Testament, above all in the book of Job. There Job is portrayed as an innocent person who suffers great reverses and affliction. He loses all his possessions, his health and his peace, and even all his loved ones. Though friends come to console him, many of their words are shallow and useless.

It is of course foolish to tell those in great pain that their pain is "all for the best," as though every evil were really directly wanted by God and therefore "secretly a blessing." Revelation does not teach that. Much suffering in this world comes from deeds of malice which are not good, deeds which God hates and forbids — though, mysteriously, He permits them, and then makes even them serve His good purposes.

It is also not right to say that those who suffer much are those who

[2]Cf. Council of Trent, Session 6, January 13, 1547, *Decree on Justification*, canon 6 (DS 1556).

have sinned much, and therefore they deserve to suffer (cf. Job. 4.7). When Jesus was asked by His disciples about a man who had been blind from birth, whether it was his sin or that of his parents that caused him to be born blind, Jesus answered: "Neither this man nor his parents sinned; he was born blind so that God's works might be revealed in him" (John 9.3). And Jesus then cured the man of his blindness (cf. John 9.6-7).

Job complains that the evils he bears are a stark mystery, while his friends have easy answers. And the divine response at the end is that it is Job who is right. Or, rather, more nearly right, for Job in his sorrows did not sufficiently reverence God's mysterious ways, assumed too readily that his own view of justice was entirely right, and thought he saw some edge of unfairness in God. So God is portrayed as asking Job questions in response to the complaining questions Job had put to Him.

"Who is this that darkens counsel by words without knowledge? Gird up your loins like a man, I will question you, and you shall declare to me. Where were you when I laid the foundation of the earth? . . ." (Job 38.2-4). Job, fundamentally good, sees God's concern and recalls that he really knows God is righteous, though He dwells in mystery, and Job replies to God: "See, I am of small account; what shall I answer You? . . . I know that You can do all things, and that no purpose of Yours can be thwarted. . . . I have uttered what I did not understand, things too wonderful for me, which I did not know. . . . I had heard of You by the hearing of the ear, but now my eye sees You; therefore I despise myself, and repent in dust and ashes" (Job 40.4, 42.2-6). God then blesses Job for all his sufferings, and He reproaches the false apologists: "You have not spoken of Me what is right, as My servant Job has" (Job 42.7).

Those who complain of God with none of Job's patience, who blaspheme God because of the pain they experience or see, may also be called to account by divine questioning. They claim for themselves a perspective and knowledge they do not and cannot have. They suggest in effect that they know the nature of the whole world and all its workings, and that they are able to fathom the mysterious plans and infinite nature of God. They say there could be no evil in the world if there were a God almighty and good. But where do they get the insight and wisdom they claim? "For who can learn the counsel of God? Or who can discern what the Lord wills?" (Wisd. 9.13).

God in His omnipotence could have made a world in which no pain or evil of any sort was tolerated. Might not such a world, however, have been less rich than this world He has made? Could there be a world with certain great goods we find in ours, a world of persons, freedom, love, generosity, forgiveness, hope, courage, if an almighty force made it impossible for anyone to do or to suffer any harm whatsoever? Could there really have been the kind of freedom we have, and the nobility of the best human characters, if no evil whatever had been tolerated?

God's questions to Job (cf. Job 38-41) are answers to the atheist's exploitation of the mystery of evil. People who would claim to understand the mystery of everything are deluding themselves or have lost perspective. There is in fact much that none of us is able to know.

Perhaps some of the good things God wills to be in this world could not be here without a real risk of genuine evils. The God who gives men freedom "neither wills evil to be done nor wills evil not to be done, but He wills to permit evil to be done, and this is a good."[3]

And when evils are brought into creation through abuses of the freedom God gives to us, He promises to turn even this toward good. "We know that all things work together for good for those who love God" (Rom 8.28). An illustration of this is the central event of salvation history: God forbade the malice of His enemies, the treachery of Judas, and the sins of all the world — and yet the bitter passion which resulted from all these was at the same time the greatest act of love and generosity ever known, and was the redemption of the world.

Light from Christ's Life

The problem of evil is a living problem. Those with sensitive hearts, who care that people not be broken, see blasphemy as no solution at all. The evils of the world can be endured with intelligent hope only by those who discover also the mercy of a God great enough to heal the wounds of all.

The problem of evil is illumined by the life of Christ. It is illumined for one thing by His tears and compassion. Many have felt that pains and sorrows are a sign of God's absence. When Jesus came to the tomb of His friend Lazarus, Martha said to Him: "Lord, if You had been here, my brother would not have died" (John 11.21). "Men have seen sin and misery around them, and whether in faith or unbelief, have said, 'If Thou hadst been here,' if Thou hadst interfered, it might have been otherwise. Here then was the Creator surrounded by the work of His hands, who adored Him indeed, yet seemed to ask why He suffered what He Himself had made to be so marred."[4] Jesus did not answer Martha in words, did not seek to voice what no language can speak. Instead, He, the Lord of all, in the presence of His creatures, revealed His heart: "Jesus began to weep" (John 11.35).

Foolish indeed are those who would curse their Creator and blas-

---

[3]St. Thomas Aquinas, *Summa Theologica* I, 19,9 ad 3, quoted in Pope Leo XIII, Encyclical, *Libertas Praestantissimum* (June 20, 1888) (DS 3251).
[4]John Henry Cardinal Newman, "Tears of Christ at the Grave of Lazarus" in *Parochial and Plain Sermons* (San Francisco, Ignatius Press, 1987), vol. 3, p. 564.

pheme Him, as though in the peace of heaven He does not care about the bruises and wounds of the frail and helpless. The life of Jesus, the whole mystery of the incarnation, is the revelation of God's earnest will to share and to heal the suffering of all. The Son of God underwent evil to overcome evil. In His passion, Christ in His humanity endured for us humiliation and abuse, loneliness, dread, anguish, and great physical pain. Not only does He wish everyone in pain in some way to have a fellow Sufferer who is able to heal those who turn to Him, but in this, as in all things, He reveals the inner heart of God eternal: God's compassion is always with us.

Evil is real in the world. We are not able to heal all of it in this life. Now God Himself is the Consoler, and in Him we can begin to grasp something of the mystery. He does not cause any moral evil, nor does He will or permit evils for their own sake. He made the world good, but free and vulnerable, and vulnerable only that it might have glorious possibilities. When evil entered the world against His command, He showed Himself to be the saving God: He draws overwhelming good out of the evil done.[5]

But it is necessary to reflect on how evil entered the world: in the malice of human persons and the work of Satan.

Sin

God created the first man and woman in a state of holiness, freedom, and peace. They deliberately sinned, and brought great sorrows on themselves and all their descendants.

"Although he was made by God in a state of holiness, from the very dawn of history man abused his liberty, at the urging of the Evil One. Man set himself against God, and sought to find his fulfillment apart from God" (GS 13). "Affected by original sin, men have frequently fallen into multiple errors concerning the true God, the nature of man, and the principles of the moral law. The result has been the corruption of morals and human institutions and not rarely contempt for the human person himself" (AA 7).

Original Sin

The account of the fall in the book of Genesis (cf. Gen. 3) presents the deep truth of the first human rebellion against God in language somewhat figurative in its details. We do not know the exact nature of the first human sin. Scripture suggests that the malice of that sin lay chiefly in its elements of pride and disobedience (cf. Gen. 3; Sir. 10.15; Rom. 5.12-14).

---

[5]Cf. Pope John Paul II, Encyclical, *Salvifici Doloris* ("On the Christian Meaning of Human Suffering," February 11, 1984) nn. 5-13 (EV 9.624-636).

The sin of Adam was in him an actual sin. He of his own free will did something he knew was in opposition to God's will. His sin, however, has affected all his descendants, the whole human family. "Therefore, just as sin came into the world through one man and death came through sin, and so death spread to all because all have sinned" (Rom. 5.12).

Basing its teaching firmly on Scripture (esp. Rom. 5.12-19), the Church teaches[6] that from Adam original sin has been transmitted to all. Not only do people tend to imitate the sinfulness that surrounds them, but each individual is born in a condition of sin, and can be freed from that condition only by the merits of Jesus Christ.

The original sin each person inherits is not an actual sin he or she personally commits. Rather, "it is human nature so fallen, stripped of the grace that clothed it, injured in its own natural powers and subjected to the dominion of death, that is transmitted to all men, and it is in this sense that every man is born in sin."[7]

The transmission of original sin means that each descendant of Adam is created without sanctifying grace, and without the special gifts that had accompanied that grace. Thus the entire human race, each person, has been wounded by original sin.

Universal human experience confirms the teaching that we are born in a sinful state. "Examining his heart, man finds that he has inclinations toward evil too, and is engulfed by manifold ills which cannot come from his good Creator. Often refusing to acknowledge God as his beginning, man has disrupted also his proper relationship to his own ultimate goal, as well as his whole orientation toward himself, toward others, and toward all created things. Therefore, man is split within himself" (GS 13).

Divine Justice

God is just. Scripture teaches that no one is to be punished because of the sins of his or her parents; it is for his or her own sins that a person incurs punishment (cf. Jer. 31.29-30). Original sin weakens us and inclines us to sin, but it is not personal sin in the descendants of Adam. Those who die in original sin, but without having committed any personal grave sins, will not suffer the pain of damnation for that.[8]

The losses that we have incurred as a result of original sin are not losses of anything due to man by right. These losses, then, are not an unfair chastisement by God. The gift of intimate, grace-stirred friendship with the Lord is more than human nature could expect on

[6]Cf. Council of Trent, Session 5, June 17, 1546, *Decree on Original Sin* (DS 1510-1516).
[7]Pope Paul VI, *Professio Fidei* ("The Credo of the People of God," June 30, 1968).
[8]Cf. Pope Innocent III, *Letter* to Ymbertus (1201) (DS 780); Pope Pius VI, Constitution, *Auctorem Fidei* (August 28, 1794) (DS 2626).

its own. Freedom from death and from the sufferings that seem to flow from our creaturely state is no clear right of ours. That we have been created at all, and have been given hope, is God's great mercy, the Creator's own free gifts to us.

Human Freedom and Responsibility

The many sorrows of human life are by no means the fruit of original sin alone. In fact, the most severe and unbearable of human evils are the fruit of our continued deliberate sins. There is special bitterness in the free and malicious hatreds, betrayals, and ingratitudes of life.

The history of the world is a record of sorrows, of sorrows arising from evils that need not have been. Our sins are not predetermined and inevitable. God gives us freedom, and it is we who choose to abuse that gift by sinning. "No one, when tempted, should say, 'I am being tempted by God'; for God cannot be tempted by evil and He Himself tempts no one" (James 1.13). Rather, God offers the help that makes resistance to temptation possible. God "will not let you be tested beyond your strength, but with the testing He will also provide the way out so that you may be able to endure it" (1 Cor. 10.13). Trials may be too great for our strength, but they are not too great for His; and we can draw upon His strength if we invoke Him. He remains present to us, a Father who cares, ready to fortify us, if we wish to respond to Him, against the terrible tragedy of doing evil, which is far worse than suffering it.

The meaning of responsibility, the gravity of sin, and something of the ways of God are revealed to us in humankind's fallen state. The result of Adam's sin makes clear how sinful failure to accept responsibility is a matter of far greater importance than we might otherwise have imagined. It reveals how God is a strong and just God, a God who is serious about the freedom and responsibility He gives to us.

Yet the whole account of original sin reveals even more the immensity of God's mercy. Though God allowed sorrows to come to us because of our sin, His permission of evil involved a plan in which the latter state of humankind would be better than the first. The redemption would be overabundant (cf. Rom. 5.15-17). Christ's redemptive love on the cross was to be a gift of such overflowing richness that it would lighten the whole burden of sin. The Church, in its liturgy for the vigil of Easter, even allows itself to sing of that first human sin: "O happy fault, O necessary sin of Adam, which gained for us so great a Redeemer!"[9]

One can sin only by freely choosing to do so. God did not make us in such a way that we would have to sin. It is true that in the cir-

[9]Roman Missal, Easter Proclamation (*Exsultet*).

cumstances of life we are subjected to many kinds of influence and pressure; even in the first sin Adam was incited toward evil by Satan (cf. GS 13; Gen. 1.1-5). These pressures and influences on us, however, are only obstacles to freedom, not exclusions of it. We do not have perfect freedom, as also we do not have perfect intelligence or perfect power. Nonetheless, God has given us sufficient insight and freedom to make us responsible in many of our acts. We choose to act or not to act, and by choosing determine our own ultimate fate. "If you choose, you can keep the commandments. . . . Before each person are life and death, and whichever one chooses will be given" (Sir. 15.15, 17).

The Devil

"Discipline yourselves, keep alert. Like a roaring lion your adversary the devil prowls around, looking for someone to devour" (1 Peter 5.8). That fallen spirits, like fallen humans, really exist and behave maliciously in this world is a teaching drawn from Scripture (cf., e.g., Luke 8.29-20; John 8.44; Rev. 12.7-9) and faithfully taught by the Church.

The Church does not teach terror of Satan. It commends only a holy fear of God, and a fear of deliberately doing evil. For the influence of Satan is decisively subordinated to the power of God. As the Second Vatican Council recalled time and again, Christ "has freed us from the power of Satan" (SC 6; cf. GS 2, 22; AG 3, 9). Because of Christ's redemptive work, the devil can genuinely harm only those who freely permit this to be done.

The Gospels speak of diabolical possession; they show Christ casting out demons and instructing His apostles to do the same (cf. Matt. 17.18; Luke 9.1-2). Far more serious than the physical harm Satan might do, however, is the moral harm. Scripture portrays Satan also as a source of temptation (cf. Gen. 3.1-5; Matt. 4.1-11). Satan is "the treacherous and cunning enchanter, who finds his way into us by way of the senses, the imagination, lust, utopian logic, or disorderly social contacts in the give and take of life, to introduce deviations. . . ."[10]

World history itself is influenced by the devil. Indeed, "a difficult struggle against the powers of darkness pervades the whole history of man; the battle was joined from the very origins of the world and will continue until the last day, as the Lord has attested (cf. Matt. 24.13; 13.24-30, 36-43)" (GS 37). "For our struggle is not against enemies of blood and flesh," says St. Paul, "but against the authorities, against the cosmic powers of this present darkness, against the spiritual forces of evil in the heavenly places" (Eph. 6.12).

Anyone sensitive to the profound and bitter depths of the mystery

---

[10]Pope Paul VI, *Address* during General Audience, November 15, 1972.

of evil can hardly be inclined to a superficial optimism, that is, to a belief that evil in the world is merely an incidental flaw in a world ever evolving toward better days. There are traces of deep malice that puzzle us. The dark mystery of Satan is that there are personal agents in the universe, poorly known to us, malicious and always ready to do evil, irrevocably alienated from God and hostile to Him (cf. Matt. 25.41). That human history is often marked by sad and irrational currents is partly due to such influences.

God remains the Lord of all. Whatever power the devils have is limited by His providence. Ultimately, all things are made to redound to the good of those who love God (cf. Rom. 8.28). Satan and the other fallen spirits are themselves mere creatures. God made them, though He did not make them to be evil or to be sources of evil. "For the devil and the other demons were created by God good by nature, but they of themselves became bad."[11]

The pattern persists. God made all things good. He forbade malice and selfishness, but He made persons free, and He does not force anyone to be loyal to Him. Those who selfishly resist God pervert themselves and bring evil into the universe. God permits this evil, not because He is helpless, but because He, the Almighty, loves freedom. He is able to draw a greater good out of every kind of evil — such greater good as loyalty in the face of hardship, patience, and charity made perfect in bitter trials.

The Faithfulness of God

The first man sinned, and his descendants have followed him in sin, but God remains merciful. "If we are faithless, He remains faithful — for He cannot deny Himself" (2 Tim. 2.13). The Church rejoices in the faithful mercy of God:

> Even when he (man) disobeyed you and lost your friendship you did not abandon him to the power of death, but helped all men to seek and find you.
> Again and again you offered a covenant to man, and through the prophets taught him to hope for salvation.[12]

The account in Genesis of the first human sin concludes with a foretelling of a divine redemption. God is portrayed there addressing the tempter: "I will put enmity between you and the woman, and between your offspring and hers; he will strike your head, and you will strike his heel" (Gen. 3.15). The faith of the Church has seen in these

[11]Fourth Lateran Council, November 1215, *The Catholic Faith* (DS 800).
[12]Roman Missal, Fourth Eucharistic Prayer.

words the first of the prophecies that Christ would come to save us (cf. LG 55; DV 3). Jesus is the "offspring" of the woman (cf. also Gal. 3.16), and "the Son of God was revealed for his purpose, to destroy the works of the devil" (1 John 3.8).

Through the ages of salvation history preceding Christ, God repeatedly called all to repentance, to renewed greatness, and to salvation. He never forgets that it was He who had made us, and He made us not only to be His creature but also to share in His own divine life and friendship. Repeatedly He speaks of His love for His chosen people as that of a faithful husband for his wife, a love that endures even if the wife is unfaithful; His is an unfathomable and eternal love that will at length lead her to faithfulness. "Therefore, I will now allure her ... and speak tenderly to her ... she will respond as in the days of her youth. ... And I will take you for my wife forever; I will take you for my wife in righteousness and in justice, in steadfast love, and in mercy" (Hos. 2.14-15, 19).

Promises of the Covenant

"In carefully planning and preparing the salvation of the whole human race, the God of supreme love, by a special dispensation, chose for Himself a people to whom He might entrust His promises. First He entered into a covenant with Abraham (cf. Gen. 15.18) and, through Moses, with the people of Israel (cf. Exod. 24.8)" (DV 14). In this covenant God pledged Himself to care for them and to save them; He required them in return to pledge themselves to faithfulness to Him.

After He had brought the Israelites out of the slavery of Egypt, God told them through Moses: "You have seen ... how I bore you on eagles' wings and brought you to Myself. Now therefore, if you obey My voice and keep My covenant, you shall be My treasured possession out of all peoples" (Exod. 19.4-5). And when Moses had "set before them all these words which the LORD had commanded him" to tell them, "all the people answered together and said, 'All that the LORD has spoken we will do' " (Exod. 19.7-8). Repeatedly, however, they and their descendants fell into sin, and experienced the sorrows and the punishment sin entails. But God's constant mercy made repentance possible, and God renewed the covenant again and again: with Joshua (cf. Jos. 8.30-35; 24.1-28), with David (cf. Ps. 89.4-5; 2 Sam. 7.8-16), at the time of Ezra (cf. Neh. 8).

God's covenants with His people are a sign of the freedom and the richness of His love. By these covenants the Lord of all creation freely binds Himself to His creatures. He enters into covenants with those whom He freely chooses to bless with special mercies. At the same time, however, His love remains universal: it is directed toward all. Even to those most specially chosen He makes it clear that they are chosen to be the ones by whom He wills to bring salvation to all. Thus He said to Abraham: "I will indeed bless you ... and by your offspring shall all the nations of the earth gain blessing for themselves" (Gen. 22.17-18).

Teaching of the Prophets

Through the prophets He sent, God taught His people how to live as they awaited His redeeming mercy. "With God Himself speaking to them through the mouth of the prophets, Israel daily gained a deeper and clearer understanding of His ways" (DV 14). These prophets were not merely sincere and fervent. They were God's people through whom God Himself spoke. God had called them, and He was able to make others recognize them as His prophets. The words of the prophets were not always accepted, however, for they demanded personal faith and inner conversion, and they insisted on faithfulness to all of God's law.

The prophets taught that all should hope for the salvation the Messiah would bring. Indeed, the Gospel Christ was to commission the apostles to preach was "promised in former times through the prophets" (DV 7). Thus the prophets of old spoke of the saving mercy to come, the good tidings of Christ who already was the salvation of those who faithfully awaited their Savior. The salvation of these is mentioned in the New Testament, in the Epistle to the Hebrews, where it says of those who were blessed with faith in the Old Testament era: "All of those died in faith without having received the promises, but from a distance they saw and greeted them ... Therefore God is not ashamed to be called their God; indeed He has prepared a city for them" (Heb. 11.13, 16).

Since the earliest days of the Church the fulfillment of Old Testament prophecies has led people toward faith or confirmed belief. This fulfillment is not merely the occurrence in Christ's life of details foretold by the prophets. The whole of the Old Testament, all its promises and expectations are seen as fulfilled in Christ. The fulfillment goes far beyond the expectations; one could not have painted in detail the mystery of Christ from the Old Testament promises. But when in the light of Christ's coming one looks back to the Old Testament, one sees how superabundantly all the hopes and promises are fulfilled in Him.

There is, to be sure, a certain obscurity in prophecy, for prophecy speaks of a mystery and addresses faith. Moreover, the language of the prophets is often the language of symbols and poetic imagery. Even so, in the centuries before Christ's coming the prophetic promises of that event confirmed God's people in hope, and at the time of that coming bore witness to Christ (cf. John 5.46). The Church teaches that the Old Testament prophecies of Christ, like Jesus' own prophecies in the Gospels, are "most certain signs of divine revelation."[13]

Preparation of the Nations

Among the pagan nations as well God kept alive the hope for salvation, and Christ brought salvation to many who did not even know His name. Through the natural gifts of the various cultures, as through the philosophy by which some of the Greeks came to speak many sublime truths about God, God was preparing the world for the advent of His Son and for the spreading of His Gospel. A saving God was able to make such gifts minister to grace and salvation. "All things necessary and profitable to life come to us from God, and philosophy more especially given to the Greeks, as a covenant peculiar to them, being, as it were, a stepping-stone to the philosophy which is according to Christ."[14]

This divine work of preparation continues even today, for there are still many who do not know Christ and His message, and some who have not yet arrived at an explicit knowledge of God. Thanks to His grace, these too can attain salvation if they strive in their lives to do what is right according to the dictates of their conscience. "Whatever of goodness and truth is found among them is looked upon by the Church as preparation for the Gospel, and as given by Him who enlightens all men so that they may finally have life" (LG 16).

Old Testament and New

Catholics are encouraged to read and meditate on the books of the Old Testament, for these books "give expression to a lively sense of God, contain a store of sublime teachings about God, sound wisdom about human life, and wonderful treasuries of prayers, and in them the mystery of our salvation is present in a hidden way" (DV 15). These books, however, are always to be read in the light of Christ, who is their fulfillment.

"God, the Inspirer and Author of both Testaments, wisely arranged that the New Testament be hidden in the Old and the Old be made manifest in the New. . . . The books of the Old Testament . . . acquire and show forth their full meaning in the New Testament (cf. Matt. 5.17; Luke 24.27; Rom. 16.15-16; 2 Cor. 3.14-16) and in turn shed light on it and explain it" (DV 16).

---

[13]First Vatican Council, Session 3, April 24, 1870, *Dogmatic Constitution on the Catholic Faith*, ch. 3 (DS 3009).

[14]St. Clement of Alexandria, *Stromata* 6.8 (MG 9.288-290).

Providence in Fallen World

The Church believes that God cares for all, wishes all to be saved, invites all to holiness, and would have His kingdom and His peace present even now on earth. The world, however, is deeply flawed. There has been no failure on the part of God. We have seen in this chapter some of the reasons for human misery and sorrow. Men and women are made in the image of God, but they are not God. The freedom God gives them is not the perfect freedom of God; it is a freedom which can be abused, a freedom in which love of God and one another can be brushed aside by pride. Though all have sinned, time and again, God in His mercy still calls them to inherit a blessing, and indeed He makes the occurrence of sin the occasion for even greater gifts.

The world, then, has a double aspect. In its sin and sorrow it mirrors the frailty and malice of creatures who resist their Creator God. In its grandeur and in the grace that yet penetrates it, however, the world continues to show the boundless bounty of God. This goodness we often see too dimly. To grasp reality in truth, we need most of all to see in the light of Christ.

6

The Son Of God Becomes Our Brother

"For you know the generous act of our Lord Jesus Christ, that though He was rich, yet for your sakes He became poor, so that by His poverty you might become rich" (2 Cor. 8.9). Through the centuries the human family in its sin and sorrow needed desperately the Savior God had promised through the prophets. When God's gift of a Savior came, it was a far richer fulfillment of the promises than anyone could have hoped for: "But when the fullness of time had fully come, God sent His Son, born of a woman" (Gal. 4.4).

In this chapter we speak of the good news of Jesus, of how He who was born on earth as our Savior is clearly one of our nature, our Brother, but is also our God; and of how He is nonetheless but one Person, the eternal Son of God. He suffered the humiliations and limitations of humanity; but in His humanity He also bore the saving gifts needed to heal our infirmities.

The Birth of Jesus

The Gospels speak with a sublime simplicity of the events surrounding the conception and birth of Jesus (cf. Matt. 1-2; Luke 1-2). The coming of Christ was quiet and gentle.

He who came to all came among the poor and the little. In view of the greatness of the divine promise, the circumstances of His coming seemed most unlikely. His mother was, in earthly estimation, an unimportant figure, as was also her husband Joseph, a carpenter.

Mary had been told: "And now, you will conceive in your womb and bear a Son, and you will name Him Jesus. He will be great, and will be called the Son of the Most High, and the Lord God will give to Him the throne of His ancestor David. He will reign over the house of Jacob forever, and of His kingdom there will be no end" (Luke 1.31-33).

Only great faith could have accepted such a promise in calm confidence. Only in faith was hope sustained in the utter poverty of Jesus' birth. Away from her home at Nazareth, at the royal city of Bethlehem, Mary "gave birth to her firstborn Son and wrapped Him in bands of cloth, and laid Him in a manger, because there was no place for them in the inn" (Luke 2.7). But in all its poverty, this first

71

Christmas was an event of supreme joy. On that day the Lord of glory appeared as our Brother.

Jesus Is Truly Man

Because He was to be our Savior, Jesus "had to become like His brothers and sisters in every respect" (Heb. 2.17). "He who is 'the image of the invisible God' (Col. 1.15) is Himself the perfect man. . . . He worked with human hands, He thought with a human mind, acted by human choice, and loved with a human heart. Born of the Virgin Mary, He has truly been made one of us, like us in everything except sin" (GS 22).

The solemn teaching of the Church[1] has always confirmed the clear teaching of Scripture that Jesus is truly a man. He did not merely appear to be a man. He truly became one of us. "And the Word became flesh and lived among us" (John 1.14). He was "born of a woman" (Gal. 4.4), and He experienced the weaknesses and frailties of human flesh.

Jesus did not merely play at being an infant and a child. He really shared our life. In the weakness of infancy He was nursed and cared for by His mother. He experienced the growth of childhood years. "And Jesus increased in wisdom and in years, and in divine and human favor" (Luke 2.52).

He had not only a human body, but also a human soul, a human mind, a human will, human emotions. He was fully and perfectly human. He shared our weakness. In His apostolic labors, He became "tired out by His journey" (John 4.6). He knew what it was to be thirsty (cf. John 4.7) and hungry (cf. Luke 4.2). He could be touched with great sadness, "greatly disturbed in spirit and deeply moved" (John 11.33). "He had to become like His brothers and sisters in every respect . . . He Himself was tested by what He suffered" (Heb. 2.17-18). His heart was moved with pity for the crowd (cf. Matt. 15.32). He wept over Jerusalem in sorrow that its people had chosen not to learn the path of peace (cf. Luke 19.42).

In His passion the reality of His humanity was clearly evident. He suffered excruciating pain of mind and body. In His agony He "began to be distressed and agitated. And said to them, 'I am deeply grieved, even to death' " (Mark 14.33-34). He suffered the sharp physical pains of scourging and crucifixion; and He truly died.

He never abandoned the humanity which for our sake He took on and made His own. After His resurrection He showed Himself in His human reality to His disciples. "Look at My hands and My feet; see that it is I Myself. Touch me and see; for a ghost does not have flesh and bones as you see that I have" (Luke 24.39).

[1]Cf., e.g., Fourth Lateran Council, November 1215, *The Catholic Faith* (DS 801).

Of no other historical person is it so important to insist that he is truly man (cf. 1 John 4.2). The humanity of Jesus is overwhelmingly important; because in Him human nature is most ennobled, and He is the perfect pattern for human living (cf. Matt. 11.29); because through His humanity He redeemed us; and because He is far more than man.

Jesus Is Truly God

The Catholic faith steadfastly professes that Jesus is literally and truly God, the eternal Son of the eternal Father. Each Sunday at the Eucharistic liturgy the Catholic family professes its belief in the central mystery of faith, belief "in one Lord, Jesus Christ, the only Son of God, eternally begotten of the Father, God from God, Light from Light, true God from true God, begotten, not made, one in Being with the Father."[2]

This is the good news of Christian faith: that He who is almighty, the eternal Lord of all, whose unseen might and mercy sustain all things, "stepped into the tide of the years"[3] and "lived among us" (John 1.14) in the visible humanity He had made His own. "The life was revealed, and we have seen it and testify to it, and declare to you the eternal life that was with the Father and was revealed to us" (1 John 1.2).

The joy of the Gospels is that we have been so loved by God that the eternal Son of God, Himself true God, has become our Brother. It is clear that the inspired authors of the New Testament rejoiced in their life-giving faith that Jesus is the Lord. "These are written that you may come to believe that Jesus is the Messiah, the Son of God, and that believing you may have life in His name" (John 20.31).

The books of the New Testament record a gradual development in the disciples' recognition of who Jesus was and is. They reflect the Church's development in Christological insight, its continuing growth in understanding the mystery of His person. Already in the New Testament, however, Jesus is explicitly called God.

In the prologue to the Gospel of St. John, for example, Jesus is identified as the Word of God, a Person who was "in the beginning" and was with the Father in the beginning. "The Word was God" (John 1.1). Through this Word "all things came into being through Him" and "without Him not one thing came into being" (John 1.3). "And the Word became flesh and lived among us, and we have seen this glory, the glory as of a Father's only Son, full of grace and truth" (John 1.14). The visible Jesus of whom the Gospel speaks is the eternal Word of the Father, the Word who is God and who has made God known to us. "No one has ever seen God. It is God, the only Son, who

---

[2]Roman Missal, The Order of Mass, Profession of Faith.
[3]St. Augustine, Sermo 191.1 (ML 38.1010 = ACW 15.107-108).

is close to the Father's heart, who has made Him known" (John 1.18).

There are a number of other passages in the New Testament in which Jesus is called God. In the joy of his Easter faith, St. Thomas cried out to Jesus: "My Lord and my God!" (John 20.28).[4] God the Father is portrayed as addressing Christ as God: "But of the Son He says, 'Your throne, O God, is forever and ever' " (Heb. 1.8). Christian life is lived in expectation, "while we wait for the blessed hope and the manifestation of the glory of our great God and Savior, Jesus Christ" (Titus 2.13; cf. also 2 Peter 1.1; Rom. 9.5).

Far more often the title "Lord" is given to Jesus. The risen Savior is called Lord in recognition of His divine glory. "At the name of Jesus every knee should bend, in heaven and on the earth and under the earth, and every tongue should confess that Jesus Christ is Lord, to the glory of God the Father" (Phil. 2.10-11). And Jesus applies to Himself names proper to God, such as the "I am" which signifies the eternal reality and presence of God: "Before Abraham was, I am" (John 8.58; cf. Exod. 3.14). The Gospel of St. John, the last of the Gospels to be written, expresses most clearly the Lordship and divinity of Jesus.

But the New Testament does more than name Jesus God. Throughout it portrays Him as doing the deeds of God, acting as One with the dignity, status, and power of God; and it presents Him as believed, trusted, prayed to, and regularly reverenced as God by those who come to faith in Him.

Thus faith proclaims that God alone created all things and sustains all things in being. But Jesus too is proclaimed the Lord of creation. "All things came into being through Him" (John 1.3). "For in Him all things in heaven and on earth were created, things visible and invisible ... — all things have been created through Him and for Him. He Himself is before all things, and in Him all things hold together" (Col. 1.16-17).

In God alone is salvation; only God can forgive sins, and give back life to soul and to body. But Jesus is the Savior of all. He personally forgives sin, out of His own compassion and on His own authority (cf., e.g., Luke 5.20-25). In language that clearly shows recognition of His divinity Jesus says of Himself: "I am the resurrection and the life. Those who believe in Me, even though they die, will live" (John 11.25-26).

In some cases, of course, we are not certain that the words attributed to Jesus in the Gospels record precisely statements made by Him, or statements made at the precise times suggested. In some cases the words attributed to Jesus by the evangelists may incorporate sub-

---

[4]The Second Council of Constantinople authoritatively declares that Christ is being called God in this passage. Cf. Second Council of Constantinople, Session 8, June 2, 553, Canon 12 (DS 434).

sequent insights into what He meant, insights gained from the experience of His passion and resurrection, and from long meditation in the light of faith and with the help of the Holy Spirit.[5] But all these statements are presented in divinely inspired texts, and therefore we are certain that the words the Gospels attribute to Jesus rightly express the truth He chose to reveal.

The power of God is seen in Jesus, power to heal the sick and to raise the dead to life. Divine wisdom rests in Him; His teaching is a wisdom that pierces the heart. "Never has anyone spoken like this!" (John 7.46).

It is God who is Judge of all (cf. Heb. 12.23). But Jesus has the divine role of judging. All the nations of the earth will assemble before the Son of Man, and He will pass judgment (cf. Matt. 25.31-46).

To God is the final glory and honor to be given; only God can be given the total assent of faith, be the foundation of hope, the object of love that truly rules our life. But because Jesus is God all this is due to Him. "But grow in the grace and knowledge of our Lord and Savior Jesus Christ. To Him be the glory both now and to the day of eternity" (2 Peter 3.18). Indeed, the same glory is given to Him and to the Father (cf. John 5.23; Rev. 1.5-6, 5.13); the same faith is given to each (cf. John 14.1; Heb. 12.2). Christ Jesus is "our hope" (1 Tim. 1.1), and we are to love Him above all, just as we are to love the Father above all (cf. Matt. 10.37; John 14.21, 23).

One with the Father

The mystery of Jesus could only begin to be grasped as the mystery of His union with the Father began to be understood. Jesus is not the Father; He was sent by the Father and He honors the Father. Though they are different Persons, they are forever together. "Do you not believe that I am in the Father and the Father is in Me" (John 14.11). Indeed, Jesus and the Father are one: "The Father and I are one" (John 10.30). They are not one Person, for He says, "The Father and I"; but they are one in sharing the same nature, the same one eternal love and wisdom and power that created and sustains the world.

True Son of God

In the eternal love that is Blessed Trinity the Father is eternally the Generator of the Son, and the Son is always the Only-begotten of the Father (cf. John 1.14). Many are called "children of God" because God gives His grace and friendship to many and adopts them as His

---

[5]Cf. Pontifical Commission for Promotion of Bible Studies, Instruction, *Sancta Mater Ecclesia* (approved by Pope Paul VI, April 21, 1964) (DS 3999-3999e; EV 2.151-161).

own. But there is only One who is Son by nature, God's own Son (cf. Heb. 1.1).

Though Sacred Scripture often calls human persons "sons and daughters of God," as enjoying divine favor or sharing by grace God's life and gifts (cf. 2 Cor. 6.17), Christ is Son of God in a unique way. The Epistle to the Hebrews, for example, proclaims that Jesus towers supremely over all others, who are indeed "sons of God," precisely because He is *the* Son of God.

The Church teaches that Jesus is Son of God not by adoption but by nature. He is not "a man bearing God in him," but "the one natural Son of God."[6] He alone is the true natural Son, possessing fully and properly with His eternal Father the full nature of God.

Jesus Is One Person

Jesus is human and Jesus is God; but Jesus is one Person. "One and the same Christ, Son, Lord, Only-begotten, must be acknowledged in two natures unconfused, unchangeable, undivided, inseparable."[7] Jesus remains always the Son of God, which He is from all eternity; He took to Himself a human nature in time, and He remains a man forever. But it is one Person, Jesus Christ, who is both God and man.

This the faith has always proclaimed. The same Christ who was born of Mary and who suffered for us in also God. The Jesus whom the apostles saw, who walked this earth, is the Lord who created all things. He who in His divine nature cannot be seen by bodily eyes or comprehended by human minds, lived and suffered in our humanity so that He might be with us, save us, and draw us to share in His divine nature and life.

Such was the strategy of divine mercy, God in His own nature dwells in eternal blessedness. That He might be with us in our trials, that He might redeem us by suffering to atone for our sins, He created in the womb of Mary a human nature in which in a very real way He could share our life. To bring creation to perfect unity and peace, God formed in the womb of the Virgin Mary a human nature that He united to the Person of the Son of God. When this human nature began to be, a new person did not begin to be; rather, the eternal Son of God then began to live in a new nature, in a humanity in which He was to unite all things to Himself.

---

[6]St. Cyril of Alexandria, Anathemas against Nestorius, n. 5 (DS 256).

[7]Council of Chalcedon, Session 5, October 22, 451 (DS 302). On the Church's doctrine about Christ, and especially on the continuing validity and relevance of the Church's early Christological formulations, cf. Pope Pius XI, Encyclical, *Lux Veritatis* (December 25, 1931); Pope Pius XII, Encyclical, *Sempiternus Rex* (September 8, 1951); Sacred Congregation for the Doctrine of the Faith, *Declaration for the Protection of Faith in the Mysteries of the Incarnation and the Trinity* (February 21, 1972) (EV 4.1558-1571).

Our Lord Jesus Christ is One Person. He is truly God, and in His divine nature dwells eternally with the Father, with whom He is "one in Being."[8] He is man as well: "He has truly been made one of us, like us in all things except sin (cf. Heb. 4.15)" (GS 22). His humanity is united with His divinity not merely by grace and friendship; there is a union in "hypostasis" or person. He who is the Son of God is this Man.[9] This Man, Jesus, is God.

"Following the Holy Fathers, therefore, we teach all with one accord to confess one and the same Son, our Lord Jesus Christ, the Same perfect in His humanity; truly God and the Same truly man composed of body and rational soul; consubstantial with the Father in His divinity and the Same consubstantial with us in His humanity, like us in all things except sin; begotten of the Father before time in His divinity, but in the last days, for our sake and for our salvation, of Mary the Virgin, the Mother of God in His humanity. One and the same Christ, Son, Lord, Only-begotten, must be acknowledged in two natures unconfused, unchangeable, undivided, inseparable."[10]

Because Jesus is one Person who lives in two distinct natures, one can truthfully say of the Son of God whatever is true of Him in either of His natures. He suffered and died in His human nature, and He is God, and so we may say that God suffered and died.[11] This is literally true, although in His divine nature Jesus could not and did not suffer. The sublime truth that Jesus is one Person, though He is both God and man, reveals much of the greatness of God's generosity in the incarnation.

"Creator of heaven and earth, He was born on earth under heaven. Unspeakably wise, He is wisely speechless; filling the world. He lies in a manger; Ruler of the stars, He nurses at His mother's bosom. He is both great in the nature of God, and small in the form of a servant, but so that His greatness is not diminished by His smallness, nor His smallness overwhelmed by His greatness. For He did not desert His divine works when He took to Himself human members. . . . Thus the food of wisdom was not taken away from the angels, and we were to taste how sweet is the Lord."[12]

"Not a Human Person"

Catholic teaching states that Jesus is one Person, and that a divine Person, "one of the Holy Trinity."[13] Thus Jesus is "not a human person."

---

[8]That is, "consubstantial," *homoousios*. Cf. Creed of the Council of Nicaea, 325 (DS 125), and Creed of the First Council of Constantinople, 381 (DS 150).

[9]Cf. Second Council of Constantinople, Session 8, June 2, 553, canon 4 (DS 424).

[10]Council of Chalcedon, Session 5, October 22, 451 (DS 301-302).

[11]Cf. St. Cyril of Alexandria, Anathemas against Nestorius, n. 12 (DS 263).

[12]St. Augustine, *Sermo* 187.1 (ML 38.1001 = 15.85-86).

[13]Second Council of Constantinople, Session 8, June 2, 553, canon 10 (DS 432). Cf. also DS 485, 561.

When we say that Jesus is not a human person, we are using the word "person" in a precise sense, important to the faith. In some senses it might be true to call Him a human person. This person, Jesus, *is* human. Certainly He is a perfect man, possessed of striking traits, most capable of being loved and cared about. But when we say He is not a human person, we are using the word "person" in its technical meaning of "distinct intelligent being." Jesus is not a being *distinct* from the Person who is the Son of God.

The point here is this: Jesus is not divided. There is no human person "Jesus" who would be other than the Person who is the eternal Son of God. In fact, this is the joyful good news of Christianity; that this Man Jesus, the One who could be seen, He who walked this earth, He is my God. He knows me, and He has always known me. In fact, devotion to the humanity of Jesus grows with full strength and force from an understanding that this Man Jesus is my Lord, and not a different person, somehow related to the Lord.

Devotion to the Sacred Heart of Jesus grows out of this sound faith. For He who is truly our Brother, because He is Himself our Lord, has loved us with an undivided love. The eternal love with which He has loved and understood us as our God is inseparably united to the ardent charity and tender human love He has had for us in His humanity. To this man Jesus we are personally known and related, because He is no mere human person, but a true man who is the Son of God.[14]

One Adoration

It is because this man Jesus is not a separate created person that He is rightly adored as God. The apostle Thomas saw the risen Jesus and greeted Him in adoration: "My Lord and my God!" (John 20.28). In the same way Catholic devotion worships the one Jesus in the Eucharist. With a single adoration and faith and love, Christian devotion salutes the one, undivided Lord Jesus. We ought to "adore with one adoration the incarnate Word of God together with His flesh, according to the tradition in the Church of God from the beginning."[15]

The Son of God Humbled Himself

The Son of God is God, of one substance with the Father, sharing forever with Him the divine nature and glory. But at the moment of His incarnation the Son of God began to exist also in our human nature. He, "though He was in the form of God, did not regard equality with God a something to be exploited, but emptied Himself, taking the

---

[14]Cf. Pope Pius XII, Encyclical, *Haurietis Aquas* (May 15, 1956) (DS 3922-3926).
[15]Second Council of Constantinople, Session 8, June 2, 553, canon 9 (DS 431).

form of a slave, being born in human likeness" (Phil. 2.6-7). He came among us as truly one of us, appearing "in the likeness of sinful flesh" (Rom. 8.3).

He who as God is Ruler of all came to share the natural frailties and humiliation of our human estate. And it was thus that He "humbled Himself and became obedient to the point of death — even death on a cross" (Phil. 2.8).

To say that God is humbled is not to speak a myth or poem or symbol. For it is a fact; it is the saving truth that is at the heart of faith. In Christ God Himself has become man; the eternal Son has begun to live in our human nature. He who made us become visible among us; His divinity indeed is not visible, but it is He Himself who is visible in His humanity, it is He who has tasted our poverty, our smallness, our pain. Daily in the Eucharistic liturgy the Church cries out in hope that we may "come to share in the divinity of Christ, who humbled himself to share in our humanity."[16]

Nothing mythical is said here, nothing unworthy of God. The Son of God remains forever infinitely perfect, unchangeable in His divine glory when in His infinite mercy He begins to exist also in a human nature. By no means does the Son of God cease to be the eternal Son of God when He begins to be the Son of Mary. Had Christ ceased to have the glory of God, it would not have been the Son of God who shared our sorrows and came to our poverty. "So the Son of God enters this lowly world, descending from His heavenly throne yet not leaving the glory of His Father."[17] The "descending" does not mean that divinity changed or moved, but that He who is the Son forever began to live on this earth the life of man.

"Let no one, therefore, believe that the Son of God was changed or transformed into the Son of man; but rather let us believe that He, remaining the Son of God, was made the Son of man, without loss of His divine substance and by a perfect assumption of the human substance. Nor do the words 'The Word was God' and 'The Word was made flesh' signify that the Word was made flesh in such a way that it ceased to be God; for in the flesh itself, because the Word was made flesh, 'Emmanuel, God with us,' was born."[18] The One who is poor and small and humbled in our midst is our God.

The Glory of His Manhood

Jesus, the Son of God, is in His human nature perfect man. He is fully God and fully man. Thus He has divine intelligence and human

---

[16]Roman Missal, Liturgy of the Eucharist, prayer at the pouring of wine and water into the chalice.

[17]Pope St. Leo I, *Letter* to Flavian ("Tome of Leo," June 13, 499) (DS 294).

[18]St. Augustine, *Sermo* 187.3 (ML 38.1002 = ACW 15.87).

intelligence, a divine will and a human will. "In accord with the teaching of the Holy Fathers, we likewise preach two natural wills and two natural operations in Him. . . . His human will follows without resistance or reluctance, but is subject rather to the divine and omnipotent will."[19] Faith teaches that His human knowledge has a wealth appropriate to His role as Savior of all, and that His human soul, heart, mind, and will are enriched with all virtues and holiness.

Knowledge of Christ

Christ's human knowledge was surpassingly rich. In His risen glory His wisdom is indescribably great. In Him "are hidden all the treasures of wisdom and knowledge" (Col. 2.3). Even in His earthly days His wisdom did nothing to make Him less human and less near us; it is a compassionate wisdom, warm with understanding and love, binding us to Him and to His Father, whom He reveals to us.

Christ has immediate and intimate knowledge of the Father. He did not need the obscure light of faith, for He was present to the Father and knew Him with total clarity: He *saw* the Father, and made Him known (cf. John 1.18). The Father "of whom you say, 'He is our God' . . . But I know Him" (John 8.54-55).

Christ also knew Himself, the mystery of his own Person, of His Messianic dignity, and the task the Father has given him.[20] Jesus, "knowing that the Father had given all things into His hands, and that He had come from God and was going to God" (John 13.3), is portrayed in full possession of Himself, confident, aware of the meaning of His life and His mission. He knew well that He was in the world to save sinners (cf. Luke 19.10), "to testify to the truth" (John 18.37), to be the "Light of the world" (John 8.12). It was in awareness of who He was that He called all men to Himself. "Come to Me, all you who are weary and are carrying heavy burdens, and I will give you rest" (Matt. 11.28). "I am the Way, and the Truth, and the Life. No one comes to the Father, except through Me" (John 14.6).

His human knowledge, even in His days on earth, extended to all He should appropriately be concerned with as Savior and Shepherd of all. The Gospels proclaim that He knew the hearts of men (cf. Matt. 9.4, 12.15, 16.8) and even future contingent things (cf., e.g., Matt. 20.18-19, 26.21-24, 24.5 ff.). In the human nature in which He appeared to us He was "full of grace and truth" (John 1.14).

---

[19]Third Council of Constantinople, Session 18, September 16, 681 (DS 556).

[20]For authentic Church teaching on Christ's knowledge of the Father and of His own divine nature and of His Messianic role, cf. Decree of the Holy Office, *Lamentabili* (July 3, 1907) nn. 32-35 (DS 3432-3435); Decree of the Holy Office, June 5, 1918 (DS 3645-3647); Pope Pius XII, Encyclical, *Mystici Corporis* (June 29, 1943) (DS 3812); International Theological Commission, *Select Questions on Christology* (October 20, 1980) n. III (EV 7.664-666); International Theological Commission, *Iam bis in Christologia* (May 31, 1986) (EV 10.681-723).

The Gospels also speak of Jesus as growing "in wisdom" (Luke 2.52), as knowing wonder about the things He came to experience humanly, and even as professing Himself unaware of the time of the last things (cf. Matt. 24.36; Mark 13.2). Of such matters theologians and Scripture scholars speak in discussing various forms of Christ's human knowledge: of beatific vision, infused knowledge, and experimental knowledge. Faith has room for various interpretations in these matters, as long as they are in accord with revealed teaching on the Person of Christ and on the explicit teaching of the Church in matters that affect an understanding of His wisdom.

Some contemporary scholars tend to emphasize very strongly those passages of the Gospels which refer to the frailties Jesus assumed in His humanity, the remarks about His growth in grace and wisdom (cf. Luke 2.52), and the words that no one knows the time of the last things, "neither the angels of heaven, nor the Son, but only the Father" (cf. Matt. 24.36; cf. Mark 13.32).

Such passages can be interpreted in various ways. Many Fathers and Doctors of the Church have felt that Jesus' words about the last days mean that He had no knowledge to communicate to us in that matter, that by natural knowledge, or knowledge rightly communicable, He did not know the time.[21] Others hold that such sayings of Jesus give a deeper insight into the reality of His humanity. These often say that some interpretations of Jesus reflect too much His risen glory, and not enough His humbled state. For He "emptied Himself" (Phil. 2.7) to become our Brother.

Further study may reveal more richly the depths of Jesus' self-humiliation. But this will never lead to a valid denial of other truths about Christ which flow necessarily from the union of His humanity with the Person of the Son of God, and which the Church has taught and teaches authoritatively.

Sinlessness of Jesus

Christ was entirely without sin all the days of His life on earth. "He committed no sin and no deceit was found in His mouth" (1 Peter 2.22). He is "one who in every respect has been tested as we are, yet without sin" (Heb. 4.15; cf. Heb. 7.26; 1 John 3.5). Indeed, to know who Christ is, that He is God and the Son of God, is to realize that He is entirely incapable of sin because of the divine dignity of His Person.

The Gospels indeed portray Christ as undergoing temptation, but never as feeling any inner inclination toward evil such as we in our concupiscence experience. Rather, He was assailed from without by Satanic malice. In His agony He felt sorrow and fear, and a desire to escape the cross the Father wished Him to endure. Yet this clear sign

21St. Robert Bellarmine, De Anima Christi 1.1.8.

of His true humanity involved no evil intent or disobedient will. Rather, in spite of every strain, His human heart was steadfastly fixed on His Father's will. "Yet, not My will but Yours be done" (Luke 22.42). Declaring that His Father remained always with him, Jesus said: "For I always do what is pleasing to Him" (John 8.29).

Holiness of Jesus

Jesus in His human nature was from the beginning uniquely holy. Clearly He had a human soul and a human will; but they were the soul and the will of a Person who is God. In all His human being, His will, heart and affections, He was filled with grace and holiness from the moment of the incarnation.[22]

Jesus was holy not only because He is the Son of God, but also because He is the crown of creation, and the source of holiness for all who are called to life. "For in Him all the fullness of God was pleased to dwell, and through Him God was pleased to reconcile to Himself all things, whether on earth or in heaven" (Col. 1.19-20).

In the human soul, heart, will, and affections of Jesus there dwelled most sublime virtue and all the gifts of the Holy Spirit. Neither Scripture nor Church teaching ever declares Jesus to have had strictly faith or hope; for Jesus did not merely believe the Father, but He knew His Father (cf. John 8.55) as "the only Son, who is close to the Father's heart" (John 1.18). As human He knew God our beginning and rejoiced in the goodness of the divine reality that is our last end. He was to be a perfect witness of divine things for us, and He Himself as man knew the truth and the good to which we must cling without vision, leaning on the witness of our Savior who knows that of which He bears witness (cf. John 3.11).

Freedom of Jesus

The gracious and saving deeds of Jesus were done in full freedom. He is true God and true man, and His deeds were works of both divine and human freedom. His human will was not overwhelmed and cancelled by the divine will; in His humanity were retained all the traits essential to man,[23] and precious among these is freedom. Only in freedom can meritorious deeds be done,[24] and in His humanity Jesus "merited for us justification by His most holy passion."[25] In His humanity He always did the will of His Father (cf. John 8.29), but He did so freely. "For this reason the Father loves Me, because I lay down

---

[22]Cf. Second Council of Constantinople, Session 8, June 2, 553, canon 12 (DS 434).

[23]Cf. Third Council of Constantinople, Session 18, September 16, 681 (DS 556-557).

[24]Cf. Pope Innocent X, Constitution, *Cum Occasione* (May 31, 1653) (DS 2003).

[25]Council of Trent, Session 6, January 13, 1547, *Decree on Justification*, ch. 7 (DS 1529).

My life in order to take it up again. No one takes it from Me, but I lay it down of My own accord" (John 10.17-18).

Power of Jesus

Jesus was "mighty in deed and word before God and all the people" (Luke 24.19). True, His humanity was created and finite; but it was enriched with remarkable wisdom and grace to serve His people, so that men exclaimed in wonder: "He has done everything well" (Mark 7.37).

In addition to the created powers that graced His humanity, Jesus, because of the personal union of His humanity with His divinity, exercised also divine power through His humanity. For His human reality served instrumentally the mercy and strength of His own divine nature (cf. LG 8). Hence Jesus, in His visible humanity, performed personally and authoritatively works that are proper to God (cf. Matt. 11.5-6; John 11.43). When a leper cried out to Him that He could heal him if He wished, Jesus replied: "I do choose. Be made clean" (Matt. 8.3). And He stated, and later showed, that He had such supreme power over even His own human life. "I have the power to lay it down, and I have power to take it up again" (John 10.18).

Such deeds of Jesus are sometimes called His "theandric" (God-man) works, deeds in which He acted through both His natures in perfect harmony. "For each nature performs the functions proper to itself, yet in conjunction with the other nature. The Word does what is proper to the Word, and the humanity what is proper to the humanity."[26]

The Mystery of Jesus

"For God so loved the world that He gave His only Son, so that everyone who believes in Him may not perish but may have eternal life" (John 3.16). It is this love that underlies the whole mystery of the incarnation, the mystery that lies at the center of Christianity.

God so loved the world that He sent His Son to be with us and to save us. The whole purpose of creation was to bring created persons into friendship with the Persons of the Blessed Trinity. So the Son of God entered into the society of man, and became our Brother. "For by His incarnation the Son of God has united Himself in some fashion with every man. . . . Born of the Virgin Mary, He has truly been made one of us, like us in all things except sin" (GS 22).

Creation is the glory of God; but nothing created so glorifies God as the humanity of Christ. The human love in Jesus' heart is the greatest of all created glories of God. He makes perfect faith possible,

---

[26]Pope St. Leo I, *Letter* to Flavian ("Tome of Leo," June 13, 449) (DS 294).

for He is the perfect witness of God, perfect in what He proclaims and what He is, God and man.

"The opening made by the Second Vatican Council has enabled the Church and all Christians to reach a more complete awareness of the mystery of Christ, 'the mystery hidden for ages' (Col. 1.26) in God, to be revealed in time in the Man Jesus Christ, and to be revealed continually in every time. In Christ and through Christ God has revealed Himself to mankind and has definitively drawn close to it; at the same time, in Christ and through Christ man has acquired full awareness of his dignity, of the heights to which he is raised, of the surpassing worth of his own humanity, and of the meaning of his existence."[27]

27Pope John Paul II, Encyclical, *Redemptor Hominis* (March 4, 1979) n. 11 (EV 6.1199).

7

The Mother Of Jesus

Everything faith teaches us about Mary is intended to draw us nearer to Jesus. He is the Son of God who has become our Brother. She is His mother; no created person is closer to Him. God surrounded her life with a variety of graces and privileges. But every special gift God gave to her centered on this essential grace: that she, though but a creature and "servant of the Lord" (Luke 1.38), was to be the mother of the eternal Son.

In a later chapter we shall speak of Mary's association with Jesus in the mystery of our redemption, and of her maternal relationship to the Church and the faithful. Here we treat the first gifts of God that bound her so closely to Jesus: the gift by which she was made the mother of God; the grace of her faithful and fruitful virginity; and the holiness that God gave her for the glory of her Son.

The Mother of God

Christian faith is more than an assent to an abstract teaching. It is a divine gift at the very heart of our following of Jesus Christ and it calls for a personal commitment to the saving God as well as an assent to His revealed word. Faith is rooted most deeply in that central saving event by which the Son of God entered history, "born of a woman" (Gal. 4.4). This woman, too, touches and illumines the saving mysteries of God's mercy. Mary is not contemplated for her own sake; she is the mother whose Child changes everything.

The historical events which provide a setting for this mystery of Mary, the mother of God, are recounted in the New Testament. The inspired word of God not only records the basic facts surrounding Mary's unique role in the birth and life of Jesus of Nazareth, but it also provides the prophetic framework that gives us insight into their deeper meaning: the mystery's saving significance for us.

This biblical revelation is much more than an historical account of the past. Within the living tradition of the Church's faith and teaching, it is a continuous testimony to belief in the good news that the same Jesus of Nazareth who was born, suffered, and died for our sins, now lives as the risen Lord and shares His new life with us.

Mary in Scripture

The New Testament does not speak at length about Mary, but the essential truths concerning her place in the mystery of Christ and His Church are rooted there. For centuries Christians have prayerfully reflected on all that Scripture says of the mother of Jesus. Our treatment begins with a brief survey of the biblical background of the Marian doctrines that are to be treated in this chapter and in chapter 15.

The Second Vatican Council introduces its discussion of Mary (LG 52-69) with a reference to one of the earliest New Testament testimonies concerning her: "Wishing in His supreme goodness and wisdom to effect the redemption of the world, 'when the fullness of time came, God sent His Son, born of a woman, . . . that we might receive the adoption of sons' (Gal. 4.4-5)" (LG 52). This very early expression of Christian faith immediately identifies Mary as the human way by which the Son of God entered history. It is St. Paul's apostolic witness to the true humanity and historical reality of the crucified and risen Lord whom he preached. In the text Mary is implicitly associated with our salvation, since by her motherhood God's Son has become one of us in order to liberate us from the bondage of sin and bestow on us adoption as free children of the Father through the Spirit.

As the early Christians in their love of Christ became more interested in the events of His life before His passion, death, and glorification, their interest in the mother of Jesus also increased. She appears more often in the later accounts of the New Testament writers.

An incident concerning Mary that seems to have found an early place in the Gospel tradition is found in the Gospel of St. Mark. One day when Jesus was in a house addressing a crowd, He was told that a number of His relatives, including His mother, were outside asking for Him. Jesus used the occasion to teach that ties of kinship are subordinate to the spiritual ties which exist among those who do the will of the Father (cf. Mark 3.31-35). The same incident is recorded in the other two synoptic Gospels (cf. Matt. 12.48-50; Luke 8.20-21), but St. Luke alone tells about a somewhat similar event when Jesus was speaking to a crowd and a woman called out with praise of His mother. Jesus acknowledged the praise, but went on to say that "blessed" are they who "hear the word of God and obey it" (Luke 11.28). Jesus was not rejecting the compliment paid to Him and His mother, but He was focusing the attention of the crowd on the basis of their spiritual excellence, the fact that they heard and followed God's word.

The fullest treatment of Mary in the New Testament is found in St. Luke's Gospel and in his Acts of the Apostles. Mary appears as a central figure at the outset of his Gospel in the infancy narrative; we also behold her persevering in prayer with the disciples in the upper room at the beginning of his Acts of the Apostles (cf. Acts 1.14). St. John opens and closes his account of the public life of Jesus with two scenes in which Mary figures very prominently, Cana and Calvary (cf. John 2.1-12; 19.25-27).

The implications for Marian doctrine and devotion of these dimensions of her biblical image will be pointed out in their proper place. They are mentioned here in order to show that even within the apostolic Church, which provides a norm for the authentic development of Christian doctrine, there was a gradual growth in the understanding of Mary's unique role in the mystery of Jesus and our salvation.

Mary in the Infancy Narratives

The so-called infancy narratives appear in the opening chapters of the Gospels of St. Matthew and St. Luke (cf. Matt. 1-2; Luke 1-2). Although both accounts exhibit Old Testament and Jewish influences, each is distinctive. For the two evangelists drew upon separate streams of tradition and each had a distinct and different theological purpose.

St. Matthew, writing the history of Jesus' origins, reflects on them in the light of the Mosaic tradition and promises. His account is largely a collation of quotations from the Old Testament whose promises are fulfilled in Jesus. He gives prominence to St. Joseph, particularly in the genealogy, as the legal father through whom Jesus properly belongs to the royal and messianic family of David (cf. Matt. 1.21). At the same time, he takes care to connect Jesus with Mary His mother, because he wished to make clear that Jesus was not Joseph's natural son, but was virginally conceived through the power of the Holy Spirit. In this virginal conception St. Matthew recognized the fulfillment of the prophecy of Isaiah: "The virgin shall be with child, and bear a son, and shall name him Immanuel" (Isa. 7.14 NAB; cf. Matt. 1.23). The substance of St. Matthew's message to his audience of Jewish origin, therefore, is that Jesus, born of a human mother, is the promised Messiah who brings His people a new presence of the saving God.

St. Luke's account provides further insight into the theological meaning of Mary's motherhood of Jesus. As with the scriptural accounts in general, St. Luke, while narrating basic facts, is much more concerned with their significance in light of God's plan of salvation history. His infancy narrative may be divided into two parts, that covering the period before the births of John the Baptist and Jesus (Luke 1.5-56) and that recounting their births (Luke 1.57-2.40). He intends both to parallel and to contrast Jesus and John, as well as Mary and Zechariah. His theological purpose is to portray Jesus as divine

Messiah and Lord. This is apparent from the very titles bestowed upon Him: Christ the Lord, Holy, Son of God, King, Light, and Savior. St. Luke also lets a special ray of Christ's splendor shine on His mother Mary, who is the true daughter of Zion.

The Annunciation

St. Luke's account of the angel Gabriel's message to Mary is the central revelation concerning our Lady in the New Testament. He artistically draws the scene against an Old Testament background of heavenly messages delivered to Hagar (cf. Gen. 16.7-15), to the wife of Manoah (cf. Judges 13.3-20), and to Gideon (cf. Judges 6.11-24). All exhibit the following similarities: God takes the initiative in the communication; difficulties arise in the course of the exchange; and the message is received with sufficient understanding before the episode ends.

The heavenly messenger greets Mary: "Greeting, favored one! The Lord is with you!" (Luke 1.28). In light of the Old Testament hopes (cf. Zeph. 3.14-17) Gabriel is inviting Mary, as the true daughter of Zion, as one who represents the best in the people of God, as one filled with longing for the Promised One, to rejoice with messianic joy. For Gabriel is announcing to her the advent of a new age, the fulfillment of the promise in the divine Messiah who will be born of her womb. She is called "favored one" or "full of grace" because of her unique role in God's saving plan as mother of the Redeemer. Luke thus discloses to us that Mary is "full of grace" as a result of her messianic motherhood, her divine maternity. "Blessed are you among women" (Luke 1.42) because she is so highly favored by the Lord's presence in her.

It is obvious from the ensuing dialogue that Mary's Son will live up to all Jewish expectations of the Messiah as "Son of the Most High" (cf. Isa. 9.6; Dan. 7.14). Mary's words, "How can this be, since I am a virgin?" (Luke 1.34), recall her commitment to serve the Lord with the undivided love of a virginal heart. A human father was not necessary for the eternal Son: "The Holy Spirit will come upon you, and the power of the Most High will overshadow you" (Luke 1.35). Once God's plan was made clear to her, Mary freely gave her consent in an act of humble faith and loving obedience: "Here I am, the servant of the Lord, let it be with me according to your word" (Luke 1.38).

Visitation, Nativity, Presentation

St. Luke's infancy narrative praises Mary's great faith through the lips of Elizabeth, mother of John the Baptist: "And blessed is she who believed that there would be a fulfillment of what was spoken to her by the Lord" (Luke 1.45). Mary's reply to her cousin's greeting comes to us in the form of her magnificent canticle, the *Magnificat* (Luke 1.46-55). This prayer beautifully sums up the spirituality of the *anawim*, the "poor of Yahweh," those saints of ancient Israel who were completely open to God's will and trusted in His covenant of love (cf. Zeph. 3.12-13; Isa. 66.2).

The nativity of the divine Messiah occurs in a setting of poverty which, by divine design, seems to call attention to the reality of the Child's humanity. And at the presentation in the temple, His parents observe the law of the Lord; they offer the least expensive of sacrifices, the offering of the poor (cf. Luke 2.24; Lev. 12.8). In the temple Simeon's prophecy links Mary with the sufferings of the Messiah (cf. Luke 2.35).

That Mary was not exempted from living by faith, with all its mystery and obscurity for the human mind, is indicated by the words of Luke after Mary and Joseph found the twelve-year-old Jesus in the temple: "But they did not understand what He said to them. . . . His mother treasured all these things in her heart" (Luke 2.50-51). Her growth in perceiving the meaning of her Son's mystery was gradual, a day-by-day growth in understanding up to the time of His crucifixion and resurrection.

Mary in the Gospel of St. John

Although the fourth Gospel speaks of Mary only twice, once at the beginning of the Lord's public life and again at the foot of the cross, the inspired author reveals much to us about this woman of faith, by implication and through his symbolic interpretation of historical events. First of all, the use of the title "Woman" when Christ addresses His mother at the wedding feast of Cana (cf. John 2.4) and from the cross on Calvary (cf. John 19.26) suggests her unique association with His redemptive mission. We may view this title as a symbolic designation of her as the "woman" of Genesis 3.15, the "New Eve," the mother of all who are called to live by the "new creation" of her divine Son.[1]

At Cana, Christ chose to anticipate the "hour" in which His glory would be manifested by working a miracle (or "sign") at her bidding. "Jesus did this, the first of His signs in Cana in Galilee, and revealed His glory; and His disciples believed in Him" (John 2.11). The structure of this Gospel, in which Mary's request came before Christ had ever worked a miracle, indicates that her faith was unparalleled among

---

[1]Cf. Pope Pius XII, Apostolic Constitution, *Munificentissimus Deus* (November 1, 1950) (DS 3901) and Encyclical, *Ad Caeli Reginam* (October 11, 1954) (DS 3915); Pope Paul VI, Apostolic Exhortation, *Marialis Cultus* (February 2, 1974) n. 6 (EV 5.26-27).

His associates. Furthermore, it was as a result of her intercession that the others "believed in Him."

The same idea is suggested by the scene on Calvary, where the words of Jesus to His mother, "Woman, here is your son" (John 19.26), point symbolically to Mary's spiritual motherhood of all the faithful. Now that the "hour" of His saving death and glorification in the Spirit by the Father has been accomplished, Mary is definitively designated as the "Woman," the "New Eve" associated with the "New Adam" in bringing forth the adopted children of God, the brothers and sisters of her divine Son.

Mary's Motherhood of God in Tradition

"The understanding of Mary in Christian history unfolded along the lines of the Scriptures. The Church saw herself symbolized in the Virgin Mary. The story of Mary, as the Church has come to see her, is at the same time the record of the Church's own self-discovery."[2] These words indicate the historical perspective in which to view the development of the dogma of Mary's divine maternity. The process by which the Church's faith-understanding of this Marian doctrine grew is an organic unfolding of the biblical revelation concerning the mystery of Mary in relation to Christ and His Church.

Theotokos, God-bearer

In accord with the biblical portrait of Mary, the basic affirmation of the faithful during postapostolic times concerned her motherhood. The first to use the title *Theotokos* ("God-bearer," or "Mother of God") in his writings may have been St. Hippolytus of Rome near the start of the third century. Prior to the Christological controversies stemming from the Arian and Nestorian heresies of the fourth and fifth centuries, however, the principal expression of Christian faith concerning Mary was the simple formula of the creeds: Christ was truly in Mary's womb and was really born of the Holy Spirit and the Virgin. During the early patristic period, the Church's primary need was to safeguard the reality of the Lord's humanity against the heresies of docetism and gnosticism, heresies which denied that Christ was really human or that He truly had a human birth from Mary. But when the truth of Christ's divinity was denied by Arius in the fourth century, the response of the Church opened the way for a more explicit understanding of Mary's role. In this context Cardinal Newman observed that the glories of the mother were always for the sake of her Son.[3] To insist on the sublimity of Mary's role was a way of glorifying Jesus. Similarly, efforts to minimize Mary's role seemed to flow from lack of faith in Jesus. Thus the Nestorian denial of the traditional teaching about Mary's motherhood of God seemed to flow from the Arian denial that Jesus, her Son, was the eternal Son of God. Nestorius wished her to be called only "mother of Christ," not "mother of God."

The entire Eastern Church rose to proclaim its faith that Mary is mother of God. To deny that seemed to be denying Christ's divine Sonship. In 431 the Council of Ephesus, the third ecumenical council of the Church, made its own the doctrine of St. Cyril of Alexandria, who had written to Nestorius: "For it was not that He was first born of the holy Virgin as an ordinary man and then the Word descended on this man; on the contrary, united from the womb itself He is said to have undergone birth according to the flesh, thus appropriating for Himself the birth of His own flesh. . . . And so (the holy Fathers) have not hesitated to call the holy virgin 'mother of God' (*Theotokos*). . . ."[4]

There is no doubt that for St. Cyril and the Council Fathers at Ephesus, *Theotokos* represented a Christological dogma, centered on the mystery of the incarnation. At the same time, the dogma asserts that Mary enjoys a unique relationship with Christ, that she is truly mother of the eternal Word who took His human flesh from her. This doctrine was clarified further at the Council of Chalcedon in 451 and at the Second Council of Constantinople in 553. Meanwhile, devotion to Mary as mother of God spread more and more, especially in the liturgy.

Theological Elaboration

In the thirteenth century St. Thomas Aquinas contributed in a special way to making the mystery of Mary's motherhood of God more intelligible and meaningful. As the Church had traditionally done, he interpreted the dogma as fundamentally Christological: "The humanity of Christ and the motherhood of the Virgin are so interconnected that he who has erred about the one must also be mistaken about the other."[5]

St. Thomas provides an extended discussion of Mary in the section of Christology in his *Summa Theologica*. He asks whether the Blessed Virgin should be called the mother of God.[6] Obviously his purpose in raising the question is not to "prove" a mystery which we accept as true by faith. Rather, he wishes to penetrate to the meaning

---

[3]Cf. John Henry Cardinal Newman, Discourse Addressed to Mixed Congregations, XVI, "The Glories of Mary for the Sake of Her Son."

[4]Council of Ephesus, 431, Letter of Bishop Cyril of Alexandria to Nestorius (DS 251).

[5]St. Thomas Aquinas, *Commentary on the Sentences of Peter Lombard* III dist. 4, 2, 2.

[6]Cf. St. Thomas Aquinas, *Summa Theologica* III, 35, 4.

of the mystery by showing theologically that the language about her divine maternity is not merely metaphorical or symbolic, but is literally true. He bases his reflections on the more fundamental mystery of the hypostatic union, that is, the mystery that in Christ the divine and human natures are united in the Person of the Word.

The traditional teaching about Christ is that the Word, the second Person of the Trinity, became incarnate from the first moment of His conception in Mary's womb. Since the woman who conceives and gives birth to a person is that person's mother, Mary is truly the mother of God because the Son of God took His human flesh from her. We cannot call our own mothers just "the mothers of our bodies," even though our souls are directly created by God. Similarly, we cannot say that Mary is only the mother of Christ's humanity, even though she did not beget His divinity. Although the divine nature of Christ is eternally begotten by the heavenly Father, by the incarnation He was conceived and born of Mary. She is, therefore, truly the mother of God.

Virginity of Mary

Closely connected with the Bible's portrait of Mary as the mother of Jesus is its treatment of her virginity. The infancy narratives in the Gospels clearly communicate the belief that Christ was conceived by the power of the Holy Spirit which "overshadowed" Mary without the intervention of any human father. St. Matthew makes this point in the context of Joseph's dream (cf. Matt. 1.20-25) and St. Luke in the angelic response to Mary's question (cf. Luke 1.34).

It is fitting that the mother of God should be a virgin: fitting because of the divine origin of Jesus who has but one Father, the first Person of the Blessed Trinity. As with all the Marian dogmas, we must reflect on the mystery of Mary's virginity in the Christological light of her role as *Theotokos*, bearer of God. What Catholic faith believes about Mary is based on what it believes about Christ. The teachings about Christ are far more central to faith than those about Mary; yet the teachings about her are precious, too, and part of an organic whole.

Virginal Conception

That Mary conceived Christ solely through the power of the Spirit is a dogma of Catholic faith. True, it has never been solemnly defined as such by the extraordinary magisterium of a pope or ecumenical council. But it is a dogma, founded on the words of Scripture, as understood and constantly taught by the universal and ordinary teaching authority of the Church.

The patristic witness to this truth is ancient and constant. As already indicated, it received expression in early creedal formulas to safeguard the mystery of the incarnation from docetist and gnostic interpretations. The Fathers provide ample testimony to Mary's virginal conception of Christ. St. Ignatius of Antioch taught it as a certain truth of the faith and even referred to it as a distinct mystery: "And the Prince of the world was in ignorance of the virginity of Mary and her childbearing and also of the death of the Lord — three mysteries loudly proclaimed to the world, though accomplished in the stillness of God."[7] The second-century apologist St. Justin Martyr interpreted Mary's virginal conception of Jesus as a fulfillment of the prophecy of Isaiah 7.14.[8] St. Irenaeus considered it to be a part of what he called the "canon of truth."[9] Later in the third century Tertullian included it in the "rule of faith," that is, a body of truth transmitted in the Church by Sacred Scripture and tradition.[10] The doctrine was incorporated into the universal conciliar creed promulgated by the First Council of Constantinople in 381. It was presupposed at the Council of Ephesus in the definition of the *Theotokos*, and Pope St. Leo the Great taught it clearly in his authoritative letter to Chalcedon.[11]

Virginity in Childbirth

The Catholic Church proclaims that Mary gave birth to Jesus in a virginal way. "She brought Him forth without the loss of virginity, even as she conceived Him without the loss of virginity . . . it was a miraculous birth."[12] His birth was exceptional. He was truly our brother and truly born of a woman; He was born to a most poor and humble life. But the gifts of grace were allowed to touch this moment. St. Augustine says: "A virgin who conceives, a virgin who gives birth; a virgin with Child, a virgin delivered of Child — a virgin ever virgin! Why do you marvel at these things, O man? When God vouchsafed to become man, it was fitting that He should be born in this way. He who was made of her, had made her what she was."[13]

Perpetual Virginity

The truth that Mary remained a virgin throughout her entire life is also a dogma of faith taught in the Church from very early times. It

[7]St. Ignatius of Antioch, *Epistula and Ephesios* 19.1 (MG 5.659 = ACW 1.67).
[8]Cf. St. Justin Martyr, *Apologia* 1.31 (MG 6.377-378).
[9]Cf. St. Irenaeus of Lyons, *Adversus Haereses* 1.10.1 (MG 7.549-552).
[10]Cf. Tertullian, *De Praescriptione Haereticorum* 13 (ML 2.26) and *De Virginibus Velandis* 1 (ML 2.889).
[11]Cf. DS 150, 252, 291-292.
[12]Pope St. Leo I, *Letter* to Flavian ("Tome of Leo," June 13, 449) (DS 291, 294). Cf. also Pope Paul VI, Apostolic Exhortation, *Marialis Cultus* (February 2, 1974) n. 19 (EV 5.44).
[13]St. Augustine, *Sermo* 186.1 (ML 38.999 = ACW 15.80).

provides a good example of the way in which the Church's understanding of Christian doctrine develops through liturgical celebration
and catechesis as well as through formal statements of the ordinary
magisterium.

The perpetual virginity of Mary is not a revealed truth which can
be clearly demonstrated from the New Testament without the light of
tradition. But what is implicit in the Scriptures concerning this dogma
gradually came to light in the Church's faith-consciousness. Thus, in
the fourth century "ever-virgin" became a popular title for Mary. The
Church has steadfastly believed that Mary remained true to God in the
intense fervor of her virginal love. By the miracle of the virginal conception He had enabled her to be both virgin and mother; and the constant witness of faith to her title "virgin" is a proclamation of faith that
she guarded His gift always.

Although the Fathers prior to the fourth century were not unani-
mous in holding that belief in this truth was binding in faith, there was
earlier patristic testimony to it. St. Irenaeus, St. Clement of
Alexandria, St. Gregory of Nyssa, and others upheld it.[14] This helped
prepare for the period of 383-392 when an abundance of testimony in
favor of her perpetual virginity came forth, especially in the work of
St. Ambrose.[15] St. Jerome vehemently refuted the arguments of Hel-
vidius against her perpetual virginity.[16] The triple formula that Mary
was a virgin "before, in, and after" the birth of Jesus is standard in St.
Augustine, St. Peter Chrysologus, and St Leo the Great.[17] Belief in the
perpetual virginity of Mary was clearly expressed by the time of the
Council of Ephesus in 431 and was accepted by all Christians until the
time of the Protestant Reformation in the sixteenth century. In 1555,
during the period of the Council of Trent but not as one of its conciliar
decrees, Pope Paul IV reaffirmed the Church's traditional faith in the
dogma of Mary's virginity "before birth, during birth, and forever
after birth."[18]

The Second Vatican Council referred to Mary as "perpetual Virgin" (LG 52), and taught that "the union of the Mother with the Son in
the work of salvation was manifested from the time of Christ's virginal conception up to His death" (LG 57) and that "this association
was shown also at the birth of Our Lord, who did not diminish His
mother's virginal integrity but sanctified it" (LG 57).

---

[14]Cf. St. Irenaeus of Lyons, *Adversus Haereses* 3.21 (MG 7.946-955); St. Clement of
Alexandria, *Stromata* 7.16 (MG 9.529-530); St. Gregory of Nyssa, *In Cantica* 13 (MG 44.1053).
[15]Cf. e.g., his *De Institutione Virginis* 13 (ML 16.325).
[16]Cf. St. Jerome, *De Perpetua Virginitate Beatae Mariae, Adversus Helvidium* (ML 23.194-215).
[17]Cf. e.g., St. Augustine, *Sermo* 186.1 (ML 38.999 = ACW 15.80); St. Peter Chrysologus, *Sermo*
117 (ML 52.520); Pope St. Leo I, *Sermo* 22.2 (ML 54.195).
[18]Pope Paul IV, Constitution, *Cum Quorumdam* (August 7, 1555) (DS 1880).

Significance of Mary's Virginity

Accepting by faith Mary's perpetual virginity as a fact, one should humbly seek out the meaning that makes it a fruitful mystery, and much more than a physical fact. Its miraculous character is only the starting point for our reflection on this aspect of God's saving plan for us. We are not dealing here with simply physiological questions, or signs and wonders; what is in question is an important part of God's plan of redemption. Unless we see this we might miss the meaning of Mary's virginity. Moreover, to interpret the dogma as a purely spiritual symbol or as a myth would be to fail to recognize the crucial historical dimension of Christian faith. Our faith seeks to contemplate the spiritual significance of real historical events.

The Fathers and saints have often spoken of the reasons why God wished the mother of Jesus to be a virgin forever. In this, as in all mysteries of faith, it is right for one reverently to seek an insight into the appropriateness of God's mighty deeds. We have already suggested that Mary's virginal conception is a fitting witness to the divine transcendence of her Child who has no human father, since God alone is His Father. At the same time, the virginal *Theotokos* gives testimony to His real immanence in the Incarnation: He truly assumed His human flesh from her. Mary's virginity also has an ecclesial and eschatological significance. For, metaphorically speaking, the Church is a virgin mother who brings forth the adopted brothers and sister of Christ through her ministry of the Word and the sacraments. Moreover, Mary is the model for those who choose chastity as priests or religious; she inspires them to bear witness to the ultimate meaning and final goal, or eschaton, of salvation history, the heavenly city where there will be no marriage (cf. Mark 12.25).

Mary's Holiness

The account of the annunciation in the Gospel of St. Luke expresses both the fact and the divine source of Mary's holiness. She is greeted by Gabriel with words which imply she has fullness of grace precisely because of her intimacy with God. Because she was predestined to be the virginal *Theotokos*, God readied her to be a fitting bearer of the Word incarnate. Her free and generous response — "Here am I, the servant of the Lord; let it be with me according to your word" (Luke 1.38) — gives the key to the secret of her sanctity. She is the highest expression of the spirituality of the "servant of Yahweh" and "anawim" of the Old Testament because of her complete openness to God's will. At the Visitation Elizabeth salutes her as "blessed" (Luke 1.45) on account of her great faith and confidence in the Lord. Mary's response, in the *Magnificat*, is that "from now on all generations will call me blessed" (Luke 1.48) only because God in His omnipotence has accomplished great deeds in her by regarding with favor her sense of utter dependence upon Him. So faithfully did Mary follow God's word that, as the Fathers of the Church were fond of saying, she conceived Christ in her heart before she received Him into her womb.

The Immaculate Conception

Mary is "the most excellent fruit of the redemption" (SC 103). This teaching climaxes a long tradition about her perfect sinlessness. The question of whether or not God's saving grace in her divine Son preserved Mary from original sin as well as from personal fault perplexed such outstanding saints of the Middle Ages as Bernard of Clairvaux and Thomas Aquinas. The crux of the difficulty was this: How could she be said to be redeemed by Christ, the Redeemer of all, if she was never touched by sin, even original sin?

William of Ware and John Duns Scotus developed the concept of "anticipatory redemption." Although as a descendent of Adam in a sinful human race Mary would naturally have incurred the guilt of original sin, a special divine decree kept her free from it in light of the foreseen or anticipated merits of Jesus Christ. Pope Pius IX solemnly defined the Immaculate Conception as a truth of revelation in 1854: "The Blessed Virgin Mary in the first instant of her conception, by a singular grace and privilege of almighty God, in view of the foreseen merits of Jesus Christ the Savior of the human race, was preserved free from all stain of original sin."[19] Mary's holiness from the first moment of her existence, therefore, makes her the first fruit of her divine Son's redemption.

Attractiveness of Mary for All Mankind

As Mary's unique graces and prerogatives in no way compete with those of her divine Son but rather make more clear His unique role as the Redeemer of every human being, including His mother, so her privileged place in salvation history does not separate her from the rest of us who are sinners. Her Immaculate Conception and virginal motherhood of God are the greatest revelation of what God's redeeming love can accomplish in a human personality. St. Thomas teaches that, along with the humanity of Christ which is united to God and the beatific vision which is the perfect enjoyment of God in heaven, the divine motherhood of the Blessed Virgin is the greatest manifestation of God's omnipotent wisdom and love. Her attractiveness is almost without limit because she shares so intimately in God's own infinite

[19]Pope Pius IX, Bull, *Ineffabilis Deus* (December 8, 1854) (DS 2803).

goodness.[20] Consequently, after the humanity of God in Jesus Christ and through its merits, Mary is the greatest outward sign of what each of us in his or her own limited way is called to become as a Christian.

Some of these thoughts will be developed further in chapter 15, when we reflect on Mary in the perfect holiness of her glorious Assumption which makes her spiritual motherhood of mankind complete. Enjoying the fullness of glory with her divine Son, she intercedes for us so that we may grow in the Christian life of faith, hope, and love. For us the grace of baptism is our "immaculate conception," our entry into the new life of Jesus Christ. We, too, can share in her "virginal motherhood" of Jesus by helping to bring forth new adopted brothers and sisters in the Lord until all the redeemed are gathered in glory with Jesus and His mother Mary.

[20]Cf. St. Thomas Aquinas, Summa Theologica I, 25, 6 ad 4; also Pope John Paul II, Letter on the 1600 anniversary of the Council of Constantinople I and on the 1550 anniversary of the Council of Ephesus (March 25, 1981) n. 8 (EV 7.1187-1189).

8

The Public Life Of Jesus

The Church's love for Jesus, flowing from faith in Him as the divine Savior, has always led it to have a special appreciation of eye-witness testimony about the Messiah. The memory of His words and deeds was guarded with affection. The most esteemed material is found in the inspired texts of the New Testament.

Here, then, we speak of the words and deeds of Jesus in His public life, that is, in the years between His baptism and His passion. This chapter treats of the truth of the Gospels, Jesus' public life, His miracles, His preaching, His self-revelation, and His first planting of the seeds of His Church.

The Gospel Truth

The earliest recorded Christian preaching stressed our Lord's death and resurrection. Clear examples of this teaching appear in St. Luke's history of the Church's early years, the Acts of the Apostles (cf., e.g., Acts 2.14-36, 3.12-26, 13.16-41), and in the pastoral letters of the apostles preserved in the Bible as Epistles (cf., e.g., 1 Cor. 15.1-11). But the faithful longed to have and preserve more details of Jesus' saving message.

To satisfy this desire the four Gospels were composed (cf. Luke 1.1-4). Ever since, the new People of God has treasured these four Gospels as historical (cf. DV 19) and divinely co-authored (cf. DV 11) narratives of Jesus' life. In our own age archaeological and historical research has confirmed the sober reliability of the Gospels, and of the other parts of the New Testament, where they speak of the geographical, legal, political, and social context of Jesus' life. This is the more striking because the Gospels were not written to be impersonal chronicles of facts. With great personal concern each of the evangelists made his selection of memories and traditions with a view to presenting the message of Jesus in his own way, guiding his treatment of materials, events, sequence, and emphasis by reference to his own personal interests and catechetical goals.

Christian scholars rightly study the structure of the Gospels, their literary origins and forms. Indeed, Catholic scholars are urged in their study of the Gospels to consider three periods in the tradition or "handing on" to us of the teaching and life of Jesus: Jesus' own teaching and life here on earth; the subsequent testimony and teaching of the apostles in the early Church; and the eventual commission of the oral tradition to writing in the composition of the four Gospels by the evangelists as indicated above.[1] But Catholics also affirm that the evangelists "told us the honest truth about Jesus" (DV 19). For, as St. Luke tells us, care was taken to search out the testimony of "those who from the beginning were eyewitnesses and servants of the word," so that the reader or hearer of the Gospel might know "the truth concerning the things about which you have been instructed" (Luke 1.2, 4).

It is, therefore, important that we study the picture of Jesus that the Gospels preserve for us.

Beginnings

The beginning of the public life and work of Jesus of Nazareth is closely connected with the preaching of His cousin, John the Baptist. Clothed in camel hair and leading a life of great self-discipline and penance in the desert, John worked to prepare his fellow countrymen for the imminent manifestation of God in their history. "Repent," he urged, "for the kingdom of heaven has come near" (Matt. 3.2; cf. Mark 1.1-8; Luke 3.3-17). Great crowds flocked to hear his call to repentance, to seek his advice, and to submit to his baptism as an outward sign of their turning back to God.

Jesus also went out to the arid Judean countryside along the Jordan to present Himself for John's baptism (cf. John 1.1-34). John recognized and greeted Jesus with the title of the classical sacrificial figure from the Old Testament, "Lamb of God" (John 1.29; cf. Isa. 53.7). Later, as Jesus rose up out of the water after being baptized, this acknowledgment was confirmed by a splendid vision. The Spirit of God was seen in the form of a dove over His head and a voice was heard from the heavens declaring: "This is My Son, the Beloved, with whom I am well pleased" (Matt. 3.17).

This event was complemented by another unique experience at the beginning of Jesus' public career. After His baptism, Jesus was led by the spirit into a desert where He fasted for forty days and nights (cf. Matt. 4:1-11; Mark 1.12-13; Luke 4:1-13). At the end of this period the devil tried repeatedly to entice Jesus into a warped and materialistic understanding of the identity revealed at His baptism. Jesus showed Himself utterly unmoved by these temptations. He showed by His constancy that He was ready and able to fulfill the divine plan for His life. At this time Jesus was about thirty years old (cf. Luke 3.23).

[1] Cf. Pontifical Commission for Promotion of Bible Studies, Instruction, *Sancta Mater Ecclesia* (approved by Pope Paul VI, April 21, 1964) (DS 3999-3999e; EV 2. 151-161).

John the Baptist, meanwhile, continued to preach his message of repentance, but his call did not meet with universal acceptance. In insisting on the requirements of the marriage code which practicing Jews were bound by the Law of Moses to follow, he incurred the enmity of the political head of Galilee, Herod Antipas. Herod was living in an incestuous union with his brother Philip's wife. Unable to silence John's insistent public denunciations of this scandal, Herod imprisoned him (cf. Matt. 14.3-12; Mark 6.17-29; Luke 3.19-21, 9.7-9).

It was after hearing about John's arrest that Jesus actually began to appear publicly. He started His preaching right in Herod's domain (cf. Mark 1.14). John's activity had met with widespread, though polarized, religious interest. From among those who had come to listen to John, a certain number had attached themselves to him in a closer way and become, in the custom of the day, disciples. When Jesus began His preaching, He also gathered around Himself a small band of close followers who accepted Him as their teacher and who traveled with Him wherever He preached (cf. Matt. 4.18-22, 10.1-4; Mark 1.6-20, 3.13-19; Luke 5.1-11, 6.12-16).

Working with this select group and accompanied by a number of women who provided them with material assistance (cf. Luke 8.2-3), Jesus began His own proclamation of the kingdom of God. Like John before Him, Jesus encountered many who were eager to hear His good news, that is, Gospel, and on occasion He addressed gatherings of over four and five thousand people (cf. Matt. 4.25, 14.21; Mark 6.31-7.37). Moving from village to village up and down the Jewish homeland, He became well-known. At times the crowds that walked with Him were so large that it became impossible for some individuals, even people of political prominence or His own relatives, to get physically near to Jesus (cf. Matt. 12.46-50; Mark 3.31-35; Luke 8.19-21).

One time as Jesus was entering the city of Jericho, a wealthy tax collector who was short in stature had to climb up into a sycamore tree simply to catch sight of Him over the throng (cf. Luke 19.3). On another occasion, as Jesus was speaking in a home in Capharnaum at the north end of the Sea of Galilee, His teaching was interrupted when a paralytic was lowered down through the roof into the midst of the hearers. The sick man's friends had broken through the top of the building because the crowd had made it impossible to approach Jesus in any other way (cf. Matt. 9.1-8; Mark 2.1-12; Luke 5.17-26). Of course many others took the less dramatic route of seeking a meeting through the mediation of Jesus' close followers. It was clear that people were drawn to Him. Even when Jesus attempted to withdraw for periods of prayer, the multitudes often came and sought Him out (cf. Mark 1.35-45; Luke 4.42).

The reaction of the religious leaders of the Jews to this popularity

was not long in turning from curiosity to hostility; there may have
been some suspicion that the new teaching of Jesus was not faithful to
the word of God long handed down, but jealousy was also evident (cf.
Luke 20.1-47). The attitude of these leaders was expressed in spying
on Jesus' activity through second-hand sources, challenging Him
directly in public debate, and, finally, in plotting to take His life. In
this those religious leaders were hampered only by their fear that the
people would side with and protect the Galilean Preacher (cf. Matt.
26.5; Mark 11.30).

What was there about Jesus which drew all this attention, both
favorable and unfavorable? The Gospels, almost the only contemporary sources available on the public life of Jesus, offer a variety of
material which helps to answer this question (cf. DV 17-20).

One reason certainly lay in the fact that Jesus combined His
preaching activity with signs of power which seemed indeed to be
seals of God's approval. As Jesus said when the disciples of His imprisoned cousin came to ask Him about Himself: "Go and tell John
what you hear and see: the blind receive their sight, the lame walk, the
lepers are cleansed, the deaf hear, the dead are raised, and the poor
have good news brought to them" (Matt. 11.4-5).

Jesus' Miracles

The first of Jesus' miracles was worked at Cana, a small village
not far from where Jesus was raised. While He was attending a wedding reception with His disciples and His mother, the wine ran out. At
Mary's request, and in order to build faith, Jesus changed ordinary
water, six large stone jars of it, into wine (cf. John 2.1-11).

It was the first of many signs. Jesus continued to exert divine
power over physical nature throughout His ministry. Once when He
was out on the Sea of Galilee with His disciples a big storm came up.
Jesus had fallen asleep on a pillow in the back of the boat. In a panic
the disciples hurriedly awakened Him. Jesus brought the wind and the
waves under control immediately by commanding them to be calm (cf.
Matt. 8.23-27; Mark 4.35-41; Luke 8.22-25).

The Church teaches that miracles are "signs of revelation that are
most certain and suited to the intelligence of all" and that Christ the
Lord "wrought many obvious miracles."[2] As signs, the miracles of
Jesus are not just wonderful or astonishing works. They are above all
sure signs of God's presence and care, making known to us that words
proclaimed in God's name will be fulfilled. Whether or not a given
miracle is beyond the power of all nature, the sort of work that only

[2]The First Vatican Council, Session 3, April 24, 1870, *Dogmatic Constitution on the Catholic
Faith*, ch. 3 (DS 3009).

God could possibly cause to be done,[3] God can and does cause miracles to be performed in such circumstances of nature and grace that those who experience them or learn of them can intelligently recognize them as signs of the presence of that infinite Love that calls all to faith and hope.

Jesus' fame spread with the reports of His miracles. But an even more urgent desire to come to Jesus was created by His many healing miracles. Coming home from the synagogue in Capharnaum one Sabbath morning with His followers, Jesus was told that the mother-in-law of His disciple Peter was ill with a high fever. Entering the house where she lay in bed, Jesus went over to her, ordered the fever to cease, and helped her up. She was cured instantly, and she was able to prepare a meal and serve them (cf. Matt. 8:14-15; Mark 1.29-31; Luke 4.38-39).

Once word got abroad of such healing power, Jesus became a symbol of hope for the afflicted. An illustration of this is an incident which occurred while Jesus was traveling south from Galilee to Jerusalem. A group of ten persons, all lepers, accosted Him on the road. The only way of effectively checking the spread of leprosy in those times was to remove from the community those who had the disease. The lepers, then, stood some distance away and called out to attract His attention: "Jesus, Master, have mercy on us" (Luke 17.13). Jesus looked up at them and told them to go and submit themselves to the examination of the priests. While on their way, they were cured of their leprosy. Later, when one of the ten came back to express gratitude for the cure, Jesus pointed out to him that his own faith had made him receptive to the power of God and thus had played an essential role in his being saved (cf. Luke 17.11-19).

Another encounter of this nature took place as Jesus was being welcomed into a city by a very large gathering. In the crowd was a woman who, despite painful and expensive medical treatment, had suffered a hemorrhaging condition over a period of twelve years. She came up behind Jesus in the crowd, and when her hand touched the hem of His clothing the bleeding stopped. Aware that the miracle had been affected through Himself, Jesus made it clear to her, as He had to the leper, that her own receptivity to what He had done had been essential: "Take heart, daughter; your faith has made you well" (Matt. 9.22; cf. Mark 5.25-34; Luke 8.43-48).

None of His signs was performed by Jesus to draw attention to Himself as a wonder-worker. Each was a response to an immediate human need and urgent human petition. Jesus did not want to stir up a taste for "signs and wonders" (John 4.48). Rather, He wished the signs

---

[3]St. Thomas Aquinas, *Summa Theologica*, I, 105, 6-8; 110,4.

to lead those who saw or heard about them to faith in a divine presence and mercy more important than any sign. In fact, He often explicitly forbade those whom He had cured to speak about it, perhaps because He did not want to encourage sensational stories about Himself (cf. Mark 1.44, 3.11, 5.43, 7.36: Matt. 12.15-21, 14.13-16). The common reaction of those cured, however, was to do just the opposite of what they were told, and the witness of those who had been healed caused an increase of public interest in Jesus — and also a deepening of the bitterness among those who refused to accept Him. As a countermeasure, the nonbelievers tried to discredit His exercise of divine power.

One of Jesus' more frequent signs was a demonstration of His superiority over the powers of darkness by driving out devils from the possessed. The reaction of those who made themselves His rivals was not to celebrate the triumph of good over evil, but to accuse Jesus of collaboration with the very demons He was exorcising: "By the ruler of the demons He casts out the demons" (Matt. 9.34; cf. Matt. 8.28-34, 9.32-34, 12.22-28). Jesus exposed the fallacy of their position by drawing the hearers' attention to those among their own people who also cast out evil spirits, and, especially, to His own consistent goodness.

Unable to humiliate Jesus in face-to-face debate, His opponents attempted to intimidate those whom He had healed (cf. John 9.24-34), or to browbeat His disciples (cf. Matt. 9.14; Mark 9.18). These efforts did not meet with much success.

Jesus' Preaching

The miracles, impressive as they were, were only one reason why people not only came to Jesus but stayed with Him. A major attraction was His preaching itself. Jesus' manner of speaking was both simple and profound. Even the illiterate crowds could grasp His message; even the most sophisticated were astounded at its wisdom and depth. Even those who went to spy on Him in a hostile spirit reported: "Never has anyone spoken like this!" (John 7.46). One of the keys to this happy combination was His skillful use of comparisons and parables. Almost all the important themes of Jesus' preaching are captured in these similes and stories. He seems to have been able to work this device into nearly all His discourses (cf. Matt. 13.34-35; Mark 4.33).

The parables reflect the agricultural background of most of the Palestinians and speak of the most ordinary activities and things of their everyday lives: the sowing and harvesting of crops, the baking of bread, the lending and losing of money, the patching of clothes, and so on. Yet He used these simple examples to teach important lessons or to show the paradoxical nature of commonplace events in a way that captures the interest of readers down to our own day.

For instance, He recalls how small the mustard seed is, and how, contrary to what one might expect, that tiny seed produces a shrub large enough for birds to nest in (cf. Mark 4.30-32). Or He tells about a woman who loses a coin of little value. She not only lights a candle and sweeps out the whole house to find it, but when she finally locates it, she calls in her friends and neighbors to share her joy (cf. Luke 15.8-10). Again, the outcome is unusual and thought-provoking.

The value of these stories, however, lies not simply in their style but in the fact that Jesus uses them to communicate the nuances of a religious message. Jesus' preaching presents the kingdom of heaven, the reign that God intends to exercise among people; the parables illustrate, in an analogous way, various aspects of that kingdom. A number of comparisons deal with the irrepressible growth of seeds which are sown or with a small piece of yeast buried in bread dough. Jesus uses these to make the point that even though He started with a smaller number of followers and His message met with limited acceptance at first, the word of God was surely going to come to fruition.

Many other parables center on the theme of the Father's great kindness and generosity in His dealings with us. In the account of the prodigal son, stress is laid on the father's initiative in welcoming back the son who had dishonored himself and his family by the folly of dissolute living. While the son was "still far off," his father "saw him and was filled with compassion; he ran and put his arms around him and kissed him" (Luke 15.20).

Jesus' parables also teach that the Father's concern for sinners requires an appropriate response and that the opportunities for this are conditioned with a deadline. He describes punishments as well as rewards. In the story of the rich man and the beggar Lazarus, it is the one who is poor who is rewarded after death by being received into a place of comfort in the company of Abraham. The one who was rich, because he failed to do good and show mercy, is condemned to separation from this happiness by a great impassable gulf and he languishes in a place of torment, tortured with flame (cf. Luke 16.19-31).

Another major theme is that of love of neighbor. When asked to identify the greatest of the commandments, Jesus ranked concern for one's neighbor second only to the obligation to love God. It is this moral which is incorporated into the story of the good Samaritan whose love for one prompts him to care for and assist a robbery victim — even though that robbery victim is a member of an ethnic group that wants nothing to do with the Samaritans (cf. Luke 10.29-37).

Going beyond the simple assertion that God requires love of neighbor, Jesus links the relationship God is willing to have with His subjects to their attitude toward one another (cf. Matt. 5.23-24; Mark

4.24, 11.26). Thus He teaches that the kingdom of God can be compared to a realm in which the king forgave a royal official a great debt for which the official and his family would otherwise have been sold into slavery. Shortly thereafter, the same royal official was petitioned by another man for time to repay what amounted to only a fraction of what the king had written off completely. Instead of showing mercy himself, the official had its debtor put into jail until he paid back what he owed. When the king learned of this, he recalled the official, rebuked him for his lack of compassion, and handed him over to the torturers until he paid back all he owed. Jesus concludes this story with its unequivocal application: "So My heavenly Father will also do to every one of you, if you do not forgive your brother or sister from your heart" (Matt. 18.35).

As Jesus presented all these teachings, the crowds were impressed not only with their content, but also with the fact that Jesus taught as one having authority, not in the manner of their professional teachers, the scribes, who could do little more than debate theological opinions (cf. Matt. 7.28-29; Mark 1.22; Luke 4.32, 7.1; John 7.15).

But just as the signs of Jesus had occasioned opposition from religious sects within Judaism, notably from the fanatically traditionalistic Pharisees, so did His teaching. In their eagerness to embarrass Jesus before the people, His opponents tried persistently to catch Him doing or saying something against the normative parts of the Old Testament, the "Law and the Prophets." Such a strategy could hardly have been more ill-conceived; Jesus did not owe any of His popularity to a proposed lessening of moral requirements (cf. Matt. 5.18). On the contrary, He went out of His way to fulfill obligations such as the payment of the temple tax and the observance of the pilgrimage feasts. This attitude even extended to a recognition of the authority of the scribes and Pharisees who occupied the "seat of Moses," that is, those who exercised a public teaching office among the Jewish people (cf. Matt. 23.2). In fact, though grace would make their burden light, Jesus made even greater demands on His own followers (cf. Matt. 5.20-48). The law, for example, held that the act of adultery was wrong, but Jesus taught that impure intentions were also immoral: "But I say to you that every one who looks at a woman lustfully has already committed adultery with her in his heart" (Matt. 5.28). General practice in first century Palestine condoned divorce in certain cases, but Jesus explained that this was a deviation from the original divine plan, a temporary concession to moral hardheartedness (cf. Matt. 19.8).

In these and similar cases Jesus showed that an important distinction was to be made between observance of the true spirit of the law and an insensitive literalism. Restrictions about what could or could not be lawfully done on the Sabbath were published in considerable detail at that time, but Jesus insisted that even these "official regulations" had to be harmonized with other, more basic principles. On the strength of this He corrected the customary interpretations of the law concerning certain Sabbath practices (cf. John 5.8-11). This He did not only because as God's true Son He was Lord of the Sabbath (cf. Matt. 12.8; Mark 2.28; Luke 6.5), but because "the sabbath was made for humankind, and not humankind for the sabbath" (Mark 2.27).

Jesus Himself

People were attracted to Jesus for a third reason, one even stronger than that of His miracles and His preaching. The external activity of this Galilean Preacher pointed to Him Himself as the strongest attraction of all.

In all His signs, Jesus never did anything merely for His own personal advantage. He showed a consistent and deep concern for others. He cared about people and their problems: the embarrassed wedding couple at Cana (cf. John 2.1-11), the sick and the possessed (cf. Luke 4.40-41), the parents of ailing children (cf. Luke 8.40-56). He had time for women with marriage problems (cf. John 4.15-30) and for mothers who wanted Him to bless their children (cf. Mark 10.13-16). He talked about loving those around Him and He accepted dinner invitations from both sinners and those who harassed Him in His work (cf. Matt. 9.11). When those who followed Him a long time to hear Him speak did not have enough to eat, He multiplied food for them (cf. John 6.1-15).

The Gospels show Jesus to be a loving Person, genuinely concerned with the will of God and the good of His brothers and sisters whose humanity He shared. If others needed rebuking, He rebuked them. If they needed forgiveness, He forgave them. Whatever He did, He did in a creative and sympathetic manner. In a word, He "has done everything well" (Mark 7.37).

Nevertheless, as His contemporaries slowly became aware, Jesus was far more than just an exemplary human being. At first, this fact was not taken by many as a serious possibility. "Is not this the carpenter's son?" they asked in Nazareth. "Is not his mother called Mary?" (Matt. 13.55; cf. Mark 6.1-6). But eventually, the mounting evidence demanded a decision one way or the other, and independently of anything else Jesus said or did, His identity became the key issue (cf. John 6.42; Matt. 16.13-16).

This was at least as apparent to His enemies as it was to His friends. In one of the attempts on His life by stoning, Jesus protested to His would-be executors: "I have shown you many good works from the Father. For which of these are you going to stone Me?" And the mob retorted: "It is not for a good work that we are going to stone you, but for blasphemy; because you, though only a human being, are making yourself God" (John 10.32-33).

Here was the enigma. God's living Word has taken on flesh and dwelt among and beside us. To those who could accept this fact, He offered Himself as the Way (cf. John 14.6). Acceptance of Jesus for what He is with all its consequences is what the arrival of the kingdom of God means.

Jesus' Church

As Jesus continued to teach and defend His doctrine, it became increasingly obvious that He was inviting people to a relationship with God that could not be contained within the religious institutions of Judaism.

In effect, Jesus was offering the possibility of a new covenant with God, the opportunity to belong to a new people, to be the subjects of God's kingdom. There were very demanding requirements for entrance into this kingdom: faith in the signs of Jesus and the realities they pointed to, faith in the teachings of Jesus about the Father and the kind of response the Father wants from people, and personal faith in Jesus as the Cornerstone of the whole arrangement (cf. LG 5, 7, 8).

Jesus looked for this faith among the band of disciples. When He found this faith among them, He strengthened and prepared it for the future. This was a gradual process which extended into the time after the resurrection, but a number of important issues were crystallized during the period of Jesus' public life as described in the Gospel accounts.

First, the disciples underwent careful and extensive education. They were not only present when Jesus spoke to larger audiences, but they had ample opportunity to ask questions about things they had not understood in the public discourses. They were tutored in the attitudes necessary for prayer through instruction, example, and sharing Jesus' own prayer life. They participated in synagogue and temple functions with Jesus, and when He withdrew to secluded places, as He often did, to speak with His Father in private, they were frequently allowed to accompany Him (cf. Luke 6.12, 6.28, 9.28, 11.1, 18.1, 22.40).

Secondly, they were directed to missionary work and their fledgling efforts in this were carefully supervised by Jesus so that they would learn what to preach and how to conduct themselves, especially in the face of opposition and adversity (cf. Luke 10.1-16). This orientation toward the service of the word which attracts people to God is evident from the time of the call of the first disciples: "I will make you fish for people" (Matt. 4.19; cf. AG 5).

Thirdly, they were given a share in Jesus' power and authority. Those who were sent out on mission participated in His ability to cure and to exorcise evil spirits (cf. Matt. 10.1). Moreover, they were promised: "Whoever listens to you listens to Me, and whoever rejects you rejects Me, and whoever rejects Me rejects Him who sent Me" (Luke 10.16; cf. LG 18-29).

At first, the disciples had difficulty in deciding just who Jesus was. Eventually they came to firm faith. The leader among them, Simon Peter, expressed it for all who believed when he confessed to Jesus: "You are the Messiah, the Son of the living God" (Matt. 16.16).

And Jesus then said to Peter: "Blessed are you, Simon son of Jonah! For flesh and blood has not revealed this to you, but My Father in heaven. And I tell you, you are Peter, and on this rock I will build My church, and the gates of Hades will not prevail against it. I will give you the keys of the kingdom of heaven, and whatever you bind on earth will be bound in heaven, and whatever you loose on earth will be loosed in heaven" (Matt. 16.17-20).

His disciples had found faith in Him. Now Christ was able to turn their eyes toward the cross, and to help them see His mission as Savior. "From that time on Jesus began to show His disciples that He must go to Jerusalem and undergo great sufferings . . . and be killed, and on the third day be raised" (Matt. 16.21).

9

By Dying He Destroyed Our Death

"We believe in our Lord Jesus Christ, who is the Son of God. . . . Under Pontius Pilate He suffered, the Lamb of God bearing the sins of the world, and He died for us on the cross, saving us by His redeeming blood. . . . We believe that our Lord Jesus Christ by the sacrifice of the cross redeemed us from original sin and all the personal sins committed by each one of us, so that, in accordance with the word of the apostle, 'where sin abounded, grace did more abound' (Rom. 5.20)."[1]

In this chapter we speak of Jesus Christ the Redeemer, of His passion and death for us, and of the meaning of our redemption. The follower of Christ glories in the cross of Christ (cf. Gal. 6.14), the cross "which is a stumbling block to the unbelievers (cf. 1 Cor. 1.23), but to us is salvation and eternal life."[2]

Jesus Came to Save Us

The Son of God became man to save us. "For us men and for our salvation he came down from heaven."[3] Christ is shown in the New Testament as one fully aware that His mission was to suffer and die for us, and to bring us to life. He Himself foretold His passion, death, and resurrection: "See, we are going up to Jerusalem, and everything that is written about the Son of Man by the prophets will be accomplished. For He will be handed over to the Gentiles; and he will be mocked and insulted and spat upon. After they have flogged Him, they will kill Him, and on the third day He will rise again" (Luke 18.31-33). But His disciples could not begin to understand this mystery of redemption (cf. Luke 18.34) until it had been accomplished (cf. Luke 24.25).

For Jesus, however, whose very name means "Savior," the cross was always before His eyes. "When the days drew near for Him to be taken up, He set His face to go to Jerusalem" (Luke 9.51). There He was to undergo the bitter and saving baptism of the cross: "I have a baptism with which to be baptized, and what stress I am under until it

[1]Pope Paul VI, *Professio Fidei* ("The Credo of the People of God," June 30, 1968) nn. 11-12, 17 (EV 3.547-548, 553).
[2]St. Ignatius of Antioch, *Epistula ad Ephesios* 18 (MG 5.660 = ACW 1.66).
[3]Roman Missal, The Order of Mass, *Profession of Faith*. Cf. Creed of the First Council of Constantinople (381) (DS 150); Creed of the Council of Nicaea (325) (DS 125).

is completed!" (Luke 12.50). But He longed for it, for only by it would the fire of His love be enkindled on earth (cf. Luke 12.49); by it He would "gather into one the children of God who are scattered abroad" (John 11.52).

The "Necessity" of the Passion

The passion of our Lord was not something which absolutely had to be. Certainly God did not have to save people when they fell into sin. And certainly God could have saved people in any of many other ways. Had God so willed, He could have accepted inadequate expressions of human repentance and atonement, or indeed He could simply have forgiven the sin.

It was God's will, however, that redemption be achieved in the most perfect and fitting way. For this, it was necessary that the Son of God should become man and suffer. It is in this sense, then, that we speak of the necessity of Jesus' passion and death.

Jesus Himself declared that He had to suffer to bring us eternal life. "So must the Son of Man be lifted up, that whoever believes in Him may have eternal life" (John 3.14-15). He had to suffer, for His eternal Father willed that His human nature, the crown and unifying bond of all creation, should receive its glory as a fruit of the cross. "Was it not necessary that the Messiah should suffer these things and then enter into His glory?" (Luke 24.26). Prophetic words had foretold Christ's sufferings; the Gospels allude to these often (esp. Isa. 53 and Ps. 22). These prophecies were expressions of God's will, and they had to be fulfilled. "Everything written about Me in the law of Moses and the prophets and the psalms must be fulfilled" (Luke 24.44).

Jesus, as man, recognized the command He had from the Father. "I have received this command from My Father" (John 10.18). Jesus freely accepted that which His Father's will required. "For this reason the Father loves Me, because I lay down My life, in order to take it up again. . . . I lay it down of My own accord" (John 10.17-18). With free and obedient love, then, He gave Himself to His Father's will in the passion (cf. Luke 22.42).

Perfect Redeemer

Jesus was sent into this world as a perfect Redeemer. Though He is God, He is also truly man, our brother. As the new Adam (cf. 1 Cor. 15.45) and Head of the Mystical Body (cf. Eph. 1.22), He has profound solidarity with all of us. He makes His disciples one with Himself, as a vine is one with its branches (cf. John 15.5). Since we are united with Him, His saving acts can be our salvation.

Because His humanity is the humanity of One who is the Son of

God, His saving acts are the acts of a Person who is God. They have, then, superabundant value (cf. Rom. 5.15-21). The man Christ Jesus, who is God's true Son, is the only One who could offer the Father a fitting atonement for sin.

Here we see the immensity of God's saving mercy. Not only does He save us, but He brings about salvation in a generous way, and in a way that honors the humanity He saves. In Christ He allows a human being to bring Him gifts worthy of salvation (cf. Rom. 5.15-21). "Man had merited death. . . . A man by His dying would conquer death. . . . It was better for us to have been delivered by Christ's passion than by God's will alone."[4]

Mediator

Jesus is our "Mediator." He who is Himself God and man rescued us from our alienation and misery and restored us to peace with the Father.

The mediation Jesus achieved through His passion is unique. Only He who is God and human being could in such a way restore us to our God.[5] Others may play a role in His saving work, but only in a secondary way, and in total dependence upon Jesus, for He is the necessary and indispensable Mediator of peace. "For there is one God; there is also one mediator between God and humankind, the man Christ Jesus, Himself human" (1 Tim.. 2.5).

Perfect Act of Redemption

That Christ should redeem us by the cross was willed by God as a most fitting way to save us. The cross of Christ teaches us the gross malice of sin. When the Son of God is seen as the appropriate sacrifice for our sin, we are taught to refrain from sin. "For you were bought with a price; therefore glorify God in your body" (1 Cor. 6.20).

In the heroism of the passion Christ gave us a pattern for the obedience, humility, and steadfastness we need to serve God faithfully, and He showed us the need to do works of justice and mercy even if we ourselves are being treated unjustly.

Most of all, the passion was the perfect form of redemption because it best reveals the greatness of God's love (cf. John 3.16). Bruised, weakened, and alienated from God by our sins, we needed to see how much we are loved by our God, so that we would learn to love God in return. "But God proves His love for us in that while we still were sinners Christ died for us" (Rom. 5.8).

"Believing in the crucified Son means 'seeing the Father' (cf.

[4]St. Thomas Aquinas, *Summa Theologica* III, 46, 3.
[5]Cf. St. Thomas Aquinas, *Summa Theologica* III, 26, 1-2.

John 14.9), means believing that love is present in the world and that this love is more powerful than any kind of evil in which individuals, humanity or the world are involved. Believing in this love means believing in mercy. For mercy is an indispensable dimension of love; it is as it were love's second name. . . ."[6]

The Passion of Jesus

Jesus was rejected by those to whom He came. "He was in the world, and the world came into being through Him, yet the world did not know Him. He came to what was His own, and His own people did not accept Him" (John 1.10-11). His passion, however, was a sign of such great love (cf. John 15.13) that people would ever after be drawn to Him. "And I, when I am lifted up from the earth, will draw all people to Myself" (John 12.32). "And you who were once estranged and hostile in mind, doing evil deeds, He has now reconciled in His fleshly body through His death . . . making peace through the blood of His cross" (Col. 1.21-22, 20).

When the early Church preached the good news of salvation, it preached, as the Church still preaches, the infinite love that shines from the cross of Christ. "We proclaim Christ crucified" (1 Cor. 1.23). His passion is the glory of the believer. "May I never boast of anything except the cross of our Lord Jesus Christ" (Gal. 6.14).

The sufferings Christ bore for us were severe, because of the greatness of His love for us. Not only did Christ wish to merit for us life in abundance; in boundless compassion He wished to share every kind of human suffering, interior and exterior, for the peace and healing of all who suffer.[7]

When the Gospels were written, the longest single section of each was the history of the passion. The Eucharist, which was and is the central liturgical act of the Christian community, is a memorial of His death (cf. Luke 22.19-20). His passion and death are recalled in devotions such as the Stations of the Cross and the Sorrowful Mysteries of the rosary. Popular Christian devotion has always stressed meditation on the sufferings of Jesus. "In the cross is salvation; in the cross is life; in the cross is protection from enemies."[8]

Last Supper

In each of the Gospels the passion narrative begins with an account of the Last Supper. Christ there clarified the meaning of His sufferings which were then imminent, though His disciples were not able

---

[6]Pope John Paul II, Encyclical, *Dives in Misericordia* (November 30, 1980) n. 7 (EV 7.903).
[7]Cf. St. Thomas Aquinas, *Summa Theologica* III, 46, 5 ad 3.
[8]Thomas à Kempis, *Imitation of Christ*, book 2, ch. 12, "The Royal Road of the Holy Cross."

to understand all thee things until after the resurrection (cf. Luke 24.25). He revealed the greatness of His saving love. "Having loved His own who were in this world, He loved them to the end" (John 13.1). He instituted the sacrament of the Eucharist, and the priesthood which serves the Eucharist. He made it clear that His death would inaugurate a new and eternal covenant between us and our God and that He, in His cross and His saving mercy, would always be present to His disciples in His sacrifice of the Mass (cf. Matt. 26.26-28; Mark 14,22-24; Luke 22.19-20; 1 Cor. 11.23-25).[9]

At the Last Supper, Christ also spoke with clarity of the Father and of the Holy Spirit, for by the cross He was to bring us to be children of God in whom the Blessed Trinity would dwell (cf. John 14.9-26). Then in words addressed to the Father He showed what the cross would accomplish: the human unity in the love of God that it would make possible (cf. John 17.1-26). There too He promulgated a new commandment: "I give you a new commandment, that you love one another. Just as I have loved you, you also should love one another" (John 13.34). In the light of the cross, the forgiving, sacrificing, utterly unselfish nature of His love is made manifest. This is the only love that brings peace to a broken world. "Peace I leave with you; My peace I give to you" (John 14.27).

Agony in the Garden

After the Last Supper, Jesus went with His disciples to the Mount of Olives, and there in a garden He prayed to His Father. He began to feel dread of the sufferings He was about to experience. "My Father, if it is possible, let this cup pass from Me" (Matt. 26.39). So great was His anguish that "His sweat became like great drops of blood falling down on the ground" (Luke 22.44). His human heart and will yet remained steadfastly loyal to the Father: "Yet not what I want but what you want" (Matt. 26.39).

Jesus' prayer in the garden, honestly expressing all the mental anguish he endured for our sake, with full commitment to the Father's will, is the perfect model for Christian prayer in times of distress.

Shortly after Jesus' prayer to His Father, a band of armed men sent by the chief priests, scribes, and elders came to the garden to arrest Him. They had been led there by Judas Iscariot, who identified Jesus for them by giving Him a traitorous embrace. Yet Jesus addressed Judas gently: "Friend" (Matt. 26.50). Jesus also showed concern for His disciples and urged that they be allowed to go their way

9Cf. Council of Trent, Session 22, September 17, 1562, *Doctrine of the Most Holy Sacrifice of the Mass*, ch. 1 (DS 1739-1742).

(cf. John 18.8). "Then all the disciples deserted Him and fled" (Matt. 26.56).

Trials and Sentencing

With great patience Jesus underwent unjust trials before the priests, Herod, and Pilate. During and between these trials He was subjected to many humiliations. He was the target of insults and mockery; He was denied, as He Himself had foretold, three times by Peter; He was scourged, spat upon, and crowned with thorns. Finally Pilate, after halfhearted attempts to spare Jesus, in the face of a crowd grown hostile, sentenced Him to die on the Cross.

The Crucifixion

Upon the cross Jesus suffered extreme physical pain, but also loneliness and desolation, and the sorrow of seeing unfathomable sorrow in one most deeply loved, His mother Mary. But even in the terrible torment of those hours, Jesus, the Son of God and High Priest of our salvation, retained patience and greatness of soul. Some insight into His mind and heart may be gained from His "seven last words" as recorded in the Gospels:

- "Father forgive them; for they do not know what they are doing" (Luke 23.34).
- To a thief who had been crucified with Him and who asked for mercy: "Truly I tell you, today you will be with Me in Paradise" (Luke 23.43).
- To His mother and to the apostle John: "Woman, here is your son . . . Here is your mother" (John 19:26-27).
- In prayerful words drawn from a prophetic Psalm: "My God, My God, why have You forsaken Me?" (Matt. 27.46; cf. Ps. 22.1).
- "I am thirsty" (John 19.28).
- "It is finished" (John 19.30).
- Again in words drawn from a prophetic Psalm: "Father, into Your hands I commend My spirit" (Luke 23.46; cf. Ps. 31.6).

Jesus then "bowed His head and gave up His spirit" (John 19.30). Thus the Son of God died for us sinners. "Indeed, rarely will anyone die for a righteous man — though perhaps for a good person someone might actually dare to die. But God proves His love for us in that while we still were sinners Christ died for us" (Rom. 5.7-8).

Mystery of the Redemption

The passion of Jesus has eternal effects. Through His suffering we were saved from sin and all its consequences, and have received every grace and gift leading to eternal life. It is Christ Jesus "who satisfied for our sins, from whom is all our sufficiency."[10]

This liberation won for us by Jesus in His passion has effects even in this world. Redemption is not only in the inner life of love and grace. Those freed from sin can transform this world also into a kingdom of greater freedom, justice, and peace, into an image and even a beginning of God's kingdom.

God Triumphs in Christ

"In Christ God was reconciling the world to Himself" (2 Cor. 5.19). It is God Himself who is always the Savior. The eternal love and power of the Father, Son, and Holy Spirit effected our redemption. God triumphed in Christ, winning victory over sin and Satan, over the bondage of the old law and of death.

Sin had reigned over us (cf. Rom. 5.21) and enslaved us (cf. Rom. 6.7). But through the passion of Jesus the Father set us free and restored us to the "kingdom of His beloved Son, in whom we have redemption, the forgiveness of sins" (Col. 1.13-14). Satan, too, was conquered. When Christ was raised up on the cross, the power of Satan was ended (cf. John 13.31); in Christ the Father "disarmed the rulers and authorities" (Col. 2.15).

Christ's death ended the bondage of the old law. Though the law itself had been holy, it did not bring life; for it revealed the duty to avoid sin, but did not give the power to do so (cf. Rom. 7.7-25). In Christ's redemptive work God inaugurated the new law of love and grace. This new covenant indeed requires even greater holiness, but the gift of God's Spirit makes it possible to serve Him with joy and love (cf. Rom. 5.5; 7.4).

Even bodily death was conquered by Christ's death (cf. 1 Cor. 15.54-57). Until the final resurrection the full scope of this victory is not seen. But even now all death can be, as Christ's death was, not simply a tragic evil, but a moment of supreme love and the threshold of life.

The passion of Jesus reveals the saving love of the Father. God the Father "so loved the world that He gave His only Son" (John 3.16). The mercy of God, in bringing about the incarnation, sanctified and transformed humanity. "Our Lord Jesus Christ . . . because of His im-

---

[10]Council of Trent, Session 14, November 25, 1551, *Doctrine on the Sacrament of Penance*, ch. 8 (DS 1690).

measurable love became what we are, so that He might bring us to what He is Himself."[11]

Jesus Redeemed Us

The Catholic faith firmly teaches that Jesus truly saved us (cf. Matt. 1.21) by deeds performed in His human nature, by His obedient love and patient endurance (cf. Heb. 5.8) and by offering His life as "a ransom for many" (Matt. 20.28). Jesus as man freed us from sin. The tragic consequences of Adam's sin had no other remedy than "the merit of the one Mediator, our Lord Jesus Christ, who reconciled us to God in His Blood."[12] It is Jesus who "merited for us justification by His most holy passion on the wood of the cross, and made satisfaction for us to God the Father."[13]

The gratuity of God's saving love is in no way denied by the doctrine that Jesus is His humanity fully atoned for our sins and truly merited for us every grace and eternal life. Rather it is the generosity of God that effects this perfect mode of salvation: a Man who is the Father's only Son won salvation for the whole human family.

Jesus the Priest

Jesus is the "great high priest" (Heb. 4.14) of the new and everlasting covenant (cf. Heb. 3-10). From the moment Jesus entered this world He was a priest (cf. Heb. 5-7). In His public life He performed the priestly work of teaching, forgiving sins, sanctifying. He applied to Himself the words of the prophetic priestly Psalm (Ps. 110; cf. Mark 12.35-37). As a priest of a new order, superior to every former priesthood (cf. Heb. 7.1-28), He announced the new covenant with God at the sacrificial banquet of the Last Supper, revealing there also the sacrificial nature of His then-impending death. By offering the one perfect sacrifice of Himself, He achieved eternal salvation for us, and abrogated the previous covenant and priesthood (cf. Heb. 9.1-10.18).

Every sacrifice is a sacred acknowledgment of God, a recognition of God's majesty. It is an act in which one asks divine forgiveness, divine favor, or gives thanks, praise, and adoration to Him to whom we wholly belong. In a sacrifice, a gift is offered to God in a way suited to express absolute recognition of God, as, for example, by the destruction of the offering. The gift Jesus offered was Himself, all His love and obedience, His body and His blood. Clearly He did not slay Himself, for others killed Him; but He as priest willingly gave Himself as the victim, in a true sacrifice. Christ appeared before the Father in

[11]St. Irenaeus of Lyons, *Adversus Haereses* 5 pref. (MG 7.1119-1120).
[12]Council of Trent, Session 5, June 17, 1546, *Decree on Original Sin*, n. 3 (DS 1513).
[13]Council of Trent, Session 6, January 13, 1547, *Decree on Justification*, ch. 7 (DS 1529).

His priestly work as the representative of all men, for He was the new Adam, the head of the redeemed human race; and His sacrificial death established a new covenant. He as priest generously offered Himself "by His death on the altar of the cross to God the Father, so that He might there accomplish an eternal redemption."[14]

We were redeemed, then, when his true "Lamb of God" (John 1.29; cf. Exod. 12; Isa. 53) offered Himself in sacrifice for us. "But when Christ had offered for all time a single sacrifice for sins, 'He sat down at the right hand of God'. . . . For by a single offering He has perfected for all time those who are sanctified" (Heb. 10.12, 14).

Reconciliation

Christ's passion was a work of reconciliation. Because Christ's saving love atoned for sin, it made possible a healing for all the divisions and hostility that had been created by sin.

For sin is the deepest root of human alienation. It separates us from God (cf. Eph. 2.13); it creates discord and enmity among us (cf. Eph. 2.14). Sin causes an inner desolation and irrational folly within the individual (cf. Rom. 7.23-24), and places the whole universe at odds with one, so that one is as a stranger in the world (cf. Gen. 3.17-19; Rom. 8.21-22).

But Christ "is our peace . . . and has broken down the dividing wall, that is, of hostility between us" (Eph. 2.14). Through Christ the Father willed "to reconcile to Himself all things, whether on earth or in heaven, by making peace through the blood of His cross" (Col. 1.20).

The Cross and Resurrection

The sufferings of Jesus and the glory of His resurrection are inseparably joined in the paschal mystery. "By dying he destroyed our death, and by rising again he restored us to life."[15] The Father saved us not only by delivering up His Son for us, but also by raising Him from the dead (cf. 1 Peter 1.3-5). The cross of Christ points toward and is fulfilled in the resurrection. Still, Christ merited all blessings for us and glory for Himself by the cross; in the resurrection God confers the graces and gifts won by Jesus through His sufferings and obedient love.

Christ Died for All

God "desires everyone to be saved" (1 Tim. 2.4), and so Christ "died for all" (2 Cor. 2.15). St. Paul speaks of the superabundance of

---

[14]Council of Trent, Session 22, September 17, 1562, *Doctrine on the Most Holy Sacrifice of the Mass*, ch. 1 (DS 1739).

[15]Roman Missal, Preface I for Easter.

His satisfaction. The sin of Adam had brought grief to all humankind, but the redeeming work of Christ was far more powerful and greater in its effects than was Adam's sin (cf. Rom. 5.15-21). The very form of the cross was seen by the Fathers as a symbol of the university of the redemption by Christ. "The form of the cross, radiating out from the center in four different directions, denotes the universal diffusion of the power and providence of Him who hung upon it."[16]

Although Christ did indeed die for all, He does not force anyone to accept eternal life. Only those to whom the merit of His passion is communicated are saved, but through His Holy Spirit He saves all who are willing. The invitation is to all, even the unwilling. "And let everyone who is thirsty come. Let anyone who wishes take the water of life as a gift" (Rev. 22.17).

Redemption Completed and Continuing

Christ has redeemed us. This is a fact. St. Paul writes to the early Christians in Corinth: "So, if anyone is in Christ, there is a new creation: everyone old has passed away; see, everything has become new! All this is from God, who reconciled us to Himself through Christ" (2 Cor. 5.17-18). But the saving work of Jesus is yet to be received in the lives of many, and the full flowering of its richness is yet to be seen. There is apostolic work yet to be done, and, as St. Paul goes on to say, God "has given us the ministry of reconciliation" (2 Cor. 5.18). God calls us to accept eternal life freely, to cling to Christ's saving work and to share in its fruit by faith and the reception of sacraments, by prayer and works of love. "We beseech you on behalf of Christ, be reconciled to God" (2 Cor. 5.20).

The Cross in Christian Life

The cross is part of every Christian life. By Christ's cross and resurrection people are saved, when they lay hold of Him through faith and love. The sacraments are sacred signs and instruments through which Jesus communicates the fruits of redemption from the tree of the cross. Nothing of Christian life can be understood apart from the cross. Anyone who wishes to grow to maturity in Christian love, to remain faithful to God, must receive light and draw strength from His saving passion.

Jesus taught His disciples ever to carry the cross: "If any want to become My followers, let them deny themselves and take up their cross daily and follow Me" (Luke 9.23). The crosses in our daily lives, the difficulties and sufferings, and the self-denials and sacrifices willingly offered, are made saving and sacred by His holy cross.

---

[16]St. Gregory of Nyssa, *Oratio in Christi Redemptionem* 1 (MG 46.624).

"Christ also suffered for you, leaving you an example, so that you should follow in His steps. He committed no sins and no deceit was found in His mouth. When He was abused, He did not return abuse; when He suffered, He did not threaten; but He entrusted Himself to the One who judges justly" (1 Peter 2.21-23).

"By suffering for us He not only provided us with an example, for us to follow in His steps (cf. 1 Peter 2.21; Matt. 15.24; Luke 14.27), but He also opened the way, and if we follow that way, life and death are made holy and take on a new meaning" (GS 22).

10

By Rising
He Restored Our Life

"This is the night when Jesus Christ broke the chains of death and rose triumphant from the grave."[1] The Church celebrates the resurrection of Jesus with surpassing joy. Not only Easter, but every Sunday of the year is a celebration of the Lord's resurrection (cf. SC 106). For the rising of Jesus not only confirms the Church's faith, but is the central mystery through which God calls us to life. The hope to which we are born in coming to faith is "a living hope through the resurrection of Jesus Christ from the dead" (1 Peter 1.3).

In this chapter we speak of the mystery of the resurrection, of what it means to believe in the resurrection, and of the reality of the Lord's rising in the flesh, in the very body which was crucified. We also speak of the ascension of Jesus, in which His enduring presence among us acquired a new form.

The Mystery of the Resurrection

"The Lord has risen indeed. . . !" (Luke 24.34). The Easter announcement is about a singular event of universal significance. It was at a particular time, "on the third day,"[2] that is, on the second day after the day of the death on the cross. It was in a particular place, in a stone sepulchre near the site of the crucifixion on Golgotha (cf. John 19.41). Then and there God raised from the dead and elevated to Himself a particular man, Jesus of Nazareth. "He is not here, but has risen" (Luke 24.6).

From the first day that the apostles preached the Gospel (cf. Acts 2.14-36) the resurrection of Jesus has been the core of the *kerygma*, the proclamation of the good news. "This Jesus God raised up, and of that all of us are witnesses" (Acts 2.32). The power that restores us to life is the "power of His resurrection" (Phil. 3.10).

Christ has been raised up, then, as He Himself had foretold (cf.

---

[1]Roman Missal, the Easter Vigil, Easter Proclamation (*Exsultet*).
[2]Apostles' Creed.

Matt. 16.21), in a true resurrection of the flesh.[3] He rose by His own power.[4]

This resurrection of Jesus plays a central part in the life of faith. It is both a life-giving mystery and a sign that confirms our faith. The resurrection is an historical fact. The apostles bore witness to the resurrection from what they had heard and seen and touched (cf. Acts 1.21-22; 1 John 1.1-3). The Catholic faith has ever taught, and ever teaches against all denials, that Christ's rising from the dead was an historical event for which there is convincing evidence. Jesus Himself gave evidence "by many convincing proofs" (Acts 1.3) to His apostles; and even up to the present day He gives signs of the resurrection, to lead all to faith.[5]

By His Own Power

Faithful to the message of Scripture, the Church teaches both that the Father raised Jesus from the dead and that Jesus rose by His own power. "But God raised Him up" (Acts 2.24). "I lay down My life in order to take it again . . . I have power to take it up again" (John 10.17-18).

The explanation is this: It was by the power of God that the humanity of Jesus was raised from the dead. This power of the one God belongs to the Father and the Son equally. When the resurrection is seen as the seal of the Father's approval, the glorification of Jesus' humanity is viewed as the work of the Father; when it is seen as a manifestation of Jesus' divine power and personality, it is viewed as the act of the Son Himself.

The Resurrection and Faith

Sincere belief in the resurrection does not spring up casually. Indeed, the pain and disillusionments of life and the skepticism of this world would almost seem to make confident faith in the resurrection foolish or impossible. To believe in the resurrection is to believe firmly that a Man who died a cruel death on the cross returned to life. It is to believe that He rose to a new kind of life, that He returned to His friends in the same flesh which was crucified and as the same person, but now glorified, no longer subject to the limiting conditions of ordinary life (cf. John 20.19; 1 Cor. 15.42-49). It is to believe that one

---

[3]Cf. Second Council of Lyons, Session 4, July 6, 1274, *Profession of Faith of Emperor Michael Palaeologus* (DS 852); Pope Innocent III, *Profession of Faith Prescribed for the Waldensians* (December 18, 1208) (DS 791).

[4]Cf. Pope Anastasius II, *Profession of Faith* (497) (DS 358); Eleventh Council of Toledo (675) (DS 539).

[5]Cf. Pope Pius X, Encyclical, *Pascendi Dominici Gregis* (September 8, 1907) (DS 3484); Decree of the Holy Office, *Lamentabili* (July 3, 1907) n. 36 (DS 3436).

who lived a mortal life here on earth has become a "life-giving spirit" (1 Cor. 15.45), bringing newness of life to all who receive Him, and promising a transformation of all creation (cf. Rom. 8.21). To believe in the resurrection is to believe that He who was crucified is truly Lord of all, and that to Him has been given "all authority in heaven and on earth" (Matt. 28.18).

Christ's death had been a devastating blow to His apostles. They had not understood His predictions concerning the paschal events, and they felt that all hope in Him was lost with His dying. They had truly had hope in Him (cf. Luke 24.21), but after the tragedy of the cross they were not prepared to believe again. When the women who first visited the tomb brought them the first reports of His rising, the apostles did not believe (cf. Luke 24.11). When the risen Jesus Himself appeared to them, they thought they were seeing a ghost (cf. Luke 24.37). The Gospels make no secret of these early doubts (cf. Matt. 28.17; Mark 16.11-24). When the risen Jesus appeared to His followers almost always additional proofs were required to identify Him. He ate with them, and He had them touch His wounds (cf. Luke 24.13-31, 24.36-43; John 20.24-29). "Look at My hands and My feet; see that it is I Myself. Touch Me and see; for a ghost does not have flesh and bones as you see that I have" (Luke 24.39).

The apostle Thomas revealed the depth of anguish that hindered him from faith in the resurrection. The testimony of the other apostles did not help. "I will not believe" (John 20.25). Unless he could see His living Lord, and himself touch and examine the wounds, to see for himself that He who had appeared to them was truly He who had died, he could not believe. But then Christ appeared to them again, and He gave Thomas the signs and the inner grace he needed, and Thomas voiced his recognition and his faith: "My Lord and my God!" (John 20.28).

By His presence, words, and gestures, Christ led His apostles toward faith. "After His suffering He presented Himself alive to them by many convincing proofs, appearing to them . . . and speaking about the kingdom of God" (Acts 1.3). By His tangible presence He made them realize that His resurrection was indeed real, not a dream or illusion. By words that made their hearts burn within them (cf. Luke 24.32) He enabled them to see the meaning of His rising, to see that it was an event that illumines all history and heals all sorrows. All previous salvation history, "Moses and all the prophets" (Luke 24.27), pointed toward it, and all future centuries would draw life from it.

But the outer signs and words were confirmed also by the inner gift of the Spirit. By valid signs they were led to faith, but by God's inner gift faith was made immovably strong. "And we are witnesses to these things, and so is the Holy Spirit whom God has given to those who obey Him" (Acts 5.32).

Belief and Unbelief

The risen Christ was not seen by all, but by "us who were chosen by God as witnesses" (Acts 10.41). Still, to all to whom His word is addressed, He gives sufficient evidence of His resurrection in forms appropriate to their circumstances.

For those in Jerusalem at the time, there was the witness of the empty tomb. But there was also much more: the transformation of the apostles and the confident testimony they gave to the risen Christ, the miraculous cures they worked in His name (cf. Acts 4.9-10; 5.12-16), and the new energy of their lives that gave evidence of the inner presence of the Spirit. Many saw these signs and believed, and they too received the gift of the Spirit and began to share in the life of the resurrection.

Others did not believe, and indeed some sought to discredit the word of Christ's rising. The Gospel of St. Matthew records how those who had worked for Jesus' death gave the soldiers who had been guarding the tomb a large bribe and instructions to say: "His disciples came by night and stole Him away while we were asleep" (Matt. 28.13). The soldiers did as they were instructed, and the evangelist, writing decades later, says their story was still circulating (cf. Matt. 28.15). And their story still circulates, though long ago St. Augustine gave a decisive answer to it: "You bring forward as witnesses men who were sleeping. Truly, it is you who have fallen asleep, you who have failed in examining such things. If they were sleeping, what could they have seen? If they saw nothing, how are they witnesses?"[6]

Through all the ages of Christian history there have been persons who have tried to explain away the Easter events. Often such persons seem to forget or ignore completely the nature of the facts and experiences to be explained. Some declare that Christ did not actually die on the cross, but in fact survived to serve as a sort of underground leader. Others say that purely subjective experiences led the apostles to a sincere but false belief that Christ had risen. Some others suggest that the apostles may indeed have had real visions, and that in some spiritual way Jesus may yet continue to be, and even manifest Himself, but that all of this is to be understood without the "scandal" of a risen body. And there are still others who more subtly insist that the proclamation of the resurrection is not to be taken as a claim that Jesus literally rose from the dead, but rather as an assertion that Jesus still lives in the sense that His cause lives on in the continuing struggle against hatred and oppression.

Clearly none of these positions explains the reality of what did in fact occur. As we have seen, doubts and misunderstandings were experienced even by Christ's own disciples. When Mary Magdalen first

[6]St. Augustine, *Enarratio in Psalmum 63 (64)* 13 (ML 36.767).

saw the empty tomb on the first Easter morning, she ran to announce: "They have taken the Lord out of the tomb" (John 20.2). When the apostles first saw the risen Christ they thought they were seeing a ghost (cf. Luke 24.37). And the apostle Thomas said he would have to see and touch for himself (cf. John 20.25). Doubts there were, but the resurrection was fact. The persistent mercy of Christ, His own show-ing of Himself (cf. Matt. 28.17), and the reasonableness of trustworthy testimony conquered the doubts.

The Test of Gamaliel

Believers today do not see all the same evidences that followers of Christ saw in apostolic times. Nevertheless, many signs of His resur-rection still shine in the Church that is built upon Christ. There is clearly the sign that the Pharisee Gamaliel said would be decisive.

Gamaliel it was who urged caution on the Sanhedrin when that group was irritated by what the apostles were preaching and wanted to kill them (cf. Acts 5.33). Gamaliel reminded the council of earlier movements which had died out quickly once their leaders were dead. The apostles were in fact making broad and startling claims. But Gamaliel gave the council this advice: "Because if this plan or this un-dertaking is of human origin, it will fail; but if it is of God, you will not be able to overthrow them — in that case you may even be found fighting against God!" (Acts 5.38-39). With these words Gamaliel in effect pointed to the ultimate reason why Christianity succeeds. If Christianity had died out long ago, if its ability to win converts had not continued through the centuries, then Christianity would have shown itself to be a human enterprise. But Christianity did not die out. It grew, and spread, and has endured. It still wins converts. Thus the position of Gamaliel converges with that of Peter and the other apostles. The truth of the claim that Jesus was not dead, bur risen and alive, that the same Jesus who had died on the cross was risen, provided the initial impetus for Christianity and also its power to last forever. For Christianity comes from God.

The Bodily Resurrection

The records of the New Testament tell what actually happened and make sense of what followed in history. Faith in Christ's rising changed the world. This faith sprang up after Jesus had died in dis-grace. His followers proclaimed not merely a religious message, but also, and fundamentally, a fact: that they had seen Christ risen and alive. They announced Him with confidence and persistence, and they showed they were prepared even to suffer pain and disgrace gladly in His name (cf. Acts 5.41). How could they have come to such a faith, a faith that nothing could crush or destroy then or ever in all the following ages?

Faith in the resurrection survived because Christ truly rose. His witnesses were truthful, and His living power remained in them and in their words. The scriptural accounts of those who saw the risen Lord are not accounts about one who had once been seen and was now merely remembered.

St. Paul speaks of the many who saw the risen Christ appear. "For I handed on to you as of first importance what I in turn had received: that Christ died for our sins in accordance with the scriptures, and that He was buried, and that He was raised on the third day in accordance with the scriptures, and that He appeared to Cephas, then to the twelve. Then He appeared to more than five hundred brothers and sisters at one time, most of whom are still alive, though some have died. Then He appeared to James, then to all the apostles. Last of all, as to one untimely born, He appeared also to me" (1 Cor. 15.3-8).

It was only about thirty years after the death of Jesus when St. Paul wrote these words, and he here refers to his earlier instruction of the Corinthians in what he himself had "received," that is, at a time earlier still. Most of those he mentions were alive when he wrote, and thus they were available to confirm or deny the accuracy of his statements about them. This passage of St. Paul shows clearly that belief in the resurrection of Jesus formed part of the earliest confessions of faith of the Christian community, and that, contrary to the opinions of the skeptics, this belief was not something that "evolved" over a long period of time. Immediately after the death and resurrection of Jesus there was an extraordinary intensity of faith and activity.

The Gospels record appearances of the risen Jesus which account for this strong faith. They provide a variety of accounts of Jesus' appearances to various followers. The evident lack of interest in harmonizing the chronology and details of all the appearances is in a sense itself testimony to the certainty of faith and the authenticity of the accounts.

The appearances of the risen Christ are recorded in varying ways by the evangelists. The differences in their narratives are due to the fact that each evangelist selected from all the memories, testimonies, and traditions available to him that which best fitted his particular purpose at the time of writing. The Gospel of St. Luke makes Jerusalem the center toward which all converges, and hence it appropriately ends with the appearances of Jesus in Jerusalem. The Gospel of St. Matthew, in which Jesus appears as the New Moses, begins its account of Jesus' preaching on a mountain of Galilee and ends with a post-resurrection appearance on a mountain of Galilee. But in spite of the variations in the formulations, the Easter message ever exhibits the same essential aspects and is based on the same facts.

The Very One Who Died

All the scriptural accounts witness to the continuity of the life of Jesus before and after the resurrection. All insist that the risen Jesus is truly the same Jesus who had died. The physical reality of His presence is stressed. The disciples not only see the risen Christ with their eyes, but they are urged to touch His solid flesh and know that He is bodily among them (cf. Luke 24.39). When doubts arise, the risen Jesus asks for food, so that by the act of eating He might convince them of the tangible reality of the resurrection (cf. Luke 24.41-43). Thomas is invited to examine the wounds (cf. John 20.27), to see that it is the very body that was crucified that is now present to give life. It was not a vision they saw. It was Jesus Himself.

To have a saving belief in the risen Lord required grace and faith. But faith was not needed to see and touch the risen Lord. Scripture reports a number of occasions on which He was seen by those who had not yet come to faith. The disciples on the road to Emmaus, for example, saw and spoke with Him before they recognized Him and believed (cf. Luke 24.13-32). Mary Magdalen saw Him at the site of the tomb and mistook Him for a gardener (cf. John 20.15).

Easter faith is newness of life, and it is firmly rooted in the personal and concrete Christ. Belief in the bodily rising of Jesus is not in itself acceptance of the fullness of the Easter mystery, but it is an indispensable grounding for the new life. That is why Scripture so emphasizes this aspect. Whereas David "both died and was buried, and his tomb is with us to this day" (Acts 2.29), Jesus of Nazareth "was not abandoned to Hades, nor did His flesh experience corruption" (Acts 2.31; cf. Ps. 16.10). David did undergo corruption, "but He whom God raised up experienced no corruption" (Acts 13:37). The Jesus who is alive now is the same Jesus who was dead before (cf. Rev. 1.18; 2.8). The witnesses of Christ understood the resurrection in the factual terms of a Man who died, was buried, and then came to life again.

The fact of the resurrection is of fundamental importance. St. Paul makes the point in stark terms: "And if Christ has not been raised, then our proclamation has been in vain and your faith has been in vain. . . . If Christ has not been raised, your faith is futile and you are still in your sins. Then those also who have died in Christ have perished" (1 Cor. 15.14, 17-18).

Fulfillment of Divine Promises

Jesus rose on the third day "in fulfillment of the Scriptures."[7] These words of the Creed of the Mass are the words of St. Paul (cf. 1

---

[7]Roman Missal, The Order of Mass, Profession of Faith.

Cor. 15.4), and they recall for us a theme stressed in the New Testament. The rising of Jesus was not merely a happy incident, nor was it simply a dramatic way of signifying Christ's divine authority. Rather, it was an event predestined from the beginning of creation. The New Testament recalls prophetic statements concerning the resurrection not only to fortify faith in the truth of Christ's rising, but also to show the centrality of this work in God's plan of salvation. In raising Christ from the dead, the Father began to give the great gifts that good people had so long hoped for.

Though the Old Testament references are not always clear, the apostolic church, aided by the Holy Spirit, saw the resurrection of Jesus as the fulfillment of prophecies such as this in Isaiah: "Out of His anguish He shall see light; He shall find satisfaction through His knowledge. The righteous one, My servant, shall make many righteous, and He shall bear their iniquities. Therefore I will allot Him a portion with the great, and He shall divide the spoil with the strong" (Isa. 53.11-12). That is, in the mind of the apostolic Church the resurrection is the response of the Father to the submission of Christ on the cross, the reward given to the Servant who has been obedient unto death (cf. Phil. 2.7-8).

"The fact that Christ 'was raised the third day' (1 Cor. 15.4) constitutes the final sign of the messianic mission, a sign that perfects the entire revelation of merciful love in a world that is subject to evil. At the same time it constitutes the sign that foretells 'a new heaven and a new earth' (Rev. 21.1), when God 'will wipe away every tear from their eyes, there will be no more death, or mourning, no crying or pain, for the former things have passed away' (Rev. 21.4)."[8]

The Father's Seal of Approval

Thus the glorified Jesus appears as vindicated in His Messianic prerogatives. His resurrection evidences the Father's approval and ratification of Christ and His work. "The God of Abraham, the God of Isaac, and the God of Jacob, the God of our ancestors has glorified His Servant Jesus, whom you handed over and rejected in the presence of Pilate, though he had decided to release Him. But you rejected the Holy and Righteous One ... whom God raised from the dead" (Acts 3.13-15; cf. 4.10; 5.30).

The resurrection of Jesus assures us that the death of Jesus was pleasing to the Father, that His miracles were performed with the power and approval of God, and that His teachings and commandments were teachings and commandments intended by God for us. Be-

[8]Pope John Paul II, Encyclical, *Dives in Misericordia* (November 30, 1980) n. 8 (EV **7**.905).

cause of the resurrection we are sure we are right when we take Christ as our way to the Father.

The resurrection points also to the transcendence of Christ. The title *Kyrios*, "Lord," is always attributed to the risen Christ. With this title the New Testament writers proclaim His sovereignty, a sovereignty which requires obedience and loyalty on the part of all. Christ acknowledged by the Father, shining in Easter glory, is recognized as Lord just as the Father is Lord. The cry "Lord Jesus!" (Rev. 22.20) is an acknowledgement of Jesus as God Himself, and of the glory of His risen humanity, now revealing the dignity of His person.

The Power of the Resurrection

The resurrection does far more than confirm the eternal value of Jesus' life and work. Jesus also appears as the new Adam (cf. 1 Cor. 15.45), the Author and Exemplar of a new humanity. "so if anyone is in Christ, there is a new creation" (2 Cor. 5.17).

The humanity of Jesus was transformed through His resurrection. He is still the same Jesus, still our Brother, still sharing our flesh, but now a "life-giving Spirit" (1 Cor. 15.45). The risen body, while truly a body, is different from and vastly superior to the body in its unperfected state (cf. 1 Cor. 15.42-54). There is mystery and power in the Lord's risen body (cf. John 20.19, 26), yet He not only appears and speaks, but also lets Himself be touched and felt.

What does it take to understand the meaning of life in the new creation? St. Paul tells us: "Those who are unspiritual do not receive the gifts of the God's Spirit, for they are foolishness to them, and they are unable to understand them because they are spiritually discerned. Those who are spiritual discern all things, but they are themselves subject to no one else's scrutiny" (1 Cor. 2.14-15). Only those who through participation in the power of Christ's resurrection have become like Him can come to terms with life in the new creation and understand something of what it is.

But Jesus by His resurrection already brings people to share in the divine life. "He was buried, and, of His own power, rose the third day, raising us by His resurrection to that sharing in the divine life which is the life of grace."[9]

It is the risen Jesus Himself who gives persons of faith the ability to experience His presence. He does this by allowing them to share in His own life, by bringing them even now, in their lives here on earth, into a real participation in His new way of existence. This He does by bringing the faithful to a true mystical death, burial, resurrection, and

[9]Pope Paul VI, *Professio Fidei* ("The Credo of the People of God," June 30, 1968) n. 12 (EV 3.548).

ascension with Him in order that they might receive, as members of His mystical body, a share in His Spirit.

Jesus came in order to lead humanity into a "spiritual incorruption" by a radical transformation. He Himself, as the new Adam, as the Head of the new generation, is both the model and the means of this transformation. The rising of Him who is the "first fruits of those who have died" (1 Cor. 15.20) is the prototype and the beginning of the transformation of humankind.

The resurrection of Jesus, then, is the foundation of the Christian life of faith, prayer, and spiritual growth. It is the pledge of the resurrection of our bodies, for Christ conforms the faithful to His own image and leads them to share in His glory. Jesus' resurrection and glorification provide the basis for our hope and faith in the immortal life of our bodies after the final resurrection at the end of time.

"The paschal mystery is Christ at the summit of the inscrutable mystery of God. It is precisely then that the words pronounced in the Upper Room are completely fulfilled: 'He who has seen Me, has seen the Father' (John 14.9)."[10]

The Ascension into Heaven

The Easter mystery approaches its culmination in the ascension of Jesus. After His appearances here on earth in His risen body, and "after giving instructions through the Holy Spirit to the apostles whom He had chosen" (Acts 1.2), Jesus "was lifted up, and a cloud took Him out of their sight" (Acts 1.9). He ascended "with the flesh in which He had risen and with His soul."[11]

The mystery of the ascension has two distinct aspects. First, it is the glorification of Jesus. The risen Christ, in the humanity He has assumed to become our Brother, returns to the Father who had sent Him. Secondly, the ascension indicates the time when Christ brought His visible ministry on earth to completion.

St. Luke notes that forty days elapsed between the resurrection and the ascension (cf. Acts 1.3). But the time is not the essential point. Nor does belief in the ascension involve any special cosmological theories, or any doctrinal positions on spatial relationships between heaven and our planet earth. When Scripture says Christ "ascended far above all the heavens" (Eph. 4.10) it is not teaching astronomy, but telling the status of the glorified Redeemer sitting at the right hand of the Father (cf. Eph. 1.20). "We say that this place of eternal joy and eternal peace is above the skies, although it cannot be perceived,

---

[10]Pope John Paul II, Encyclical, *Dives in Misericordia* (November 30, 1980) n. 8 (EV 7.909).
[11]Second Council of Lyons, Session 4, July 6, 1274, *Profession of Faith of Emperor Michael Palaeologus* (DS 852).

described or defined in terms of place. . . . Thus Christ has ascended above every place and every time, since He is Truth Itself and does not sit, as it were, at the edge of the cosmos, but at the center."[12]

The ascension is not an event which changes the relationship of Jesus to heaven, but it does affect His relationship to the world. Jesus in His ascension is not turning away from the earth, but His relationship to earth is no longer limited to specific times and places. In His glorified life He makes all times and places present to Himself.

He had died for us and risen again, and now He "entered into heaven itself, now to appear in the presence of God on our behalf" (Heb. 9.24). In His risen body He had plainly showed Himself to His disciples, and now He "was taken up to heaven in their sight to claim for us a share in his divine life."[13]

He has ascended, but He has not abandoned us. He comes to the Father as the eternal High Priest, "able for all time to save those who approach God through Him, since He always lives to make intercession for them" (Heb. 7.25). Scriptural accounts of the ascension relate the event to the sending of the Holy Spirit and to the mission of the Church. Through His Holy Spirit and the life the Spirit nourishes in the Church, the risen Christ will be present to those who belong to Him. Though He deprives us of His visible presence for a time that He might send the gift of the Spirit (cf. John 16.7), Christ will be with the Church always (cf. Matt. 28.20). He is present in the Church's life of faith and prayer, and especially in the sacramental meetings with His glorified body. He is present also in our life of charity.

Christ Himself will remain with us through the gift of the Holy Spirit. "When the Spirit of truth comes, He will guide you into all the truth. . . . He will glorify Me, because He will take what is Mine and declare it to you" (John 16.13-14).

---

[12]Nicholas of Cusa, *De Docta Ignorantia* (ed. A. Petzelt, 1.107).
[13]Roman Missal, Preface II for Ascension.

11

The Holy Spirit

"We believe in the Holy Spirit, the Lord, the giver of life, who proceeds from the Father and the Son."[1] The Holy Spirit is a Person of the Blessed Trinity, truly and eternally God. He is the Paraclete, the Counselor that Christ promised the apostles would be given "to be with you forever" (John 14.16). "God's love has been poured into our hearts through the Holy Spirit that has been given to us" (Rom. 5.5).

In this chapter we speak of the Holy Spirit, of His work in the Church, of His presence in each member of the faithful, and of the gifts He gives, distributing them to each one as He wills (cf. 1 Cor. 12.11).

The Spirit of God

Catholic faith believes that God dwells with us most intimately by the gift of the Holy Spirit. The Spirit is sent by the eternal Father and by Jesus to give light, comfort, and strength, and to stir up within us a newness of life. The Holy Spirit seals our friendship with God (cf. 2 Cor. 1.22), and He unites us with one another by the divine love He pours into our hearts (cf. Rom. 5.5).

The Holy Spirit is not simply a name given to warm movements of grace within us. The Spirit is God. He is a distinct Person of the Blessed Trinity, co-eternal and co-equal with the Father and the Son.[2]

The centuries of salvation history saw a gradual revelation of the Holy Spirit. The Old Testament shows a developing awareness and understanding of the working of God's Spirit in this world. The prophets taught that God was present in the world by His Spirit, and that in Messianic days the life and joy given by the gift of God's Spirit would be abundant. But the mystery of the Trinity, one God in three divine Persons, was not yet revealed to the chosen people of God living in the polytheistic world of antiquity and guarding faith in the true God by an intense witness to His oneness. Not until the era of the New Testament, in the paschal mystery and in the joys of Pentecost, was the Holy Spirit revealed as a distinct divine Person.

[1]Roman Missal, The Order of Mass, Profession of Faith.
[2]Cf. Creed of Constantinople I (DS 150); Council of Florence, Bull, *Cantate Domino* (February 4, 1442) (DS 1331).

In the Old Testament

The presence of God through His Spirit is suggested through several analogies in the Old Testament. The prophets used the word *Shekinah* to describe God's presence among His people, a presence sometimes manifested visibly by a light, a cloud, or a wind. The Hebrew word for Spirit, *Ruah*, has many closely interrelated meanings: it is spirit, and breath; it is the source of life breathed forth by God; through it God is present and active in this world.

Breath and spirit signified also the dynamic force under which a person acts, whether for good or for evil. We read, for example, that "the spirit of the LORD came mightily upon David" when he was anointed by Samuel (cf. 1 Sam. 16.13), and that "the Spirit of the LORD departed from Saul, and an evil spirit sent from the LORD tormented him" (1 Sam. 16.14). The last clause here may, of course, mean that God permitted Saul, who had turned from the Lord (cf. 1 Sam. 15.11), to be moved by a force hostile to God.

The Spirit of God is a charismatic force when it comes upon those holding office in Israel, as judges (cf. Judges 3.10; 11.29) and kings (cf. 1 Sam. 11.6). The Spirit of the Lord descended upon the prophets (cf. Isa. 61.1; Jer. 1.4); under His impetus they could proclaim the word of the Lord with courage and absolute faithfulness.

The Old Testament belief in the Spirit looked forward to a future fulfillment. The days would come when God would pour out His Spirit on all humankind. "I will pour My spirit upon your descendants, and My blessing on your offspring" (Isa. 44.3). "A new heart I will give you, and a new spirit I will put within you. . . . I will put My spirit within you, and make you follow My statutes and be careful to observe My ordinances" (Ezek. 36.26-27). "Then afterward I will pour out My spirit on all flesh; your sons and your daughters shall prophesy, your old men shall dream dreams, and your young men shall see visions. Even upon the male and female slaves, in those days, I will pour out My spirit" (Joel 2.28-29).

Most of all, the Messiah who was awaited would be entirely filled with the Holy Spirit. "For a child has been born for us, a son given to us; authority rests upon His shoulders, and He is named 'Wonderful Counselor, Mighty God, Everlasting Father, Prince of Peace.' . . . And the Spirit of the LORD shall rest on Him, the spirit of wisdom and understanding, the spirit of counsel and might, the spirit of knowledge and the fear of the LORD. . . . Here is My servant, whom I uphold, My chosen, in whom My soul delights: I have put My Spirit upon Him" (Isa. 9.6; 11.2; 42.1).

Thus the Old Testament speaks of the coming of the Spirit of God as a presence of God, acting with living energy from within. But the

Old Testament does not speak of the Holy Spirit as a divine Person distinct from the Father.

In the Gospels

It is through Jesus that the mystery of the inner life of God is revealed to us. He it is who made us know more fully the Father, by being in their midst as the divine Son sent by the Father. It is also through Jesus that the Spirit of God is revealed most richly, as a Person distinct from the Father and the Son, as the personal Love within the Trinity that is the source and pattern of all created love (cf. GS 24).

Much about the Spirit of God began to be experienced and understood only after Jesus had been glorified (cf. John 7.39). But the Gospels teach us that the Holy Spirit was active in the saving work of Jesus even before the paschal and Pentecostal mysteries made His special mission better known.

The Gospels speak often of the Spirit in describing the events surrounding the conception and birth of Jesus. The Gospel of St. Matthew tells us that Mary "was found to be with child of the Holy Spirit" (Matt. 1.18), and that Joseph was told by an angel: "Do not be afraid to take Mary as you wife, for the child conceived in her is from the Holy Spirit" (Matt. 1.20). In the Gospel of St. Luke we read of the earlier Annunciation to Mary. When Mary had asked how she, a virgin, could conceive, the angel had replied: "The Holy Spirit will come upon you, and the power of the Most High will overshadow you" (Luke 1.35). When Elizabeth was visited by Mary, Elizabeth was "filled with the Holy Spirit" (Luke 1.41). Zechariah too was "filled with the Holy Spirit" (Luke 1.67) when he uttered his prophecy at the time of John's circumcision. When Simeon held the infant Jesus in his arms, he was able to speak of Jesus' saving work, for he had received a special revelation from the Holy Spirit (cf. Luke 2.25-35).

While the Gospels speak often of the Holy Spirit, the words that speak of Him most clearly as a Person distinct from the Father and the Son are those of Christ at the Last Supper and after His resurrection. Jesus refers to Him as a "paraclete," or "counselor," or an "advocate," that is a comforter or helper; the word "paraclete" was used in profane Greek of a person called to assist or speak for another, especially in legal processes. "And I will ask the Father, and He will give you another Advocate, to be with you forever. This is the Spirit of truth" (John 14.16). "When the Advocate comes, whom I shall send to you from the Father, the Spirit of truth who comes from the Father, He will testify on My behalf" (John 15.26). "Go therefore and make disciples of all nations, baptizing them in the name of the Father and of the Son and of the Holy Spirit" (Matt. 28.19).

In these passages the Holy Spirit is clearly presented as One who is a Person as the Father and the Son are Persons, and yet One who is distinct from the Father and the Son, and sent to us by the Father and the Son.

In Faith and Doctrine

When the Advocate descended on the apostles on Pentecost, Peter was able to testify to the Spirit in order to explain the prodigies and charisms that accompanied the Pentecostal event. Addressing the crowd which had assembled, Peter spoke first of Jesus. "This Jesus God raised up, and of that we all are witnesses. Being therefore exalted at the right hand of God, and having received from the Father the promise of the Holy Spirit, He has poured out this that you both see and hear" (Acts 2.32-33). The people in the crowd were deeply moved and they asked Peter what they should do. He told them: "Repent, and be baptized every one of you in the name of Jesus Christ so that your sins may be forgiven; and you will receive the gift of the Holy Spirit" (Acts 2.38).

Jesus and the Holy Spirit together were always believed, loved, and adored in the Christian community. Absolute confidence was always placed in Jesus and in His Holy Spirit. Although Scripture nowhere uses the word "Trinity" to express the mystery of the Triune God, the Trinity itself was certainly known and adored before that word was adapted into special Christian usage.

As the early councils of the Church faithfully expressed the true and eternal relationship between the Father and the Son, so also they expressed the truth about the Holy Spirit. The ancient profession of faith still recited or sung each Sunday at Mass summarizes the Church's belief in the Holy Spirit:

> We believe in the Holy Spirit, the Lord, the giver of life, who proceeds from the Father and the Son.
> With the Father and the Son he is worshiped and glorified.
> He has spoken through the Prophets.[3]

Thus the Church proclaims belief in the Holy Spirit is precisely the same way in which it proclaims belief in the Father and in the Son. The Holy Spirit is a divine Person to be equally adored and honored.

The temporal missions of the Son and the Holy Spirit in this world reflect for us also Their eternal role in the Blessed Trinity, of which we shall speak further in the next chapter. The Son is the Word of the Father, eternally begotten; all that the Father is, is perfectly expressed

---

[3]Roman Missal, The Order of Mass, Profession of Faith. The creed used in the Mass is essentially the creed of the First Council of Constantinople in 381 (cf. DS 150), to which the Church subsequently added "and the Son" (*Filioque*) after "proceeds from the Father."

in the eternal Word who is His Son, so that the Son is forever equal to the Father. The Father and the Son love each other with an eternal Love that fully expresses everything that each of Them is, and is eternally equal to each; this Love which proceeds from the Father and the Son is a Person, the eternal Holy Spirit.

The Church has proclaimed much of its teaching on the Holy Spirit in its ordinary teaching, in its creeds, and in solemn declarations. There has not, however, been as great a development of the theology of the Holy Spirit over the centuries as there has been reflection on the eternal Son who has become incarnate among us. In many of the Eastern Fathers there is a rich theology of the Holy Spirit. The growing devotion to the Holy Spirit in our times, and the deepening interest in the theology of the Eastern thinkers, may lead to fruitful developments in reflection on the Holy Spirit in the Church of our time.

Devotion to the Holy Spirit

Faith is the personal and distinct reality of the Holy Spirit is ever reflected in the prayer of the Church. Something of the nature of this faith is seen in the rich array of titles given the Holy Spirit in worship. In the Sequence of the Mass for Pentecost, for example, the Holy Spirit is addressed as Father of the poor, Giver of gifts, Light of human hearts, Comforter, Guest of the soul, Consolation, and Most Blessed Light. In the hymn *Veni, Creator Spiritus*, the Holy Spirit is called Creator, Paraclete, Living Spring, Fire, and Love. Under these and many other names the Holy Spirit is adored.

The warm prayers of the Church to the Holy Spirit, especially on the feast of Pentecost and in administering the sacrament of confirmation, reflect the adoration and devotion to Him that have lived in the Church since earliest times. The witness of the ancient writers of both East and West to this devotion is supported by the evidence of Christian art and archaeology, hymnology, and liturgy. Surges of devotion to Holy Spirit have marked many periods of Church history, as in the Middle Ages, in the seventeenth century, and in modern times. Papal encyclicals of the past century have done much to encourage this devotion.[4]

The Holy Spirit and the Church

Jesus told the apostles that the richest outpouring of the Holy Spirit would come only after His own mission had come to its perfec-

---

[4]Cf. Pope Leo XIII, Encyclical, *Divinum Illud Munus* (May 9, 1897); Pope Pius XII, Encyclical, *Mystici Corporis* (June 29, 1943); Pope John Paul II, Encyclical, *Dominum et Vivificantem* (Lord and Giver of Life, May 18,1986) (EV 10.448-631).

tion and He had returned in His glorified humanity to the Father (cf. Acts 1.4-9). The decisive coming of the Spirit on Pentecost is described in the second chapter of the Acts of the Apostles. It is in the scriptural books that record the experiences of the early Church that the meaning and mission of the Holy Spirit are most clearly portrayed. The Acts of the Apostles, which chronicles much of the early life of the Church, has been called by some the "Gospel of the Holy Spirit." The Epistles of St. Paul are records of the intense activity of the Spirit in the life of the early Christians. St. Gregory of Nazianzus said that the Father is revealed in the Old Testament, the Son in the Incarnation, and the Holy Spirit in the Church.[5]

The Church recognizes all the books of the Bible as sacred because, "having been written under the inspiration of the Holy Spirit (cf. John 20.31; 2 Tim. 3.16; 2 Peter 1.19-21; 3.15-16), they have God as their Author" (DV 11). God chose the writers and used them in such a way that they "made use of their powers and abilities," so that "with Him acting in them and through them, they, as true authors, consigned to writing everything and only those things which He wanted" (DV 11). Since "everything asserted by the inspired authors or sacred writers must be held to be asserted by the Holy Spirit," it must be acknowledged that the books of Scripture "teach firmly, faithfully, and without error that truth which God wanted put into the sacred writings for our salvation" (DV 11).

The early Fathers of the Church insisted that the Church and the Holy Spirit are inseparable. "Where the Church is, there also is the Spirit of God; and where the Spirit of God is, there is the Church."[6] Today as well the Church proclaims that it is the Holy Spirit who gives life and being to the Church. "What was once preached by the Lord, or what was once wrought in Him for the saving of the human race, must be proclaimed and spread abroad to the ends of the earth (Acts 1.8), beginning from Jerusalem (cf. Luke 24.47), so that what was accomplished once for the salvation of all may in the course of time come to achieve its effect in all. To accomplish this goal, Christ sent the Holy Spirit from the Father. The Spirit was to carry out His saving work inwardly and to impel the Church toward her proper expansion. Doubtless, the Holy Spirit was already at work in the world before Christ was glorified. Yet on the day of Pentecost, He came down upon the disciples to remain with them forever (cf. John 14.16). On that day the Church was publicly revealed to the multitude, the spread of the Gospel among the nations by means of preaching began, and finally there was foreshadowed the union of peoples in a universal

---

5Cf. St. Gregory of Nazianzus, *Oratio* 31.26 (MG 36.161).
6Cf. St. Irenaeus of Lyons, *Adversus Haereses* 3.24.1 (MG 7.966).

faith, through the Church of the New Covenant. . ." (AG 3-4; cf. DV 8).

The Holy Spirit is the "soul" of the Church,[7] that is, of the Body of Christ. It is the Holy Spirit "who, with His heavenly breath of life, is to be considered the Principle of every vital and truly saving action in all parts of the Body. It is He who, though He is personally present in all the members and is divinely active in them, yet also works in the lower members through the ministry of the higher ones."[8]

The gifts of Christ are poured out upon the Church by the Holy Spirit. All the charisms, free gifts, are intended to increase faith, hope, and love, "for building up the body of Christ, until all of us come to the unity of the faith and of the knowledge of the Son of God" (Eph. 4.12-13).

Of primary importance, therefore, are those gifts that minister to the faith, love, and unity of the whole Church, that is, the hierarchical and sacramental gifts of Christ and His Spirit to His people. "The whole flock of Christ is preserved and grows in the unity of faith through the action of the same Holy Spirit" who gives the "charism of the Church's infallibility" (LG 25) to the successor of Peter and the "sure charism of truth" (DV 8) to the successors of all the apostles. Indeed, the personal coming of the Spirit to individual Christians first of all enables them to grasp as God's word the message spoken by those sent to speak in His name. For it is the Holy Spirit who "calls all men to Christ by the seeds of the word and by the preaching of the Gospel, and stirs up in hearts the obedience of faith" (AG 15). It is one and the same Spirit who enables the Church to proclaim the word of God faithfully and who enables hearers of the word to recognize the divine origin of the word proclaimed. "Under the guiding light of the Spirit of truth, revelation is religiously preserved and faithfully expounded in the Church" (LG 25).

But the ministry of the word is aimed ultimately at love. We are to recognize and believe God's word, that we might begin to share His love. As we share in His love we participate in His life. To share in the divine life won for us by Jesus Christ is a gift imparted through His sacraments, in which the Holy Spirit also exercises His sanctifying influence.

Baptism is conferred by water and the Holy Spirit (cf. John 4.5). In confirmation, the Christian receives a strengthening in the power of the Holy Spirit. When the sacrament of penance is administered, the very form of absolution notes the role of the Holy Spirit in the forgive-

---

[7]Cf. Pope Leo XIII, Encyclical, *Divinum Illud Munus* (May 9, 1897) (DS 3328), with quotation there from St. Augustine, *Sermo* 267.4 (ML 38.1231).
[8]Pope Pius XII, Encyclical, *Mystici Corporis* (June 29, 1943) (DS 3803).

ness of sins. The formula for the anointing of the sick calls down the grace of the Holy Spirit. Eucharistic prayers of the Mass invoke the sanctifying power of the Holy Spirit that the bread and wine may become the body and blood of Christ.[9]

The Holy Spirit in the Faithful

"Do you not know," asks St. Paul, "that you are God's temple and that God's Spirit dwells in you?" (1 Cor. 3.16).

The Holy Spirit works in the People of God corporately as the Church, but His warmth and love are directed also to each individual Christian. With personal concern He wills to sanctify each and lead each to the perfection of charity. In each person who is thirsty for the waters of grace (cf. Rev. 22.17) He wishes to make faith and love personal and strong.[10] Indeed, only the presence of the Spirit binds the Christian closely to Christ. "Anyone who does not have the Spirit of Christ does not belong to Him" (Rom. 8.9). "And . . . we know that He (Christ) abides in us, by the Spirit that He has given us" (1 John 3.24).

The essential task of the Holy Spirit within the souls of the faithful is this: to make them holy. To become holy, the Christian must be enlivened and guided by the Spirit. The process of becoming holy begins at baptism, when the Holy Spirit begins to dwell in the soul, to endow it with sanctifying grace, to implant in it faith and love and other rich gifts. "Those who love Me," Jesus said, "will keep My word, and My Father will love them, and We will come to them and make Our home with them" (John 14.23).

Gifts of the Holy Spirit

All the generous gifts by which God calls to holiness are attributed to the Holy Spirit, the "Sanctifier." The expression "gifts of the Holy Spirit" is used also in a particular sense, however, to refer to a special set of endowments which are most conducive to growth in the life of grace. These gifts of the Spirit are traditionally enumerated as wisdom, understanding, counsel, fortitude, knowledge, piety, and fear of the Lord (cf. Isa. 11.2-3). Of these gifts, and of the divine indwelling and of the other sanctifying activities of the Holy Spirit, more will be said in a later chapter, in a treatment of grace.

Charismatic Gifts

In addition to the hierarchical and sacramental gifts given to the whole Church to make unity and holiness possible, and in addition to

---

[9]Cf. Roman Missal, The Order of Mass, Eucharistic Prayers II, III, IV.
[10]Pope John Paul II, Apostolic Exhortation, *Catechesi Tradendae* (October 16, 1979) n. 72 (EV 6.1929-1938).

the inner gifts that make individuals holy, there are also many charismatic gifts, or "charisms." These charisms are not given for the sake of their individual recipients alone, but for the benefit of others, "for building up the body of Christ" (Eph. 4.12). Charisms have an appropriate place in the life of the Church. A mature faith must evaluate them carefully (cf. 1 Cor. 14). Authentic spiritual gifts are the work of the Holy Spirit (cf. 1 Cor. 12.4), and God's favor is received "according to the measure of Christ's gift" (Eph. 4.7). St. Paul always insists that the charisms are intended to unite the Church, not to divide it, though each member may have a special gift, he is to use it for the benefit of all in the unity of faith and love (cf. 1 Cor. 12.22-26).

One may rightly desire to have a charism, for authentic charisms serve the good of the Church. All the charisms are of their nature ordered toward "a still more excellent way" (1 Cor. 12.31), that is, the way of Christian love.

By the end of the second century, extraordinary and miraculous charisms had largely disappeared from the Christian communities. St. Gregory the Great, who lived in the sixth century, noted this fact and explained it by pointing out that such charismatic signs were necessary in the first days of faith, but not in later years.[11] When a visible family of faith had become rooted in the world, then the Church itself with its marks of unity, faith, and love became the principal sign of God's presence.[12]

Prophecy

One of the most important charisms is that of prophecy. Prophets are moved by the Holy Spirit to speak His words and His will rather than their own. Often "prophecy" is used for "foretelling the future." Under God's inspiration people can do this, and have done so. But the charism of prophecy is more frequently concerned with proclaiming God's will for the present. Prophecy calls people earnestly to faithfulness to God and to performance of deeds of justice and mercy.

Prophecy serves the "upbuilding and encouragement and consolation" (1 Cor. 14.3) of the Church, and it will not be absent from a community that is strong in faith.

Discernment of Spirits

Among the gifts listed by St. Paul is "the discernment of spirits" (1 Cor. 12.10).[13] Such a gift is necessary in the Church. For it is pos-

---

[11]Cf. St. Gregory the Great, *Homiliae in Evangelia*, hom. 29.4 (MG 76.1215-1216).

[12]Cf. First Vatican Council, Session 3, April 24, 1870, *Dogmatic Constitution on the Catholic Faith*, ch. 3 (DS 3013-3014).

[13]Cf. Pope John Paul II, Apostolic Exhortation, *Familiaris Consortio* (November 22, 1981) n. 5 (EV 7.1536-1540).

sible for us to be deceived, and to believe that the Holy Spirit is urging us when really we are being moved merely by some deep desire of our own, or even by hidden and unworthy motives, or by a spirit of the world or an evil spirit. The spirits, then, are to be tested. "Beloved, do not believe every spirit, but test the spirits to see whether they are from God; for many false prophets have gone out into the world" (1 John 4.1).

Jesus Himself gave the basic criterion for the discernment of spirits: "You will know them by their fruits" (Matt. 7.16). Utterances and deeds that exhibit obedience to faith and lead to unity and peace in faith and love, these are the works of the Holy Spirit; those that turn from faith and disturb the unity of Christian love are not from the Holy Spirit (cf. 1 John 4.2-6; 1 Cor. 12.3). Charisms are not to be used in disorder, but in peace and obedience. "The spirits of prophets are subject to prophets, for God is a God not of disorder but of peace" (1 Cor. 14.32-33).

Charismatic gifts are to be evaluated and their use governed by those to whom God has entrusted the care of the community of faith. "These charismatic gifts, whether they be the most outstanding or the more simple and more widely diffused, are to be received with thanksgiving and consolation, for they are exceedingly suitable and useful for the needs of the Church. Still, extraordinary gifts are not to be rashly sought after, nor are the fruits of apostolic labor to be presumptuously expected from them. In any case, judgment as to their genuineness and proper use belongs to those who preside over the Church, and to whose special competence it belongs, not indeed to extinguish the Spirit, but to test all things and hold fast to that which is good (cf. 1 Thess. 5.12, 19-21)" (LG 12).

The Mission of the Spirit

The mission of the Holy Spirit in salvation history is summarized in the following words of the Second Vatican Council:

"When the work which the Father had given the Son to do on earth (cf. John 17.4) was accomplished, the Holy Spirit was sent on the day of Pentecost in order that He might forever sanctify the Church, and thus believers would have access to the Father through Christ in the one Spirit (cf. Eph. 2.18). He is the Spirit of life, a fountain of water springing up to life eternal (cf. John 4.14; 7.38-39). Through Him the Father gives life to men who are dead from sin, till at last He revives in Christ even their mortal bodies (cf. Rom. 8.10-11). The Spirit dwells in the Church and in the hearts of the faithful as in a temple (cf. 1 Cor. 3.16; 6.19). In them He prays and bears witness to the fact that they are adopted sons (cf. Gal. 4.6; Rom. 8.15-16, 26). The Spirit guides the Church into the fullness of truth (cf. John 16.13) and gives her a unity of fellowship and service. He furnishes and directs her with hierarchical and charismatic gifts, and adorns her with His fruits (cf. Eph. 4.11-12; 1 Cor. 12.4; Gal. 5.22). By the power of the Gospel He makes the Church keep the freshness of youth, perpetually renews her, and leads her to perfect union with her Spouse. The Spirit and the Bride say to the Lord Jesus, 'Come!' (cf. Rev. 22.17)" (LG 4).

12

The Holy Trinity

The central mystery of Christian faith is the mystery of the Holy Trinity. "The history of salvation is identical with the history of the way and the plan by which God, true and one, the Father, the Son, the Holy Spirit, reveals Himself to men, and reconciles and unites with Himself those turned away from sin."[1]

In this chapter we speak of the mystery of the Trinity, and of what it means to believe in the Trinity, "three Persons equal in majesty, undivided in splendor, yet one Lord, one God, ever to be adored."[2] We discuss how the mystery of the Trinity transcends human reason but is not contrary to it; how the works of the Trinity in salvation history reveal to us something of the inner life of the Triune God; and how in Its saving deeds for us the Trinity works in unity.

The Mystery of the Trinity

The mystery of the Blessed Trinity is the mystery of God in Himself. Because it illumines so many other teaching of the faith, and because belief in it is presupposed by so many other revealed truths, it stands clearly as the most basic and essential of teachings in the "hierarchy of the truths of faith."[3]

The key importance of the Trinity in Christian doctrine is evident from the beginning. When Christ commissioned the apostles to go forth and "make disciples of all the nations" (Matt. 28.19), He instructed them to baptize in the name of the Trinity: ". . .baptizing them in the name of the Father and of the Son and of the Holy Spirit" (Matt. 28.19). From the earliest centuries the Church's professions of faith have proclaimed belief in the Trinity of the Father, the Son, and the Holy Spirit. "Now the Catholic faith is this: that we worship one God in the Trinity, and the Trinity in unity. . . . The Father is a distinct Person, the Son is a distinct Person, and the Holy Spirit is a distinct Per-

[1]Sacred Congregation for the Clergy, *General Catechetical Directory* (April 11, 1971), n. 47 (EV 4.523).
[2]Roman Missal, Preface for Masses of the Holy Trinity.
[3]Sacred Congregation for the Clergy, *General Catechetical Directory* (April 11, 1971) n. 43 (EV 4.519). Cf. UR 11-12.

son; but the Father and the Son and the Holy Spirit have one divinity, equal glory, and coeternal majesty."[4]

To believe in the Trinity is to believe that there is only one God, and that there are three distinct Persons who possess eternally the same divine nature. To say that there is only one God or only one divine nature is to say that there is no plurality of divine beings. Thus there is only one Wisdom, one Love, one Life that is God, the source and goal of all. The one only God exists in three Persons, the Father, the Son, and the Holy Spirit, three who are distinct, but who know us with one infinite wisdom and who love us with one eternal love, and with whom we can enter into personal relationships through grace.

Mystery of Faith

The Trinity is in the strictest sense a mystery of faith. It is one of those "mysteries hidden in God which, unless divinely revealed, could not come to be known."[5] Some truths of revelation are open to rational investigation and discovery, but mysteries like that of the Trinity can be grasped only by believing God, and only by those who have recognized His testimony in the message of faith.

The fact that mysteries such as that of the Trinity can be grasped only by faith is in no way an affront to human reason. The divine mysteries are not contrary to human reason, nor are they incompatible with the principles of rational thought. Even in our relationships with other human persons we must fall back upon faith — a human faith — to know the truth of their intimate lives and of their love for us. The things God tells us of His intimate life are above reason, although reason, enlightened by faith, can come to some understanding of them.

"And indeed reason, illumined by faith, when it seeks earnestly, devoutly, and prudently, does attain by a gift from God some understanding of mysteries, and that a most fruitful one."[6] By analogy with truths which are naturally known, and by discovering the close and illuminating interrelationships of mysteries, one can gain insight into the depth of their richness. But the human mind can never fully grasp the divine mysteries in the way it can comprehend finite and created things. "For the divine mysteries by their very nature so surpass the created intellect that even when delivered by revelation and accepted by faith, they yet remain covered by the veil of faith itself and shrouded as it were in a sort of obscurity so long as in this mortal life

---

[4]Creed "Quicumque," often called "Athanasian Creed" (DS 75).

[5]First Vatican Council, Session 3, April 24, 1870, *Dogmatic Constitution on the Catholic Faith*, ch. 4 (DS 3015).

[6]First Vatican Council, Session 3, April 24, 1870, *Dogmatic Constitution on the Catholic Faith*, ch. 4 (DS 3016).

'we are away from the Lord, for we walk by faith and not by sight' (2 Cor. 5.6-7)."[7]

At Center of Faith

The dogma of the Trinity is the central dogma of Catholic faith. Only with belief in it can one grasp and explicitly believe other central Christian teachings.

"It is impossible to believe explicitly in the mystery of Christ without faith in the Trinity, for the mystery of Christ includes that the Son of God took flesh, that He renewed the world through the grace of the Holy Spirit, and again, that He was conceived by the Holy Spirit."[8] Clearly one could not believe that Jesus is the Son of God, and true God, sent by the Father, if one did not believe in the plurality of Persons in one God. Nor could one grasp the meaning of eternal life, or of the grace that leads to it, without believing in the Trinity, for grace and eternal life are a sharing in the Trinitarian life.

All the teachings and sacraments and hopes of Christian life are related to the personal life of the Trinity, to the infinite and eternal love which forever unites the three divine Persons, and which calls all human persons to share in the life of the Trinity.

The basic importance of the doctrine of the Trinity is that it communicates to us light on the inner life of God. God reveals to us primarily Himself (cf. DV 2), and all of God's merciful deeds in salvation history are aimed at uniting our lives with the life of the Trinity.

The Trinity in Revelation

The doctrine of the Trinity was not revealed with full clarity at the start of salvation history. Only gradually did God make known to His people the truth about Himself (cf. DV 2-4). In the Old Testament there were foreshadowings, but the mystery of the Trinity was not formally revealed. In the New Testament the mystery is revealed; the Son and the Holy Spirit are made known, and are recognized as God and as Persons distinct from the Father. But for the Church to attain a clearer synthesis of these truths with the enduring truth that there is only one God, took prayer and reflection, and the guidance of the Holy Spirit, through the first generations of Christian faith.[9]

The word "Trinity" does not appear in the New Testament; and the meanings of the words "person" and "nature," in the precise sense

---

[7]First Vatican Council, Session 3, April 24, 1870, *Dogmatic Constitution on the Catholic Faith*, ch. 4 (DS 3016).
[8]St. Thomas Aquinas, *Summa Theologica* II-II, 2, 8.
[9]Cf. John Henry Cardinal Newman, *An Essay on the Development of Christian Doctrine*, ch. 4, sect. 2.

in which these words are used to bear the message of God, had to be carefully refined to bear the message rightly. But what the New Testament teaches is in truth captured with care and reverence in the exact statements of the early councils of the Church.[10]

Old Testament

The Old Testament proclaims clearly part of the mystery of the Trinity, for it proclaims clearly that there is only one God. But it does not speak of a plurality of Persons in God or reveal the inner life of God. The Old Testament writers declare rather the external works and manifestations of God. They use various names for Him (El, Elohim, Shaddai, Adonai), but the revealed name most properly His is Yahweh, for He is the great "I AM" (cf. Exod. 3.13-16). He is the one and only God. "Hear, O Israel: The LORD is our God, the LORD alone. . . . See now that I, even I, am He; there is no god beside Me" (Deut. 6.4, 32.39).

Yet there are some passages in the Old Testament which seem to be veiled references to, or in a way preparations for the revelation of, distinct Persons in God. Many of the Fathers saw such suggestions in the frequent use of the plural noun (Elohim) and plural personal pronoun for the one God (cf. Gen. 1.26; 3.22; 11.7) and in the triple repetitions of the divine name or attributes (cf. Deut. 6.4; Ps. 67.7-8; Isa. 6.3). More significant are the special names and titles that suggest some distinction in divinity (cf. the uses of "Wisdom" and "Spirit" in reference to God in Wisd. 7; Prov. 8.22f.; Isa. 32.15, 42.1).

New Testament

Jesus Christ, by His presence, by His promise of the Holy Spirit, and by His teaching, revealed the mystery of the Trinity. In earlier chapters we have seen how the Gospels proclaim what is essential to the Trinitarian mystery: that there is one God; that Jesus is the true Son of God, truly God, a divine Person distinct from and sent by the Father; and that the Holy Spirit is God, a divine Person sent by the Father and the Son to console and enlighten the faithful.

At times the New Testament speaks in compact sentences the mystery of the Trinity. Christ instructs the apostles to baptize "in the name of the Father and of the Son and of the Holy Spirit" (Matt.28.19). In His discourse at the Last Supper Jesus talks with warmth of the Persons of the Trinity. He, the Son, has been sent by the Father; in turn He will ask the Father, and the Father "will give you another Advocate, to be with you forever. This is the Spirit of truth"

[10]Cf. Congregation for the Doctrine of the Faith, *Declaration for Protection of Faith in the Mysteries of the Incarnation and the Trinity* (February 21, 1972) (EV 4.1558.1571).

(John 14.16-17). The divine mission that has been Christ's will be completed by the divine gift of the Holy Spirit (cf. John 12.49; 15.26; 14.9-21).

In the Gospel of St. John there are several passages that imply the Father, Son, and Holy Spirit are distinct Persons (cf. John 1.29-35; 14.16; 14.26; 16.15). St. Paul often refers to the three Persons of the Trinity in a single passage: "The grace of our Lord Jesus Christ, the love of God, and the communion of the Holy Spirit be with all of you" (2 Cor. 13.13); "Now there are varieties of gifts, but the same Spirit; and there are varieties of service, but the same Lord; and there are varieties of working, but it is the same God who activates all of them in everyone" (1 Cor. 12.4-6; cf. also 2 Thess. 2.13-14; Gal. 4.6; Rom. 15.30). In this text, as often in the New Testament, "God" is used to name the Father, the first Person of the Trinity.

The revelation of the Blessed Trinity is reflected also in many other passages of the New Testament, as, for example, in this phrase from the First Epistle of Peter: "chosen and destined by God the Father and sanctified by the Spirit to be obedient to Jesus Christ" (1 Peter 1.2; cf. also Titus 3.4-6; Heb. 10.29; Jude 20-21).

The Eternal Trinity and History

Jesus did not reveal the mystery of the Trinity in abstract language but in the context of God's saving deeds for humankind. In His presence and in His words He spoke of His own "mission" in the world and of "sending" the Holy Spirit. He Himself had been sent forth by His Father (cf., e.g., John 4.34; 5.23) into history at a certain place to save His people. He said that after His glorification the Father would send in His name another divine Advocate, the Spirit of truth (cf. John 14.16-17; 15.26). But the temporal missions of the Son and of the Holy Spirit reflect also the eternal "processions" within God. Through His saving deeds among us, God reveals His inner life to us.

The Eternal Trinity

By His saving deeds and words God reveals to us first of all Himself (cf. DV 2). When the Father sent His Son into the world, and when the Holy Spirit was sent by the Father and the Son (cf. John 14.16-17; 15.26), something of the inner life of God was revealed to us. Within the Trinity the Son proceeds eternally from the Father, and the Holy Spirit proceeds eternally from the Father and the Son. Faith in the Trinity is faith in three eternal, equal, infinite Persons, each distinct from the others, yet each the same one God. Faith in the Trinity is faith in three divine Persons living in the deep eternal relationships of the Trinity. The Father is always the Father to the eternal Son, who is ever His only-begotten and uncreated Son. The Holy Spirit lives always as the Person who expresses the eternal love that binds the Father and the Son.

Scripture speaks in two ways of the relationship between the first two persons of the Blessed Trinity. The second Person is Son to the first, the Father. He is also the Word of the Father, who dwells with the Father eternally, with Him "in the beginning" as the Word through whom all created things come to be (cf. John 1.1-3). The Son is the perfect image of the Father (cf. 2 Cor. 4.4), perfectly mirroring and expressing all that the Father is.

The Father is absolutely without origin. The Son is uncreated, eternal, equally God; but without beginning and eternally He proceeds from the Father. He enjoys a uniquely divine knowledge and revelatory power. He is truly the Father's Son, but the eternal, unchanging, infinite Son who is God equally with His Father.

The Holy Spirit, a Person distinct from the Father and the Son, is equally truly God. In God there is infinite wisdom and infinite love. The Father eternally knows Himself with a perfect Word, an expression of wisdom that fully speaks God's full reality, and this Word is the Son (cf. John 1.1, 14). The Father and the Son love one another with a boundless love, a love that fully expresses all Their reality, a love which is personal and living as are the Father and the Son, and this personal Love proceeding from the Father and the Son is the Holy Spirit. The Spirit is not created; He is a Person co-equal and co-eternal with the Father and the Son.

Intimately present to one another, bound together in inexpressible love, distinct Persons dwelling in perfect unity, the Blessed Trinity is the model and goal of every personal society. "The Lord Jesus, when He prayed to the Father, 'that all may be one . . . as We are One' (John 17.21-22), opened up vistas closed to human reason. For He implied a certain likeness between the union of the divine Persons and the union of God's sons in truth and charity" (GS 24).

Here we see one of the basic reasons why the doctrine of the Trinity is central for Christian faith. While there is but one God, and He is the Source of all else that is, God is not an utterly solitary God, nor is He an impersonal sea of being. The Trinity, the one true God, is a community of Persons eternally bound together in perfect understanding and love. In knowing the mystery of the Trinity, we realize that divine life can be shared, and shared even by us created persons, who as adopted sons and daughters can be brought into the joy of the perfect community.

The ancient creed from which we quoted earlier in this chapter speaks of the relations among the Persons of the Trinity. "The Father is not made by anyone, nor created, nor begotten. The Son is from the Father alone, not made, not created, but begotten. The Holy Spirit is from the Father and the Son, not made, not created, not begotten, but proceeding. ... But the entire three Persons are co-eternal with one another and co-equal, so that, as has already been said above, both Trinity in Unity and Unity in Trinity are to be adored."[11]

Inadequacy of Analogies

Many have tried to find ways of expressing at least something of the mystery of the Trinity by analogy with created things. Some have sought as comparison the human person as an image of the Trinity, for from our mind spring forth both the "word" which expresses one's understanding and the inspiration which bears one's love. Others have used the example of fire with its flame, heat, and light. On a different level, still others have cited the shamrock, the three-leaf clover. Some contemporary authors seek analogies in I-Thou relationships, in the presence in friendship of understanding and love.

However helpful these various analogies may be to some, they are all inadequate. The mystery of the Triune God so far transcends creation that no analogies from created things can express it adequately. The heat of a fire is not the fire, nor is the light the fire. But the Father is God, the Son is God, and the Holy Spirit is God, and each of the three distinct Persons is the one God.

Yet those ways of speaking of the Trinity that are commended by the Fathers, and especially those rooted in Scripture, are to be profoundly respected. Terms that Scripture uses to express the inner life of the Trinity are certainly true and not without foundation in reality. We can certainly say that the two divine processions (of the Son from the Father, and of the Spirit from the Father and the Son), whose existence is guaranteed by Scripture, are related to the two basic acts which we know belong to persons: knowledge and love. This is firmly rooted in God's word. Even there, of course, there is less than full and perfect expression of that Reality which is greater than all else. Because of the limitations of human knowledge, our present understanding of the infinite God must be expressed in human concepts. The divine gift guarantees that the words proclaimed in His name are true. The divine mysteries themselves remain for us here on earth shrouded in obscurity; but faith remains confident, resting on the authority of the Triune God making Himself known to us.

Councils and the Trinity

The first councils of the Church sought to express more clearly and precisely as well as faithfully the message God has given of Him-

---

[11]Creed "Quicumque," often called "Athanasian Creed" (DS 75).

self. For human pride, unwilling to recognize the majesty of God and the truth of mysteries that are beyond full human comprehension, was beginning to lead many away from the faith, and there was need to reject erroneous versions of the divine message.

Thus the heresies of Arianism and Macedonianism were rejected, for they failed to admit the co-equality and co-eternity of the Persons who are God. Sabellianism and other kinds of Modalism were rejected, for they held that there are not really three distinct Persons, but only One, and that the Father, in coming to save us, would be named the Son, and thus that there is no eternal Son distinct from Him and eternally loved by Him in the Spirit. Also rejected were rationalistic theories that were really tritheisms, holding that there are three divine substances or gods rather than only one divine wisdom and love, in which three Persons subsist, who are the one God.

All these heresies the Church steadfastly denies, because there is a literal truth which God has revealed to us. And this is a truth central to human hope, for the life of the Trinity is the model of all perfect love, and is the beatitude we were created to share in. The Church steadfastly professes faith in three Persons who are distinct, but are the one God. "We believe in one God, the Father almighty. . . . And in one Lord Jesus Christ, the only-begotten Son of God, born of the Father before all ages, Light from light, true God from true God, begotten, not made, consubstantial with the Father; through Him all things were made. . . . And in the Holy Spirit, the Lord and giver of life, who proceeds from the Father, and who together with the Father and the Son is adored and glorified, who spoke through the prophets. . . ."[12]

The truths of the Trinity are ever defended with fervor by the Church, for only orthodox Trinitarian beliefs sustains faith in Jesus and keeps alive the heavenly hope of the community of faith.

The Saving Works of God

Since the Father, Son, and Holy Spirit subsist in the one divine nature, the creative and conserving and saving acts of God are acts of all the Persons of the Blessed Trinity. "The three Persons are not to be considered as separable, since it is our belief that none existed or acted before or after another or without another. For they are inseparable both in what They are and in what They do."[13]

The three Persons have "one substance, one essence, one nature, one divinity, one immeasurableness, one eternity, and all things are one where there is no distinction by opposition of relation."[14] The last

---

[12]Creed of the First Council of Constantinople, 381 (DS 150). In later forms of this creed, and in the liturgical use of it, "and the Son" is added after the words "proceeds from the Father."
[13]Creed of the Eleventh Council of Toledo, 675 (DS 531).
[14]Council of Florence, Bull, *Cantate Domino* (February 4, 1442) (DS 1330).

words here refer to what are called "the divine relations," that is, the relationships of the three Persons to one another in the life of the Trinity. The Father, Son, and Holy Spirit are indeed distinct Persons, and in God's inner life They are present to each other with intimate personal presence. Thus, what is done by the Father in works outside the Trinity, in creating and conserving the universe and in deeds of salvation, is done by all three Persons together. It is not the Father alone who creates, but the Father with the Son and the Holy Spirit. So also it is God the Blessed Trinity who guards and saves us in all things. What is done by one Person through the divine nature is shared by the three Persons who subsist in one nature, one wisdom, one love.

Still, certain works done by the Trinity, and thus literally by all the Persons, are fittingly attributed to one of the Persons when the work or action in question reflects that which is, in God's inner life, most proper to one Person. The technical word for such attribution is "appropriation." To the Father are appropriated especially the works of power, like creation; to the Son, the works of wisdom; to the Holy Spirit, the works of love.[15]

Some truths are spoken literally of one Person and not of the other Persons. It is the Son, "one of the Holy Trinity,"[16] who became man and suffered for us, not the Father or the Holy Spirit. Hence it would be incorrect to say that the Father or the Holy Spirit suffered for us on the cross. For what Jesus did and suffered for us in His human nature was done by the Son of God rather than by the Father or the Holy Spirit. But the eternal divine love of the Son for us is shared equally by the Father and the Spirit.

The Trinity and Christian Life

"Those who love Me," said Jesus, "will keep My word, and My Father will love them, and We will come to them and make Our home with them. . . . But the Advocate, the Holy Spirit, whom the Father will send in My name, will teach you everything, and remind you of all that I have said to you" (John 14.23, 26).

The Father sent His only Son that we might have supernatural life. It is only in and through the Son, Jesus Christ, that we receive this life and become adopted children of God our Father. The Spirit sent by the Father and the Son is to complete the work of the soul's sanctification, even to the point of transformation in Christ. In this sense the just soul enjoys a special relationship with each of the Persons of the Trinity. The Father regenerates and adopts us through the redemptive merits of

---

[15]Cf. Pope Leo XIII, Encyclical, *Divinum Illud Munus* (May 9, 1897) (DS 3326).

[16]Second Council of Constantinople, Session 8, June 2, 553, *Anathematisms concerning the Three Chapters*, canon 10 (DS 432).

Jesus Christ, the Son, and He leads us to the perfection of grace and charity through the power of the Holy Spirit.

Through the gift of sanctifying grace the soul is admitted to the fellowship of the three divine Persons, who dwell in the soul of the just. The soul then becomes a mirror of the Trinity — the Father generating the Word in the soul and the Father and the Word together infusing the Spirit of love.

This "indwelling" of the Trinity is in Scripture attributed in a special way to the Holy Spirit. When the Holy Spirit enters the soul, He comes with all His gifts, so that if the soul responds it can be led to the perfection of the life of grace and charity. By the Holy Spirit all baptized Christians are called to the fullness of life which constitutes Christian perfection.

In this life it is not possible for our human minds to comprehend the mystery of the Trinity. Human language, fashioned to speak of the visible realities of our experience, is strained to speak of this sublime truth about God. Much that is said in these pages concerning the Trinity may seem paradoxical and puzzling. What has been said with great care by saints and by councils of the Church to guard this central mystery of faith may seem at first entirely opaque. But in prayer and reflection and love we can grow in the knowledge of the eternal Father, and of Jesus His son, and of the Spirit who dwells in us.

The goal of all Christian life is to know the Blessed Trinity, to know the Father, the Son, and the Holy Spirit even as They know us, and so to share in God's inner life of wisdom and love (cf. 1 John 3.2). This the just will do in the eternal life to come, and they will be eternally happy "with a joy very similar to that with which the most holy and undivided Trinity is happy."[17]

---

[17]Pope Pius XII, Encyclical, *Mystici Corporis* (June 29, 1943) (DS 3815). See also, Pope John Paul II, Encyclical, *Dominum et Vivificantem* (May 18, 1986), Part III, 6.

13

The Catholic Church

The Catholic Church belongs entirely to Christ. He is the Head of the Church, its Founder, its Spouse and Savior. He continues to do His saving work in and through the Church. In the New Testament we see His preparation for the Church, His promises concerning it, and the beginning of their rich fulfillment.

In this chapter we speak of the Church as the continuation of Christ in the world and as the sacrament of His presence; as a reality illumined in Scripture by many titles and images; as a visible family of faith sealed with many marks to show that it is Christ's; and as a community having a design and structure fashioned by Christ Himself.

Christ in the Church

Christ is the Light of the world. The Church receives its being and mission from Him. The Church is not merely a society of men and women; it has a certain sacred dimension because of the inseparable union which Christ established between it and Himself. Only in the light of that union can the Church be seen in proper perspective.

For it is not the Church as such that is the primary object of Catholic faith. The Catholic believes in Christ, and in His Father, and in the Holy Spirit. In the creed he or she professes belief in "the holy Catholic Church," but precisely because one sees the Church as a presence of Christ and of His Spirit. The Catholic believes what the Church teaches, but precisely because one recognizes Christ's authority in the Church. The Catholic recognizes a duty to further the work of the Church, but precisely because the mission of the Church is seen as a continuation of Christ's work in the world. Always Catholic faith sees the Church in relation to Christ.

Our faith and our hope, including our hope in the Church, are in Christ. He organized the Church to carry on His work in the world, bringing His ministry and truth to all and always. It is Christ who accomplishes all that is done in the Church for our salvation. The institution which is the Church survives because it comes from Christ, and He promises to be with it to the end of time (cf. Matt. 28.20).

The Church Is a Sacrament of Christ

"By her relationship with Christ, the Church is a kind of sacrament or sign and instrument of intimate union with God, and of the unity of the whole human race" (LG 1).

A sacrament is a sacred sign. In Catholic usage the word "sacrament" has been used especially for baptism, or the Eucharist, or any of the seven sacraments in which visible realities are, by the will of Christ, made effective signs of His saving gifts. The Church is as it were a more universal and comprehensive sacrament: it is a visible reality that Christ has formed in this world as a sacred sign of His presence, a sign and also the means He uses to give the unity and holiness He actually confers through it.

As a family called to share in the life of the Trinity, the Church has an eternal destiny. But in its time of pilgrimage on earth it has also visible, sacramental dimensions: it exists also as a sign. The very purpose of a "sign" is to lead beyond itself. Because the Church is a sign, it must lead us to what it signifies, that is, to Christ, to God. And when we come finally to God, with Christ, in eternity, the Church in this aspect of a sign will have no further reason to exist. It will have accomplished what God put it on earth to do. When we speak of the Church in heaven, we no longer mean the Church in the condition in which it is a sign, with ministers and sacraments. These will cease; as signs and instruments they will be absorbed into the heavenly realities they serve. When we speak of the Church in heaven, therefore, we mean the union of the saints with Christ, the life they have in Him with the Father and the Holy Spirit. That reality is already present on earth because of the faith and love God pours into our hearts. Its full glory does not appear here, however; that is for the next world.

In this sense, the Second Vatican Council describes the mission of the Church: "The Church, 'like a pilgrim in a foreign land, presses forward amid the persecutions of the world and the consolations of God,' announcing the cross and death of the Lord until He comes (cf. 1 Cor. 11.26). By the power of the risen Lord, she is given strength to overcome patiently and lovingly the afflictions and hardships which assail her from within and without, and to show forth in the world the mystery of the Lord in a faithful though shadowed way, until at the last it will be revealed in full light" (LG 8).[1] The church must work "until through the Cross she arrives at the light which knows no setting" (LG 9).

The sacrament which is the visible Church is now, in time, a precious and indispensable gift of Christ. It is the work of Christ, and will last, as He promises, until the end of the world when it reaches its ful-

[1]The interior quotation is from St. Augustine, *De Civitate Dei* 18.51.2 (ML 41.614).

fillment in glorious union in Christ. Its task on earth will not be finished until Christ brings His redemptive work to completion and God has become, as St. Paul put it, "all, and in all" (Col. 3.11).

The Spirit comes to us only because Christ sends Him, and Christ sends the Spirit for the express purpose of guiding His Church and safeguarding it from error, and sanctifying its members in truth (cf. John 17.17). He sends the Spirit with the promise that the Spirit "will guide you into all the truth" (John 16.13) and "remind you of all that I have said to you" (John 14.26). The life of the Church and the life of the Spirit among those who love God are joined together and are inseparable from Christ. It is not possible to neglect the Church, through which the Lord gives His most precious gifts, if we wish to receive those gifts. One of the earliest Fathers of the Church, St. Irenaeus, expressed this truth beautifully: "Where the Church is, there is the Spirit of God, and where the Spirit of God is, there is the Church and all grace, and the Spirit is truth."[2]

The Mystery of Christ in the Church

The Church is a living continuation on earth of its divine Founder. Jesus is indeed the Son of God, but He is truly an individual Man, too, the Son of Mary. Similarly, the Church is the presence of Christ and His Holy Spirit, a bearer of heavenly gifts, yet is also very human, very much of the earth. Its sublime mission is carried out by human agents. In doing their work these human agents perform sacred ceremonies (entrusted to them by Christ) that are linked, in what we commonly call the sacraments, with ordinary realities of human life: bread, water, wine, oil. As Christ in His humanity could appear unattractive to those who did not understand the mystery concealed by His humanity (cf. Isa. 53.3), so the visible humanness of the Church might lead many to undervalue it.

But many came to faith in Jesus because the signs He gave, most of all His resurrection, made them able to recognize Him as Lord and Maker of all. So also those who love Him can come to recognize His visible Church. The signs with which He has marked the Church, and the inner graces by which He makes Catholics able to understand these signs, enable them to see the saving presence of Jesus in the works He does in the Church.

To come to the Catholic faith is to see that the Church acts for Christ. It is to understand that when a priest gives us a sacrament, it is Christ who gives us the sacrament through him. It is to know that when the Church speaks His word to us, it is Christ who speaks and calls to faith. It is to recognize in the teaching and ruling authority of the Church the shepherding of Christ.

---

[2]St. Irenaeus, *Adversus Haereses* 3.24.1 (MG 7.966).

The essential activity of the Church is its spiritual life: its believing, hoping, and loving, and its services of teaching and shepherding that nourish such life in Christ. All the external structures and activities of the Church exist to serve the spiritual purposes.

There are not two churches, one visible and external, the other invisible and spiritual. There is one Church of Christ. It is the visible Church in which and through which Christ acts.

The visible Church and the spiritual presence of Christ "form one interlocked reality, which is comprised of a divine and a human element. For this reason, by an excellent analogy, the reality is compared to the mystery of the incarnate Word. Just as the assumed nature inseparably united to the divine Word serves Him as a living instrument of salvation, so, in a similar way, does the communal structure of the Church serve Christ's Spirit, who vivifies it by way of building up the body (cf. Eph. 4.16)" (LG 8).

The Mystery Is Taught by Images

We can learn best about the Church from the images and titles Our Lord and His apostles used to illumine its nature. No one image or title can exhaust the mystery.

The People of God

The Second Vatican Council chose especially to speak of the Church as the "People of God" (cf. LG 9-17). The Church is not an abstraction, and it certainly is not merely a group of officials in important positions. The Church is made up of all the members of the family of faith. We are all together the Church, all blessed with the gifts of the Spirit. As one united people, we are called to do Christ's work in the world.

"This was to be the new People of God. For, those who believe in Christ, who are reborn not from a perishable but from an imperishable seed through the Word of the living God (cf. 1 Peter 1.23), not from the flesh but from water and the Holy Spirit (cf. John 3.5-6), are finally established as 'a chosen race, a royal priesthood, a holy nation, a purchased people. ... You who in times past were not a people, but are now the people of God' (1 Peter 2.9-10)" (LG 9).

Pope, laymen, bishops, religious, priests, and members of every degree and vocation, all gathered together in Christ, are the Church. We are Christ's people, the "People of God." Though each person has some special call, a particular mission with its own responsibilities and functions, still all together in Christ make up a single, united people. All receive the same Spirit in baptism, all are nourished with the one Eucharist, all share the same hope of our calling. A fundamental equality in the new dignity of children of God is a basic note of the people of God.

Old Testament Origins

The phrase "People of God" was first applied to Israel, and it has to be understood in the light of our dependence on the Old Testament. In effect it characterizes the Church as the fulfillment of the Old Testament prophecies. Christ is the fulfillment of the prophecies and promises given to the world through the Jewish people. Because we possess Him, and His new gifts, and the enduring heritage of the Old Testament, we can speak of ourselves as "the People of God."

A People Called Together by Christ

The very phrase, with its Old Testament origins, serves to keep us aware that we are all alike in being members of the "assembling" of God's people. The people are the Church. All members share in the dignity, and all are to carry on, each in his proper way, the heavenly mission of its Founder, Christ, "Priest, Prophet and King" (cf. LG 11-13).

The Old Testament doctrine of the calling of God's people made it abundantly clear that they were a "*qāhāl*" (the Hebrew word which lies behind our word "church"), a "congregation called together," only because God has made them that. The same is true of the Church; it had to be "called together" by Christ. "The people" can be a Church only because they are united by the grace of Christ. The Church is not so much people joining together as people joined together. The Joiner, the Builder, is the Lord Jesus. All this makes it clear that Christ has determined how His people are to be united and gathered together.

Just as authority among the chosen people in the Old Testament came from God, so it is with the Church. For authority and ministry in the Church are concerned with giving to people and guarding for them the gifts of Christ. Christ has chosen the ways to do this, sending His apostles and teachers. All "mission" in the Church comes from Christ, who is its true Author and the only One who can give any valid share in His own unique priesthood and prophetic office.

The Kingdom of God

God rules in the midst of His people. The Church and the kingdom of God are not precisely synonymous. But the Church is a realization on earth of God's kingdom, the final fulfillment of which is in eternity (cf. LG 5).

The Gospels tell us that Jesus "went throughout Galilee ...

proclaiming the good news of the kingdom" (Matt. 4.23). He was teaching a reality that was part of the Messianic hopes of the Jews. In some Old Testament books (cf. Dan. 7; Isa. 40-45; Ezek. 34) and in a number of other Jewish writings in the centuries before Christ, much was written that led to the expectation of a Messiah who would save Israel. Many hopes centered on the glorious kingdom the Messiah would establish. When Christ spoke of the kingdom of God, or the kingdom of heaven, He was using language familiar to His Jewish hearers. In His teaching Christ was careful to free the idea of the "kingdom" from the nationalistic hopes of the people among whom He lived. To do this He often emphasized the heavenly aspect of the kingdom, and its interior, religious character.

The Church and the Kingdom

Aware of the intimate bond between the kingdom of God on earth and the Church, we can consider some of what Jesus taught about His kingdom. Like the reign of God, the kingdom is spiritual and will be perfected in the last days. It is not a political kingdom: "My kingdom is not from this world" (John 18:36). Yet His kingdom is planted in this world. Christ shows it to us as something visible, a community called together by Him and of which He is the Good Shepherd (cf. John 10.11-16).

In one of His parables the kingdom of God is likened to a mustard seed which, tiny at first, grows until it becomes a large shrub or tree in which "the birds of the air come and make nests in its branches" (Matt. 13.32). To explain the kingdom He told a parable of someone who sows good seed in a field. At night an enemy comes and sows weeds. In the kingdom both the good and evil are allowed to grow until the harvest. For everyone must have abundant opportunity to be saved (cf. Matt. 13.24-30). He also said that the kingdom is like a net let down into the sea. The net gathers all kinds of things, both good and bad. At the judgment the angels will separate the good from the bad. And Christ makes clear that there will be a judgment (cf. Matt. 13.47-52).

The Church Is Visible

From these and other parables, we can see that the kingdom, or the Church on earth, is something visible. It can be recognized by us. It contains both good and bad. It exists side by side with a hostile kingdom which works against it. The growth of the kingdom will be slow but certain. In it the word of God must be sown and cultivated; it will bear fruit in different measures in different hearers, and will even fail to have any effect on some who hear it (cf. Matt. 13.3-23). The kingdom must be in contact with the world, and like a leaven convert and transform it (cf. Matt. 13.33).

The Church was made in reality a visible Church when Christ sent the apostles to preach the kingdom in His name. He made it evident that their work was His: "And they went out and proclaimed the good news everywhere, while the Lord worked with them and confirmed the message by the signs that accompanied it" (Mark 16.20). The early growth of the visible Church is traced in the Acts of the Apostles and in the Epistles. Its established reality is celebrated in the work of the earliest Fathers, like St. Ignatius of Antioch, who writes so forcefully of the duty of a Christian to be united visibly with the visible Church.[3]

The Bride of Christ

One of the most beautiful images used by St. Paul to portray the nature of the Church and its relation to Christ is that of a bride whom Christ deeply loves. So much does He love the Church that He "gave Himself up for her" (Eph. 5.25). Through His gifts, sacraments and saving words, He cares for her and makes her holy, "by cleansing her with the washing of water by the word" (Eph. 5.26). His love makes her a resplendent bride, "the church . . . in splendor, without spot or wrinkle or anything of the kind. . . holy and without blemish" (Eph. 5.27).

When the side of the dead Christ was pierced by a soldier's lance, there immediately flowed forth blood and water (cf. John 19.34). These still flow in the Eucharistic sacrifice and in baptism: in these life-giving streams the Savior gives life to His bride, the Church. She is the new Eve, faithful spouse of the new Adam (cf. 1 Cor. 15.45); she was formed from the side of Christ as He slept in death upon the cross.[4]

The Church is a faithful bride of Christ. It is necessary always to distinguish what the Church is because of Christ's loving presence to her, and what her frail and sinful members are. By virtue of Christ's never-failing love, she is a faithful spouse, ever teaching the truth, ever calling to holiness, the fruitful source of all His saving gifts. "By the power of the Holy Spirit the Church has remained the faithful spouse of her Lord and has never ceased to be the sign of salvation on earth. Still she is well aware that among her members, both clerical and lay, some have been unfaithful to the Spirit of God. . ." (GS 43).

---

[3]Cf. St. Ignatius of Antioch, *Epistula ad Philadelphenses* proem. (MG 5.699 = ACW 1.85); *Epistula ad Ephesios* 4 (MG 5.648 = ACW 1.61-62).
[4]Cf. Gen. 2.21-22. For patristic commentaries on this, see St. Thomas Aquinas, *Catena Aurea* 19.10.

The Church Is Our Mother

"Holy Mother Church" is a term which has its roots in the earliest years of Christian history.

The Church is called a mother because, in virtue of Christ's love, she gives birth to many children (cf. LG 12). All the faithful are born of her: "By her preaching and by baptism she brings forth to a new and immortal life children who are conceived of the Holy Spirit and born of God" (LG 64). Moreover, Christ is to "be born and grow in the hearts of the faithful through the Church" (LG 65). This is achieved only by the solicitous maternal love Christ arouses in those who teach in His name. Thus St. Paul wrote to his flock in Galatia: "My little children, for whom I am again in pain of childbirth until Christ is formed in you" (Gal. 4.19).

Because Christ continues to nourish our life through the Church, we ought to honor her as a mother and a teacher.[5] Those who are enlightened by the grace of God to recognize the Church as Christ's faithful bride with whom He is inseparably united, and in whom He cares for His people, owe unfailing loyalty to her. St. Cyprian has expressed this forcefully: "You cannot have God for your Father if you have not the Church for your mother."[6] It is not enough to be born of her in baptism. As her faithful children, we must learn from her the mind of Christ her Spouse, and be schooled by her in the ways of life.

The Mystical Body of Christ

The Church is not only dear to Christ and the bearer of all His saving gifts. In a real way, the Church is Christ. She is made one with Him as His Mystical Body (cf. LG 7).[7]

Christ often identified Himself with His followers, with His Church. To the disciples, as He sent them to preach in His name, He said: "Whoever listens to you listens to Me, and whoever rejects you rejects Me" (Luke 10.16). To those who did deeds of charity for His little ones He proclaimed: "Just as you did it to one of the least of these who are members of My family, you did it to Me" (Matt. 25.40). Of St. Paul, who had been vigorously persecuting the Church before his own conversion, Christ asked: "Why do you persecute Me? . . . I am Jesus, whom you are persecuting" (Acts 9.4-5). At the Last Supper He spoke of the intense unity that makes Him one with those who are united by faith and love to Him. "I am the vine, you are the branches" (John 15.5). The vine and branches are one living reality. So it is also with Christ and His Church, Christ and those who love Him.

[5]Cf. Pope John XXIII, Encyclical, *Mater et Magistra* ("Mother and Teacher," May 15, 1961).
[6]St. Cyprian, *De Ecclesiae Catholicae Unitate* 6 (ML 4.502 = ACW 25.48-49).
[7]See Pope Pius XII, Encyclical, *Mystici Corporis* (June 29, 1943).

St. Paul develops the teaching on the Mystical Body in a number of his Epistles. Writing to the faithful at Corinth, he says: "Now you are the body of Christ and individually members of it" (1 Cor. 12.27). In baptism Christ gave each of us His Holy Spirit. The Holy Spirit is thus the soul of the Catholic Church (cf. LG 7),[8] a single soul that binds into a unity that overcomes every kind of division. "For in the one Spirit we were all baptized into one body — Jews or Greeks, slaves or free. . ." (1 Cor. 12.13).

It is true that we have diverse roles to play in the Church, just as in the natural body eyes and ears and feet have diverse functions. So in the body of Christ some are apostles, some are teachers, some are administrators, and some have more humble roles (cf. 1 Cor. 12.28-31). All, however, are called to the greatest gifts and duties, to the glory of believing, hoping, loving (cf. 1 Cor. 13). The diversity of roles does not harm, but serves the unity of the body. "But as it is, God arranged the members in the body, each one of them, as He chose. If all were a single member, where would the body be? As it is, there are many members, yet one body" (1 Cor. 12.18-20).

The Eucharist in a special way brings about the unity of Christ's body. "The bread that we break, is it not a sharing in the body of Christ? Because there is one bread, we who are many are one body, for we all partake of the one bread" (1 Cor. 10.16-17). Thus it is precisely through our union with Christ that we become members of one another in the Church (cf. Rom. 12.5). So united, the members are to love one another as themselves, even to love one another as Christ. "If one member suffers, all suffer together with it; if one member is honored, all rejoice together with it" (1 Cor. 12.26).

Christ is the Head of this body. "He is the head of the body, the church" (Col. 1.18). To live as a Christian is to grow up in Christ, to be more and more identified with Him, more and more to have His rich life penetrate and be our life. "But speaking the truth in love, we must grow up in every way into Him who is the head, into Christ, from whom the whole body, joined and knit together by every ligament with which it is equipped, as each part is working properly, promotes the body's growth in building itself up in love" (Eph. 4.15-16).

As we learn to understand that the Church is the Body of Christ, we can learn to love the Church more earnestly.

"That such a love, solidly grounded and undivided, may abide and increase in our souls, we must accustom ourselves to see Christ in the Church. It is Christ who lives in the Church, who teaches, governs,

---

[8]Cf. also Pope Pius XII, Encyclical, *Mystical Corporis* (June 29, 1943) (DS 3808), quoting there Pope Leo XIII, Encyclical, *Divinum Illud Munus* (May 9, 1897) (DS 3328).

and sanctifies through her. It is Christ too who manifests Himself differently in different members of His society. Once the faithful try to live in this spirit of conscious faith, they will not only pay due honor and reverence to the higher members of this Mystical Body, especially those who by Christ's mandate will have to render an account of our souls, but they will take to their hearts those members who are the object of our Savior's special love: the weak, the troubled, the wounded and sick, who are in need of natural or supernatural assistance; children whose innocence is so easily exposed to danger these days and whose little hearts are wax to be molded; and finally the poor, in helping whom we touch, as it were, through His supreme mercy, the very person of Jesus Christ."9

The Marks of the Church

In many ancient creeds the Catholic Church identifies itself as "one, holy, catholic, and apostolic."10 These words refer to what are traditionally known as the "marks" of the Church, that is, traits that make it possible for one to recognize it for what it truly is.

"Each of these marks is so linked to the others that it cannot be separated from them."11 Each quality we call a "mark" is so joined with the others that all of them form one coherent and interrelated idea of what Christ's Church must be. For example, the unity of the Church is more remarkable because it is a Catholic unity, that is, a unity of faith and hope in all places and ages; it is an apostolic unity, guarding the one faith first proclaimed by the apostles; and it is a unity ministering to holiness of life.

Many Catholics who write about the Church today refer to "signs of the Church" rather than to its "marks." This flows from a growing realization of how important it is to see the Church as a "sacrament" of the presence of Christ (cf. LG 1). These qualities, "one, holy, catholic, and apostolic," are seen as being of the essence of the Church as a sacrament, that is, a "sign" of Christ and His presence.

The Signs Are Paradoxes

The signs of the Church strengthen the faith of the believer and can attract the attention to the unbeliever and lead him to investigate the Church. But they also have a puzzling aspect. For they are found in the Church side by side with human imperfections. Their effectiveness as signs is sometimes lessened by the scandals which arise from the imperfection of the human members who are the Church. Or, to

9Pope Pius XII, Encyclical, *Mystici Corporis* (June 29, 1943) 104-105.
10Creed of the First Council of Constantinople (381) (DS 150).
11Letter of the Holy Office to the Bishops of England (September 16, 1864) (DS 2888).

put it another way, their "sign-value" can be also a puzzle for believers and nonbelievers since the perfections of the Church, divine in their origin, are found in this human family which is richly blessed by God but is still made up of sinners.

That the Church is made up of sinners is amply evident from history. One thinks, for example, of the scandalous lives of some Church leaders in the Renaissance, or of the excesses of the Inquisition, or of other periods and events. Today as well there are many signs of the human weaknesses of members of the Church, and Catholics can expect to be shocked at times by the actions and behavior of their fellow Catholics. For we are sinners, and we are the Church; and yet the Church is holy.

Indeed, the Church ever remains one, holy, catholic and apostolic in spite of its sinner membership. That fact should attract our attention, calling on us, as it were, to perceive the presence of Christ in the Church. The presence of sinners in the Church is enough to explain its flaws; but people alone could not account for the qualities to which the marks refer.

The marks are more than signs. They are rich gifts Christ promised to give His Church. Catholic creeds profess firm faith in His word, that the Church will never cease to be one, holy, catholic, and apostolic. The Church is confident, for it has Christ's promise: "I am with you always" (Matt. 28.20).

The Church Is One

Christ's Church is one in the faith its members believe and profess. It has an essential unity of worship. All are united to one saving sacrifice of Christ in the Eucharist, and eat of the one Bread that unites all in Christ. They receive the same sacraments. There is also a unity in our communion with other parts of the Church throughout the world. The "local churches" (or dioceses), each under its own bishop, are united in a common allegiance to the Pope, who is a sign and servant of unity. It is a living unity, springing spontaneously from the gifts of Christ's grace.

The Church Is Holy

The Creed proclaims that the Church is holy. This holiness is to be found first of all in its Founder, Jesus Christ. From Him, and from His Holy Spirit, comes all holiness. Because of Him the doctrine the Church teaches is holy; it remains unchangeably His doctrine. The Church's worship is holy, and the sacraments it ministers to the members of the Church make it possible for them to live Christian lives.

The Church invites all to a holy life (cf. LG 39-42). In this it has remained constant despite the many sins of its members. Wherever the Catholic faith is lived sincerely, Christ brings forth fruits of holiness. Without ignoring the scandals and sins of some of the Church's members, we can say in all confidence that there is holiness in the Church because so many of its members have shown eminent holiness, even to the point of martyrdom. There is such holiness in the Church in the present age as in ages past. Possibly no era of Christian history has been as blessed as the present one by so many faithful who witness the faith in suffering, and in suffering even to death. These are modern martyrs.

The Church Is Catholic

Christ's Church must be "catholic." The word "catholic" means "universal." The Catholic Church is a Church for all peoples in all places and in all times.

Moreover, the Church is universal, or catholic, in that it continues to teach all of what Christ taught. And it regards itself as obliged by Christ to teach that doctrine to all.

The Church Is Apostolic

Finally, the Church is apostolic. It is the same community as the Church of the apostolic age.

Christ founded His Church on the apostles. They in turn had successors, and the Church is apostolic because it continues to be governed by such successors. It is apostolic also because it teaches the same doctrine and way of life as the apostles taught. When we call the Church "apostolic" we mean that the teaching of Jesus Christ, which was first preached to the world by the apostles, and the Christian community, in which that apostolic faith has lived and grown, continue to have their existence in the Catholic Church (cf. LG 8).

The Church in History

The Church in its heart remains ever unchanged, always sealed with the marks that identify it as Christ's. But it is also a Church immersed in history. It is called always to speak and live in a way that best serves each succeeding age and culture.

Christ's Church "does not hover formlessly over the cities or exist unseen among the nations of the world. ... If one reflects on how detached from human history and how inconsistent with the human condition an invisible Church would be, he realizes how necessary is that visibility, which Catholics have always believed to be Christ's provision for His Church."[12] In every age the Catholic Church in this visible church, living here and now on earth. The Church is not an abstraction fashioned by scholars; it is a reality living in history.

It is a duty of the Church in each passing age to be the instrument through which Christ brings His truth and His gifts to people of that age. It must speak the language of each age; it must live in the circumstances of very diverse times. Because the same Christ always dwells in the Church, and teaches and sanctifies in it, and calls all through it to one hope, the Church is essentially the same always. But much in the Church reflects its historical reality. The special characteristics of each age are mirrored in the Church at the time of the Fathers, in the high Middle Ages, during the Renaissance and the Enlightenment.

The world's great cultures all pass away in time. The Church lives in each one of them in its day. But when a culture perishes and its great culture institutions die, the Church continues. The Church survives every transition, for the Lord of history has promised the Church that it will endure until the end of time.

The Hierarchy in the Church

The Church is a hierarchical community by the will of Christ (cf LG 18-29). A hierarchy is a "sacred leadership." To say that Christ willed the Church to have a hierarchy is to say that Christ Himself chose to rule His people through the bishops and pastors He has appointed to care for it.

While all the people of God share the same essential call to faith, love, and eternal life, different members of the community have different tasks. There is a service of leadership. Christ by His divine authority appointed men to teach, sanctify, and rule the Church in His name. The Church teaches that those who succeed in the office of the those chosen directly by Christ are equally rulers and guardians of the Church by the will of God Himself (cf. Acts 20.28). For Christ promised that He would be with those teaching and shepherding His flock, not for a single generation but until the end of time (cf. Matt. 28.20).

The Scriptural Foundation

The New Testament was written in the Church by those who lived in this new community of faith. We find in the New Testament many remembrances of the words and works of Jesus that had shaped the reality of the young Church. While our Lord yet lived, before the Paschal mysteries and the coming of the Holy Spirit, much of His message concerning the Church might well have escaped the clear

---

[12]United States Bishops, Pastoral Letter, *The Church in Our Day* (November 1967) ch. 2.

understanding of His hearers. But the Gospels and Epistles, written under the inspiration of the Holy Spirit, bear strong witness to the truth that the Church is of Jesus' own making, and carries on His work.

Early in His public life Jesus called together a special group of privileged associates who would be the foundation of the new household of God (cf. Eph. 2.20). "And when day came, He called His disciples and chose twelve of them, whom He also named apostles: Simon, whom He named Peter, and his brother, Andrew, and James, and John, and Philip, and Bartholomew, and Matthew, and Thomas, and James the son of Alphaeus, and Simon who was called the Zealot, the Judas son of James, and Judas Iscariot, who became a traitor" (Luke 6.13-16).

During His public life Jesus prepared the apostles for leadership roles. To them He committed the tasks of teaching, baptizing, forgiving sin, celebrating the Eucharist. At the Last Supper He promised that He would send them the Spirit of Truth to guide and guard their work (cf. John 16.13). In the account of Pentecost (cf. Acts 2) and the further history of the Church, the New Testament recalls the fulfillment of that promise. In His last words to His apostles, Jesus gave them a rich share of the "full authority" that He possesses: "Go therefore and make disciples of all nations . . . teaching them to obey everything that I have commanded you. And remember, I am with you always, to the end of the age" (Matt. 28.19-20).

The New Testament's witness concerning the hierarchy in the Church is not a matter of isolated passages, but rather a rich vision of the Church itself in which the members of the hierarchy (the apostles, their associates, and those they appointed to roles of leadership) have special functions to perform. Anticipations of this are seen throughout the Gospels; the early exercise of leadership is traced in the Acts of the Apostles and in the New Testament Epistles.

The Promises to Peter

Some of the central passages deserve special notice. At a climactic movement in St. Matthew's Gospel, Simon makes a stirring profession of faith in Jesus as the Messiah. Because Simon had recognized His identity, Jesus conferred on him a sacred new role and identity, giving him a new name, Peter. The name Peter means "Rock," and Jesus promised Peter that he would be the rock or foundation on which He would build His Church. The corrosive power of time and even death itself would have no power over the Church: it would endure. And to Peter, the Rock, He would give the keys of government and the power to bind and to loose with authority. "Blessed are you, Simon son of Jonah! For flesh and blood has not revealed this to you, but My Father in heaven. And I tell you, you are Peter, and on this rock I will build

My church, and the gates of Hades will not prevail against it. I will give you the keys of the kingdom of heaven, and whatever you bind on earth will be bound in heaven, and whatever you loose on earth will be loosed in heaven" (Matt. 16.17-20).

The fulfillments of these promises is recorded as well. During the passion of Jesus, Peter proved frail. Three times he denied his Master. After the Resurrection Jesus recalled Peter to a threefold profession of atoning love, and in so doing confirmed Peter in the role of shepherd and leader of all the flock: " 'Simon, son of John, do you love Me more than these?' He said to Him, 'Yes, Lord; You know that I love You.' Jesus said to him, 'Feed My lambs.' A second time He said to him, 'Simon son of John, do you love Me?' He said to Him, 'Yes, Lord; You know that I love You.' Jesus said to him, 'Tend My sheep.' He said to him the third time, 'Simon son of John, do you love Me?' Peter felt hurt because He said to him the third time, 'Do you love Me?' And he said to Him, 'Lord, You know everything; You know that I love You.' Jesus said to him, 'Feed My sheep' " (John 21.15-17).

The shepherding role conferred on Peter was that of ruling and guiding the Church. The symbolic meaning of shepherding goes back to Jewish history at least as far as David: "It is you who shall be shepherd of My people Israel, you who shall be ruler over Israel" (2 Sam. 5.2). But the same image is also used by Christ to describe His own ministry: "I am the good shepherd. I know My own and My own know Me" (John 10.14).

In many ways the New Testament suggests the entirely exceptional role of Peter in the Church. At the Last Supper Jesus said to Peter: "I have prayed for you that your own faith may not fail; and you, when once you have turned back, strengthen your brothers" (Luke 22.32). Through Peter all the faithful were to be fortified in faith in the hours of difficulty.

To the apostles as a group, in association with Peter, Christ gave a similar commission to exercise authority in His Church (cf. Matt. 18.18; LG 22). The mission of the apostles as a group was compared by Christ to the mission of Christ Himself received from the Father (cf. John 17.18). The apostles were sent forth as a group to convert the world. "Go into all the world and proclaim the good news to the whole creation" (Mark 16.15).

After Pentecost the apostles planted the seeds of the Church. As they felt the need, they designated men of the local churches to preside over the rule the flock (cf., e.g., Acts 14.23).

Successors of the Apostles

St. Peter and the other apostles were mortal, but the mission given them was to be carried out until the end of time (cf. Matt. 28.20). "For this reason the apostles took care to appoint successors in this hierarchically structured society" (LG 20; cf. Acts 20.25-27; 2 Tim. 4.6). This is noted by the earliest Fathers of the Church, who lived at the end of or immediately after the apostolic age. Thus Pope St. Clement of Rome, writing around the year 96, says that the apostles themselves "laid down a rule once for all to this effect: when these men die, other approved men shall succeed to their sacred ministry."[13]

From these first days of the Church, bishops appointed by or succeeding to the apostles were recognized as shepherds who rightly ruled and guarded the Church in the name of Christ. Loyalty to Christ was visibly expressed by loyalty to the bishops. Thus St. Ignatius of Antioch, in a letter written in or about 106, praises the church at Philadelphia in Asia as "a source of everlasting joy, especially when the members are at one with the bishop and his assistants, the presbyters and deacons, that have been appointed in accordance with the wish of Jesus Christ, and whom He has, by His own will, through the operation of His Holy Spirit, confirmed in loyalty."[14]

A Hierarchy of Service

The Second Vatican Council presents the hierarchy as a "diakonia," a ministry of service. "Those ministers who are endowed with sacred power are servants of their brethren, so that all who are of the People of God, and therefore enjoy a true Christian dignity, can work toward a common goal freely and in an orderly way" (LG 18).

Christ insisted that those who had authority in His Church were to exercise it with a humility patterned on His own (cf. Matt. 20.28). But He taught all to recognize legitimate authority, and to profit by the divine gifts conferred through it, even if those who in fact have the authority should personally live lives unworthy of it (cf. Matt. 23.3). At the Last Supper, by a dramatic gesture, Christ made it clear that authority is to be exercised in service. "If I then, your Lord and Teacher, have washed your feet, you also ought to wash one another's feet" (John 13.14). But the leaders of the Church are to be active in their service. A pope or bishop who failed to serve his people by protecting them in their faith and guiding them in moral matters would be derelict in his duty (cf. 2 Tim. 4.1-5; 1 Cor. 9.16).

St. Augustine, who was bishop of Hippo in North Africa, told the people entrusted to his care: "What I am for you terrifies me; what I am with you consoles me. For you I am a bishop; with you I am a

---

[13]St. Clement of Rome, *Epistula ad Corinthios* 44 (MG 1.296 = ACW 1.36).
[14]St. Ignatius of Antioch, *Epistula ad Philadelphenses* proem. (MG 5.699 = ACW 1.85).

Christian. The former is a title of duty; the latter, one of grace. The former is a danger; the latter, salvation."[15]

Authority and diversity of functions are indispensable for human cooperation in any common effort. It is not surprising, then, that authority was incorporated by Christ into the structure of His Church. It was a Church for human beings. Moreover, in His mercy He wished to enable them not only to have the fruits of redemption, but to share in many ways in His saving work.

The Hierarchy Today

The roles of St. Peter and the other apostles were in many ways unique. They were privileged personal associates of Jesus. Many of their duties, however, were to persist in the Church. Their enduring responsibilities, the tasks of teaching, ruling, and sanctifying the flock, are borne in the Church today by the pope, who succeeds to St. Peter's office as the first shepherd and bishop, and by the whole body or "college" of bishops, who inherit the tasks of the "apostolic college." The pope and the other bishops, like the apostles themselves, are not substituted for Christ, but are persons in and through whom Christ continues to care for His own. "In the bishops . . . our Lord Jesus Christ is present in the midst of those who believe" (LG 21).

The Pope

After recalling the words of Scripture noted above concerning the privileged place Christ gave Peter in ruling His Church, the First Vatican Council explained the enduring nature of the primacy in Peter's successors.

"Now, what Christ the Lord, the Prince of Shepherds and Great Shepherd of the Sheep, established in the person of the blessed apostle Peter for the perpetual welfare and everlasting good of the Church must, by the will of the Same, endure without interruption in the Church, which, founded on the Rock, will stand firm to the end of the world. Indeed, 'no one doubts, in fact it is known to all ages, that the holy and most blessed Peter, prince and head of the apostles, the pillar of faith and foundation of the Catholic Church, received the keys of the kingdom from our Lord Jesus Christ, the Savior and Redeemer of the human race; and even to this time and forever he lives' and governs 'and exercises judgment in his successors,'[16] the bishops of the Holy Roman See, which was founded by him and consecrated by his blood. Therefore, whoever succeeds Peter in this Chair holds

---

[15]St. Augustine, *Sermo* 340.1 (ML 38.1483). These words of St. Augustine are quoted in LG 32.
[16]These are the words of Philip, papal legate to the Council of Ephesus (431), in an address to the council fathers.

Peter's primacy over the whole Church according to the plan of Christ Himself. 'Therefore, the disposition made by Truth endures, and blessed Peter, persevering in the rocklike strength he received, has not given up the government of the Church undertaken by him.'[17] Hence, 'because of its greater sovereignty' it has always been 'necessary for every church, that is, the faithful who are everywhere, to be in agreement'[18] with the Roman Church, that, in the See from which 'the rights of sacred communion'[19] flow to all, they might, as members joined in the head, coalesce into one compact body."[20]

The council then solemnly defined the doctrine that by the will of Christ there has been a continuous line of successors to the office of St. Peter, and that the Roman Pontiff does succeed in Peter's primacy over the universal Church.[21]

The council then described the nature and extent of the pope's jurisdiction, that is, his right and duty to rule or shepherd the Church.[22] The pope has jurisdiction over the entire Church. He is bishop not only of Rome, but of the universal Church. His authority as bishop is "immediate," that is to say, each member of the flock, of whatever rank, is required to accept the pastoral direction of the first shepherd. He is bishop of all the Church, of his fellow bishops and all the faithful, individually and collectively. The pope's authority and duty extend not only to the teaching of faith and moral doctrine, but also to whatever pertains to the discipline and government of the Church throughout the world.

The pope is known by a variety of titles: Roman Pontiff, Supreme Pontiff, Holy Father, Vicar of Christ. In signing official documents, however, he usually adds the most appropriate and honorable of his titles: Servant of the Servants of God.

Eastern Churches and Patriarchtes

The richness of the Catholic heritage is manifested by the diversity of rites that she enoys. While all Catholics have the same faith, the same sacraments, and are all shepherded by the same successor to St. Peter, they are also gathered into a variety of rites. These rites are bearers of a variety of liturgical forms, patterns of Church discipline, and expressions of spiritual life. The largest rite is the Latin rite, the

---

[17]Pope St. Leo I, *Sermo 3 de Natali Ipsius* 3 (ML 54.146B).

[18]St. Irenaeus, *Adversus Haereses* 3.3.2 (MG 7.849A).

[19]St. Ambrose of Milan, *Epistula* 11.4 (ML 16.986B).

[20]First Vatican Council, Session 4, July 18, 1870, *First Dogmatic Constitution on the Church of Christ*, ch. 2 (DS 3056-3057).

[21]First Vatican Council, Session 4, July 18, 1870, *First Dogmatic Constitution on the Church of Christ*, ch. 2 (DS 3058).

[22]First Vatican Council, Session 4, July 18, 1870, *First Dogmatic Constitution on the Church of Christ*, ch. 3 (DS 3059-3064).

rite of the Western Church. There are also several Eastern Catholic Rites, which shape their forms of worship in accord with ancient traditions, but in full harmony with the faith of the whole Church.

An Eastern Patriarch is a "bishop who has jurisdiction over all bishops (including metropolitans), clergy, and people of his own territory or rite" (OE 7). Each patriarch is given "exceptional respect" since he serves as "father and head" of all those within the rite (cf. OE 9).

"All Eastern rite members should know and be convinced that they can and should always preserve their lawful liturgical rites and their established way of life" (OE 6). The universal Church wishes all these rites to flourish and to guard the special gifts God has entrusted them for the enrichment of the whole Church. Where there is contact between the Latin Church and other rites, it is important that all with responsible roles "be carefully trained to know and respect the rites, discipline, doctrine, history, and characteristics of Easterners" (OE 6).

The College of Bishops

"By the Lord's will, St. Peter and the other apostles constitute one apostolic college" (LG 22). Though Christ gave a true primacy to Peter, he was to shepherd the Church not in isolation, but in fraternal collegial unity with his fellow apostles. In a similar way, the Pope, as successor to St. Peter, governs the Church in collegial unity with his fellow bishops, successors of the apostolic college. Fully respecting the special role Christ wishes the Holy Father to undertake in His name, the bishops over the whole world cooperate with him in the care for all the Church.

This "collegiality" has always been recognized in the living practice of the Church. Even in the earliest years of the Church, when dangers threatened the purity and unity of faith, the bishops gathered together in councils to make, with the assistance of the Holy Spirit (cf. Acts 15.28), decisions for the direction of the whole Church.

Another expression of collegiality in antiquity was the great concern for "communion" among the various local churches and between each of them and the Roman See. They were linked together "in a bond of unity, charity, and peace" (LG 22). The "communion" of bishops with one another was a sign and expression of the communion binding together the whole Church.

Collegiality at Work

"In spite of all appearances, the Church is now more united in the fellowship of service and in the awareness of apostolate. This unity springs from the principle of collegiality, mentioned by the Second Vatican Council...."[23]

The collegial nature of the bishops taken as a whole is seen in a vivid way when they come together for an ecumenical council. Such councils, of which there have been twenty-one, bring together bishops from every part of the Church to discuss some part of the Church's doctrine or discipline. The most recent such council, which was the second to be held in St. Peter's Basilica at the Vatican, was the Second Vatican Council. It began in 1962 and ended in 1965.

In 1965, during the final session of the Second Vatican Council, Pope Paul VI instituted a new form of collegial cooperation in the Church: the Synod of Bishops.[24] Consisting of a group of bishops representing bishops from all over the world, the Synod of Bishops is called together by the Holy Father to discuss certain matters and pastoral questions facing the Church. In their consultations the bishops collegially assist the Pope in his work, and they keep him informed of the mind and concerns of bishops and people throughout the world. The first session of the Synod of Bishops was convened in 1967; others have been held at regular intervals since then.

The Bishop in His Diocese

In the Catholic Church there are many local churches or dioceses. Each of these is entrusted to an individual bishop, who has the responsibility to care for the Church in that particular place. The bishop in charge of a diocese is called the Ordinary, a title which refers to his authority in the diocese. Sometimes the Ordinary of a diocese is assisted by one or more auxiliary or coadjutor bishops in the care of his flock.

The bishop is the authentic teacher of the faith in his own diocese; he is a sign and center of unity; he is the "administrator of the mysteries of God" (cf. 1 Cor. 4.1) for the people committed to his care. To be a true teacher of his flock, the bishop must, of course, be in harmony with the pope and the other members of the college of bishops. Within his diocese, the bishop works together with and through his priests and deacons. Their mission in the Church depends upon the bishop; they have been made "co-workers" with him by ordination (cf. LG 28).

The bishop shepherds his flock as a true ambassador and vicar of Christ. When he is consecrated into the order of bishops by others who have preceded him in that office, and is assigned by proper authority to care for a particular diocese, he governs his flock as a true succes-

---

[23]Pope John Paul II, Encyclical, *Redemptor Hominis* (March 4, 1979) n. 5 (EV 6.1178).
[24]Cf. Pope Paul VI, Apostolic Letter, *Apostolica Sollicitudo* (September 15, 1965) (EV 2.444-457).

sor of the apostles, with an authority given by Christ Himself. This authority is to be exercised in the spirit of Christ, to assist the faithful in guarding unity and in growing in love (cf. LG 26-27; CD *passim*).

Salvation through the Church

The Catholic Church steadfastly believes that it is the one and only Church of Jesus Christ. To say this is certainly not to say that other Christian communities are without value, or insincere, or that their members are not deeply devoted to Christ. Rather, it is a concise way of expressing many of the truths mentioned in this chapter. It is to profess that Jesus indeed willed to remain present among those in the Church that grew up, through the grace of the Holy Spirit, from the preaching of the apostles He sent. It is to say that the one community of faith He planted through His apostles continues to live, as He said it would, through all the ages, sealed with sacred marks: "one, holy, catholic, apostolic." It is to say that Christ, dwelling in the Catholic Church, invites all to complete unity of faith and the close communion of love in this visible, living Church; and that in saving mercy Christ requires all who come by grace to recognize this Church as the sacrament of His presence to join it, and rejoice in the life He gives through it.

"This is the unique Church of Christ which in the creed we avow as one, holy, catholic, and apostolic. After His resurrection our Savior handed her over to Peter to be shepherded (cf. John 21.17); He committed her to him and to the other apostles that they might propagate and rule her (cf. Matt. 28.18 ff.). Her he erected for all ages as 'the pillar and bulwark of the truth' (1 Tim. 3.15). This Church, constituted and organized in this world as a society, subsists in the Catholic Church, governed by the successor of Peter and the bishops in communion with him" (LG 8). To say that Christ's Church "subsists" in the Catholic Church is to say that Christ's Church is a concrete historical reality, and that that concrete reality is found in the living, visible Catholic Church.

Separated Brethren

Many who are not members in the full sense of the Catholic Church are surely Christ's own, and linked to the saving sacrament of His Church by many bonds. "The Catholic Church accepts them with respect and affection as brothers. For these who believe in Christ and have been properly baptized are brought into a certain, though imperfect, communion with the Catholic Church" (UR 3). Even though they are not bound to it by a full sharing in the joy of Catholic faith, nor by a full communion with those in whom Christ shepherds His flock, they do share many true gifts of Christ, as faith in Him and baptism, gifts that "possess an inner dynamism toward Catholic unity" (LG 8). The Catholic should honor God's gifts in them, and so live his or her own Catholic life as to make more apparent its real nature, that others may come to know the blessings of full unity with Christ in His Church.

Salvation in the Church Alone

From its earliest days the Church has proclaimed that Christ is the only Savior, and that people lay hold of eternal life only by coming to Him. To come to Him in a fully explicit way is to enter the Church, the family of faith; it is to receive new birth at the baptismal font, and to live in communion with those in whom He teaches and sanctifies His people.

"For there is no salvation outside the Church," St. Cyprian taught in the third century.[25] The Church has always taught this doctrine. But this is no fierce proclamation that those who, through no fault of their own, have not come to recognize Christ's presence in the Church and His command to come to this life (cf. Mark 16.16) will be excluded from salvation. Certainly those who earnestly intend in their hearts to do all that God requires of them are not excluded from the hope of eternal life, as they are not excluded from a certain membership by desire in the Church.[26]

There is, however, a note of urgency in the classic expression of St. Cyprian. The Catholic Church is not an organization which is merely optional. Christ cares deeply that we believe His whole word, that we obey His saving commands, that we be bound together in the unity of His family. If one were to recognize the reality of the Catholic faith and the personal will of Christ that we live in it, and yet deliberately disobey so important a call, he would be turning himself away from the Savior and from salvation. "For this reason, those who, aware of the fact that the Catholic Church was made necessary by God through Jesus Christ, would yet refuse to enter her or persevere in her, could not be saved" (LG 14).

This is not a matter of human loyalty, but of faithfulness to Jesus Christ. It is He who invites all to life, and there "is no other name under heaven given among mortals by which we must be saved" (Acts 4.12).

---

[25]St. Cyprian, *Epistula* 73.21.2 (ML 3.1169A = ACW 47.66).
[26]Cf. Letter of the Holy Office to the Archbishop of Boston (August 8, 1949) (DS 3870).

14

Christ Shepherds His People

The Church traditionally has spoken of three offices of Christ the Savior. He is Prophet or Teacher of truth; he is King or Ruler who shows the way; and He is above all the Sanctifier who gives His people abundant life (cf. John 14.6). Christ performs His work not only personally, but also through the Church. He is with His Church, acts in it, and enables the whole Church, each member in his own role and task, to share actively in His saving work.

Jesus is present in a special way in His bishops. Through them His teaching, ruling, and sanctifying care still touches the whole flock. "In the bishops ... our Lord Jesus Christ, the supreme High Priest, is present in the midst of those who believe" (LG 21). Pope St. Leo the Great spoke of this in a homily in the fifth century: "The Lord Jesus Christ is in the midst of those who believe in Him; though He sits at the right hand of the Father. ... He who is the supreme Bishop is not separated from the full assembly of His bishops."[1]

In this chapter we speak of how Christ teaches, rules, and sanctifies in His Church. The chapter treats especially the teaching mission of the Church: why sacred teaching is needed, to whom this teaching is committed, and the various ways in which the teaching office of the Church guides the life of the faith.

Christ Teaches His People

Christ is the Teacher of His people. A major part of His saving mission was to free us from the despair of ignorance and doubt, from the frightening fear that perhaps nothing makes sense at all. "For this I was born, and for this I came into the world, to testify to the truth" (John 18:37).

Jesus was concerned so much with truth because He is Himself the Truth, as He is the Way and the Life (cf. John 14.6). Much of His public life on earth was spent in teaching. The common title He received was "Teacher." He is a unique witness of divine truth; for as the mystery of the incarnation shows, He alone both dwells as Son forever with the Father, sharing entirely His infinite wisdom, and lives

[1]Pope St. Leo I, *Sermo* 5.3 (ML 54.154). This passage is referred to in a note to LG 21.

as a man, able to speak as no one else can the truth of which He is the perfect witness.

Jesus teaches also through those He sends. When sending disciples to preach the word during His lifetime, He sent them to "every town and place where He Himself intended to go" (Luke 10.1). When He sent the apostles forth in the hour of His ascension, after which He would no longer be visible to people in His humanity, He said He would be with them always in their teaching (cf. Matt. 28.20). And when the apostles "went out and proclaimed the good news everywhere," Christ "worked with them and confirmed the message by the signs that attended it" (Mark 16.20). Anyone who did not accept the word of those He sent would be rejecting not mere people, but Christ Himself, whereas acceptance of their word would be acceptance of Christ (cf. Luke 10.16).

Human Need for Divine Teaching

We human beings have a need to be taught by God. Although God is revealed in all the things He has made, human folly and worldliness would keep us from clear and confident knowledge of God, if our fallen state were left to our own resources. Though human reason can come to a sure knowledge of God, our knowledge from purely natural and philosophical insights does not extend to that personal grasping of God as a Father who loves and gives Himself (cf. DV 6).[2]

"No one knows the Father except the Son and anyone to whom the Son chooses to reveal Him" (Matt. 11.27). We have heard of God, but none of us has known Him with the saving, loving understanding of faith except through the gift of Jesus. "No one has ever seen God. It is God the only Son, who is close to the Father's heart, who has made Him known" (John 1.18). Christ dwelt frequently on this theme. Christ came to give us personal and saving knowledge of God.

Even the knowledge revealed to us by Christ is not immediate acquaintance with God or direct vision of Him. Though Jesus speaks the truth about God, and in His own person and reality reveals the goodness of God, we see His divinity only in seeing Him as a man, a human being, and we hear the divine, infinite truth spoken in human and finite language. "For now we see in a mirror dimly" (1 Cor. 13.12). Faith gives life, certainty, and joy, but we will not see God clearly until the day of eternal life dawns and we see "face to face" (1 Cor. 13.12). "Now I know only in part; then I will know fully, even as I have been fully known" (1 Cor. 13.12). "Even though we know that while we are at home in the body, we are away from the Lord — for we walk by faith, not by sight" (2 Cor. 5.6-7).

[2]Cf. also First Vatican Council, Session 3, April 24, 1870, *Dogmatic Constitution on the Catholic Faith*, ch. 2 (DS 3004-3005).

Nevertheless, the wisdom of faith is itself a splendid reality. It does not give us that vision of God we hope to enjoy in heaven, but it does give us truth. It provides us, on the authority of Jesus the perfect Witness, with sure and liberating access to the Father.

Human Language and Faith

We see only created, finite things. All our language and ideas are conditioned by them. Our words, therefore, cannot worthily and fully express the reality of the infinite God as He is in Himself. Yet it is possible in a number of ways to speak of God truthfully.

God is not like us in our flawed and finite existence. God is not mortal, ignorant, battered by time. We may say to Him truly that He is immortal, all-knowing, eternal — that is, that He lives without the flaws we know too well in human life. True statements can be made of God also in expressing awareness that all flows from Him, and that all good has its origin and roots in Him. Truth, goodness, life, wisdom — it is true to say that God has all these perfections, even though these dwell in Him in a way that exceeds the power of our language completely to capture or of our minds fully to possess, until we see Him as He is.

When Jesus and the prophets before Him spoke to us of God, they claimed to speak the truth about the infinite Lord of all. They used human language. But Scripture has also insisted that such language did not bear the fullness of that truth. "What no eye has seen, nor ear heard, nor the human heart of man conceived" (1 Cor. 2.9; cf. Isa. 64.3), what is the splendor of that God who shall be our eternal beatitude?

Still human language is able to bear the message God wishes it to bear. The doctrines of creation and of the incarnation are relevant to this. We are finite, and the world we experience only inadequately reflects God. Still, the heavens and earth are "telling the glory of God" (cf. Ps. 19.1).

The word of God, the expression in language of divine truth, is not the creation of man working alone. The Father is Himself the source of revealed knowledge. Christ, who is the Lord, receives all truth from the Father; at the same time He is a man who uses human language, and speaks truly in human language the message He came to give.

How the Divine Message Is Grasped

Any act of teaching proposes some message or truth to be grasped and considered, to be accepted or rejected. In much human teaching, arguments or reasons are given to prove the truth of what is said. Then the hearer may judge for oneself, in the light of one's own experience and insight, the strength of the argument and the truth of what is said. One will hold a view not on the "authority" of the teacher, but on the authority of one's own intelligence. Other human teaching involves human faith. When the hearer has come, for a variety of reasons, to consider the teacher truthful, informed, and competent, one accepts as true what the teacher declares to be true. In principle at least, the things so taught may be checked out; but in reality human education does not proceed far without such trust.

The teaching of faith, which is a "witnessing," has a pattern different from that of ordinary human teaching. The word of God does not begin with men and women. It is a gift of God. The central mysteries of the faith are not open to our checking. God is not a teacher who announces to us the inner mystery of His nature and the saving plan of His mercy and then points out to us various evidences lying about from which we can prove the truth of what He has said. For the world does not contain adequate signs of all those divine things God wishes to speak to us. It is a personal revelation He makes, and the truth of the word He gives can be known only on His word. Only by divine faith can we grasp this message with certainty. To enter the vision of God would be to go beyond faith; but the vision of nothing else provides a proof for what faith offers. So until one enters the blessed vision of God, it is only testimony, or witnessing, that makes possible a knowledge of the word of faith.

But witnessing is sufficient here, as it would not be in any other case. True, we cannot have complete certainty in believing other people, even good people, for they as well as we are imperfect in many ways. But God's witnessing is altogether different. "If we receive human testimony, the testimony of God is greater; for this is the testimony of God that He has testified to His Son. Those who believe in the Son of God have the testimony in their hearts" (1 John 5.9-10). God is able so to place His message in history, surrounded by signs that He chooses, and so to move the apprehension of one from within, that one can with full certainty come to recognize that it is indeed God who speaks in those He has sent.

If it were only a long argument that led us to recognize a prophet as authentic, we might continue to have doubts. But God is able to lead those whom He calls to know with great certainty that it is He who speaks in those He sends. It was not through long arguments but by gifts of grace that the apostles came to find God in Christ (cf. John 6.69; Matt. 16.16-17). Similarly, it was with a deep certainty that the Thessalonians came to realize that what St. Paul preached was in fact God's word (cf. 1 Thess. 2.13). For faith is the gift of a present God. Through grace He gives us an obscure but certain sharing in His own wisdom, so that we acquire in faith a certainty that is in many ways puzzling but nonetheless more sure than all else we know.

The Work of the Church Is to Teach

Only God can make known to us the truths we most need to know, the mysteries hidden in God, the purposes and plans of Him who in the source and final goal of all that is real. God stirred up people of His own choosing to speak in His name (cf. Rom. 10.14-15), and in His providence He made it possible for hearers to recognize that these chosen ones, called prophets, did speak for Him. But most of all it is Christ who reveals God to the world. "Long ago God spoke to our ancestors in many and various ways by the prophets, but in these last days He has spoken to us by the Son' (Heb. 1.1-2). God's Son continues to speak to us through those He chooses to send in His name (cf. John 15.16). They must not be self-appointed; they must be called in His name (cf. Jer. 23.13-28).

God's Word and the Apostles

Christ committed to the apostles the task of preaching His word in His name, that is, authoritatively. He assured them of the assistance of the Spirit who would guard them in all truth in speaking (cf. John 14.16,26). He commanded them to teach His word to all nations, binding the hearers to the duty of believing their words as the words of God (and thus implicitly promising that He would make those He called to faith able to recognize Him in His spokespersons), and He promised to be with them in their preaching until the end of time (cf. Matt. 28.20).

In their preaching the apostles had special gifts. Not only did the Spirit guard them in keeping the word of Jesus that they had heard from Him, but He also enriched their possession and grasp of sacred truth.

Preserving the Deposit of Faith

With the end of the apostolic age the time of new public revelation came to an end (cf. DV 4). The task of the Church thereafter was to hand on the word which had been entrusted to the apostles, the deposit of faith, to grow in it, to nourish its development, and to make it living and effective, a leaven to renew the earth. We say that revelation continues in the sense that the living God remains present to His people, and by His continuing care and His gifts of grace enables them to recognize and love Him and the good news of the Gospel. But Jesus proclaimed the full saving message and gave it to His people, "and now no new public revelation is to be expected before the glorious manifestation of our Lord Jesus Christ (cf. 1 Tim 6.14 and Titus 2.13)" (DV 4).

In the Epistles to Timothy and to Titus there is stress on the need to serve the deposit of faith with loving care, to guard "the good treasure entrusted to you" (2 Tim. 1.14; cf. 1 Tim. 6:20; Titus 1.9). Christ is the one Savior; there will never be a Gospel other than that which He has given us (cf. Gal. 1.6-8), the message the Church has always preached. His word is to be guarded by those who, as successors to the apostles, are authentic teachers and witnesses of the faith. The bishops who are to guard the truth will be assisted by the Spirit of God. They will not have special revelations, but by God's mercy, for the sake of His people, they will be enabled to preach the word with unfailing truth (cf. DV 8).

Bishops must be vigilant and active to fulfill their tasks. God calls them to serve Him and His word with personal love. In the inspired words of St. Paul's message to his disciple Timothy, whom Paul had appointed as leader or bishop of the Church at Ephesus, the task of teachers in the Church for all centuries to come is made clear: "In the presence of God and of Christ Jesus, who is to judge the living and the dead, and in view of His appearing and His Kingdom, I solemnly urge you: proclaim the message; be persistent whether the time is favorable or unfavorable; convince, rebuke, and encourage with the utmost patience in teaching" (2 Tim. 4.1-2). This is the work of apostolic love: to care that people hear the saving words of God.

The task of the bishops is a difficult one. Hungry as some are for the saving truth of Christ, they may feel that this truth makes unwelcome demands on them. Until the weaknesses of the flesh are healed by grace, there is also an inclination to reject the Gospel, or at least to revise it in terms that do not call for such a radical newness and integrity in ways of thinking and living. "For the time is coming when people will not put up with sound doctrine, but having itching ears, they will accumulate for themselves teachers to suit their own desires" (2 Tim. 4.3).

These words recall a regrettable fact, experienced by the apostles themselves and in the many centuries of Church history. Many people would like to compromise. Having caught sight of the hope in Christ, they would like to have it, but to have it without giving for it their whole lives and minds and hearts. They would seek out versions of the Gospel that are not so demanding. Against such rejection of the purity of faith St. Paul writes often, as in his Epistle to the Galatians.

Pastoral care is not all strain and labor. It is endlessly buoyed up by the great love that flourishes among the many who recognize God's words in His spokespersons and who give generous love and loyalty to the agents through whom God gives them saving light. Though the task of bishops is demanding, and to be a faithful bishop is to suffer much for the faith (cf. 2 Cor. 11.28-29), yet the charisms with which God surrounds their preaching give it an effectiveness and make it a joy. The divine Shepherd always causes His own to hear His voice in the created shepherds in whom He speaks, and it is a blessed vocation to have the service of God's word as the meaning of one's life. For preachers of the word also taste the joy of seeing the fruits of the Holy Spirit's assistance. They see the words they speak accepted with faith. "We also constantly give thanks to God for this, that when you received the word of God that you heard from us, you accepted it not as a human word but as what it really is, God's word, which is also at work in you believers" (1 Thess. 2.13).

Development of Doctrine

The Church does not hand on doctrine in a static way; it teaches and believes a living faith. As centuries pass, the prayer and study of the Church, and the guidance of the Holy Spirit, lead the Church into an ever-greater understanding of the divine word. Mary and the apostles may well have grasped the mystery of Jesus, in their post-resurrection faith, far more richly than we, though not in the technically articulated ways to which centuries of reflection on the faith have led. But for the whole community of faith there has been a growing penetration into the revealed word.

Development of doctrine never means abandonment of doctrine, or the substitution of new doctrine for old; it never means that what the Church once firmly assents to it will ever deny. "Hence also that meaning of the sacred dogmas which has once been declared by holy Mother Church must always be retained."[3]

Genuine development of doctrine always proceeds along consistent lines; it is growth from partial to fuller vision, so that what has been believed continues to be believed, though its depths and consequences are more and more fully realized. Moreover, what is implicit in the faith, and not fully realized because of temporary obstacles, may become resplendently clear as truly present in the Gospel message. This is not by virtue of a new revelation, but because of a clearer insight into the message that has been handed on. This growth of "understanding, knowledge, and wisdom" is always to be "in the same doctrine, in the same meaning, and in the same sense."[4]

For example, Christian faith has always believed the Gospel teaching about Mary's singular holiness (cf. Luke 1.28). But it was not always clear whether or not she had contracted original sin. Some felt that she had, for the universality of Christ's redemptive work and the

---

[3]First Vatican Council, Session 3, April 24, 1870, *Dogmatic Constitution on the Catholic Faith*, ch. 4 (DS 3020). Cf. Pope Benedict XV, Encyclical, *Ad Beatissimi Apostolorum* (November 1, 1914) (DS 3626); Pope Pius XII, Encyclical, *Humani Generis* (August 12, 1950) (DS 3886).
[4]Vincent of Lerins, *Commonitorium primum* 23 (ML 50.668), quoted in First Vatican Council, Session 3, April 24, 1870, *Dogmatic Constitution on the Catholic Faith*, ch. 4 (DS 3020).

doctrine that "all have sinned" (cf. Rom. 5.12) seemed to demand this. Others felt that Mary could not have contracted original sin, because the unequivocal Gospel witness to her holiness, as the Fathers and saints understood it, and her sublime dignity as Mother of God seemed to make it unthinkable that she could ever have lived outside of the friendship of God. For many years it was not fully clear what faith really taught on this subject.

With the passage of time, the reflections of saints and theologians (not without divine guidance) caught sight of a possibility not realized before. It was seen that Mary could have been redeemed by Jesus from the universal debt of original sin in a special way, that is, by being kept free from original sin. It became evident that there were no obstacles to accepting the Gospel teaching on Mary's holiness in its full, traditional breadth, and it became clear also that the teaching on her Immaculate Conception was implicit in the word of faith that had been received from the beginning. It had always been divinely revealed, but the realization of its divine revelation was only gradually acquired.

Authentic Teachers in the Church

It was primarily to Peter and the other apostles that Christ entrusted the preaching of the Gospel. The Catholic Church teaches that just as the Holy Father and the other bishops are the successors of the apostles in ruling His flock, so also are they the apostles' successors as the authentic teachers and witnesses of the faith. They are the witnesses that Christ has established to teach the Church; and to the word of the Holy Father and of the college of bishops as teachers God has given the charism of truth that does not fail (cf. LG 25; DV 8). For in them especially He causes the word He sent the apostles to speak to be faithfully spoken; in them He guards the word with divine care, not to glorify them, but to make them centers of unity and truth for those He calls to faith. Clearly the Catholic bishop has a duty to teach collegially, in unity of faith with the Holy Father and his brother bishops.

Other teachers assist the bishops in their work. Priests preach the Gospel, as officially sent by their bishops to the task. They are committed to speak faithfully the word that Christ preserves pure and untainted in the successors of the apostles.

Theologians and scholars teach the word, and help the Church to grow in penetrating its depths. To be sure, they are not official teachers, as bishops, the successors of the apostles, are; and theologians do not as such receive with the bishops that "sure gift of truth" (DV 8) which the apostolic witnesses of faith receive. But they are important helpers of the bishops; for bishops are not exempt from the responsibility of seeking appropriate assistance for the understanding of divine revelation. The official magisterium of the Church needs the scholarly help of theologians, whose study and work make it possible for the Church's judgment to mature more readily. To be able to do their work in the Church properly, theologians must of course reverently accept the witness of bishops. For the principles of faith are not founded on mere scholarship, but on the word of Christ, and the authentic teachers of that word are the Holy Father and the other bishops.[5]

Other teachers are parents, "the first and foremost educators of their children" (GE 3).[6] St. Augustine referred to parents as "bishops" in the home.[7] Very important teachers also are those who teach the faith in schools and in centers of catechetical learning. All these too draw their certainty and sureness not from mere scholarship, from human philosophies and sciences, but from the word Christ causes to be proclaimed by those He has sent. They find a sure guide for their teaching in the voice of the Pastors of the Church.

Christ is the source of all belief. In its purity and authentic meaning Christ's word is ministered to us through His apostles, and through those who have succeeded to the place of the apostles.

The Message to Be Taught

On the day of his death, Pope John Paul I stated: "Among the rights of the faithful, one of the greatest is the right to receive God's word in all its entirety and purity. . . ."[8]

The Holy Father and the other bishops are servants of the word of God. They have a duty to believe the Scriptures and the word that has been handed down to them in the Church, by the bishops and apostles who proceeded them. There is a continual "handing on" of faith. It has a human dimension, because the Church is a family of people united in Christ. But to enable the people of God to guard divine faith purely, to have unshaken faith in it, and to remain unified in their understanding and love of it is not merely human work, but the work of God. It is the Spirit of God who gives the charism of truth to authentic teachers and the charism of faith to these teachers and to those who hear them.

[5]Cf. Pope Paul VI, *Addresses* to Theological Commission (October 6, 1969, and October 11, 1973).
[6]Cf. Pope John II, Apostolic Exhortation, *Familiaris Consortio* (November 22, 1981) nn. 36-41 (EV 7.1638-1661).
[7]Cf. St. Augustine, *In Ioannis Evangelium Tractatus* 51.13 (ML 35.1768).
[8]Pope John Paul II, *Address* at Catholic University of America, to professors and theologians (October 7, 1979).

Tradition, Scripture, and the Magisterium

Bishops and those who assist them in teaching the word of God are to hand on all the saving word of Christ, the message in its entirety. "Tradition" means "handing on," and the Church is responsible for handing on faithfully all that it has received from the Lord. "Tradition" also means "that which is handed on." "Now that which was handed on by the apostles includes everything which contributes to holiness of life, and the increase in faith in the people of God; and so the Church, in her teaching, life, and worship, perpetuates and hands on to all generations all that she herself is, all that she believes" (DV 8).

There can also be in the Church human traditions, which may be of only temporary value. It is only by Christ's gift of the Spirit, guarding the living teachers He sets over the Church, that the Church is able rightly to distinguish that which is enduring word of God, and unfailingly to be handed on, from that which is only of passing worth.

Sacred tradition is inseparably united with the Sacred Scriptures, which were written under the inspiration of the same Holy Spirit who guides the Church in handing on sacred tradition (cf. DV 8). Among all the Scriptures the Gospels "have a special preeminence, and rightly so, for they are the principal witness of the life and teaching of the incarnate Word, our Savior" (DV 18). These four Gospels, together with an account of the events of the young Church, that is, the Acts of the Apostles, and with twenty-one letters or epistles and the book of Revelation, make up the New Testament. These inspired writings of the Christian family, joined with the sacred books of the former, or Jewish, dispensation which are known collectively as the Old Testament, make up the entire canon of the Bible.

The writings of the New Testament had their origin in the Church. They were written to confirm and enrich faith (cf. Luke 1.1-4; John 20.31) and meet the questions and problems that the apostles met in the life of the Church. They were written, by divine inspiration (cf. 2 Tim. 3.16; cf. DV 11), to preserve for coming generations rich insights into the Gospel message, which had been preached and was being preached by the apostles, and lived in the whole Church. From the beginning, then, they have been proclaimed by the Church's own teachers, and have been believed and understood in the light of the whole living tradition and faith of the Church.

Thus it is "not from Sacred Scripture alone that the Church draws its certainty about everything which has been revealed" (DV 9). Sacred tradition and Sacred Scripture form "one sacred deposit of the word of God, which is committed to the Church" (DV 10), and both "are to be accepted and venerated with the same sense of devotion and reverence" (DV 9).

Interpreting this word of God is a task of the magisterium or teaching office in the Church. "The task of authentically interpreting the word of God, whether written or handed on, has been entrusted exclusively to the living magisterium of the Church, whose authority is exercised in the name of Jesus Christ" (DV 10). This does not mean that the authentic teachers of the Church are above the word of God. They are servants of God's word. By being faithful to God's word as faithfully taught and lived under the inspiration of the Holy Spirit, and guarded by the charism of truth the Holy Spirit gives to the continuing apostolic office, they serve in helping the faithful ever to understand each element of God's word in the light of the whole message of salvation.

The gifts of tradition, of Scripture, and of the living magisterium, with the presence of the Spirit guiding the faithful to be open to the truth, are all gifts of God. The close union of these gifts cannot be forgotten. "It is clear, therefore, that sacred tradition, Sacred Scripture, and the magisterium of the Church, in accord with God's most wise design, are so linked and that all together, each in its own way under the action of the one Holy Spirit, contribute effectively to the salvation of souls" (DV 10).

Infallibility and Faith

Christ promised to send His Holy Spirit to those who believed in Him to guide them in all truth (cf. John 16.13). An important gift to the whole believing Church, and to the teaching Church, is the gift of infallibility, that is, a certain inability to err in believing or teaching revealed truth.

"Christ Himself, concerned for this fidelity to divine truth, promised the Church the special assistance of the Spirit of truth, gave the gift of infallibility to those whom He entrusted with the mandate of transmitting and teaching that truth — as has besides been clearly defined by the First Vatican Council and has then been repeated by the Second Vatican Council — and He furthermore endowed the whole of the People of God with a special sense of the faith."[9]

The Church may teach infallibly any element in the whole deposit of divine revelation which Christ has entrusted to His Church (cf. LG 25). Theologians generally point out that infallibility extends also to other truths not actually contained in revelation, but intimately associated with revelation. Thus the Church could not only teach infallibly in a general council some aspects of revealed truth; it could also infallibly declare that the council itself is a true ecumenical council.

[9]Pope John Paul II, Encyclical, *Redemptor Hominis* (March 4, 1979) n. 19 (EV 6.1245).

Infallibility in Believing

God alone is completely infallible. People are by nature capable of falling into error. Obviously faith does not give believers certain knowledge of all things. But it does give light and certainty in some matters that are of essential importance for their salvation. The God who gives the Church a share in the light of His own knowledge by the gift of faith grants to the Church also a certain participation in His own infallibility. What the whole Church believes, instructed by Christ and those whom He has sent, and strengthened by the Holy Spirit, is certainly true. "The body of the faithful as a whole, anointed as they are by the Holy Spirit (cf. 1 John 2.20, 27), cannot err in matters of belief. Thanks to a supernatural sense of the faith which characterizes the People of God as a whole, it manifests this special quality when 'from the bishops to the last members of the laity' it shows universal agreement in matters of faith and morals" (LG 12).[10]

The unerring faith of the Church is a gift of the Holy Spirit who dwells in the faithful. He enlightens the eyes of their hearts (cf. Eph. 1.18) so that they may recognize and obediently acknowledge as the word of God, certain and entirely reliable, the word that He causes to be spoken definitively in His Church (cf. 1 Thess. 2.18). Hence the infallibility of the believing Church is essentially related to the infallibility of the teaching Church.

Infallibility in Teaching

As we have seen, Christ commanded St. Peter and the other apostles to proclaim His Gospel until the end of time. The teaching office He gave them has by His will been handed on to their successors, the pope and the other bishops. This teaching office is exercised in two ways in the Church, through the "ordinary magisterium" and through the "extraordinary magisterium."

Ordinary Magisterium

The bishops normally teach the Church in simple pastoral ways. They preach the Gospel; they see to the catechetical instruction of the faithful in their care; they watch over the forms of prayer and worship in which the faith is lived and exercised; in their instructions and pastoral letters they guide the faithful on what they are to believe and do to attain salvation, in accord with the revelation that has been entrusted to them in their pastoral office. This is their "ordinary magisterium."

Infallibility does not extend to all the teaching of each individual

---

[10]The interior quotation is from St. Augustine, *De Praedestinatione Sanctorum* 14.27 (ML 44.980).

bishop. But the bishops, as authentic teachers of Christ's people, can proclaim His teaching infallibly. "This is so, even when they are dispersed around the world, provided that while maintaining the bond of unity among themselves and with Peter's successor, and while teaching authentically on a matter of faith and morals, they concur in a single viewpoint as the one which must be held conclusively" (LG 25).[11]

Long before special councils had solemnly defined that Jesus is truly God, or had specifically and solemnly proclaimed that God knows us and loves us, these and many other essential elements of Catholic faith and life were taught by bishops everywhere in their ordinary magisterium as the revealed word of God. To say that the bishops teach infallibly in such cases is in effect to say that they do what Christ commanded them to do: they serve as recognizable witness of a meaningful faith, so that people, hearing them, can believe God.

When the bishops throughout the world teach that any matter of faith or morals is revealed by God, their unified witness is a certain sign of the authenticity of their message. What they proclaim is a part of Catholic faith, and part of the Church's infallible teaching (cf. LG 25).

Extraordinary Magisterium

The "extraordinary magisterium" of the Church, which is also infallible, has two forms. The first of these is found in the ecumenical councils. In such councils, known also as general councils, the college of all the bishops, together with the pope as the head of that college, may make definitive statements concerning the faith of the whole Church. The second form is the *ex cathedra* ("from the chair") definition of doctrine by the Holy Father.

Ecumenical Councils

The authority of ecumenical councils was foreshown in the Acts of the Apostles by what is said there of a council of apostles and apostolic co-workers not many years after the resurrection of Jesus (cf. Acts 15.1-28).

At a time of great tension in the early Church, when some people were teaching doctrines that were in fact opposed to the central points of Christianity (though the fact of that conflict had perhaps not been clear to all), Church leaders gathered to discuss the matter. After Peter and others had spoken, there was agreement on the decision to be made: the Gentiles would not be bound to observe the whole Mosaic code. The announcement of this decision was made with great confidence: "It has seemed good to the Holy Spirit and to us to lay upon

---

[11]Cf. also First Vatican Council, Session 3, April 24, 1870, *Dogmatic Constitution on the Catholic Faith*, ch. 3 (DS 3011).

you no greater burden then these necessary things" (Acts 15.28). That is, they taught confidently that the Spirit's guidance, which had been promised to the leaders of the Church, was in fact being given. When these leaders solemnly and publicly proclaimed that something was an element of the true faith, it certainly was so. To them it was clearly a joyful gift of God, a blessing freeing them from anxiety and doubt, to be able thus to be sure of God's will and His message.

Since that apostolic period, when major heresies and discords have arisen the Church's bishops have gathered in ecumenical councils. There have been twenty-one such councils in the course of the Church's history. The first was the Council of Nicaea in 325; the most recent was the Second Vatican Council, from 1962 to 1965.

Anyone who wishes to be a true Christian has always been held required to accept what the ecumenical councils teach as matters of faith. What is taught as divinely revealed by all the teachers of Christ's Church together is the word of God, and therefore it has the infallible certainty of His word. As the Second Vatican Council declared, the infallible teaching office of the bishops "is even more clearly verified when, gathered together in an ecumenical council, they are teachers and judges of faith and morals for the universal Church. Their definitions must then be adhered to with the submission of faith" (LG 25).

Not everything said by ecumenical councils is meant to be infallible teaching.[12] Some conciliar statements are directed rather at offering pastoral considerations or disciplinary legislation.

But ecumenical councils have often made exact formulations of doctrine, and taught these solemnly to the whole Church as infallibly true. These solemn "definitions" state the revealed truth in a way that is "irreformable" and "unalterable." This does not mean the same truth could not also be expressed in other ways, even in more adequate ways; nor does it mean that as language changes in time more appropriate ways of communicating the enduring truth might not be found.[13] But it does mean that the dogmatic formulations of the Church's magisterium express revealed truth aptly, and in such a way that "as they are they remain forever suitable for communicating this truth to those who interpret them correctly,"[14] that is, in the sense in which they were solemnly made.

---

[12]Cf. Declaration of March 6, 1964, by the Second Vatican Council's Doctrinal Commission (text included in "Announcements" document printed in AAS as an appendix to LG): cf. also the Council's note appended to the title of GS.

[13]Cf. Pope John XXIII, *Address* at opening of the Second Vatican Council, October 11, 1962. (EV 1.26* - 69*). Cf. also GS 62.

[14]Sacred Congregation for the Doctrine of the Faith, *Mysterium Ecclesiae* ("Declaration in Defense of the Catholic Doctrine on the Church against Certain Errors of the Present Day," June 24, 1973) n. 5 (EV 4.2576-2581). Cf. Pope Paul VI, Encyclical, *Mysterium Fidei* (September 3, 1965) (EV 2.408-443).

Papal Magisterium

The Holy Father has a special teaching office among the bishops. Succeeding to St. Peter's role as shepherd of the whole flock, he has a duty to care for the faith of the entire Church. Christ Himself wills the chief shepherd of all to have this personal concern.

The pope does not drive his authority and power from other bishops, or by delegation from the Church, but from Christ. Hence he has an independent responsibility to guard the faith. Because it is a personal duty of his office to teach the whole Church, his words have authority from his own sacred office, and do not need approval or acceptance by others to deserve reverent hearing and acceptance from each member of the Church (cf. LG 25). Still, it is the regular practice of the Holy Father to consult widely with other bishops, and with theologians and other scholars, before giving authoritative teaching to the Church.

Christ, having committed the chief pastoral care of the Church to Peter and his successors, Himself teaches the Church through the pope. He does not remove freedom from the pope, nor does He assure us that all popes will be holy men. There have been unworthy popes. Indeed, the possibility of such is suggested in the Gospels themselves. Hardly had Christ promised St. Peter primacy when the apostle foolishly spoke against the cross and received a severe reproach from Christ (cf. Matt. 16.22-23). Moreover, at the time of Christ's passion, Peter fell gravely in denying his Lord (cf. Matt. 26.69-75; Mark 14.66-72; Luke 22.55-62; John 18.17, 25-27). Yet Peter's pastoral role was confirmed by Christ (cf. John 21.15-17).

Even when a pope is unworthy of his office, the Lord guards the Church from false teaching at his hands. Through the Holy See, Christ has wonderfully guarded the purity and consistency of faith over the centuries. Christ's prayer for Peter at the Last Supper was efficacious: "But I have prayed for you that your own faith may not fail; and you, when once you have turned back, strengthen your brothers" (Luke 22.32). In his successors as in his life (cf. Acts 15.7-11), St. Peter has, by the support of Christ, ever confirmed the faith of his brothers. Papal teaching has not been singular, and apart from the faith of the Church. It has spoken that which is the faith of all, and been the center of unity and peace in guarding Christ's truth.

Papal Infallibility

The Holy Father is infallible in certain of his pronouncements. The ancient Catholic teaching in this matter, rooted in the scriptural texts concerning St. Peter noted in the preceding chapter, and affirmed with growing clarity through the centuries, was solemnly defined by the First Vatican Council.[15]

The Holy Father has infallibility because of his role in an infallible Church, that is, in a Church which Christ has made capable of preaching the faith in such a way that His word can be recognized in it, and known to be true because it is His. In that Church St. Peter and his successors were given in perpetuity the duty of confirming and supporting faith; and all members of the flock have had the duty to recognize Christ's pastoral care in the pope's. That the Church itself may be a secure witness, and men and women may have access to faith with confidence, Christ gives to the chief shepherd the ability to witness with recognizable validity in His name. Christ guards the chief shepherd whom He places in charge of His flock from leading His own astray.

The First Vatican Council, after showing how securely this teaching of faith is rooted in the Gospel, how through the centuries God had guarded the faith and unity of the Church through the successors of St. Peter, and how the Church had constantly acknowledged that the supreme teaching authority for the faith rests with the Bishop of Rome as St. Peter's successor, gave its solemn definition of papal infallibility: "Therefore, faithfully adhering to the tradition received from the beginning of the Christian faith . . . we teach and define that it is a dogma divinely revealed: that the Roman Pontiff, when he speaks *ex cathedra*, that is, when acting in the office of shepherd and teacher of all Christians by virtue of his supreme apostolic authority he defines doctrine concerning faith or morals to be held by the whole Church, by the divine assistance promised him in Blessed Peter, is possessed of that infallibility with which the divine Redeemer willed His Church to be endowed in defining doctrine concerning faith or morals; and that therefore such definitions of the Roman Pontiff are of themselves, and not from consent of the Church, irreformable."[16]

The infallibility of the pope, like that of the believing Church and that of the whole body of bishops, is not the same thing as revelation or inspiration. It does not imply any special supernatural insight or wisdom. But it is a precious safeguard for the whole Church. Through the gift of papal infallibility the Holy Spirit guards the faith of the whole Church from error.

Papal infallibility does not extend to matters of natural science and human wisdom. It applies to the same matters as the infallibility of the whole Church, that is, in the words of the definition quoted above, to

---

[15]Cf. First Vatican Council, Session 4, July 18, 1870, *First Dogmatic Constitution on the Church of Christ*, ch. 4 (DS 3065-3075).
[16]First Vatican Council, Session 4, July 18, 1870, *First Dogmatic Constitution on the Church of Christ*, ch. 4 (DS 3074). Cf. also LG 25.

"doctrine concerning faith or morals to be held by the whole Church."

The pope teaches infallibly with the other bishops when he and they exercise the infallible ordinary or extraordinary magisterium of the college of bishops. His individual infallible magisterium is exercised only in his *ex cathedra* statements. Such statements are rarely made by the Holy See; but the pope's teaching role remains to confirm the faith of his brothers (cf. Luke 22.32).

Authoritative Teaching

Catholic teaching is far more than the proclamation of a limited number of infallibly defined dogmas or articles of faith. The Catholic knows that Christ is present in His Church, and is teaching there, making known a rich mystery that needs always to be more richly learned. The faith of the Catholic is rooted in the living God, and it extends to whatever God bears witness to through the Church in which He causes the saving truth to be proclaimed.

Faith in the dogmas of the Church themselves means more than acceptance of the formulas in which the dogmas are expressed. To believe an article of faith rightly one must hold it in the very sense in which the Church means it, as expressing a truth the Church has believed and does believe.[17] The meaning of Christian teachings is grasped only by an attentive person who wishes to understand the mind of the Church in all its teachings and life.

The Catholic is expected to assent to all the authoritative teachings of the Church, even when the Church is not using its full infallible authority. "Bishops teaching in communion with the Roman Pontiff are to be respected by all as witnesses to divine and Catholic truth. When their bishop speaks in the name of Christ in matters of faith and morals, the faithful are to accept his teaching and adhere to it with a religious assent of soul. This religious submission of will and of mind must be shown in a special way to the authentic magisterium of the Roman Pontiff even when he is not speaking *ex cathedra*. That is, it must be shown in such a way that his supreme magisterium is acknowledged with reverence, and the judgments made by him are sincerely adhered to, according to his manifest mind and will. His mind and will here may be known chiefly either from the character of the documents, from his frequent repetition of the same doctrine, or from his manner of speaking" (LG 25).

The encyclical letters of the Holy Father, in which he addresses the Church in an especially solemn and serious manner, have a special claim to reverent assent, even when they are not intended to announce any solemn definitions of faith. In them the chief pastor of the whole

---

[17]Cf. First Vatican Council, Session 3, April 24, 1870, *Dogmatic Constitution on the Catholic Faith*, ch. 4 (DS 3020).

Church is addressing in Christ's name the whole flock of the Lord. "Such teachings belong to the ordinary magisterium, of which it is true to say: 'He who hears you, hears Me' (Luke 10.16). For the most part, what is expounded and stressed in encyclical letters already belongs to Catholic doctrine for other reasons. But if the supreme pontiffs in their acts give attention to and pass judgment on a matter up to that point controverted, it is obvious to all that the matter, according to the mind and will of the same pontiffs, can no longer be considered a question for free debate among theologians."[18]

The proper interpretation of an encyclical or other Church document is not always easy to determine. Careful study of the text is required, in the context of other papal pronouncements and of relevant theological writings. Popes do not settle theological controversies hastily or without pressing reasons. But the sublime office they hold requires them at times to make firm judgments in order to safeguard the faith and to care for the common good of the Church.

The assent to authentic teachings which are not clearly infallible teachings is called a "religious assent." Because a Catholic believes that God gives the successors of the apostles authority to guide the faith and religious life of the Church, the Catholic "abides not only by the extraordinary decision of the Church, but by its ordinary life as well where faith and discipline are concerned."[19]

Such religious assent is required of all who profess faith in the Catholic Church. It is required of the Holy Father and bishops, of priests and theologians, as well as of the laity. The confidence is placed not in human resources, but in Christ, whose care constantly guards the Church. Saints and scholars of all centuries in the Church have affirmed the importance of this heeding of Christ in His Church. And they have regularly proclaimed that this is fully in accord with the highest intellectual integrity as well as with the duties of personal faith, and that it liberates rather than binds the spirit of those who love Christ.

Those who instruct others in the faith must be careful to teach the authentic message of the Church. For the Catholic there should never be any doubt about what the Church teaches. The Catholic deserves as teacher a priest who is in accord with his bishop, and a bishop who is in unity of faith with the college of bishops and with the pope.

Christ Rules in His Church

It is in Christ that all authority of the Church natively dwells. "All authority in heaven and on earth has been given to Me" (Matt. 28.18).

---

[18]Pope Pius XII, Encyclical, *Humani Generis* (August 12, 1950) (DS 3885).
[19]United States Bishops, Pastoral Letter, *The Church in Our Day* (November 1967). Cf. also Congregation for the Doctrine of the Faith, *Instruction on the Ecclesial Vocation of the Theologian* (May 24, 1990).

Because He is strong and merciful in His possession of authority, He chooses to exercise it through human agents He has chosen. On earth Christ rules through people whom He selects, whom He makes visible as His own spokesmen and shepherds, and to whom He gives the duty to give His commands and directives to His people. "Go therefore and make disciples of all nations, baptizing them . . . , teaching them to obey everything that I have commanded you. And, remember, I am with you always, to the end of the age" (Matt. 28.19-20).

Those to whom this commission was spoken had earlier been given promises that they would have authority in His name. It was to be an authority used in love with the strength of love, but also with humility and personal concern (cf. Matt. 20.25-28; John 13.12-17).

The authority was given in a special way to one of the apostles. To Peter, the Rock, there was specially assigned the role of bearer of the keys, of the symbols of the ruler in the house. To him the shepherding care for all the flock was entrusted.

This ruling office in the Church which is exercised by the pope and the other bishops has been discussed in the preceding chapter. Often called the power of jurisdiction, the office of ruling exists to serve the growth of faith and holiness in the Church. The laws of the Church are issued with the authority Christ gave to the Church (cf. Matt. 16.19; 18.18) for the good of the People of God. The Code of Canon Law is a collection of laws promulgated by the Holy See to guide the Universal Church in questions of faith, morals, worship, and discipline. Canon Law was first codified in 1917; a new code was issued in 1983. The bishops of each country generally list the most notable of special duties of Catholics which are known as precepts of the Church.[20] These cover such obligations as those to attend Mass on Sundays and holy days of obligation, and to avoid unnecessary and inappropriate work on such days; to lead a regular sacramental life; to observe the marriage laws of the Church; to strengthen and support the Church; to do penance at the appointed times.

Christ Sanctifies in His Church

Christ's sanctifying work is the most comprehensive and important of all. He came to give us the life that is love and holiness. He came to bind us to the Father in friendship, to join us together in Himself as a priestly people, and to associate us personally with the acts by which He redeems and makes holy the universe.

Teaching and ruling in the Church are each ordered to the more important task of sanctifying. Sacred teaching is not aimed at satisfy-

[20]Cf., e.g., United States Catholic Conference, *Sharing the Light of Faith — National Catechetical Directory for Catholics of the United States* (1979) Appendix B.

ing curiosity, but at giving the saving truth, love of which is both a part of holiness and a guide to doing the will of God in love. All ruling in the Church is directed toward holiness, to be used for edification, and not for any personal gratification or glory of those called to serve by allowing Christ to rule in them (cf. LG 39-42).

But there are certain most precious specifically sanctifying powers Christ gave to the Church. For example, He instructed His apostles to baptize, to celebrate the Eucharist, to forgive sins.

Some of the sanctifying forces Christ gave to the Church He gave to all. The whole Church is to be "a royal priesthood, a holy nation" (1 Peter 2.9; cf. LG 9). In baptism and confirmation His people is to be made suitable to share in His perfect worship, the one sacrifice that is the healing of the world (cf. Heb. 10).

Some of the sanctifying works of Christ are to be done through the shepherds of His flock, the bishops and priests. Not to every Christian is there given the call or the ability to make present the Eucharistic sacrifice of Christ, and His bodily presence, by speaking His sacred words. Not to everyone is given the task and the power to forgive sins in Christ's name (cf. John 20.22-23). Only those called, sealed with the sacrament of orders as priests or bishops, can be instruments by which Christ confers many of His gifts on His people. The powers of orders are not personal honors for those who hold them, and do not, of themselves, make those who are ordained better persons. It is the intensity of one's Christian love that is the measure of one's greatness before God and in reality; and everyone in the Church is called equally to be holy, to become perfect. But as servants of the holiness of others, some are called to special posts that minister the greater gifts. These sanctifying gifts in the Church are discussed in the third part of this book, especially in chapters 26 to 30.

The labor of all faithful bishops will be directed to the same aims as those toward which St. Paul directed his concern: ". . .we have not ceased praying for you and asking that you may be filled with the knowledge of God's will in all spiritual wisdom and understanding so that you may lead lives worthy of the Lord, fully pleasing to Him, as you bear fruit in every good work and as you grow in the knowledge of God" (Col. 1.9-10).

15

Mary, Mother
And Model Of The Church

Mary, the mother of Jesus, was with Him in the hour of His passion (cf. John 19.25). In many ways she was associated with His redemptive work. Jesus has shared with her also, in her Assumption, the glory of His risen life. Because of all that this intimate nearness to Jesus' work implies, Mary has close ties with all those who have been redeemed and called to be members of her Son's Mystical Body.

The first part of this chapter treats Mary's role as Mother of the Church and of each of the faithful. Though she was herself redeemed by Jesus, she shared with great love in His saving work; she is spiritually our mother, and a mediatrix of grace. The chapter then treats Mary's position as model of the Church, the pattern of what the Church should be as the mother of the faithful and as a holy servant of the Lord. The final part of the chapter speaks of the role of St. Joseph, Mary's husband, in Christian life.

Mother of the Church

Catholic devotion salutes Mary as "Mother of the Church."[1] Mary deserves this title because she is the mother of Jesus, and because of her special association with His saving work, which is continued in the Church. The title aptly expresses the spiritual maternity she exercises in the life of the faithful. It suggests her role as model of the Church in the way she shows forth the Christian virtues.

Mary Redeemed by Christ

Christ alone is the Redeemer of all. Mary, then, was redeemed by Him. Her redemption, however, like the rest of her role in God's plan, was unique. Christ did not take away His mother's sins, for she had none; rather, by His redemptive mercy He kept her from incurring sin, so that she was conceived without original sin and was guarded by His grace against falling into sin.

---

[1]Cf., e.g., Pope Paul VI, *Address* at the close of the third session of the Second Vatican Council (November 21, 1964) (EV 1.319*); Pope John Paul II, Encyclical, *Redemptor Hominis* (March 4, 1979) n. 22 (EV 6.1262-1268).

We are redeemed not only by Christ's saving mysteries but also in Him. When the Son of God took our human nature, He so identified Himself with us that His saving deeds counted for us. There is a solidarity in humankind. When Adam sinned, we, his children, became members of a fallen race. When Jesus, the second Adam (cf. 1 Cor. 15.45), our Brother and Savior, gave His life on the cross for us, we became a redeemed people. By His life, death, and resurrection Jesus has already reconciled our race with the Father. This is "objective redemption": the guilt of our sins has already been objectively atoned for by the saving mercy of Christ.

"Subjective redemption" is the application of the saving gifts of Christ to each one of us personally. This application is not automatic. Redemption is not forced upon us. Each individual must participate actively in receiving God's gift. As grace won by Jesus makes it possible, the one called must reach out in faith to receive the gift. Only infants and others who, like them, are incapable of an active response can receive the fruits of redemption without a free act of their own.

We received the fruits of redemption as God's pure gift in our baptism. Mary received this gift at the moment of her immaculate conception. Those who receive baptism in infancy must offer their free response later. So Mary, too, as her personality developed, gave her free consent to this gift.

Mary belonged to the sinful human race. She therefore stood in need of redemption. The fact that she did not actually incur original sin is not due to her action but Christ's. He truly suffered and died for her; in fact, in a certain sense He suffered and died more for His mother than for the rest of us, for He redeemed her so thoroughly as to preserve her from all sin and to give her the fullness of grace. Because she shared in a unique way in His redemptive grace, she led a life free from any personal sin or evil inclination. The totality of her cooperation with grace corresponded with the abundance of Christ's gifts to her, so that she is the first fruits of redemption.

Mary's Share in Our Redemption

The perfection of her redemption by Christ is the basis for Mary's special role in our redemption. In an earlier chapter we saw something of what was significant by her words at the Annunciation: "Let it be to me according to your word" (Luke 1.38). At the deepest level of her personality she opened herself to the mysterious will of God. In humble and obedient faith she freely accepted the grace of divine motherhood. This was an expression of her own personal or subjective redemption growing out of the unique grace of her immaculate conception. Her free agreement in faith to be the Redeemer's mother expressed her willingness to play her part in the redemption of humankind.

St. Thomas Aquinas says that the Blessed Virgin gave her consent "in place of the whole human race."[2] Because Mary accepted God's will for her, we are able to accept the fruits of Christ's redemption into our own lives.

Mary's consent to be the mother of Yahweh's suffering Servant was an implicit acceptance of His Crucifixion. Certainly she did not understand this fully from the beginning; but the "let it be to me" she uttered at the Annunciation was never retracted, and her words reached their fullest meaning at the foot of the cross. Then, when the sword of sorrow pierced her heart, as had been prophesied (cf. Luke 2.35), her obedience to the Father's will that she suffer with the Redeemer reached its highest expression. With compassionate and sacrificial love she accepted in freedom and pain her Son's passion and death for the redemption of the world. This acceptance made her most completely mother both of the Savior and of us as members of His Mystical Body, which was born from His redeeming death. She alone was His mother. No one else could become so directly involved in His redemptive suffering as Mary.

After her Son's ascension, the Acts of the Apostles tells us, Mary was among those gathered together with the apostles in prayer (cf. Acts 1.14). Scripture thus portrays her in the midst of the infant Church, awaiting in faith the first Pentecost. The Holy Spirit of the risen Lord would soon come upon those in the upper room of the Cenacle and enlighten their understanding concerning all Christ had taught them. Mary's unique grace among the redeemed made her most responsive to the inspirations of her divine Spouse, the Holy Spirit, and her motherly presence influenced the infant Church to grasp more fully its apostolic mission of preaching the Gospel to the ends of the earth. She may well have had a role in the composition of the Gospels, as a source of knowledge about Christ; this at least seems to be one possible interpretation of St. Luke's words that Mary "treasured all these words and pondered them in her heart" (Luke 2.19; cf. Luke 2.51).

Mary's unique role in our redemption follows from her complete cooperation in her own personal redemption. Because she received the Redeemer into her own life with such deep faith, especially at the moments of the Annunciation, Calvary, and Pentecost, Mary cooperated maternally in Christ's objective redemption of the human race. Her "let it be" in the name of all humankind accepted Christ's saving grace for the benefit of every human being. Though Christ alone is our Redeemer reconciling us with the Father, she, by virtue of her faith and divine maternity, is both the spiritual and bodily mother of our

[2]St. Thomas Aquinas, *Summa Theologica* III, 30, 1.

redemption in her divine Son. Her free act of identification with His objective redemption of humankind has a redemptive meaning and value for all of us. This is the basis for Mary's "spiritual motherhood" of all men and women, insofar as all are called to be members of her Son's Mystical Body, the Church.

Mary's Spiritual Motherhood

"Our Blessed Mother" is a title especially dear to Catholics. With a rich heritage of our religious history, it is at once simple and profound in meaning. Mary is our spiritual mother because of her special role in communicating to us our life in Christ.[3] As we have seen, this role is based upon her real motherhood of the Lord, our Savior and Head of the Body to which we belong as His members. Mary is spiritual mother of the whole human family because Christ suffered, died, and rose for the redemption of all. In a special way, however, she is the mother of all the faithful who are actually members of His Body the Church. For this reason she is called "Mother of the Church."

What does it mean to say that Mary was really Jesus' mother? It means that she physically conceived Him and brought Him into the world. It means also that she received Him into her own spiritual life and raised Him to fulfill the mission He had come to accomplish. Her faith is the foundation for understanding her spiritual motherhood of humankind. "At the message of the angel, the Virgin Mary received the Word of God in her heart and in her body, and gave Life to the world. Hence she is acknowledged and honored as being truly the Mother of God and Mother of the Redeemer" (LG 53). As mother of our Redeemer she heard God's word and kept it.

Concerning her continuous association with Christ our Savior, the Second Vatican Council stated: "Thus the Blessed Virgin advanced in her pilgrimage of faith, and loyally persevered in her union with her Son unto the cross. There she stood, in keeping with the divine plan (cf. John 19.25), suffering grievously with her only-begotten Son. There she united herself with a maternal heart to His sacrifice, and lovingly consented to the immolation of this Victim which she herself had brought forth. Finally, the same Christ Jesus dying on the cross gave her as a mother to His disciple. This He did when He said: 'Woman, there is your son' (cf. John 19.26-27)" (LG 58).

"But since it pleased God not to manifest solemnly the mystery of the salvation of the human race until He poured forth the Spirit promised by Christ, we see the apostles before the day of Pentecost 'continuing with one mind in prayer with the women and Mary, the mother of Jesus, and with His brethren' (Acts 1.14). We see Mary

---

[3]Cf. Pope John Paul II, Encyclical, *Dives in Misericordia* (November 30, 1980) n. 9 (EV 7.911-916).

prayerfully imploring the gift of the Spirit, who had already over-shadowed her in the Annunciation" (LG 59). From her voiced "let it be" at the Annunciation through her silent "let it be" on Calvary to her prayer for the Spirit of the risen Lord at Pentecost, the New Testament pictures Mary as the woman of faith who helps both to beget and to nurture us in the life of Christ.

The Second Vatican Council borrowed the words of St. Augustine to speak of Mary's spiritual maternity. She is "clearly the mother of the members of Christ ... since she cooperated out of love so that there might be born in the Church the faithful, who are members of Christ their Head."[4] St. Augustine adds that even being Christ's mother according to the flesh would have had no spiritual significance for Mary if she had not borne Christ before all in her heart. Spiritual kinship with Christ belongs to all who do the Father's will. Thus Mary's outstanding faith gives her physical motherhood of Christ a deep meaning in salvation history, a meaning which justifies speaking of her "spiritual motherhood" of all humankind.

"In an utterly singular way she cooperated by her obedience, faith, hope, and burning charity in the Savior's work of restoring super-natural life to souls. For this reason she is a mother to us in the order of grace" (LG 61).

Mary's Mediation and Intercession

Mary's spiritual motherhood must be considered not only in the light of the Church's traditional and growing understanding of the biblical message about her association with Christ on earth, but also in the light of the Church's teaching about her special relationship to the risen Lord and to us in the communion of saints. "This maternity will last without interruption until the eternal fulfillment of all the elect. For, taken up to heaven, she did not lay aside this saving role, but by her manifold acts of intercession continues to procure for us gifts of eternal salvation" (LG 62).

One of the titles under which Mary is invoked in the Church is "Mediatrix" (cf. LG 62). This title, as the Second Vatican Council ex-plained, is understood in such a way that it "neither takes away from nor adds anything to the dignity and efficacy of Christ the one Mediator" (LG 62). On the other hand, while all of the faithful receive in baptism the grace of sharing in the priestly mission of mediating salvation to mankind. Mary's life of perfect faith on earth and her spe-cial union with the risen Lord in glory make her the highest example of mediation within the communion of saints. She who took part in His redeeming labors as his mother and as sharer of His sorrows par-ticipates as mediatrix in His will to bestow salvation upon all. She is a

4St. Augustine, *De Sancta Virginitate* 6 (ML 40.399), quoted in LG 53.

pattern for all: the more one enjoys the fruits of the redemption, the more one is united with Christ, and the more one will share in Christ's redeeming work.

Mary's role in the distribution of graces does not compete with the centrality of Christ as the one Mediator between God and humankind (cf. 1 Tim. 2.5-6). "The maternal duty of Mary toward men in no wise obscures or diminishes this unique mediation of Christ, but rather shows His power. For every saving influence of the Blessed Virgin on men originates, not from some inner necessity, but from the divine pleasure. It flows forth from the superabundance of the merits of Christ, rests on His mediation, depends entirely upon it, and draws all its powers from it. It in no way impedes, but rather fosters the immediate union of the faithful with Christ" (LG 60).

Mary's mediating role, then, fosters the immediacy of our union with Christ. "Since Mary is rightly to be regarded as the way by which we are led to Christ, the person who encounters Mary cannot help but encounter Christ likewise."[5] Expressions such as the council's "immediate union of the faithful with Christ" and the Holy Father's "encounter Christ likewise" make it clear that Mary in her mediation does not stand between us and a remote Christ.

Confusion about Mary's role has not only been the cause of much misunderstanding between Catholics and other Christians but, more fundamentally, has for some obscured the most important meaning of the Incarnation, the mystery that God has truly become one of us in Jesus Christ and so is intimately present to each of us, offering His saving grace. Mary is great because she is close to Christ and draws us close to Him. Her mediation continues to create the spiritual climate for our immediate encounter with Christ. It would be a great mistake to consider her as a separate and intermediate agency between the Redeemer and ourselves. That would not glorify her role, but rather minimize it. The power of her spiritual motherhood is rather this: she serves to effect a direct, intimate, and most fruitful meeting between her Son and her spiritual children.

Jesus, having entered glory as the eternal High Priest, continues to pray for us. He "holds His priesthood permanently, because He continues for ever. Consequently He is able for all time to save those who approach God through Him, since He always lives to make intercession for them" (Heb. 7.24-25). Mary, ever associated with her Son, prays for us with him. She is not alone in this. The whole community of the blessed in heaven imitate Christ in continuing their concern for us. As we pray for one another upon earth and for the souls in purgatory, so our brothers and sisters in heaven intercede for us. We are

[5]Pope Paul VI, Encyclical, *Mense Maio* (April 29, 1965).

united with all of them by intimate bonds of Christian love. But Mary, our spiritual mother, has an altogether exceptional role in this. Among those redeemed by her Son, her intercessory power is by far the most extensive and effective.

Catholic devotion speaks of invoking or "praying to" the saints, "on whose constant intercession we rely for help."[6] We do not address the saints as though they were God. To invoke the intercession of the saints, including Mary, is really to pray that, together with them, we may grow in the love of the triune God who wills the salvation of all. It is to express the longing that the saints, living in personal love of God, will also embrace us in that personal God-given love, and will by their prayers assist us in obtaining benefits from God.

Mary's intercession has the same meaning and purpose as that of the other saints. The profound difference lies in its intensity and universality. Mary's love, inspired by her close union with her Son, embraces the whole human family and the needs of all. She cares with intense personal love for the entire fulfillment of his work of salvation. That is why, under Jesus, she is said to be the mediatrix of graces.[7]

Special Devotion to Mary

While it would be wrong to say that it is absolutely necessary to be devoted to Mary in order to be saved, one who does not invoke her special intercession misses a valuable opportunity for grace to grow in Christ. The Blessed Mother wishes to show her spiritual children how to know, love, and serve her divine Son more generously. Without her maternal guidance, received through some form of devotion to her, one will not mature as fully in Christian worship and mission as Christ wishes.

Honor has always been shown to Mary in the Church, and the faithful have persistently had a devoted love for her. Devotion to Mary, of course, "differs essentially from the cult of adoration" (LG 66) which is given to God alone. Though Mary has sublime dignity as the Mother of God, she is a fellow creature. In devotion to her one should avoid both exaggeration and minimalization. "True devotion consists neither in fruitless, passing emotion, nor in a certain vain credulity. Rather, it proceeds from faith, by which we are led to know the excellence of the Mother of God, and are moved to a filial love toward our mother and to the imitation of her virtues" (LG 67).

At times devotion to Mary has been stimulated by word of her appearance to devout suppliants, as at Lourdes, Fatima, and Guadalupe.

6Roman Missal, The Order of Mass, Eucharistic Prayer III.

7Cf. Pope Pius X, Encyclical, *Ad Diem Illum* (February 2, 1904) (DS 3370); Pope Pius XII, Encyclical, *Ad Caeli Reginam* (October 11, 1954 (DS 3914-3917); Pope John Paul II, Encyclical, *Redemptoris Mater* (March 25, 1987) nn. 38-41 (EV 10.1375-1386).

The Church does not give any definitive teaching on the authenticity or nature of such apparitions. But the Church does study them carefully, and if the fruits of an event breathe of the presence of God's providential designs, it approves the consequent devotions. Wherever such approved devotions to Mary develop, they lead to a deeper appreciation of the meaning and spirit of the Gospel. "These providential happenings serve as reminders to us of basic Christian themes: prayer, penance, and the necessity of the sacraments."[8]

Personal devotion to Mary ought to imitate the patterns found in the Church's liturgy, in its joyful worship of God and praise of her in the feasts in which the honoring of Mary leads us to a warmer love of her Son, and in the daily recognition that the liturgy gives to her closeness to Jesus. Liturgical worship is always rooted securely in the doctrines of faith, as are the traditional private Marian prayers most honored and most warmly encouraged in the Church, such as the Angelus and the rosary.

The Church has long recommended the rosary as a convenient and effective way of meditating on the great mysteries of our salvation.[9]

Mary, Model of the Church

Mary is truly a member of the Church founded by her divine Son Jesus Christ. But she occupies a special place in that community. Not only is she "mother" of the Church, communicating the life of Christ the Head, but she is also "model" of the Church in the unique example she gives of Christian virtue. "Through the gift and role of divine maternity, Mary is united with her Son, the Redeemer, and with His singular graces and offices. By these, the Blessed Virgin is also intimately united with the Church. As St. Ambrose taught,[10] the mother of God is a model of the Church in the order of faith, charity, and perfect union with Christ. For in the mystery of the Church, which is itself rightly called mother and virgin, the Blessed Virgin Mary stands out in eminent and singular fashion as exemplar of both virginity and motherhood" (LG 63).

Motherhood of Mary and of the Church

The Church is both a saved community and a saving community. It has been endowed by Jesus Christ with the ministry of the word and the sacraments, and these make it a saving community. On the other

---

[8]United States National Conference of Catholic Bishops, Pastoral Letter, *Behold Your Mother: Woman of Faith* (November 21, 1973) n. 100.

[9]Cf. Pope Paul VI, Apostolic Exhortation, *Marialis Cultus* (February 2, 1974) nn. 40-55 (EV 5.71-87).

[10]Cf. St. Ambrose, *Expositio Evangelii secundum Lucam* 2.7 (ML 15.1555).

hand, the Church is a saved community of faith and worship, made holy by the grace of Jesus Christ. These two aspects should not be understood as incompatible opposites. It is the one Church which is saving, because it bears the activity of Christ, and which is saved, because it receives it. In the former sense, the Church has always been saluted as mother of the faithful.

There is a close relationship between Mary's spiritual motherhood and the motherhood of the Church. As a number of the Fathers of the Church observed, what is said of Mary is also to be said of the Church. The Church, too, is both mother and virgin, holy and sanctifying. Mary is the model of the Church as the great sacrament, the efficacious sign of the saving presence of Jesus Christ. She is also a pattern for all whose task in the Church is to assist in Jesus' saving work. Her maternal concern for all that leads fallen humanity to redemption in her divine Son gives the greatest example of the fidelity to continuing Christ's mission to which the Church is called. Every pope, bishop, priest, deacon, religious, and lay person can look to Mary as the exemplar of fidelity to his or her special vocation of mediating salvation.[11]

Holiness of Mary and of the Church

The most basic truth about the mystery of the Church is that it is a community of brothers and sisters in the Lord. In this community Mary also is our sister, just as every member, whether pope or lay person, whether scholar or simple unlettered believer, is our brother or sister in the Lord. The basis of our Christian community is that we share the totally unmerited gift of God's saving love. Our very ability to respond freely by committing ourselves to the service of Christ is itself rooted in grace.

Mary's example of complete openness to God's will is a constant source of edification for our growth in Christian holiness. A unique lay person in the Church, she did not possess the ministerial powers of the priesthood. Yet her life of deep faith, humble obedience, persevering hope, fruitful poverty of spirit, and courageous love provides a model for every member of the Church. Married couples and parents can be enlightened and inspired by her selfless love of Joseph and Jesus; celibate priests and religious, by her virginal consecration to God's plan of redemption in Christ; single persons in the world, by her spirit of prayer and dedicated service. In our own times she shows all who seek or enjoy a new liberation how to use freedom in such a way that it does not degenerate into the slavery of sinfulness but becomes

---

[11]Cf. Pope John Paul II, Encyclical, *Redemptoris Mater* (March 25, 1987) nn. 42-47 (EV 10.1387-1405).

instead a source of energy for self-fulfillment and transformation of the world.

Mary's Assumption and the Church in Heaven

After her life on earth had ended, Mary was reunited with her Son. She was taken up to heaven in body as well as in soul. There is no explicit reference in Scripture to the Assumption of Mary. But the doctrine has deep roots in the Scripture's teaching on the holiness and dignity of Mary, and on the meaning of a human being, sin, death, and the resurrection of the body.[12]

Because she was the mother of God she had been kept holy always by a singular gift of God. As the fruits of the redemption were anticipated to preserve her from original sin, so they were anticipated to bring her bodily to heaven before the general resurrection at the end of time. Since she had never been subject to sin, she, like her divine Son, was not to remain in the grave, subject to the empire of death that sin had brought into the world. It was fitting, then, that she who gave bodily birth to Jesus should be with Him bodily in heaven as she adores Him in the glory of His risen body.

Devotion to Mary in the glory of her Assumption is ancient in the Church. As early as around the year 500 the Eastern Church celebrated on August 15 the feast of Mary's "Dormition," her "falling asleep" in the Lord. By the end of the eighth-century the feast was celebrated throughout the Western Church. Toward the middle of the eighth-century St. John Damascene, in three magnificent homilies on Mary's Dormition, summed up the traditional faith and teaching of the Eastern and Western Church concerning her glorious Assumption and mediation of graces in heaven.[13]

Thus many centuries of belief and devotion were crowned when the doctrine of the Assumption was formally defined by Pope Pius XII on November 1, 1950: ". . . we proclaim, declare, and define it to be a dogma revealed by God that the immaculate Mother of God, Mary ever Virgin, when the course of her earthly life was finished, was taken up body and soul into the glory of heaven."[14]

Like all the special graces and privileges bestowed on Mary through the merits of Christ's redeeming love, the Assumption does not separate Mary from the rest of the redeemed People of God, but unites her more intimately with each one of us. The ways in which she is unique in salvation history should not be thought of as setting her apart but rather as creating for her a closer relationship with Christ and

---

[12]Cf. Pope Pius XII, Apostolic Constitution, *Munificentissimus Deus* (November 1, 1950).

[13]Cf. St. John Damascene, *Homiliae in Dormitionem Beatae Virginis Mariae* (MG 96.699-762).

[14]Pope Pius XII, Apostolic Constitution, *Munificentissimus Deus* (November 1, 1950) (DS 3903). Cf. also LG 59.

His Church. "In the bodily and spiritual glory which she possesses in heaven, the Mother of Jesus continues in this present world as the image and first flowering of the Church as she is to be perfected in the world to come" (LG 68). As Jesus did not abandon us by ascending to heaven but continually sends His Holy Spirit to sustain His Church, so Mary, in the Assumption, has not been separated from us but instead remains a sign of sure hope that each one of us is called to share as she has in the fullness of Christ's glory. As the most faithful spouse of the Holy Spirit, she is the model of all that the Church and humankind hope to become in heaven.

St. Joseph in Our Christian Life

One cannot adequately consider Mary's place in Christian life without reference to St. Joseph's special role in our salvation. As guardian of the Holy Family, most chaste spouse of our Lady, and foster father of our Savior, he received from God one of the highest vocations in the plan of redemption.

Although the Gospels say little about this man of faith, they bear ample witness to his virtue and reverence for the divine will. Like Mary, he was in the Old Testament tradition of the "poor of Yahweh," entirely open to God's revealing word. After Mary had conceived Jesus virginally, while she was engaged to Joseph, he was pained and puzzled; but in his nobility of heart he behaved, in the words of Scripture, as "a righteous man" (Matt. 1.19). Convinced of her virtue, he would not expose her to the penalty of the law. Yet, as a righteous man who looked for God's will in the law, he could not take Mary as his wife. His painful decision to "dismiss her quietly" (Matt. 1.19) was the most prudent path until his faith and patience were rewarded by an angelic message concerning Mary's virginal conception and her Son Jesus, who "will save His people from their sins" (Matt. 1.21).

Joseph was truly married to Mary, in a virginal marriage, but a marriage of devoted personal love. Jesus was not merely Joseph's adopted Son; He was born of Joseph's wife. God chose to make the deep personal love of the Virgin Mary and of the chaste Joseph provide the human context for the birth of the Savior of all. It is true that Joseph was not naturally or physically the father of Jesus, "yet to the piety and love of Joseph a Son was born of the Virgin Mary — He who was also the Son of God."[15] Like Mary, Joseph must have had a profound influence upon the Child who was "obedient to them" (Luke 2.51).

Many aspects of devotion to St. Joseph trace their source from the desire during the Middle Ages to know more about Jesus and Mary.

---

[15]St. Augustine, *Sermo* 51.30 (ML 38.351 = ACW 15.64).

This motive of devotion should be ours as well. On December 8, 1870, Pope Pius IX proclaimed St. Joseph Patron of the Universal Church,[16] a title which aptly described his special place in Christian life. His special virtues of justice and fidelity are particularly appropriate for imitation by fathers of families. But for every person devotion to St. Joseph can lead to a deeper faith in the new life of Christ communicated through Mary.

---

[16]Cf. Pope Piux IX, Decree, *Quemadmodum Deus Josephum* (December 8, 1870). Cf. also Pope John Paul II, Apostolic Exhortation, *Redemptoris Custos* (August 15, 1989).

16

Faith Lived In A Divided World

The Catholic Church, "God's only flock" (UR 2), carries on Christ's work in a world in which people profess many different religions and indeed many people profess no religion at all. The Church does not despise other religions, but rather respects all that is good and true in all religions. It knows that faith is a gift of God, and that the Holy Spirit distributes His gifts as He will (cf. 1 Cor. 12.11); and it knows that God in His mercy and love gives grace to all sufficient for salvation if they but respond. For Christ "died for all" (2 Cor. 5.15) and God wills that all be saved (cf. 1 Tim. 2.4).

Yet the Church, "missionary by her very nature" (AG 2), can never forget its mission to proclaim the Gospel to all creation (cf. Mark 16.15). "All men are called to belong to the new People of God. Wherefore this People, while remaining one and unique, is to be spread throughout the whole world and must exist in all ages, so that the purpose of God's will may be fulfilled" (LG 13). In this chapter we discuss the Catholic response to the multiplicity of religions in the world today. The chapter also discusses the responsibility of the Church to the world, and the meaning and importance of true religious freedom.

Judaism

Of the non-Christian religions, Judaism holds a unique place in the history of salvation. The Old Testament records the history of the Jews and it shows how God chose them in a special way and revealed Himself to them. This was part of the divine plan and preparation for salvation.

God Himself entered into a covenant, a pact or agreement, with Abraham (cf. Gen. 15.16) and, through Moses, with the people of Israel (cf. Exod. 24.8). He "taught this nation to acknowledge Him as the one living and true God, provident Father and just Judge, and to wait for the Savior promised by Him, and in this manner He prepared the way for the Gospel down through the centuries" (DV 3). When the Son of God became man, He came on earth as a Jew. Those He chose as apostles were Jews. Most of the early disciples were Jews.

Christians should always remember that the beginnings of their faith are found already among the patriarchs, Moses, and the prophets. The books of the Hebrew Bible are found also in the Catholic Bible. It was through God's chosen people of old that the Church received the revelation of the Old Testament. The Old Testament yields its ultimate meaning only in the light of the New Testament, but the books of the Old Testament have permanent value in themselves (cf. DV 15-16). All who believe in Christ are included in the call of Abraham, and are "the descendants of Abraham" (Gal. 3.7). "Indeed, the Church believes that by His cross Christ, our Peace, reconciled Jew and Gentile, making them both one in Himself (cf. Eph. 2.14-16)" (NA 4).

Thus there is a spiritual bond linking the people of the New Covenant, the new People of God, with the people of the Old Covenant. The fact that most of the Jews at the time of Christ did not accept Him as the Messiah and rejected His message in no way meant a rejection of God by the Jews. "The history of Judaism did not end with the destruction of Jerusalem, but rather went on to develop a religious tradition. And, although we believe that the importance and meaning of that tradition were deeply affected by the coming of Christ, it is still nonetheless rich in religious values."[1] Certainly the Jews "still remain most dear to God because of their fathers, for God does not repent of the gifts He makes nor of the calls He issues (cf. Rom. 11.28-29)," and, together with the prophets and St. Paul, the Church "awaits that day, known to God alone, on which all people will address the Lord in a single voice and 'serve Him with one accord' (Zeph. 3.9; cf. Isa. 66.23; Ps. 65.4; Rom. 11.11-32)" (NA 4).

Christian-Jewish Relations

In addressing the question of relations between Christians and Jews, the Second Vatican Council recalled the great heritage common to both and encouraged "that mutual understanding and respect which is the fruit above all of biblical and theological studies, and of brotherly dialogues" (NA 4).

This clearly requires truth and sincerity. The Commission for Religious Relations with the Jews established by the Holy Father in 1974 reminds us what real dialogue means: "Dialogue presupposes that each side wishes to know the other, and wishes to increase and deepen its knowledge of the other. . . . Dialogue demands respect for the other as he is; above all, respect for his faith and his religious convictions." Christians must reflect on and make clear the meaning of their own faith, and "must strive to learn by what essential traits the

[1]Commission for Religious Relations with the Jews, *Guidelines and Suggestions for Implementing Conciliar Declaration 'Nostra Aetate' (n. 4)* (December 1, 1974) III (EV 5.786).

Jews define themselves in the light of their own religious experience."[2]

The urgings of the Council and of the Commission in no way deny or alter the Church's mission to the whole world; nor indeed do they in any way call for a rewriting of history. It remains true that authorities of the Jews and those who followed their lead did press for the death of Jesus (cf. John 19.6). But what happened in Christ's passion and death cannot be blamed without distinction on all the Jews who were then living, and even less can the events of that time be blamed on the Jews of today. The truth of this has obvious significance for the way in which the message of Christ is to be presented and taught.

There have been Christians who with sincere but misguided zeal have used various scriptural passages (e.g., Matt. 23.37-39; 27.25; 1 Thess. 2.14-16) to "justify" a view that the Jews, because they do not accept Jesus as the Messiah, are truly an accursed race, rightly and permanently punished because of their treatment of Christ.[3] This is not the view of the Church. Indeed, the Church firmly warns against such use of God's word: "Although the Church is the new People of God, the Jews should not be presented as repudiated or cursed by God, as if such views followed from the Holy Scriptures. All should take pains, then, lest in catechetical instruction and in the preaching of God's word they teach anything out of harmony with the truth of the Gospel and the spirit of Christ" (NA 4).

All sinners share in the guilt for Christ's passion and death. As the Church holds and has always held, Christ "in His boundless love freely underwent His passion and death because of the sins of all men, so that all might attain salvation" (NA 4). A passage in the so-called *Catechism of the Council of Trent for Parish Priests*, known also as *The Roman Catechism*, reminds us that guilt for Christ's death is in fact perhaps greater in us Christians than in the Jews. "This guilt of us sinful Christians takes a deeper hue of enormity when contrasted with that of the Jews: according to the testimony of the Apostle, if they had known the hidden wisdom of God, 'they would not have crucified the Lord of glory' (1 Cor 2.8). But we, on the contrary, both profess to known Him and yet deny Him by our actions. Hence we too seem, so to speak, to lay violent hands on Him (see Titus 11.16)."[4]

---

[2]Commission for Religious Relations with the Jews, *Guidelines and Suggestions for Implementing Conciliar Declaration 'Nostra Aetate' (n. 4)* (December 1, 1974) Introduction and I (EV 5.774-775).

[3]This view is found even in some of the Fathers. Cf. the eight homilies against the Jews delivered by St. John Chrysostom in 386-387 (MG 48.843-942): also, the very strong polemics against the Jews in some of St. Cyril of Alexandria's paschal letters (MG 77.401-982).

[4]*The Roman Catechism* (Boston, St. Paul Editions, 1985) is quoted here from the translation of R.I. Bradley and E. Kevane, p. 60.

Anti-Semitism

It is clear, then, that anti-Semitism, that is, hostility toward Jews or discrimination against them, is unchristian. Nonetheless, it is true that Jews have suffered much abuse and even savage persecution from Christian individuals and from nations called Christian; and certainly there have been many times in history when Jews could hardly have been expected to recognize the Christ witnessed by some Christians as indeed the Prince of Peace.

The harsh facts of history should of course never be allowed to mute the facts of joy and salvation in the saving actions of Christ. But they can serve as a constant reminder to us to repent for any injustice we have done to the Jews and to purge ourselves of any anti-Semitic attitudes we may have. The teaching of the Church on this is unequivocally clear: The Church, "mindful of her common patrimony with the Jews, and motivated by the Gospel's spiritual love and by no political considerations, deplores the hatred, persecutions, and displays of anti-Semitism directed against the Jews at any time and from any source" (NA 4).

Separated Christians

"That they may all be one," Christ prayed for all who would believe in Him and in His message, "as You, Father, are in Me, and I am in You" (John 17.21). Although unity, or oneness, is an essential mark of the one true Church, there are in fact many Christian communions today which present themselves to the world as the true heritage of Jesus Christ. "To be sure, all proclaim themselves to be disciples of the Lord, but their convictions clash and their paths diverge, as though Christ Himself were divided (cf. 1 Cor. 1.13). Without doubt, this discord openly contradicts the will of Christ, provides a stumbling block to the world, and inflicts damage on the most holy cause of proclaiming the good news to every creature" (UR 1).

The divisions among Christians are in truth a scandal to the world. There have been many efforts in the past to heal these divisions. Recent decades have seen new efforts, with new vigor, and the growth of what is known as the Ecumenical Movement. The Second Vatican Council took account of these various efforts and desires, and called on all Catholics to work for what it said was one of the chief concerns of the council: promoting the restoration of unity among all Christians (cf. UR 1,4).

Separations: Schism and Heresy

To separate oneself deliberately and culpably from the Church is to fall into "schism" or "heresy." Although neither of these words is in great use today, what they are and stand for is relevant for understanding the present situation and how it came about.

The sin of schism is formal and willful separation from the unity of the Church. The sin of heresy is formal denial or doubt about one or more elements of the Catholic faith. Schism does in fact always involve some heresy, at least in regard to Catholic teaching on the unity and authority of the Church. As St. Augustine observed many centuries ago, there cannot be a schism unless those in question "follow something contrary."[5] In many writers, both ancient and modern, a sharp distinction between schism and heresy is not maintained.

Because the sins of schism and heresy are both willful acts, it is not really appropriate to use the words "schismatic" and "heretic" in reference to the Christians who through no fault of their own do not have the fullness of Catholic faith. Although the words "schism" and "heresy" are sometimes used in another sense, simply to describe the fact of separation, it is abundantly clear that those born into communities long since separated from the Church are not themselves guilty of that separation. They may in a sense be said to be "in schism" or "in heresy," but the sin of willful separation is not theirs. This point as well was noted by St. Augustine, who wrote that those whose false opinion was received from parents led astray and fallen into error, and who themselves seek the truth, ready to be corrected when they find it, "are by no means to be counted among the heretics."[6]

The Early Centuries

From the very beginnings of the Church there appeared certain rifts (cf. 1 Cor. 11.18-19; Gal. 1.6-9; John 2.18-19). These were censured strongly by St. Paul (cf. 1 Cor. 1.11-13; 11.22), and throughout the history of the Church the seriousness of separation from the Church and its teaching has been recognized. For it is Christ Himself who speaks in His Church, and those whom He sends speaks His word: "Whoever listens to you listens to Me, and whoever rejects you rejects Me, and . . . the One who sent Me" (Luke 10.16).

The early Christian writers speak of heresy and schism in various ways and in various figures. Separation from the Church is as it were a rent in the seamless robe of Christ (cf. John 19.23), this robe itself being seen as a symbol of unity. Very common among the early Fathers is the concept that contaminated faith, or heresy, debauches the faith and attacks the Church's virginity. The embracing of false doctrine is compared to adultery: "Whoever breaks with the Church and enters on an adulterous union, cuts himself off from the promises

5St. Augustine, *Contra Cresconium* 2.7.9 (ML 43.471).
6St. Augustine, *Epistula* 43.1 (ML 33.160).

made to the Church; and he who turns his back on the Church of Christ shall not come to the rewards of Christ: he is an alien, a worldling, an enemy."[7]

Drawing upon the words of St. Paul (cf. 1 Cor. 11.19), the Fathers could see a certain usefulness of heretics — "usefulness, of course, in the sense that God makes good use even of bad people."[8] St. Augustine observes that the false charges of heretics lead members of the faithful to search into, and to learn, more about the mysteries of the faith. "And thus it happens that while these people practice their sophistries for the purpose of seducing others into error, they actually prove themselves useful for the discovery of truth. For the quest of truth would be conducted less zealously, were it not for the lying adversaries it has. 'For,' Scripture says, 'there must be also heresies'; and, as though we might ask why this should be so, it immediately adds, 'that they who are approved may be made manifest among you' (1 Cor. 11.19)."[9] Similarly also St. Cyprian: "Heresies have often arisen and still arise. . . . But these things the Lord allows and endures, leaving man's freedom unimpaired, so that our minds and hearts are tested by the touchstone of truth, the unswerving faith of those who are approved may appear in the clearest light. This is foretold by the Holy Spirit through the Apostle. . . ."[10]

The number of heresies and schisms which arose during the course of the first centuries of the Church was large. St. Augustine, in a work written in 428 or 429, listed eighty-eight heresies, from that of Simon Magus to that of Pelagius.[11] Even the names of the early heresies will seem strange to many people today: Abelites, Arians, Circumcellions, Docetists, Donatists, Monophysites, Monothelites, Montanists, Pelagians, and so on. The life-spans of these early separations varied greatly. Some died out quickly. Others developed and spread, then seemingly disappeared, only to flare up again under different names. Some indeed have continued, in one form or another, under one name or another, from the early days of the Church to the present. Certainly there are few if any doctrinal errors current in modern times which cannot be found in some form in the heresies resisted by the Church in the days of the Fathers.

Divisions Today

The principal divisions in Christendom today are the result of separations which took place hundreds of years ago. We are speaking

---

[7]St. Cyprian, *De Ecclesiae Catholicae Unitate* 6 (ML 4.507 = ACW 25.48).
[8]St. Augustine, *Sermo* 51.11 (ML 38.339 = ACW 15.36).
[9]St. Augustine, *Sermo* 51.11 (ML 38.339 = ACW 15.36).
[10]St. Cyprian, *De Ecclesiae Catholicae Unitate* 10 (ML 4.509 = ACW 25.52).
[11]Cf. St. Augustine, *De Haeresibus ad Quodvultdeum* (ML 42.21-50).

here primarily of the break between the Holy See and the Eastern Patriarchates in the eleventh century and, in the West, of the separation of various communions, both national and denominational, in what is commonly called the Reformation, largely in the sixteenth century. Neither in the case of the Orthodox Churches in the East nor in the case of Protestantism in the West was the separation a single historical event; the separations we know today in fact evolved over long periods of time, from different causes, resulting in divisions different in nature.

The Eastern Orthodox Churches, although they are not in ecclesiastical communion with the Holy See, and thus are separated from the Catholic Church, nonetheless "possess true sacraments, above all — by apostolic succession — the priesthood and the Eucharist, whereby they are still joined to us in a very close relationship" (UR 15).

The Second Vatican Council reminds us that many of the local churches of the East "glory in having their origins from the apostles themselves" (UR 14), and that the Eastern churches have had from their beginnings "a treasury from which the Church of the West has amply drawn for its liturgy, spiritual tradition, and jurisprudence" (UR 14). A number of basic dogmas of the faith were defined at Ecumenical Councils held in the East,[12] and "to preserve this faith, these churches have suffered much, and still do so" (UR 14). Variety in liturgy, customs, and traditions is by no means a bar to Church unity; nor indeed is variety in theological expressions of doctrinal truth. "With regard to the authentic theological traditions of the Easterners, we must recognize that they are admirably rooted in Holy Scripture, fostered and given expression in liturgical life, and nourished by the living tradition of the apostles and by the writings of the Fathers and spiritual authors of the East; they are directed toward a right ordering of life, indeed, toward a full contemplation of Christian truth" (UR 17).

There are of course many Catholics who, in the Eastern Catholic churches, or rites, are preserving the rich heritage of the East while living in full communion with the Holy See and with all who follow the tradition of the West. The true riches of the East are in truth part of the riches of the Church as a whole. "The Catholic Church holds in high esteem the institutions of the Eastern churches, their liturgical rites, ecclesiastical traditions, and Christian way of life. For, distinguished as they are by their venerable antiquity, they are bright with that tradition which was handed down from the apostles through the

---

[12]The first eight General Councils of the Church were held in Nicaea (325), Constantinople (381), Ephesus (431), Chalcedon (451), Constantinople (553), Constantinople (680-681), Nicaea (787), and Constantinople (869-870).

Fathers, and which forms part of the divinely revealed and undivided heritage of the universal Church" (OE 1). The Eastern Catholic churches "have a special role to play in promoting the unity of all Christians, particularly Easterners . . . , first of all by prayer, then by the example of their lives, by religious fidelity to ancient Eastern traditions, by greater mutual knowledge, by collaboration, and by a brotherly regard for objects and attitudes" (OE 24).

The divisions which developed in the West in the Reformation and in the post-Reformation period are of a different type. Here the non-Catholic Christian communions "differ not only from us but also among themselves to a considerable degree" (UR 19), and it is difficult to speak of them in a collective way. But the separations in the West were, and are, more than rupture of Church unity. For there are genuine differences in doctrine (not merely differences in expressions of doctrine), in the interpretation of revelation and in the ways of considering Holy Scripture (cf. UR 21). Although baptism provides a sacramental bond of unity linking all who are reborn by means of it (cf. UR 22), these separated Christians "lack that fullness of unity with us which should flow from baptism, and we believe that especially because of the lack of the sacrament of orders they have not preserved the genuine and total reality of the Eucharistic mystery" (UR 22).

Nonetheless, these separated churches and ecclesial communities remain close to us. They "are bound to the Catholic Church by a special affinity and close relationship in view of the long span of earlier centuries when the Christian people lived in ecclesiastical communion" (UR 19). Their Christian way of life is nourished by faith in the one Christ and is strengthened by the grace of baptism and the hearing of God's word; and the faith by which they believe in Christ does bear fruit in a number of ways (cf. UR 23).

Promoting Christian Unity

All Catholics are called to share in the task of ecumenism, the fostering of unity among Christians. Few are equipped or in positions to participate in all phases of ecumenical work, but all can contribute to the effort. "Concern for restoring unity pertains to the whole Church, faithful and clergy alike. It extends to everyone, according to the potential of each, whether it be exercised in daily Christian living or in theological and historical studies" (UR 5). Indeed, this concern itself "already reveals to some extent the bond of brotherhood existing among all Christians, and it leads toward that full and perfect unity which God lovingly desires" (UR 5).

The divisions rooted in centuries past did not come about without fault on both sides. This needs to be recognized and understood. Pope Paul VI set an example, in an address opening the second session of the Second Vatican Council, asking pardon of God and of our fellow Christians for the faults committed by Catholics and extending pardon from the heart for whatever injuries the Church has suffered in the past.[13] The council followed the example (cf. UR 7), noting that the words of St. John hold also for offenses against unity: "If we say that we have not sinned, we make Him a liar, and His word is not in us" (1 John 1.10).

Catholics have an obligation to bear witness to their Catholic faith, and they assist the cause of unity to the extent they do this well. Certainly Catholics must be concerned for their separated brethren, praying for them, communicating with them about Church matters, and making the first approaches to them. But there is a primary duty to see that the Catholic family of faith bears witness more faithfully and more clearly in its life to those things which have been handed down from Christ through the apostles (cf. UR 4). "For although the Catholic Church has been endowed with all divinely revealed truth and with all means of grace, her members fail to live by them with all the fervor they should. As a result, the radiance of the Church's face shines less brightly in the eyes of our separated brethren and of the world at large, and the growth of God's kingdom is retarded" (UR 4).

At the same time, Catholics "must joyfully acknowledge and esteem the truly Christian endowments derived from our common heritage which are to be found among our separated brethren" (UR 4). For they too bear witness to Christ in their lives and share in some of His riches. Their faith and religious convictions are to be respected. We should be willing to be edified by God's grace in them, for "whatever is wrought by the grace of the Holy Spirit in the hearts of our separated brethren can contribute to our own edification" (UR 4).

Ecumenical dialogue, especially by competent representatives, can contribute much to the mutual understanding and clarification of points of agreement and points of difference. Recent years have seen many such exchanges which have been fruitful in terms of new understanding and increased awareness of what it is that each believes. Discussions of this sort, entered into in a spirit of charity and humility and conducted with honesty and frankness and mutual respect, have in some important matters shown that actual areas of difference are often smaller than had been believed. This assists the search for unity and encourages prayerful hope that by the grace of God the distance of separation may be narrowed to the point of nonexistence.

There is wide room for cooperation between Catholics and non-Catholic Christians, and this too promotes understanding and the cause

---

[13]Cf. Pope Paul VI, *Address* opening second session of the Second Vatican Council (September 29, 1963) (EV 1.176*).

of unity. "Since in our times cooperation in social matters is very widely practiced, all men without exception are summoned to united effort. Those who believe in God have a stronger summons, but the strongest claims are laid on Christians, since they have been sealed with the name of Christ" (UR 12). Cooperation among all Christians "vividly expresses that bond which already unites them" (UR 12). Through cooperation in applying Gospel principles to social life, in advancing the arts and sciences in a Christian spirit, in providing relief services of various sorts, and so on, "all believers in Christ are able to learn easily how they can understand each other better and esteem each other more, and how the road to the unity of Christians may be made smooth" (UR 12).

"True ecumenical activity means openness, drawing closer, availability for dialogue, and a shared investigation of the truth in the full evangelical and Christian sense; but in no way does it or can it mean giving up or in any way diminishing the treasures of divine truth that the Church has constantly confessed and taught."[14]

In no way does the practice of ecumenism call for any submergence of Catholic identity or any suppression of Catholic truth. In ecumenical dialogue, doctrine is to be presented clearly in its entirety. "Nothing is so foreign to the spirit of ecumenism as a false conciliatory approach which harms the purity of Catholic doctrine and obscures its assured genuine meaning" (UR 11). Catholics believe that "it is through Christ's Catholic Church alone, which is the all-embracing means of salvation, that all fullness of the means of salvation can be obtained" (UR 3), and "are bound to profess that through the gift of God's mercy they belong to that Church which Christ founded and which is governed by the successors of Peter and the other apostles, who are the depositaries of the original tradition, living and intact, which is the permanent heritage of doctrine and holiness of that same Church."[15] Catholic ecumenical activity should be devoid of all "superficiality or imprudent zeal" and be always "fully and sincerely Catholic" (UR 24).

Still, the Church realizes "that the holy task of reconciling all Christians in the unity of the one and only Church of Christ transcends human energies and abilities. It therefore places its hope entirely in the prayer of Christ for the Church, in the love of the Father for us, and in the power of the Holy Spirit. 'And hope does not disappoint, because the charity of God is poured forth in our hearts by the Holy Spirit who has been given to us' (Rom. 5.5)" (UR 24).

[14]Pope John Paul II, Encyclical, *Redemptor Hominis* (March 4, 1979) n. 6 (EV 6.1184).

[15]Congregation for the Doctrine of the Faith, *Mysterium Ecclesiae* ("Declaration in Defense of the Catholic Doctrine on the Church against Certain Errors of the Present Day," June 24, 1973) n. 1 (EV 4.2566).

Other Religions and Cultures

A large part of the world's population does not know or has had minimal exposure to the Gospel of Christ and His Church, and looks to various religions for answers to the profound questions about good and evil, about the origins of humankind and our ultimate fate.

Islam

The Second Vatican Council spoke in a special way about the Moslems. They, "professing to hold the faith of Abraham, along with us adore the one and merciful God, who on the last day will judge mankind" (LG 16). Though the Islamic faith does not acknowledge Jesus as God, it does revere Him as a prophet, and also honors His virgin mother. Moslems "prize the moral life, and give worship to God especially through prayer, almsgiving, and fasting" (NA 3). Noting that there have been many quarrels and hostilities between Christians and Moslems, the council urged that all "forget the past and strive sincerely for mutual understanding, and, on behalf of all mankind, make common cause of safeguarding and fostering social justice, moral values, peace, and freedom" (NA 3).

Other Non-Christian Religions

The non-Christian religions, including Hinduism, Buddhism, and many others besides Islam, differ in many ways from the Catholic Church. This, however, does not put their followers in good conscience outside the plan of salvation. For "the divine design of salvation embraces all men; and those who without fault on their part do not know the Gospel of Christ and His Church, but seek God sincerely, and under the influence of grace endeavor to do His will as recognized through the promptings of their conscience, they, in a number known only to God, can obtain salvation."[16]

The Catholic Church rejects nothing which is true and holy in these non-Christian religions, and indeed "looks with sincere respect upon those ways of conduct and of life, those rules and teachings which, though differing in many particulars from what she holds and sets forth, nevertheless often reflect a ray of that Truth which enlightens all men" (NA 2). The Church exhorts Catholics that they "prudently and lovingly, through dialogue and collaboration with the followers of other religions, and in witness of Christian faith and life, acknowledge, preserve, and promote the spiritual and moral goods found among these men, as well as the values in their society and culture' (NA 2).

---

[16]Pope Paul VI, *Professio Fidei* ("The Credo of the People of God," June 30, 1968) (EV 3.559). Cf. LG 16; NA 2.

Atheism

In this world of many religions there are also many people who have no religious belief and profess atheism. The mystery of unbelief has been discussed in an earlier chapter.

Some contemporary forms of atheism, as Marxism, have some of the characteristics of Christian heresy. They promise confidently a kingdom of justice and peace, and their promise seems in a way to mirror the confident Christian hope; but they seek for such a kingdom only on this earth, and as effected by blind historical laws. The strength and attractiveness that many find in their positions flow in large part from what they derive from Christianity; but they clearly reject large and essential areas of Christian teaching.

The Church rejects atheism completely. Here also, however, some dialogue is useful. For the Church strives to detect in the atheist's mind the reasons for the denial of God, and it invites the atheist to examine the Gospel with an open mind. Moreover, the Church believes that all of us, believers and unbelievers alike, ought to work for the rightful betterment of this world in which all alike live, and this cannot be brought about without "sincere and prudent dialogue" (GS 21).

Missionary Task of the Church

In the pluralistic world in which it works, and in which it seeks good relations with all, the Church is ever mindful of the charge given it by Christ:"Go into all the world and proclaim the good news to the whole creation" (Mark 16.15; cf. Matt. 28.19). In obedience to this mandate from its Founder, the Church "strives to proclaim the Gospel to all men" (AG 1).

The Church is "missionary by her very nature" (AG 2). The Gospel message has not yet been heard, or scarcely so, by many in this world, and there is still a "gigantic missionary task" (AG 10) to be accomplished. Every follower of Christ has an obligation to do what one can in spreading the faith (cf. LG 17; AG 23, 35); indeed, "by its very nature the Christian vocation is also a vocation to the apostolate" (AA 2). But some are called specifically by Christ to work in mission fields, and they dedicate themselves to this task (cf. AG 23). "Sent by legitimate authority, they go out faithfully and obediently to those who are far from Christ. They are set apart for the work to which they have been called (cf. Acts 13.2) as ministers of the Gospel, so 'that the offering up of the Gentiles may become acceptable, being sanctified by the Holy Spirit' (Rom. 15.16)" (AG 23).

The mission of the Church and the necessity of the Church for salvation have been discussed in earlier chapters. The Church has an obligation ever to proclaim the message of Christ, and those who come to awareness that the Catholic Church was made necessary by God through Jesus Christ have an obligation to enter the Church and persevere in it (cf. LG 14). Although God "in ways known to Himself can lead those inculpably ignorant of the Gospel to that faith without which it is impossible to please Him (cf. Heb. 11.6), yet a necessity lies upon the Church (cf. 1 Cor. 9.16), and at the same time a sacred duty, to preach the Gospel. Hence missionary activity today as always retains its power and necessity" (AG 7).

Religious Freedom

Among the basic human rights flowing from the dignity of the human person is the right to religious freedom. This right to immunity from external coercion in matters religious is a right which governments as well as individuals must respect.

The Second Vatican Council declared that the right to religious freedom "has its foundation in the very dignity of the human person" (DH 2), for human beings are by nature endowed with reason and free will and therefore privileged to bear personal responsibility. This right in civil life does not in any way negate or alter the moral obligation we have to seek the truth, especially religious truth, and to adhere to that truth when it is known, and to order our lives in accord with the demands of truth. But the right to religious freedom is so basic that it is had even by those who do not live up to their obligation to seek and to follow truth.

Although revelation does not affirm in so many words the right to immunity from external coercion in matters religious, it does disclose the dignity of the human person in its full dimensions, and it gives evidence of the respect which Christ showed toward the freedom with which one is to fulfill one's duty of belief in the word of God (cf. DH 9).[17]

God calls people to serve Him, but He does not force them. "It is one of the major tenets of Catholic doctrine that man's response to God in faith must be free. Therefore no one is to be forced to embrace the Christian faith against his own will. This doctrine is contained in the word of God and it was constantly proclaimed by the Fathers of the Church. The act of faith is of its very nature a free act. Man, redeemed by Christ the Savior and through Christ Jesus called to be God's adopted son (cf. Eph. 1.5), cannot give his adherence to God revealing Himself unless the Father draw him (cf. John 6.44) to offer to God the reasonable and free submission of faith" (DH 10).

[17]Cf. Pope John Paul II, Encyclical, *Redemptor Hominis* (March 4, 1979) n. 12 (EV 6.1202-1205).

Thus it is completely in accord with the nature of the faith that in matters religious every manner of coercion should be excluded. Indeed, the principle of religious freedom "makes no small contribution to the creation of an environment in which men can without hindrance be invited to Christian faith, and embrace it of their own free will, and profess it effectively in their whole manner of life" (DH 10).

Part Three

With Christ:
Sharing The Life Of God

17

Christ Comes To Give Life

Jesus came to give us life. "I came that they may have life, and have it abundantly" (John 10.10). He offers a life richer than any we could ever otherwise have, a life so radically new that we must be born again to have it (cf. John 3.3-8).

This new life fulfills our deepest longings. It makes what is good in human life far better and richer. It makes our broken lives authentically human; it causes us to share in God's life as well. From the beginning God made us not merely to be His creatures, but to be His friends (cf. John 15.15). This is indeed the reason why God created the world, why He did all the merciful deeds of salvation history, why He permitted all the sorrows of human history: the ultimate purpose of all things is that, in Christ, all persons made by God's creative love might freely come to Him and share the abundant life of the Blessed Trinity.

The rest of this book speaks of the life that Christ offers us, and of how that life is to be received, increased, and expressed.

This chapter first discusses how this new life is an entirely free gift of God in Christ. It notes some of the basic elements of the new life, and outlines the major ways in which one obtains this new life and grows in it.

The New Life Given Us by God

The good news of Jesus is proclaimed to the world by those who have already tasted the new life He has given us through the Holy Spirit. "Blessed be the God and Father of our Lord Jesus Christ, who has blessed us in Christ with every spiritual blessing in the heavenly places" (Eph. 1.3). Just as the sins and sorrows from which He has called us are very real, so the life Christ has given is very real. Loneliness and despair, inability to believe and to love, the utter frustration of human efforts — all these are terribly real in the world. But even more real and present are the life, faith, freedom and healing that Christ brings.

Because they have already lived the new life, the disciples of Jesus can bear witness to its reality and accessibility. They do not merely report Jesus' words: "Come to Me, that are weary and are carrying heavy burdens, and I will give you rest" (Matt. 11.28). They have themselves experienced that faith which "throws a new light on everything" (GS 11) and have learned in some measure to live in His love. Thus it is not to an utterly unknown mystery that they call their hearers. Rather, they speak "so that you also may have fellowship with us" (1 John 1.3).

Christ in God's Eternal Plan

The Apostle Paul was always grateful that he had been called to make known to the nations God's merciful plan. "Although I am the very least of all the saints, this grace was given to me to bring to the Gentiles the news of the boundless riches of Christ, and to make everyone see what is the plan of the mystery hidden for ages in God who created all things" (Eph. 3.8-9). For the world had seemed a bitter mystery. The abundance of pain, of heartache, the tragedies of human life and history endlessly tempt people to denounce everything, the world and even their own existence, as meaningless. But the "mystery of Christ" (Col. 4.3), the "mystery that had been hidden throughout the ages and generations" (Col. 1.26), reveals with a splendid light the meaning of the world.

God "chose us in Christ before the foundation of the world to be holy and blameless before Him in love. . . . With all wisdom and insight He has made known to us the mystery of His will, according to His good pleasure that He set forth in Christ, as a plan for the fullness of time, to gather up all things in Him, things in heaven and things on earth" (Eph. 1.4, 9-10).

Christ is the reason why there is a world. The love He freely gave to His Father on the cross and the generous love He makes possible in our human hearts, binding us to Himself and to the Father in friendship, freedom, and life, explain the why of the world. God made the world so that the love which is the inner life of the Trinity might be shared by other persons, whom He would call to Himself in Christ. Christ "is the image of the invisible God, the first-born of all creation; for in Him all things, in heaven and on earth were created . . . all things have been created through Him and for Him" (Col. 1.15-16).

The love and the goodness of Christ's humanity give more glory to God than all else that has been made. But it is not simply the individual Christ for whom the world was made, but Christ in His saving glory as Redeemer and Head of a Mystical Body. It is for this Christ, who unites to Himself all who respond freely to God's call, that everything is. "For in Him all the fulness of God was pleased to dwell, and through Him God was pleased to reconcile to Himself all things, whether on earth or in heaven, making peace through the blood of His cross" (Col. 1.19-20).

The world was made, then, so that created persons might, in Christ, come to share the life of the Trinity. But they were to come to God only freely. The freedom God gave created persons also made it possible for them to reject His call and to sin. But "we know that all things work together for good with those who love God, who are called according to His purpose" (Rom. 8.28). He is able to overcome in Christ all the evil that sin creates, and to make even suffering and pain instruments of His healing love.

The story of creation is told anew at the beginning of the fourth Gospel, now in the light of Christ's revelation. In the very beginning, we are told, the Word was creatively present with the Father. This was the Word, the Son of God, who was to become our brother. Everything that was created was made through Him, so that through Him we might also become children of God.

"In the beginning was the Word, and the Word was with God. All things came into being through Him, and without Him not one thing came into being. What has come into being in Him was life, the life was the light of all people. ... The true light which enlightens everyone, was coming into the world. ... To all who received Him, who believed in His name, He gave power to become children of God. ... And the Word became flesh and lived among us, and we have seen His glory, the glory as of a Father's only Son, full of grace and truth. ... From His fullness we have all received, grace upon grace" (John 1.1-4, 9, 12, 14, 16).

God's Free Gift

St. Paul often reminded the early Christians that this new life is a free gift of God. To convey the message of revelation, he took a secular Greek word, *charis* ("favor," "grace"), and gave it religious meaning. It is from *gratia*, the Latin for *charis*, that we get our word "grace." This new life is a grace, a free gift of God, not something deserved by us at all. "For by grace you have been saved through faith, and this is not your own doing, it is the gift of God — not the result of works, so that no one may boast. For we are what He has made us, created in Christ Jesus for good works, which God prepared beforehand" (Eph. 2.8-10).

Those who come to faith should not imagine that God's blessings are due to their merits. Absolutely everything is due to God's generous, free love. In His infinite power and mercy He chose us and blessed us. Sensitive to our helplessness to do anything by ourselves alone to acquire the new life of the Spirit, Jesus said: "Apart from Me you can do nothing" (John 15.5). "No one can come to Me unless drawn by the Father who sent Me" (John 6.44).

He predestines us; He gives without our prior deserving. "He destined us for adoption as His children through Jesus Christ, according to the good pleasure of His will, to the praise of His glorious grace that He freely bestowed on us in the Beloved" (Eph. 1.5).

But God's predestination of us does not mean that He treats us as controlled puppets or robots. He calls us as free persons, and He desires from us a free response of love and friendship. He does not call any to life in such a way that they are forced to come; neither does He exclude any from His favor arbitrarily, simply willing that they be lost forever. He "desires everyone to be saved and to come to the knowledge of the truth" (1 Tim. 2.4). Christ died for all, and His grace is offered to all. Those who in fact accept His grace do so not because they are good; their ability to respond freely to him is itself a gift of grace. Those who refuse His grace do not do so because He has abandoned them, but because they themselves choose to reject His gifts.

Life in Christ

Christ is the life of the world in many ways. "For in Him all the fullness of God was pleased to dwell, and through Him God was pleased to reconcile to Himself all things" (Col. 1.19-20). First, God has graced the humanity of Jesus with the fullness of all divine gifts. Jesus is always attractive, an invitation to life, for all who come to know Him. In Him the "goodness and loving kindness of God" (Titus 3.4) were made visible.

He is also the Teacher of life, and the Exemplar of life. In His words and in His actions men can find the best guide and model for the way we ourselves most wish to live. Even more, He is the Fountain and Source of life. We are not merely to imitate Him, but to live in Him and from Him. "Abide in Me, as I abide in you. Just as the branch cannot bear fruit by itself unless it abides in the vine, neither can you unless you abide in Me. I am the vine, you are the branches" (John 15.4-5).

The whole teaching of the Mystical Body of Jesus is a reminder that our life is to be transformed by our union with Him. His life, His mind, His Spirit are to be ours. For "we are members of His body" (Eph. 5.30).

We are made one with Him by the gift of His Spirit. Regarding Jesus' words that the thirsty who came to Him to drink would have living waters in abundance, the evangelist notes: "Now He said this about the Spirit, which believers in Him were to receive" (John 7.39). "Any one who does not have the Spirit of Christ does not belong to Him" (Rom. 8.9). But to have this Spirit is to be a new person. For it is to have faith, hope, and at least some measure of true love of God; and these are transforming gifts.

Elements of This New Life

This newness of life involves both a healing of our wounds and an elevation of our lives to a sharing in divine life.

Human integrity has been wounded by sin, and so it is in our very humanity that we are is healed by the new life Jesus brings. Grace does not make one any less human, any less concerned with the personal and social good of humankind and true temporal values. It makes one more human; one should be more concerned. "Indeed nothing genuinely human fails to raise an echo in the hearts of followers of Christ" (GS 1).

But the gift of Christ's life does far more than restore humankind's full humanity. Through Christ we are called to a true friendship with the Trinity, with the God who chooses to dwell within those one who love Christ (cf.John 14.23); they are called to share in the very nature of God (2 Peter 1.4). They are called to be God's children now (cf. 1 John 3.2), to live already on earth in a divine way, sharing God's knowledge in unshakable faith, and sharing in God's inmost life by the gift of His love (cf. Rom. 5.5).

Healing and Freedom

In his Epistle to the Romans, St. Paul speaks of the dehumanizing consequences of sin in human life. These effects could be seen with brutal clarity in the pagan society in the midst of which the young Church lived (cf. Rom. 1.18-32). There one saw people who were "foolish, faithless, heartless, ruthless" (Rom. 1.31), who had made for themselves on earth a life that was a beginning of hell.

The life Christ gives frees one from the deep wounds inflicted by sin; it enables one to be more authentically human.

St. Paul had himself tasted bitter helplessness before he received Christ's mercy and the gift of the Spirit. The grace of realizing how one should live does not of itself give power to live that way. "I am of the flesh, sold into slavery under sin. I do not understand my own actions. For I do not do what I want, but I do the very thing I hate. ... For I know that nothing good dwells within me, that is, in my flesh. I can will what is right, but I cannot do it. For I do not do the good I want, but the evil I do not want is what I do" (Rom. 7.14-15, 18-19).

Here St. Paul is describing a situation that has been experienced by many. St. Augustine wrote of similar anxious struggles just before his own conversion, of his disgust with the evil he himself did, and of his powerlessness to avoid it.[1] Such indeed is the constant experience of the world living without grace: the wars that no one wants, the in-

[1]Cf. St. Augustine, *Confessiones* 8.11-12 (ML 32.760-764).

justices that all despise, the entanglement of human life in frustration and pretense. When fallen human beings seek within themselves, from mere human strength and wisdom, resources to overcome evil consistently, they find they are helpless. "I can will what is right, but I cannot do it" (Rom. 7.18).

This precisely is the gift of Christ: power to do the good. "Wretched man that I am! Who will rescue me from this body of death? Thanks be to God through Jesus Christ our Lord!" (Rom. 7.24-25). "But to all who received Him, who believed in His name, He gave power to become children of God" (John 1.12).

God's grace liberates; it gives us freedom. Grace supposes freedom of choice, for grace is not forced on us, but offered to us.[2] But there is a kind of freedom which grace itself gives: an ability to do the good and saving acts that one could not do before, to share in the strength of Christ, to be fortified by the gift of the Spirit.

This liberation is precious. Without the grace of Christ, we are hard-pressed in every way. Unruly desires, fears, and anger incline one toward sin. To yield is to degrade oneself and to generate conflict. To resist is to struggle against deep disorders within oneself, and one's resistance often collapses. But the freedom grace offers is rich and real, if one chooses to accept and grow in it. "For sin will have no dominion over you, since you are not under law but under grace" (Rom. 6.14).

When, by the gift of a new life in Christ, God heals us and gives us freedom, He effects a profound transformation within our inmost being. This change is sometimes slow to come to completion; though conversion may at times be instantaneous, growth in grace is generally gradual over time. St. Paul speaks of this change in a variety of ways: it is a transition from bondage to freedom (cf. Rom. 6.12-20), from condemnation to acquittal (cf. Rom. 5.18), from death to life (cf. Rom. 6.6-7), from the old man to the new man (cf. Eph. 4.21 f.), from darkness to light (cf. Col. 1.12-13), from slavery to salvation (cf. Titus 3.3-5). Indeed the justifying act by which God so brings us to life is one in which He makes us sharers in His own life, children of God, heirs of heaven.

Acquiring and Living the New Life

The new life won for us by Jesus in His redemptive work is, as we have noted, never forced on those whom God calls. Only freely can they receive and grow in the life that lifts them to the sublime freedom of children of God. Only freely can they cling to Christ, the true Vine, and learn to bear richer fruit in Him (cf. John 15.4-5).

---

[2]Cf. Council of Trent, Session 6, January 13, 1547, *Decree on Justification*, ch. 6 (DS 1526).

In the chapters which follow we shall speak chiefly of three main ways of coming to, growing in, and expressing the new life of Christ. Here we note them only briefly. These three ways, all closely related, are: by works of love, by prayer, and by sharing in the sacramental acts of Christ.

By Works of Love

Christ tells us that "only the one who does the will of My Father in heaven" will enter the kingdom of God (cf. Matt. 7.21). It is by leading a life pleasing to God, obeying His commandments, all rooted in the demanding commandments of love, that we live in the world the life we have received.

"For once you were darkness, but now in the Lord you are light. Live as children of light — for the fruit of the light is found in all that is good and right and true.. . . . Take no part in the unfruitful works of darkness" (Eph. 5.8-9, 11). By doing the will of God in charity we grow in the divine life we have received.

By Prayer

Prayer is a part of the Christian life. Jesus tirelessly taught, both by word and by example, the importance of prayer. Prayer is itself a gift of God, the work of the Spirit within us (cf. Rom. 8.26); only because God's mercy arouses us to prayer can we fruitfully cry out to Him to save us. Prayer is realistic; it shows a heart ready to confess that "every generous act of giving, with every perfect gift, is from above" (James 1.17).

But prayer is far more than a plea for life. It is an essential way of living the Christian life and of seeking perfection in it. In later chapters we discuss further what prayer is and how it nourishes and expresses our relationship with God.

By the Sacraments

Moved by the mystery of Jesus, Nicodemus came to Him by night to learn the way to life. Jesus told him: "Very truly, I tell you, no one can enter the Kingdom of God without being born of water and Spirit" (John 3.5).

By baptism we are born to newness of life. Though human ministers serve as agents for Christ, Christ Himself is the principal minister of baptism and of every sacrament. For this reason the Church declares that the sacred signs we call sacraments are deeds of Christ in

His Church. Sacraments are outward signs instituted by Christ to give grace.[3]

Sacramental participation underscores both aspects of the mystery of grace. The initiative is entirely the Lord's. The sacraments are His actions, His saving deeds, performed by Him through His ministers. But they are fruitful, in an adult, only when there is in the recipient a free inner disposition, a willing response to grace. The sacraments implant and nourish faith and love. Christ causes this faith and love to grow; but the acts of faith and love are also the free acts of the Christian.

This is one of the mysteries of grace. Divine mercy enables us to do freely acts that are far above our human power. God makes us capable of believing Him with the utter certainty of faith, and of loving Him and one another with divine charity. As we have been brought into unity with Christ, we are made able to take part in divine activity by His favor. Christian faith and love are not acts that we can of ourselves draw forth from our own heart. "This is not your doing, it is the gift of God" (Eph. 2.8). Yet one who is moved by grace truly can believe and love. The saving actions by which we cling to Christ and express our sharing of His life are both the work of God and our own free, joyful deeds.

Growing Up in Christ

The Christian is not called merely to conversion, and to a static preservation of a gift once received. Christ has given us life, a life that must grow. "But speaking the truth in love, we must grow up in every way into Him who is the head, into Christ" (Eph. 4.15). We must seek to grow toward a fulfillment so splendid that it cannot be fully achieved in this world. "Be perfect therefore, as your heavenly Father is perfect" (Matt. 5.48).

Merit

By ever becoming more intensely alive in Christ, and by exercising this life in union with Jesus in personal prayer and in liturgy and in deeds of love, we also prepare for and truly merit the heavenly life to which all earthly sharing in Christ's life is ordered as its final crown and final perfection.

All our prayer, worship, and works of love in this world are imperfect. We live in a state of faith and obscurity, and in a world still suffering, awaiting final redemption (cf. Rom. 8.22-23). While the works of a Christian may bring this world ever closer to conformity

---

[3]Cf. Council of Trent, Session 7, March 3, 1547, *Decree on the Sacraments*, canons on the sacraments in general (DS 1601-1608).

with the plan of God's kingdom, that kingdom cannot be perfected here. What we strive after in living now the life of Christ will be fully realized only when we have come to see God face to face, and in His light learn to love Him and one another perfectly, and to rejoice in the utter victory of Christ over all sin, death, and imperfection (cf. 1 Cor. 15.24-28).

Our good deeds, moved by the grace of Christ, build up the Body of Christ and merit eternal life for us. It is not, however, our own power which makes our good deeds so effective, so fruitful. We ourselves could never initiate or draw out our own resources acts meriting life forever with God. It is Christ who merited for us all the good we hope for.

But it is also His gift that He treats us as persons, and calls us to serve Him freely. It is His generosity that enlarges our life by His grace, so that we may truly believe and love, that we may truly share in the work of God. When He has given us the power to do freely such sublime deeds, then, in virtue of God's promises and of the genuine abilities He has given us by His graces, those deeds genuinely merit eternal life.

Scripture commends the justice of God in bestowing eternal life on those who have served Him with love. "From now on there is reserved up for me the crown of righteousness, which the Lord, the righteous judge, will give me on that day, and not only to me but also to all who have longed for His appearing" (2 Tim. 4.8). God is truly just to reward those who were freely faithful to grace when they might have failed Him, though they also know that the glory is rightly His. It is His gift that we have seen and cared and served. "When God crowns our merits, is He not crowning precisely His own gifts?"[4]

---

[4]St. Augustine, *Epistula* 194.5.19 (ML 33.880).

18

God's Plan For Human Living

Called to a new life, Christians must live their lives on this earth and in the midst of their brothers and sisters. As creatures made children of God, and as co-workers of God in bettering the world, they are called to live freely and responsibly. With their natural talents and the gifts of grace they are to chart out for themselves and live a life pleasing to God.

In this chapter we discuss first the problems involved in the shaping of a good human life. Then we speak of Christ's place in solving these problems. The chapter treats of what conscience is and how it is to be guided; how God makes known the natural law and the commandments; and how the grace-rooted virtues we have as His gifts enable us to grow in freedom in doing His will.

The Shaping of Human Life

To be a person is to be free. We human beings can make choices, and because we can, we must. Thus our freedom presents us with a problem: How should we live?

Some starting points are clear enough. Intelligent reflection and the teaching of Scripture assure us that many things are authentically good. Anyone can appreciate that life and health and safety, considered simply in themselves, are good. Death, disease, injury, and pain, on the other hand, are bad. The play of the senses, the exercise of human capacities and skills, the appreciation of beauty, and the knowledge of truth are good. Stupor, insensitivity, ignorance, and error are bad. The sharing of goods with others, peace and harmony within oneself and with others, freedom to pursue goods in ways which seem reasonable —these, too, are basic forms of goodness.

These basic forms of human goodness mark out the whole field of human action, the broad range of human possibilities. All personal growth and all enrichment of community life are realizations of one or more of these basic forms of goodness. It is the attractiveness of these values, of life and friendship and truth and the rest, in one form or another, that stimulates all human efforts, all historical movements.

When we consider the full realization of any of these values, we see that their goodness is in its way as real as this book in our hands or that tree in the field. When we say that creation manifests God's glory, we need not think only of majestic stellar space (cf. Ps. 19.1), or of the wonderful hidden structure of matter, or of the flowers which outshine Solomon in all his splendor (cf. Matt. 6.28-29). For the image of God shines even more clearly in a human life that participates richly in these basic forms of goodness. A person is not meant simply to exist, but to flourish and be "like trees planted by streams of water" (Ps. 1.3), flourishing in health and friendship and every manner of good.

The Song of Songs in the Old Testament celebrates the purposeful work, the loving play, the joyful friendship, sexual union, procreation, and fidelity of man and woman. But God's glory also is reflected in Job's heroic concern for truth when everything else has failed.

We see many kinds of human flourishing and fulfillment in the lives of others. We see them portrayed imaginatively in fiction; and we can project them as possibilities which we might realize for ourselves and others by and in our own free acts. When we reflect on them, appreciating their solid and unquestionable goodness in themselves, we are understanding, humanly, a real aspect of God's creative intention, an aspect of God's plan for human life.

The Moral Problem

But as soon as one begins to think about what to do oneself, many questions arise. For there are many kinds of good that one might pursue, and many ways of realizing these basic goods in one's life. Also, my own life is not the only life that might be enriched as a result of my choices; there are many lives which I could enhance. Am I my neighbor's keeper? and who is my neighbor? What forms of good should I now be realizing? How much? For whom? With whom? Of all the choices I could make, which are the ones I really ought to make? What are the proper standards to use in choosing?

Questions of this sort indicate the moral problem. When a person wrestles with them in order to decide what to do, we may say that he or she is exploring the paths of conscience.

The variety of moral systems and approaches to morality suggests the complexity of the moral problem. Still, the problem is far from being altogether beyond human ability to deal with. Straightforward human reasonableness and simple human friendship can carry one far toward a solution.

Reasonableness requires one to reject sheer arbitrariness in the pursuit of the various forms of good. Reasonableness demands that like cases be treated alike and that different cases be treated differently. Thus it suggests a notion of fairness or justice. Since the same goods can be realized as much in one person as in another, reasonableness urges one to avoid preferring one person to another without some real reason. The Golden Rule, "Do to others as you would have them do to you" (Luke 6:31; cf. Matt. 7.12), emerged in human conscience long before Christ revealed its full weight (cf. Tobit 4.16).

In carrying one beyond mere self-interest, the call of reason reinforces the call of friendship. Friendship leads one to broader concerns, and establishes a new practical perspective. Each of us can see that true friendship is part of our own well-being. But our friendships would be neither true nor really valuable if we entered into them solely for the sake of our own well-being. To be a true friend, we must seek our friends' well-being for our friends' sake. We must care to see our friends prosper because in unselfish love we wish them to be happy. Each friend wishes to see good befall his or her friends. Thus friendship establishes a kind of impartiality, of shared unselfishness, in the pursuit of goods.

One's perspective can be shifted still further from immediate self-interest by reflection on one's life as a whole, not merely as a set of separate moments. Viewed in its entirety, it can make more or less sense. Looking back on this life at the moment of one's death, one presumably would see many choices one made which now seem irrational, a waste of opportunities, a stunting of one's own free development, a failure, a shame. The parable of the rich man appeals to conscience by appealing to intelligence: "You fool! This night your soul is being demanded of you. And the things you have prepared, whose will they be?" (Luke 12.20).

"In all you do, remember the end of your life" (Sir. 7.36). These words are a reminder not so much of the life hereafter as of the proper perspective for living this life. Wise men in every age have realized that the right measure of the pursuit of values is established by finding the proper viewpoint. Then the full range of human possibilities comes into view, the many aspects of human good more or less fall into place, and the vice and worthlessness of arbitrariness and selfishness become clear.

Thus, even without God's revelation human reflection has found and can always find in reason an inward guide for the exercise of freedom. Pagan philosophers, reflecting on the inwardness and force of this guidance, called it the "law of nature" or the "law of reason." St. Paul seems to have adopted their vocabulary and their insight when he said: "When Gentiles, who do not possess the law, do instinctively what the law requires, these, though not having the law, are a law to themselves. They show that what the law requires is written on their hearts, to which their own conscience also bears witness. . ." (Rom. 2.14-15).

The Doubts about Morality and Freedom

Each of us can make the shift from concentrating exclusively on our own pain and pleasure to thinking in terms of what is really worthwhile in itself. Judgments about what is worthy, just, and right, we call judgments of conscience.

But new questions arise. Why should I do what is worthy? Why should I respond to the voice of conscience? Why should anyone take seriously his spontaneous inclination to seek truth, to be reasonable, to be a friend? How can one be sure that the moral good is really good? Is conscience really anything more than an inborn inhibition, a voice of one's subconscious, an effect merely of heredity and environment, perhaps an image of the parental discipline of one's childhood or of the standards of society?

And with these questions comes doubt about the authenticity of one's freedom. If there is nothing really good, truly worthy, for one to know, is not one simply the creature of one's psychology, one's upbringing, one's society? Or else is not one the prisoner of one's passions? How real is a "freedom" which can "choose" only by following an illusion or a compulsion?

God has given us an answer to these doubts about human life and actions. It is in Christ.

Shaping One's Life in Christ

Christ's call to each of us is an appeal to our desire for truth. If we follow this desire it will lead us to acknowledge the man Jesus as the Word of God. Then He calls upon our capacity for gratitude and love; these, if we allow them, will spur us to follow His way and imitate Him. Thus His call is a call to *faith*.

Christ's call is an appeal to our intelligent sense that nothing could be more desirable and worthwhile than to attain what would be ours if we could contemplate the depths of God's creative purpose and of His own being. Thus it is a call to *hope*, a hope that through friendship with God we may overcome all difficulties, see Him face to face, and know even as we are known (cf. 1 Cor. 13.12).

Christ's call is a call to apply our intelligence and all of our talents to discovering and furthering the loving purpose of His Father, the purpose for which He became man. Thus it is a call to *love*.

What is involved in following the call of Christ? This chapter seeks to answer this question and to show how Christ's call is God's response to the human doubts and fears about the worth of conscience and the reality of freedom. In the next three chapters, then, the signposts along the way of Christ are pointed out more precisely.

In these chapters on the moral life we consider Christ's call only insofar as it is an appeal and guide to choice and action, an answer to the question, "What shall I do?" We take for granted all that has been and will be said in other parts of this book about the direct action of God's grace in us. We take for granted that in the last analysis the message of Christ is "written not with ink but with the Spirit of the living God, not on tablets of stone but on tablets of human hearts" (2 Cor. 3.3). The message of Christ can be received and acted upon only if God moves within us to transform our hearts of stone into hearts of flesh (cf. Ezek. 11.19; 36.26). God does this by stimulating within us love of truth, concern for the good we should seek, and willingness to do whatever such love and concern require of us. The priority of a personal turning to God through grace and the sacramental life in the community of faith, hope, and love are assumed throughout these chapters.

Conforming to the Mind of Christ

Christ "fully reveals man to man himself and makes his supreme calling clear" (GS 22). How? "By the revelation of the mystery o the Father and His love" (GS 22). Apart from the life and teaching of Jesus, God's purposes are only dimly known. "No one has ever seen God. It is God the only Son, who is close to the Father's heart, who has made Him known" (John 1.18) by becoming flesh and by living among us, to give light to everyone (cf. John 1.14, 9).

The value of Christ's life and teaching consists in their conformity to the intention of God the Father. "My judgment is just, because I seek to do not My own will but the will of Him who sent Me" (John 5.30). Christ's own prayer in the face of the terror of death was: "Father . . . , not My will but Yours be done" (Luke 22.42). Christ lived and died in the spirit of the prayer He taught us: "Our Father . . . , Your will be done, on earth as it is in heaven" (Matt. 6.9-10). He makes this the very meaning of His Sonship, through which we become sons of God: "For whoever does the will of My Father in heaven is My brother and sister and mother" (Matt. 12.50).

To conform to the mind of Christ is to conform to the mind of the Father. If we ask what we must do to "perform the works of God," Jesus replies: "This is the work of God, that you believe in Him whom He has sent" (John 6.28-29). But "not every one who says to Me, 'Lord, Lord,' will enter the kingdom of heaven, but only the one who does the will of My Father in heaven" (Matt. 7.21).

As St. Paul teaches, we can know "the mind of the Lord" as those who are "unspiritual" do not, because "we have the mind of Christ" (1 Cor. 2.14-16). This, then, enables St. Paul to answer the question of what we ought to do. His answer is that we should conduct ourselves in a way pleasing to God (cf. 1 Thess. 4.1). This expresses the mind of Christ, for Christ does only what pleases the Father (cf. John 8.29).

When Christ rejects Peter's advice to Him as sheer temptation, His reason is: "You are setting your mind not on divine things but on human things" (Matt. 16.23). Peter's advice was to avoid the cross; but Christ went to the cross "so that free from sins, we might live for righteousness" (1 Peter 2.24).

Judging by God's Standards

We see correctly when we see with the eye of God. On this principle every part of Christian moral teaching depends. When what we choose to be or to do conforms to God's plan, then and only then is that choice good.

In the search for the worthwhile, the right, the morally good, the only way to satisfy wholly the demands of reasonableness is to see as God sees, to judge as God judges, to love as God loves. The struggle to reach up to this divine perspective and purpose is first a struggle of one's questioning intelligence, but it comes to involve one's whole character. It corrects the arbitrariness of biased self-love and the mere prejudices of one's community. "Do not be conformed to this world but be transformed by the renewing of your minds, so that you may discern what is the will of God — what is good and acceptable and perfect" (Rom. 12.2; cf. Col. 1.9-10).

The struggle to attain this standard of judgment, to put it into practice in one's life, and to return to it when one has fallen away from it, is simply the struggle to judge and act conscientiously.

Conscience as the Voice of God

Conscience is one's practical judgment about the rightness or wrongness of one's acts. Judgments of conscience are the outcome of a person's effort to avoid being arbitrary and unresponsive in pursuing the values which attract human love. When this effort succeeds, then the answers are right. Then the conscience is true and upright, and a person attains what he was implicitly or explicitly seeking: the knowledge of God's design and will. That is why St. Paul not only observes the universality and naturalness of the phenomena of human conscience in all times and places, but also insists on the fact that conscience bears witness to the demands of God's law (cf. Rom. 2.15).

"The Creator of the world has stamped man's inmost being with an order which his conscience reveals to him and strongly enjoins him to obey."[1] The Church has constantly taught that to say that a conscience is correct is to say that its judgments are right and correspond

---

[1]Pope John XXIII, Encyclical, *Pacem in Terris* (April 11, 1963) (DS 3956).

to God's judgments. When one "enters into his own heart," sincerely seeking the true direction and standard for love, then "God, who probes the heart, awaits him there" (GS 14). If one really cares for the search for the true and good, then, in the quiet reflection of conscience, "he is alone with God, whose voice echoes in his depths" (GS 16).

"In the depths of his conscience, man detects a law which he does not impose upon himself, but which holds him to obedience. Always summoning him to love good and do it and to avoid evil, the voice of conscience can when necessary speak to his heart more specifically: do this, shun that. For man has in his heart a law written by God. To obey it is the very dignity of man; according to it he will be judged" (GS 16).

Conscience, then, is not a device for making exceptions to objective requirements of morality. On the contrary, "through the mediation of conscience man perceives and acknowledges the imperatives of the divine law" (DH 3; cf. GS 16).

This "divine law" is "eternal, objective, and universal," and is the "highest norm of human life" (DH 3). Fidelity to conscience is fidelity in the search for truth, and insofar as our search is successful we turn aside from blind choice and wishful thinking; we are guided by "objective norms of morality" (GS 16).

Conscience and Error

Even when one's quest for the truly good is sincerely motivated and intelligently pursued, it is possible for the judgments of conscience to be mistaken. The mind may be waylaid by inattention, oversight, deep structures of prejudice in one's education, and so on. Conscience is peculiarly exposed to error. For when we work from the grasp of basic principles of good toward particular decisions, we are working in the midst of our passions and inclinations even as we seek to make a reasonable judgment about them.

"Conscience frequently errs from invincible ignorance without losing its dignity" (GS 16). "Everyone of us is bound to obey his conscience" (DH 11). These words of the Second Vatican Council summarize the constant teaching of the doctors of the Church. St. Thomas Aquinas, for example, taught that we are obliged to follow our conscience even when, unknown to us, it is quite mistaken; for we necessarily construe our own conscientious judgment as expressing the authentic demands, if not of God Himself, then at least of truth, reason, goodness, and love. To defy one's conscience is to turn one's back, if not consciously on God Himself, as least on moral authenticity.[2]

Ignorance or error is not excusable, however, when it results from negligence in the pursuit of truth and goodness. When the Second Vatican Council said that an erring but sincere conscience need not

2Cf. St. Thomas Aquinas, *Summa Theologica* I-II, 19, 5.

lose its dignity, it immediately added: "But the same cannot be said of a man who cares but little for truth and goodness" (GS 16). If, therefore, one's conscience errs because of one's complacency, prejudice, rashness, or self-centeredness, one will be in the wrong whether one rejects or follows its dictates.

Conscience and Authority

Conscience is not a matter of "seeing" what is right by a special personal intuition. Judgments of conscience have the authority of objectivity only if they are the judgments that would be made by one who is reasonable and who has reached the impartiality that comes with full friendship with God and neighbor. Can we be sure that we ourselves are just such persons? If one had to rely on one's own search for truth, without a guide, who could be sure that the voice heard is the voice of God rather than the voice of the multitude, or of a particular group, or even of one's own biased self-love?

Again we find that the conscientious search for a moral standard of action is a search for that all-seeing and all-loving impartiality which takes everything into account. Such impartiality exists on a small scale between one friend and another. In its fullest reality it is the viewpoint of God.

A conscience which knows its own power and dignity does aspire to attain "the contemplation and appreciation of the divine plan" (GS 15). But even St. Paul, who exhorts us to renew our minds so as to judge what is God's will (cf. Rom. 12.2), writes: "How unsearchable are His judgments and how inscrutable His ways! 'For who has known the mind of the Lord?' " (Rom. 11.33-34; cf. Wisd. 9.13). It is Christ above all who makes known to us the will of God. For this reason, it would be foolish for a Christian not to guide his conscience by the teaching of Christ.

A Christian conscience cannot be individualistic. We must conform our consciences to the teaching of Christ. The Christian can find significant guidance on this in the example and teachings of saints and doctors whose unequivocal love of truth and goodness has been shown in deed as well as word. Most of all, however, the Christian heeds Christ by conforming his conscience to the teaching of those who teach all nations all that He commanded (cf. Matt. 28.20). For the teaching of the apostles and their successors is not their own, but that of Christ who sent them.

The Second Vatican Council stated: "In the formation of their consciences, the Christian faithful ought carefully to attend to the sacred and certain doctrine of the Church. The Catholic Church is, by the will of Christ, the teacher of the truth. It is her duty to give utterance to, and authoritatively to teach, that Truth which is Christ

Himself and also to declare and confirm by her authority those principles of the moral order which have their own origin in human nature itself" (DH 14). Thus a Christian has the right and duty to follow the judgments of conscience, but also the responsibility to form conscience in accord with truth and in the light of faith.

"It is [the pope's and the bishops'] office and duty to express Christ's teaching on moral questions and matters of belief. This special teaching office within the Catholic Church is a gift of the Lord Jesus for the benefit of all His followers in their efforts to know what He teaches, value as He values, and live as free, responsible, loving, and holy persons. (Cf. Luke 10.16). The authoritative moral teachings of the Church enlighten personal conscience and are to be regarded as certain and binding norms of morality."[3]

The Natural Law

When the Church speaks of "those principles of the moral order which have their origin in human nature itself" (DH 14) her words remind us of the language of the ancient Greek philosophers. The Church has made much use of such language. The Second Vatican Council, for example, in a section on international hostilities, says: "Contemplating this melancholy state of humanity, the Council wishes to recall first of all the permanent binding force of universal natural law and its all-embracing principles" (GS 79).

As many passages in documents of the Church show, however, the language of "natural law" is not used by the Church in the same sense in which it was used by the Greek philosophers or the Roman lawyers of old; nor is it used by the Church in the sense in which one might speak of "laws of nature" in the physical or biological sciences. The Church uses "natural law" in a classical Christian sense. In this sense, "natural law" signifies the plan of God in relation to human life and action, insofar as the human mind in this life can grasp that plan and share with God the role of directing human life according to it (cf. DH 3).[4]

When we know any truth at all, we know it by sharing in the light of God's understanding. We are speaking here of the mysterious but commonplace light by which we pass from the facts of perception and experience to understanding, and from understanding to reasonable judgment. Among the facts of human experience are built-in inclinations toward the basic forms of human flourishing. When we consider the practical question of what one ought to do, we see at once, without

---

[3]United States Catholic Conference, *Sharing the Light of Faith — National Catechetical Directory for Catholics of the United States* (1979) n. 104.
[4]Cf. also Pope Leo XIII, Encyclical, *Libertas Praestantissimum* (June 20, 1888) (DS 3247); Pope John XXIII, Encyclical, *Pacem in Terris* (April 11, 1963) (DS 3956, 3973). See also St. Thomas Aquinas, *Summa Theologica* I-II, 91, 2.

reasoning or further proof, that these forms of goodness ought to be pursued and that what is at odds with them ought to be avoided.[5]

These basic practical insights are the starting points of all sound moral reasoning. They are frequently called the first principles of "natural law." In this initial sense, the natural law is simply the starting point, taught us by God in the very formation of our native tendencies and our natural ability to understand, for directing our lives toward our own fulfillment. This fulfillment is the complete good which God plans for us.

Why, then, does the Church speak of "natural law" as well as of "the will of God" and "God's plan," and of the conscience which discerns that plan?

First of all, the expression "natural law" emphasizes that the fundamental moral principles are not extrinsic commands, arbitrarily imposed on us by God. The Creator does not impose anything on His creatures in making them be what they are, for apart from their being as creatures they are nothing at all. Fundamental moral principles follow from our being what we are. The law of God, which we can discern by an upright conscience, is not the command of a master of slaves. It is rather like a composer's directions to the musicians who collaborate in attaining the purpose of the composer's art.

Moreover, by speaking of "natural" law the Church recalls that in this life we do not in fact share God's full understanding of all the details of His divine plan. In particular, we do not understand how it is that God will bring greater good out of every evil and failure.

Such secrets of providence we do not know. But we do know for certain that the basic forms of human self-realization are good. We can grasp the certainty and constant relevance of the principles which express that goodness, such as, for example, the principle that human life is a good to be realized, preserved, and favored, and that whatever threatens life is to be feared, avoided, defended against. We also recognize the principle of reasonableness, which provides all the goods and principles with their moral force, and which illumines the path from basic principles to particular decisions.

Human life is lived, then, in the midst of this ignorance and this knowledge of God's plan. What follows from this mingled knowledge and ignorance will be elaborated when, in the chapters which follow, we consider how the love of God guides us in this life.

Principles for All

The expression "natural law" is also used by the Church to emphasize that the moral principles taught by Christ and by the Church are principles for all men and women, for all times and places, for all

[5]Cf. St. Thomas Aquinas, *Summa Theologica* I-II, 94, 2.

cultures and situations. The natural law must be distinguished from the precepts which Christ made concerning the structure and sacraments of the Church. The natural law also must be distinguished from the ecclesiastical or canon laws which the Church itself makes and unmakes as circumstances urge for the well-being of the faithful.

The principles of natural law are recognizable by all. Our intellect is naturally inclined toward this understanding of human well-being. But our response in applying these principles is variable and varied. The Church never has supposed that what is naturally reasonable is in fact consistently seen as such by all or even by most.

The Church always has considered that we normally come to an adequate knowledge of natural law only through revelation, above all through the example and teaching of Christ. He alone perfectly reflects what God meant human persons to be when He created them in their first innocence and goodness. This is why it is a function of the magisterium of the Church to interpret the moral natural law. "It is in fact indisputable, as our predecessors have many times declared, that Jesus Christ, when He communicated His divine authority to Peter and the other apostles and sent them to teach all nations His precepts, constituted them authentic guardians and interpreters of the whole moral law, that is, not only of the law of the Gospel but also of the natural law, which is also an expression of the will of God, the faithful fulfillment of which is equally necessary for salvation."[6]

The Commandments

What is right can be known by the natural light of reason. But it is crystallized in the Decalogue, the Ten Commandments of the old covenant with Israel, and is brought to full clarity in the new law of Christ.[7] This theme is suggested by St. Paul, taught by many Fathers of the Church, and elaborated by St. Thomas Aquinas. The Second Vatican Council took up the same theme, pointing out that at all times God has welcomed those who fear Him and do what is right, that He manifested His will to His covenanted people Israel, but that all this was in preparation for a more luminous revelation and the perfect covenant, ratified in Christ, with its new law of love (cf. LG 9).

The Gospel, which had been "promised in former times through the prophets" and which Christ Himself "fulfilled and promulgated with His own lips," and which He commissioned His apostles to preach to all, is "the source of all saving truth and all moral teaching" (DV 7). Christ, as St. Paul says, "is the end of the law" (Rom. 10.4),

[6]Pope Paul VI, Encyclical, *Humanae Vitae* (July 25, 1968) no. 4 (EV 3.590). Similarly GS 89; DH 14.
[7]United States National Conference of Catholic Bishops, *To Live in Christ Jesus* (November 11, 1976).

the "end" here meaning not the finish, but the completion or perfection.

The Decalogue

The fundamental moral commands or laws given by God to Israel through Moses are listed in two places of the Old Testament, in Exodus (20.2-17) and in Deuteronomy (5.6-22). In summary form the Ten Commandments are:

1. I, the Lord, am your God. You shall not have other gods before Me.
2. You shall not take the name of the Lord, your God, in vain.
3. Remember to keep holy the Sabbath day.
4. Honor your father and your mother.
5. You shall not kill.
6. You shall not commit adultery.
7. You shall not steal.
8. You shall not bear false witness against your neighbor.
9. You shall not covet your neighbor's wife.
10. You shall not covet anything that belongs to your neighbor.

What does God teach us in these commandments? First, He teaches the absolute priority of loving service of God. The Deuteronomist, after setting out the Decalogue, says: "The LORD is our God, the LORD alone. You shall love the LORD your God with all your heart, and with all your soul, and with all your might" (Deut. 6.4-5). Christ called this "the greatest and first commandment" (Matt. 22.38).

Second, God teaches that serving Him requires unconditional respect, in deeds and thoughts and words, for one's neighbor. We must honor our parents, who are the source of our life. We must respect human life itself, in ourselves and in others. We must respect the sexual relations by which, within marriage, life is transmitted. We must respect property, which is to be used in the service of persons. We must respect the truth about persons.

Third, the Decalogue teaches that certain types of acts, and even, as the last two commandments show, the inner disposition to such types of acts, are incompatible with love of God and respect for neighbor. Acts of such types are thus always and everywhere wrong; they may not be done in any situation.

The Decalogue does not identify these types of acts with complete precision. This identification is in some respects made in other parts of Scripture, but it is in many respects left to the consciences of the people of God as they move through history, guided by the saints and doctors who strive to see as God sees and to love as He loves, and by "the Church's teaching office, which authentically interprets the divine law in the light of the Gospel" (GS 50), and thus by Christ Himself.

The Law of Christ

Christ ratified the Decalogue, both as a whole and in its parts (cf. Matt. 19.17-19; Mark 10.17-19; Luke 18.18-20).[8] He also ratified the Deuteronomist's summary on love of God (cf. Matt. 22.37-38), and He added a summary of the last seven commandments: "You shall love your neighbor as yourself" (Matt. 22.39).

This command of love of neighbor was not new (cf. Lev. 19.18), and Christ did not say it was new. But Christ did give a new commandment of love: "I give you a new commandment, that you love one another. Just as I have loved you, you also should love one another" (John 13.34).

What is new in Christ's commandment of love is the standard which He sets, the standard which He Himself is. This standard demands the maximum of human love, and it transforms human love into a love which is divine.

Christ loves us with the maximum of human love. He is the Lord at whose name "every knee should bend" (Phil. 2.10; cf. Isa. 45.23) because, although divine by nature, He "did not regard equality with God as something to be exploited, but emptied Himself, taking the form of a slave" and "humbled Himself and became obedient to the point of death — even death on a cross" (Phil. 2.6-8). Precisely in the greatness of His self-sacrifice, Christ set the example St. Paul emphasizes: "Let the same mind be in you that was in Christ Jesus" (Phil. 2.5). Jesus Himself said: "You are My friends if you do what I command you" (John 15.14).

But Christ's love for us is not only the maximum of human love. Jesus loves us in the way the Father loves Him. "As the Father has loved Me, so have I loved you; abide in My love. If you keep My commandments, you will abide in My love, just as I have kept My Father's commandments and abide in His love" (John 15.9-10). The Father's love for the Son is divine; Jesus' love for us is divine; our love for one another is to be divine.

The standard is that of children of God. "Like obedient children, do not be conformed to the desires that you formerly had in ignorance. Instead, as He who called you is holy, be holy yourselves in all your conduct" (1 Peter 1.14-15). We are summoned to "be imitators of God, as beloved children, and live in love, as Christ loved us. . ." (Eph. 5.1-2). By following this way we are given title to become sons and daughters of God (cf. John 1.12). And as adopted children of God

---

[8] Cf. also Council of Trent, Session 6, January 13, 1547, *Decree on Justification*, canon 19 (DS 1569).

we are called to share Christ's entire lot, both His suffering as man and His glorification as Son of God (cf. Rom. 8.16-17). St. Paul summed up "the law of Christ" as the demand that we not merely respect our neighbor but actually "bear one another's burden" (Gal. 6.2).

For "the truth is in Jesus. You were taught to put away your former way of life, your old self, corrupt and deluded by its lusts, and to be renewed in the spirit of your minds, and to clothe yourselves with the new self, created after the likeness of God in true righteousness and holiness" (Eph. 4.21-24).

Virtues and Graces in the Moral Life

Thus the law of Christ more than completes our grasp of the natural law, our sharing in the principles of God's universal plan. But how can this law be lived? As human beings we drift constantly and all too easily toward the arbitrary and the unloving.

We can live the law of Christ only because, by God's utterly free grace, we can live in Christ. He is not only our Teacher, Master, Leader, and Model; He is God's Son who sends us the Spirit, the Spirit who pours God's love into our hearts (cf. Rom. 5.5), the Spirit by whom we are adopted children of God (cf. Rom. 14.16).

St. Thomas Aquinas, following St. Augustine, teaches that "in its primary significance, the new Law is the grace of the Holy Spirit, given to those who believe in Christ."[9] St. Paul had said of the law that "the letter kills, but the Spirit gives life" (2 Cor. 3.6). St. Thomas takes up St. Augustine's commentary and dares to affirm that "even the letter of the Gospel — the written moral precepts contained in it — would kill were it not for the healing grace of faith present within."[10]

The life of grace will be the theme of a later chapter. What concerns us here is the newness of life generated within us by the grace of the Spirit. Through grace we acquire a second self, a second nature. This new nature is to express itself in new ways of living. Christian theologians, following the language of pagan philosophers but the thought of the New Testament, call these new ways of living "virtues."

A virtue is a settled disposition characteristic of the good person, a tendency toward the altogether good, truly loving, and therefore morally right action in any relevant situation. A virtue is an aspect of the identity which a good person establishes for himself by his love and responsible pursuit of what is good. It is evidenced in good works, as the goodness of the tree is evidenced by good fruits.

[9]*Summa Theologica* I-II, 106,1.
[10]*Summa Theologica* I-II, 106, 2. Cf. St. Augustine, *De Spiritu et Littera* 14, 17 (ML 44.215, 219).

In one respect, law and conscience are prior to virtue. Virtue is the disposition to do good; the plan of God, expressed in moral law and known through conscience, defines what counts as virtues. In another respect, virtue is prior to law and conscience. Only the person who loves truth, pursues friendship, and thus *strives* toward God can attain through his own conscience an authentic understanding of God's plan for human life. And any such established love, pursuit, striving, is a virtue.

Law and virtue go together as call and response. The specifically Christian understanding of virtue flows from recognition that our response to God's call is itself initiated by the grace of God moving us, within us, prior to any cooperation on our part.

Thus the virtues natural to us, good as they are, are insufficient for the life of full friendship with God and with our neighbors. They are perfected and given a new orientation by God "working in us without us."[11] When transformed in this way, the virtues are called by theologians "infused virtues," the "infused" here meaning that they are poured into our hearts with the love of God by the Spirit (cf. Rom. 5.5).

Primary among the virtues of the new life are those which dispose us in a special way toward God. All virtues, insofar as they are dispositions toward human goods, are dispositions toward that sharing in divine goodness which is naturally open to men. But faith, hope, and love dispose human persons to a life destined to be lived in everlasting friendship with God. These virtues are called "theological virtues," not because they pertain to the study of theology, but because they orient us toward God directly.

Freedom and the Christian Moral Life

A person's response to God's call is not really a personal response if it is not free. God's call is a call to completely authentic freedom, as freedom to do with joy and spontaneity what one's heart most desires. Morality is the pattern of a growth from freedom to freedom.

"Since man's true freedom is not found in everything that the various systems and individuals see and propagate as freedom, the Church, because of her divine mission, becomes all the more the guardian of this freedom, which is the condition and basis for the human person's true dignity."[12]

Growth in freedom is rooted in our freedom to respond or not to respond reasonably to the call of the good, and so to the call of Him who is their creative source. It is called "free will," or "freedom of

---

[11]On this classic phrase and the thought here, cf. St. Thomas Aquinas, *Summa Theologica* I-II, 55, 4; 63,2.

[12]Pope John Paul II, Encyclical, *Redemptor Hominis* (March 4, 1979) n. 12 (6.1203).

choice." Moral growth is growth toward the fuller freedom to which everyone is called, the freedom of the children of God in their Father's household, the freedom of friend with friend, the freedom of a personality without stunting and without compulsions (cf. GS 17).

The Epistle of St. James describes the word of God on which we must act as "the law of liberty" (James 1.25). The First Epistle of St. Peter underlines what might seem contradictory, that to live "as servants of God" is to "live as free people" (1 Peter 2.16). St. Paul sums up the whole matter: "For you were called to freedom, brothers and sisters; only do not use your freedom as an opportunity for self-indulgence, but through love become slaves to one another. . . . Live by the Spirit, I say . . . But if you are led by the Spirit you are not subject to the law" (Gal. 5.13, 16, 18).

In these and all the New Testament writings we find an awareness of moral obligation which could scarcely be more intense, yet with it an awareness that in the final analysis obligation is not what morality is all about.

That is why St. Augustine put forward his summary of Christian morality — "Love and do what you will"[13] — in his commentary on the equivalent summary in the First Epistle of John: "By this we know that we love the children of God, when we love God and obey His commandments. For the love of God is this, that we obey His commandments. And His commandments are not burdensome" (1 John 5.2-3). The mystery of love is this: there is a command of love, but, as St. Thomas says, "no one can fulfill a precept of love except of his own free will."[14] Since the will of God is the rule of goodness, those who are united with God also have freedom to do as they please, for what pleases them is to please God.

The Christian Nature of Morality

Christ came to set us free, by the truth of His call to us and the spirit of His life within us; free not only from our own failure, inertia, compulsiveness, misdirection of effort, and waste of opportunity, but also from enslavement to public opinion, to the standards and taboos of a merely human culture, to the image and upbringing of perhaps all-too-human parents.

Christian morality is not a morality for Christians only. It is for all, for all are called to follow Christ. Christian morality is the authentic, central, and integral form of morality. Apart from Christian understanding and Christian life, every element of morality and of moral language loses something of its vitality and meaning. Apart from faith in Christ, the great questions about the reality of freedom, the

---

[13]St. Augustine, *In Epistulam Ioannis ad Parthos* 6.4.8 (ML 35.2033).
[14]*Summa Theologica* II-II, 44, 1 ad 2.

rationality of conscience, and the value of pursuing human goods unselfishly cannot be fully answered.

In Christ we find the questions answered, answered with a divine Word who tells us more than we asked, who surpasses our expectations. In Christ we see that questioning itself is a part of the movement of His grace within us. If we respond to this movement, we will question and reject every form of arbitrariness and inertia in the pursuit of good as unworthy — unworthy of the dignity of the human person created in the image of God and re-created as a new creature in the image of His Son, unworthy in the sight of God who through His Word summons us out of nothing and makes us all that we can freely choose to be.

19

Living Faith, Hope, and Love

"And now faith, hope, love abide, these three" (1 Cor. 13.13).

The personal response to Christ's call has a variety of aspects, not necessarily separable in time. First, there is recognition that it is God who calls us, and acknowledgment that He is trustworthy and His word is true and good. This is faith. Second, there is lively confidence that in responding to Him we approach One whose will it is to fulfill our needs and longings more fully than we could otherwise have imagined. This is hope. Finally, there is the fullest response, the gift to Him of one's whole self, of mind and heart and strength, accepting His call to membership in God's family, to friendship with the Trinity and with all created persons. This is charity, or love.

The preceding chapters have said much of faith, hope, and love. These are, as we have already seen, principles of a life lived according to God's plan. Here all that needs to be added is further clarification of the place of these theological virtues in the moral life, and of the special obligations that they imply.

The Life of Faith

The first duty of one to whom God addresses His word is faith. When the Lord who has created us invites us to faith and makes it possible for us to know that it is He who calls, the "obedience of faith" (Rom. 16.26) is required for us. Only if we believe Him can we trust and love Him. Faith "is the beginning of human salvation."[1] Without faith it is impossible for us fallen creatures in the course of our lives not to fail morally, not to become arbitrary, or selfish, or unresponsive (cf. AA 4). For it is faith that raises the mind toward God's perspective on human affairs (cf. GS 15). "And without faith it is impossible to please God" (Heb. 11.6).

Often "faith" is used in a comprehensive sense, that is, for full response to the word of God, a response lived in hope and in love. But "faith" is also used at times in a narrower sense, for an aspect of

---

[1]St. Fulgentius, *De Fide, ad Petrum* prolog. 1 (ML 65.671), quoted by the Council of Trent, Session 6, January 13, 1547, *Decree on Justification*, ch. 8 (DS 1532), and by the First Vatican Council, Session 3, April 24, 1870, *Dogmatic Constitution on the Catholic Faith*, ch. 3 (DS 3008).

Christian life distinct from (though closely related to) hope and love. Such faith is a true gift of God; it enables one to believe God and cling freely to His word.

Because we are free, it is possible for us who received faith as a gift of God not to respond in hope and love to the call which faith recognizes. In such a case, the faith is real, but it is dormant and fruitless.

The Church teaches that it is possible for a sinner to have faith. The Church has flatly denied that "with the loss of grace through sin faith is also always lost."[2] When a Christian commits a serious sin, one which is not itself a sin of denial or rejection of faith, he does not lose the gift of faith.

But "faith without hope and charity neither unites a man perfectly with Christ nor makes him a living member of His body. Therefore it is most rightly said that 'faith without works is dead' (cf. James 2.17 ff.) and unprofitable, and that 'in Christ Jesus neither circumcision nor uncircumcision is of any avail, but faith working through love' (Gal. 5.6, 6.15)."[3]

The personal, grace-moved act of believing God is at the very roots of the moral life. Faith provides the plan of Christian living. The one whom God calls to know and serve Him must first of all be a hearer and believer of the word.

Duty to Believe

Faith is a virtue infused by the Holy Spirit. It is the enduring gift of a faithful God. One who has been brought by God to the gift of and explicit Christian and Catholic faith has the duty never to abandon it (cf. Heb. 10.26-31). Those who have never received the gift of explicit faith may indeed believe God and serve Him generously outside the visible Church; but those who have received the gift of a full Catholic faith must not reject it.

"Those whom He has brought out of darkness into His own admirable light (cf. 1 Peter 2.9) He strengthens with His grace, so that they may persevere in that light, deserting none who do not desert Him. Therefore, the condition of those who by the heavenly gift of faith have embraced the Catholic truth is by no means the same as that of those who, led by human opinions, follow a false religion. For those who have received the faith under the teaching authority of the Church can never have a just reason to change this same faith or to call it into doubt."[4]

[2] Council of Trent, Session 6, January 13, 1547, *Decree on Justification*, canon 28 (DS 1578).
[3] Council of Trent, Session 6, January 13, 1547, *Decree on Justification*, ch. 7 (DS 1531).
[4] First Vatican Council, Session 3, April 24, 1870, *Dogmatic Constitution on the Catholic Faith*, ch. 3 (DS 3014).

These words of the First Vatican Council are no invitation to judge others, whose apparent falling from faith may be the result of trials, emotional pressures, and weaknesses no one but God is able to evaluate. But they are a strong reminder to all who have been blessed with the light of faith that they have a duty never to give up the gift God has given them.

Of course, a believer always has questions. The gift of faith is a partial answer to our search for truth. It does not remove all problems. In what it teaches us, it gives full assurance, but this is not the clear vision proper to eternal life. "For now we see in a mirror dimly" (1 Cor. 13.12). Those who love the saving truth may well ask further questions, but they will ask in the light of faith, thereby straining toward that perfect knowledge which we are to enjoy in heaven.

Worldly wisdom will have its own questions to put to faith, and its own spirit in asking them. Even those questions which are tinged with hostility or muddled by worldly wisdom's lack of the true perspective must be given a Christian response.[5]

These, then, are the primary duties of faith: to believe what we are enabled to recognize as God's word (cf. John 6.29); to seek to have an informed faith; to hold fast to the word of God in its purity, refusing to be "tossed to and from and blown about by every wind of doctrine, by people's trickery" (Eph. 4.14). Similarly, pastors and parents who have responsibility for the care of little ones in Christ must be tireless to the truth God has revealed, guarding the faith in its entirety and "with the utmost patience in teaching" (2 Tim. 4.2).

Faith and Fidelity

As the Second Vatican Council teaches, "the disciple is bound by a grave obligation toward Christ his Master ever more adequately to understand the truth received from Him, faithfully to proclaim it, and vigorously to defend it" (DH 14). Our Lord demands of us that we shape our life by our faith. But He also demands that we are prepared to profess and acknowledge our faith when it is called into question seriously, or whenever silence on our part would give bad example to others.

Christ states these obligations in no uncertain terms: "Everyone therefore who acknowledges Me before others, I also will acknowledge before My Father in heaven; but whoever denies Me before others, I also will deny before My Father is in heaven" (Matt. 10.32-33; cf. Luke 10.8-12).

The Second Vatican Council summarizes the duty of fidelity: "All must be prepared to confess Christ before men, and to follow Him

[5]Cf. Pope John Paul II, Apostolic Exhortation, *Catechesi Tradendae* (October 16, 1979) nn. 56-61 (EV 6.1894-1907).

along the way of the cross through the persecutions which the Church will never fail to suffer" (LG 42).

Not all persecutions are bloody. Today, as always, Christians must be ready to make great sacrifices to be true to the moral demands of faith.

Confident Hope

"Now faith is the assurance of things hoped for, the conviction of things not seen" (Heb. 11.1). Here the essential link between faith and hope is indicated. In faith, we believe not only what God tells us about Himself, but also what He promises for us. By hope we look forward with confidence to the fulfillment of those promises.

Hope and Self

It might seem to some more Christian, at least as an ideal, to think not at all of oneself. This "ideal," however, is not Christian. Christ teaches us to hope for our own salvation. Each person seeks eternal life as one of many brothers and sisters who will inherit the kingdom together (cf. Rom. 8.29, 8.18; 1 Peter 1.4-5). Christ holds self-love and forgetfulness of self in perfect balance: "Those who love their life lose it, and those who hate their life in this world will keep it for eternal life. . . . Whoever serves Me, the Father will honor" (John 12.25-26; cf. Matt. 16.24-27).

It is right to hope for the reward which Christ promises. The fulfillment of oneself in the community of the divine family is the glory of God and the fulfillment of His will (cf. GS 32). To hope for the one and for the other is to hope for the same reality, described from different points of view.

Hope and This World

Just as there is no real conflict between hoping for one's salvation and hoping for God's glory, so there is no real conflict between hoping for heaven and hoping for the redemption of human life in this world. The Church teaches that "a hope concerning the end of time does not diminish the importance of intervening duties, but rather undergirds the acquittal of them with fresh incentives" (GS 21). "Human fulfillment constitutes, as it were, a summary of our duties," and this fulfillment is not merely individual self-fulfillment, but the development and progress of all humankind.[6]

But this Christian hope for a better world is quite different from mere optimism. Our duty to our neighbor is a duty in love, and it is

---

[6]Cf. Pope VI, Encyclical, *Populorum Progressio* (March 26, 1967) nn. 16-17 (EV 2.1061-1062).

equally insistent whether the life of the neighbor, or the life of us, or the life of the human family, seems to be waxing or waning. The Lord urges us to feed the hungry, give drink to the thirsty, welcome the stranger, clothe the naked, comfort the ill, visit the prisoner, and to attend to all human needs — and at the same time He warns us against any assumption that the humanity we are to serve will in fact be in fit state to greet Him when He comes again (cf. Matt. 24.36-25.45).

Christians of course hope that the future of this world will be one of development, not ruin. But this is not the Christian hope which comes from the Holy Spirit and which alone "does not disappoint us" (Rom. 5.5). Christians are free to speculate about the course of the world and human progress in it in the years ahead. Christians as biologists, for example, may reasonably speculate about possible evolution of the human race through future millennia; Christians as political scientists may reasonably speculate about war and peace and the likelihood or unlikelihood that the race will before long destroy itself. But the Christian message does not itself sponsor such speculations or depend upon them. The Christian message teaches that "the People of God has no lasting city here below, but looks forward to one which is to come" (LG 44), for "the structure of this world is passing away" (LG 42; cf. 1 Cor. 7.31).

That which Endures

Yet not everything passes away. The words of Christ remain. Love remains. And, in some way, the good works of humankind in this world remains. "For after we have, in obedience to the Lord and in His Spirit, nurtured on earth the values of human dignity, brotherhood, and freedom, and indeed all the good fruits of our nature and enterprise, we will find them again, but freed of stain, burnished and transfigured. This will be so when Christ hands over to the Father an eternal and universal kingdom, 'a kingdom of truth and life, a kingdom of holiness and grace, a kingdom of justice, love, and peace.' On this earth the kingdom is already present in mystery. When the Lord returns it will be brought into full flower" (GS 39).[7]

Thus, the solution to the tension between this-worldly and otherworldly hope is that the Christian should not regard life on this earth as isolated from the eternal life to come. Rather, eternal life somehow begins here. Our good works done in love of Christ build up this world, but at the same time they accumulate as a kind of hidden treasure, invisible at present to us. The world which passes away is the world in which evil abounds, the world misshapen by the sins of creatures.

Time passes, and Christ is calling us to fullness of life. In Him the world has been redeemed. In the risen Savior the many forms of

[7]The internal quotation is from the Roman Missal, Preface for the Feast of Christ the King.

human flourishing are already abundantly realized. Already He has begun to transform the lives of those who love Him. His kingdom already among us gives us confident assurance that at the end of time He will exert fully His jurisdiction, gather His whole kingdom into Himself, and hand it over to the Father. Living a good moral life is our part in this great design and work of the Lord (cf. LG 36).

Not Doing Evil to Achieve Good

The distinctions between more optimism and hope, and between progress of this world and progress in building eternal life in this world, help us to understand why we may not do evil that good may come of it (cf. Rom. 3.8). Some kinds of "new morality" hold that a very important end or goal justifies the use of any means necessary, even acts otherwise deemed evil. They would permit or even encourage direct attacks on the most basic human goods, even the killing of an unborn child or of an aged infirm person, if in some impossible calculation of goods and evils it is judged that some greater amount of measurable "good" would be achieved. They count only the good which can be humanly seen and "foreseen" in a world which is passing away. But Christ's Church remembers that the future is hidden with God and that "we do not know the day or the hour" (LG 48; cf. Matt. 25.13). The truly new morality, the morality of Christ, counts the good which cannot be seen, the good which is hidden but is known to us by faith. This good, the kingdom already present, demands that all of its aspects — truth, life, holiness, grace, justice, love, and peace — be respected in every human action.

One who lives in Christian hope will not do even a "small evil" for the purpose of achieving a great good or avoiding a great hardship. For even a small sin is, in the eyes of faith, more grievous than any amount of physical evil. Never is one in a situation in which, whatever one does, one must commit sin. For even the person with weighty responsibilities is never obliged to do the evil deed, to tell the lie, to perform the unchaste act that may seem needed to bring about some great good.

Hope, Fear, and Perseverance

We hope in God when we confidently expect from Him all that we need to attain eternal life: grace, mercy, forgiveness, and the overcoming of obstacles and temptations. The Our Father, the prayer taught us by our Lord Himself, is a perfect act of hope.

The confidence of Christians in their own salvation is not based on any supposition that no one can lose his soul. One who has turned to God is still free to turn away from Him. The assurance of the hope of Christians lies in God's fidelity to His promises. But we, too, must be faithful. We cannot be absolutely certain that we will persevere; all must firmly trust in God. "For, unless they themselves are unfaithful to His grace, God, who began the good work, will bring it to completion, effecting both the will and the execution (cf. Phil. 2.13)."[8]

"Pride goeth before a fall" is a sound Christian saying (cf. 1 Cor. 10.12). We must work for our salvation "with fear and trembling" (Phil. 2.12). "The fear of the LORD," says the psalmist, "is the beginning of wisdom" (Ps. 111.10).

A right fear of God is essential to Christian living, a reverent fear that knows His justice and almighty power. But this fear is not to be a slavish fear, or a childish fear. We cannot lose God's help as we lose money, by having it stolen, or taken from us by some accident. We can lose God's help only by disregarding it, ignoring it, refusing it.

Overwhelmed by the disproportion between ourselves as we are and ourselves as we hope to be in heaven, we are all too likely to become discouraged. Sorrow for sin is necessary, but sin should not be the central focus of a Christian's life. Instead, the central focus should be what God already has done and what we can confidently expect He will do. Christ is risen. Mary has been assumed into heaven. She, as we, depended upon her Son for redemption. We, as she, are redeemed, not by any sufficiency of ourselves, but by the superabundant merit of Christ. Thus, we can heed the injunction of St. Paul: "Rejoice in the Lord always; again I will say, Rejoice" (Phil. 4.4).

Lasting Love

St. Paul drew together many of the themes of this chapter and the preceding one when he wrote to the Philippians: "And this is my prayer that your love may overflow more and more with knowledge and full insight to help you to determine what is best, so that in the day of Christ you may be pure and blameless" (Phil. 1.9-10). The first teaching of one of the earliest Christian writings after the New Testament is: "Now, the way of life is this: 'First, love the God who made you; secondly, your neighbor as yourself.' "[9] The order of priority is that underlined by the Second Vatican Council: "The first and most necessary gift is this charity by which we love God above all things and our neighbor because of God" (LG 42).

The Love of God

Love of God is the heart of Christian life. It is true that the goodness of life and truth and friendship give energy to our lives and stir us into action. But when God revealed Himself in Christ, we came to

---

[8]Council of Trent, Session 6, January 13, 1547, *Decree on Justification*, ch. 13 (DS 1541).
[9]*Didache* 1.2 (= ACW 6.15).

know more confidently the perfect Goal of all striving, the Goodness all human goods can only dimly reflect. But Christ reveals to us not only that God is infinitely good. In Christ, God is seen as our Friend, calling us to be children of God and to share His life forever.

God's love for us is prior to our love for Him. He created us. He redeemed us. He pours His love into our hearts. In gratitude we say: "We love because He first loved us" (1 John 4.19). "We know love by this, that He laid down His life for us — and we ought to lay down our lives for one another" (1 John 3.16). As St. Paul exhorts: "Be imitators of God, as beloved children, and live in love, as Christ loved us" (Eph. 5.1-2). God's love is the supreme model for us. We could never have known this model by reason alone. But the limitations of our wisdom and the extent of God's love are made clear in the folly of the cross.

The life of the Trinity is for us the model of love. The Father, Son, and Holy Spirit eternally love one another with that boundless love which is Their Being and the creative force that made and sustains the universe. We were created for the very purpose of sharing in the personal life and love of the divine family. Thus, the Second Vatican Council sums up the basis of love of neighbor according to the new law of Christ: "The Lord Jesus, when He prayed to the Father, 'that all may be one ... as We are one' (John 17.21-22), opened up vistas closed to human reason. For He implied a certain likeness between the union of the divine Persons and the union of God's sons in truth and charity. This likeness reveals that man, who is the only creature on earth which God willed for itself, cannot fully find himself except through a sincere gift of himself" (GS 24).

If one loves God, one keeps His commandments, just as one who loves another person seeks to do what is pleasing to that person. If we love our neighbor, we will try to do good to and for our neighbor. This takes on an eternal significance in that humankind has been called to share in divine life. The highest act of Christian love is the effort to help others attain eternal life. "Indeed, the law of love, which is the Lord's greatest commandment, impels all the faithful to work for the glory of God through the coming of His kingdom and for eternal life for all men, so that they may know the only true God and Him whom He sent, Jesus Christ (cf. John 17.3). On all Christians therefore is laid the splendid burden of working to make the divine message of salvation known and accepted by all men throughout the world" (AA 3).

The Church does not regard unloving obedience to God's law, or the doing of what is right toward one's neighbor for merely humanistic reasons, as something worthless.[10] Still, without love one cannot

---

[10]Cf. Pope St. Pius V, Bull, *Ex Omnibus Afflictionibus* (October 1, 1567) (DS 1916).

effectively serve Christ's kingdom or do anything to merit eternal life. "If I give away all I have, and if I deliver my body to be burned, but have not love, I gain nothing" (1 Cor. 13.3). The Christian must live a life based upon an explicit commitment to God, and must renew this act of love from time to time.[11]

Sin

The central focus of our new life is Christian love. Sin is the opposite of this love. Above all, it is hostile to that great love of God which calls us to growth in what is good.

Just as we can strive freely to see things from God's point of view and to act in accord with His will, so we can freely choose to ignore God's plan and the role He invites us to play in it. We can be grateful to God, our Creator and Redeemer, and stand in awe of His power and holiness, or we can be ungrateful, despise God, and violate His plan and holy will. We can determine to model our life on the life of Christ, or we can reject that model in favor of a cheap pattern of our own making. In short, just as we can accept the invitation God has made to adopt us as members of His own family, so we can refuse this offer in favor of a selfish and isolated life. Such a refusal of God's gift to us of Himself is sin. The refusal of a creature to recognize what one is, to acknowledge the authority of the Love that made one and calls one to life, is pride, which is the root of all sin.

Sin is basically a personal offense against God, a turning from God. For this reason it is important to distinguish between actions which are done with knowledge and freedom and those which are not. Some actions which are in themselves wrong are done without personal guilt because the doer acts in ignorance or without freedom. The actions in these cases are to be distinguished from sin in the strict sense, sometimes called formal sin, in which one freely and knowingly does what he judges to be wrong. A formal sin is a deliberate violation of the known will of God.

"Sin is the greatest obstacle human beings face in their efforts to love God and their brothers and sisters and work out their salvation. . . . In addition to the effects of original sin, there is personal sin, committed by the individual. . . . Personal sin resides essentially in interior rejection of God's commands of love, but this rejection is commonly expressed in exterior acts contrary to God's law. A grave offense (mortal sin) radically disrupts the sinner's relationship with the Father and places him or her in danger of everlasting loss. Even lesser offen-

---

[11]Cf. Decree of the Holy Office (August 24, 1690) (DS 2290).

ses (venial sins) impair this relationship and can pave the way for the commission of grave sins."[12]

Mortal Sin

Formal sin may be either mortal or venial. A mortal sin is a sin that separates one from friendship with God, or deepens alienation from God. There is a sharp distinction between mortal and venial sin. Formal mortal sin, which is incompatible with divine love, destroys the life of grace in the soul. Venial sin weakens but does not destroy the life of grace. "There is no middle way between life and death."[13] Everyone is in the state of grace and in friendship with god, or is separated from the grace of God and not on the way toward eternal life. "Some sins are intrinsically grave and mortal by reason of their matter. That is, there exist acts which, *per se* and in themselves, independently of circumstances, are always seriously wrong by reason of their object. These acts, if carried out with sufficient awareness and freedom, are always mortal."[14]

Certain specific kinds of actions are in themselves always materially mortal. These are so seriously wrong that they exclude one who does them deliberately from the kingdom of heaven. "Do not be deceived! Fornicators, idolaters, adulterers, male prostitutes, sodomites, thieves, the greedy, drunkards, revilers, robbers — none of these will inherit the kingdom of God" (1 Cor. 6.9-10; cf. also Gal. 5.19-21; Eph. 5.5; 1 Tim. 1.9-11; Rev. 21.8, 22; 22.15). The Church does not teach that such passages of Scripture provide complete "lists" of mortal sins, or that the precise meaning and range of mortal sins can be determined from isolated scriptural texts. But in each age the Church performs its duty of clarifying God's law; and it persistently teaches that there are kinds of gravely evil acts which are strictly forbidden by God, and that one who knowingly and deliberately does such acts is deliberately turning away from God.

Not only those sins which express a formal contempt for God or neighbor can be mortal sins. For mortal sin can be found in "every act of disobedience to God's commandments in a grave matter."[15] Thus mortally sinful are not only deliberate acts of blasphemy or hatred of

---

[12]United States Catholic Conference, *Sharing the Light of Faith — National Catechetical Directory for Catholics of the United States* (1979) n. 98.

[13]Pope John Paul II, Post-Synodal Apostolic Exhortation, *Reconciliatio et Paenitentia* (December 2, 1984) n. 17 (EV 9.1126).

[14]Pope John Paul II, Post-Synodal Apostolic Exhortation, *Reconciliatio et Paenitentia* (December 2, 1984) n. 17 (EV 9.1124). The Holy Father here cites the Council of Trent, Session 6, January 11, 1547, *Decree on Justification*, chap. 15 (DS 1544) as a solemn witness to this teaching.

[15]Pope John Paul II, Post-Synodal Apostolic Exhortation, *Reconciliatio et Paenitentia* (December 2, 1984) n. 17 (EV 9.1125).

God, but also those of abortion, fornication, adultery, perjury, and the like.

The degree of knowledge and deliberateness required to constitute a mortal sin cannot be stated with precision. Comprehensive knowledge and absolute freedom are never had in human affairs, and are not needed. To commit mortal sin one must be substantially aware that what one is doing is gravely wrong, and one must be substantially free in one's conduct. Catholic teaching readily recognizes that emotional problems and the influence of external conditions can reduce and even take away one's freedom and responsibility. But the Church does not teach that people are rarely free to choose, that only seldom are they really able to do something seriously good or to do something seriously evil.

Mortal sin is sometimes spoken of as a disposition, or orientation of life, rather than as a single action. There is a sense in which that is clearly true. For mortal sin is not merely an episode; it alters the direction of one's life. One can be in the "state of mortal sin," that is, living a life in which one is not committed to love of God and faithfulness to Him. One can fall from the friendship of God to this sad state only by free and deliberate action. Such an action is an actual mortal sin. The action by which one who is a child of God places oneself in hostility to God will not be a casual or slight one. Normally the gravely sinful act by one who has really loved God will be preceded by many failings in loyalty. One certainly does not pass thoughtlessly from love of God to mortal sin and back to love. Only serious and deliberate sin turns one from God; only a genuine conversion returns divine life and love to one who has sinned gravely.

If we deliberately and knowingly offend God in a serious matter, we thereby lose our share in divine life and give up our title to a place in heaven. To die having forfeited the friendship of God is to face the terrifying prospect of God's judgment and the eternal separation from God of which He has warned us (cf. Matt. 25.41).

Mortal sin need not take away all of one's natural dispositions to goodness, but the special gifts implanted by the Holy Spirit to make a person's life truly a life in Christ are forced out by even a single mortal sin.

One who has sinned mortally is dead to all that abundant new life Christ came to win for all of us (cf. John 17.10). There remains in that sinner no power one can oneself exercise that might make possible a return to God. Sinners can do nothing to begin to bring themselves back to life without God's first moving them to repent. God's merciful acceptance of their consequent repentance, God's gracious forgiveness of those who promise to act once more as His friends — only these acts of God can heal the breach caused by mortal sin.

Fundamental Option

In recent years many Christian thinkers have adopted the expression "fundamental option" as a name for the persistent will or attitude that shapes a person's life; the basic intent to live as one who believes God's word and accepts His call to a new life, or to decline to do so. The expression is an apt one to the extent that it highlights those basic stances which in fact determine many choices that we must make.

The expression underlines another important point also. The act of faith and love by which one turns to God is not an isolated act. It has roots in prior responses to grace, and it establishes a friendship with God that is the fundamental orientation of one's life. Similarly, a mortal sin ordinarily has roots in prior acts of unfaithfulness, and it endures in a deliberately chosen life without God.

There are important differences between the way we turn to God and the way we turn from Him. A conversion or fundamental turning toward God is a creative act in which God's grace and human freedom meet. Mortal sin is a destructive act, which one can do by oneself. We are capable of bringing about our own destruction, but not our own salvation.

Turning toward God requires more explicit consideration of God than does sinning. Even in human friendships, to fall in love and to be in love involve turning one's mind and heart toward the object of one's affections. But one who betrays a friend, and remains unfaithful, may hide in bad faith; one can make oneself hardly aware of the friend being betrayed.

Human lives tend to have a basic orientation, that is, to become established in a rooted loyalty to God or to become more set in the selfishness that turns one from God. But this does not mean that those who would wish to serve God simply cannot commit mortal sins. We have many frailties. If we deliberately choose to be unfaithful in small things, we can drift toward an act of disloyalty and disobedience so radical that it brings about and reveals a very different orientation. It would be presumptuous to claim that one's life has been so steadfastly turned toward God that it would not be possible for a single act of lust or abortion or blasphemy to change the direction of one's life. For if one is prepared to do, and does, an action that is gravely evil and known to be opposed to the demanding will of God, and does this with sufficient awareness and freedom, one reveals that one is not firmly devoted to God, and expresses the spirit of one who does not love Him (cf. John 14.15).

"According to the Church's teaching, mortal sin, which is opposed to God, does not consist only in formal and direct resistance to the commandment of charity. It is equally to be found in this opposition to authentic love which is included in every deliberate transgression, in serious matter, of each of the moral laws."[16]

Venial Sin

We use the word "sin" in another sense when we speak of venial sin. For venial sin does not deprive one wholly of the life of grace and of friendship with God; it is not a conscious and free decision to do what is gravely wrong. Venial sin is a less serious offense against the law of God. It is not a turning away from God, but a shortcoming, a hesitation or misstep as it were, in one's efforts to follow after Christ.

Although venial sin is an offense less serious than mortal sin, it disposes one toward mortal sin, and is the greatest of all evils except for mortal sin.

It is clear from Scripture that not all sins are equally serious (cf. John 19.11; Ezek. 16.44; Jer. 7.26; Lam. 4.6). St. James referred to venial sin, that is, to sin that does not separate one from friendship with God: "For all of us make many mistakes" (James 3.2; cf. LG 40). Even the closest disciples of Jesus were taught by Him to ask forgiveness: "Forgive us our trespasses. . . ."

Care is needed in distinguishing venial from mortal sin. Sometimes a sin is venial because the wrong done is not so base or serious a disorder that it involves turning from the love of God. An example would be carelessness about keeping a promise to do some slight service for a friend, when such carelessness might disappoint but not really hurt. Sometimes a sin is venial because it violates a serious responsibility in only a slight degree. An example is the theft of a quite trivial item. Sometimes a sin is venial because, although the violation is of something central and is significant, still one is not acting with full awareness and willingness. No human action, however evil it might appear to be, can be a mortal sin in the strict formal sense, with all the grave consequences that that implies, unless the action is done with an awareness that it is evil and a willingness to do it despite that.

The First Three Commandments

Faith, hope, and love imply a number of specific duties. The first three commandments of the Decalogue make more explicit the duties that flow from these virtues and from the natural virtue of religion.

The first commandment obliges us to recognize only the one true

---

[16]Sacred Congregation for the Doctrine of the Faith, *Declaration on Certain Questions regarding Sexual Ethics* (December 29, 1975) n. 10 (EV 5.1736).

God as God, and to worship Him alone. We worship Him first by faith, hope, and love. An act of these virtues can be expressed in many ways, especially by participation in Christ's perfect sacrifice, renewed in the Mass. We worship Him also by praying to Him in our needs, thereby acknowledging His power and providence. By seeking to keep all His commandments we acknowledge His divine authority.

By sincere prayers of faith, hope, and love, we elicit acts of such worship. We have a duty to live in faith, hope, and love, and actually to express these commitments at certain times: early in life, when they become aware of the duty to be so related to God; often in life, to keep this disposition alive and real; in times of temptation, when these expressions of commitment are needed to guard loyalty to Him. The act of love is by far the most important. At the hour of death, as often in life, we should if possible express explicitly our love for our heavenly Father.

Sins against faith, hope, and love are violations of the first commandment. Sins against faith include apostasy, or the abandoning of faith entirely, and heresy, the deliberate denial of some revealed truth or truths that He has given us grace enough to be able to recognize.

One would sin against hope by presumption, that is, by supposing one could find salvation without God's help and without prayerfully seeking this help, or by pretending that salvation can be had without personal cooperation with His grace. Despair is a sin more directly opposed to hope. It is a deliberate refusal to trust that God will enable one to be saved.

The most bitter sin against love is hatred. Envy, or sadness at another's good fortune, and sloth, or distaste for things that lead to growth of charity because of the efforts required, also are enemies of love. Of special social importance are scandal (that is, any behavior which not only has the appearance of evil but also tends to lead others into sin) and cooperation in the sins of others.

Sins of superstition and sacrilege also are directly opposed to faithful worship of God. In superstition one seriously attributes to created persons or things powers to shape events or to foresee the future which are proper only to God. Sacrilege is a mistreatment of what is sacred, of persons or things consecrated to divine worship. Especially serious in sacrilegious reception of sacraments, approaching those sacraments which signify and demand love of God in one's heart, as the Eucharist, confirmation, orders, or matrimony, when one has committed grave sin and not repented.

The second commandment requires reverence for God's name. God's name is dishonored in especially grave ways in false oaths, or perjury, that is, when one lies after calling upon the name of God as a pledge that one will speak the truth. God's name is dishonored if one is false to one's vows, that is, if one does not fulfill promises made to God and sealed with His name. One dishonors God by cursing, that is, by calling on Him who is Savior of all to do harm to others; and especially by blasphemy, that is, by any words or behavior intended to insult or express contempt for almighty God.

The third commandment requires an expression of one's worship of God: keeping the Lord's day holy. Church law specifies for the Catholic certain fundamental duties in this matter. Attendance at Mass ought to be counted a joy and a privilege; but the Catholic has also the serious duty to attend Mass on Sundays and on certain holy days. Such days are to be kept holy also by avoiding needless labor and unnecessary commercial dealings, that is, activity of a kind that hinders the spirit of celebration and joy in the Lord that should mark such days. At times, of course, one in dispensed from these precepts on worship and rest, if some real necessity requires this. The necessity might be an urgent demand of charity. Worship is a great duty, but charity a greater one. "The sabbath was made for humankind, not humankind for the sabbath" (Mark 2.27).

Sin and Self-Love

Christian hope, as has already been noted, includes a perfectly legitimate concern for oneself. There is nothing Christian in the attitude of one who has no interest in eternal life with God.

There is a proper order of love. After love of God comes love of self. Christ commanded: "You shall love your neighbor as yourself" (Mark 12.31; cf. Luke 10:27; Rom. 13.9; Gal. 5.14; James 2.8). But the love of self that is set as the standard for love of one's neighbor is a right love of self, a love that is governed and guided by love of God. One who does not have a right love of self, a love that flows from a grateful love of God, is not able to love one's neighbor rightly. All of us should think of our own salvation, our own pursuit of the truly good, as our first responsibility. While we can help each other to build up the kingdom of God, each of us can and must do for ourselves in this pursuit much that our neighbor cannot do for us.

On the other hand, disordered self-love is the root of all sin. There can be only one center of a person's life. Everything else will revolve about that center. That center can be God, or it can be oneself. The second choice is pride, the root of sin.

Human life and society are radically affected by the kind of love that rules the hearts of men. If we love ourselves with a love that flows from and is ordered to a prior love of God, we can build a community of charity. If we love ourselves first, we foolishly build a city of discord. "And so the two cities have been fashioned by two loves. . . ."[17]

In sinning mortally, one turns not only away from God but

[17]St. Augustine, *De Civitate Dei* ("The City of God") 14.28 (ML 41.426).

towards some lesser good. This finite good becomes a substitute for the divine goodness when one takes it as the objective in which one seeks fulfillment (cf. GS 13). The replacement of God by something else is what goes wrong in serious sin. Then one is refusing the divine call to be open to every manner of good, and to pursue good in ways that enable one to draw toward complete fulfillment in God. Sin is arbitrary, self-stunting. Thus, we can see, sin is a failure to love oneself rightly.

Love and the Moral Virtues

Christian self-love, which grows out of a grateful love of God and blossoms into unselfish love of neighbor, is supported by certain indispensable virtues. The first of these is humility, one of the most distinctive of Christian virtues. Paradoxically it exalts us by leading to acknowledge our true status: we are creatures, and every good in us is God's gift and should glorify God, not our own small ego (cf. Luke 14.11). Humility does not require pretense or sham; rather, it recognizes and is grateful for God's gifts of every sort, even extraordinary talents one may happen to possess. Christ ceaselessly taught humility by words (cf. Matt. 5.3, 18.4) and by example. "Learn from Me; for I am gentle and humble in heart" (Matt. 11.29). Humility liberates one from the folly of pride.

Patience, or endurance, is equally needed. To love oneself rightly in an existence in which the entire fulfillment of one's hopes is not immediately possible, in which the cross precedes the resurrection, in which one must await the time of God's appointing, requires patience. "And let endurance have its full effect, so that you may be mature and complete, lacking in nothing" (James 1.4). Tertullian and St. Cyprian considered this virtue a great Christian innovation in a pagan world. There is no need to stress how central it is in the perfect character of Jesus. It has obvious links with humility, poverty in spirit, temperance, self-control, fortitude, and perseverance.

We cannot truly love ourselves or others if we do not have temperance or self-control. This virtue inclines us to moderate our excessive inclination to seek pleasures of the senses and to flee what is painful. Those who are temperate will seek what intelligent thought and the light of faith point out as really good, rather than be instinctively driven to conduct that mere craving for immediate satisfaction demands, behavior that can destroy their friendships and their hopes. By a false love of self catering to immediate cravings, intemperance destroys the better self one should love. "For I do not do the good I want, but the evil I do not want is what I do" (Rom. 7.19). Sins against temperance include such self-destructive ones as gluttony, drunkenness, drug abuse, lust. Such sins can destroy one's freedom. Sometimes the circumstances that lead human frailty toward such sins reduce personal responsibility for them very much.

But even the weak, sustained by God's grace (cf. Rom. 7.24), can acquire the virtues we have mentioned. Growth in virtue requires generous effort in response to grace. Mature people nourish such virtue by deliberately doing the kind of deeds that humble, patient, and temperate people do. Out of motives of faith and love, they freely do acts which are not strictly required and forgo goals not strictly forbidden. Gradually a new nature, a new life, a new spontaneous and free ease is acquired in so acting. Thus it is possible to "clothe yourselves with the new self, created according to the likeness of God" (Eph. 4.24).

Unless these virtues are fostered in one's character, one will hardly be able to live a life worthy of the calling we have received, "with all humility and gentleness, with patience, bearing with one another in love" (Eph. 4.2; cf. GS 8), a life in "purity, knowledge, patience, kindness, holiness of Spirit, genuine love" (2 Cor. 6.6), perhaps seeming to have nothing and yet "possessing everything" (2 Cor. 6.10).

Love of Neighbor

We approach the end of this chapter without seeming to have said much about love of neighbor. After all, the reader may ask, has not this discussion of love of God and love of self left out the really practical consideration, that is, love of neighbor?

Love of neighbor certainly is important, and indeed is treated in the last seven commandments of the Decalogue. Love of neighbor is in one sense the whole of Christian morality. "For the one who loves another has fulfilled the law" (Rom. 13.8; cf. Rom. 13.10; Gal. 5.4). One cannot read the New Testament without being struck by its emphasis on love of others. "The commandment we have from Him is this: those who love God must love their brothers and sisters also" (1 John 4.21).

But the discussions here and in the preceding chapters have not omitted love of neighbor. These chapters have laid the groundwork for treating it, and the next two chapters will discuss the moral significance of the basic forms of human good for self and neighbor alike.

Moreover in dealing with Christian love, and with the life based on it, the sharp distinctions sometimes made between love of God, love of self, and love of neighbor begin at a certain point to break down. In Christ, God has become our neighbor. Through Christ we become more than neighbors to God; we become His children, brothers of one another and of Christ. In this family of God, love of neighbor becomes love of a brother or sister in Christ, love of one who shares or is called to share in divine life. Therefore, love of neighbor, proper love of oneself, and love of God in Christ become one.

Charity and the Body of Christ

St. Paul's most thorough and most beautiful word on charity is in his letter responding to problems of order in the church at Corinth. Members of that church with diverse gifts and duties were contending with one another instead of cooperating. For example, some claimed that their particular gift of speaking in tongues was superior, others that their particular gift of prophecy was better.

Paul explained that just as each part of the human body has its own function, so each member of the Church has one's own role to play. No part of the body is independent. Each part needs the rest; even the noblest needs the least noble. God has designed the body to function as a harmonious whole. So it is with the Church, which is the Body of Christ. The members of the Church must not contend for themselves as if they were living by and for themselves.

Therefore, the gifts over which members of the church at Corinth were contending, gifts which will pass away, are far less important than the gifts which unify them, gifts which will last. "Now faith, hope, and love abide, these three; and the greatest of these is love" (1 Cor. 13.13).

Love vivifies the unity of the Body of Christ: "If I speak in the tongues of mortals and of angels, but have not love, I am a noisy gong or a clanging cymbal. And if I have prophetic powers, and understand all mysteries and all knowledge, and if I have all faith, so as to remove mountains, but do not have love, I am nothing" (1 Cor. 13.1-2). The gifts the Christians at Corinth were arguing about were thus reduced to their proper value on the scale of love.

Today, as then, charity, the love which should bind the Church together, is far more important than any lesser considerations which would divide us. For this love, as we have seen, is participation in divine life.

20

A Life Worthy Of Our Calling

Only by cultivating "natural goods and values" can a person come to "an authentic and full humanity" (GS 53). If human values are to be promoted and protected as they should be, we must have the "perspective of humanity redeemed by Christ" (GE 2) and those "higher principles of the Christian life" (AA 7) that we have sketched in the preceding two chapters. For "faith throws a new light on everything, manifests God's design for man's total vocation, and thus directs the mind to solutions which are fully human" (GS 11). Only in that light can we make sound judgments on all that concerns our daily life.

In this chapter we consider how, in the light of faith, Christian hope and love should heal and perfect our attitudes toward three basic human values: life, procreation (the transmission of life), and truth.

Human Life

The Church has always proclaimed the dignity of each human person. Because we are images of our Maker and are called through Christ to share in the personal life of the Trinity, each of us has a transcendent worth. In many ways the Second Vatican Council addressed a special need of our age when it stressed anew how human life must be honored and upheld, fostered and respected.

"Through his bodily composition man gathers to himself the elements of the material world. Thus they reach their crown through him, and through him raise their voice in free praise of the Creator (cf. Dan. 3.57-90 V). For this reason man is not allowed to despise his bodily life" (GS 14).

There is a "growing awareness of the exalted dignity proper to the human person, since he stands above all things, and his rights and duties are universal and inviolable," and therefore there should be made available to him "everything necessary for leading a life truly human, such as food, clothing, and shelter. . ." (GS 26). "Coming down to practical and particularly urgent consequences, this Council lays stress on reverence for man . . . taking into account first of all his life and the means necessary to living it with dignity" (GS 27).

"Furthermore, whatever is opposed to life itself, such as any type of murder, genocide, abortion, euthanasia, and willful self-destruction ... all these things and others of their like are infamies indeed. They poison human society, but they do more harm to those who do them than to those who suffer the injury. Moreover, they are a supreme dishonor to the Creator" (GS 27).

"For God, the Lord of life, has conferred on man the surpassing ministry of safeguarding life — a ministry which must be fulfilled in a manner which is worthy of man. Therefore, from the moment of its conception life must be guarded with the greatest care; abortion and infanticide are unspeakable crimes" (GS 51).

Among the actions which "deliberately conflict" with the universal principles of natural law "must first of all be counted those actions designed for the methodical extermination of an entire people, nation, or ethnic minority" (GS 79).

Finally, the Second Vatican Council, "making its own the condemnations of total war already pronounced by recent Popes," declared: "Every act of war which tends indiscriminately to the destruction of entire cities or of extensive areas along with their populations is a crime against God and man himself, and is to be condemned firmly and without hesitation" (GS 80).

Respect for Human Goods

To assist in understanding the structure of Christian concern for life and every basic human value, several points may be noted here.

First, a human value is realized and fostered only in concrete acts of love and justice. In the case of life, for example, it is not "human life" in the abstract we are speaking about, but the life and flourishing of people, of individual persons. Life can be loved and furthered in an endless variety of ways; no concrete act or set of acts could exhaustively realize any such basic value. Yet life is the same value loved and realized in and for each, however varied the acts and persons involved. To realize, respect, and foster human life, or any other form of goodness, is to glorify the Creator of all persons and to honor His transcendent and creative goodness.

Thus all of us ought to realize this value of life both in our own person and in the person of others. We must not despise our own bodily life, and we must not despise bodily life in others. We have a solemn duty to preserve our own life by our own labor, and we have a solemn duty to feed the hungry and to help a neighbor in distress (cf. Matt. 25.41-46; Luke 10.30-37). We are not to commit suicide, and we are not to murder; both types of acts are "opposed to life itself" (GS 27). The call to love God through active concern for the opportunities for good which He has created goes beyond justice and even beyond natural love of neighbor. In the way of Christ, one is to love one's neighbor as one loves oneself. The flourishing life of each and every person manifests God's glory.

The call of the basic values for realization in one's action is, then, fundamentally positive. To be a mature Christian requires more than not doing certain things. It is not enough simply to restrict one's activity, to do no murders, to tell no lies, and so on. Rather, we are called to show personal and positive love by causing the basic values to flourish concretely in our own lives and in the lives of others.

There is, of course, more than one basic value. It is not possible for each of us to be always and everywhere actively engaged in realizing each one of them, and certainly we are not bound to try to do so. What is expected of us is that we make a realistic commitment to a harmonious set of purposes, which may be more or less specialized. We Christians must remain open to all of the basic human goods, but we may in our individual lives be particularly dedicated to a specific one. Thus some will dedicate themselves, temporarily or permanently, especially to the service of life, perhaps as doctors or nurses, or ambulance drivers, or hospital employees, or firemen, or, less directly, as farmers, and so on. But all of us are obliged to reverence life through care for the safety of others and through works of mercy. Moreover, each of us is strictly bound never to choose directly against life.

The teaching of the Second Vatican Council on actions "opposed to life itself" (GS 27) is in the unwavering Christian tradition. It insists that there are certain kinds of acts that one who loves God must never do. The Christian must never do evil that good may come of it (cf. Rom. 3.8); particularly he must not do the direct evil of attacking directly a basic human value, such as human life, for any motive whatever, or in any circumstances. The council rejects the approach of weighing, balancing, or attempting to calculate the expected consequences in such cases. It leaves no room for the suggestion that there might be situations and circumstances that could justify a free and deliberate act of murder, genocide, abortion, or suicide. Such acts directly attack a basic form of human goodness, and they are evil and wrongful, "infamies indeed" (GS 27).

Acts "Opposed to Life Itself"

There are many ways in which we can fail to fulfill our responsibility to respect and pursue a basic value. Often it is difficult to see clearly in a particular case the measure of concern that should be shown. For example, one may be in doubt about the extent of social reform required to provide each person with the resources needed to make life flourish as it should. At the same time, however, there are some types of action that are so directly opposed to a basic value that they are certainly incompatible with love of God and neighbor.

In the case of war, for example, the Church does not ask whether many lives might in the end be saved by the killing of such a large number of civilians that the enemy would quickly surrender. Rather, the Church affirms that "every act of war which tends indiscriminately to the destruction of entire cities or of extensive areas along with their populations is a crime against God and man himself. . ." (GS 80).

On the other hand, the Church does not consider that every act which causes or might cause death is opposed to life itself. "You shall not kill": the language and context of the fifth commandment (Exod. 20.13; Matt. 5.21; 19.18; Mark 10.19; Luke 18.20; Rom. 13.9), and its interpretation by Israel and the Church, show that the general formulation can be made more precise: "Do not kill the innocent and those in the right" (Exod. 23.7; cf. Jer. 7.6; 22.3).

Thus, though war is undoubtedly as great human tragedy, the Church does not condemn every act of war as evil. Since war "has not been rooted out of human affairs" and there is at this time no "competent and sufficiently powerful authority at the international level," when "every means of peaceful settlement has been exhausted" governments "cannot be denied the right to legitimate defense" through "military action for the just defense of the people" (GS 79; cf. Heb. 11.33-34).

Those who are attacked unjustly have a right to resist. Those responsible for defending justice in a community may have a duty to defend the helpless when they are assailed; under certain conditions they might even be called upon to perform defensive actions that result in the death of the assailants. Indeed, in times when there has seemed to be no other way of preventing the unjust violence of a criminal, the Church has not condemned the execution of a criminal according to law by properly constituted authority.[1]

But this does not mean that public authorities, or anyone else, can rightly do anything and everything, without exception, to prevent the triumph of an unjust attack. Indiscriminate destruction of whole populations is always wrong, wrong even if a nation could defend its freedom in no other way. If an unjust attack could be prevented only by killing innocent hostages, one would still be obliged to refrain from such killing. While making every morally permissible effort to prevent the evils which flow from the triumph of the unjust, we must leave the outcome to God's providence rather than directly attack innocent life to attain our ends.

---

[1]Cf. Pope Innocent III, *Profession of Faith Prescribed for the Waldensians* (December 18, 1208) (DS 795); Pope Pius XI, *Casti Connubii* (December 31, 1930) (DS 3720, 3722). Without declaring capital punishment intrinsically wrong, the bishops of the United States have urged the end of capital punishment; cf. United States Bishops, *Statement on Capital Punishment* (November 1980).

Providence and Human Choices

The foreseeable consequences of a morally upright decision may at times seem harsh. The results of a decision not to kill the innocent will often seem to many to be worse, sometimes much worse, than the death of the innocent. Many more persons may seem certain to die, or perhaps to suffer spiritual harm.

Here the Christian faith helps our understanding. It reminds us that certain kinds of acts "do more harm to those who do them than to those who suffer the injury" (GS 27). For ultimately nothing matters so much as remaining in friendship with God. All the perceptible evils and suffering in a situation are outweighed by the moral evil of dishonoring God's goodness by choosing against the basic values of His creation. It is basic in Christian morality that the deliberate doing of an immoral act, even a single venial sin, is a worse evil, because it is a far graver kind of evil, than the occurrence of any physical evils whatever.[2]

Our faith also reminds us of the limits of our vision. We are unable to see all the good or evil which may result from our choices. We know that God in His providence brings good out of evil, but we do not know how. We can foresee only a tiny fraction of the consequences of any action, and we can hardly see at all the part that tiny fraction plays in the total scheme of things.

Faith further reminds us that we are not morally responsible for harm and suffering which we could have averted only by doing evil. If a person suffers a martyrdom which could have been avoided only by killing the innocent or by apostatizing from the truth, that is person not to blame either for the death or for the harm which might come to the family or others as a result, even if these consequences were foreseeable. Heroic people like St. Thomas More have known this well, for such are the implications of the clear-sighted Christian recognition of the mystery of God's good will and providence. Such also are the implications of the Christian hope for a friendship with God, a hope which will begin by striving for and clinging to good in this world but which is destined for fulfillment in eternal life in the home of God our Father.

Nevertheless, moral problems can often be extremely complex. What Christian faith demands is steadfast faithfulness to certain basic principles. We must care about doing good; we must do no evil whatever, not even to achieve noble objectives or to avoid terrible losses.

Refusing to Do Evil

Men of great goodness instinctively, not without the light of the Holy Spirit, find the solution to deep moral problems in ways that do

---

[2]For one of the most famous expressions of this truth, see John Henry Cardinal Newman's *Apologia pro Vita Sua*, Part VII.

not involve the doing of evil. The Church in its pastoral teaching expresses the principle for such solutions in terms of the distinction to be made between the direct and the indirect consequences of an act. An understanding of this distinction, which is referred to in the principle of double effect, can help one avoid moral confusion and the despairing conclusion that in some situations it is impossible to avoid doing evil.

The case of martyrs as discussed above can be illuminating here. There is something martyrs directly do, what they directly achieve or intend to achieve. What they choose to do is to proclaim the truth and to remain loyal to their God. These are the direct consequences of their choices. On the other hand, there is the death of the martyrs, and there may be other quite foreseeable effects, perhaps death or ruin for others, as a result of the choices they make. But it is not the martyrs' own deeds that directly cause these results. They do not desire or intend the evil effects either in themselves or for the sake of achieving anything else. They do not want the evil effects, though they may know they will follow if they act faithfully.

Thus, martyrs know that they will die; but they are not suicides. They know perhaps that others will die whom they could save by denying the faith; but they are not murderers. Their decision to remain steadfast has for them and perhaps for others a death-dealing effect; but their choice is clearly not a choice "opposed to life itself."

The distinction between direct and indirect consequences makes it clear that, while there are difficult situations in which any choice a person makes will have painful consequences, there are no situations of ultimate moral dilemma, in which every possible choice a person can make is immoral. Christ does not command the impossible.

The actions of persons in military service may also be seen better in the light of the distinction between direct and indirect effects. A soldier can be doing an upright deed when, acting in the defense of his country, the soldier brings about the death of others. How is this so? On the one hand, there are the direct consequences of the behavior of conscientious soldiers; they are doing deeds reasonably aimed at thrusting back an unjust attack, and so defending the lives and liberty of their fellow citizens. In so doing, they "can and should regard themselves as agents of security and freedom on behalf of their people" (GS 79; cf. Heb. 11.33-34).

On the other hand, their decision to uphold justice will often and foreseeably result in the death, not only of those actively taking part in the unjust assault, but also of persons neither engaged in nor assisting that attack. Such persons are innocent in the sense of the divine commandment; they should not be slain. A direct attack on the lives of such persons, even if one could dishearten the enemy and hasten victory by such action, would be immoral. Still, a military decision to do an act aimed at resisting an unjust attack would not of itself be an act aimed against life, even if it is foreseen that some who are innocent may die as a result of that defensive action.

In a complex world the support of justice and other essential values will at times have bad side-effects. To maintain purity of heart one must indeed care about those unwanted bad effects, and seek to create a world order in which they do not occur. But even in a sinful world one is able to act without doing evil oneself.

Suicide and Euthanasia

Those who are very ill, suffering much, or severely disabled may be tempted to feel that their lives are useless, and others too may count their lives worthless. But to God every human life is most precious and very dear, "in every condition, whole or disabled, rich or poor."[3] Even severe trials can be sources of grace and salvation for those who bear them and for others, especially when the Christian community shows full respect to suffering people, and gives them due support.[4]

Not all those who end their own lives do so deliberately. Pain and anxiety can take away freedom and sinfulness from behavior at times, and compassionate attention should be given to those tempted to suicide, and to the families of those who have taken their own lives. Still, objectively it is very wrong for those who are sick or debilitated to kill themselves, and it is wrong for others to help them do so ("mercy killing," or euthanasia). It is always wrong to choose to kill an innocent person. Neither does it make such difference what means one chooses to bring about the death. One can kill by a positive act, as by giving an overdose of drugs. One can kill also by omitting acts that one has a duty to do. This would be the case when one deliberately starves oneself to death (even if there is a good motive, such as seeking to call attention to some noble cause); it would be the case also if one withheld food and water from a baby whose parents reject him or her because of some birth defect.

While we may never take our lives or those of others to escape pain or distress, reverence for life does not demand that we do everything possible to sustain bodily life. We do have a duty to use ordinary means to guard our life and health. But one does not need to use extraordinary means for this: one is not obliged to take medical steps that are excessively expensive, painful, or burdensome. Thus, if one could save one's life only by surgery that could well now end one's life, there would be no obligation to undergo that immediate risk. And one is not required to impoverish one's family by recourse to very expen-

[3]Pope John Paul II, Post-Synodal Apostolic Exhortation, *Christifideles Laici* (AAS 81 [1989] 463) n. 38.

[4]Pope John Paul II, Apostolic Letter, *Salvifici Doloris* (February 11, 1984) (EV 10.572-667).

sive treatments, or empty the last months of life by leaving loved ones for recourse to a more healthy climate.[5]

Abortion

Christ's law concerning attacks on human life has been proclaimed most fully by the Church on the subject of abortion.[6] The victims of abortion are clearly innocent and are particularly helpless.

Though the reasons that prompt people to kill the unborn are not always negligible, the insufficiency of the reasons is usually clear. A desire to escape burdens, for example, or to maintain a higher standard of living, is understandable, but it clearly is not reasonable to kill for that. No one who wishes to act according to the mind of God could fail to discern the contempt for a basic human value, the lack of love of neighbor, and the glaring lack of justice that are involved here.

It sometimes happens that two lives seems to be at stake, the life of a mother and the life of her unborn child. How is one to act in such situations? Pope Pius XII treated this question in some detail:

"Any direct attempt on an innocent human life as a means to an end — in this case to the end of saving another human life — is unlawful. Any direct deliberate attack on innocent human life, in whatsoever condition it is found from the very first moment of its existence, is wrong. This principle holds good both for the life of the child and for that of the mother. Never and in no case has the Church taught that the life of the child must be preferred to that of the mother. . . . No, neither the life of the mother nor that of the child can be subjected to an act of direct suppression. In the one case as in the other, there can be but one obligation: to make every effort to save the lives of both. . . .

"Deliberately, we have always used the expression '*direct* attempt on the life of the innocent person,' '*direct* killing'; because if, for example, the saving of the life of the mother-to-be, independently of her pregnant condition, should have as an accessory consequence, in no way desired or intended, but inevitable, the death of the fetus, such an act could no longer be called a *direct* attempt on an innocent life. Under these conditions the operation can be lawful, like other similar medical interventions, granted always that another good of high worth is concerned, such as life, and that it is not possible to postpone the operation until after the birth of the child, nor to have recourse to other efficacious remedies."[7] Such an operation, then, can be a morally

---

[5]Congregation for the Doctrine of the Faith, *Declaration on Euthanasia* (May 5, 1980) (EV 7.346-373).

[6]Cf. e.g., Sacred Congregation for the Doctrine of Faith, *Declaration on Abortion* (November 18, 1974) (EV 5.662-688). The tradition of the Church is summarized in nn. 6 and 7. Cf. also *Declaration on Euthanasia* (May 5, 1980) (EV 7.346-373).

[7]Pope Pius XII, *Address* to the Family Associations (November 26, 1951).

good act. It is aimed entirely at saving life, and is in no way directed against innocent life. The death of the unborn is neither desired nor intended.

Here, as in the military and police situations referred to above, the lines are finely drawn. But they are drawn precisely where the Christian conscience has always drawn them, and in a way that rings true for all who have reverence for every kind of basic value. They are not determined by a weighing and calculating of expected consequences; such weighing and calculating in an effort to "justify" a direct attack on human life for a "sufficient" reason can only be a cloak for arbitrariness. Clearly it is not enough to have good intentions. What is needed is a resolute will to honor God by respecting the basic forms of human goodness whenever we are confronted with a direct choice to do so or not. Here Christian faith, hope, and love are in tension with the immediate interests of self or of some set of persons arbitrarily defined by peering into an imagined future. Here indeed the gate through which we must enter after Christ seems narrow, and rough His road (cf. Matt. 7.13-14).

Even though the moral judgments which must be made are not always easy, it is possible to reach correct conclusions by keeping in mind the fundamental perspective of our hope in Christ: "Do not fear those who kill the body but cannot kill the soul; rather fear him who can destroy both soul and body in hell" (Matt. 10.28). Help in these difficult areas can be found in various guidelines presented by authentic teachers in the Church.[8]

Transmission of Life

"When a woman is in labor, she has pain. . . . But when her child is born, she no longer remembers the anguish, because of the joy of having brought a human being into the world" (John 16.21).

Parents rightly rejoice when a child is born as a fruit of their love. The procreative good is one of the basic human values. To have children and help them grow to a rich maturity is one of the strongest motivating forces. From end to end the Bible celebrates full realization of this good in positive images of courtship, betrothal, weddings, conjugal love, sexual intercourse, procreation, childbirth, and the family life in which children grow to full maturity.

In the following chapter we discuss the family as a community, and in a later chapter we discuss the sacrament of matrimony. Here, then, we shall do no more than sketch the shape and demands of that rich human value to which Christian marriage is a full response.

[8]Cf., e.g., *Ethical and Religious Directives for Catholic Health Facilities*, approved November 16, 1971, by the United States National Conference to Catholic Bishops as the national code, subject to the approval of the bishop for use in the diocese.

The Importance of Sex

The Church has always considered sex a precious and sacred reality. For that very reason it has condemned the abuse and degradation of sex. Faithful to Scripture,[9] the Church insists that love of God is incompatible with every form of fornication, sexual promiscuity and uncleanness, sensuality and licentiousness, lustful desires, incest, homosexual acts, and other sexual perversions. Christ warns solemnly that fidelity to God can be broken even by a lustful look (cf. Matt. 5.28).

Clearly sex is important. But how can it be so important? How can sexual desire, excitement, and climax, even when there are no further or lasting consequences, have such moral significance? One can understand that quantitative excess could amount to a morally damaging obsession or imbalance. But the concern for chastity expressed in many passages of the New Testament is far deeper than that.

At the time the New Testament was written, its teaching regarding sexual morality must have been striking indeed. Certainly it is strikingly at variance with many attitudes toward sex today.

Sex in Marriage

For a first answer to the question on the importance of sex we can look to the significance of sexual intercourse for the love of man and wife.

"It is not good that the man should be alone" (Gen. 2.18). When some Pharisees asked Christ whether a man might divorce his wife for any reason whatever, Christ replied: "Have you not read that the One who made them from the beginning 'made them male and female,' and said, 'For this reason a man shall leave his father and mother and be joined to his wife, and the two shall become one flesh'? So they are no longer two, but one flesh. Therefore what God has joined together, let no one separate" (Matt. 19.4-6; cf. Mark 10.7-9). St. Paul quotes the same passage of Genesis after stating: "Husbands should love their wives as they do their own bodies. He who loves his wife loves himself" (Eph. 5.28).

In this perspective, marriage calls for a total giving of oneself to one's partner, in body as in other ways. Sexual intercourse represents and expresses the mutual gift of self. Thus sexual activity is deformed if separated from this mutual self-giving.

Sexual intercourse is important, then, because through it conjugal love "is uniquely expressed and perfected" (GS 49). For, "expressed

---

9See Matt. 15.19; Mark 7.21; Rom. 1.24,26-27; 13.13; 1 Cor. 5.1; 6.13, 16, 18; 7.2; 10.8; 2 Cor. 12.21; Gal. 5.19; Eph. 5.3, 5; Col. 3.5; 1 Thess. 4.3-4; 1 Tim. 1.10; Heb. 13.4; 1 Peter 4.3; Jude 4.

in a manner which is truly human, the actions within marriage by which the couple are united intimately and chastely, signify and promote that mutual self-giving by which spouses enrich each other with a joyful and thankful will" (GS 49). Through this "mutual gift of themselves, which is properly theirs and exclusive to them alone," husband and wife "develop that union of two persons in which they perfect one another. . . ."[10]

Hence, a person's capacity for sexual intercourse fits him or her in a quite special way for that form of companionship which "produces the primary form of interpersonal communion" (GS 12). This potentially great significance provides a first answer to the question why virtuous sexual conduct is so important in the way of Christ.

Sex and Procreation

Why, however, is sexual intercourse so special as an expression of mutual self-giving and communion between man and wife? Why, even within marriage, is it something more than a pleasurable release of tension or an agreeable mutual diversion like dining out or dancing? Why indeed is sexual intercourse a good which may not be enjoyed with many partners? Why may it not be enjoyed freely before marriage? Why must it be engaged in only within marriage?

The answer to all these questions — and the fundamental reason for the human and moral significance of sex — is based on the fact that sexual intercourse naturally tends to transmit human life. This fact need not be uppermost in the minds of those who join in sexual union or who exchange the promises of marriage. It need be no more present to their awareness than it is in those most delicate evocations of fruitfulness at the climax of the Song of Songs (cf. Song 7.11-13).

But even when it is most playful and most expressive of love, sexual intercourse is suited to transmit human life. How otherwise could sexuality have its profound human significance? Those who engage in sexual intercourse thereby bring themselves, whether it occurs to them or not, within the range of a basic human good, the procreative good.

Knowing the biological fact, a couple can choose to foster the value, by trying or hoping to have a child. Or they can simply proceed without regard for the possible outcome, neither acting against nor deliberately seeking the procreative good. Another possibility is that they can choose against the procreative good as it is at stake in their action, and so engage in sexual intercourse in such a way that it is not, as a human action, open to the transmission of life. Sexual activity thus cannot fail to be morally significant, because for anyone who

10Pope Paul VI, Encyclical, *Humanae Vitae* (July 25, 1968) n. 8 (EV 3.594).

knows it biological potential it cannot fail to express, either immediately or mediately, an attitude of respect or disrespect toward a basic human good.

Procreation in Marriage

To join fully with another person in passing on to children both life and fullness of life is a basic form of human self-realization. Indeed, this is the value which primarily makes sense of that exclusive and lifelong form of association which we call marriage.

"By their very nature, both the institution of matrimony itself and conjugal love are ordained for the procreation and education of children, and find in them their ultimate crown" (GS 48).

"Marriage and conjugal love are by their nature ordained toward the begetting and educating of children. Children are really the supreme gift of marriage and contribute very substantially to the well-being of their parents. The God Himself who said, 'It is not good for man to be alone' (Gen. 2.18), and 'who made man from the beginning male and female' (Matt. 19.4), wishing to share with man a certain participation in His own creative work, blessed male and female, saying: 'Increase and multiply' (Gen. 1.28). Hence, while not making the other purposes of matrimony of less account, the true practice of conjugal love, and the whole meaning of family life which results from it, have this aim: that the couple be ready with stout hearts to cooperate with the love of the Creator and the Savior, who through them will enlarge and enrich His own family day by day. Spouses should regard as their proper mission the task of transmitting human life and educating those to whom it has been transmitted" (GS 50).

Christian marriage is the expression of a richly developed care and concern both for the wonderful dignity of human love and for the special cooperation of human beings with God the Creator in the transmission of human life.

The double aspect of marriage, and of sexual intercourse within marriage, is expressed in a sentence of Pope Paul VI which sums up the whole Christian tradition and above all the teaching of the Second Vatican Council: "Husband and wife, through that mutual gift of themselves which is properly theirs and exclusive to them alone, develop that union of two persons in which they perfect one another, in order to cooperate with God in the generation and education of new lives."[11] Friendship is a basic value in all human relations; the special forms and requirements of conjugal friendship derive from the demands of the value of procreation, demands to which marriage and marital sexual acts are a fully human response.

---

[11]Encyclical, *Humanae Vitae* (July 2, 1968) n. 8 (EV 3.594).

A child is a precious gift. But even children are not to be sought by means that fall short of what love requires. If a couple's hope for a child is not fulfilled, they may of course seek medical advice and treatment to overcome the conditions that prevent conception. But children should be brought into this world through acts of love between the parents. No one should seek to bring about pregnancy by any method, such as artificial insemination or *in vitro* fertilization, which substitutes some sort of technology for the marital act, or alters that act's nature as a mutual gift of complete sexual communion open to new life.[12]

Sins Against Marital Values

From its first preaching of the Gospel to the present day the Church has drawn from Christ's insistent teaching practical conclusions that flow from our duty to reverence the goods associated with sex. These same conclusions could also be reached by truly conscientious reflection on the relations between basic values and the biological and psychological facts of sex.

Often particular human acts are essentially related to some basic human value. The writing of history, for example, is closely related to the value of truth. This is why it is wrong to write history without care as to its truth. For writing history brings one inescapably within the range of the value of truth, and in disregard of truth there is a form of attack on that basic value. In a similar way, the practical conclusions that Christian morality draws concerning sex flow from the fact that every sexual act inescapably brings a person within the range of at least two basic human values, those of friendship and procreation.

The ties between sex and the values of friendship and procreation are so close that any sexual act will be objectively wrong if it is performed outside that friendship adapted to procreation, that is to say, if it is performed outside marriage. Similarly wrong will be any sexual act performed in such a way that one is equivalently separating it from the good of procreation or the good of friendship between man and wife.

The Church has constantly taught that specific kinds of sexual activities which obviously involve a departure from either or both of these values at stake in human sexuality are forbidden by God. This is so not only because such acts are forbidden by name in Scripture. They are wrong because they amount to attacks on basic human values persistently upheld by Scripture, and are opposed to principles which we can discern even without revelation. Such acts as masturbation, fornication, and adultery, homosexual acts, and other like sexual vices,

12Congregation for the Doctrine of the Faith, Instruction, *Donum Vitae* (February 22, 1987) (EV10.1150-1253).

have throughout the centuries been condemned by the ordinary teaching of the Church and by formal judgments of the magisterium.[13]

Thus the Church, basing her teaching on Scripture, has constantly taught that homosexual acts are objectively always gravely wrong.[14] A homosexual orientation or tendency, however, is to be distinguished from homosexual activity. Such an orientation is not in itself a moral fault. It is, however, a reality which interferes with the complete human fulfillment of those who experience it. Those who have a homosexual orientation have as much personal dignity as others do. They are not to be mistreated or subjected to discrimination on that account. Homosexuals have a duty to maintain self-possession and to abstain from objectively wrong behavior, as all who suffer inclinations to wrong conduct must. But in their efforts they deserve pastoral care and the support of the Christian community.[15]

Clearly, human frailty is such that we can fall into these sins without clear realization of their malice and without full freedom. Acts of masturbation, for example, especially in the case of the young, are at times engaged in with little understanding of the malice and without the freedom necessary for full moral responsibility. Similarly limited may be the vision and freedom of a person with a psychosexual orientation toward homosexuality as a result of causes for which one was not fully responsible. For these reasons it is extremely difficult to assess the personal guilt involved in some disordered sexual acts.[16] Nonetheless, these acts are such evident departures from respect for basic human values that the Church has, as we have noted, clearly and persistently taught that the performance of such acts deliberately and freely is a mortal sin, a sin which excludes one from the kingdom of God.

Even the deliberate intention to perform such acts is seriously wrong (cf. Matt. 5.28). Clearly, not all thoughts about sex are wrong, for sex is good and can be considered and studied in many excellent ways. But the deliberate intention to commit sexual sins, or a deliberate will to delight in them in the imagination, is sinful, just as a serious intent to perform or approve of any gravely wrong act would be. Other sexual fantasizing, when it is deliberate, may be sinful for

---

[13]Cf., e.g., Pope St. Leo IX, *Letter* to Peter Damian (1054) (DS 687-688); Pope Innocent IV, *Letter* to the Bishop of Tusculum (March 6, 1254) (DS 835); Council of Vienne, Session 3, May 6, 1312, Constitution, *Ad Nostrum Qui* (DS 897); Pope Pius II, *Letter* (November 14, 1459) (DS 1367); Decrees of the Holy Office (September 24, 1665; March 2, 1679; July 24, 1929) (DS 2044-2045; 2148-2150; 3684).

[14]Congregation for the Doctrine of the Faith, Instruction, *Persona Humana*, n. 8.

[15]Congregation for the Doctrine of the Faith, Letter, *On the Pastoral Care of Homosexual Persons* (October 1, 1986), n. 7 (EV 10.902-948).

[16]Cf. *Principles to Guide Confessors in Questions of Homosexuality* (1973) approved by the Bishops' Committee on Pastoral Research and Practices, United States National Conference of Catholic Bishops.

another reason: to the extent that it tends to stir up the passions un-reasonably and becomes an occasion of sin.

Modesty

Modesty is an important safeguard to chastity. Forms of dress, dancing, conversation, entertainment, and other external things can have a strong influence in shaping one's attitude and behavior in sexual matters. Christian modesty inclines one to govern his conduct in all these areas in an intelligent way, properly responsive to one's Christian vocation.

Specific standards of modesty will vary. In matters of dress, for example, that which is suitable for the beach is not suitable for the office. A style of clothing that would in one culture be considered scandalous and lust-provoking might in another culture be entirely appropriate. But this does not mean that one may rightly conform to any standards of modesty accepted in one's own culture. For the Christian lives in a world that is often hostile to the spirit of Christ. Fashions and amusements that notable numbers in a society find desirable and pursue are often deliberately calculated to promote attitudes and conduct that the Christian must reject (cf. Eph. 5.3-20).

Christian chastity and modesty are by no means impossible to achieve even in an age and atmosphere of great sexual laxity. Growth in these virtues, which will be assisted by a spirit of prayer, faithful reception of the sacraments, and devotion to the Blessed Virgin Mary, leads not to prudery and narrowness, but to joy and peace. Chastity and modesty establish conditions that make possible enduring and un-selfish love.[17]

Contraceptive Birth Control

Marriage is to be a fully human and thus Christian response to the call to foster a special kind of friendship, one open to the responsible transmission of life. Since friendship and life come into question in every sexual act, there should be a fully human response to them, not only in marriage as an institution and in each marriage as a whole, but also in each marital act of sexual intercourse.

As we have already seen, the way of Christ always and everywhere demands respect for the basic forms of goodness in each and every one of our actions. A general orientation in favor of these values is not enough. When these values come directly into question, Christian faith and hope make it clear to us that it is wrong to attack a basic good for the sake of some other good or goods. At all times,

---

[17]Cf. Pope Pius XII, Encyclical, *Sacra Virginitas* (March 25, 1954); Pope Paul VI, *Address* during General Audience (September 13, 1972).

then, implicitly in Scripture and explicitly since the early patristic age, it has been Christian doctrine that "preserving the full sense of mutual self-giving and of human procreation" (GS 51) is demanded in each and every act of sexual intercourse within marriage.

As Pope Pius XI put it: "Each and every marriage act which in its exercise is deprived by human interference of its natural power to procreate life is an offense against the law of God and of nature."[18] As Pope Pius XII put it: "Any attempt on the part of the husband and wife to deprive their marital act of its inherent force or to impede the procreation of a new life, either in the performance of the act itself or in the course of the development of its natural consequences, is immoral."[19] And Pope Paul VI: "Every act that intends to impede procreation must be repudiated, whether that act is intended as an end to be attained or as a means to be used, and whether it is done in anticipation of marital intercourse, or during it, or while it is having its natural consequence."[20]

And Pope John Paul II: "The Church is certainly aware of the many complex problems which couples in many countries face today in their task of transmitting life in a responsible way; she also recognizes the serious problem of population growth in the form it has taken in many parts of the world and its moral implications. However, she holds that consideration in depth of all the aspects of these problems offers a new and stronger confirmation of the importance of the authentic teaching of the Church reproposed in the Second Vatican Council and in the encyclical *Humanae Vitae*."[21]

The Second Vatican Council, following in this all Christian tradition, instructed: "Sons and daughters of the Church . . . may not undertake methods of regulating procreation which are found blameworthy by the teaching authority of the Church in its unfolding of the divine law" (GS 51).

Excluded from Christian behavior, then, will be all acts that are performed with the purpose of directly preventing conception. Similarly excluded will be all forms of direct sterilization for this purpose.[22]

Responsible Family Limitation

Natural family planning is very different from contraception. Couples who use natural family planning do not thereby act against

---

18Encyclical, *Casti Connubii* (December 31, 1930) (DS 3717).

19*Address* to a meeting of the Italian Society of Midwives (October 29, 1951).

20Encyclical, *Humanae Vitae* (July 25, 1968) n. 14 (EV 3.600).

21Apostolic Exhortation, *Familiaris Consortio* (November 22, 1981) n. 31 (EV 7.1617).

22Cf. e.g., Pope Pius XI, Encyclical, *Casti Connubii* (December 31, 1930) (DS 3722-3723); Pope Pius VI, Encyclical, *Humanae Vitae* (July 25, 1968) n. 14 (EV 3.600). Cf. also Sacred Congregation for the Doctrine of the Faith. Response to questions of the Bishops' Conference of North America on sterilization in Catholic hospitals (March 13, 1975) (EV 5.1199-1202).

the procreative good. They do not judge it appropriate to count the sacred act of marital love as something trivial, which one may casually separate from the great goods of love and new life, toward which sexual activity is ordered by God.

Providentially, more effective forms of natural family planning have been learned in recent years, when social and economic pressures to regulate births have become greater. The Church "notes with satisfaction the results achieved by scientific research aimed at a more precise knowledge of the rhythms of women's fertility."[23]

Those who use natural family planning do not emerge in an act that is of its nature life-giving and then engage in other acts to repress the possible beginnings of life. Rather they treat each other and marital activity with full respect. Understanding well their own fertility, they know when conception is likely to result from intercourse and when it is not. With self-possession and responsible love for all the goods that sexual activity is related to, they make their free choices in the light of this knowledge.

For while a child is a great blessing, it is sometimes very important for parents to give careful thought to the size of their families. Husband and wife "will thoughtfully take into account both their own welfare and that of their children, those already born and those which may be foreseen. For this accounting they will reckon with both the material and the spiritual conditions of the times as well as of their state of life. Finally, they will consult the interests of the family group, of temporal society, and of the Church herself. The married partners themselves should make this judgment, in the sight of God" (GS 50).

Provided it is not the expression of a wrong attitude toward the good of procreation, the practice of periodic abstinence to regulate human birth not only is completely right and reasonable, but also can have a real value of its own. Such natural family planning can avoid procreation which would be irresponsible. Moreover, it can give the relationship of man and wife a more humanly loving character, foster their consideration for one another, and help them to avoid excessive self-love which would profane their love for each other (cf. GS 47).

A sound marriage requires in each of the partners a strong possession of marital chastity. There are times when love demands restraint even when passions are insistent. Mature married love requires the ability to forgo intercourse willingly when the good of the partner, or some other important consideration, demands this. A society in which self-discipline in marriage is replaced by technological control of

[23]Pope John Paul II, Apostolic Exhortation, *Familiaris Consortio* (November 22, 1981) n. 35 (EV 7.1636).

reproduction will be one in which the humanly disciplined and chaste attitudes toward sex are generally undermined.

The ecclesial community has the duty to help couples escape the many moral and physical evils associated with contraception by making accessible knowledge about natural family planning by "offering practical help to those who wish to live out their parenthood in a truly responsible way."[24] Those who have experienced the human goodness and the personal fruits of self-possession found in natural family planning are called to be witnesses to others: "To them the Lord entrusts the task of making visible to people the holiness and sweetness of the law which unites the mutual love of husband and wife with their cooperation with the love of God, the Author of human life."[25]

Truth

Jesus Christ came into this world "to testify to the truth" (John 18.37). His revelation of "the deepest truth about God and the salvation of man" (DV 2) in an aspect of God's invitation to man to enter into a fellowship so complete that it amounts to sharing in the divine nature.

Understanding the truth and living in contact with reality are basic aspects of the full human freedom which Christ came to restore to us. Indeed, understanding is possible at all only because the created person "shares in the light of the divine mind" (GS 15). And the ultimate value of intelligence is that, through "wisdom's gentle attraction of the human mind to a quest and a love for what is true and good, man passes through visible realities to those which are unseen" (GS 15) and so comes to understand the truth about truth, reality, and oneself.

Precisely because this search for truth is central to human dignity, and because an authentic grasp and personal acceptance of truth, especially the truth about God, are so precious, human persons have a right to religious freedom.

The Second Vatican Council declared that the right to religious freedom has its foundation in the very dignity of the human person. "It is in accordance with their dignity as persons — that is, beings endowed with reason and free will and therefore privileged to bear personal responsibility — that all men should be at once impelled by nature and also bound by a moral obligation to seek the truth, especially religious truth" (DH 2).

[24]Pope John Paul II, Apostolic Exhortation, *Familiaris Consortio* (November 22, 1981) n. 35 (EV 7.1636).
[25]Pope Paul VI, Encyclical, *Humanae Vitae* (July 25, 1968), n. 25 (EV 3.611); this is quoted by Pope John Paul II in *Familiaris Consortio* (November 22, 1981) n. 35 (EV 7.1637).

People have a right to religious freedom because they have a serious duty to pursue religious truth in a personal, human way, and freedom is the indispensable condition for such a pursuit (cf. DH 1-2).

Rights and Duties Connected

Throughout the moral teachings of the Church, "natural rights are joined together, in the very person who is their subject, with an equal number of duties. ... Therefore, to cite some examples, with the right to life there is the duty to preserve one's life; with the right to a decent standard of living there is the duty to live in a becoming fashion; with the right to be free to seek out the truth there is the duty to devote oneself to an ever-deeper and wider pursuit of it."[26] And this does not exhaust the demands of a basic natural good, such as attaining truth.

For instance, besides the right to immunity from unreasonable interference in pursuing, expressing, and propagating what one considers to be true (cf. DH 2; GS 59, 60, 62), one enjoys the right to be given appropriate information (cf. IM 5, 12; GS 26, 59).[27] And since information is useless unless one is ready to receive it, there is a right to education: "Since every human being of whatever race, condition, and age is endowed with the dignity of a person, he or she has an inalienable right to an education corresponding to his or her proper destiny and suited to his or her talents, sex, cultural background and ancestral heritage" (GE 1; cf. GS 26, 60).

Learning truth, even religious truth, requires effort and personal involvement. Modern scientific culture serves the value of truth in a variety of ways. It stresses "scientific study and strict fidelity to truth in scientific research, the necessity of working together with others in technical groups, a sense of international solidarity. . ." (GS 57); these are so evidently "values of intellect, will, conscience, and fraternity, . . . rooted in God the Creator" (GS 61), that they can "provide some preparation for the acceptance of the message of the Gospel" (GS 57). Christians, therefore, in whom the seed of the Word has already taken root, ought to excel in pursuing and respecting such values.

Christians "need that undeviating honesty which can attract all men to the love of truth and goodness, and finally to the Church and to Christ" (AA 13). Without interior honesty, even the most brilliant intellectual life is inwardly corrupted by hypocrisy such as that which the Lord vehemently condemned (cf. Matt. 23.27-28; Luke 16.15). Without such honesty, native intelligence, even brilliance, will not be enough to attain reality rather than a counterfeit. Catholic scholars or students, young or old, must put away any self-centered pride, any im-

---

[26]Pope John XXIII, Encyclical, *Pacem in Terris* (April 11, 1963) (DS 3970).
[27]Cf. Pope John XXIII, Encyclical, *Pacem in Terris* (April 11, 1963) (DS 3959, 3970).

moderate desire to dominate, detestation of those who disagree with them. They will need to cultivate self-discipline, diligence, patience, perseverance, gratitude for abilities they did not give themselves, humility before the truth to be learned about creation, appreciation of the reflection of God in this creation.

Lying

We have a duty to seek the truth and to speak the truth. We must be honest with ourselves and with others.

Truth is attained primarily in an interior judgment of the mind. Hence, one way of dishonoring truth is by an inward obscurantism, a willful blindness, a determination to think only what is convenient, a willingness to rest in and rationalize one's prejudices and, perhaps, one's lusts. Refusal to pursue truth can amount to one of those forms of sin that tend to cut one off from the very possibility of reaching or returning to the friendship of God, a "sin against the Holy Spirit" (cf. Matt. 12.31-32; Mark 3.29; Luke 12.10).[28]

Communication is the heart of life in community with others, and truth is, of course, dishonored by the lie. A lie is an assertion, in a context in which genuine communication is reasonably expected, of something which one considers to be false.

Lying is wrong. It is forbidden by the eighth commandment: "You shall not bear false witness against your neighbor" (Exod. 20.16; cf. Deut. 5.20). "Clothe yourselves with the new self, created according to the likeness of God in true righteousness and holiness," St. Paul wrote to the Ephesians, adding: "So then, putting away falsehood, let all of us speak the truth to our neighbors" (Eph. 4.24-25; cf. Mark 7.22; Rom. 1.29; Col. 3.9; 1 Tim 1.10).

As in the case of the other basic human goods, Christian doctrine rejects the notion that a choice directly against truth can be justified by an appeal to expected good consequences. The direct lie is forbidden even if one could thereby avert an injury or loss, or even save a life.

Lying under oath is a particularly serious wrong. In swearing an oath one calls on God, the Source of all truth, to witness the truth of one's testimony, assertions, or intentions. In accord with the injunctions of Scripture (cf. Lev. 19.12), the Church has faithfully taught that deliberate perjury is always a grave sin, whatever the reason or occasion.[29]

As was indicated in the preceding chapter, the Christian tradition has always insisted that when one is questioned about one's faith by

28Cf. St. Thomas Aquinas, *Summa Theologica* II-II, 14, 2; 15,2-3.
29Cf. Pope Martin V, Bull, *Inter Cunctas* (February 22, 1418) n. 14 (DS 1254); Decree of the Holy Office (March 2, 1679) n. 44 (DS 2144); Pope Pius IX, *Syllabus* (December 8, 1864) n. 64 (DS 2964).

public authorities, it is wrong to keep silent. "All must be prepared to confess Christ before men. . ." (LG 42). In this way the truth of faith, which is of supreme importance, is given an exceptional significance in Christian life.

But there are circumstances in which one must show concern for the proper keeping of secrets (which itself can be a serious obligation), for allowing reasonable privacy, and for maintaining authentic interpersonal harmony. One must not lie. In contexts in which the communication of truth is reasonably expected, one must honor the basic value of truth by avoiding any direct affirmation of a statement known to be false. But one who improperly volunteers information may at times be betraying a friend or showing contempt for other values that one should safeguard. Hence there can be situations in which one may remain silent, or may rightly allow others to be deceived, or fail to point out the way in which one's reply is restricted or otherwise affected by the context.[30] No simple rule can provide the right answer for all such cases. In each instance one must carefully consider what kinds of silence, or forthrightness, or evasive or partial response, would fairly serve all the interests rightly involved, and at the same time avoid any direct contradiction of what one judges to be the truth.

At times, of course, statements do not really come within the range of the value of truth at all. Clearly one does not come within that range in the ordinary writing of fiction. The novelist, for example, can invent facts and adapt historical events to fit the story he is telling. Conventional greetings and phrases are also commonly neither meant nor understood as meant to be serious communications of truth. "You look well today" can be a word of encouragement rather than an expression of one's considered judgment.

In all situations Christians must not only be sincere and authentic in themselves, but also be trustworthy and honest in their representation of reality to others.

"Do not lie to one another," for you "have stripped off the old self with its practices and have clothed yourself with the new self, which is being renewed in knowledge according to the image of its creator" (Col. 3.9-10).

---

[30]Against laxity in assessing appropriate occasions for evasive or ambiguous answers, cf. Decree of the Holy Office (March 2, 1679) nn. 26-28 (DS 2126-2128).

21

Building A Just And Good Society

We are social beings. Community with others not only helps us secure such basic goods as knowledge and life itself, but is itself a basic element in our well-being and fulfillment as persons. Each of our lives is deeply affected by the society in which we live; each has a duty to share in the task of shaping and conserving a just and humane social order.

As we saw in an earlier chapter, the social nature of the human person is evident to common sense as it reflects on self-love and friendship. But, beyond that, "vistas closed to human reason were opened up by the Lord Jesus when He prayed to the Father, 'that all may be one . . . as We are one' (John 17.21-22). For He implied a certain likeness between the union of the divine Persons and the union of God's sons in truth and charity. This likeness reveals that man . . . cannot fully find himself except through a sincere gift of himself" (GS 24).

The first part of this chapter discusses the principles that underlie our social life. The chapter then treats of the basic forms of this social life: the family, economic society, the political community, and the family of nations.

The Person and His Communities

The social teaching of the Church is an essential part of its message.[1] Christ Himself has taught us that we should not selfishly seek earthly treasure, that as children of one Father we should share property generously, show special solicitude for the poor and afflicted, and seek to structure our earthly life in such a way that the kingdom of God may begin to appear in our midst. The Church's social teaching is a working out of certain elementary requirements of Christian faith, hope, and love. This whole social teaching rests on two fundamental principles.

First, we cannot find fulfillment unless we have some community with others, community in which we serve and are served, love and

[1]Cf. Pope John XXIII, Encyclical, *Mater et Magistra* (May 15, 1961) Part IV, esp. nn. 218, 222. The Second Vatican Council stressed the importance of Christian social teaching; cf., e.g., GS 43, 76, and *passim*; AA 31 and *passim*.

are loved. Second, we cannot find personal fulfillment without making our own deep personal commitment to God. That is, we are indeed social beings, but we are much more than that. We are social beings who are also persons with transcendent dignity, persons called to an immediate personal relationship with God.[2]

So, "the beginning, the subject, and the goal of all social institutions is and must be the human person, who for his part and by his very nature stands completely in need of social life. This social life is not something added on to man. Hence, through his dealings with others, through reciprocal responsibilities and through conversation with his brothers, he develops all his gifts, and is able to rise to his destiny" (GS 25).

This destiny of the person is not limited to the goods a temporal society can provide. "While living in history he fully maintains his eternal vocation" (GS 76). Even in relation to the fullest temporal community, the political community, the human person has a "transcendence" (GS 76).

It is precisely because of our supra-temporal destiny that no person can be simply subordinated to the good of any society and that all persons are basically equal. "True, all men are not alike from the point of view of varying physical power and the diversity of intellectual and moral resources. Nevertheless, with respect to the fundamental rights of the person, every type of discrimination, whether social or cultural, whether based on sex, race, color, social condition, language, or religion, is to be overcome and eradicated as contrary to God's intent" (GS 29; cf. DH 6). Why? "Because all men, having a rational soul and being created in God's image, have the same nature and origin, and because all men, having been redeemed by Christ, enjoyed the same divine calling and destiny" (GS 29).

Those who suffer from unjust discrimination, whose lives are bruised by the unjust attitudes and structures that sin has implanted in our society, are persons of transcendent worth. They are our brothers and sisters. We owe them a realistic and active love. We have a duty to accept personal responsibility for concrete action toward the shaping of a society in which there will be justice, freedom, and peace.[3] To despise the fraternal and social implication of the Gospel is to fail in basic responsibilities. "Those who say, 'I love God,' and hate their brothers and sisters, are liars; for those who do not love a brother or sister whom they have seen, cannot love God whom they have not seen. The commandment we have from Him is this: those who love God must love their brothers and sisters also" (1 John 4.20-21).

---

[2]Cf. Pope Paul VI, Encyclical, *Populorum Progessio* (March 26, 1967) nn. 15, 16 (EV 2.1060-1061).
[3]Cf. Pope Paul VI, Apostolic Letter, *Octogesima Adveniens* (May 14, 1971) nn. 48-51 (EV 4.774-779).

The Common Good

A community is bound together by the pursuit of a "common good." God's goodness can be called the common good for all, since His goodness is the common source and goal of all creatures. God's goodness is also common in the sense that He shares it in common with all those created persons He has called to life with Himself. Life in heaven will be the joy of a perfect community, a community rejoicing in the goodness which God communicates to all who respond to His call.

Human goods reflect God's goodness, and basic human goods are common goods in the sense that they pervade all of human life. They are common, too, in the sense that all men and women can share in them. Finally, it is because we have a good in common to which we can be dedicated together that we can be joined in authentic friendship, in unselfish shared pursuit of what is truly good.

In its social teaching the Church uses the term "common good" in the sense that the common good of society "consists chiefly in the protection of the rights and the performance of the duties of the human person" (DH 6). Many of one's rights and duties flow from the demands of the good of living in community, and some forms of social life protect rights and fulfill duties more adequately than others. The Church therefore often speaks of the common good as "the sum of those conditions of social life which allow not only groups but also their individual members to achieve their own fulfillment more fully and more readily" than they otherwise could (cf. GS 26, 79; DH 6).

Man and Socialization

Some of the social ties that bind us together spring immediately from the demands of our human nature. To live well we clearly need such societies as the family and the political community. Other social ties are made and developed by free human decisions.

In our own era a sensitive awareness of the need for many social ties and groups has given rise to a great variety of public and private organizations and associations: cooperatives, unions, corporations, professional, cultural, and recreational societies, international institutions, and so on. "This development, which is called socialization, while certainly not without its dangers, brings with it many advantages with respect to consolidating and increasing the qualities of the human person, and safeguarding his rights" (GS 25).[4]

---

[4]Cf. Pope John XXIII, Encyclical, *Mater et Magistra* (May 15, 1961) Part II, esp. nn. 59-67.

The Principle of Subsidiarity

The Church's accounts of the common good often refer specifically to the fulfillment of families and other associations as well as to the self-fulfillment of individuals. These groups help the individual further his ends; even more, they themselves can be part of the well-being of a creature born to friendship.

Implicit in these accounts of the common good is that principle which Pope Pius XI, Pope John XXIII, and the Second Vatican Council call the principle of subsidiarity. This principle is expressed as follows: "Just as it is wrong to withdraw from the individual and commit to the community at large what private initiative and endeavor can accomplish, so it is likewise an injustice, a serious harm, and a disturbance of proper order to turn over to a greater society, of higher rank, functions and services which can be performed by smaller communities on a lower plane. For any social undertaking, of its very nature, ought to give aid to the members of the body social, and ought never to destroy and absorb them."[5]

In accord with the principle of subsidiarity, decisions should be made at the lowest reasonable level in order to enlarge freedom and to broaden participation in responsible action. Only when an individual or small social unit cannot properly fulfill a task should that task be taken over by a wider society.

The Family

The principle of subsidiarity may be illustrated first in relation to the family. The marital companionship between a man and woman is "the primary form of interpersonal communion" (GS 12). Moreover, it is "the beginning and basis of human society," and its mission is to be "the first and vital cell of society" (AA 11; cf. GS 52). "It is the cradle of life and love, the place in which the individual 'is born' and 'grows.' Therefore a primary concern is reserved for this community, especially in these times when human egoism, the anti-birth campaign, totalitarian politics, situations of poverty, material, cultural and moral misery, threaten to make these very springs of life dry up."[6]

Although each marriage is contracted by the free decision of the two persons involved, it is neither they nor the laws and customs of their community that determine what marriage is.

To be sure, there are all sorts of individual choices and social con-

[5]Pope Pius XI, Encyclical, *Quadragesimo Anno* (May 15, 1931) n. 79 (DS 3738); quoted in Pope John XXIII, Encyclical, *Mater et Magistra* (May 15, 1961) Part II, n. 53 (DS 3943); cf. Pope John XXIII, Encyclical, *Pacem in Terris* (April 11, 1963) Part IV (DS 3995); GS 86; GE 3,6.
[6]Pope John Paul II, Post-Synodal Apostolic Exhortation, *Christifidelis Laici* (December 30, 1988) n. 40.

ventions that shape the ways in which people do in fact engage in sexual relations. All these are subject to a critique by Christian doctrine. For certainly these ways do not all equally support and further the values which, faith teaches, must be respected in every sexual act: the good of that special personal union that is marital friendship, and the procreative good to which that friendship is ordered. Only in the family are these values fully guarded. For this reason, the family "is a society in its own original right" (DH 5). The family is not the product of artificial convention; it is not established by, nor is it subject to essential change by, any higher human authority.

It follows that "public authority should regard it as a sacred duty to recognize, protect, and promote the authentic nature" of marriage and the family, "to shield public morality, and to favor the prosperity of domestic life" (GS 52). In particular, "attention is to be paid to the needs of the family in government policies regarding housing, the education of children, working conditions, social security, and taxation" (AA 11).

Needs of Families

The needs of many families today are urgent and great. "The modern Christian family is often tempted to be discouraged and distressed at the growth of its difficulties; it is an eminent form of love to give it back its reasons for confidence in itself, in the riches that it possesses by nature and grace, and in the mission that God has entrusted to it."[7] Families that are victims of economic change and a long-standing social injustices often must struggle for existence in intolerable living conditions in crowded urban centers. Those that belong to racial minorities or to migrant groups find it especially difficult to claim their legitimate social rights. Even when problems are so great that social, political, and economic changes seem urgently needed, measures often are not taken unless concerned persons press for effective social action. Christians should cooperate with others of good will to ensure that the policies of their governments give attention to these ills (cf. AA 11).

Those in public authority also "have rights and duties with regard to the population problems of their own nation," but only "within the limits of their own competence" (GS 87).[8] It is not the function of governments and public authorities to supplant the essentially personal roles of husband and wife. Marriage and the family have a significance and value beyond the goods which can be shared in civil

---

[7]Pope John Paul II, Apostolic Exhortation, *Familiaris Consortio* (November 22, 1981) n. 86 (EV 7.1806). Cf. also Holy See, *Charter of Rights of the Family* (November 24, 1983) (EV 9.538-552).

[8]Cf. Pope Paul VI, Encyclical, *Populorum Progessio* (March 26, 1967) n. 37 (EV 2.1082).

society. The interest the state has in the number of children born in a family is by no means the only or primary interest at stake.

Thus, for example, "in view of the inalienable human right to marry and beget children, the question of how many children to have belongs to the right judgment of parents and can in no way be committed to the decision of public authority" (GS 87). As was noted in the preceding chapter, the common good of their society is one of the things to be considered by parents in making their decision (cf. GS 50).

Education of Children

The education of children is also a basic parental concern. "Since the parents have conferred life on their children, they have a most solemn obligation to educate their offspring, and so must be acknowledged as the first and foremost educators of those children" (GE 3; cf. GE 6; AA 11; GS 48). Civil society does indeed have rights and duties in relation to the education of children, but this is because the family needs help in its educative task (cf. GE 3).

Here civil society plays its part "by guarding the duties and rights of parents and of others who have a role in education, and by providing them with assistance; by implementing the principle of subsidiarity and by completing the task of education, with attention to parental wishes, whenever the efforts of parents and of other groups are insufficient; and, moreover, by building its own schools and institutes, as the common good may demand" (GE 3). The principle of subsidiarity requires that "no kind of school monopoly arise" (GE 6). Governments "must acknowledge the right of parents to make a genuinely free choice of schools and of other means of education" (DH 5).

Parents have authority to determine the course of their children's education because for many years children cannot reasonably make their own decisions in this important matter. When young people are mature enough to decide their own vocation and the education required to pursue it, they should exercise the rights hitherto exercised on their behalf by their parents. Civil society must then deal with the education of these persons with full recognition of the fact that they are free and equal members of the community.

Relationships within the Family

The sexes are equal in human dignity and fundamental rights (cf. GS 29; DH 6).[9] This fact is particularly significant for a husband and

---

[9] Cf. also Pope Pius XI, Encyclical, *Casti Connubii* (December 31, 1930) n. 76. Cf. Pope John Paul II, Apostolic Letter, *Mulieris Dignitatem* (August 15, 1988) esp. ch. 3.

wife, for theirs is a union in marital love and friendship. Each has an equal claim on the other's respect, affection, sexual attentions, and assistance of every kind. In all these matters, "the wife does not have authority over her own body, but the husband does; likewise the husband does not have authority over his own body, but the wife does" (1 Cor. 7.4).

Marriage usually requires a specialization of function. Ordinarily one partner works in the wider community for the support of the family while the other devotes time more directly to the upbringing of the children. No one can do or be everything. To note the difference between the sexes is not to suggest that woman is inferior to man, or man to woman. St. Paul certainly insists upon the difference between the two, but he also teaches: "Nevertheless, in the Lord woman is not independent of man or man independent of woman. For just as woman came from man, so man comes through woman; but all things come from God" (1 Cor. 11.11-12).

In distinguishing between the permanent reality and the changing expressions of the family, the Church teaches that the mother has a "domestic role which must be safely preserved" (GS 52). Young children in particular normally need their mother at home (cf. GS 52). In the family, the mother ordinarily has a certain priority of responsibility in caring for the children, while the father has the prior responsibility in deciding the basic fortunes of the family. If the husband is the head of the family, the wife is its heart.[10] Ideally, decisions will be made in mutual understanding and with joint deliberation (cf. GS 52).

All Christians ought to be "subject to one another out of reverence for Christ" (Eph. 5.21), honoring the various forms of priority and dignity that each has in his or her own role. Thus when St. Paul speaks of the way in which a wife should be subject to her husband, he does not compromise her dignity. She is not related to her husband as a child is to parents, but as the Church is related to Christ, who Himself lived in our midst as the servant of all (cf. Luke 22.27). "Wives, be subject to your husbands as you are to the Lord. For the husband is the head of the wife just as Christ is the head of the church, the body of which He is the Savior. . . . Husbands, love your wives, just as Christ loved the church and gave Himself up for her. . ." (Eph. 5.22-23, 25; cf. Col. 3.18-19; Titus 2.5; 1 Peter 3.1, 7).

Sincere personal love should be the basic form of relationship between husbands and wives. Marriage is a union of essentially equal persons, but in some way the two partners fulfill and perfect each other, and each has a proper role. Neither nature nor revelation excludes some cultural variations in these roles. Moreover, if either

[10]Cf. Pope Pius XI, Encyclical, *Casti Connubii* (December 31, 1930) nn. 27-29 (DS 3709), n. 74.

partner is unable to fulfill his role, or otherwise fails to fulfill it, the other must shoulder appropriate responsibilities. But for the Christian family the love between Christ and the Church forms the ideal pattern for the relationship between husband and wife.

Obedience in the Christian Family

"Children, obey your parents in the Lord, for this is right. 'Honor your father and mother' — this is the first commandment with a promise: 'so that it may be well with you. . .' " (Eph. 6.1-3; cf. Exod. 20.12; Deut. 5.16). The commandment to honor one's parents is included in the reply Jesus gave to the man who asked what he must do to share in everlasting life (cf. Mark 10.17-19).

Children owe parents more than compliance with expressed parental directions. Children have a duty to honor their parents and to have concern for them all their lives (cf. GS 48; Sir. 2.12-13). "And whoever does not provide for relatives, and especially for family members," says St. Paul in considering the condition of widows, "has denied the faith and is worse than an unbeliever" (1 Tim. 5.8).

Christian obedience in childhood lays a foundation for responsible Christian self-commitment as one matures. Again and again the Church, as in the Second Vatican Council, "urges everyone, especially those who are charged with the task of educating others, to do their utmost to form men who, respecting the moral order, will be obedient to legitimate authority and lovers of authentic freedom — men, in other words, who will come to decisions on their own judgment and in the light of truth, govern their activities with a sense of responsibility, and strive to pursue whatever is true and right, by willingly joining with others in cooperative effort" (DH 8).

The obedience of children should be motivated not by fear but by love, gratitude, and humility (cf. Sir. 7.27-28). Such attitudes equip one for free and responsible cooperation with other people and with Christ Himself. When young children have grown into young men and young women, they must make decisions which their parents have no right to make for them. They alone can rightly decide the path for their mature life. Each must choose personally the vocation he or she wishes to follow, religious or secular (cf. GS 52).

Economic Life

To support his family and himself the father of a family ordinarily works "in the production and exchange of goods or in the performance of economic services" (GS 67). In this way, he is "joined to his fellow men and serves them, and is able to exercise genuine charity and to be a partner in the work of bringing God's creation to perfection" (GS 67). Indeed, by offering their labor to God, every person "can become associated with the redemptive work itself of Jesus Christ, who conferred an eminent dignity on labor when at Nazareth He worked with His own hands" (GS 67). All elements of economic life other than human work are merely instrumental (cf. GS 67). An expanded development of the significance of human work is provided by Pope John Paul II in his encyclical *Laborem Exercens.*[11]

The main elements of the Church's teaching on socio-economic matters are rooted in the sublime dignity of the person and the destiny of the person. They are rooted in the principle's of freedom, personal development, equality, subsidiarity, and participation.

Freedom and Personal Development

Ownership and other forms of private control over material goods are to serve the development of personality. Their purpose is to provide everyone with a necessary area of independence; private ownership should be regarded as "an extension of human freedom" (GS 71).[12]

Indeed, the principal original source of private property lies in the exercise of human freedom. Thus, for example, there is that exercise of freedom whereby "the person stamps the things of nature with his seal and subdues them to his will" (GS 67), as when on our own initiative we cultivate what was barren waste, or shape what was without humanly relevant form. Then there is the free decision of a person to accumulate savings out of the payment for work done, payment which in justice "must be such as to furnish a man with the means to cultivate his own and his dependents' material, social, cultural, and spiritual life worthily. . ." (GS 67).

Fundamental Equality of Economic Rights

"God intended the earth and all that it contains for the use of all human beings and all peoples. Therefore, created goods ought equitably to flow to all, with justice as the guide, accompanied by charity" (GS 69).

Prior to our natural right to own private property, then, whatever the forms of ownership may be in particular times and places, is the right of every person to have a share of material goods for needed subsistence (cf. GS 60).[13]

[11]Pope John Paul II, Encyclical, *Laborem Exercens* (September 14, 1981) (EV 7.1388-1517).
[12]A development of ownership and of its limitations is given by Pope John Paul II in his encyclical, *Laborem Exercens* (September 14, 1981) n. 14 (EV 7.1450-1456).
[13]Cf. John Paul XXIII, Encyclical, *Mater et Magistra* (May 15, 1961) n. 43 (DS 3942), citing there Pope Pius XII, Broadcast (June 1, 1941), AAS 33 (1941) 199. On the individual and social aspects of property, cf. also Pope Leo XIII, Encyclical, *Rerum Novarum* (May 15, 1891); Pope Pius XI, Encyclical, *Quadragesimo Anno* (May 15, 1931); Pope Paul VI, Encyclical, *Populorum Progressio* (March 26, 1967) (EV 2.1046-1132); etc.

"In using his lawful possessions, therefore, a man ought to regard them not merely as his own, but also as common property in the sense that they can be of benefit not only to himself but also to others" (GS 69). This is what the Fathers and Doctors of the Church meant when they taught that all were obliged to come to the relief of the poor, "and to do so not merely out of their superfluous goods" (GS 69).

Moreover, "if a person is in extreme necessity, he has the right to take care of his needs for himself from the riches of others" (GS 69).[14]

Subsidiarity and Participation

Economic activity and production, like private property, should serve the common good. Their fundamental purpose is "the service of man, and indeed of the whole man, viewed in terms of his material needs and the demands of his intellectual, moral, spiritual, and religious life; and when we say man, we mean every man whatsoever..." (GS 64).

Economic growth "must not be allowed merely to follow a kind of automatic course resulting from the economic activity of individuals" (GS 65), for private individuals as such cannot effectively organize the pursuit of the common good. So, "the spontaneous activities of individuals and of independent groups must be coordinated with the efforts of public authorities" (GS 65). Corporations, banks, and other powerful economic forces have a duty to serve the common good, not merely the narrow interests of management or owners. Theories which in the name of a false liberty deny the need for any social planning are to be rejected (cf. GS 65).

At the same time, however, economic activity "must not be entrusted solely to the authority of government" (GS 65).[15] The proper role of public authority, however comprehensive it may need to be in certain stages of development or in conditions of emergency, is to be auxiliary. Theories which "subordinate the basic rights of individual persons and groups to the collective organization of production" are to be rejected (cf. GS 65). Among the basic rights relevant here is the right (and duty) of individual persons under normal circumstances to provide for the support of themselves and of their families.[16]

Hence, "at every level the largest possible number of people should ... have an active role in the directing" of economic development (GS 65). The Church recognizes the right of private ownership of productive goods,[17] as it acknowledges the right to form corpora-

---

[14] On the application of this principle, cf., e.g., St. Thomas Aquinas, *Summa Theologica* II-II, 66,7.

[15] Pope John XXIII, Encyclical, *Mater et Magistra* (May 15, 1961) n. 51 (DS 3943).

[16] Cf. Pope John XXIII, Encyclical, *Mater et Magistra* (May 15, 1961) n. 55.

[17] Cf. Pope John XXIII, Encyclical, *Mater et Magistra* (May 15, 1961), nn. 108-121.

tions, to establish trade unions, and to set up ways of assisting the participation of workers in the economy as a whole.[18] The principle of participation applies not only to the economic system as a whole, but also within each economic enterprise. It also applies within the institutions which, at a higher level, make decisions affecting those enterprises and their employees, and in the unions which represent the workers of one company or of one industry (GS 68).

All this, in the mind of the Church, derives from the same transcendence of the human person. "In economic enterprises it is persons who work together, that is, free and independent human beings created to the image of God. Therefore . . . the active participation of everyone in the running of enterprises should be promoted" (GS 68).

Political Community

Each person's active participation in community affairs is a good as relevant in political life as in other forms of community. A fully human political community will give all citizens "the chance to participate freely and actively in establishing the constitutional basis of a political community, governing the state, determining the scope and purpose of various institutions, and choosing leaders" (GS 75). The particular ways in which a given state will structure itself and regulate public authority may, of course, vary "according to the particular character of a people and its historical development" (GS 74; cf. GS 31).

Again, the common good is the criterion of good and bad in the public order. "Individuals, families and various groups which compose civil society are aware of their own insufficiency in the matter of establishing a fully human condition of life. They see the need for a wider community in which each would daily contribute his energies toward an ever better attainment of the common good. And so they constitute political community, in a variety of forms. It is for the common good that political community exists" (GS 74).

Legitimate Political Authority

From the very nature of things it is essential that there be real authority in the political community. Many different people go to make up a political community, and inevitably there will be different opinions about how things should be done. "Now, if the political community is not to be torn to pieces as each person follows his own viewpoint, authority is needed in order to direct the energies of all citizens toward the common good — not mechanically or despotically, but

18Cf. Pope John XXIII, Encyclical, *Mater et Magistra* (May 15, 1961), nn. 82-103.

primarily as a moral force which depends on freedom and on the conscientious discharge of the burdens of any office which has been undertaken. It is therefore obvious that the political community and public authority are based on human nature and hence belong to an order of things preordained by God, though the choice of government and the designation of leaders is left to the free choice of the citizens" (GS 74; cf. Rom. 13.1-5).

Governments have a certain right to command. When legitimate public authority is exercised within the limits of the moral order and on behalf of the common good, citizens "are conscience-bound to obey" (GS 74; cf. Rom. 13.5). This moral obligation can extend even to laws which might reasonably have been different (such as speed limits and tax rates) but which nonetheless are intelligibly related to the needs of the common good and established in good faith (cf. GS 30; Rom. 13.5-7). Indeed, even where public authority oversteps its bounds, the people should in some circumstances obey. Unjust authorities as such do not deserve obedience, and unjust laws do not oblige; obedience is due only to the extent that the common good in particular cases requires it (cf. GS 74).

"Obedience to just laws and reverence for legitimately constituted authorities" is part of the Christian faith (cf. CD 19; DH 8). "Give therefore to the emperor the things that are the emperor's, and to God the things that are God's" (Matt. 22.21). Obedience to civil authorities is not obedience paid to them as human persons; rather, as Pope John XXIII said, by our obedience we "pay homage to God, the provident Creator of the universe, who decreed that men's dealings with one another be regulated in accordance with that order which He Himself established."[19]

But God, of course, does not command immoral actions. Certainly moral evils do not become justified because civil law permits or demands them. If civil authorities issue laws or decrees which are in contravention of the moral order, "and therefore against the will of God," these "cannot be binding on the consciences of the citizens, since 'one ought to obey God rather than men' (Acts 5.29)."[20] Moreover, "if any government does not acknowledge human rights, or violates them, not only does it fail in its duty, but its orders are wholly lacking in binding force."[21] And, as the Second Vatican Council taught, it is lawful for citizens to defend their own rights and those of their fellow citizens against abuse of public authority, provided that in so doing they observe the limits set by natural law and the Gospel (cf. GS 74).

19Pope John XXIII, Encyclical, *Pacem in Terris* (April 11, 1963) (EV 2.21).
20Pope John XXIII, Encyclical, *Pacem in Terris* (April 11, 1963) (EV 2.21).
21Pope John XXIII, Encyclical, *Pacem in Terris* (April 11, 1963) (EV 2.24).

Human Rights and Public Order

Since the Church has expressed so much of its social teaching in terms of human rights, it must be noted that these rights are of two kinds. First, there are those rights which are inalienable and which must be supported in every situation whatsoever. An example is the right of an innocent person to life. To such rights correspond unqualified duties. One must never take the life of an innocent person directly, not for any reason whatsoever.

There are also many rights which are inalienable and inviolable in a somewhat different sense. An example here is the right to a good education (cf. GE 1). These rights belong to all persons as such, and may never be discounted or treated as irrelevant by other persons or by public authority (cf. DH 6). But the positive fulfillment of these rights is subject to other moral considerations, for it is not always possible to provide for the full realization of all such rights. The government has a duty to assist citizens in the exercise of these rights in ways compatible with the common good and with what is possible in all the circumstances of time and place.

Governments have the duty to assist citizens in countering racism, a false teaching and a sinful stance which treats members of some races as inferior because of their race, as without full human dignity and all human rights. "The Church rejects, as foreign to the mind of Christ, any discrimination against men or harassment of them because of their race, color, condition of life, or religion" (NA 5).[22]

It is also a duty of government to provide protection against the abuse of rights, whether the abuse is of the rights of property or economic initiative (cf. GS 64), or of the right to communicate with others in speech and art (cf. IM 12), or of the right to express religious beliefs (cf. DH 7). In providing protection against abuse of rights, public authority is itself to act fairly and "in conformity with the objective moral order" (DH 7).

Civil authority has no right to direct consciences or to control actions which are truly private. The political community is a "complete society" in that it has all the means necessary for advancing the temporal good of human society. It is true that a good temporal order provides a context in which each person may more readily glorify God and attain the eternal and supernatural vocation of friendship with Him. But the political society is not the only complete society, and it has no legitimate supremacy over the spiritual life of its citizens. It is the Church which has all the means necessary for advancing the life of the spirit. Because Christ rules in the Church, the Church can rightly

[22]See Pope Pius XI, Encyclical, *Mit Brennender Sorge* (March 14, 1937); Pope John XXIII, Encyclical, *Mater et Magistra* (May 15, 1961) and *Pacem in Terris* (April 11, 1963).

speak directly to conscience, and can exercise jurisdiction over even one's interior life.[23]

When a government makes regulations to direct the exercise of natural rights, it is to be guided by "that basic component of the common good which is called 'public order' " (DH 7). Public order can be considered to have three components: "the effective safeguard of the rights of all citizens and the peaceful settlement of conflicts or rights," "adequate care for that genuine public peace which exists when men live together in good order and in true justice," and "a proper guardianship of public morality" (DH 7).

A Christian must be faithful to every human value and to sound moral principles not only in private decisions, but also in the choices and activities of public life.

Concern for Justice

Justice is a virtue which disposes a person "to render to everyone his due."[24] The form of justice that governs relationships between individuals is called commutative justice. Each person is required to respect all the rights of his neighbor. The commandments speak of the basic duties we have in justice toward our neighbor; each person is required not to kill, or slander, or steal from another. Should one person violate the rights of another, a duty to make restitution arises. Thus, one who has taken the property of another must return the property, or its equivalent, as far as possible; one who has injured the neighbor in other ways should find suitable ways to atone for the offense. The form of justice that deals with fair divisions of the goods and burdens of life in society may be called social justice.

Catholics "should feel themselves obliged to promote the true common good. Thus, they should, make the weight of their opinion felt, so that civil authority may act with justice and laws may conform to moral precepts and the common good" (AA 14). "Let the laity by their combined efforts remedy any institutions and conditions of the world which are customarily an inducement to sin, so that all such things may be conformed to the norms of justice and may favor the practice of virtue rather than hinder it" (LG 36).

To create a more just and compassionate society, Christians should work together in solidarity. Solidarity "is not a feeling of vague compassion or shallow distress at the misfortunes of so many people. On the contrary, it is a firm and persevering determination to commit

[23]On the teaching of the Church that the ecclesiastical authority and civil authority are distinct, and that both are supreme, each in its own domain, cf. esp. Pope Leo XIII, Encyclical, *Immortale Dei* (November 1, 1885) (DS 3165-3172). Cf. DH 13.

[24]St. Thomas Aquinas, *Summa Theologica* II-II,58, 1.

oneself to the common good, that is to say, to the good of all and of each individual because we are all really responsible for all."[25]

Often injustices have complex roots and the corrective measures needed require intelligent planning as well as good will. Education for justice is an integral part of Christian education. This education for justice "demands a renewal of heart, a renewal based on the recognition of sin in its individual and social manifestations. It will also inculcate a truly and entirely human way of life in justice, love and simplicity. It will likewise awaken a critical sense, which will lead us to reflect on the society in which we live and on its values; it will make men ready to renounce these values when they cease to promote justice for all men."[26] This education should be a liberating education, enabling us to establish truly human communities. It is a continuing education. "It is also a practical education: it comes through action, participation and vital contact with the reality of injustice."[27]

Catholics will also remember, however, that even God in His providence does not seek at the cost of freedom to extirpate all the evils which flow the from abuse of human freedom. Subject to the requirements of public order (to the extent that these can with reasonable effectiveness be satisfied by lawful means), "the usages of society are to be the usages of freedom in their full range," and this means that "the freedom of man is to be respected as far as possible, and curtailed only when and insofar as necessary" (DH 7); cf. LG 37).

While the Church thus asserts the value of freedom, it also asserts that it is generally the function of the well-formed Christian conscience of the laity to see "that the divine law is inscribed in the life of the earthly city" (GS 43; cf. AA 14).

International Community

Instantaneous communication, rapid transportation, and a host of economic and cultural ties today bind ever more closely all the citizens and peoples of the world (cf. GS 84). The whole human family on earth constitutes a society which must be the concern of all persons and of all nations. The common good of the state "cannot be divorced from the common good of the entire human family."[28] There

[25] Pope John Paul II, Encyclical, *Sollicitudo Rei Socialis* (December 30, 1987) n. 38 (EV 10.2650).

[26] Second General Assembly of the Synod of Bishops, 1971, *Justice in the World*, Part III (EV 4.1283).

[27] Second General Assembly of the Synod of Bishops, 1971, *Justice in the World*, Part III (EV 4.1285).Cf. Congregation for the Doctrine of the Faith, Instruction, *Liberatis Nuntius* (August 6, 1984) (EV 9.866-987) and Instruction, *Libertatis Conscientia* (March 22, 1986) (EV 10.196-344); these stress the liberating nature of Catholic social teaching, flaws in some, and the true nature of an authentic liberation theology.

[28] Pope John XXIII, Encyclical, *Pacem in Terris* (April 11, 1963) (EV 2.35).

is a "universal common good" which "needs to be intelligently pursued and more effectively achieved" (GS 84).

The problems and the opportunities that face us on the international level require an international organization with real authority to care for them. "Today the universal common good poses problems which are worldwide in their dimensions. Problems of this sort cannot be solved except by a public authority with power, structure, and means which are in scope equal to the problems, and with a worldwide sphere of activity. Consequently, the moral order itself demands the establishment of some general public authority . . . set up with the consent of all nations."[29]

Nations and their leaders are not above the demands of morality and the natural law.[30] The same principles that govern the dealings of individuals with one another and call for a just organization within states must also govern the relations of political communities with one another.[31] The nation state is today in many respects tending to become a subordinate group; it would be a form of injustice for it to cling to prerogatives and functions it can no longer properly exercise.

Thus, the principle of subsidiarity is to be respected on the international level. Some world problems are so large and complex that only an international organization with real authority will be able to deal effectively with them. Such an organization, however, must not be allowed to destroy the proper independence, diversity, and separate functioning of smaller groups. "There are questions which, because of their extreme gravity, vastness, and urgency, must be considered too difficult for the rulers of individual states to solve with any degree of success. But it is no part of the duty of this universal authority to limit the sphere of action of the public authority of other states, or to arrogate to itself their proper functions. On the contrary, its purpose is to create world conditions in which not only the public authorities of all nations but also the individual persons and the intermediate groups can carry out their tasks, fulfill their duties, and claim their rights with greater security."[32]

True Nature of Our Hope

Everyone must be concerned with the pursuit of world peace, and of the justice without which peace cannot endure. Peace cannot be secured simply by acquiring more, bigger, and more sophisticated weapons. "The arms race is an utterly treacherous trap of humanity, and one which injures the poor to an intolerable degree" (GS 81). Far

[29]Pope John XXIII, Encyclical, *Pacem in Terris* (April 11, 1963) (EV 2.46-47).
[30]Cf. Pope John XXIII, Encyclical, *Pacem in Terris* (April 11, 1963) (EV. 2.32).
[31]Cf. Pope John XXIII, Encyclical, *Pacem in Terris* (April 11, 1963) (EV 2.32).
[32]Pope John XXIII, Encyclical, *Pacem in Terris* (April 11, 1963) (EV 2.49).

more radical means are needed. But what is hoped for is so great a good, and what must be feared is so great an evil, that every effort must be made in pursuit of world peace. Unless peace is secured, all other efforts for an earthly common good may come to naught.

Mankind needs to redirect its thoughts and attitudes toward peace. In the education of our young, we must emphasize ways to pursue peace. The international organizations that now exist should be used well. We have a duty "to strain every muscle as we work for the time when all war can be completely outlawed by international consent" (GS 82). This goal "undoubtedly requires the establishment of some universal public authority acknowledged as such by all, and endowed with effective power to safeguard, on the behalf of all, security, regard for justice, and respect for rights" (GS 82).

Peace can only be the fruit of justice and the fruit of love. The radical causes of dissension must be overcome if there is to be peace. Among the causes of tension are the excessive economic inequalities among nations. Other causes stem from the quest for power and the contempt for personal rights. Deeper explanations lie within the hearts of men, "in human jealousy, distrust, pride, and other egotistic passions" (GS 83). "These conflicts and disputes among you, where do they come from? Do they not come from your cravings that are at war within you?" (James 4.1).

To have peace, humankind needs most of all a profound change of heart. "Let us not be deceived by a false hope. For unless enmities and hatreds are put away and firm, honest agreements are concluded regarding universal peace in the future, humanity, which is already in the midst of a grave crisis, although endowed with marvelous knowledge, will perhaps be brought to that mournful hour in which it will experience no peace other than the dreadful peace of death. But while it says this, still the Church of Christ, standing in the midst of the anxiety of this age, does not cease to hope with the utmost confidence" (GS 82).

What is the Church's hope? It is a rich, complex hope. Its basic aspect is that "lively hope," and gift of the Holy Spirit, that people "will finally be caught up in peace and utter happiness in the fatherland radiant with the glory of the Lord" (GS 93).

Christian hope looks forward also to God's mercy in this world, to the gift of Christ's peace to the nations on earth. This peace, however, is not promised to us unconditionally; it certainly is not offered as a mere fruit of human progress. The future of this world is "as uncertain as it is changing."[33]

The ultimate concern of Christians is for eternal life. But eternal

---

[33]Pope Paul VI, Apostolic Letter, *Octogesima Adveniens* (May 14, 1971) n. 7 (EV 4.722).

life begins in this world. Christians, then, have a serious duty to bring the spirit of Christ to social life at every level, to bring mercy, justice, and peace. "Christians . . . have shouldered a gigantic task demanding fulfillment in this world. Concerning this task they must give a reckoning to Him who will judge every man on the last day. Not everyone who cries, 'Lord, Lord,' will enter the kingdom of heaven, but those who do the Father's will and take a strong grip on the work at hand. Now, the Father wills that in all men we recognize Christ our brother and love Him effectively, both in word and in deed, thus giving witness to the Truth, and that we share with others the mystery of the heavenly Father's love" (GS 93).

22

Ways Of Living A Christian Life

"I came to bring fire to the earth; and how I wish it were already kindled!" (Luke 12.49). There are many vocations in which God can be served, but there is basically only one Christian vocation: to serve God's saving plan by loving Him and one another, and to share God's life in holiness and joy. "All the faithful of Christ of whatever rank or status are called to the fullness of the Christian life and to the perfection of charity" (LG 40). It is within that one call that there is a variety of forms of Christian life.

In other chapters we speak of the special duties and blessings in the lives of those called to holy orders or to matrimony. Here we treat of the universal call to perfection, of minimal service to God, on the vocation of the Christian in the world, and of the vocation of the religious.

Unity and Diversity

In a sense, there is only one way of living the Christian life. Charity is the life and the perfection of the believer. "You shall love the Lord your God with all your heart, and with all your soul, and with all your strength, and with all your mind; and your neighbor as yourself" (Luke 10.27).

We live, however, in a world of immense complexity, a complexity which reflects the richness of the world's Creator. Each of us is a unique and distinct person. The basic human condition is the same for us all, but we live our lives in a vast number of different actual situations and circumstances.

The sanctification of this world so complex calls for many ministries. The twofold law of love — of God and of neighbor — remains sufficient. But in carrying out that law we have a great deal of freedom and a large variety of choices. These choices exist that the redemptive work of Christ might be carried into every sphere of human activity, and the Gospel brought to people everywhere, so that every person will be able to come in contact with Christ through the words and works of the believer living and working side by side.

The two great commandments of love are complementary. Love of God comes first: "This is the greatest and first commandment"

(Matt. 22.38). But "those who love God must love their brothers and sisters also" (1 John 4.21). In the Christian vocation, brotherly love is bound inseparably to love of God. The goods we will for our brothers and sisters are chiefly the supreme blessings which the Gospel promises. But Christian love cares also for the neighbor's earthly needs. Secular labors too are to contribute "to a better ordering of human society, very much in the interest of the kingdom of God" (GS 39). The converse is also true. "No human law can provide such secure ground for man's dignity and liberty as the Gospel entrusted to Christ's Church" (GS 41).

Christian Love and Joy

Christian love, as it is lived in the pilgrim conditions of this life, must be correctly understood. This love indeed bears fruit in the joy which St. Paul lists among the fruits of the Spirit (cf. Gal. 5.22). But neither the love nor the joy here is to be understood in shallow ways. "Love" in particular might easily, though mistakenly, be identified with emotional feelings of affection. Christian love involves a firm will to give what is truly good to others. It requires generosity. If we who care only for our own self-interest, we are false to ourselves and lose everything; if we who give all out of unselfish love we attain fulfillment, and bear much fruit (cf. John 12.24-25).

Christian joy as well has a paradoxical character. It can flourish along with great suffering. "Blessed are the poor in spirit. . . . Blessed are those who mourn. . . . Blessed are those who are persecuted for righteousness' sake. . ." (Matt. 5.3-4, 10). The blessedness or happiness to which Christ here refers is not merely that of a bright disposition, nor is it the shallow gratification of sensible pleasures. There is profound joy in love strong enough to bear the cross. Christian joy does not need to escape pain or the realities of this life in order to know happiness. It is a rejoicing in the midst of trials (cf. Rom. 5.3) and in unshakable hope (cf. Rom. 5.5). For those who share Christ's unselfish love know that He is calling us to life together in God, a life that shall finally be purified of all sorrows (cf. Rev. 7.17).

Minimal Love of God

Unfortunately, most Christians do not live lives of intense holiness. Some have no real love of God at all; some have a love which is real, but too undeveloped to give the joy of Christianity lived fully.

We have no love of God if we are not resolved to do the will of God. "They who have My commandments and keep them are those who love Me" (John 14.21). Professions of piety and loyalty amount to nothing if we do not actually do God's will. One who has com-

mitted a mortal sin and has not properly repented of it, does not love
God even minimally (cf. 1 John 4.20). There are those who would be
pleased to be God's friends if that did not require turning from their
evil and selfish deeds. But friendship with God does demand that; and
those who refuse to accept the minimal demands do not rise to any
level of genuine love at all (cf. Matt. 21.28-31).

Some of us are satisfied with a minimal love of God. Because it is
love, it will involve faith in God and reverence for Him. Because it is
minimal, it is willing to let the relationship with God remain simply as
it is, and it does not strive to cultivate intimate friendship with God.
The person of minimal love understands the basic love of God (cf.
Luke 19.18-20). He gives some worship and he offers some prayer.
He knows that deliberate disobedience and failure to honor the precious values through which one ought to love others are sufficient to
exclude one from divine love and from the kingdom. Hence, even one
who has only minimal love resolutely tries to maintain a level of faithfulness and to shun serious wrong. He is not eager to share fully now
in the divine favor and life, though he at least seeks to avoid mortal sin
and somehow to reach eternal life. One who lives with such minimal
love does not live the Christian life in glad generosity, but stingily.

God's Call

The real challenge of living a Christian life begins when we seem
to hear the quiet voice of the Lord calling to us: "Friend, move up
higher" (Luke 14.10). This call may come to us in prayer, even in
prayer less than fervent, or in our hearing of the word of Scripture. We
can never be entirely safe from it, even if we are slack and inattentive
in religious matters. It can reach us in all manners of ways — through
literature, through human love, through happiness or suffering or both,
through the unconscious witness of some holy friend, through a sud-
den outpouring of compassion for all the world's afflicted.

In one way or another the call will come. God is patient (cf. 2
Peter 3.9), but because He loves us He is hard to satisfy. Though He
allows us to drift along for a while in our unsatisfactory ways, He also
invites us to respond more generously and so to find joy in the
generous giving of self which charity demands. We cannot do this
without His call and His grace. Even with grace the Christian realizes
how weak he or she is. One is weak, but grace enables. "My grace is
sufficient for you, for power is made perfect in weakness" (2 Cor.
12.9).

Meanwhile, we must live our daily lives in the old familiar trials,
weaknesses, and crosses, but now in this new spirit, seeing our lives as
the medium in which we respond to God's call, our own particular
vocation.

Vocation

The word "vocation" means "calling." Some people tend to think of it only in terms of a call to the ministerial priesthood or the religious life. This is not correct, for we do appropriately speak of "the lay vocation." In fact, the lay vocation is the proper, the best vocation for most persons. It is not a second-class vocation.

Some people also tend to think of "vocation" in excessively dramatic ways. St. Paul indeed did experience a soul-searing inward illumination on the road to Damascus (cf. Acts 9.1-9). Miraculous events can accompany vocation. Ordinarily they do not.

Every Christian has a vocation. That is to say, every Christian is called by God to some particular way of carrying out the one great service or ministry of love. All believers are called by the Lord to "abide in His love" (John 15.10). Moreover, this vocation is usually made known through the actual circumstances in which one finds oneself.

"There are varieties of gifts, but the same Spirit; and there are varieties of service, but the same Lord" (1 Cor. 12.4-5). The one God calls us to a thousand different tasks and lifestyles. In some senses, one vocation may have an excellence beyond that of another, a call to greater service and sacrifice (cf. Acts 9.15).[1] But concretely the call which God gives to each person is the best for that person. No one's vocation is an inferior version of any other. Every vocation can be a road to the height of holiness.

The Lay Christian Vocation

In discussing vocations, there is a danger of giving disproportionate emphasis to those vocations which are explicitly and professionally religious, that it, vocations to the priesthood and religious life. The Christian called to serve God in the world also has a vocation of surpassing importance.

The law of love, which is the Lord's great commandment, is addressed to all, and invites all to share the liberating and saving task of making the kingdom of God flourish on earth. "On all Christians therefore is laid the splendid burden of working to make the divine message of salvation accepted by all men throughout the world" (AA 3).

The Church wishes to stress that each member of the laity has an important vocation in the Church. "The voice of the Lord resounds in the depths of each of Christ's followers, who through faith and the sacraments of Christian initiation is made like to Jesus Christ, is incor-

[1]Cf. Council of Trent, Session 24, November 11, 1563, *Doctrine on the Sacrament of Matrimony*, canon 10 (DS 1810). Cf. also LG 42; OT 10.

porated as a living member in the Church and has an active part in her mission of salvation."[2]

Laity and the Temporal Order

Christ's redemptive work is of itself aimed at our eternal salvation; but it involves the renewal of the whole temporal order. Laity are called to participate in both the spiritual and temporal aspects of the apostolate; but they "must take on the renewal of the temporal order as their own special obligation" (AA 7).[3]

The world made by God is loved by Him. Every element of the temporal order ought to be affected by Christ's saving work. The laity, moved by faith and love, should use their own particular skills and act on their own responsibility to assist in healing a world marred in many ways by sin, and to establish a temporal order based on justice and love.

To care for the temporal order is to care for the goods of life and of the family, for culture and business, for the arts and professions, for political and social institutions (cf. AA 7). "This order requires constant improvement. It must be founded on truth, built on justice, and animated by love" (GS 26). Immediate concern for the temporal order is the proper concern of laymen, because it requires all the knowledge, skills, and insight they acquire and exercise in their varied secular tasks. The temporal order must be renewed with reverence by those who respect its own "stability, goodness, proper laws, and order" (GS 36), while bringing it into conformity with the higher principles of Christian life (cf. AA 7).

Every Christian, then, according to the circumstances of his or her particular situation, has a duty to try to shape the world in accord with justice and charity. Christians must accept the fact that sometimes this may make them extremely unpopular in some quarters. Jesus was aware that not everyone would react favorably to His teaching or to His followers. "If the world hates you, be aware that it hated Me before it hated you" (John 15.18).

With these things in mind, Christians should be prepared to weigh very carefully their vocational choices. Many careers offer promise of high income and prestige, but in some circumstances one cannot pursue them or succeed well in them without participating in dishonesty, or cruelty, or exploitation of the weak, or assertion of false witness. To seek success at such a cost is to abandon Christ. "For what will it

---

[2]Pope John Paul II, Post-Synodal Apostolic Exhortation, *Christifideles Laici* (December 30, 1988) n. 3.

[3]The traditional teaching that detailed and political plans and activities to achieve a just social order should have lay leadership has frequently been restated in our time. See *Address* of Pope John Paul II to the Latin American Episcopal Conference (June 2, 1980) n. 6; also *The Final Document of the Pueblo Conference* (1980) nn. 526 and 789-793.

profit them, if they gain the whole world but forfeit their life?" (Matt. 16.26).

Laity and the Apostolate

Baptism gives each believer an apostolic vocation. "Go therefore and make disciples of all nations, baptizing them ... teaching them to obey everything that I have commanded you" (Matt. 28.19-20). The apostolate of "spreading the kingdom of Christ everywhere for the glory of God the Father" is not for the clergy alone, but is carried on by the Church "through all its members" (AA 2). All believers must proclaim their faith by the way they live. But the lay apostolate "does not consist only in the witness of one's way of life; a true apostle looks for opportunities to announce Christ by words addressed either to non-believers with a view to leading them to faith, or to believers with a view to instructing and strengthening them, and motivating them to a more fervent faith" (AA 6).

The task of proclaiming and spreading the faith is not always easy. Living in an age of aggressive secularism, we may be tempted at times to view it as an impossible task. The Lord, however, never promised it would be easy. He warned us that not everyone would have ears to hear the good news (cf. Mark 4.9).

On the other hand, the need for God is still as widely felt in the world as ever it was. The great difference is that in our time this need for God is often not recognized for what it is. An enormous amount of "idealism" — that is, hunger for the Perfect — coexists today with indifference and even hostility toward religion, especially institutional religion. Duty to God and compassion for our neighbor require that here also we feed the spiritually hungry. The need is there: "Many people, including many of the young, have lost sight of the meaning of their lives and are anxiously searching for the contemplative dimension of their being."[4]

Distinctive Traits of Lay Witnessing

Each believer must be an active witness to God and the faith. His principal duties as a witness to the faith are two: to carry the words of life to those who are to believe and have no other way of coming to them (cf. Rom. 10.14), and to testify to those words by words and by acts.

Jesus, speaking of His role as the incarnate Witness of the Father, noted that He did nothing on His own authority but taught only what He had been taught by the Father. "I ... speak these things as the

---

[4]Pope Paul VI, Apostolic Exhortation, *Evangelica Testificatio* (June 29, 1971) n. 45 (EV 4.1046).

Father instructed Me" (John 8.28). "My teaching is not Mine but His who sent Me" (John 7.16).

The witness, therefore, having received the message with joy, remains always subject to it and obedient before it. The message is not a personal possession to alter or distort. The faith to which Christ has called us, and which we are to hand to those we love, has not been given in secret whisperings to each individual. However personal the graces by which God calls us to Himself, He calls us to the publicly proclaimed Gospel which is to unite in one faith the whole family of God.

The more actively one works as apostle — perhaps as a writer or teacher, or as a parent, or in some other capacity — the more important it is that one's work be rooted in the obedience of faith, in full openness and assent to what Christ constantly teaches in His Church.

Young Catholics and Vocations

A realization that every person has a vocation must be inculcated especially in the young. "In fact the Church sees her path towards the future in the youth, beholding in them a reflection of herself and her call to that blessed youthfulness which she constantly enjoys as a result of Christ's Spirit."[5]

Young Catholics are not to be seen simply as people whom the Church should serve in a variety of ways, but also as people who come to realize what they are and are called to be by being invited themselves to do in the Church the important tasks to which Christ calls them. "Young people are and ought to be encouraged to be active on behalf of the Church as leading characters in evangelization and participants in the renewal of society."[6]

Formation for the Apostolate

Suitable preparation is necessary for the effective exercise of the lay apostolate. Spiritual formation is most important. One can advance in the kingdom effectively only if one's life is firmly rooted in faith. Lay apostles must love the world in their love for the Creator, and care to save it in their love for Christ. If we treat our neighbor's need as less important than our luxuries, our claim to love God will lack plausibility (cf. 1 John 3.17).

[5]Pope John Paul II, Post-Synodal Apostolic Exhortation, *Christfideles Laici* (December 30, 1988) n. 46.
[6]Ibid. Cf. also Pope John Paul II, Apostolic Letter, *Parati Semper* (March 31, 1985) (EV 9.1452-1531).

In addition to spiritual formation, the laity need doctrinal instruction in the faith, and in the sciences and skills relevant to their apostolate. They should learn to "view, judge, and do all things in the light of faith" (AA 29).

The lay apostolate can be exercised by individuals, and preparation for it can be acquired in many ways. But there are valuable group forms of the apostolate also. Many are assisted in their formation for the apostolate by membership in a sodality, charitable association, apostolic guild, or third order. Especially to be noted are those associations which have received the title of "Catholic Action." In such groups, the laity cooperate more directly and immediately with the hierarchy, offering their own skills and experience to further the Church's apostolic aims, in a way that symbolizes fittingly the unity and community nature of the Church (cf. AA 20).

Some formal commitment will be involved in almost every serious response to God's call to an apostolic Christian life. Some will make the basic Christian commitment to faithfulness in daily prayer and Sunday Mass and devotedness in one's work and family responsibilities. Others will join an association like those we have noted above. A more solemn commitment can be in a "secular institute." In joining such an institute one consecrates the work of one's ordinary life to God through such means as profession of poverty, chastity, and obedience, and the following of a common rule.[7]

Spontaneity is good. But true human spontaneity is aided by a rule of life and self-discipline. Human spontaneity is not merely doing what impulse suggests; it flows more richly from an ordered life, in which one has rooted out what is false and selfish, so that the whole man, brought to inner peace, may gladly and from the whole heart do what is grasped as really good. For this reason, the rule of life for a religious or devoted layman is no legalistic prison. It is a work of love, a freely adopted and strengthening commitment, as marriage can be for those who truly love each other.

In love of God and neighbor each of us is called to serve the Gospel and to make it bear fruit in the world. When the lay vocation is lived well, then alone will other worthy vocations flower in Christian homes and provide both the religious and secular commitments needed in the world and Church today. In living out the faith in dedicated love, the lay people in their homes, with their families, and with their friends will become the source of encouragement to those whom God calls to the priesthood or religious life. In this sense, the fostering of vocations is largely a lay person's task.

[7]On secular institutes, see Congregation for Religious and for Secular Institutes, *Informative Document, Since 1947* (January 6, 1984) (EV 9.566-604).

Gospel Counsels and Religious Life

Christ taught the rich young man that everyone is obliged to love God and his neighbor in the faithful observance of the commandments (cf. Luke 18.10-20). But those in whom God's grace stirs a hunger for a more excellent life are called to share with Christ a generous will to give up much that they may cling to God in a richer freedom. Christ's invitation to many to close discipleship endures in the Church in a special way in the religious life. Those who enter religious life bind themselves, "either by vows or by other sacred bonds which are like vows in their purpose" (LG 44), to observance of the evangelical counsels of perfection, that is, the Gospel counsels of chastity, poverty, and obedience.

"The evangelical counsels of chastity dedicated to God, poverty, and obedience are based upon the words and example of the Lord. They were further commended by the apostles and the Fathers, and other teachers and shepherds of the Church. The counsels are a divine gift, which the Church has received from her Lord and which she ever preserves with the help of His grace" (LG 43).

The Christian who undertakes to bind himself solemnly to these Gospel counsels has through baptism already "died to sin and been consecrated to God" (LG 44). But, "in order to be able to gather more abundant fruit from this baptismal grace, he intends, by the profession of the evangelical counsels in the Church, to free himself from those obstacles which might draw him away from the fervor of charity and the perfection of divine worship," and one is "more intimately consecrated to divine service" (LG 44). Acceptance of the evangelical counsels involves giving up things which are by no means evil in themselves. The merchant who wants to buy a pearl of great price must sell other perfectly innocent possessions in order to do so (cf. Matt. 13.46). The athlete who hopes to excel must live rather austerely (cf. 1 Cor. 9.25). The same is true in the world of spiritual exercise.

The word "decide" comes from a Latin word which means "cut away." A decision to follow Christ closely through the observance of His evangelical counsels involves cutting away many perfectly laudable objectives which one might otherwise pursue: sexual and domestic fulfillment in marriage, ownership of property, legitimate self-concern. Yet the giving up of these things can be counted as nothing (cf. Phil. 3.8) by those who long to share emptying of self with Christ, so that they might cling to him immediately with a full and freer heart (cf. 1 Cor. 7.32-35).

The Witness of Religious Life

It is in the context of our long, slow, stumbling march to another, more perfect home that religious life makes sense. Knowing we have a destination — life with our Father — the religious gladly offers himself or herself as a sign pointing the way. By a visible, dedicated life he or she shows all who will look and can see that God has already begun His final work on earth and that this divine labor will culminate in glory in the life to come.

In words addressed to religious, Pope Paul VI refers to the "grandeur of this self-giving, freely made by yourselves, after the pattern of Christ's self-giving to His Church," a self-giving "total and irreversible." He continues: "It is precisely for the sake of the kingdom of heaven that you have vowed to Christ, generously and without reservation, that capacity to love, and need to possess, and that freedom to regulate one's own life, which are so precious to man. Such is your consecration, made within the Church and through her ministry — both that of her representatives who receive your profession and that of the Christian community itself, whose love recognizes, welcomes, sustains, and embraces those who within it make an offering of themselves as a living sign 'which can and ought to attract all the members of the Church to an effective and prompt fulfillment of the duties to this Christian vocation ... more adequately manifesting to all believers the presence of heavenly goods already possessed in this world' (LG 44)."[8]

Thus the vows of religious are to be understood positively. They are made "for the sake of the kingdom of heaven." They are a way of bearing witness to values that transcend private possessions, marital love, independent action.

Religious Poverty

By consecrated poverty, a religious renounces personal possession or control of property in order to imitate Christ, who made Himself poor for our sake (cf. 2 Cor. 8.9). The religious withdraws far from too great a love of earthly things, to become a consolation and support to the many poor and little ones of Christ. Religious commitment to poverty is a constant reminder to the whole Church of the Gospel demand that all believers free their hearts from the treacherous charm of riches and acquire poverty of spirit. "At a time when there is an increased danger for many of being enticed by the alluring security of possessions, knowledge, and power, the call of God places you at the pinnacle of the Christian conscience. You are to remind men that their true and complete progress consists in responding to their calling 'to share as sons in the life of the living God, the Father of all men.' "[9]

---

[8]Pope Paul VI, Apostolic Exhortation, *Evangelica Testificatio* (June 29, 1971) n. 7 (EV 4.1005).
[9]Pope Paul VI, Apostolic Exhortation, *Evangelica Testificatio* (June 29, 1971) n. 19 (EV 4.1019). The interior quotation is from Pope Paul VI, Encyclical, *Populorum Progressio* (March 26, 1967) n. 21 (EV 2.1066).

Consecrated Chastity

Another challenge to prevailing habits of thought in the world is the virtue of dedicated chastity. The celibate offers something to God that is in fact a good. More profoundly, he or she is bearing witness that human sexuality, although good in itself, is only one form of love. By their chastity religious "give witness to all Christ's faithful of that wondrous marriage in which the Church has Christ as her only Spouse, a marriage which has been established by God and which will be fully manifested in the world to come" (PC 12).

Not all are called to a life of consecrated chastity. But those who are called by grace and embrace this life out of the love of Christ and in the desire to serve His kingdom with greater freedom and single-heartedness (cf. 1 Cor. 7.32-35) find in chastity a means to profound self-fulfillment and growth in grace. The Church has learned by experience and from the words of Christ (cf. Matt. 19.11-12) that virginity for Christ is a vocation of "surpassing excellence."[10]

Christ-like Obedience

Consecrated obedience also challenges many present-day habits of thought. Various factors, including misleading popularizations of psychology, have led many to suppose that genuine self-fulfillment is opposed to the selfless generosity required to imitate the heroic obedience of Jesus (cf. Phil. 2.8). Modern demands for autonomy sometimes go far beyond all rational limits, urging us to view any authority, even that of the saving God, as a threat to our dignity. Thus many today find it difficult to see genuine obedience as a virtue at all, and they fail to see that when obedience imitates the obedience of Christ, it enlarges the human spirit.

Christ's obedience was not cringing or slavish. With a firm will He did that which was bitterly difficult out of love for Him who sent Him. There is a grandeur in Christ's self-forgetting obedience to His Father — "For Christ did not please Himself" (Rom. 15.3) — as there is in the mature obedience of the servant of Christ.

In a sense, obedient Christians, like Christ, both do and do not do their own will. For those who live in obedience have put their hearts at peace. Their deep will is to do what God wishes them to do, through whatever means His will is made known. It pleases good religious to do even that which does not please them, when God calls to generous

---

[10]Cf. Pope Paul VI, Apostolic Exhortation, *Evangelica Testificatio* (June 29, 1971) n. 13 (EV 4.1013). Cf. also OT 10; Pope Pius XII, Encyclical, *Sacra Virginitas* (March 25, 1954); Council of Trent, Session 24, November 11, 1563, *Doctrine on the Sacrament of Matrimony*, canon 10 (DS 1810).

service. By obedience the religious bears witness to a principle the world needs ever to relearn: it is not through indulgent self-will but through self-restraint that one lays holds of freedom.

Religious life normally is lived in religious community. Those living this common life can help each other in faithfulness to the Gospel generosity to which they are called. Such a common life is expected to provide a pattern of community also for the other faithful. Those freed from the burdens of secular life are expected to make the sacrifices of forgiveness and magnanimity that build community in such a way as to give heart to all the faithful.

Religious Community as a Sign

Thus we see that within the Church, itself a sign, the consecrated religious is a sign. His or her life must point out to others the love, understanding, compassion, and truth of Christ. This type of life is a sign within the great sacramental sign which is the Church. By being a light, as it were, it illuminates the way for others within the Church.

Religious must reach out to God in order to enrich their own personal relationship with Him. At the same time, through his or her works and love the religious is a visible and effective sign, one greatly needed in the Church today. "Without this concrete sign there would be a danger that the charity which animates the entire Church would grow cold, that the salvific paradox of the Gospel would be blunted, and that the 'salt' of faith would lose its savor in a world undergoing secularization."[11]

Religious commitment makes sense only to one who lives by faith. Total commitment of one's self, one's life, energies, love, and talents to a life of disciplined service in community is unintelligible and impossible without the eyes of faith. St. Paul reminds us that to the world sacrifice in apostolic love seems foolish (cf. 1 Cor. 4.9-10). One must be willing to seem foolish.

Personal holiness is part of the holiness of the whole Christian community. The activity of a religious, therefore, must not be directed solely toward one religious community, but toward the good of the whole Church and, through the Church, to the entire human family. The "new creation" of which St. Paul speaks (cf. Gal. 6.15) demands truth, justice, love, peace and all the beauty and holiness of the Gospels. It cannot be brought about by merely turning inward. It is the result of the work of the entire Christian community working together, confident that we can build a "new world."

[11]Pope Paul VI, Apostolic Exhortation, *Evangelica Testificatio* (June 29, 1971) n. 3 (EV 4.998).

Special Blessing of Contemplative Religious

The importance of the religious life, especially its contemplative aspect, can hardly be exaggerated. Every Christian knows that God is to be found and loved and served in one's neighbor. It is often forgotten, however, that one's neighbor is also to be found and loved and served in God, and that for some this will be the most practical approach to the task of even temporal charity.

Active works are essential, but their effort is particular and limited. One who realistically wishes to do something for the world and the human race on a large scale might best devote oneself to a life of prayer, obedience, penance, solitude, and silence. That is how the Church has always embarked on "renewal." That is how the great efforts launched by the saints started, as witness the hermits of the Thebaid, Benedict at Subiaco, Francis at La Verna, Ignatius at Manresa, Teresa of Jesus, and many more. Jesus Himself fasted in the desert. Whenever there has been in the Church what subsequent generations have recognized as a major renewal, it has started with individuals or small groups who have cared enough to go out into the desert or to the hermitage or to the cloister to wrestle alone with God and Satan, in the solitude of contemplative prayer.

For these reasons, the Church insists that communities of contemplative religious "will always have a distinguished part to play in Christ's Mystical Body" (PC 7). Contemplative religious contribute to the building up of the kingdom of God by the witness of their lives, and their communities are a source of "hidden apostolic fruitfulness' (PC 7).

A special contemporary danger, or temptation, is that of excessive activism. External acts can of themselves never "save" the world; the religious had no ultimate hope apart from the cross and resurrection of Christ. The life of the hermit and the enclosed life of the contemplative religious are among the most "relevant" of the lives to which Christians are called.

Vocation and Wisdom

"Let nothing be put before the Work of God," said St. Benedict. He was referring to the ordered worship of God in the Divine Office. But whatever our vocation in life, it is in prayer and worship, especially in liturgical worship, that we are most fully human, since we are then doing the particular thing for which we were made. It may at times seem a burden, but contemplation of God is in the end the goal of our life, the whole point and purpose and joy of existence.

We must learn to care and not to care. Each of us must respond to God's particular calls, and must live accordingly. On the other hand, there is a sense in which the outward pattern or form of our lives is a matter of complete unimportance. In any situation holiness is an option available to us; in no situation will it be easy for us. Yet nothing else really matters. It is wisdom to seek first of all the kingdom of God. Everything else good flows from that pursuit (cf. Matt. 6.33).

23

To Share In The Divinity Of Christ

The Son of God became our Brother so that we might share in the life of God. This is the great mystery of God's love in the Incarnation. "What has revealed the love of God among us is that the only-begotten Son of God has been sent by the Father into the world so that, being made man, the Son might by His redemption of the entire human race give new life to it and unify it" (UR 2). Daily the Church prays that we may "come to share in the divinity of Christ, who humbled himself to share in our humanity."[1]

In this chapter we speak of the ways in which we share in the life of God. The chapter discusses the various kinds of grace, how God Himself dwelling in us is the uncreated grace, and how God transforms His people with the created gifts of grace. Finally, it shows why it is necessary for those who have been justified to grow in the life of grace.

The Meaning of Grace

The word "grace" (or "favor") is commonly used in the New Testament to speak of the generosity by which God gives us new life. On the one hand, the word is used to suggest the pure mercy and freedom with which God so blesses us. It is also used of the gifts themselves that flow from that mercy.

Every gift of God that is related to the new life Christ came to give is called a grace. The new life itself is a grace. Certainly everything God enriches us with is a gift. Our very existence and all the things of nature that sustain and enrich our lives are His gifts. But some of His gifts are doubly gratuitous. In sublime freedom God chose to call us to be not only His creatures, but His friends. We are invited to know Him by faith and to love Him and one another with a divine love bestowed by Him. All these special gifts are aimed at our coming to full possession of God in the blessed vision of eternal life. The gifts God gives us to arouse, nourish, and fulfill this life in us are called "supernatural" gifts, or graces.[2]

---

[1]Roman Missal, Liturgy of the Eucharist, prayer at the pouring of wine and water into the chalice.

[2]Cf. First Vatican Council, Session 3, April 24, 1870, *Dogmatic Constitution on the Catholic Faith*, ch. 2 (DS 3004-3005).

Justification

We are called to this new life from a sinful state. Each person is born in original sin, and born into a world damaged by sin. But God "has rescued us from the power of darkness and transferred us to the kingdom of His beloved Son, in whom we have redemption, the forgiveness of sins" (Col. 1.13-14). St. Paul speaks of this justifying mercy of God often, especially in his Epistle to the Romans (cf. Rom. 6-8).[3]

Freedom is the keynote of justification. God does not justify us out of necessity, but because He chooses to. The grace with which He draws us to new life is utterly unmerited by us. But He treats us as free persons, not as puppets or as programmed robots. Grace is given to our freedom. In all the stages of justification of an adult, from the first invitation of grace to its full flowering, divine freedom arouses human freedom. If we do not reject His gift, God moves us in such a way that we come to have a holy and useful fear of His justice, to have hope in His mercy, and to begin to love Him, and so to hate and turn away from sin, so that we repent and come to the new birth of baptism. Then, in justification itself, we receive "not only remission of sins, but also a sanctification and renewal of the inner man through the voluntary reception of the grace and gifts whereby an unjust man becomes just and from being an enemy becomes a friend, that he may be 'an heir according to the hope of life everlasting' (Titus 3.7)."[4]

God's Gift of Himself: Uncreated Grace

The first of all God's gifts is the gift of Himself. He desires to give Himself to us perfectly in eternal life. Then we shall join those who already "are in glory, beholding 'clearly God triune and one, as He is' " (LC 49),[5] and share forever the richness of infinite life.

Even in this present life God gives Himself in many ways. He gives Himself to us as a friend in the gifts of revelation and charity; He gives Himself to us in Christ in whom "the whole fullness of deity dwells bodily" (Col. 2.9). At the Last Supper, however, Christ spoke of a special gift that God makes of Himself to us in time, a gift or grace known as the divine indwelling. "Those who love Me will keep My word, and My Father will love them, and we will come to them and make our home with them" (John 14.23). The Father and Son will dwell in those who love Christ, and They will cause the Holy Spirit to dwell there as Advocate. "The Holy Spirit, whom the Father will send

---

[3]Cf. Council of Trent, Session 6, January 13, 1547, *Decree on Justification*, esp. chs. 1-8 (DS 1521-1532) for an authentic Catholic interpretation of this teaching.

[4]Council of Trent, Session 6, January 13, 1547, *Decree on Justification*, ch. 7 (DS 1528).

[5]The interior quotation is from Council of Florence, Bull, *Laetentur Caeli* (July 6, 1439) (DS 1305).

in My name, will teach you all things" (John 14.26). Because the Triune God will be in them, and because they will know that He who infinitely loves them is with them, it will be well with them. "Peace I
leave with you; My peace I give to you" (John 14.27). Though visibly
Jesus departs from the disciples they will have peace, for the Persons
of God will dwell in them, until the day when they will see the Trinity
face to face in the eternal home prepared for them (cf. John 14.2-3).

This dwelling of God in the hearts of the faithful is a central truth
of faith. St. John and St. Paul speak of this frequently and urge us to
live lives worthy of so great a grace. "God abides in those who confess that Jesus is the Son of God, and they abide in God. ... God is
love, and those who abide in love abide in God, and God abides in
them" (1 John 4.15-16). "Do you not know that you are God's temple
and that God's Spirit dwells in you?" (1 Cor. 3.16).

This presence of God is far more than the ordinary presence of
God as Creator and Lord of all that is. To those who love and believe
Him He is present in a richly new way. He is present as Friend, with
personal affection; He is present transforming them, making them
children by adoption and sharers in His nature. He is present to unite
them to Himself (cf. John 17.22-23). He is present that He may be
known. He wishes men to grow in holiness and the life of prayer that
they may more and more taste His presence, as saints and mystics of
every age have proclaimed.[6] Faith teaches the true meaning of this
tremendous mystery. Though we are closely joined with God and
share His life as He dwells in us, He remains God and we remain creatures. While we share His life, we remain always finite and distinct
from Him who is the infinite Lord of all.[7] But it is a mystery that
transcends our understanding; it is truly a beginning of a heavenly life.
"This marvelous union, known by the special name of indwelling, differs only by reason of our condition or state from that union in which
God embraces and beatifies the citizens of heaven."[8] Such is the uncreated grace: God Himself is within us to save us.

Created Grace and Gifts

When God dwells in those who love Him, He changes them. "He
has given us, through these things, His precious and very great
promises, so that through them you may escape from the corruption
that is in the world because of lust, and may become participants of
the divine nature" (2 Peter 1.4). God does not merely regard us in a
different light; His love is powerful and transforms those who love

---

[6]Cf., e.g., St. Teresa of Avila, *The Interior Castle*, "Seventh Mansion," ch. 1.
[7]Cf. Pope Pius XII, Encyclical, *Mystici Corporis* (June 29, 1943) (DS 3814).
[8]Pope Leo XIII, Encyclical, *Divinum Illud Munus* (May 9, 1897) (DS 3331).

Him. In justifying us He causes us to "clothe ourselves "with the new self, created according to likeness of God in true righteousness and holiness" (Eph. 4.24). We who have been aliens and outcasts because of sin become sons by adoption, truly sharing in His life. "See what love the Father has given us, that we should be called children of God; and that is what we are" (1 John 3.1).

All this reveals a profound change in our being, that "sanctification and renewal of the inner man" of which the Council of Trent spoke. God truly gives us new life when He justifies us. This change in the heart of our being, the created gift by which He binds us personally to Himself, the uncreated Gift, and makes us be His sons and daughters and heirs of heaven, is called sanctifying grace.

State of Grace

Sanctifying grace is meant to be an enduring gift. For that reason, it is also called "habitual grace." Once we receive this grace it remains with us, unless we separate ourselves from God by deliberate mortal sin. To keep sanctifying grace means to preserve one's friendship with God; to lose sanctifying grace means to separate oneself from personal friendship with the Lord.

One is said to be in the "state of grace" when one possesses this sanctifying grace, and the personal relationships with God that are its inner meaning. This "state" is spoken of in various ways. "Justification from sin and God's indwelling in the soul are a grace. When we say a sinner is justified by God, is given life by the Holy Spirit, possesses in himself Christ's life, or has grace, we are using expressions which in different words mean one and the same thing, namely, dying to sin, becoming partakers of the divinity of the Son through the Spirit of adoption, and entering into an intimate communion with the most Holy Trinity."[9]

It is a prime duty of the Catholic to retain and develop this friendship with God. Only in the state of grace can one merit further blessings and eternal life. The Church speaks often of the need to remain always in this friendship with God, especially when one draws near to Him in certain of the sacraments and as one approaches the hour of death. It is a serious sin to receive any of the "sacraments of the living" (confirmation, Eucharist, marriage, holy orders) if one is not in the state of grace, that is, if one does not have inwardly the friendship with God that reception of these sacraments outwardly proclaims. Only those who die in God's grace enter the kingdom of God; indeed the blessed vision of God is a flowering of the life which begins with the possession of grace.

[9]Sacred Congregation for the Clergy, *General Catechetical Directory* (April 11, 1971) n. 60 (EV 4 544).

The state of grace, as we have seen, is lost by a deliberate mortal sin. For such sin is a personal turning away from God, a refusal to remain a son or daughter of God, a rejection of one's right to eternal life, the loss of infused gifts and virtues, the forfeiture of all acquired merits. But God can and does call sinners back to life; He moves them to "exert themselves to obtain through the sacrament of penance the recovery, by the merits of Christ, of the grace lost."[10]

This return to grace also is a serious and decisive step. An insincere confession of sins will not achieve it. There must be a change of heart, made possible by God's grace, and sincerely exercised in earnest repentance.

Virtues and Gifts

Together with sanctifying grace God gives us the virtues of faith, hope, and love, so that, having become children of God, we may do the works of God. These virtues orient our new life directly to God.

By the virtue of faith, God enables us to share in the light of His own knowledge, so we may know Him and His saving word. The certainty of the believer is not founded on merely human wisdom, but on the life given by God which causes one to whom He is present to recognize Him and His testimony in revelation (cf. John 5.9-10). By the virtue of hope, God gives an unshakable confidence in Himself. St. Paul speaks in the name of every Christian: "I am convinced that neither death, nor life . . . nor height, nor depth, nor anything else in all creation, will be able to separate us from the love of God in Christ Jesus our Lord" (Rom. 8.38-39). But the greatest of these three theological virtues is love (cf. 1 Cor. 13.13). "Poured into our hearts through the Holy Spirit" (Rom. 5.5), it enables us to cling with our whole hearts to God with an energy and life that He Himself communicates. All Christian moral life is grounded on these theological virtues.

But there are other virtues. Every good person should grow in the "cardinal virtues" of justice, fortitude, temperance, and prudence (cf. Wisd. 8.7), and in the many virtues that flow from these. To the extent that these virtues are merely human and natural, they do not of themselves minister to grace or lead men to friendship and eternal life with God. But grace and charity can transform natural virtues, and plant in the heart dispositions to do all humanly good deeds in a way that makes them expressions of divine love. Thus it is that supports for every kind of good action are planted in the soul with sanctifying grace.

Gifts of the Holy Spirit are also given with grace. A familiar Messianic prophecy of the Old Testament declared that the Spirit would

---

[10]Council of Trent, Session 6, January 13, 1547, *Decree on Justification*, ch. 14 (DS 1542).

bring to the Redeemer gifts of wisdom, understanding, counsel, fortitude, knowledge, piety, and fear of the Lord (cf. Isa. 11.2-3).[11] The Fathers and saints of the Church have persistently taught that these same gifts are conferred on Christ's members, on all the faithful who are in grace. By the gifts of the Spirit "the soul is furnished and strengthened to be able to obey God's voice and impulse more easily and promptly."[12] Those who are weak and unpracticed in serving Christ often find it hard to recognize and do God's will; for, though grace be present, the whole person is not yet attuned to receiving well the gentle guidance of the Spirit. But faithful service develops a sensitivity, so that the mature Christian is able to respond with greater ease and joy to the Spirit's call. The more one is led by the mysterious quiet direction of God rather than by one's own calculation and determination, the more perfect one's acts become. One reward of faithfulness to grace in times of difficulty is the growing ease and joy with which the mature Christian lives with assurance of the Holy Spirit's guidance.

"By means of these gifts the soul is excited and encouraged to seek after and attain the evangelical beatitudes."[13] These beatitudes were pronounced by our Lord at the very beginning of His public preaching (cf. Matt. 5.3-10):

- Blessed are the poor in spirit, for theirs is the kingdom of heaven.
- Blessed are those who mourn, for they will be comforted.
- Blessed are the meek, for they will inherit the earth.
- Blessed are those who hunger and thirst for righteousness, for they will be filled.
- Blessed are the merciful, for they will obtain mercy.
- Blessed are the pure in heart, for they will see God.
- Blessed are the peacemakers, for they will be called children of God.
- Blessed are those who are persecuted for righteousness' sake, for theirs is the kingdom of heaven.

By the gifts of the Holy Spirit one is led toward the sublime dispositions that the beatitudes praise and the blessedness that they promise. These, together with the fruits of the Holy Spirit, "are the signs and harbingers of eternal beatitude."[14] "The fruit of the Spirit is love, joy, peace, patience, kindness, generosity, faithfulness, gentleness, self-control" (Gal. 5.22-23).

[11]"Piety" is not in the Hebrew text, but is in the Septuagint and Vulgate versions.
[12]Pope Leo XIII, Encyclical, *Divinum Illud Munus* (May 9, 1897), AAS 29 (1896-97) 654.
[13]Pope Leo XIII, Encyclical, *Divinum Illud Munus* (May 9, 1897), AAS 29 (1896-97) 654.
[14]Pope Leo XIII, Encyclical, *Divinum Illud Munus* (May 9, 1897), AAS 29 (1896-97) 654.

Actual Grace

God is also ever present to us with what we call "actual" graces. These are the helps which God gives us so that we may actually do deeds of love. By actual graces God enlightens our minds to see His ways and strengthens our resolve to walk in them, or to return to them if we have gone astray.

The Catholic faith steadfastly proclaims that every saving act, every action that leads to or expresses love of God or the work of His saving mercy, is made possible only by God's gift. It likewise proclaims that God treats us as persons endowed with free will and responsibility. His grace does not lessen, but increases, our freedom.

Actual graces can be internal or external. Internal actual graces are gifts by which God assists and animates us from within, so that we may perform free and saving actions. External graces are infinitely varied. Every kind of gift by which God moves us toward knowing Him and sharing His life is a grace. Devoted parents, faithful friends, good books, great music — indeed anything at all may be used by God to lead toward life. Even sickness and trials may be mercies by which God is directing toward salvation those whom He loves.

Dying to Sin

Catholic Faith proclaims that the gifts of God are very real. God truly makes holy those whom He justifies by faith, baptism, and the life of the Spirit. Yet even after justification their remains in us something of sin. It is not possible at the same time both to have and not to have the new life of Christ, both to love God and to be separated from Him by the present guilt of a deliberate mortal sin. But it is possible to be in the state of grace and at the same time to experience concupiscence, the inclination to sin. St. Paul sometimes calls his tendency toward evil that we discover in ourselves "sin" (cf. Rom. 6.12-13; 7.7; 7.14-20). But this is something very different from a deliberate rejection of God; it is not an actual mortal sin. It is called "sin" only because of its source and tendency: "it comes from sin and inclines toward sin."[15]

As Christians, grateful for God's grace, we must nonetheless acknowledge that we are sinners. We were born in original sin, and we experience tendencies toward sin. We are able to remember well our personal, deliberate sins, and we know how much they have intensified concupiscence. Frequently we are guilty of selfish and ungrateful deeds, even if the mercy of God guards us from the tragic malice of mortal sin.

The Christian must struggle against sin. While the grace of God

---

[15]Council of Trent, Session 5, June 17, 1546, *Decree on Original Sin* n. 5 (DS 1515).

guarantees our final victory unless we reject God's help, grace does not excuse us from faithful and serious effort. "Do not let sin exercise dominion in your mortal bodies, to make you obey their passions" (Rom. 6.12). Some who were called by God and given grace neglected to respond energetically to grace and "have suffered shipwreck in the faith" (1 Tim. 1.19). To be a Christian demands dying to sin, dying with Christ to something deep within oneself, so that one may rise to newness of life (cf. Rom. 6.4). The new life is God's gift, but it is not secured without efforts responding to His grace. As athletes must deny themselves much in training if they desire victory, so we must discipline ourselves if we truly care about eternal life. "Run in such a way that you may win it. . . . I do not run aimlessly, I do not box as though beating the air; but I punish my body and enslave it" (1 Cor. 9.24, 26-27). The matter is vital; nothing is more urgent. Within and without are forces to be conquered. The Lord Himself came to "free and strengthen man" (GS 13); but we ourselves must act in the "dramatic struggle between good and evil" (GS 13).

The Flesh

Concupiscence inclines us to every capital sin, that is, to pride, covetousness, lust, anger, gluttony, envy, and sloth,[16] and to their dismal fruits. We must persevere in penance and self-denial if we are to destroy the perverse tendencies in our hearts and make room there for the new gifts of God to take root and grow. "If any want to become My followers, let them deny themselves and take up their cross and follow Me" (Matt. 16.24). Only in this way do disciples of Christ find their true selves and eternal life (cf. Matt. 16.25-26). "And those who belong to Christ Jesus have crucified the flesh with its passions and desires" (Gal. 5.24).

The World

The struggle is also against the world. God indeed is its Creator and His world is "very good" (Gen. 1.31), and "God so loved the world" (John 3.16) that He sent His Son to save it. But Scripture also speaks of the "world" in another and very different sense, of the "world" as an alignment of forces that do not believe and love God. This is the "world" Christ refused to pray for as the hour of His passion approached (cf. John 17.9).

"The love of the Father is not in those who love the world" (1 John 2.15). Christians must guard themselves from the fascinating attractions of the world, while yet retaining an unselfish love of persons in the world, for whom Christ died.

---

[16]Cf. St. Gregory the Great, *Moralia in Iob* 31.45 (ML 76.621).

The Devil

Our life in Christ has cosmic dimensions as well. Although we do not understand fully what role God permits the devil and other demons to have on this earth, the reality of malign spiritual forces is only too evident in the despondent pain of the unbelieving world and in the tragic sorrows in the record of history. "For our struggle is not against enemies of blood and flesh, but against the rulers, against the authorities, against the cosmic powers of this present darkness, against the spiritual forces of evil in the heavenly places" (Eph. 6.12).[17]

Growing in Grace

Grace is a gift of life, and we must grow in it. Even the first gifts of grace, when one first comes to justification, are sublime gifts; but with them we are really only infants in a new life (cf. 1 Peter 2.2). We are to grow up in faith (cf. 2 Cor. 10.15), in doing deeds of love (cf. 1 Thess. 3.4), growing up in every way to mirror the splendid maturity of Christ our Head (cf. Eph. 4.15).

Faith, hope, love, and all the gifts of the new life are not deeply rooted or perfectly expressed in us at first. In the Epistle to the Colossians, St. Paul tells his converts, already rich with Christ's life, what they should look forward to. "We have not ceased praying for you and asking that you may be filled with the knowledge of God's will in all spiritual wisdom and understanding, so that you may lead lives worthy of the Lord, fully pleasing to Him, as you bear fruit in every good work and as you grow in the knowledge of God. May you be made strong with all the strength that comes from His glorious power, and may you be prepared to endure everything with patience, while joyfully giving thanks to the Father, who has enabled you to share in the inheritance of the saints in light" (Col. 1.9-12).

Christ has called us to a perfection that is not quickly reached (cf. Matt. 5.48), to an intense living of all His gifts, especially of love, which "binds everything together in perfect harmony" (Col. 3.14). Joy in the life received ought to make one gladly strain forward to what is ahead. "One thing I do: forgetting what lies behind and straining forward to what lies ahead, I press on toward the goal for the prize of the heavenly call of God in Christ Jesus" (Phil. 3.13-14).

This growth which is expected of every Christian is not something to be achieved by individuals in isolation, but is a growth in love with the whole family of faith. We allow God to build us together into a dwelling place of His presence: "Like living stones let yourselves be built into a spiritual house" (1 Peter 2.5). This growth requires effort

---

[17]Cf. the study commissioned by the Sacred Congregation for the Doctrine of the Faith, *Christian Faith and Demonology* (June 26, 1975) (EV 5.1347-1393).

on our part, but it is God who gives the growth (cf. 1 Cor. 6.6). By accepting His call and allowing His gifts to bear fruit in us (cf. Matt. 5.8), we can become more generous in keeping His commands of love, drawing near to Him in prayer, and associating ourselves with Christ's life-giving mysteries through His sacraments. In such living of faith one experiences the joy and richness of the new life which becomes more and more the eternal life of heaven anticipated already in time.

To live this divine life ever more fully is to become certain that its entire fulfillment in the blessed vision of God will be a good beyond all imagining. "No eye has seen, nor ear heard, nor the human heart conceived, what God has prepared for those who love Him" (1 Cor. 2.9; cf. Isa. 64.3).

24

Christ And The Life Of Prayer

"Lord, teach us to pray" (Luke 11.1). The disciples, seeing our Lord so long at prayer, asked that they might learn to pray. And Jesus taught them.

In this chapter we treat of prayer in the life of one who has accepted Jesus as Lord and Teacher. Here we discuss Christ as Model and Teacher of prayer, the necessity of prayer for the Christian life, the effects of prayer, the definition and types of prayer, and the necessity of grace for prayer.

Christ as Model and Teacher of Prayer

The person converted to Jesus Christ will pay careful attention to the Master's pattern of living as well as to His teachings. Both the lifestyle and the words of Jesus Christ show that prayer should have priority in the allocation of one's time.

The Gospels, especially St. Luke's, often describe Christ at prayer (cf. Luke 3.21; 5.16; 9.29; 10.21; 11.1; 22.32). He prayed, publicly as well as privately, before the most important acts and decisions of His ministry (cf. Luke 4.1; Matt. 14.23; Heb. 5.7). Mark, after describing a day of intense activity by Christ, notes: "And in the morning, while it was still very dark, He got up and went out to a deserted place, and there He prayed. And Simon and his companions hunted for Him. When they found Him they said to Him, 'Everyone is searching for You,' He answered, 'Let us go on to the neighboring towns, so that I may proclaim the message there also; for that is what I came to do' " (Mark 1.35-38). Luke seems to indicate a consistent pattern in Christ's life: withdrawal, prayer, activity. Prayer was the constant background of the Lord's life. This continuous prayer is explained by the evangelist John as flowing from Jesus' special relationship to the Father (cf. John 1.51; 4.34; 8.29; 11.41).

In His prayer life, the Lord showed Himself an heir to the treasures and traditions of the Hebrews concerning prayer. He prayed the Psalms (cf. Matt. 27.46), especially the Hallel, the great hymn of praise formed by Psalms 113-118 (cf. Matt. 26.30). He knew well the Shema, the ritual prayer said by the Jews twice a day: "Hear, O Israel! The LORD is our God, the LORD alone. . ." (Deut. 6.4; cf. Matt. 22.37).

The teaching of Jesus about prayer was a teaching which He was already living. In many ways Jesus showed the disciples how to pray. To show them what to pray for, He gave them the Our Father, which was His prayer, the perfect prayer, as a model. Yet even the Our Father is given to us in different words in the Gospels of Luke (11.2-4) and Matthew (6.9-13). This suggests that the spirit of a prayer is more important than any exact set of words. Jesus taught His disciples to be sincere and unostentatious in their prayer.

The Sermon on the Mount includes His instruction to pray in private (cf. Matt. 6.6). That directive is followed by a reminder not to "heap up empty phrases as the Gentiles do" (Matt. 6.7).

Jesus Himself prayed in simple and direct words. He addressed God the Father as "Abba," the simple, familiar address used by a child to his father. Jesus uses the title "Abba" at Gethsemani (cf. Mark 14.36). St. Paul refers to it twice (cf. Rom. 8.15; Gal. 4.6), as if by that time it had gained usage in liturgical prayer. It is thought that Jesus used this distinctive form of addressing God in prayer, and that the earliest Aramaic-speaking community formally adopted it. There are no indications that Judaism at the time of Christ made use of this title in prayer.

Necessity of Prayer for Christian Life

Jesus Himself lived always in a prayerful spirit and blossomed easily into explicit prayer. Such prayerfulness He taught the apostles also. They should "watch and pray." The Lord seems even to have commended prayer as a constant activity: "Then Jesus told them a parable about their need to pray always and not to lose heart" (Luke 18.1).

From the example and teaching of Jesus Christ, it is clear that a Christian should be a person of prayer. All who know that their existence and life of grace come from God can recognize the need to remain in communion with God.

This point is important because there are always people who find prayer worthless. There are the lazy or distracted who do not have the generosity to follow the Master in praying, and who try to excuse themselves. There are the contentious who say that God already knows what we need, the deists who say God has no personal interest in this world. There are some who see prayer as selfishness.

Against such errors the Church teaches that God indeed does know everything, and that prayer is not an attempt to inform God of our needs.[1] Prayer can be an acknowledgment of one's weakness and

---

[1]For a classic treatment on the usefulness of prayer and how this is not excluded by God's providence, cf. St. Thomas Aquinas, *Summa Contra Gentiles* III, 95-96.

dependence on God. Further, prayer is not selfish, because one prays — if one prays as Christ teaches — with humble submission to God's will and in obedience to His command (cf. Luke 11.9-13). We cannot reach salvation without graces from God — and some graces according to God's plan are granted only in answer to prayer.[2]

Prayer, therefore, is neither useless nor selfish. It flows from one's filial relationship with God. It is the loving, obedient response of a child to a Father's love. Any life lived in faith, hope, and love will have to express itself to God in prayer.

The Second Vatican Council repeatedly taught the necessity of prayer. Prayer is presented as an identifying mark of the Church and of the genuine Christian (cf. LG 10, 12, 40, 41). Its necessity for the laity as well as for priests and religious is made clear: "Since Christ in His mission from the Father is the fountain and source of the whole apostolate of the Church, the success of the lay apostolate depends upon the laity's living union with Christ. . . . This life of intimate union with Christ in the Church is nourished by spiritual aids which are common to all the faithful, especially active participation in the sacred liturgy" (AA 4).

Effects of Prayer on Christian Life

St. Thomas Aquinas teaches that prayer brings about three effects: it merits graces from God, it obtains other benefits from God, and it brings a certain spiritual refreshment of the mind.[3]

It is certainly true that prayer, when it follows the pattern of Christ's prayer, has a transforming effect on one's life. Genuine prayer is bound into the totality of life as it is lived, affects the rest of life and is affected by the rest of life. We cannot pray well unless we are prepared to change in our lives those things which hold us back from God. We do not set our lives in order first and then pray. We pray — and we are prepared to discover that as we go on praying we shall find more and more things that have to be changed.

The person who has learned to pray, and who actually does pray, can reach a point where his whole life is penetrated by prayer. This connection between prayer and all of life was also described by the Second Vatican Council (cf. AA 4).

The Christian must be careful to avoid the trap of activism. To say, "My work is my prayer," is wrong if it implies that one need not pray explicitly at times. For those who never, or hardly ever, pray, it is simply not true that their work is part of their prayer. The experience of many Catholics confirms this. Those who truly pray by their work

[2]Cf. St. Thomas Aquinas, *Summa Theologica* II-II, 83, 2.
[3]Cf. St. Thomas Aquinas, *Summa Theologica* II-II, 83, 13.

are the very ones who are careful to pray to the Father in secret (cf. Matt. 6.6), who take time to be alone with the Lord.

What is the "certain spiritual refreshment of the mind" that comes from a life of prayer? As the general words used by St. Thomas Aquinas suggest, this is not something easy to describe in specific terms. Prayer does make radical demands on one. But it ultimately leads to a refashioning of oneself according to the plan of God. One's personality, viewed as a complex of attitudes and values, must be trimmed and cultivated, and trained to the mind of Christ. "Let the same mind be in you that was in Christ Jesus" (Phil. 2.5). The end result is the peace of Christ: a harmonious order and balance within oneself; a view of this world from the perspective of God and of eternity; a strength to hold oneself together despite change about and within one; a growing closeness to God through Jesus Christ.

Definition and Types of Prayer

The traditional Catholic definition of prayer is "the raising of one's mind and heart to God." When we pray, we turn our minds and hearts to God, to adore Him and thank Him or ask favors or forgiveness of Him.

It is not easy to give a brief, satisfactory definition of prayer. The verb "to pray" means literally to ask for something — and yet prayer is much more than just asking God for something. Any definition of prayer must show that it is more than an activity of the intellect. A person's will, affections, and activities are all to be lifted up to God, bringing about an intimate personal relationship with Him.

St. John of Damascus described prayer as "the ascent of the mind to God, the request for fitting things from God."[4] St. Thomas Aquinas pointed out that there is an element of petition in all prayer; indeed, according to St. Thomas, the ultimate prayer of petition is the quest for God, in accord with Psalm 27: "One thing I asked of the LORD, that will I seek after: to live in the house of the LORD all the days of my life" (Ps. 27.4)[5] Definitions of the word "prayer" came in time to cover also meditation and various degrees of contemplation.

At the present time there is a preference for the broad definition of prayer as "speaking with God." This definition has advantage. It includes all types of prayer. At the same time, it indicates that prayer is not a monologue but a dialogue, a conversation. By prayer we respond to God who first spoke to us, especially through His unique Word made flesh.

---

[4]St. John of Damascus, *De Fide Orthodoxa* 3.24 (MG 94.1089-1090).
[5]Cf. St. Thomas Aquinas, *Summa Theologica* II-II, 83, 17;83, 1 ad 2.

Purposes of Prayer

There are four general types of prayer, according to the reasons or purposes for which one prays: adoration, thanksgiving, petition, and contrition. All other kinds of prayer — love, praise, abandonment to God's will, atonement, reparation, and so on — can be included in one or the other of the four general types. Praise, for example, is a way of adoring God with joy. The four general types express the motives of one's prayer: to express God's excellence and our absolute dependence (adoration); to express gratitude for benefits received (thanksgiving); to express a request for something (petition); and to express sorrow for sins (contrition).

These motives are often interconnected in actual prayer. In every true petition to God there is at least a virtual expression of adoration, thanksgiving, and contrition. In the Our Father, expressions of adoration ("hallowed be Thy name") and contrition ("forgive us our trespasses") themselves become petitions.

Here on earth our prayers are frequently expressions of sorrow and petition. But the Christian life requires also prayers of adoration and thanksgiving. In heaven the prayers of the blessed will be chiefly expressions of adoration and thanksgiving.

Prayers of Petition

It is important for the praying follower of Christ to have a correct, balanced understanding of the prayer of petition. There is a tendency to turn to God only when we want something, and to pray only prayers of petition, and then to be displeased with God if we do not promptly get what we have asked for. This is clearly not a Christian attitude.

On the other hand, Christ Himself told us to ask God for things: "Very truly, I tell you, if you ask anything of the Father in My name He will give it to you. Until now you have not asked for anything in My name. Ask and You will receive, so that your joy may be complete" (John 16.23-24; cf. Matt. 7.7). This promise is fulfilled for every Christian who truly prays in Christ's name, with the proper dispositions and for something that will be helpful to eternal salvation.[6] God always hears our prayers. He knows how to give good things to His children (cf. Luke 11.13). Sometimes, however, we ask for foolish or even harmful things. For what, then, should one pray? It seems fitting to pray to God for anything one needs or might reasonably desire. Though prayer is a spiritual activity, we may ask our heavenly Father for physical and material things: our "daily bread." Everything we care about is worthy of prayer, for nothing which is important to us is insignificant to God, who loves us.

[6]Cf. St. Thomas Aquinas, *Summa Theologica* II-II, 83, 15 ad 2.

There is undoubtedly a certain order of priorities in what is worth praying for. For some things, we must pray. For other things, we are free to pray. In keeping with the Our Father, we should ask for God's glory, the coming of His kingdom, the fulfillment of His will on earth, and the graces necessary and useful for salvation.

The Christian must be careful in praying for specific material goods and possessions. These can be asked for, if they are helpful towards salvation. The poverty of Christ and His warnings about riches should make us cautious about praying for superfluous material goods. No Christian would expect God to give something that might be detrimental to salvation. Consequently God does not grant every petition for improved health, employment, material possessions, and the like, for these might be spiritually harmful. Nevertheless, all prayers for worldly goods are heard by God. It may be that the answer is often in a spiritual form.

It is proper for the Christians to pray for themselves, that they accomplish God's will in life and reach eternal salvation. They should also pray for their neighbors, in keeping with the requirements of Christian charity. The Church tells us to use the "Prayer of the Faithful" at Mass to pray for (a) the needs of the Church, (b) public authorities and the salvation of the world, (c) those oppressed by any need, and (d) the local community.[7] Our private prayer as well should have wide range. We pray for our families, for the people we work with, for our friends and neighbors. Prayers should also be offered for the Holy Father, one's bishop and all bishops, one's pastor and all priests and deacons, religious women and men, for all in the Church, for all outside the Church that there may be one flock and one shepherd, for those in authority, for relatives and benefactors, for the deceased whom one has known and for all souls in purgatory (cf. LG 50), and even for enemies and persecutors (cf. Matt. 5.44).

Qualities Essential in Genuine Prayer

Christian prayer should have certain qualities. Among these are attention, devotion, confidence, and perseverance.

Attention. Christ requires that we pray with an absolute inner sincerity, not with the hypocritical externalism of the Pharisees (cf. Matt. 6.5-8). The devout Christian, consequently, will pray thoughtfully. "I will pray with the spirit, but I will pray with the mind also; I will sing praise with the spirit, but I will sing praise with the mind also" (1 Cor. 14.15). Involuntary distractions may come and go, because of human weakness. These do not destroy the value of prayer.

Devotion. Prayer is more than an exercise of the mind. It is also a

---

[7]Cf. General Instruction of the Roman Missal, n. 46.

genuflection of the will to God. Genuine devotion should not be confused with a feeling of satisfaction or with emotion. For devotion is properly a total dedication to God. As a mother's devotion to her family is shown chiefly in her generous action, devotion to God is shown in freely choosing to give Him our mind and heart. At times devoted acts are accompanied by peace and joy. At times they are not. Yet even when prayer comes hard, the will can submit to God: "Thy will be done. . . ." Even a sinner, though lacking in devotion, is obligated to pray. But the more devoted to God one is, the closer one's friendship with Him, and the more likely that a prayer will be heard.[8]

Confidence. The Lord has told us to pray with an unshakable confidence born of faith (cf. Matt. 11.24; Luke 17.5; James 1.5). We do this by praying "in the name of Jesus" our Mediator with full confidence in His redemptive love and in the power of His merits to obtain from the Father what is asked (cf. John 16.23-24). To approach God with little or no hope is to offend Him (cf. James 1.6). For this reason the official prayers of the Church which are addressed to the Father end the petition with the words "through Christ our Lord."

Perseverance. We learn from the Gospels to pray with perseverance. "And will not God grant justice to His chosen ones who cry to Him day and night?" (Luke 18.7; cf. also Matt. 7.7-11; 15.21; Luke 11.1-13; Eph. 6.18; 1 Thess. 5.17). The Christian should never be discouraged in prayer, should never give up, never lose heart (cf. Luke 18.1).

To Whom We Pray

The Christian prays to the one, triune God. Ordinarily in the New Testament all prayer, private as well as public, is addressed to God the Father through Christ and in the Spirit. One may direct prayer to all three Persons or to one of Them. Thus occasionally in the New Testament (cf. John 14.14; Acts 7.59; 1 Cor. 1.2; 2 Cor. 12.8; 1 Tim. 1.12) and in the Mass, prayers are directed to Christ. Similarly some prayers, as the "Come, Holy Spirit," are addressed to the Holy Spirit.

The Second Vatican Council expressed clearly how our prayers are ultimately addressed to God, and how prayers to the Blessed Virgin and to the angels and saints in heaven ask them to intercede before God for us (cf. LG 50). "At the same time, let the faithful be instructed that our communion with those in heaven, provided that it is understood in the more adequate light of faith, in no way weakens, but rather on the contrary more thoroughly enriches, the supreme worship we give to God the Father, through Christ, in the Spirit" (LG 51).

So to God we give absolute worship, and to Him we pray: "Have

---

[8]Cf. St. Thomas Aquinas, *Summa Theologica* II-II, 83, 15-16. 9.

mercy on us." To the Blessed Mother and to the saints we show a different kind of honor or devotion, and we ask them: "Pray for us" (cf. LG 67).

Prayer and Grace

Christian prayer is supernatural. In prayer the mystery of God and the mystery of man meet in discourse — and the Holy Spirit works to bring this communication about. "The Spirit helps us in our weakness; for we do not know how to pray as we ought, but that very Spirit intercedes with sighs too deep for words. And God, who searches the heart, knows what is the mind of the Spirit, because the Spirit intercedes for the saints according to the will of God" (Rom. 8.26-27).

Prayer is beyond what we human beings can do by ourselves. Prayer cannot be mastered by human efforts or human techniques alone. There is no true prayer which is not the effect of grace. No matter how difficult or studied or how spontaneous one's prayer may be, it is always God who raises up the heart which lifts itself to Him.

Ultimately, then, prayer is possible only because God makes it possible. As an expression of the supernatural virtues of faith, hope, and love, prayer itself is of the realm of grace. It is the work of the Holy Spirit within us — and yet it is we who pray.

Filial Prayer

In the New Testament, the basis for prayer is the new relationship by which Christians come to the Father through Jesus Christ. We are adopted sons and daughters of God. The Christian, joyfully aware of this, can pray with childlike confidence and tender intimacy to the loving Father, to "Abba" (Rom. 8.15; Gal. 4.6). This new relationship gives a special quality to the prayer of a Christian in the name of Christ. So also it gives a distinctive flavor to Christian mysticism.

Prayer a Response to God's Word

Prayer, as we noted earlier in this chapter, is a dialogue in which God has already spoken and has expressed the first word. The books of Sacred Scripture are in a particular way the word of God. "For in the sacred books, the Father who is in heaven meets His children with great love and speaks with them; and the force and power in the word of God is so great that it remains the support and energy of the Church, the strength of faith for her sons, the food of the soul, the pure and perennial source of spiritual life" (DV 21). Moreover, "Christ is present in His word, since it is He Himself who speaks when the Holy Scriptures are read in the Church" (SC 7).

The prayer of a Christian, consequently, is a response to God's word. This is shown in the Mass: first God speaks to the assembled Church in the Liturgy of the Word; then the Church responds in the Profession of Faith and joins Christ in the Eucharistic Prayer.

The same approach is important in private prayer. Catholic tradition has strongly recommended the reading of Scripture as the basis of prayer, and has considered prayer and contemplation to be the proper response to God's word. This explains the traditional emphasis on "spiritual reading" in Catholic spirituality. In the Bible and also through other spiritual writings God's word comes to us. This word calls for our response, and the first response is prayer.

Discipline in Prayer

The hard work of persevering prayer demands faithfulness to other graces from God. Only one trying to lead a good life will have the appropriate dispositions to pray.

The state of soul that permits prayer does not come about without preparation through an entire range of circumstances. One prepares for a life of prayer by leading a good life, and prayer is an expression of that life. So every sacrifice which detaches us from the world, everything which conforms us to the image of God, every movement of love that puts us in harmony with the triune God — all this is preparation for prayer.

Every Christian who seeks to pray faithfully learns that perseverance in prayer requires self-discipline. Saints who have loved and enjoyed prayer have often reminded us that faithfulness in prayer requires effort and discipline. In the well-balanced *Rule* of St. Benedict, the recitation of the choir office of Psalms and prayers is called "the work of God." In *The Sayings of the Fathers*, a collection of sayings or maxims of Egyptian monks of the fourth and fifth centuries, there is the wise saying of Father Agatho: "The brothers asked Abba Agatho: 'Father, which virtue in our way of life needs the most effort to acquire?' And he said to them: 'Forgive me, I think there is nothing that needs so much effort as prayer to God. If a man wishes to pray, the demons infest him in the attempt to interrupt prayer, for they know that prayer is the only thing that hinders them. In all the other efforts of a religious life, whether they are made vehemently or gently, there is room for a measure of rest. But we need to pray till we breathe out our dying breath.' "[9]

[9]*Apophthegmata Patrum* 12.2.

25

Private And Liturgical Prayer

All prayer is personal. In it we are to be personally involved mind and heart, in speaking with God. There are, however various forms of prayer. Sometimes prayer is individual or private; sometimes it is shared with others; sometimes it is public or liturgical.

In this chapter we discuss each of these various forms of prayer and offer some suggestions on learning to pray.

Individual Prayer

Prayer is often addressed to God by an individual in private. This form of prayer was commended by the Lord in His Sermon on the Mount: "Whenever you pray, go into your room and shut the door and pray to your Father who is in secret; and your Father who sees in secret will reward you" (Matt. 6.6).

These words of the Master expressed a cherished Old Testament tradition. A quiet room in the house, with a window facing Jerusalem, was a favorite place for private prayer (cf. Tobit 3.11; Dan 6.10; 1 Kings 8.38; 2 Chron. 6.34). Thus the biblical roots of private prayer are found in the Old Testament as well as in the New.

For prayer in private there are no particular rules. Any place is adequate, and any posture is suitable. There are no requirements on length of time, or on the use of vocal or mental prayer. There are no firmly fixed hours of the day, though Christian custom strongly favors morning and evening prayers and prayers at meals, and the Christian has a duty to pray in times of danger and temptation. But the individual has complete freedom in judging the way one will pray, in being completely oneself while speaking with God.

Personal prayer is of basic importance in leading the Christian life, as the words of the Lord clearly indicate. This is the daily link to God which transforms character and life. Personal prayer helps prepare the Christian for liturgical prayer. The Catholic with no discernible private prayer life may find Sunday Mass an isolated, unsatisfactory prayer experience; the Catholic with a vigorous private prayer life will appreciate the Mass more and be better prepared to participate fruitfully.

Vocal Prayer

A vocal prayer is one expressed in words, or occasionally in gestures. It may be a fixed formula or in one's own words; it may be said aloud or silently. In any case, the words should express the thoughts of the one praying. Jesus warned against sheer multiplication of words while praying (cf. Matt. 6.7), and He quoted Isaiah to rebuke the Pharisees: "This people honors me with their lips, but their hearts are far from me" (Matt. 15.8; cf. Isa. 29.13).

Vocal prayer may be a personal, spontaneous cry that springs from the heart of a person in joy or in danger. But vocal prayer is usually the recitation of a fixed formula — such as the Our Father, the Hail Mary, and Glory Be; or a Psalm or hymn; or a repetitive prayer such as a litany, the Angelus, or the rosary.[1] That Christ made use of prayer formulas is clear from the Gospels. The Lord quoted the great prayers of the Old Testament. When asked by the disciples for instruction in prayer, Jesus gave them the Our Father as a model and as the greatest vocal prayer of Christianity (cf. Matt. 6.9-13; Luke 11.2-4).

Guided by the example and teaching of Jesus and the strong tradition of the Church, the Catholic should know and say memorized prayers. Memorization has had "a special place in the handing-on of the faith throughout the ages and should continue to have such a place today, especially in catechetical programs for the young."[2] Prayers considered here are such as the Sign of the Cross, the Lord's Prayer, Hail Mary, Apostles' Creed, Acts of Faith, Hope and Charity, and Act of Contrition.

The validity and usefulness of vocal prayer for every state of the spiritual life have been formally taught by the Catholic Church.[3]

Brief vocal prayers, according to long tradition, can be an effective way of praying. Both the Eastern and the Western traditions of Christianity know methods of praying through short, memorized formulas. For some, this use of prayerful ejaculations has been a considerable help in learning prayer and drawing close to God. The early monks of the desert, for example, commended the practice of repeating often in the day the first verse of Psalm 70: "Be pleased, O God, to

---

[1]On the Angelus and the rosary, cf., e.g., Pope Paul VI, Apostolic Exhortation, *Marialis Cultus* (February 2, 1974) nn. 40-55 (EV 5.71-87).

[2]United States Catholic Conference, *Sharing the Light of Faith — National Catechetical Directory for Catholics of the United States* (1979) n. 176.

[3]Cf., e.g., Decree of the Holy Office (August 28, 1687) and Pope Innocent XI, Constitution, *Caelistis Pastor* (November 20, 1687) (DS 2221, 2269).

deliver me. O LORD, make haste to help me." St. Francis of Assisi regularly made similar use of "My Lord and my God!"

The so-called "Jesus Prayer" is another ejaculation. It seems to have originated in the desert of Sinai, and since the fourteenth century has been used by many Christians of the East. The prayer is simple: "Lord Jesus Christ, Son of God, have mercy on me, a sinner."

The use of such brief, intense prayers is helpful for maintaining a spirit of prayerfulness when one is unable to establish regular times for longer prayer. The Psalms are a source of many such brief prayers, suited to the needs and moods of the individual. Such prayers can also be drawn from the liturgy, as, for example, the familiar "Lord have mercy . . . Christ have mercy."

Spontaneous Prayer

Spontaneous prayer is a type of vocal prayer which comes to one's lips because of a situation in which one finds oneself. This is the prayer that gushes forth from one at certain moments in life. Generally speaking, spontaneous prayer is possible in two kinds of situations. The first is when we become vividly aware and appreciative of God, and this awareness evokes a response of joy and worship. The other is when we are in serious difficulty. These are the times when we cry out to God in fear and anguish, from the depths of discouragement and loneliness. We sense there is no hope for us unless God rescues us: we turn to God and we pray.

We must recognize, however, that it is not sufficient to pray only when one is in danger or experiencing great happiness. We must pray regularly. It is a mistake to think a person can sustain spontaneous prayer on a daily basis throughout life. There are long periods of life, especially in the adult, when one is neither at the top nor at the bottom of the emotional scale. Yet the Christian must pray in those periods, even when he does not feel like praying. Conviction should sustain prayer when spontaneous fervor does not.

This point is important. Most people who begin a life of prayer come sooner or later to times when all spontaneity is gone. They may think that unless they feel strongly or emotionally about the words and phrases they use, they are not sincere. But this is not true. The spiritual writers note that there can be periods of monotony, even aridity, without affecting the value of prayer. The mature Christian, then, continues to work at prayer, following a daily program in spite of any feeling of dryness.

Mental Prayer: Meditation and Contemplation

In general, mental prayer is characterized by the absence of external words or gestures. The intellect and will, however, are truly attentive to God. In both vocal and mental prayer the most characteristic functions are praise, adoration, and thanksgiving. In both vocal and mental prayer an element of petition is present. There is a difference, however, in that mental prayer is a more personal approach to God.

Mental prayer may be either formal or informal. It is formal when one devotes a definite period of time to making these internal acts of prayer, and does nothing else at the same time. It is informal when one prays internally while also doing something else — such as cooking, sewing, or driving.

The process of mental prayer is a major means of developing spiritual life. The vocation of every Christian is to be a saint. Sanctity means acquiring the mind of God and reaching intimacy with God. The means of reaching God is to become intimate with Jesus, who, though He is God, is also like us in all things but sin. By studying Jesus and imitating Him, we eliminate our pride and learn from Him who is "gentle and humble in heart" (Matt. 11.29). We gradually "put on the Lord Jesus Christ" (Rom. 13.14), and in the process make God central in our lives. Formal mental prayer is the technique of putting off the old self and putting on the new (cf. Col. 3.9-10), of trying to become perfect as our heavenly Father is perfect (cf. Matt. 5.48).[4]

Without earnest prayer one cannot progress far in paths of holiness. There may indeed be many simple followers of Christ who reach a high degree of spiritual perfection through a devout practice of thoughtful vocal prayer and disciplined lives of charity. Therefore, it cannot be said that formal mental prayer is necessary for all who strive for Christian perfection. Formal mental prayer is, however, a suitable means of Christian perfection for most followers of Christ. Such prayer cannot be neglected without spiritual loss. Its daily practice is recommended most strongly to the clergy and religious. St. Thomas Aquinas says that meditation is necessary for devotion.[5] Canon Law makes it clear that the clergy and religious should engage in mental prayer.[6] The Second Vatican Council called for "faithful meditation on God's word" as part of the spiritual formation of seminarians (cf. OT 8).

Methods and Divisions of Mental Prayer

Many methods of mental prayer have been developed within Catholic tradition. All these methods aim at helping us gather together our human powers and concentrate our attention where it is needed.

---

[4]At times forms of meditation based on principles not faithful to the Gospel tend to become popular. Cf. the Congregation for the Doctrine of the Faith, *Letter to the Bishops of the Catholic Church on Some Aspects of Christian Meditation* (October 15, 1989). This urges the use of forms of prayer entirely faithful to Catholic teaching.

[5]Cf. *Summa Theologica* II-II, 82,3.

[6]Cf. *Code of Canon Law*, canons 276.2 n. 5, 663.3.

But all the spiritual guides tell us not to become preoccupied with method.

If a person needs a method to start mental prayer — and many people of today do — then it is helpful for one to know something of the stages of growth in prayer life and the approaches to prayer used by others. It is wise to use a method which corresponds to one's own psychological makeup. Individuals with active, analytical minds may be helped by a method such as that developed by St. Ignatius Loyola. Others who are less analytical and more emotional of temperament might benefit more from methods developed by St. Francis de Sales. In any case the individual should keep in mind that the purpose of a method of prayer is not to develop interesting and fresh ideas about God, but actually to raise one's mind and heart to God and to converse with Him.

Since the seventeenth century it has been usual for spiritual writers to describe three stages of formal mental prayer. Though various terms are used, we here call them (1) meditation, (2) affective prayer, and (3) contemplation. There is a normal course of development in the spiritual life. Those who grow in a life of prayer normally advance from the more structured meditation to the more simple and direct contemplation.

Meditation

Meditation is also called "discursive prayer," because it calls for a good deal of thinking and reasoning. Meditation is strongly encouraged for beginners in the spiritual life. It is thoughtful prayer, and it involves communion with God and the saints and it leads to resolutions. During the course of the Christian centuries various methods and techniques for meditation were developed. All of them have the same general purpose of helping the individual become more Christlike through regular mental prayer.

The early Fathers and monks of the Church had definite periods for holy reading. During these set times they read the Scriptures, meditated and prayed. This was one of the earliest forms of meditation, and it remains one of the simplest.

In the Middle Ages, St. Bernard of Clairvaux taught his followers to focus their meditations on Christ in His humanity. This was a helpful development, as was Bernard's formula for meditation. Later the Franciscans popularized meditation on the life of Christ, particularly on His poverty and His passion.

The new religious orders of the sixteenth and seventeenth centuries tried to develop a practical prayer technique adapted to their apostolic life. The *Spiritual Exercises* of St. Ignatius Loyola was written to guide spiritual directors in fostering mental prayer. The influential Carmelite tradition descended from Louis of Granada and Peter of Alcántara to Teresa of Jesus.

In his *Introduction to the Devout Life*, St. Francis de Sales aimed at helping lay people to pray, whatever their occupation or state of life. He drew generously on the wisdom of the past, but adapted the older techniques to new situations and states of mind. Thanks to his common sense and good humor, St. Francis de Sales is still a helpful guide in the life of serious prayer.

St. Alphonsus Liguori in similar fashion developed the method of St. Teresa in a way that his Redemptorist descendants have used with good effect. Also deserving of mention is the influential tradition of the French Oratory, formed by the intellectual Cardinal de Berulle, and the Christocentric method of Father Jean Olier, developed by the Sulpicians and taught to many generations of seminarians.

Structure of Meditation

In every method attention is called to three elements: the preparation, the mental prayer itself, and the conclusion.

In Christian meditation, the person is deliberately and carefully trying to study the life and teaching of Jesus Christ in such a way that he will be transformed and grow in holiness. This is no small task. The remote preparation for meditation is the whole pattern of one's life. The immediate preparation consists of such things as withdrawing to quiet, reading the selected text of Scripture or other religious book, placing oneself in God's presence, and asking Him to enable one to meditate well.

The body of the meditation consists chiefly in devout reflection on a chosen theme. One seeks in this prayer to give to God one's whole attention; one's memory, imagination, understanding, and all one's affections. The immediate purpose of meditation is to deepen one's faith, spiritual insight, and convictions, so that the mysteries of faith reflected on begin to be appreciated in their overwhelming richness, and so that one's commitment to God and love of Him may acquire deep and lasting roots.

A considerable amount of the time in meditation is given to thinking about Christ and His saving mysteries and message. Here we lay the foundation for future spiritual growth. We are seeking to gain fuller personal possession of the mysteries of faith, seeking to love God with our whole mind (cf. Matt. 22.27), so that we might have the motives to pursue a more earnest love of God with our whole heart.

The conclusion of the meditation may include a more familiar discussion with God, the Blessed Mother, or some particular saint. Some firm, practical resolution should be made, so that the activity of prayer may help one direct one's life more earnestly in the way of Christ.

Many spiritual guides recommend selecting a key idea from the meditation to keep gently in one's thoughts throughout the day.

Affective Prayer

A more advanced form of mental prayer is called "affective prayer." Here probing reflections play a smaller part. One's mind and heart are already rooted firmly in God, and are turned more easily and immediately to God. One has already learned much of Christ and His mysteries, but longs for a deeper kind of knowing and a closer presence of love.

Scripture often speaks of friendship with God as analogous with the friendship between human persons who love one another. When a man and woman are first attracted deeply to each other, they would like to talk with each other extensively. There are many things to learn, and each wishes to know all that concerns the other. But there comes a time when much speaking is superfluous. Quiet being together, and caring, is now more important. A glance, a gesture, a presence can be eloquent enough. This degree of friendship and love normally needs considerable preparation. So, too, it is with those advancing in friendship with God.

Affective prayer is normally found in those who have already rooted themselves in God by meditation and resolute faithfulness in Christian life. Of course, affective elements are present in all prayer, even that of beginners. But the distinctive simplicity and depth of this kind of affective prayer reveal that one has made considerable progress.

Most serious followers of Christ can advance to this stage of prayer, can move from meditation to more simple prayer. In mental prayer certain signs are often noted: though one remains faithful to times of prayer, and faithful to God in one's life, one's prayer begins to seem dry and pointless. For one not yet sufficiently schooled in meditation it may be important to endure this trial patiently, while desiring and seeking to come to more fruitful meditation. In other cases, however, the sense of aridity itself may be a sign that one is ready for the richer joy of a more simple prayer.

Contemplation

The highest stage of mental prayer is contemplation, which itself has many stages. Contemplation is God's most generous gift in this life to those who have loved Him with great faithfulness. In its highest forms, this prayer draws one as near to God as it is possible to come before one reaches the beatific vision. It gives a certain rich experience of the divine presence, and it brings great joy and peace.

When this contemplative prayer is authentic, it is the expression of a whole life given to God with excelling generosity. One comes to such great love through the cross, through dark nights and faithfulness in trials. Yet in contemplation one comes to the overwhelming peace of Christ. This is not a peace free of trials, but a peace born to great love. "For just as the sufferings of Christ are abundant for us, so also our consolation is abundant through Christ" (2 Cor. 1.5).

The writings of the Catholic mystics show the great variety of ways in which God unites Himself in mystic prayer to His close friends. Persons of every state of life have been blessed with this kind of prayer. Observance of the evangelical counsels helps to purify the heart and prepare it for the love such prayer requires. Indeed, many religious orders seek above all to help their members to advance toward the service of God and the Church in this heroic way.

The Church speaks of religious orders of contemplatives as a "glory of the Church and an overflowing fountain of heavenly graces" (PC 7). The charter for the contemplative life has often been seen in the words of Christ about one who gave Him the total gift of her mind and heart in preference even to giving Him the service of external labor. Christ pointed out the surpassing excellence in the focused love of the contemplative: "There is need of only one thing. Mary has chosen the better part, which will not be taken away from her" (Luke 10.41).[7]

Growth in Prayer and Christian Living

In our approaches to mental prayer we may be surprised to realize that we are almost strangers to Christ and to spiritual values. The words of the Gospel and of spiritual writers seem to us distant and strange. The soul must do much work in meditation. But gradually one grows in knowledge and love of the Lord. Christ assists our efforts.

With persistent care the soul purifies itself of other attachments and becomes more free to concentrate on God. In time the soul knows that of itself it is nothing — but this leads only to greater confidence in God. There are slips and failures, but these need not cause discouragement. Prayer then becomes simple and easy; suffering is valued; the Holy Spirit works much. Contrition is deep and sincere; the soul shrinks from anything approaching sin. There is a remarkable tolerance of the faults and weaknesses of others, as if the person, sharing in God's forgiveness, finds it easier to forgive others. The liturgy is loved. The soul has God's viewpoint on all things, lives in a supernatural atmosphere, and is an apt instrument to accomplish God's will.

Growth in prayer essentially requires growth in all of Christian

---

[7]Cf. Pope Pius XI, Apostolic Constitution, *Umbratilem* (July 8, 1924).

life. The life of prayer, then, is the way to reach that holiness to which every follower of Christ is called (cf. Matt. 5.18).

Shared Prayer

Shared prayer has become popular in some Catholic circles in the period since the Second Vatican Council. This is actually private vocal prayer addressed to God but voiced aloud while gathered together with others.

Shared prayer is somewhat different from simply praying together with others. In an atmosphere of faith a group of Christians assembles. Various individuals singly express to God their deepest thoughts and feelings in prayer. The prayer is addressed to God, but each is conscious that those who are with one are sharing a prayer. Each person may benefit from the testimony of faith and commitment shown in the prayer of the others.

In some of its forms shared prayer is encouraged by the charismatic movement. Pope Paul VI noted some of the strengths such a movement can have. It can encourage "the taste for deep prayer, personal and in groups, a return to contemplation and emphasizing of the praise of God, the desire to give oneself completely to Christ, a great availability for the calls of the Holy Spirit, more assiduous reading of the Scripture, generous brotherly devotion, the will to make a contribution to the service of the Church."[8]

Care is of course needed to guard these advantages, and to guard against pride and ostentation. Discernment of spirits is necessary, as St. Paul had already noted in writing about early charismatic prayer (cf. 1 Cor. 14.26-33); there is need to maintain great love for the whole family of the Church and its ordinary, indispensable means of grace and forms of liturgical prayer, lest any separatism or elitism impair full unity with the Church.[9] Pastoral concern for such a movement "devolves upon those who are in charge of the Church, 'to whose special competence it belongs not indeed to extinguish the Spirit, but to test all things and hold fast to that which is good (cf. 1 Thess. 5.12, 19-21).' "[10]

Liturgical Prayer

Liturgical prayer is the prayer of the whole Church, of the family of God united together in Christ. "The sacred liturgy is the public wor-

[8]Pope Paul VI, *Address* to participants at a meeting of prayer groups, at Grottaferrata, October 10, 1973.
[9]Cf. Pope Paul VI, *Address* at General Audience, February 28, 1973, and *Address* to the Congress of Catholic Charismatic Renewal, May 19, 1975.
[10]Pope Paul VI, *Address* to participants at a meeting of prayer groups, at Grottaferrata, October 10, 1973. The internal quotation is from LG 12.

ship which our Redeemer as Head of the Church renders to the heavenly Father and which the community of the faithful renders to its Founder and through Him to the eternal Father. It is, in short, the entire public worship rendered by the Mystical Body of Christ, that is, by the Head and His members."[11]

It is important to make a clear distinction between liturgical prayer and private prayer. In private prayer, individuals or groups approach God as their own fervor and their own personalities urge them. In liturgical prayer, the individual participates not as a private individual, but as a member of the Lord's Church. The liturgy is the prayer of the Church community headed by Christ. Often called the "official" prayer of the Church, liturgical prayer is subject to regulations to which private prayer is not.

The word "liturgy" comes from a Greek word for the public work, public service, or duty undertaken by the citizen for the good of the country. The basic idea of the word is that of a service performed for community purposes. Today the term liturgy is applied to the public worship of the Church, and is generally distinguished from private devotion or private prayer. Liturgy is the Church's sacramental-priestly worship, as distinct from other devotions of individuals or of groups.

The Mass, the other sacraments, the Divine Office, and public ritual are all part of the Church's liturgy. The Stations of the Cross, the rosary, prayer services, and so on, even when said by a group of people together, are devotions distinct from the liturgical, or public, prayer of the Church.

Private Prayer Ordered towards Liturgical

Because liturgy is the Church's prayer, community worship, it must be both exterior and interior. Liturgical acts of worship are exterior expressions of shared interior attitudes. The chief element in worship must be interior, in order to guarantee the sincerity and genuineness of the exterior words and actions. Otherwise, "religion clearly amounts to mere formalism, without meaning and without content. . . . It should be clear that God cannot be honored worthily unless the mind and heart turn to Him in quest of the perfect life."[12]

Private prayer is ordered towards this official, public prayer of the Church community. It is God's plan that Christians relate to Him not merely as individuals, but as a family united in Christ. It is, then, God's plan that we relate to Him as a praying community, not only as praying individuals. As members of the Mystical Body we join especially in the prayer led by our Redeemer.[13]

[11]Pope Pius XII, Encyclical, *Mediator Dei* (November 20, 1947), n. 20 (DS 3841).
[12]Pope Pius XII, Encyclical, *Mediator Dei* (November 20, 1947) nn. 24, 26.
[13]Cf. Pope Pius XII, Encyclical, *Mediator Dei* (November 20, 1947) n. 20 (DS 3841).

A life of private prayer prepares us for effective liturgical worship of God. At the same time, participation in the liturgy is at the heart of each individual's personal life of prayer. Neither private prayer nor liturgical prayer may be omitted.[14]

Excellence of Liturgical Prayer

The excellence of liturgical prayer comes not only from the devotion of the human persons united in it, but especially from the fact that this is the prayer and action of Christ and of His Mystical Body, the Church.

The liturgy is "the outstanding means by which the faithful can express in their lives, and manifest to others, the mystery of Christ and the real nature of the true Church" (SC 2). "Christ is always present in His Church, especially in her liturgical celebrations" (SC 7). "Rightly, then, the liturgy is considered as an exercise of the priestly office of Jesus Christ. In the liturgy . . . full public worship is performed by the Mystical Body of Jesus Christ, that is, by the Head and His members. From this it follows that every liturgical celebration, because it is the action of Christ the priest and of His Body the Church, is a sacred action surpassing all others. No other action of the Church can match its claim to efficacy, nor equal the degree of it" (SC 7). The liturgy is "the summit toward which the activity of the Church is directed; at the same time it is the fountain from which all her power flows" (SC 10).

The Highest Form: The Eucharistic Sacrifice

The first, highest, and central form of all Christian liturgy is the Eucharistic sacrifice, the Mass. Within the setting of a Jewish Passover meal, the Lord instituted the Eucharistic sacrificial meal of the New Covenant. It was from this rite that the New Testament liturgy was born.

The Passover meal was a ritual. It called for certain foods, including bread and wine, as well as certain prayers and explanations. On the night before He died, Jesus took some of the unleavened bread, offered it to the Father, and said: "This is My Body." He gave His Body to the apostles to eat. He took a cup of the Passover wine and said: "This is My Blood, the Blood of the New Testament." He gave His Blood to the apostles to drink. And He told them: "Do this in remembrance of me" (cf. Matt. 26.26-29; Mark 14.22-25; Luke 22.19-20; 1 Cor. 11.23-27).

Obedient to Christ, the Church does what Christ did, in remembrance of Him. The worship of the Church and its whole inner

---

[14]Cf. Pope Paul VI, Apostolic Exhortation, *Marialis Cultus* (February 2, 1974) n. 31 (EV 5.58-60).

life has always centered on the Eucharistic sacrifice, the Mass. In a later chapter we shall speak of this memorial of the Lord, of the inner reality of the sacrifice in which Christ's saving death is made present again. Here we shall only briefly note something of the form in which this great action is expressed.

The ceremonies of the Mass have their roots in the Old Testament liturgies that foreshadowed it. The ceremonies have developed through the ages. Even today there are somewhat different expressions of the same reality in the various rites of the Church. But the same general outline is adhered to everywhere.

There are two chief parts. In the Latin rite these are called the "Liturgy of the Word" and the "Liturgy of the Eucharist."

The Liturgy of the Word is made up of prayers, songs, and, chiefly, readings from Scripture. There are also moments of quiet reflection and a homily to illumine the meaning of God's word.

The Liturgy of the Eucharist has three stages. In the offertory rite, the gifts of bread and wine are brought to the altar and offered to the Lord. In the Eucharistic Prayer, the saving mysteries of the Lord's passion and resurrection are recalled by a sacramental action which makes these mysteries present again in the midst of His people. In the Communion rite, the Body and Blood of Christ are received in a sacred meal, to gather into closest unity with Christ those who have received life through Him.

The Other Sacraments and Liturgical Prayer

Each of the seven sacraments, as instituted by Christ, is part of the liturgy of the Church. Sacraments are acts of worship and the principal actions through which Christ gives His Spirit to Christians and makes them a holy people. In the chapters which follow we present a treatment of the sacraments.

The Divine Office

Another liturgical act of the entire Church is the Divine Office, or "Liturgy of the Hours." The word "office" here means duty or obligation. Prayer of praise and thanksgiving is a constant duty of the Church. "For Christ Jesus continues His priestly work through the agency of His Church, which is ceaselessly engaged in praising the Lord and interceding for the salvation of the whole world. This she does not only by celebrating the Eucharist, but also in other ways, especially by praying the Divine Office" (SC 83).

The Divine Office "is arranged so that the whole course of the day and night is made holy by the praises of God" (SC 84). It consists of (1) an Hour of Readings, (2) Morning Praises, (3) Mid-day Prayers,

(4) Vespers, or Evening Prayers, and (5) a short Night Prayer, or Compline. This Office or Liturgy of the Hours is predominantly scriptural, the Psalms holding a prominent place in it. There is a separate pattern of prayer for each day, following the rhythms of the liturgical year and of the feasts of the saints.

This is the Church's prayer, and some, especially those who are in holy orders or who have made solemn religious vows, are delegated and required to pray it faithfully in the name of the whole Church. But because it belongs to the whole Church, the faithful too are invited to participate in the Divine Office, especially in Morning Praises and Vespers. The Divine Office is a treasury of prayers — scriptural, ancient, modern. Ordinarily it takes time to learn to appreciate and love this form of prayer. But the person who schools himself or herself in this prayer of the Church will profit greatly from it.

Characteristics of Liturgical Prayer

Liturgical prayer requires the following three conditions: (1) it must be prayer in a format or formula which has been approved by those responsible for Church worship; (2) it must be prayer recited in the name of the Church; (3) it must be led or presided over by a person properly assigned.

Many misunderstandings have developed because individuals have confused liturgical prayer and private prayer. There is in fact considerable difference between the two. In the liturgy, the individual becomes an integral part of the praying community and the praying Christ. In an age of individualism, the idea of liturgical prayer is not always easily grasped and accepted.

A cleric who recites the Divine Office by himself is still praying liturgical prayer because he prays it in the name of the entire Church. A priest who celebrates Mass without a congregation is joined liturgically with the entire praying community of Christ.

There are several characteristics of the Church's liturgical worship. It is always based on the priestly, redemptive work of Jesus Christ: Christ is the supreme Celebrant of all liturgical worship. It is associated with the Church hierarchy: those bound to Christ precisely through holy orders preside over the liturgy. It is always communal in nature: it unites the members of the Church and calls for their participation. It is sanctifying: liturgy is the sign and source of the true Christian spirit.

Pope Pius XII stated that the liturgy is the most effective way of reaching sanctity and that private devotions would be sterile if they caused a person to neglect the liturgy. At the same time, however, he strongly insisted that a life of interior dedication and prayer is necessary if the liturgy is to have its proper effect and not become an empty ritualism.[15] The spiritual life, to be fully Christian and fully sincere, must be a prayer life leading up and into liturgical prayer, and from the liturgy into all the days of the week and all the hours of the day.

Because liturgy is the worship of Christ and all His Church, responsibility for directing this public prayer rests with those to whom Christ has entrusted the care of the Church, to the Holy Father and the bishops. One who takes part in liturgical prayer is acting in the name of the whole Church; those in holy orders who act as liturgical ministers are required to use the approved forms established for Church prayer (cf. SC 22). Certain parts of the liturgy are rightly left open to optional forms, to permit appropriate adaptations and allow suitable elements of spontaneity. Certain elements, in reading, prayers, vestments, and sacred gestures are required, to express the unity in faith and worship of the whole community. It would be unfair for those without authority to do so to modify the prayer of the Mystical Body, for liturgy belongs to the whole Church, not merely to the individual ministers, cantors, or others assigned special roles in it.

Learning to Pray

Prayer is necessary for us. It is a richly rewarding gift. But faithfulness in prayer also requires patient effort. The adult who wishes to pray should recognize the need for discipline, the need to develop the habit of prayer. One way to begin is to concentrate on morning prayers, evening prayers, and daily meditation.

A pattern of morning prayer might include praise of God, thanks for past goodness, an act of faith in God and His saving word, an act of hope in God above this world, an act of love of God, a resolution to imitate Jesus Christ today, and an offering to Him of all the prayers, works, and sufferings of the day ahead.

Appropriate for inclusion in prayer before retiring for the night are expressions of thanksgiving for the gifts God has given and of sorrow for one's failings during the day, and then a commending of oneself and one's loved ones to God. The official "Night Prayer" of the Church always ends with an anthem to the Blessed Mother. This is a practice which all the faithful could well follow.

Daily meditation will present the greatest challenge. Those who would grow strong in their Christian life would do well to reserve a period of time, perhaps fifteen to thirty minutes, for mental prayer each day. For some, the devout and thoughtful recitation of vocal prayers may be a useful first step in mental prayer.

An ability to manage time is important. It is difficult if not impossible to pray attentively and well when one is tense, pressured, feeling

---

[15]Cf. Pope Pius XII, Encyclical, *Mediator Dei* (November 20, 1947) nn. 31, 32, 175.

behind schedule. One should make an effort to stop the rush and be in the present now in order to pray.

Teaching Prayer to Children

Parents should of course be mindful that their children should have education in prayer. This is so even for the very young, "so that the little child may learn to call upon the God who loves us and protects us, and upon Jesus, the Son of God and our brother, who leads us to the Father, and upon the Holy Spirit, who dwells within our hearts; and so that this child may also direct confident prayers to Mary, the Mother of Jesus and our mother."[16]

Children should be taught by example the habit of praying — at morning, at night, at meals. They should be instructed in the liturgy of the Mass so that they will know what the Mass is, understand its parts, participate in it well.

The teaching of prayer should take place through experiences of prayer, through the example of prayer, and through the learning of common prayers. The part of parents should be great.

"The concrete example and living witness of parents is fundamental and irreplaceable in educating their children to pray. Only by praying together with their children can a father and mother — exercising their royal priesthood — penetrate the innermost depths of their children's hearts and leave an impression that the future events in their lives will not be able to efface."[17]

---

[16]Sacred Congregation for the Clergy, *General Catechetical Directory* (April 11, 1972) n. 78 (EV 4.577).
[17]Pope John Paul II, Apostolic Exhortation, *Familiaris Consortio* (November 22, 1981) n. 60 (EV 7.1711).

26

Liturgy: The Paschal Mystery
And Sacramental Life

Religion at its core is the quest for God. "One thing I asked the LORD, that will I seek after: that I may dwell in the house of the LORD all the days of my life" (Ps. 27.4). All that we have learned so far is given to help us in our quest. In a special way this personal quest for God is concentrated in prayer; and our personal prayer widens out to join with that of our fellowmen in community prayer. When community prayer is the prayer of the living Church itself, gathering people into one in new ways, it becomes liturgy. Liturgy is "the full public worship performed by the Mystical Body of Jesus Christ, that is, by the Head and His members" (SC 7).

In this chapter we discuss the liturgy and Christ's presence therein, the paschal mystery, the meaning of "sacrament," the seven sacraments instituted by Christ (each of which will be treated in detail in the chapters which follow), and the use of sacramentals in the Church.

Christ Present in Liturgy

Liturgical prayer is more than community prayer. The Second Vatican Council, in its Constitution on the Sacred Liturgy, showed anew how the realities of prayer and community — and sacramentality — converge in the liturgy. The Council did not speak of only a quest, or of only an encounter, but of a presence, that is, the presence of God in Christ in the liturgy. Indeed, we seek and find God only if He first comes to us. "In this is love, not that we loved God but that He loved us. . ." (1 John 4.10). God therefore is present. It is we who are absent and must seek the encounter; the obstacles to be removed are in ourselves.

"Christ is always present in His Church, especially in her liturgical celebrations. He is present in the sacrifice of the Mass, not only in the person of His minister, 'the same one now offering, through the ministry of priests, who formerly offered Himself on the cross,'[1] but especially under the Eucharistic species. By His power He is present

---

[1]Council of Trent, Session 22, Sept. 17, 1562, *Doctrine on the Most Holy Sacrifice of the Mass*, ch. 2 (DS 1743).

in the sacraments, so that when a man baptizes it is really Christ Himself who baptizes. He is present in His word, since it is He Himself who speaks when the holy Scriptures are read in the Church. He is present, finally, when the Church prays and sings, for He promised: 'Where two or three are gathered together in My name, there am I in the midst of them' (Matt. 18.20)" (SC 7).

Christ, then, is present even as His members gather together in communal prayer. In the liturgy we see the Church assembled for its central purpose of worship. Here the Head and members are gathered together before the Father. Here we are enveloped by the covenant which God Himself has made, not with isolated individuals but with His people united in Christ. Worship calls for the cooperation of the whole community, not merely as spectators but as participants.

Again, Christ is present in His word. It is "Christ Himself who speaks when the holy Scriptures are read in Church" (SC 7). Because the Church wishes to make the riches of God's word more accessible, the celebration to every sacrament now begins with a Liturgy of the Word. This liturgy includes, in addition to readings, pauses for meditation and prayer. The Liturgy of the Word is in effect a veritable school of prayer, an ascent through hearing, meditation, and devotion to intimacy. Since the quest for God is the heart at once of all prayer and especially of liturgy, prayer must indeed direct and form liturgical acts. Ritual without prayer is not liturgy.

In the liturgy Christ is yet more wonderfully with us in His Eucharistic presence; and He is present in the saving power by which He acts in all the sacraments.

All these presences are part of what St. Paul calls the mystery of God, the mystery of Christ, the paschal mystery, or simply the mystery (cf. Col. 2.2, 4.3).

The Paschal Mystery

Indeed, the Church locates the center of the whole Christian religion in the paschal mystery. Christ redeemed mankind "principally by the paschal mystery of His blessed passion, resurrection from the dead, and glorious ascension, whereby 'dying, He destroyed our death and, rising, He restored our life' " (SC 5).[2] "The Church has never failed to come together to celebrate the paschal mystery: reading also 'in all the Scriptures those things which referred to Himself' (Luke 24.27), celebrating the Eucharist in which 'the victory and triumph of His death are again made present,'[3] and at the same time giving thanks 'to God for His indescribable gift' (2 Cor. 9.15) in Christ Jesus, 'to the

[2]The interior quotation is from the Preface for Easter in the Roman Missal.
[3]Council of Trent, Session, 13, Oct. 1, 1551, *Decree on the Most Holy Eucharist*, ch. 5 (DS 1644).

praise of His glory' (Eph. 1.12), through the power of the Holy Spirit" (SC 6).

Only by realizing that in the liturgy the victory and triumph of Christ's death are made present, can we understand two statements of the Second Vatican Council which might otherwise seem unintelligible: "The liturgy is the summit toward which the activity of the Church is directed; at the same time it is the font from which all her power flows" (SC 10), and, "It is the primary and indispensable source from which the faithful are to draw the true Christian spirit. . ." (SC 14). If the liturgy were mere symbolic ritual, such claims could not be made for it. They are true only because the liturgy (which includes all the sacraments but is centered in the Eucharist) continues and makes present the paschal mystery of Christ.

The Unfolding of God's Plan

The paschal mystery is the heart of God's saving plan for us. This plan, of which Christ is the center and summit, unfolds gradually in the history of God's dealings with the human family and reaches its climax in bringing all things into one in Christ, uniting "all things in Him, things in heaven and things on earth" (Eph. 1.10).

Of this redeeming plan we have spoken earlier. It culminates in "the fullness of time" (Eph. 1.10) with the death and resurrection of Christ. By dying He destroys our death, and by rising He restores our life. At this point a marvelous transformation takes place. What appeared at the time as a cruel and unjust execution is placed by the Epistle to the Hebrews in its true perspective, in a cosmic liturgical setting. Calvary is seen as a towering mountain, a sanctuary where a new High Priest offers a sacrifice for all the nations of the world. The naked and crucified Servant, now replacing Aaron, appears as the High Priest of mankind according to the order of Melchizedek (cf. Heb. 7; Gen. 14.18). "But when Christ came as a high priest of the good things that have come, then through the greater and perfect tent (not made with hands, that is, not of this creation) He entered once for all into the Holy Place, not with the blood of goats and calves, but with His own blood, thus obtaining eternal redemption. . . . For Christ did not enter a sanctuary made by human hands, a mere copy of the true one, but He entered into heaven itself, now to appear in the presence of God on our behalf" (Heb. 9.11-12, 24).

The Book of Revelation also describes this liturgy as the climax of history. "Then I saw between the throne and the four living creatures and among the elders, a Lamb standing as if it had been slaughtered. . . . 'Worthy is the Lamb that was slaughtered to receive power and wealth and wisdom and might and honor and glory and blessing!' " (Rev. 5.6, 12). So Jesus crucified, then rising in the glory of the resurrection and ascending into the sanctuary of heaven, offers an acceptable sacrifice in a universal liturgy that joins all the redeemed to one another as they are united by Christ to Himself and the Father.

Christ in Sacrament

This liturgy, this single sacrifice that redeems all, this most perfect act of worship, is then given to the Church. "Rightly, then, the liturgy is considered as an exercise of the priestly office of Jesus Christ" (SC 7). In this liturgy Jesus Himself is the Source of every sacrament, and of every visible sign of salvation. He *is* humankind's encounter with God. He is the Word made flesh (cf. John 1.14). "In Him we see our God made visible and so are caught up in love of the God we can not see."[4] He thus shows us in His person, by the humanity He has assumed, what sacrament is: God giving His life to us, God acting redemptively on us through His visible creation. Jesus further extended this principle when He established His Church, the fundamental sacrament, in which human beings of flesh like Himself, in fact His brothers and sisters, are marked by the formative influence of the hidden Spirit. The other sacraments are means whereby Christ reaches out to humankind, and whereby the Church also, joined to Him as His Body, extends His healing and sanctifying action to all His members.

The word "sacrament" comes from the Latin word for the Greek "mysterion," the mystery of God in Christ in which St. Paul sees the vast unfolding plan and action of God among us (cf., e.g., Col. 1.26). In this mystery, Christ poured into the Church, the great sacrament which issued from Him, all the riches of grace and truth gained through His death and resurrection. The Church, we have seen, was born "from the side of Christ as He slept the sleep of death upon the cross" (SC 5). The Preface of the Sacred Heart includes: "His wounded side, flowing with blood and water, is the fountain of grace renewing the Church with sacramental life."

The Seven Sacraments

Through the sacraments the faithful cling to Christ, and draw from Him this grace and life. The Church declares that in the New Law there are seven sacramental rites instituted by our Lord Jesus Christ.[5] These seven are: Baptism, Confirmation, Holy Eucharist, Penance, the Sacrament of the Sick, Holy Orders, and Matrimony.

Each of these rites has a visible material element or elements, like bread, wine, water, oil, or visible human actions. These material ele-

---

[4]Roman Missal, Preface I for Christmas.

[5]Cf. Council of Trent, Session 7, March 3, 1547, *Decree on the Sacraments*, canon 1 on the sacraments in general (DS 1601).

ments are illumined by sacred words to become signs of faith and instruments of Christ's own saving action on humankind. The visible sign of each sacrament symbolizes the gift of grace conferred by Christ in the sacrament.

These seven sacraments, then, are actions of Christ and of His Church. They are symbols and signs that we are blessed by God and saved by Christ's redeeming mercy. They are signs of faith by which we cling in worship to Christ to share the fruits of His paschal gift; they are instruments by which Christ, through the liturgical acts of His Church, in fact confers the graces symbolized by the sacraments.

The Material Signs

Jesus shows at once His power and His compassion in meeting our human needs and aspirations, and in doing this in a way we can see and understand. He further shows wisdom and understanding in choosing elements that are almost universally recognized by the religious spirit of created persons as having a character of quasi-sacredness; and this because of their connection with life, whose source is God. Christ often drew upon the powerful symbolic force of these material realities, as water (cf. John 4.10-14) and bread (cf. John 6.27-58). True, these elements can be, and in paganism have been, deflected into superstitious and magical practices. But they can also be caught up in Christ's and humankind's effort to glorify the Father.

Sacraments are thus gifts of Christ by which He confers divine life and exercises divine power through expressive signs adapted to our human nature. In the sacraments Christ reaches out to all people of every place and in every area. In His earthly life Christ shared our finite limitation to one place and one time. Through the sacraments the glorified Christ puts aside these limitations and draws us by visible signs appropriate to our condition to the new world of eternal life, already present but hidden. His sacramental action will continue everywhere until all His promises are fulfilled.

Sacramental Encounter

Our sacramental encounter with God through Jesus Christ is a veiled encounter. Nonetheless, it is also revealing, because the sacramental elements symbolize the character of God's action upon us. Water symbolizes cleansing and life. Bread and wine signify nourishment. Oil means healing and strength. And what they signify, according to Catholic teaching, is what Christ brings about through them. Hence, even though our meeting with God in the liturgy is veiled, it is nonetheless real. Through it we are drawn in all of the sacramental rites into the mystery of the Lord's death and resurrection and ascension.

In every sacrament we rise to God in praise, petition, and thanksgiving. At the same time, God comes to us bearing life and other gifts. One may think here of Jacob's dream of the stairway on which God's messengers were moving up and down (cf. Gen. 28.12). Each liturgy is, as a prayer of the Christmas season expresses it, an "admirable exchange."[6]

Liturgical Celebration

Because sacraments are symbolic actions with very real effects, care must be taken to administer them validly, that is, in such a way that the full sign is present and its purpose is achieved. For all symbolic actions, even secular ones, concern for validity is basic. When one buys a house, the symbolic act of signing a contract has important rules for validity; for example, it may be essential that the signing be witnessed or dated for the contract to be a valid instrument. If a symbolic action is not valid, it becomes useless and meaningless. It may reflect a sincere intent, but it does not achieve the desired effect.

Sacraments have conditions for validity. The sacraments are signs of faith and acts of obedience to Christ, and one may not arbitrarily choose signs other than those He appointed and entrusted to His Church. It is for the Church to state the conditions of validity for sacraments. This the Church does. For example, the Church, faithful to Scripture, insists that baptism can be validity administered only with water, not with other liquids, and that only bread and the fruit of the vine, not other materials, can be validly used in the Eucharist. It is not that these material signs have any sacramental power in themselves. Their fruitfulness here comes from the passion of Christ and His present care. But in the sacraments Christ works mighty deeds for the public good of the Church, and His deeds must be done faithfully in the Church if they are to be His saving actions.

It is true that God's generosity is not limited to the sacraments. If in good faith a minister should fail to administer sacraments validly, God is able to supply in other ways the needs of those who seek Him. Still, a sacrament itself is simply not administered if the conditions established by Christ personally or through His Church are not fulfilled.

Sacraments are sacred actions, and the human minister should celebrate them with great faith and charity. As the Church has always taught, however, the validity of a sacrament does not depend on the worthiness of the minister. It is not from the goodness or power of

6Liturgy of the Hours, Feast of Solemnity of Mary, the Mother of God, the Octave of Christmas (January 1), first antiphon at vespers.

human ministers that the faithful hope to draw the fruits of salvation, but from Christ Himself, who is always the principal minister of the sacraments. The efficacy of sacraments is drawn from Him; sacraments are basically actions of Christ. "When Peter baptizes, it is Christ who baptizes; when Paul baptizes, it is Christ who baptizes; when Judas baptizes, it is Christ who baptizes."[7]

Certain human dispositions, made possible by grace, are necessary for valid reception of a sacrament. A context of faith and a personal willingness to accept Christ and receive the gift must be present in any adult who wishes to receive a sacrament effectively.

The Church is responsible for reverent care of the sacraments. It makes laws for their licit celebration and for their proper reception, so that the reverence due these gifts and the good of the faithful may be preserved. Thus the Church may insist on reasonable requirements of place and circumstances for these acts of public worship.

But far more is required in administration of the sacraments than observance of minimal demands for validity and lawfulness. Each sacramental liturgy should be fully celebrated as an act of worship. "Pastors of souls must therefore realize that, when the liturgy is celebrated, more is required than the mere observance of the laws governing valid and licit celebration. It is their duty also to insure that the faithful take part knowingly, actively, and fruitfully" (SC 11).

The hurried, lifeless observance of a bare rite is scarcely a celebration. Our liturgy commemorates and proclaims the death and resurrection of the Lord. The Church wants the faithful to take part "knowingly, actively, and fruitfully." It states that the nature of the liturgy calls for full, conscious, and active participation (cf. SC 14).

The sacramental rites, then, are not to be handled mechanically, but with faith and with joyful celebration. Past, present, and future come together in the joyful celebration of each rite. Every sacrament recalls the paschal mystery in which Christ won redemption; each symbolizes a grace He now confers; the sacraments point always toward the fullness of eternal life.[8]

Sacramentals

Jesus Himself, as we have already observed, designated the basic material signs around which the sacramental celebrations revolve. The Church reaches further into the material universe and appropriates many other objects, indeed potentially all, into the direct service of God and also as signs in His worship. These the Church calls sacramentals, distinguishing them by name so that they will not be

[7]St. Augustine, *Tractatus in Ioannis Evangelium* 6.7 (ML 35.1428).
[8]Cf. St. Thomas Aquinas, *Summa Theologica* II-II, 60,3.

confused with the signs that are Christ's sacraments. They differ in this, that the spiritual efficacy of sacramentals depends on the faith and devotion of the users, whereas the sacraments are, as it were, arms of the Savior Himself by which He extends His action throughout place and time to give life, to bless, to renew, to heal, and to multiply the bread of life.

Many of the secondary signs — for example, the altar, the font, the sacred vessels — are also drawn directly into worship, supplementing the primary signs, indeed forming with them a constellation of signs for each sacrament whereby the meaning of the sacrament may be revealed, expressed, and shared by the worshippers. It is the task of a full, conscious, and active participation to explore, even to exploit, these signs. All the riches of ritual language should be called upon to clarify and enhance these signs and thus to proclaim the mystery of Christ with fervor, conviction and gladness.

In Sum: The Grain of Wheat

A description of the paschal mystery was given by the Lord Himself on the eve of His death and resurrection. It contains His theological explanation of what was about to happen, but He gave it to us in an image drawn from nature. "The hour has come for the Son of Man to be glorified. Very truly, I tell you, unless a grain of wheat falls into the earth and dies, it remains just a single grain; but if it dies, it bears much fruit" (John 12.23-24). Jesus Himself is the Grain of Wheat who dies in order to "bear much fruit." This fruit, issuing from the paschal mystery, comes to us in the sacramental liturgies.

The same law applies to His followers, who are also grains of wheat: "Those who love their life lose it, and those who hate their life in this world will keep it for eternal life" (John 12.25). So the paschal mystery becomes a way of life for all the followers of Jesus. "While we live we are always being given up to death for Jesus' sake," says St. Paul, "so that the life of Jesus may be made visible in our mortal flesh" (2 Cor. 4.11). And it is to the sacramental liturgies, especially to the Eucharist, that we bring our own daily dyings and risings to be drawn into the paschal mystery of the Savior. In this way we can also say with the Apostle: "In my flesh I am completing what is lacking in Christ's afflictions for the sake of His body, that is, the church" (Col. 1.24).

27

The Eucharist — Center Of Life

The Eucharist is at the heart of the Church's life. In the Eucharist Christ Himself is present to His people in the paschal mystery. Rich in symbolism and richer in reality, the Eucharist bears within itself the whole reality of Christ, and mediates to us His saving work.

"At the Last Supper, on the night He was betrayed, our Savior instituted the Eucharistic Sacrifice of His Body and Blood. He did this to perpetuate the sacrifice of the cross throughout the centuries until He should come again, and so to entrust to His beloved spouse, the Church, a memorial of His death and resurrection: a sacrament of love, a sign of unity, a bond of charity, a paschal banquet in which Christ is received, the mind is filled with grace, and a pledge of future glory is given to us" (SC 47).

This chapter has two major parts. The first treats of the Eucharist and its central role in Christian life, of how it is the sacrifice of the new covenant and our saving Food, of its rich effects, and of Christ's real presence in the sacrament. The second major part treats of holy orders, the sacrament in which men are consecrated to serve the Eucharistic ministry.

The Eucharist

Center of Christian Life

The center of all Christian life is Christ Himself. By His incarnation and His work of redemption we are healed, and called to share in a new life, a life that binds us together as children of God and sharers in the life of the Trinity.

It is for this very reason that the Eucharist is the center and crown of Christian life. For in the Eucharist Christ gives Himself to us, and we lay hold of Him. The Eucharist is not merely a symbol and ceremony; it is the sacrament in which, most of all, the saving works of Jesus and the gifts of God are made accessible to men.

The existence of the local or the universal Church would be unthinkable without the Eucharist. "No Christian community can be built up unless it has its basis and center in the celebration of the Most Holy Eucharist" (PO 6).

"The other sacraments, as well as every ministry of the Church and every work of the apostolate, are linked with the Holy Eucharist and are directed toward it. For the Most Blessed Eucharist contains the Church's entire spiritual wealth, that is, Christ Himself, our Passover and living bread. Through His very flesh, made vital and vitalizing by the Holy Spirit, He offers life to men. They are thereby invited and led to offer themselves, their labors, and all created things together with Him" (PO 5).

The graced relationship begun in baptism and strengthened in confirmation is ordered to union with the Eucharistic Christ and a sharing in His saving sacrifice in the Mass. The Eucharist is the "medicine of immortality"[1] which complements the healing effects of penance and the anointing of the sick. Holy orders confers a priesthood devoted to the altar of the Eucharist. Marriage symbolizes the union of Christ and Church which is the fruit of the Eucharist.

New Sacrifice of the New Covenant

Because the Eucharist is the most sacred presence of Christ and His paschal mysteries in the Church, it is both the "source and summit" (PO 5) of all the Church's ministries and apostolates. It threads a beauty, meaning, and purpose through all the varied activities involved in loving God, ourselves, and our fellow human beings. It offers a contact with the transcendent on which we can orient ourselves in the cosmic and timeless dimensions of our existence. In celebrating the Eucharist with and in Christ, the faithful are not only offered a share in His life, they are "invited and led to offer themselves, their labors, and all created things together with Him" (PO 4).

Long before Christ was born, God taught His people through the prophets to long for the life that He would bring. "The days are surely coming, says the LORD, when I will make a new covenant with the house of Israel. ... I will make an everlasting covenant with them, never to draw back from doing good to them" (Jer. 31.31, 32.40).

We have seen that it is by His cross and resurrection that Jesus brought us to newness of life. By these He inaugurated a new covenant in which He gives us His Spirit and makes us children of God, sharers of His life. We are made into a new community, a new people of God, able to worship God "in spirit and truth" (John 4.23), able as a family of God to join in the one sacrifice which is the hope and salvation of all forever.

These gifts of God are mediated to us chiefly through the Eucharistic Sacrifice. This memorial sacrifice was foreshadowed in the Old Testament, was instituted by Jesus, and is lived in His Church.

---

[1]St. Ignatius of Antioch, *Epistula ad Ephesios* 20.2 (MG 5.66 = ACW 1.68).

Foreshadowed in Old Testament

In one of the Eucharistic Prayers of the Roman liturgy the history of salvation is recalled:

Father. . . ,
You formed man in your own likeness. . . .
Even when he disobeyed you and lost your friendship
you did not abandon him to the power of death,
but helped all men to seek and find you.
Again and again you offered a covenant to man. . . .[2]

In the ages before Christ's incarnation, God enabled His people to seek Him and to find mercy. In various ways God taught them also to hope, and to offer sacrifices by which they acknowledged His Lordship and bound themselves together as His people. Especially among God's chosen people, who were favored by the guidance of His special revelation, there were sacrifices that foreshadowed the one sacrifice which would truly merit salvation from all nations and all ages.

Every authentic sacrifice is a sacred offering directed to God alone, to acknowledge that He is Lord of all. The very acknowledgment of His transcendent glory and supreme dominion helps the worshiper to draw near to Him who is greater than all. In many Old Testament sacrifices a sacred meal was an element in the worship. In many sacrifices part of the offering was destroyed to symbolize utter dedication to God; but part, made holy by its use in the sacrifice, was returned to the one offering it to be consumed. By this sharing, a kind of communion with God was accomplished.

From the first pages of Genesis onward, we see that the initiative to "share" was clearly and consistently God's. Again and again God called men to sacred worship in which they might share His presence and His mercy. All these gifts of God were to be climaxed in the institution of the Eucharist.

With both Noah (cf. Gen. 8.20, 9.9) and Abraham (cf. Gen, 15.9, 18) covenants were made in the context of a food-sacrifice. Later, when their descendants refused to respect these covenants, God did not abandon them. Rather He entered into the greatest of the Old Testament alliances in the complexus of events known as the Exodus. Again, the covenant was associated with a sacred meal.

On the eve of the liberation of the chosen people from slavery under the Pharaohs the Lord spoke to Moses and Aaron: "Tell the whole congregation of Israel that on the tenth of this month they are to take a lamb for each family, a lamb for each household. . . . Your lamb shall be without blemish, a year-old male. . . . You shall keep it until the fourteenth day of this month; then the whole assembled congregation of Israel shall slaughter it at twilight. They shall take some of the

[2]Roman Missal, The Order of Mass, Eucharistic Prayer IV.

blood and put it on the two doorposts and the lintel of the houses in which they eat it. They shall eat the lamb that same night; they shall eat it roasted over the fire with unleavened bread and bitter herbs" (Exod. 12.3, 5-8).

There were further instructions: "This is how you shall eat it: your loins girded, your sandals on your feet, and your staff in your hand; and you shall eat it hurriedly. It is the passover of the LORD. For I will pass through the land of Egypt that night, and I will strike down every first-born in the land of Egypt. . . . The blood shall be a sign for you on the houses where you live: when I see the blood, I will pass over you. . ." (Exod. 12.11-13).

The meal was thus integrally connected with the circumstances of the liberation. The symbols of nourishment taken in community and of eating in haste while prepared for flight both captured in ritual what God was about to effect in history.

Added to this was the Lord's special command to repeat these ceremonies in the future: "This day shall be a day of remembrance for you. You shall celebrate it as a festival to the LORD; throughout your generations you shall observe it as a perpetual ordinance . . . for on this very day I brought your companies out of the land of Egypt: you shall observe this day throughout your generations as a perpetual ordinance" (Exod. 12.14, 17).

Historically, the great Exodus covenant was completed only with the giving of the Law on Mount Sinai. Here the people received their obligations under the covenant, and Moses sealed the agreement by sprinkling an altar of sacrifice with calves' blood. Half the blood he sprinkled on the people with these words: "See the blood of the covenant that the LORD has made with you in accordance with all these words" (Exod. 24.8).

The whole series of saving events was ritually preserved in the annual repetition of the Passover meal in what was called a "memorial feast." As generation after generation shared the paschal lamb and the unleavened bread, fathers told their children of the wonders Yahweh had worked on behalf of His chosen people. In this "memorial feast" they understood and celebrated far more than a community festival. The Passover meal was not looked upon simply as an opportunity to review past history. In this meal the people of God knew they were with their Lord, and they renewed the covenant He had made with them.

Instituted by Christ

At the Last Supper the Lord instituted a new memorial sacrifice. The true "Lamb of God" (John 1.29) was about to be slain. By His cross and resurrection He was to free not just one nation from bondage, but all humankind from the more bitter slavery of sin. He was about to create a new people of God by the rich gift of His Spirit. There was to be a new law of love, a new nearness to God, a new promised land. All was to be new, when God fulfilled the promises of the centuries in the paschal mysteries. It was right, then, that there should also be a new memorial sacrifice, in which through all the ages till the final fulfillment God's people might be united to the saving deeds of this hour.

Jesus first carried out the rubrics of the Passover ritual. But in this holy night He spoke of the new gifts to come, of which the treasures of the past were only shadows and images. He promulgated the new law of the new covenant: "This is My commandment, that you love one another as I have loved you" (John 15.12). He spoke of the saving work He was about to do for them out of loving obedience to the Father (cf. John 14.31) and out of love for us (cf. John 15.13). Then He made that redemptive sacrifice present in the institution of the Eucharist, in the memorial rite He would command them to perform always in His memory.

During the supper, at one of the ceremonial eatings of the un-leavened bread, Jesus "took the bread, and after blessing it He broke it, and gave it to the disciples and said, 'Take, eat; this is My body' " (Matt. 26.26). Picking up a ceremonial cup of wine, He gave thanks and passed it to His disciples, saying: "This cup that is poured out for you is the new covenant in My blood" (Luke 22.20). Finally, He commanded them: "Do this in remembrance of Me" (1 Cor. 11.24). Then, after singing songs of praise (cf. Matt. 22.30; Mark 14.26), they walked down across the valley to where Jesus was arrested.

The interplay that took place in the Exodus between ritual and history was repeated at the New Pasch. Christ's crucifixion and resurrection, which are the sacrificial offering that frees us from sin, took place after the Last Supper, just as the flight from Egypt and the events of Sinai followed the first Passover meal. But Jesus' command to repeat this as a "memorial" of Himself established the Last Supper as the ceremonial setting for the representation of the events of our salvation. In this memorial sacrifice the new covenant could and would be constantly renewed with every succeeding generation.

Like the Passover meal, this memorial sacrifice of the new law is both sacrifice and sacred meal. "Both sacrifice and sacrament pertain inseparably to the same mystery. In an unbloody representation of the sacrifice of the cross and in application of its saving power, the Lord is immolated in the sacrifice of the Mass when, through the words of consecration, He begins to be present in a sacramental form under the appearance of bread and wine to become the spiritual food of the faithful."[3]

---

[3]Pope Paul VI, Encyclical, *Mysterium Fidei* (September 3, 1965) (EV 2.421).

As with many of the sacrifices of the ancient world, Christ's covenantal sacrifice was completed by the shedding of blood. This was not, as the New Testament reminds us, the blood of goats or calves, but rather the blood of the Priest Himself who presided in the cenacle and on Calvary (cf. Heb. 9.12). Jesus died only once and shed His blood only once, but, because of the command for a memorial, that Blood is made available for all time.

The Eucharist and the Church

In describing the life of the early Church, Christian writers of that time gave special attention to the Eucharist. For the Eucharist was the community's essential celebration; it signified, and kept most real, the presence of Christ in the community. In the Acts of the Apostles, St. Luke says of the converts at Jerusalem that they "devoted themselves to the apostles' teaching and fellowship, to the breaking of bread and the prayers" (Acts 2.42).

The phrase "breaking of bread" appears also elsewhere in the New Testament (cf. Acts 2.46; 20.7, 11; 27.35; 1 Cor. 10.16) and in the oldest non-scriptural liturgical instructions we know of.[4] In describing the Church's activity in such terms, the writers were already witnessing to the essentially ecclesial nature of the Eucharist. The Church today remains the Eucharistic community. The celebration of the paschal mystery is the reason for the Church's existence.

As Christianity was first spreading, the worship of the faithful commonly included participation in the Scripture services of neighboring Jewish synagogues, and then, at another time and place, they gathered in one another's homes to celebrate the Lord's Supper. But this arrangement did not last long. Faith in Christ and the Good News and new life he had brought were the center of the Christian community's life; but many Jews rejected these and began to harass the Christians (cf. Acts 8.1-3). The Christians formulated their own programs of Scripture readings and prayer, and before long these were joined directly to the memorial-sacrificial meal. This combination of a liturgy of the Word and a liturgy of the Eucharist remains present in all the Eucharistic services Christians celebrate today.

The liturgical form of Eucharistic worship developed in many places at the same time. There naturally arose a variety of forms, which reflected the cultures of the various faith communities as well as the different theological insights and devotional preferences of their people. This variety in external ceremonial still exists; each type is called a "rite."

In the western half of the Roman empire this variety eventually

---

[4]Cf. *Didache* 14.1 (= ACW 6.23).

merged into a basic unity in the Latin rite. In the East a variety of regional heritages was preserved. The two approaches resulted in a liturgical richness which the universal Church guards and treasures (cf. OE 1-6).[5]

Unity of Faith

With all the variety of ceremony in the Church there is the wonderful uniformity of belief in the single reality which is celebrated. Together, the crucifixion and resurrection of Jesus are responsible for our redemption: "Jesus our Lord . . . was handed over to death for our trespasses and was raised for our justification" (Rom. 4.24-25). Unlike the repetitious sacrifices of the Old Law, the single sacrifice of Jesus' obedient death was completely sufficient in itself. As the Epistle to the Hebrews stresses, He did not have to "offer Himself again and again, as the high priest enters the Holy Place again and again with blood that is not his own; for then He would have had to suffer again and again repeatedly since the foundation of the world. But as it is, He has appeared once for all at the end of the age to remove sin by the sacrifice of Himself" (Heb. 9.25-26).

The One Sacrifice

Jesus does not die and rise again every time the Eucharistic liturgy is enacted, but His one sacrifice is made present to all in every celebration of Mass. The God-Man instituted the Mass with an ecclesial dimension — its ability to be carried on everywhere in the Church — so that "the bloody sacrifice which was once offered on the cross should be made present, its memory preserved to the end of the world, and its salvation-bringing power applied to the forgiveness of the sins which are daily committed by us."[6]

At Mass, as upon the cross, Jesus is the chief Priest and also the Victim, giving unending and infinite praise and satisfaction to the Father. But in the Mass His Church joins Him in the sacrifice. With Him the Church also performs the role of priest and victim, making a total offering of itself together with Him.[7]

Christ commanded His apostles to celebrate this sacrifice. "Do this in remembrance of Me" (1 Cor. 11.24). This is a sacred task: to act in the person of Christ, to be His minister, to speak words that

---

[5]Cf. Congregation for the Sacraments and Divine Worship, Instruction, *Inaestimabile Donum* (April 3, 1980) (EV 7.288-323).

[6]Council of Trent, Session 22, September 17, 1562, *Doctrine on the Most Holy Sacrifice of the Mass*, ch. 1 (DS 1740). Cf. Pope John Paul II, Letter to all the bishops of the Church on the mystery and cult of the Eucharist, *Dominicae Cenae* (February 24, 1980) n. 9 (EV 7.190-198).

[7]Cf. Congregation of Rites, Instruction, *Eucharisticum Mysterium* (May 25, 1967) n. 3 (EV 2.1296-1303).

make present the living Christ and renew the paschal mysteries. This can be done only at the will of Christ, by those whom He has empowered so to act as His ministers by calling them and sealing them in the sacrament of holy orders. When, in the person of Christ, bishops and priests pronounce the words of consecration, the sacrifice of the new covenant is made present to the faithful in such a way that they too can participate in it.

Mass Offered for All

Priests are called to offer the Eucharistic sacrifice to the Father, with Christ, in the Holy Spirit, for the living and the dead, for the salvation of all, for the many needs of the people of God. Because the Eucharistic sacrifice is the supreme act of worship, it can be offered only to God.

A Mass may be offered on the occasion of a saint's feast, and give incidental honor to the saint. But the sacrifice of Christ is offered only to God, for He alone is worthy of this perfect adoration and praise. Masses may be offered for the needs of an individual person, living or deceased, but no Mass can be offered exclusively for such a limited intention. Every Mass is offered chiefly by Christ, and His ministerial priest must share His universal saving purposes. The Mass is offered to glorify God, to bring salvation to all, to make present and accessible the limitless riches of Christ.

Often the faithful ask that a Mass be said for a special intention of theirs: for the eternal rest of one who has died, for some spiritual or temporal need, or to express thanks to God. Ordinarily they give a financial offering when they make such a request. When a Mass offering or stipend is given that a Mass be said for a special intention, it is in truth only a plea that part of the fruits of the Mass might come to one who is loved in Christ. A Mass offering or stipend is to be understood as an expression of a desire on the part of those who give it to participate more intimately in the Eucharistic sacrifice by adding "to it a form of sacrifice of their own by which they contribute in a particular way to the needs of the Church and especially to the sustenance of its ministers."[8]

Holy Communion

It is the privileged responsibility of the celebrant of each Mass to distribute the Sacrament to himself and the people. He may be assisted by other ordained ministers (bishops, priests, deacons) if they are available, or, when necessary, by auxiliary ministers (acolytes or specially appointed lay persons).

[8]Pope Paul VI, Apostolic Letter on Mass stipends (June 13, 1974) (EV 5.534).

The Eucharist as received sacramentally is called "Holy Communion." The name is appropriate, since, as the word "communion" indicates, it is the sharing of a gift God gives to all; it is a coming into close union with Christ, and with one's brothers and sisters in Him.

Because of its intimate connection with the sacrificial aspect of the Mass, Holy Communion is most fittingly received by those attending. One who has received Communion the same day may receive it a second time only within a Eucharistic celebration in which that person participates.[9] Catholics of the Latin rite have normally received the Eucharist only under the form of bread, though there are many occasions and circumstances in which they may receive under the forms of both bread and wine. Whether one receives under one species or both, one receives the whole Christ in Holy Communion.[10] This is true since, in the Sacrament, it is the living, risen Christ who is present whole and entire under the appearance of bread, and also under the appearance of wine.

"To touch the Sacred Species and *to share them with one's own hands* is a privilege of the ordained, which indicates *active participation in the ministry of the Eucharist.* But it is clear that the Church can give such power to men who are neither priests nor deacons, of any sort, whether they are acolytes following their ministry, especially if they are destined for future ordination, of if they are other laypeople who have accepted the faculty from just necessity, but always after a suitable preparation."[11]

Participation

The ministerial priest, acting in the person of Christ, brings about the Eucharistic sacrifice and offers it to God in the name of all the people. The faithful, too, by virtue of their "royal priesthood" (cf. 1 Peter. 2.9), join in the offering (cf. LG 10). They do this not only by the reception of Holy Communion, but by fully exercising their status as members of the Mystical Body, "offering the victim and themselves not only through the hands of the priest but also with him."[12]

"The celebration of Mass is the action of Christ and the people of God hierarchically assembled. . . . It is of the greatest importance that

---

[9]Cf. *Code of Canon Law,* canon 917. In danger of death one could, of course, receive Communion as Viaticum even if one had received Communion earlier in the same day; cf. the *Code of Canon Law,* canon 921, 2.

[10]Cf. Council of Constance, Session 13, June 15, 1415, *Decree on Communion under the Species of Bread Only* (DS 1198-1200); Council of Trent; Session 21, July 16, 1562, *Doctrine on Communion under Both Species and Communion of Children,* ch. 1 and canons 1-3 (DS 1726-1727, 1731-1733).

[11]Pope John Paul II, Letter to all the bishops of the Church on the mystery and cult of the Eucharist, *Dominicae Cenae* (February 24, 1980) n. 11 (EV 7.215).

[12]Roman Missal, General Instruction, n. 62.

the celebration of the Mass, the Lord's Supper, be so arranged that the ministers and the faithful may take their own proper part in it and thus gain its fruits more fully. This is why Christ instituted the eucharistic sacrifice of his body and blood and entrusted it to his bride, the Church, as a memorial of his passion and resurrection. This purpose will be accomplished if the celebration takes into account the nature and circumstances of each assembly and is planned to bring about conscious, active, and full participation of the people, motivated by faith, hope, and charity. Such participation of mind and body is desired by the Church, demanded by the nature of the celebration, and is the right and duty of Christians by reason of their baptism."[13]

Necessity of Communion

Jesus Himself stressed our need to receive Communion. "Unless you eat the flesh of the Son of man and drink His blood, you have no life in you" (John 6.53).

The divine precept does not state how often one must receive Communion. The Church commands the faithful to receive Communion at least once a year, in the paschal season, unless there is just cause for another time.[14] The Church speaks also of the duty to receive Communion when one is in danger of death.[15] But one who loves Christ naturally wishes to deepen one's friendship with Him by frequent reception of this sacrament.

Lawful Reception

To receive this sacrament worthily, one must be a baptized Catholic in the state of grace and believe what the Church teaches about the sacrament. One conscious of having committed a mortal sin must make a sacramental confession before approaching the Eucharist.[16] If one who has sinned gravely has a pressing need to receive the Eucharist and has no opportunity to confess, he should first make an act of perfect contrition, an act which includes in it a promise to confess as soon as possible.[17]

It is not merely Church law that demands that one who approaches this sacrament be in the state of grace. The New Testament reminds us of the grave duty we have to receive worthily: "Whoever, therefore, eats the bread or drinks the cup of the Lord in an unworthy manner

[13]Roman Missal, General Instruction, nn. 1-3.
[14]Cf. *Code of Canon Law*, canon 920.
[15]Cf. *Code of Canon Law*, canon 921.1
[16]Cf. Council of Trent, Session 13, October 11, 1551, *Decree on the Most Holy Eucharist*, ch. 7 (DS 1647).
[17]Cf. *Code of Canon Law*, canon 916.

will be answerable for the body and blood of the Lord. . . . For all who eat and drink without discerning the body, eat and drink judgment against themselves" (1 Cor. 11.27-29).[18]

As an outward and communal sign of this respectful awareness of who it is we receive in the Eucharist, and as a penitential preparation, the Church directs us to abstain from solid food and drink one hour before receiving Holy Communion. The sick and elderly and those caring for them are not obliged to fast. Drinking water and taking medicine do not break the Eucharistic fast.[19]

When instituting this milder form of Eucharistic fast, Pope Pius XII encouraged those of the faithful who can do so to observe the old and venerable form of the fast before Communion, that is, complete abstinence from all food and drink, even water, from midnight.[20]

Baptism also readies a person to communicate by conferring membership in the Church. Since the entire Eucharistic service is the most characteristic and important activity of the Church, it is an expression of a common belief, not only in the presence of Christ in the Eucharist, but in all that the Church is and teaches in the name of Christ. Fully participating in the sacrificial banquet is itself an act of faith; through it Christians confirm and strengthen the belief that unites them to God and to one another.

It is because of this signification that non-Catholics may receive Communion in the Catholic Church only under exceptional circumstances. These are: (1) recipients must have the same faith in the Eucharist as is professed by Catholics; (2) they must have a deep spiritual need for the Eucharist; (3) they must have been unable, over a prolonged period, to communicate in their own church; (4) of their own accord they must request the sacrament of Communion. The local Catholic bishop is to pass judgment in each such case.[21]

---

[18]Pope John Paul II has noted certain modern pressures toward unworthy reception of Communion and has urged pastoral care to guard the faithful from so great an evil; see Letter to all the bishops of the Church on the mystery and cult of the Eucharist, *Dominicae Cenae* (February 24, 1980) n. 11 (EV 7.208-209); Encyclical, *Redemptor Hominis* (March 4, 1979) n. 20 (EV 6.1251-1256).

[19]Cf. *Code of Canon Law*, canon 919.1 and 3.

[20]Cf. Pope Pius XII, Apostolic Constitution, *Christus Dominus* (January 5, 1953).

[21]Secretariat for Promoting Christian Unity, Instruction, *De Pecularibus Casibus Admitendi Alios Christianos ad Communionem Eucharisticam* (June 1, 1972) (EV 4.1626-1640). — The *National Conference of Catholic Bishops* has issued the following "Guidelines for Receiving Communion": "—*For Catholics:* Catholics fully participate in the celebration of the Eucharist when they receive Holy Communion in fulfillment of Christ's command to eat His Body and drink His Blood. In order to be properly disposed to receive Communion, communicants should not be conscious of grave sin, *have fasted for an hour,* and seek to live in charity and love with their neighbors. Persons conscious of grave sin must first be reconciled with God and the Church through the sacrament of Penance. A frequent reception of the sacrament of Penance is encouraged for all. —*For Other Christians:* We welcome to this celebration of the Eucharist those Christians who are not fully united with us. *It is a consequence of the sad divisions in Chris-*

Symbol and Realities

Sacraments are outward signs instituted by Christ that symbolize what they effect and effect what they symbolize. This is true in a special way of the Eucharist when the faithful receive the sacrament at the Table of the Lord.

Eucharist as Food

The most obvious sign of this sacrament is the image of nourishment. The elements used in the Passover meal were staples of the Palestinian diet in Biblical times. Bread was available to everyone, the most common of foods. Wine was served as the normal table beverage even in the homes of the poor.

The Western Church uses unleavened bread, because unleavened bread was used at the Last Supper. The bread is to be of wheat only.[22] St. Paul saw unleavened bread as a symbol of purity and newness (cf. 1 Cor. 5.6-8). Unleavened bread was also more quickly prepared than bread with yeast, and hence it fit in with the "pilgrim people" idea associated with the Exodus. We are a pilgrim Church, and we receive our spiritual Bread in a form that reminds us that we are still on the way to our promised land.

Wine was associated in popular thinking with joyful exuberance (cf. Ps. 104.15). The reference to the Good Samaritan's pouring of wine on the injured traveler's wounds (cf. Luke 10.34) and St. Paul's advice to Timothy that a little wine is good for the stomach and recurring illness (cf. 1 Tim. 5.23) suggest that the ancient world also considered wine to be somewhat therapeutic. This symbolism is retained in the Mass, where grape wine is still used.

The commands at the Last Supper to eat and drink fit in with the same symbolism. Jesus had even foretold the nourishment aspect of this sacrament in His preaching: "I am the bread of life. Whoever comes to Me will never be hungry, and whoever believes in Me will never be thirsty. . . . For My flesh is true food and My blood is true drink" (John 6.35, 55).

---

tianity that we cannot extend to them a general invitation to receive Communion. Catholics believe that the Eucharist is an action of the celebrating community signifying a oneness in faith, life, and worship of the community. Reception of the Eucharist by Christians not fully united with us would imply a oneness which does not yet exist, and for which we must all pray. —For Those Not Receiving Communion: Those not receiving sacramental Communion are encouraged to express in their hearts a prayerful desire for unity with the Lord Jesus and with one another. — For Non-Christians: We also welcome to this celebration those who do not share our faith in Jesus. While we cannot extend to them an invitation to receive Communion, we do invite them to be united with us in prayer."

[22]Cf. Congregation for the Sacraments of Divine Worship, Instruction, Inaestimabile Donum (April 3, 1980) n. 8 (EV 7.298); Code of Canon Law, canon 924.2.

The Eucharist brings about the nourishing effect it symbolizes. This is achieved through the presence of Jesus Himself and the bestowal of grace on those who receive Him according to their individual needs and the needs of the community. Insofar as we have been wounded by sin, Christ and His power work in a remedial way; to the extent that we are making progress in holiness, He strengthens and fosters our growth.

"And, although it is true that the Eucharist always was and must continue to be the most profound revelation of the human brotherhood of Christ's disciples and confessors, it cannot be treated merely as an 'occasion' for manifesting this brotherhood. When celebrating the Sacrament of the Body and Blood of the Lord, the full magnitude of the divine mystery must be respected, as must the full meaning of this sacramental sign in which Christ is really present. . . ."[23]

Symbol of Unity

The Eucharist symbolizes also the unity of the Church. Christ prayed for that unity at the first Eucharistic sacrifice (cf. John 17.20-21). The bread and wine He used were themselves symbols of unity; the family of God is to be gathered into one, as many grains of wheat are brought together to make bread and many grapes are brought together to make wine. An ancient Eucharistic prayer recalled this: "As this broken bread was scattered over the hills, and then, when gathered, has become one mass, so may Thy Church be gathered from the ends of the earth into Thy kingdom."[24]

Unity is also symbolized by community sharing in the one Bread which is Christ. "Because there is one bread, we who are many are one body, for we all partake of the one bread" (1 Cor. 10.17).

By the sacrament of the Eucharist "the unity of the Church is both signified and brought about" (UR 2). The unity of the Church, the Mystical Body of Christ, is effected chiefly by love. "The liturgy inspires the faithful to become 'of one heart in love'[25] when they have tasted their full of the paschal mysteries; it prays that 'they may put into action in their lives what they have received with faith.'[26] The renewal in the Eucharist of the covenant between the Lord and man draws the faithful into the compelling love of Christ and sets them afire" (SC 10).

The union that worthy reception of Communion strengthens is first of all personal union with Christ. At the Last Supper Christ said: "Abide in Me as I abide in you. Just as the branch cannot bear fruit by

[23]Pope John Paul II, Encyclical, *Redemptor Hominis* (March 4, 1979) n. 20 (EV 6.1254).
[24]*Didache* 9.4 (= ACW 6.20).
[25]Roman Missal, Postcommunion in the Easter Vigil Mass and the Mass of Easter Sunday.
[26]Roman Missal, Prayer of the Mass for Monday within the Octave of Easter.

itself unless it abides in the vine, neither can you unless you abide in Me" (John 15.4). But through union with Him we are bound together with one another, and thus made able to bear fruit for one another in works of love.

Eucharist and Eternal Life

A third symbolism is that of our heavenly inheritance. "In the earthly liturgy, by way of foretaste, we share in that heavenly liturgy which is celebrated in the holy city of Jerusalem toward which we journey as pilgrims, and in which Christ is sitting at the right hand of God, a minister of the sanctuary and of the true tabernacle" (SC 8).

The entire Eucharistic service should symbolize the kingdom of God in its final fulfillment. Then the community of the faithful, gathered around the throne of the Father with their loved ones, will join with overwhelming gladness in Christ's perpetual praise and receive, as Abraham was once promised (cf. Gen. 15.1), God Himself as their everlasting reward.

In the earthly celebration there is an anticipatory experience of all these elements. Its peace, beauty and order, though always imperfect in this life, are still a foreshadowing of the conditions of heaven.

Participation at Mass not only unites us with the living Church on earth but also with those who have gone before us marked with the indelible character of faith. "Celebrating the Eucharistic sacrifice, therefore, we are most closely united to the worshiping Church in heaven as we join with . . . all the saints" (LG 50).

Most wonderfully of all, we experience a foretaste of the greatest reward, the presence of God within us. In the Eucharist we see Him, albeit indistinctly with our weak faith, as in the dark metal mirrors of antiquity; yet it is the same Lord now whom we shall see in heaven "face to face" (1 Cor. 13.12).

Real Presence

The faith of the Church about the presence of Jesus in the Eucharist under the appearances of bread and wine goes back to the preaching of Jesus Himself recorded in the Gospel of St. John. In the Eucharistic discourse after the multiplication of the loaves (cf. John 6.22-71), our Lord contrasted ordinary bread with a Bread that is not of this world but which contains eternal life for those who eat it.

"I am the bread of life. . . . I am the living bread that came down from heaven. Whoever eats of this bread will live forever; and the bread that I will give for the life of the world is My flesh" (John 6.48, 51).

The immediate reaction of the crowd to this claim was a mixed one. Some found this promise too much to believe. Their aversion to so puzzling a teaching was so strong that many disciples broke away and refused to follow Jesus any longer. Others, including the Twelve, did accept it. Even though such a notion was for them as much as it was for those who rejected it something beyond their personal experience, they gave their assent to His words because they recognized Jesus to be the Holy One of God and they trusted in His assurance more than in the appearance of things (cf. John 6.69).

On one point, however, the two groups were in clear agreement. All of the hearers understood that Jesus was making a statement that was to be taken quite literally. Nor did He wish it to be understood in any other way. As Christian commentators have noted repeatedly, when the unbelievers walked away Jesus did not retract the promise or try to change their understanding of His words. He did not call them back to say He had been speaking poetically or metaphorically.

We are constantly reminded in the liturgy that the Eucharist is "the mystery of faith." This mystery can be approached only "with humility and reverence, not relying on human reasoning, which ought to hold its peace, but rather adhering firmly to divine revelation."[27] Thus St. John Chrysostom follows the example of the faith of St. Peter (cf. John 6.68) in the Eucharist when he says: "Let us submit to God in all things and not contradict Him, even if what He says seems to contradict our reason and intellect. . . . Let us act in this way with regard to the mysteries, not limiting our attention to those things which can be perceived by the senses, but instead holding fast what He says. For His word can never deceive."[28]

Presence in Fullest Sense

The presence of Jesus in the Eucharist is not the only form of His presence within the Church, but the wonder of His Eucharistic presence is unique. Certainly He is also with the Church in a special way as the Church believes, prays, and does works of mercy, and in its faith; He is with the bishops and priests of the Church when they preach God's word, govern His people, and administer His other sacraments. But the sacramental presence of Jesus which is brought about in the Mass has special claim to the description "real presence" — not because the other types of presence are not "real," but because it is "presence in its fullest sense."[29] The other six sacraments are rites in which the faithful encounter Christ in His action and power. Only the Eucharist, however, *is* Jesus Christ.

The way in which Jesus is present in the Eucharist cannot be ex-

27Pope Paul VI, Encyclical, *Mysterium Fidei* (September 3, 1965) (EV 2.411).
28St. John Chrysostom, *Homily on Matthew* 82.4 (MG 58.743).
29Pope Paul VI, Encyclical, *Mysterium Fidei* (September 3, 1965) (EV 2.424).

plained in physical terms because it transcends the ordinary necessities of space and measurement. It is not as though Jesus took on a miniature body to be present in the Eucharist, or as though He were present in a natural way but hidden beneath a thin layer of bread and wine. It is a supernatural mystery that the Person who becomes fully present at Mass is the same risen Savior who is seated at the right hand of the Father. In becoming present on the altar Christ's condition does not change. He does not have to leave heaven to become present on earth.

The same is true when many Masses are celebrated simultaneously. What changes is not Jesus, but the number of places in which He is present. When the Eucharistic liturgy is celebrated throughout the world, as it is daily "from the rising of the sun to its setting" (Mal. 1.11), Jesus is not multiplied; nor is He diminished when His sacred Body and Blood are consumed in Holy Communion. Similarly as the flame of the paschal candle is shared among the faithful on Easter night without becoming itself brighter or dimmer, and as the message of God in the Gospel is shared with all the members of a congregation at Mass without being itself enlarged or contracted, so Jesus' Body and Blood are not changed in any way in the continuous pulse of Eucharistic celebrations throughout the universal Church.

Meaning of Eucharistic Presence

The Eucharistic presence of Jesus is so rich in meaning that it can be spoken of in many ways. When the words of consecration are spoken over the bread and wine, there is a great change in meaning or significance, a "transsignification." That which had meant to us only earthly food and drink now means far more, and speaks to us the presence of Jesus. There is also a change in the purpose of what we see, a "transfinalization." The purpose of earthly bread is to minister to natural bodily life; when the words of Jesus have touched this visible gift of the Eucharist, its whole thrust and dynamism are different. It has become a Food that nourishes the life of God in us and strengthens us for eternal life.

But deeper than all these changes, underlying them and their foundation, is the change in being, the "transubstantiation." The appearance of bread and wine "take on this new significance, this new finality, precisely because they contain a new reality."[30] Faith is concerned deeply with this reality; Jesus *is* here. He is present not merely spiritually, by His knowledge, His care, His activity, but He is present "in a unique way, whole and entire, God and man, substantially and permanently."[31]

---

[30]Pope Paul VI, Encyclical, *Mysterium Fidei* (September 3, 1965) (EV 2.427).
[31]Congregation of Rites, Instruction, *Eucharisticum Mysterium* (May 25, 1967) (EV 2.1309).

Over what had been bread and wine Jesus said: "This is My Body. ... This is My Blood. ..." With firm faith in Christ, the Church has ever believed that what He gives us in the Eucharist is indeed His Body and His Blood. When His priest says His sacred words over the gifts, the bread and wine "have ceased to exist," and it is "the adorable Body and Blood of the Lord Jesus that from then on are really before us under the sacramental species of bread and wine."[32] With Easter faith we recognize that it is the Lord. "Instructed in these matters and certain in faith that what seems to be bread is not bread — though it tastes like it — but rather the Body of Christ, and that what seems to be wine is not wine — though it seems so to the taste — but the Blood of Christ ... strengthen your heart by receiving this Bread as spiritual food and gladden the countenance of your soul."[33]

The change that occurs when Christ becomes sacramentally present in the Eucharist is enduring because it is so radical, so real a change. After the consecration Jesus remains bodily present as long as the appearances of bread and wine remain. Back in the fifth century St. Cyril of Alexandria was once confronted with the false opinion that if a part of the Eucharist were left over until the following day it would lose its power to sanctify. He rejected the opinion and replied with the belief that the faith has always proclaimed: "For Christ is not altered and His holy Body is not changed, but the power and force and life-giving grace of the blessing remain in it forever."[34]

Adoration of the Blessed Sacrament

Faith in the enduring presence of Christ in the Blessed Sacrament prompted the gradual development of devotions to Christ in the Eucharist even apart from Mass.

In the earliest centuries of the Church the chief reason for preserving the Sacred Species was to assist those unable to attend the liturgy, especially the sick and the dying. The Sacrament of the Lord was reverently taken to them so that they too could communicate.

With the passage of time, reverent reflection led the Church to enrich its Eucharistic devotion. Faith that Jesus is truly present in the sacrament led believers to worship Christ dwelling with us permanently in the sacrament. Wherever the sacrament is, there is the Christ who is our Lord and our God; hence He is ever to be worshiped in this mystery.[35] Such worship is expressed in many ways: in genuflections, in adoration of the Eucharist, in the many forms of Eucharistic devotion that faith has nourished.

[32]Pope Paul VI, *Professio Fidei* ("The Credo of the People of God," June 30, 1968) (EV 3.561).
[33]St. Cyril of Jerusalem, *Catechesis* 22(myst. 4).9 (MG 33.1104).
[34]St. Cyril of Alexandria, *Epistula ad Calosyrium* (MG 76.1075).
[35]Cf. Pope Paul VI, Encyclical, *Mysterium Fidei* (September 3, 1965) (EV 2.433-434).

In the thirteenth century, when the charisms of saints like Francis of Assisi and Thomas Aquinas had intensified the Church's gratitude for the enduring presence of Jesus, the feast of Corpus Christi ("Body of Christ") was established. The popularity of this feast, with its joyful hymns and public processions, encouraged further developments of Eucharistic devotion.

The Blessed Sacrament is at times removed from the tabernacle in which it is ordinarily kept, and placed upon the altar for adoration. Usually the Host is placed in a monstrance, so that the Sacred Species can be seen by the faithful adoring their present but unseen Lord. These periods of exposition are sometimes extended into Holy Hours. Catholic parishes often celebrate Eucharistic Days, or the Forty Hours Devotion, in which the Sacrament is exposed upon the altar continuously for a full day or longer, to intensify the Eucharistic life of the parish. When such exposition is terminated, the priest raises the Sacred Host before the people in blessing. From this closing act has come the name "Benediction of the Blessed Sacrament."

In some dioceses and certain religious communities perpetual adoration is maintained before the continuously exposed Host. But every Catholic Church is a place in which the faithful are invited to worship the present Christ. Visits to the Lord in the tabernacle are still another form of devotion to the Real Presence that the Church warmly commends.[36]

Since the latter half of the nineteenth century, Eucharistic Congresses have drawn Catholics to international gatherings marked by liturgical functions, conferences, and other events. All these are designed to render our united gratitude and praise for the Father's great gift to us in this life: His beloved Son present among us under the appearances of bread and wine.[37]

Holy Orders

Origin of Priestly Office

On the same first Holy Thursday on which He instituted the sacrament of the Eucharist, Christ conferred priesthood on the apostles: "Do this in remembrance of Me."

In instituting the sacrament of the Eucharist He created what would be a living re-presentation of His own death and resurrection. At the same time He charged some to see that this sacred mystery

[36]Cf. Congregation of Rites, Instruction, *Eucharisticum Mysterium* (May 25, 1967) part III (EV 2.1331-1341).

[37]Cf. Pope John Paul II, Letter to all the bishops of the Church on the mystery and cult of the Eucharist, *Dominicae Cenae* (February 24, 1980) n. 3 (EV 7.163-164).

would be performed thenceforth in His memory. Thus the origin of holy orders lies in the will of Christ and His explicit acts on that first Holy Thursday.

Holy orders and the great Christian paschal sacrifice are inseparable. Christ the Priest offered Himself for our salvation; the Eucharist is the continued re-presentation of that sacrifice; the priesthood is a special human participation in that divine work.

On the first Easter, the risen Christ breathed on His new priests and gave them the power to forgive sins: "Receive the Holy Spirit. If you forgive the sins of any, they are forgiven; if you retain the sins of any, they are retained" (John 20.22-23).

The new priesthood established by Christ was a "visible and external priesthood," and "Sacred Scripture shows, and the tradition of the Catholic Church has always taught, that this was instituted by the same Lord our Savior, and that the power of consecrating, offering, and administering His Body and Blood, as also the power of forgiving and retaining sins, was given to the apostles and their successors in the priesthood."[38]

Holy orders do not take their origin from the community, "as though it were the community that 'called' or 'delegated.' The sacramental priesthood is truly a gift for this community and comes from Christ Himself, from the fullness of His priesthood. This fullness finds its expression in the fact that Christ, while making everyone capable of offering the spiritual sacrifice, calls some and enables them to be ministers of His own sacramental Sacrifice, the Eucharist — in the offering of which all the faithful share — in which are taken up all the spiritual sacrifices of the People of God."[39]

The sacrament of holy orders is rooted in Christ's incarnation. In order to carry out the mission given Him by the Father, the Son of God became man. His work here culminated in His death, resurrection, and ascension. The priesthood, then, is based on the person and mission of Christ. Through the priesthood He was to continue to make visible His saving action.

Identification with Christ

Central to an understanding of how Christ's work is transmitted to His Church is the notion of participation in the person and actions of Christ. Such participation touches the very life of Christ as shared through grace. By ordination a believer is chosen from among the faithful to share more fully in Christ's priestly mission.

[38]Council of Trent, Session 23, July 15, 1563, *Doctrine on the Sacrament of Order*, ch. 1 (DS 1764).
[39]Pope John Paul II, *Letter* to all the priests of the Church as Holy Thursday approaches (April 8, 1979) n. 4 (EV 6.1297).

When a person is ordained a priest, he becomes a sign of God's presence and power in the world. His consecration represents Christ's total self-emptying, and also prefigures the day when Christ's kingdom will be fully realized. Since the priest is intimately identified with Christ, his priesthood is in some way a permanent part of his being. In philosophical terms, the priesthood is not merely a role one has, but it is an aspect of what one is. In theological terms, the priesthood is an irrevocable gift of God. "You are a priest forever according to the order of Melchizedek" (Ps. 110.4).[40]

In explaining how the priest can function as Christ, the Church speaks of the priesthood as an identification with Christ on the most fundamental level. In their reception of orders priests are "consecrated to God in a new way," and they become "living instruments of Christ the eternal Priest," so that they may be able to "carry on through the ages His wonderful work, which has with heavenly power reunited the whole society of men" (PO 12). The priestly office "is conferred by that special sacrament through which priests, by the anointing of the Holy Spirit, are marked with a special character and are so configured to Christ the Priest that they can act in the person of Christ the Head" (PO 2; cf. LG 10).

Christ lives and acts in many ways in the priest. The priest's identification with Christ is the theme of many works of the Fathers. St. John Chrysostom, for example, says that to disregard the teaching of the priest is to disregard God;[41] he also says that the hand of Christ moves through the hand of the priest, and that Christ's healing works are accomplished only through the priest.[42] The priest's power as "another Christ" is rooted in his unique ability to perform certain actions which are the works of Christ alone. "When you behold the priest offering the consecrated Bread, see in his hand the hand of Christ Himself."[43]

The priest's union with Christ is expressed by exercising the unique power which permits him to perpetuate Christ's work (cf. LG 10). This work is the essential work of the apostles: proclaiming the Gospel, gathering together and leading the community, remitting sin and anointing the sick, celebrating the Eucharist, exercising Christ's work of redeeming mankind, and glorifying God. In brief, those ordained to the priesthood are "sharers in the functions of sanctifying, teaching, and governing."[44]

---

[40]In the ordination liturgy, Ps. 110, including the verse quoted here, is recited immediately after the actual ordination.

[41]Cf. St. John Chrysostom, *Homilia 2 in Epistulam II ad Timotheum* 2 (MG 62.610).

[42]Cf. St. John Chrysostom, *De Sacerdotio* 3.6 (MG 48.643-644).

[43]St. John Chrysostom, *Homilia 50 in Matthaeum* 3 (MG 58.507-508).

[44]Second General Assembly of the Synod of Bishops, *The Ministerial Priesthood* (1971) Part One, n. 4 (EV 4.1165).

Identification with Christ's Work

As Christ is teacher, witness, and means of saving sacrifice, so also is the priest. The source of all priestly existence and activity is Christ. Through the priest Christ makes His own priestly life and work present here and now.

The priest is differentiated from all others precisely by the way he is identified with Christ's unique work. The Church notes how certain powers identified with carrying on Christ's work were handed on. St. Paul clearly was conscious of his acting by Christ's mission and mandate (cf. 2 Cor. 5.18-20; 6.4). This mandate was being passed on, with the obligation that it be handed on further. There is a warning: "Do not ordain anyone hastily" (1 Tim. 5.22). The two Epistles to Timothy and the Epistle to Titus express the sacramental aspects of the laying on of hands, and they point up the fact that ordination is not just a call to community service, but a consecration.

Permanence of Priesthood

The priestly consecration is such that it cannot be lost. Once ordained a priest, a man remains a priest forever. The sacrament of holy orders touches the very being of the recipient: he belongs to Christ in an enduring way. "This special participation in Christ's priesthood does not disappear even if a priest for ecclesial or personal reasons is dispensed or removed from the exercise of his ministry."[45]

The permanence of the priesthood flows from the way in which the priest is united to Christ by his ordination. Christ's mission will be completed only in the glory of God's kingdom. Until the final realization of the kingdom, the priest remains the living sign and the promise of its completion in glory.

Thus ordination is an "eschatological sign," that is, a sign pointing to the coming of Christ's kingdom. The priest's free giving of himself points to the day when Christ's kingdom will be fully realized. In that kingdom all will freely give themselves irrevocably to Christ. By accepting priestly orders, the priest helps convert human freedom to God by uniting himself irrevocably with Christ in faith and grace. The priest is a sign of the kingdom to come and a pledge of the salvific presence of Christ.

"The Church has ever more closely examined the nature of the ministerial priesthood, which can be shown to have been invariably conferred from apostolic times by a sacred rite (cf.1 Tim. 4.15; 2 Tim. 1.6). By the assistance of the Holy Spirit, she recognized more clearly as time went on that God wished her to understand that this rite con-

---

45Second General Assembly of the Synod of Bishops, *The Ministerial Priesthood* (1971) Part One, n. 5 (EV 4.1170).

ferred upon priests not only an increase of grace for carrying out ecclesiastical duties in a holy way, but also a permanent designation by Christ, or character, by virtue of which they are equipped for their work and endowed with the necessary power that is derived from the supreme power of Christ. The permanent existence of this character, the nature of which is explained in different ways by theologians, is taught by the Council of Florence and reaffirmed by two decrees of the Council of Trent. In recent times the Second Vatican Council more than once mentioned it, and the second General Assembly of the Synod of Bishops rightly considered the enduring nature of the priestly character throughout life as pertaining to the teaching of faith."[46]

To accept ordination, then, is to make a permanent commitment. But at times the Church does permit priests to cease exercising their ministry. For serious reasons the Church may dispense them from the special priestly obligations, as that of celibacy and that of praying daily the Liturgy of the Hours. To some people it may seem strange that the Church can permit a priest to leave his priestly commitment and enter marriage, while it does not permit a person in an unhappy marriage to leave the commitment and marry again. But the cases are different. The Church may dispense from its own law of priestly celibacy; it does not have the power to dispense from Christ's prohibition of divorce and remarriage. There is some likeness in the cases, however; and all in the Church should pray that in every vocation, even in these times of widespread rootlessness, a spirit of faithfulness may grow.

Sacramental Ministry

A priest is pre-eminently a means of sacramental contact with Christ. The Christian meets God in the sacraments. And it is through the priest that Christ maintains His sacramental presence.

The priest is called to act in the very person of Christ.[47] In the sacrament of penance he says: "I absolve you. . . ." And in the Eucharistic sacrifice: "This is My Body. . . . This is My Blood. . . ." In anointing the sick, the priest continues in a special manner Christ's healing mission. By administering the sacraments the priest builds up

---

[46]Congregation for the Doctrine of the Faith, *Mysterium Ecclesiae* ("Declaration in Defense of the Catholic Doctrine on the Church against Certain Errors of the Present Day," June 24, 1973) n. 6 (EV 4.2586). Cf. Council of Florence, Bull, *Exsultate Deo* (November 22, 1439); Council of Trent, Session 7, March 3, 1547, *Decree on the Sacraments*, canon 9 (DS 1609), and Session 23, July 15, 1563, *Doctrine on the Sacrament of Order*, ch. 4 and canon 4 (DS 1767 and 1774); Second Vatican Council, LG 21 and PO 2; Second General Assembly of the Synod of Bishops, *The Ministerial Priesthood* (1971) Part One, n. 5 (EV 4.1169).

[47]For an explanation of "in the very person of Christ," cf. Pope John Paul II, Letter to all the bishops of the Church on the mystery and cult of the Eucharist, *Dominicae Cenae* (February 24, 1980) n. 8 (EV 7.186).

the community of faith. By bringing human life into contact with divine life, he continues and extends Christ's work of establishing God's kingdom among us.

Priesthood of Christ Shared in Different Ways

All members of the Church share one faith and one mission. But the nature of a member's participation in the mission depends on the member's sacramental life and calling. By baptism every Christian is joined to Christ and made a sharer in His divine life and mission. The sacrament of orders, however, makes one participate in Christ's mission in a unique way; it makes the recipient an authentic, authoritative, and special representative of Christ. For Christ at the Last Supper instituted the ministerial priesthood as a distinct sacrament, and the priesthood of the ordained is different and distinct from the common priesthood of the faithful.

The priest, then, has a distinct role in the Church. "Though they differ from one another in essence and not only in degree, the common priesthood of the faithful and the ministerial or hierarchical priesthood are nonetheless interrelated. Each of them in its own special way is a participation in the one priesthood of Christ. The ministerial priest, by the sacred power he enjoys, molds and rules the priestly people. Acting in the person of Christ, he brings about the Eucharistic sacrifice, and offers it to God in the name of all the people. For their part, the faithful join in the offering of the Eucharist by virtue of their royal priesthood. They likewise exercise that priesthood by receiving the sacraments, by prayer and thanksgiving, by the witness of a holy life, and by self-denial and active charity" (LG 10).

St. Paul points out that the Holy Spirit is the source of the division of labor in the Church, and that the offices are quite distinct (cf. 1 Cor. 12.4-11; Rom. 12.4-8). The division of work follows a design set by God. Some are called to serve as priests, others to serve in other roles — and all are called to build up the Church of Christ (cf. 1 Cor. 12.27-31).

Ministries within the Church

All mission with the Church is rooted in Christ's original sending of the apostles to teach His way to all (cf. Matt. 28.19; Mark 3.14). All Christians share this task.

Within the Church certain people must be chosen for particular functions. This is necessary in any organization. The selection and ordination of certain people is the means by which Christ's priestly work is carried on. Like all baptized persons, these people — bishops, priests, deacons — share in Christ's mission. Because they are set apart in a unique manner, they are appointed to share in Christ's work in a special way.

The Holy Spirit uses all ministries to build up the Church as a reconciling community for the glory of God and the salvation of all (cf. Eph. 4.11-13). In the New Testament ministerial actions are varied and functions and titles are not all precisely defined. Explicit emphasis is given, however, to the proclamation of God's word, the safeguarding of doctrine, the care of the flock, and the witness of Christian living. By the time of the Epistles to Timothy and to Titus and the First Epistle of St. Peter, some ministerial functions are more clearly discernible. This suggests that as the Church matured the importance of certain functions caused them to be located in specific officials of the community. Here we can already see elements which remain at the heart of what we today call "ordination." The laying on of hands by a bishop seals a man as a priest. This ceremony in its essence is found in the pages of Scripture.

New Testament and Now

In the Church today the sacrament of orders has three hierarchical grades, or orders: bishops, priests, deacons. Such offices were distinct in the infant Church, as we learn from the writings of the earliest Fathers of the Church.[48] In the New Testament itself there is frequent mention of bishops ("overseers"), priests ("elders"), and deacons (cf., eg., Phil. 1.1; Titus 1.5-7). However, the Greek words for bishop and priest seem at times to have been used interchangeably. It is not altogether clear from the books of the New Testament that in ordaining their first associates to the ministerial priesthood the apostles distinguished the office of priest from that of bishop. It is possible that the distinction of orders appeared as the Church developed and it became useful to have not only ministers enjoying the fullness of the sacramental priesthood, that is, bishops, but also assistants to them, ministers having a real but more limited participation in the same priesthood. But the three orders of bishop, priest, and deacon did emerge in the early Church and have continued in it ever since.

It is quite clear from the New Testament that Christ chose leaders for His Church and gave them powers of teaching, ruling and sanctifying. The apostles, it is true, had certain gifts and duties associated with their unique role as Christ's companions and as the foundation on which the Church was built at the start. But they had other roles which, by the will of Christ, and in accord with the continuing guidance of His Spirit, were to be carried on in the Church through all the ages.

---

[48]Cf., e.g., St. Ignatius of Antioch, *Epistula ad Magnesios* 6.1 (MG 5.668 = ACW 1.70-71) and *Epistula ad Trallianos* 3.1 (MG 5.667 = ACW 1.76).

There was to continue in the Church the ministry of forgiveness of sins (cf. John 20.21-23), as also the offering of the Eucharistic Sacrifice. Various powers that could be given men by God alone were to be continued in the Church. In the Epistle to Titus, this companion of St. Paul who had been placed in charge of a local church is told: "I left you behind in Crete for this very reason, that you should put in order what remained to be done, and should appoint elders in every town as I directed you . . ." (Titus 1.5). While Paul and his associates were on their missionary journeys, they "appointed elders . . . in each church" (Acts 14.23). The Greek word for "elder" is "presbyter"; this came to be the common term for "priest."

As the Church developed, her priests continued to do divine things, things that men may not do except with the authorization of God. The Church taught that Christ had called men to do these things, because He had chosen apostles and sent them upon a mission that was to endure until He comes again. Those the apostles chose to carry on their work were confirmed in Office by Christ and the Holy Spirit. To those so appointed to rule the Church in Asia Minor St. Paul could say: "Keep watch over yourselves and over all the flock, of which the Holy Spirit has made you overseers" (Acts 20.28).

Thus it is an essential part of the faith of the Church that there is a continuity in mission. As Christ sent the apostles, so the apostles in His name chose associates and successors, and they in turn laid hands on others in Christ's name. By the guidance of the Spirit of Christ the hierarchical priesthood emerged in the Church, and it continues at His will (cf. LG 18-22).

Orders are found in their fullness in bishops, in a secondary manner in priests, and finally in the diaconate. "Bishops enjoy the fullness of the sacrament of orders, and all priests as well as deacons are dependent upon them in the exercise of authority. For the 'presbyters' are prudent fellow workers of the episcopal order and are themselves consecrated as true priests of the New Testament, just as deacons are ordained for service and minister to the people of God in communion with the bishop and his presbytery. Therefore bishops are the principal dispensers of the mysteries of God, just as they are the governors, promoters, and guardians of the entire liturgical life in the Church committed to them" (CD 15; PO 2).

Bishops and Apostolic Succession

Bishops are successors of the apostles. By the will of Christ they carry on a task first done by the apostles, and they are needed always in the Church. Apostolic succession, then, is a reality found in bishops, who trace their mission back to the apostles, and to Christ.

The incarnational character of the Church requires that Christ's powers be transmitted through individuals, not just through "the Church" in some abstract sense. The transmission of sacred power in the Church reflects the reality of the incarnation and requires that real, living individuals in the Church be bearers of Christ's power.

Certainly historical, cultural, or social influences have shaped the style in which priestly office within the Church has been expressed. When the Church defines the priesthood as a sharing in Christ's saving mission, it prescinds from these historical variations. But there will be such accidental differences. The incarnational principle requires that any mission must be clothed in the cloth of the day. Christ's acceptance of the human condition sets the pattern for the Church.

Bishops are to the Church today what the apostles were to the early Christian community. Bishops are ordained to be the focal point of the local church and its source of unity. This unity appears especially when they offer the Eucharistic sacrifice in the midst of their priests and people. Bishops are ordained only by other bishops (cf. LG 21), and long-standing venerable tradition in the Church restricts to them also the ordination of priests and deacons. Bishops are also the ordinary ministers of the sacrament of confirmation, and, as the source and sign of the unity of the Christian community on the local level, they are the leaders in the Church's liturgical worship, just as they are the principal teachers within their dioceses.

"That divine mission entrusted by Christ to the apostles will last until the end of the world (cf. Matt. 28.20). . . . Just as the role that the Lord gave individually to Peter, the first among the apostles, is permanent and was meant to be transmitted to his successors, so also the apostles' office of nurturing the Church is permanent, and was meant to be exercised without interruption by the sacred order of bishops" (LG 20). The Church teaches "that by divine institution bishops have succeeded to the place of the apostles as shepherds of the Church, and that he who hears them, hears Christ, while he who rejects them, rejects Christ and Him who sent Christ (cf. Luke 10.16)" (LG 20).

Priests

Bishops share their priestly orders with others. Priests "are called to share in the priesthood of the bishops and to mold themselves in the likeness of Christ, the supreme and eternal Priest. By consecration they will preach the Gospel, sustain the people of God, celebrate sacred rites, especially the Lord's sacrifice."[49]

Priests are ordained to continue the saving action of Christ in and through the sacraments. A priest gathers the faithful for the Eucharistic sacrifice which only a priest can offer in the person and in the place

[49]Roman Pontifical, *Rite of Ordination of Priests*, n. 14.

of Christ. He forgives sins in the sacrament of penance, again acting in the name and person of the Lord. His other specifically priestly functions are preaching, praying for the Church, anointing the sick, administering the other sacraments, and caring in every way for Christ's flock (cf. PO 2).

The priesthood must be viewed in the context of Christ and His Church. It is the Church which has primary responsibility for continuing Christ's work. Each bishop in charge of a local church is responsible for the sacramental life of his flock. He is in charge of a certain area of the Church, and within that area, usually a diocese, he is obliged to see that faith and Christian order are maintained. In charging others to help him, he gives them permission to exercise the orders they have received. When a priest is given this permission, he is said to "receive faculties." By his ordination a priest becomes a proper minister of the sacraments. But to perform priestly work, especially to hear confessions and to preach, he must also receive permission from the bishop in the area in which he is to function.

Women in the Ministry

The service of women in the Church has enriched the Christian community from earliest times. A number of women served Jesus in His ministry (cf. Luke 8.1-3), and Mary, His mother, shared in the saving work of Jesus more intimately than any other human person. The Church has always been blessed with women saints. In the life of the Church, women have been involved in countless indispensable ways, in teaching, in the care of the sick and the poor, in administration, and in other areas.

But women have never been ordained priests or bishops in the Church. Even the Blessed Virgin, whose role in the Church is more sublime than that of any other human person, was not called to any priestly office. Over the centuries the Church has believed and taught that only male baptized persons may be validly ordained. It "has never felt that priestly or episcopal ordination can be validly conferred on women,"[50] and "this norm, based on Christ's example, has been and is still observed because it is considered to conform to God's plan for His Church."[51]

In all these considerations it is clear that no Catholic ever has a *right* to orders. For the sacrament of orders is not a gift required for one's spiritual growth or personal fulfillment. The sacrament of orders

---

[50]Congregation for the Doctrine of the Faith, *Declaration* on the Question of the Admission of Women to the Ministerial Priesthood (October 15, 1976) n. 1 (EV 5.2115). Cf. also *Code of Canon Law*, canon 1024.

[51]Congregation for the Doctrine of the Faith, *Declaration* on the Question of the Admission of Women to the Ministerial Priesthood (October 15, 1976) n. 4 (EV 5.2131).

is not intended as a means of enriching the recipient, but for the good of the Church community. The Church has a duty to call to orders those — and only those — whom it judges right for the good of the family of faith, in accord with the will of Christ.

Deacons

The diaconate is traditionally traced back to the apostles and to a time when the infant Church needed an expanded ministry. "Therefore, friends, select from among yourselves seven men of good standing, full of the Spirit and of wisdom, whom we may appoint to this task. . . . They had these men stand before the apostles, who prayed and laid their hands on them" (Acts 6.3, 6). The existence of the diaconate as a distinct office in the Church is often noted in Scripture (cf. Phil. 1.1; 1 Tim. 3.8-13) and is confirmed by the witness of the first Fathers.[52] Like the bishopric and the priesthood, the diaconate is a sacramental order and of divine institution;[53] it has an enduring place in the Church of Christ.

The title "deacon" comes from a Greek word meaning "service." The deacon gives service to the Church. Already in the time of the apostles the richness of the ministry of the diaconate is suggested. Deacons serve at table, notably at the table of the Eucharistic meal. They are ministers of the charity of the Church (cf. Acts 6.1-4). They are witnesses to the faith, and defenders of it. Thus the deacon St. Stephen became the first Christian martyr; and he proclaimed the faith with courageous eloquence and forgiving love before he was slain (cf. Acts 7). Deacons take part also in the Church's task of evangelization, as the deacon Philip did in Samaria (cf. Acts 8.4-13).

In the first centuries of the Church the office of deacon was a permanent one of great importance in the community. There was a gradual decline in the scope of its ministry and influence. At length it became in the Western Church an order exercised by an individual for only a brief time; it was an office filled by one who intended shortly thereafter to become a priest. The Second Vatican Council called for a renewal of the permanent diaconate (cf. LG 29), so that this ancient vocation of service could again shine in the Church.

The Latin Church has decided in our time to permit married men to become deacons. One effect of this decision has been that in many places an important ordained leader in a parish is drawn from the parish family itself. Still the ancient witness to celibacy attached to holy orders remains. Anyone accepting the office of permanent

---

[52]Cf. St. Justin Martyr, *Apologia* 1.65 (MG 6.428); St. Ignatius of Antioch, *Epistula ad Philadelphenses* 4 (MG 5.700 = ACW 1.86).

[53]Cf. Council of Trent, Session 23, July 15, 1563, *Doctrine of the Sacrament of Order*, chs. 2-3 (DS 1765-1766).

deacon, if he is single, promises in the name of Christ not to marry; and if he is already married, he commits himself not to marry again should his wife die before him.

The ancient services of the deacon are continued in the Church today, with added tasks appropriate to our time. The deacon assists at the liturgy; he distributes Communion, and he baptizes. He proclaims the Gospel and preaches. Deacons are invited to assist in many tasks of the Church: in catechesis, in caring for the poor, and in ministering to the sick (though it is the task of the priest to administer penance and to anoint the sick). It is the deacon's office to assist bishop and priest in all the tasks of caring for Christ's flock.

Vocation and Priestly Qualities

Only those who are called by Christ should enter the priesthood. Christ directs His call, or vocation, to those He wishes. Young men are said to have the "signs" of a vocation if they are blessed with the health, the intellectual ability, and the strengths of character required for the priesthood, and if they find in their hearts a desire to do priestly work for God's glory and the salvation of people. But the individual may only offer his service to the Church. The inner inclination must be confirmed by an ecclesiastical call. The Church has the task of confirming the reality of the vocation, and in Christ's name it ordains those selected. The choice is always Christ's. "You did not choose Me but I chose you" (John 15.16).[54]

No one can demand ordination. The imposition of hands in the sacrament of orders is not a recognition of merit or a response to individual preference. It is the recognition of God's special call and the Church's unique role in salvation.

A priestly vocation is a call to a state of life requiring one to serve God for the spiritual welfare of others. Ordination is not a mere ceremony designating one for a particular position or profession in the Church. It is a sacrament which bestows not only the powers of administering the sacraments and preaching God's word, but also the grace which enables one to exercise these powers in a holy manner. The sacrament imparts a special grace of office.

One who accepts the call to serve as a priest must prepare himself to do priestly work. Like the secular professions, the priesthood requires natural aptitudes of body and mind. One who feels he has a vocation should also become aware of the qualities, particularly spiritual, that he must develop and maintain. Modeled on the example of the great High Priest, his must be a life of prayer, humility, and study. Furthermore, a priest gives up home and family life, because he

---

[54]Cf. Pope Pius XII, Apostolic Constitution, *Sedes Sapientiae* (May 31, 1956).

has found a higher joy in devotion to God's work, in labor for the salvation of all.

Celibacy

When speaking of the sacrifices a man might make in order to follow Him, Christ spoke of those who would give up wives and homes for the sake of the Gospel (cf. Matt. 19.29). From the first days of the Church there were priests who were celibate, that is, who did not marry, so that they might give their lives and hearts even more undividedly to the service of Christ (cf. 1 Cor. 7.32-35; 9.5). Different practices developed in different parts of the Church. In the Eastern Church it was customary to permit the ordination of married men; in the West it became the practice to ordain only those who felt they were able and willing to live celibate lives for Christ. Neither in the East nor in the West was a man permitted to marry after he had received holy orders.

Celibacy is loved in the Church for many reasons. It makes the priest more like Christ. St. Paul noted that it gives one great freedom in the service of Christ, and it deepens personal attachment to Him (cf. 1 Cor. 7.32-35). Moreover, the Church desires priests, who preach the duty to bear the cross and to be obedient to God's commands even in the most difficult circumstances, to live in such a way that it is obvious that they are making great personal sacrifices for the Gospel. Priestly celibacy has also been called an eschatological sign, a sign pointing toward eternal life, for one who lives a celibate life in the world is living in a style appropriate to the reality of the next life, in which there will be no marrying (cf. Mark 12.25), and so manifests his faith in eternal life.

In recent years many have urged that the Western Church drop its insistence on celibacy for priests, either to permit the ordination of married men or even to permit men already ordained to marry. This question was discussed at length at the Second General Assembly of the Synod of Bishops (1971), which concluded that "the law of priestly celibacy existing in the Latin Church is to be kept in its entirety."[55] This conclusion was confirmed by the Holy Father.[56]

Certainly no human rights are violated by the requirement of celibacy for priests, for no one is required to become a priest. And the Church may rightfully retain the practice so commended by saints through the centuries, a practice which is so strong a support to the faith of the Catholic people, and continue to call to the priesthood only

[55]Second General Assembly of the Synod of Bishops, *The Ministerial Priesthood* (1971) Part Two, n. 4 (EV 4.1219).
[56]Cf. Rescript of the Audience given by the Holy Father to the Cardinal Secretary of State, November 30, 1971 (EV 4.1134).

those who judge they can willingly live celibate lives for the sake of the kingdom.

The requirement of celibacy is one the Church has power to relax should it judge this appropriate. But it is no arbitrary requirement. The New Testament message and the experience of the Church have shown how fruitful for the people of God has been this charism lived by its priests.

Life of Prayer

The priest should be a man of prayer. On the day of ordination, the candidate receives the special obligation to recite daily the Liturgy of the Hours. The Church thus appoints its priests to a ministry of praise, adoration, petition, and thanksgiving. They are a "voice" of the Church petitioning our heavenly Father to bless the whole world.

Meditation and reflection on what he is and what he is called to be should be part of every priest's life. Without deep spiritual convictions, without a spirit of prayer and sacrifice, he cannot lead the flock entrusted to his care to God. A priest, called to be always a man of God, must interpret the problems of the world and of his parishioners in the light of spiritual realities.

Witness

The priest's identification with Christ is clearly not limited to the dispensing of the sacraments in His name. The mission of the priest is also to represent Christ to the world and to be active in completing Christ's work in the world. In Christ's name he is to serve the word of God, bearing witness and evangelizing in His name, and to lead the Christian community and build Christian unity.

All these tasks of the priest are aspects on one integrated ministry. To preach Christ's message, to make His saving work present in the sacraments, and to build community in His name must all be parts of his ministry. Priests are to carry out the whole mission entrusted to them by Christ.

Service of Authority

In order to bring about unity, a priest is endowed with authority. Both evangelization and sacramental life demand a *diaconia* (service) of authority. The Church is the context for this priestly authority, and the Church's well-being limits and guides the exercise of it. Priestly authority at all times must work in harmony with the Church's purpose for the spiritual good of all believers and their unity in the Church.

The exercise of the *diaconia* of authority falls into two categories: the teaching of truth with authority, and the directing of the community in the path of unity. The first requires that the priest authoritatively interpret the word of God for his people in ways appropriate to his day. The second is centered in the priest's mission to maintain and build Christian community, acting with the authority conferred by Christ's wish that all may be one (cf. John 17.11).

The nature of the priest's authority to build community is conditioned by the nature of the community of faith which the priest undertakes to confirm and build. "The proper mission entrusted by Christ to the priest, as to the Church, is not of the political, economic, or social order, but of the religious order (cf. GS 42); yet, in the pursuit of his ministry, the priest can contribute greatly to the establishment of a more just secular order, especially in places where the human problems of injustice and oppression are more serious. He must always, however, preserve ecclesial communion and reject violence in words or deeds as not being in accordance with the Gospel."[57]

Politics and the Priest

The priest's witness will always touch the political, social, cultural, and economic orders. His message must reach people where they are. The question is one of how he is to make his witness felt.

The work of the priest should affect notably the social and political life of the community. The priest is both a part of the political community and a spokesman for some of its most cherished principles. In his preaching and in other situations he should make clear the moral imperatives contained in the Gospel message that concern the social order. Like all Christians, the priest has a responsibility to help make the political community just. But the means a priest would use are ordinarily different from those appropriate for the layman, whose more immediate role it is to sanctify earthly structures. The extent of priests' engagement in secular political activity must be limited, and guided by the judgment of their bishops.[58] Similarly, while priests should preach on the public duties of Christians, they should not abuse their preaching role by insisting on a particular political, social, or economic option when there is more than one option in harmony with the Gospel.[59]

[57]Second General Assembly of the Synod of Bishops, The *Ministerial Priesthood* (1971) Part One, n. 7 (EV 4.1175).

[58]Cf. Second General Assembly of the Synod of Bishops, *The Ministerial Priesthood* (1971) Part Two, n. 2 (EV 4.1192).

[59]Cf. Second General Assembly of the Synod of Bishops, *The Ministerial Priesthood* (1971) Part Two, n. 2 (EV 1195-1197).

Proclaiming the Gospel

A priest must continually announce the coming and presence among us of the kingdom of God. He is to pass on to others in word and deed the good news that he has received. Priestly witness takes place within the Church. It participates in the authenticity of the Church's witness, because, through the bishop, a priest shares in the call of the Church to spread the message.

The first "witnessing" task of the priest is to proclaim the Gospel. In accepting this task and carrying it out, a priest participates in the mission of Christ as the Truth, the Light of the world. Thus he brings people to faith, upon which they depend to reach God. A priest as witness is "guarantor" of the Gospel.[60]

The patristic tradition on witness is strong. St. Cyprian writes that priests are to witness to Christ in their words and deeds so that others may come to see and know Christ.[61] St. John Chrysostom notes that priestly witness must be "zealous" to be efficacious; he also notes the exclusive nature of a priest's work in devoting himself expressly to the eternal salvation of others.[62] St. Gregory the Great writes of the danger that arises when a priest devotes his time and energies to activities other than the care of the faithful and the works of the Church; regarding political engagement of a priest he remarks that it leaves "his flock without a shepherd" and places the faithful in a position where they "cannot see the light of truth because the mind of their pastor is intent on earthly cares."[63]

The function of the witness is indispensable to faith. The world will not learn of the kingdom unless others tell them of it; God's people must hear of grace, redemption, and eternal life if they are to know of them.

The priest, then, must testify not only to the Person of Jesus Christ, but to the content of the faith, carrying the words of life to those who are to believe and have no other way of coming to them, and testifying to the truth by words and acts.

In this aspect of his priesthood, the priest reflects the work of Christ. Jesus, speaking of His role as the witness of the Father, said He did nothing of His own authority, but said only that which he had been taught by the Father (cf. John 8.28). The priest as witness should absorb the message and remain obedient to it, passing it on as it is. The mission remains the same: to testify to the truth of God as revealed, that through the truth all may live.

60Cf. Second General Assembly of the Synod of Bishops, *The Ministerial Priesthood* (1971) Part One, n. 4 (EV 4.1167).

61Cf. St. Cyprian, *Epistula* 63.14 (ML 4.385-386 = ACW 46.105f.).

62Cf. St. John Chrysostom, *Homilia 86 in Ioannem* 4 (MG 59.471-472).

63St. Gregory the Great, *Regula Pastoralis* 2.7 (ML 77.39 = ACW 11.68-74).

28

Sacraments Of Initiation

Three of the sacraments — baptism, confirmation, and the Eucharist — are concerned with Christian initiation: "The three sacraments of Christian initiation closely combine to bring the faithful to the full stature of Christ and to enable them to carry out the mission of the entire people of God in the Church and in the world."[1]

The Eucharist, which is the center of all sacramental life, has already been treated at length in the preceding chapter. In this chapter we discuss the sacraments of baptism and confirmation.

Baptism

Salvation History and Baptism

We may best approach the sacrament of baptism through the Holy Saturday Vigil liturgy, which is the masterpiece of the Church's liturgical-catechetical teaching art. In the fullest sense this rite is religious pedagogy. It goes beyond an abstract presentation of the Church's teaching by drawing on the prophetic symbolism of the Old Testament, which in turn leads to the teaching of the New Testament. Then all is brought together in a rite which richly expresses the meaning of baptism.

The first scriptural reading of the vigil liturgy is the creation story from the Book of Genesis (cf. Gen. 1.1-22). It illustrates the power of God, culminating in the creation of human life. This narrative of divine power is seen here as a symbol of what St. Paul will call a "new creation," the creation effected by Jesus Christ through His passion and death. "So if anyone is in Christ, there is a new creation: everything old has passed away; see, everything has become new" (2 Cor. 5.17). "For neither circumcision nor uncircumcision is anything, but a new creation is everything" (Gal. 6.15). This new creation actually takes place at the climax of the vigil — in baptism.

The second reading (Gen. 22.1-18) recounts Abraham's faith as shown in his readiness to sacrifice his son Isaac. This is a foreshadow-

---

[1]Congregation for Divine Worship, *Rite of Baptism for Children*, published by authority of Pope Paul VI, May 15, 1969, General Introduction, n. 2 (EV 3.1093). A second typical edition, published on August 29, 1973, lists several significant changes in the text on page 6.

ing of Christ's sacrifice, from which baptism, like all the other sacraments, receives its power. Isaac, spared, rose from the altar alive; Jesus died — the Father "did not withhold His own Son" (Rom. 8.32) — but rose again in a resurrection far greater than Isaac's.

The third reading (Exod. 14.15-15.1) tells of the deliverance of the Jews at the Red Sea. This is linked with the account of the paschal sacrifice, anticipated on Holy Thursday. At this point the concern is with the idea of deliverance through water, a necessary background for understanding the Lord's use of water and the power of baptism. Later He will say to Nicodemus; "Very truly, I tell to you, no one can enter the Kingdom of God without being born of water and Spirit" (John 3.5). Indeed, already in the Genesis account, the Spirit entered the waters creatively: "And the Spirit of God hovered over the surface of the water" (Gen. 1.2 REB).

The water is at once destructive, in Genesis, part of the wasteland and darkness, and also the source from which life arises. This double symbolism of water — death and life, destruction and salvation — becomes ever clearer in the history of Noah, which is alluded to in the fourth reading (Isa. 54.5-14). Water is used by God to destroy His enemies and save His friends. But the classic instance of this divine use of water is the passing of the Jews through the Red Sea, which, together with the paschal sacrifice, became central in Jewish life and salvation history, pointing forward to Christ "our paschal lamb" (1 Cor. 5.7). Once more God's enemies are destroyed by water, vindicating the divine justice, while in the same act His chosen people are delivered and pass over to the Promised Land.

The remaining readings (Isa. 55.1-11; Bar. 3.9-15, 32-44; Ezech. 36.16-17a, 18-28) are from the prophetic writings and point to the spiritual effects of baptism, still celebrating God's wonderful use of water, as Jesus would use it afterwards: "The water that I shall give will become in them a spring of water gushing up to eternal life" (John 4.14). The final reading, from Ezekiel, anticipates the "new creation" by promising a new heart and a new Spirit.

Thus the stage was set for "when the fullness of time had come" (Gal. 4.4). When John the Baptist made his appearance in the Judean desert, he proclaimed a "baptism of repentance for the forgiveness of sins" (Mark 1.4). Jesus Himself, going down into the waters of the Jordan, brings this long, dramatic sequence of water-events to completion. Sinless Himself, He leads His people from sin through the waters of baptism to a new covenant with the Father.

St. Paul evidently had all this in mind when he wrote: "Do you not know that all of us who have been baptized into Christ Jesus were baptized into His death?" (Rom. 6.3). But he has more in mind than the saving of the people at the Red Sea. He sees also the ultimate signification of baptism. Jesus Himself had said: "I have a baptism with which to be baptized, and what stress I am under until it is completed!" (Luke 12.50; cf. Mark 10.38). And so Paul continues: "Therefore we were buried with Him by baptism into death, so that, just as Christ was raised from the dead by the glory of the Father, so we too might walk in newness of life" (Rom. 6.4).

By the waters of baptism, sin and evil are destroyed and we rise to a new life, sharing in the resurrection of Jesus. "You have stripped off the old self with its practices and have clothed yourselves with the new self..." (Col. 3.9). Indeed, "our old self was crucified with Him so that the body of sin might be destroyed, and we might no longer be enslaved to sin" (Rom. 6.6). Then the whole paschal mystery, the dying and the rising of Christ as it envelops the baptized, is summarized by St. Paul in a passage read on Easter morning: "So if you have been raised with Christ, seek the things that are above, where Christ is, seated at the right hand of God. Set your mind on things that are above, not on things that are on earth. For you have died, and your life is hidden with Christ in God" (Col. 3.1-3).

The Baptismal Liturgy

Against this background of salvation history culminating in Christ, we can appreciate the baptismal liturgy. Certainly in the case of adults the preparation has started long before Easter; the Easter liturgy completes it. Easter is the most appropriate time for baptism and full participation in the Eucharist, since then above all we celebrate our sharing in the death and resurrection of the Lord. It follows that Lent is a most suitable time for preparing for baptism (or for preparing for renewal of baptismal pledges), as it was in the ancient catechumenate, the period of instruction prior to baptism. A major feature of the Church's *Rite of Christian Initiation of Adults*[2] is emphasis on the community aspect of baptism.

The vigil itself begins with a Light Service. From a new fire, the paschal candle is lighted; it stands for the risen Christ, His wounds now glorified: "The light shines in the darkness, and the darkness did not overcome it" (John 1.5). While the candle is carried in procession to the sanctuary, the light is gradually diffused as first the celebrant, then the ministers, and finally all others in the congregation light their candles from the paschal candle. The Easter Proclamation (*Exsultet*) is sung, all rejoicing in the victory of God's light at this climax of salvation history. Then come the scriptural readings described above.

[2]Congregation for Divine Worship, *Ordo Initiationis Christianae Adultorum (Rite of Christian Initiation of Adults)*, published by authority for Pope Paul VI, January 6, 1972; a new edition of the *Rite of Christian Initiation of Adults*, with modifications was approved for use in the dioceses of the United States of America by the National Conference of Catholic Bishops on November 11, 1986, and was confirmed by the Apostolic See on February 19, 1988.

The emphasis now turns to the joy of the resurrection. Altar candles are lighted, the Gloria is sung, church bells are rung. All is ready for baptism. First, the water is blessed with a prayer that sums up the salvation history just heard in the readings. The paschal candle is lowered into the water. Through the risen Christ, whom the candle signifies, the font will now become life-giving. The font, the womb of the Church, will bring forth children of God, as once more the Spirit of God is hovering "over the surface of the waters."

The baptismal promises are now pronounced. Then follows a profession of faith. Finally there is the baptism itself. Those baptized are then anointed with chrism, recalling Christ's anointing by the Spirit, which is now shared by the new Christian. This foreshadows and anticipates the anointing of confirmation, which may take place here. The baptized are thus admitted to God's covenanted people and will now be allowed to share in the "holy priesthood, to offer spiritual sacrifices acceptable to God through Jesus Christ" (1 Peter 2.5). The ceremony is completed by investing those who have been baptized with a symbolic white garment, the token of their baptismal innocence. They now are ready to share in the Eucharist in which we celebrate and renew the death and resurrection of the Lord.

Lent

The catechumens were (and are) an important part of the community during Lent. They vividly dramatize in their conversion and baptism the meaning of dying and rising with Christ at Easter. Nevertheless, Lent, as it developed, belongs to the whole community, for whom it has become an annual period of penance and renewal. Although Lent has not always consisted of forty days as it does now, the present number of days in Lent is based on the length of our Lord's own fast (cf. Matt. 4.2).

Lent is a period for the instruction of catechumens, but it is a period for the baptized as well. The baptized Christian is encouraged to approach each Easter as one should when solemnly preparing for baptism. Today also we have in Lent the opportunity to relive our baptism experience and deepen the realization of its meaning as we renew our baptismal vows at the Easter Vigil.

All this helps us understand the Lenten discipline of the Church today.[3] All acts of penance are part of that total conversion called for by baptism, a whole inner renewal leading one to think, judge, and arrange one's entire life under the impulse of the charity revealed to us in Christ. Acts of penance without this inner spirit are lifeless. Still, the inner spirit ought to be incarnated in deeds. There must be bodily penances, not because the body, so consecrated by Christ, is evil, but

---

[3]Cf. Pope Paul VI, Apostolic Constitution, *Paenitemini* (February 16, 1966) (EV 2.625-654).

because we must take the flesh seriously and seek to liberate it also. To share Christ's cross is to be freed by Him ever more fully from the consequences of the Fall.

Christian penance traditionally involves prayer, fasting, and works of charity. In our times it may be appropriate, even necessary, in many instances to put less emphasis on fasting and more on the penance necessarily involved in faithful prayer and in doing charitable works. But the witness of Scripture and the life of the Church will not let us abandon corporal penances. Fasting and abstinence are encouraged in Lent, but Church law does not require a great deal of us in this regard. Specific regulations vary in different countries. In the United States of America, for example, all Fridays of Lent are days of abstinence, that is, days on which no meat is to be eaten; and Ash Wednesday and Good Friday are days of fast as well as abstinence. On fast days one is to abstain from solid foods except at the one full meal and the two smaller meals permitted. Fasting binds those between the ages of 21 and 59; those who have reached the age of fourteen are bound by abstinence. For sufficient reasons, the faithful may judge themselves excused or seek a dispensation from these particular regulations. But we can never be excused from the duty of doing penance. Because the Church is a family of faith, it is called in Lent to do penance collectively.

Fasting and abstinence are by no means the only types of penance. "Let us witness to our love and imitation of Christ, by special solicitude for the sick, the poor, the underprivileged, the imprisoned, the bedridden, the discouraged, the stranger, the lonely, and persons of other color, nationalities, or backgrounds than our own."[4] In the Scriptures fasting is commonly associated with almsgiving (cf. Tobit 12:8; Matt. 6). When the well-fed fast, they are thereby able to share with the hungry; and this sharing by almsgiving is surely an act of love.

Easter Customs

In Europe the custom grew (and was sometimes transplanted to other areas) as bringing "Easter water" into the home to bless and renew everything. Food, which represents the resurgence of nature in the spring, was especially set aside to be blessed. All this is done to acknowledge the "new creation" spoken of by St. Paul and to rejoice that "the old has passed away" and "the new has come" (2 Cor. 5.17).

Such simple customs have a large significance. If our Easter liturgy is to be really a joyous celebration, setting in high relief the culminating liturgy of the year, it must have a human dimension, must take root in our human lives.

---

[4]United States National Conference of Catholic Bishops, *Pastoral Statement on Penance and Abstinence* n. 15(November 18, 1966).

Some have observed that although Easter is the greatest Christian feast, Christmas is in fact celebrated with greater joy. The reason seems plain. Christmas has more human resonances. There are family gatherings and reunions, children take the center of the stage, gifts are exchanged. To accomplish something like this for Easter, we need more than theological explanation. If a parish community could be brought to recognize Easter as the annual celebration of the baptism and first communion of all the parishioners, then there might also be rejoicing and family gatherings, with sponsors as well as parents and grandparents.

Rite of Baptism

Baptism is in fact celebrated not only at Easter but at all times of the year. Still the spirit of the paschal mystery must always penetrate its celebration. Baptism may be administered either by pouring baptismal water over the candidate's head three times, or by immersing the candidate three times in the baptismal water. While the water is applied, the celebrant speaks the baptismal formula: "N., I baptize you in the name of the Father, and of the Son, and of the Holy Spirit." The water and the words symbolize the new life of the Trinity to which one is called, by sharing in the death and resurrection of Christ.

Bishops, priests, and deacons are the ordinary ministers of baptism. Anyone, however, even a non-Christian, can validly administer this sacrament by performing the rite with the serious intent to baptize in accord with the mind of the Church. Every Catholic should be able to administer this sacrament should an emergency demand this. For such cases the Church has prepared a suitable brief ceremony. If this cannot be used, it is sufficient to recite the Apostles' Creed (and even this may be omitted if necessary), and to pour water over the one to be baptized while saying the baptismal formula noted above. Children baptized in emergencies are to be greeted by the Church community with the special ceremonies prepared for the time when they are able to come to the church.

Each baptismal candidate should have at least one godparent, but may have a godfather and godmother. The godparent chosen by or for the one being baptized should be a mature person (ordinarily at least sixteen years of age), a Catholic living the faith, one who is able and willing to fulfill a role of spiritual concern for the one baptized. In special circumstances, as in the case of children of mixed marriages, a baptized and believing Christian of a separated community may serve as an additional witness to the baptism.[5]

The name to be given at baptism should not be out of harmony

---

[5]On this paragraph, cf. *Code of Canon Law*, 873-874.

with the Christian calling of the person. The name of a saint is ordinarily given. Ideally, the saint whose name is chosen should become well known to the one baptized, as a patron and friend.

Effects of Baptism

The effects of baptism have been indicated in the scriptural passages cited and also in the liturgical signs of the Church described above. What remains is to bring these teachings together. In this we are aided by the *Rite of Baptism for Children*, for it crystallizes the Church's teachings on the sacrament. One of these, which is a basis for understanding all sacraments, concerns the manner of justification through grace. We are justified, the Church teaches, by God's grace and gifts, and this is "not only a remission of sins, but also the sanctification and renewal of the inner man. . . ."[6] This teaching refutes the error that justification, although accomplished by God's grace, is only an outward cloak. The Church insists that it is an interior sanctification, a true inward renewal which is accomplished "when, by the merit of the same most holy passion, the charity of God is poured forth through the Holy Spirit in the hearts (cf. Rom. 5.5) of those who are justified and inheres in them."[7]

By baptism people "are plunged into the paschal mystery of Christ: they die with Him, are buried with Him, and rise with Him. . ." (SC 6). The ritual adds: "Far superior to the purifications of the old law, baptism produces all these effects by the power of the mystery of the Lord's passion and resurrection."[8] What are "all these effects" comprehended in the paschal mystery?

Dying with Christ

In our review of the Old Testament signs of baptism we saw that water is at once destructive and life-giving. So in baptism there is a destructive process: "Those who are baptized are engrafted in the likeness of Christ's death. They are buried with him. . . ."[9] St. Paul explains: "We know that our old self was crucified with Him so that the body of sin might be destroyed, and we might no longer be enslaved to sin" (Rom. 6.6).

How are we engrafted in the likeness of Christ's death? How are we buried with Him that we may pass from death to life? How do we put off the old self? By cleansing us from sin, the waters of baptism set us on a new way of life. When adults are baptized their sins are

---

[6]Council of Trent, Session 6, January 13, 1547, *Decree on Justification*, ch. 7 (DS 1528).
[7]Council of Trent, Session 6, January 13, 1547, *Decree on Justification*, ch. 7 (DS 1530).
[8]*Rite of Baptism for Children*, General Introduction, n. 6 (EV 3.1097).
[9]*Rite of Baptism for Children*, General Introduction, n. 6 (EV 3.1097).

forgiven even as they receive the new life of grace; for divine grace, in virtue of Christ's passion and death, has a forgiving and healing effect. Accordingly, baptism remits original sin and, for those baptized after infancy, also all personal sins which are sincerely repented of. "Repent, and be baptized every one of you in the name of Jesus Christ so that your sins may be forgiven; and you will receive the gift of the Holy Spirit" (Acts. 2.38). Converts to Christ need not submit themselves to the power of the keys by confessing their sins; in baptism they are forgiven by an act of divine amnesty.

Since original sin involves all the members of our race, in this respect infants as well as adults must "die" with Christ and come to a new life of grace. This is made clear by the prayer of exorcism in the baptismal ceremony:

> Almighty and ever-living God,
> you sent your only Son into the world
> to cast out the power of Satan, spirit of evil. . . .
> We pray for these children:
> set them free from original sin,
> make them temples of your glory,
> and send your Holy Spirit to dwell within them.[10]

Although the guilt of original sin is removed, some of its effects remain. So the Church prays also:

> We now pray for these children
> who will have to face the world with its temptations,
> and fight the devil in all his cunning.[11]

St. Paul speaks of the effect of sin as feverish desire, or concupiscence, which he at times also calls "sin."

This inclination to sin remains in those who have been reborn in baptism. It is "left for us to wrestle with," but it "cannot harm those who do not consent but manfully resist through the grace of Jesus Christ."[12] This "wrestling," this agonizing struggle with our own desires, involves a lifelong sharing in the dying of Jesus. God permits us to undergo this struggle that we may more fully share in the great work of our own redemption. Sometimes this struggle seems almost too much for us. But steadfastness is made possible by the healing and quickening grace of the risen Jesus, which also assures victory to those who desire victory.

Rising with Christ

The baptized die with Christ only to rise with Him and share His life: "They are buried with him, they are given life again with him,

---

[10]*Rite of Baptism for Children*, n. 49.

[11]*Rite of Baptism for Children*, n. 49.

[12]Council of Trent, Session 5, June 17, 1546, *Decree on Original Sin*, n. 5 (DS 1515).

and with him they rise again. For baptism recalls the effects the paschal mystery itself, because by means of it men and women pass from
the death of sin into life."[13] It is the risen life of Christ we share.
When St. Paul says: "I have been crucified with Christ; and it is no
longer I who live, but it is Christ who lives in me," he is writing of the
risen life, for he adds: "And the life I now live in the flesh I live by
faith in the Son of God, who loved me and gave Himself for me" (Gal.
2.19-20). The interior renewal we spoke of above is effected by this
sharing in Christ's risen life.

Baptism makes us members of the Church. But to become a member
of the Church is to be radically changed; it is to be grafted on the
vine (cf. John 15.4-6) and joined vitally to the Body of Christ. Through
an all-pervading bond of life we become members of God's covenanted
people. All this is effected in the paschal mystery: "This cup that is
poured out for you is the new covenant in My blood" (Luke 22.20).

Children of God

"Baptism, the cleansing with water by the power of the living
Word, makes us sharers in God's own life and his adopted children."[14]
Baptism is both a rising with Christ and a new birth. As St. Peter
wrote: "Blessed be the God and Father of our Lord Jesus Christ! By
His great mercy He has given us a new birth into a living hope through
the resurrection of Jesus Christ from the dead. . ." (1 Peter 1.3). But
that we become children of God through baptism is told to us by Jesus
Himself: "Very truly, I tell you, no one can enter the Kingdom of God
without being born of water and Spirit" (John 3.5).

Since Jesus Christ is "the only Son of God" (John 3.18), we
receive our status by "adoption" (Gal. 4.5). Still, as St. John assures
us, this adoption is no legal fiction, as when children are legally
adopted: "See what love the Father has given us, that we should be
called children of God; and that is what we are" (1 John 3.1). Offspring share the nature of their parents. If we are truly children of
God, we must in some way share in the nature and life of God. Scripture assures us that we do: "Thus He has given us through these things
His precious and very great promises, so that through them you may
escape from the corruption that is in the world because of lust, and
may become participants of the divine nature" (2 Peter 1.4).

A Royal Priesthood

The first Epistle of St. Peter is largely a meditation on baptism, its
effects, and its practical implications. It brings many of the above

---

[13]*Rite of Baptism for Children*, General Introduction, n. 6 (EV 3.1097).
[14]*Rite of Baptism for Children*, General Introduction, n. 5 (EV 3.1096).

themes together and yet says its own distinctive word: "And like living stones, let yourselves be built into a spiritual house, to be a holy priesthood, to offer spiritual sacrifices acceptable to God through Jesus Christ" (1 Peter 2.5). In studying the sacrament or orders we have seen the difference between the priesthood of the laity and the ministerial priesthood. St. Peter here speaks of baptism, by which all become worshipers of God in Spirit and in truth: "But you are a chosen race, a royal priesthood, a holy nation, God's own people, in order that you may proclaim the mighty acts of Him who called you out of darkness into His marvelous light. Once you were not a people, but now you are God's people" (1 Peter 2.9-10). The apostle is recalling Exodus where the Jewish people were spoken of as a royal priesthood (cf. Exod. 19.6) although only the Levites were specially designated for divine service.

In a similar way, while a new order of priests, sharing Christ's High Priesthood, has been instituted to continue and renew His sacrifice, all the baptized are now called to join in worshiping God fully, consciously, and actively. As the context shows also, St. Peter is speaking here of the worship of the people not only in the sense of its liturgy but in the wider sense of embracing and sanctifying all the duties of life. The *Rite of Baptism for Children* brings these ideas together when it says that " baptism is the sacrament by which men and women are incorporated into the Church, built into a house where God lives, in the Spirit, into a holy nation and a royal priesthood."[15]

Baptism of Infants

So far we have been concerned largely with adult baptism. Now turn to infant baptism.[16] The practice of baptizing infants, questioned by some in the past, is again being questioned by some today. "Why baptize an infant, who has no understanding, who can make no personal commitment?" "Is it not unwise and even unjust for parents to predetermine the religion of a child, thus removing or diminishing later freedom of choice?"

The Church has solemnly defined the validity of infant baptism.[17] In fact, Church law commands Catholics to have their children baptized within the first weeks after birth.[18]

Almost from the beginning, if not from the very beginning of

---

[15]*Rite of Baptism for Children*, General Introduction, n. 4 (EV 3.1095).

[16]Cf. Congregation for the Doctrine of the Faith, *De Baptismo Parvulorum* (20 October 1980) (EV 7.587-630).

[17]Cf. Council of Trent, Session 7, March 3, 1547, *Decree on the Sacraments*, canon 13 on the sacrament of baptism (DS 1626).

[18]Cf. *Code of Canon Law*, canon 867.

Christianity, infant baptism was practiced when whole families were baptized. Among the "relatives and close friends" (Acts 10.24) whom Cornelius invited to hear St. Peter preach, and who were afterwards baptized with him (cf. Acts 10.48), there may well have been children. In any case, infant baptism clearly was practiced very early. Origen, writing in the third century, expressly states that the Church's tradition of baptizing infants came from the apostles.[19] St. Augustine cites the universal practice of infant baptism as evidence of the Church's traditional belief in original sin.[20]

The theological reason for infant baptism is given by Jesus Himself: "Very truly, I tell you, no one can see the Kingdom of God without being born of water and the Spirit" (John 3.5). There could be no stronger statement of the need for baptism. After the resurrection Jesus summarized the whole history of God's salvific power working through water when He placed all under the obligation of receiving baptism: "Go into all the world and proclaim the good news to the whole creation. The one who believes and is baptized will be saved; but the one who does not believe will be condemned" (Mark 16.15).

Moreover, would not parents, converted to Christianity, especially when the conversion was a profound spiritual experience, desire to share this with their own children? Would they not be most anxious that their children also become citizens of God's kingdom and have their whole lives directed towards Him as their true last end and supreme good? Would they not also wish them to receive this orientation while they are most open to guidance from those they love?

Indeed, society itself is concerned with the birth of a child. A birth is a momentous event in the life of a family, and also in the life of society, which is receiving a new member who may be creative or may be destructive.

Children born of Christian parents are introduced by baptism into the covenanted people of God. They are given a place, not only in their families, but in the community of the Church, and also in the universe; they are provided with a purpose, a key to the meaning of life, and a place in the economy of salvation in which these can be realized. The baptized child is introduced into "a chosen race, a royal priesthood, a holy nation, God's own people" (1 Peter 2.9). At baptism we are welcomed on earth by the very God who created us, received through the Son and at once made members of the Body whose Head is Christ.

The parents, in bringing their child to be baptized, are also acting

---

[19]Cf. Origen, *In Romanos Commentarii* 5.9 (MG 14.1047). Cf. also St. Cyprian, *Epistula* 64.5.2 (ML 3.1018 = ACW 46.112).

[20]Cf., e.g., St. Augustine's *Contra Iulianum Opus Imperfectum* 1.50 (ML 45.1073).

as members of God's covenanted people; they are exercising their royal priesthood by introducing their child into God's holy nation.

The Necessity of Baptism

The Church, heeding the words of the Gospel (cf., e.g., John 3.3,5), teaches that no one can enter the kingdom of heaven unless he or she is baptized.[21]

This insistence on the need for baptism for salvation may seem puzzling to many. Does it not follow that salvation is impossible for those who have never heard of Christ or baptism? This is by no means a new question. Nor is the answer new. Not all baptism is sacramental baptism with water. There is also "baptism of blood" and "baptism of desire."

Baptism of blood is received by dying for Christ. The Holy Innocents (cf. Matt. 2.16-18) received such a baptism, as did the early catechumens who were martyred for Christ.

Baptism of desire has a far wider scope. It is most clearly present in those who explicitly wish to be baptized but who die before their intention can be carried out. Moreover, the desire for baptism does not have to be explicit. Baptism of desire can be present in one who, in response to God's grace, has faith in God and loves Him. Baptism of desire is certainly received by those who, implicitly or explicitly, desire baptism but for some reason are unable to receive it sacramentally. Even those who through no fault of their own do not know Christ and His Church may be counted as anonymous Christians if their striving to lead a good life is in fact a response to His grace, which is given in sufficient measure to all (cf. LG 16).[22]

Even this anonymous faith is implicitly directed toward the Church. There is only one Christ in whom people are saved. Those who love Him without knowing Him do wish in an obscure way to do His whole will. Implicitly, then, they do desire baptism, and this we call baptism of desire.

The Baptismal Character

The Church teaches that baptism, like confirmation and orders, imprints a permanent character or sign.[23] St. Augustine, who intro-

---

[21]Cf., e.g., Council of Florence, Bull, *Exsultate Deo* (November 22, 1439) (DS 1314); Council of Trent, Session 6, January 13, 1547, *Decree on Justification*, ch. 4 (DS 1524) and Session 7, March 3, 1547, *Decree on the Sacraments*, canon 5 on the sacrament of baptism (DS 1618). Cf. also *Code of Canon Law*, canon 849.

[22]Cf. also Holy Office, *Letter* to the Archbishop of Boston (August 8, 1949) (DS 3866-3873).

[23]Council of Trent, Session 7, March 3, 1547, *Decree on the Sacraments*, canon 9 on the sacraments in general (DS 1609). Cf. also *Code of Canon Law*, canon 849.

duced this use of the word "character" into Christian theology, took it from the mark by which soldiers were identified as belonging to a particular commander, owing him their allegiance. In the Scriptures the word used is "seal," which also marks or identifies. Yet the sacramental character is visible only in that it is conferred in a visible rite.

In order to understand the spiritual reality which the word "character" here expresses symbolically, we must note a significant difference between these sacraments and the others. The other sacraments may be received more than once, but baptism, confirmation and orders may not. There is a reason for this. Apart from the grace which they confer, which can be lost through sin, the sacraments of baptism, confirmation, and orders also have a lasting effect. This endures even if the recipient sins gravely. It remains in eternity. St. John in his vision of heaven sees an angel with "the seal of the living God," which was to be used in marking "the servants of our God with a seal upon their foreheads" (Rev. 7.3). On the other hand, St. Paul speaks of our being sealed already in accepting the Gospel: "In Him you also, when you had heard the word of truth, the gospel of your salvation, and have believed in Him, were marked with the seal of the promised Holy Spirit" (Eph. 1.13). The seal is also associated with anointing and the Holy Spirit (hence the use of chrism in the baptismal ceremony and in confirmation): "It is God who establishes us with you in Christ, and has anointed us, by putting His seal on us and giving us His Spirit in our hearts as a first installment" (2 Cor. 1.21-22). Like St. John, St. Paul also sees this seal enduring into eternity: "Do not grieve the Holy Spirit of God, with which you marked with a seal for the day of redemption" (Eph. 4.30).

The character points to the stability and permanence of the Church. It cries out that God's gifts are enduring, and that He will continue to work His mercy in and through those He has chosen. "You belong to Christ, and Christ belongs to God" (1 Cor. 3.23). As priests share fully in the priesthood of Christ, and are ordained to make His sacrifice present everywhere, so by baptism, all participate in a basic way in the royal priesthood of Christ, are designated for divine worship, and are rendered capable of offering their whole lives in union with His sacrifice. Even if they fail, they can be reconciled to the Church by the sacrament of penance without a repetition of baptism.

Christ marks out His own. He has chosen us. We belong to Him. He prays, indeed He dies, that He will keep all of us. "Father, I desire that those also, whom You have given Me, may be with Me where I am. . . . This is the will of Him who sent Me, that I should lose nothing of all that He has given Me" (John 17.24, 6.39). The baptismal character is the sign at once of the Christian's permanent vocation, of his call by Jesus Christ, and, in the first place, of God's initial and undiscourageable love.

Confirmation

Divine Origin of Confirmation

Confirmation (like the anointing of the sick and matrimony) is a sacrament which we first learn about in New Testament passages that speak of its use in the Church's liturgy. The Gospels contain no direct teaching on it, as they do on the Eucharist, baptism, and penance. When we first hear of this sacrament in the New Testament it is already being administered — Christ having already ascended — in the infant Church. There are two places in the Acts of the Apostles where this is recorded.

"When the apostles at Jerusalem heard that Samaria had accepted the word of God, they sent Peter and John to them. The two went down and prayed for them that they might receive the Holy Spirit (for as yet the Spirit had not come upon any of them; but they had only been baptized in the name of the Lord Jesus). Then Peter and John laid their hands on them, and they received the Holy Spirit" (Acts 8.14-17). The other passage is Acts 19.5-7.

That we learn of confirmation through its liturgy is significant. This highlights the importance of liturgy as a means of knowing and transmitting religious teaching.[24]

Some Christians have denied the Church's firm teaching that confirmation is a distinct sacrament instituted by Christ. Their denial could stem from a misinterpretation of the way in which faith is transmitted. Not everything the Church believes is explicitly articulated in abstract statements. The faith can be embodied in its attitudes and rites before it is explicitly formulated. This is certainly the case with the sacrament of confirmation (and also the anointing of the sick and matrimony). We must start with the sacrament as celebrated, then go back to the Gospels and to the Old Testament types to discover the rich meanings that have been brought together in this sacramental rite.

Anointing in Scripture

To the laying on of hands described in the Acts of the Apostles there was added an anointing with oil. The oil of olives was a valued product in Palestine as in most of the ancient world. Because of its many uses it was also rich in significance. It was a food condiment, a beauty preparation, a medicine, an unguent for athletes and, mixed with perfume, for refreshment after bathing; and it was a sign of joy. It was the ordinary fuel for lamps, even in the sanctuary. A special sacred oil for anointing was prepared at the direction of Moses (cf. Exod. 30.25 f.). Aaron was anointed as high priest, and then Aaron's

---

[24]Cf. Pope Pius XII, Encyclical, *Mediator Dei* (November 20, 1947) nn. 47-48.

sons (cf. Lev. 8.12, 30). Later Samuel anointed Saul as king, then David (cf. 1 Sam. 10.1 f., 16.13 f). In these instances, anointing brought the Spirit on those who received it, resulting in extraordinary actions: Saul prophesied and "the Spirit of the Lord came mightily upon David" (1 Sam. 16.13).

Since Jesus in the line of David was the Messiah, He would certainly be anointed. So Isaiah had foretold (cf. Isa. 61.1), and this was the very prophecy that Jesus read and commented upon in teaching at Nazareth: "The Spirit of the Lord is upon Me, because He has anointed Me. . ." (Luke 4.18). To be sure, Jesus was anointed directly by the Spirit, following His baptism by John. Yet the Epistle to the Hebrews applies to Jesus, at least symbolically, a passage of the Old Testament which speaks of an anointing with oil: "But of the Son He says, '. . . You have loved righteousness and hated lawlessness; therefore God, your God, has anointed you with the oil of gladness beyond your companions' "(Heb. 1.8-9; cf. Ps. 45.7-8).

Sacrament of the Holy Spirit

Thus oil came to symbolize the coming of the Spirit, as a sharing of the Gift sent first to the apostles. At times the laying on of hands was absorbed into the act of anointing (as in the Eastern Churches), and at other times both actions were retained distinctly. Today the Latin Church has a laying on of hands separate from the anointing. It should be noted that the anointing of the forehead is done by the laying on of the hand.

In the administration of the sacrament olive oil perfumed with balsam is used (although other suitable plant oils and other fragrances are acceptable, according to availability). In consecrating this chrism, the bishop recalls that it takes its name from Christ, who is the Messiah, the "Anointed One." He goes on to pray that those who receive the sacrament may be given "the fullness of royal, priestly, and prophetic power." With chrism the Christian is, so to speak, Christified.

Confirmation exists to extend to the Church of every time and place the Gift of the Holy Spirit sent to the apostles on Pentecost. The Holy Spirit is the gift of Christ. "I will ask the Father, and He will give you another Advocate, to be with you forever. This is the Spirit of truth. . . . But the Advocate, the Holy Spirit, whom the Father will send in My name, will teach you everything, and remind you of all that I have said to you. . . . When the Advocate comes, whom I will send to you from the Father, the Spirit of truth who comes from the Father, He will testify on my behalf" (John 14.16-17, 26; 15.26).

Christ's promise was fulfilled for the apostles on Pentecost. "When the day of Pentecost had come, they were all together in one place. And suddenly from heaven there came a sound like the rush of a violent wind, and it filled the entire house where they were sitting. Divided tongues, as of fire, appeared among them, and a tongue rested on each of them. All of them were filled with the Holy Spirit and began to speak in other languages, as the Spirit gave ability" (Acts 2.1-4).

Marvels accompany the Spirit's coming — the mysterious wind, the tongues of fire, the gift of tongues, the bold proclamation, and the numerous conversions. But perhaps the most notable effect was the transformation of this frightened, cowardly group of men into inspired and fearless witnesses to their Lord's resurrection: "Their voice has gone out to all the earth, and their words to the ends of the world" (Rom. 10.18; cf. Ps. 19.5).

Confirmation is thus the sacrament whereby the apostles and their successors, by the laying on of hands and anointing with chrism, communicate to the whole Church and all its members the gift of the Spirit received at Pentecost. It is Pentecost extended throughout the world, perpetuated, and made ever present in the Church. It is a call to spread the kingdom of Christ, to spread the message of salvation.

Although any priest is authorized, as need urges and the Church delegates him, to administer the sacrament of Confirmation, there is a special propriety in its being conferred by a bishop: "The original minister of confirmation is the bishop. Ordinarily the sacrament is administered by the bishop so that there will be a more evident relationship to the first pouring forth of the Holy Spirit on the day of Pentecost. After they were filled with the Holy Spirit, the apostles themselves gave the Spirit to the faithful through the laying on of their hands. In this way the reception of the Spirit through the ministry of the bishop shows the close bond which joins the confirmed to the Church and the mandate of Christ to be witnesses among men."[25]

Sacrament of Christian Maturity

In the early centuries of the Church, confirmation was administered soon after baptism. It became part of the Holy Saturday Vigil service following baptism and preceding the Eucharist. Baptism, although a rebirth and a new creation, was assumed to require completion by the Spirit. Those who have been baptized still need the further pledge of guidance, inspiration, courage, and growth. Pope Paul VI writes: "The sharing in the divine nature which is granted to men through the grace of Christ has a certain likeness to the origin, development, and nourishing of natural life. The faithful are born anew by baptism, strengthened by the sacrament of confirmation, and

[25]Congregation for Divine Worship, *Rite of Confirmation*, published by authority of Pope Paul VI, August 22, 1971, Introduction, n. 7 (EV 4.1093).

finally are sustained by the food of eternal life in the Eucharist."[26] The Pope is here adopting the language of classical theology, especially that of St. Thomas Aquinas, who taught that the divine life of grace in which the Christian shares parallels the stages of human growth.[27] The three sacraments of initiation give birth, growth, and nourishment to this life. Penance and anointing are for its healing and renewal. Marriage and orders are concerned with its continuance and transmission.

Anthropologists, studying the ritual behavior of various peoples, have arrived at a view of ritual that in a remarkable way confirms the teaching of St. Thomas. They find that religion, utilizing ritual, intervenes in life at certain critical moments and periods of its development. Birth is a critical time; adolescence is another; so likewise are marriage, sickness, death. The Christian sacraments correspond with such critical times and help both individuals and the community through them. Once again we see how the Christian religion responds also to our deepest human needs.

There is, however, some uncertainty about the place of confirmation in this process of human development. Some would wish to see in confirmation a sacramental sign of coming to spiritual maturity or of adult commitment to Christ. In this they are supported by the New Testament examples of confirming adults. They also seem to be supported by the teaching that confirmation confers strength and belongs to Christian growth.

On the other hand, precisely because confirmation is a sacrament of initiation following baptism, Eastern Catholics confirm even infants after their baptism. Others are concerned that confirmation, because it is a sacrament of initiation, should at least precede full participation in the Eucharist, which is the climax of initiation. Some liturgical considerations therefore seem to favor early confirmation; some psychological factors seem to urge postponement until at least the threshold of maturity.

The Holy See has left the matter somewhat open. *The Rite of Confirmation* states that with regard to children in the Latin Church "the administration of confirmation is generally postponed until about the seventh year" yet allows that it may, for pastoral reasons, be postponed to "a more mature age."[28] In many places the tendency is to postpone confirmation at least until early adolescence. If we see the Christian life as a whole, progressing from rebirth to mature manhood in Christ (cf. Eph. 4.13), there is no difficulty in regarding confirma-

---

[26]Pope Paul VI, Apostolic Constitution, *Divinae Consortium Naturae* (August 15, 1971) (EV 4.1067).

[27]Cf. St. Thomas Aquinas, *Summa Theologica III*, 65, 1.

[28]*Rite of Confirmation*, Introduction, n. 11 (EV 4.1099-1100). The *Code of Canon Law*, canon 891, says that ordinarily it is conferred around the age of discretion but allows for exceptions.

tion, even when administered in adolescence or later, as a sacrament of initiation.

The sponsor for confirmation should be like the godparent chosen for baptism. In fact, it is appropriate that the same person be used.[29]

Lasting Effects of Confirmation

Confirmation implies growth, and it is a continual challenge to the recipient to cultivate growth. Life is required for this growth, and the recipient must be in the state of grace. Yet confirmation cannot be counted on to produce instantaneous growth; nor is it intended to do this. As one of the sacraments which are administered to a person only once, and whose effect is therefore permanent, confirmation confers a permanent character. This is shown by the words with which it is administered: "Be sealed with the gift of the Holy Spirit." We have heard St. Paul speak of this seal; his words to the Corinthians already quoted above seem especially applicable to confirmation: "It is God who establishes us with you in Christ and has anointed us, by putting His seal on us and giving us His Spirit in our hearts as a first installment" (2 Cor. 1.21-22). "Signed with the perfumed oil by the bishop's hand, the baptized person receives the indelible character, the seal of the Lord, together with the gift of the Spirit, which conforms him more closely to Christ and gives him the grace of spreading the Lord's presence among men."[30]

Growth in the Spirit

As Pentecost follows Easter and is the fruit of the paschal mystery, so confirmation makes Pentecost permanent in the Church and in the lives of its members. The Holy Spirit is God's unrepented gift; one who receives this gift becomes a "temple of the Holy Spirit" (1 Cor. 6.19). Even if one strays from the fold, the seal remains, an ever-present invitation to return.

Meanwhile, as the feast of Pentecost brings to completion one part of the liturgical year and dominates the liturgical time that follows it, so does the Spirit rule the lives of those who have received this first of God's gifts. His presence is life, and life is growth. St. Paul describes this growing process as issuing from "the mystery": "This mystery, which is Christ in you. . . . It is He whom we proclaim, warning everyone and teaching everyone in all wisdom, so that we may present everyone mature in Christ" (Col. 1.27-28).

Jesus Himself requires growth of us. He compares His teaching to living things — a vine, a seed that produces a crop, a mustard seed

---

[29]*Code of Canon Law*, canon 893.
[30]*Rite of Confirmation*, Introduction, n. 9 (EV 4.1096-1097).

that becomes a large plant (cf. John 15.1-8; Mark 4.3-20, 31-32; Matt. 13.31-32). He astonishes the apostles by cursing a barren fig tree even though it is not the season for figs (cf. Mark 11.5, 20). In His parable of the talents He makes the same point, although in a different way. The man who buries his talent is condemned. "You wicked and lazy slave! You knew, did you, that I reap where I did not sow, and gather where I did not scatter" (Matt. 25.26). "Be perfect, therefore," Jesus says to His followers, "as your heavenly Father is perfect" (Matt. 5.48). The seal of confirmation does not let us forget this challenge, this destiny.

Growth in the Christian life, precisely because it is a life, cannot be programmed. Here is the difficulty of taking confirmation as a rite of adult commitment. Grace indeed brings about growth. Yet growth also depends on many personal factors, and even perhaps on the experience of spiritual crises, to bring about a realization of what it means to be a child of God and a temple of the Holy Spirit. The grace of confirmation, though it does not immediately effect such full personal realization, can help to bring it about. The real tragedy is when there is no growth, when the baptized — and perhaps confirmed — live out their Christian vocations in routine mediocrity.

To Witness and Defend the Faith

Christ Himself associated the gift of the Holy Spirit and the Christian apostolic mission. "You will receive power when the Holy Spirit has come upon you; and you will be My witnesses ... to the ends of the earth" (Acts 1.8). The Church declares that those who have received this special strength of the Holy Spirit in confirmation "are more strictly obliged to spread and defend the faith both by word and by deed as true witnesses of Christ" (LG 11). The call of the laity to apostolic tasks in the world, and to their role in shaping the kingdom on earth, is related to this sacrament. For the laity, "strengthened by the power of the Holy Spirit through confirmation, are assigned to the apostolate by the Lord Himself" (AA 3).

Confirmation and the Paschal Mystery

Confirmation, like all the other sacraments, derives its efficacy from the paschal mystery of the Lord's death and resurrection. This is indicated in that "ordinarily confirmation takes place within Mass. . . ."[31] But even if confirmation is celebrated apart from Mass, its source is still the paschal mystery. The chrism, too, signifies the recipient's sharing in this mystery. It recalls the Lord's own anointing (cf. Isa. 42.1; Mark 1.11).

---

[31]*Rite of Confirmation*, Introduction, n. 13 (EV 4.1104).

Yet the chrism also signifies our sharing in the destiny of the Son as the Lord's Anointed, the Messiah. God's revelation of the mysterious Suffering Servant told us something new and startling about the Messiah. Instead of a splendid conqueror, He was to be, and was, "a man of suffering, and acquainted with infirmity . . . despised, and we held Him of no account" (Isa. 53.3). As the Master, so the disciple: "Remember the word that I said to you, 'Servants are not greater than their master' " (John 15.20).

No Christian can grow to maturity in Christ without accepting His invitation: "If any want to become my followers, let them deny themselves and take up their cross daily and follow Me" (Luke 9.23). With St. Paul we must be able to say, "I have been crucified with Christ," if we also wish to say, "It is no longer I who live, but it is Christ who lives in me" (Gal. 2.19-20). "Share in suffering," Paul wrote to Timothy, "like a good soldier of Christ Jesus" (2 Tim. 2.3).

The manner of the Holy Spirit's anointing, to inspire and sustain Christians throughout the long Pentecostal season of life, has been told by St. John. The Spirit is the Paraclete, our Advocate, our Counselor.

Isaiah had already told us how the Holy Spirit who dwells in us works through His gifts. "A shoot shall come out from the stump of Jesse, and a branch shall grow out of his roots. The Spirit of the LORD shall rest upon Him, the spirit of wisdom and understanding, the spirit of counsel and might, the spirit of knowledge and the fear of the LORD" (Isa. 11.1-2). Wisdom, understanding, counsel, fortitude, knowledge, piety, and fear of the Lord are commonly known as the gifts of the Holy Spirit.

Finally, the indwelling Spirit will produce in those receptive to His presence what are known as the fruits of the Holy Spirit: love, joy, peace, patience, kindness, generosity, faithfulness, gentleness, faith, modesty, self-control, and chastity (cf. Gal. 5.22-23).

29

Sacraments Of Healing

"Those who approach the sacrament of penance obtain pardon from the mercy of God for offenses committed against Him, and at the same time are reconciled with the Church, which they have wounded by their sins, and which by charity, example, and prayer seeks their conversion. By the sacred anointing of the sick and the prayer of her priests, the whole Church commends those who are ill to the suffering and glorified Lord, asking that He may lighten their suffering and save them (cf. James 5.14-16)" (LG 11).

In this chapter we discuss the sacraments of penance and anointing of the sick, each of them a sacrament of healing instituted by Christ our Physician.

Penance

Gospel Signs

Jesus promulgated the sacrament of penance on Easter, thus showing clearly how it arises from the paschal mystery of His death and rising.

"While it was evening on that day, the first day of the week, and the doors of the house where the disciples had met were locked for fear of the Jews, Jesus came and stood among them and said, 'Peace be with you.' After He said this, He showed them His hands and His side. Then the disciples rejoiced when they saw the Lord. Jesus said to them again, 'Peace be with you. As the Father has sent Me, so I send you.' When He had said this, He breathed on them, and said to them, 'Receive the Holy Spirit. If you forgive the sins of any, they are forgiven them; if you retain the sins of any, they are retained' " (John 20.19-23). Thus was the sacrament of penance instituted.[1]

"...Our Savior, Jesus Christ, when he gave to his apostles and their successors power to forgive sins, instituted in his Church the sacrament of penance. Thus the faithful who fall into sin after baptism may be reconciled with God and renewed in grace."[2]

---

[1]Cf. Council of Trent, Session 14, November 25, 1551, *Doctrine on the Sacrament of Penance*, ch. 1 (DS 1670) and canon 3 on the sacrament of penance (DS 1703).
[2]Congregation for Divine Worship, *Rite of Penance*, published by authority of Pope Paul VI, December 2, 1973, Introduction, n. 2 (EV 4.2677).

Earlier, as is recorded in the Gospel of St. Matthew, Jesus had anticipated this gift. To Peter, who had just professed Him to be the Messiah and who was rewarded by being made the firm foundation of the Church, He said: "I will give you the keys of the kingdom of heaven, and whatever you bind on earth will be bound in heaven, and whatever you loose on earth will be loosed in heaven" (Matt. 16.19). A little later, after the promise to Peter, He extended this power of binding and loosing to "the disciples": "Truly I tell you, whatever you bind on earth will be bound in heaven, and whatever you loose on earth will be loosed in heaven" (Matt. 18.18).

Through the centuries the Church has exercised this authority to forgive sins. The sacrament of penance, the liturgical rite in which the Church does this, has had a variety of forms. But Catholic faith has always believed that Christ continues to forgive sins in His Church.

The Sacramental Sign

The graces of Christ are conferred in the sacraments by means of visible signs — signs which are acts of worship, symbols of the grace conferred, and recognizable gestures through which the Lord confers His gifts. The forgiveness of sins and the restoring of baptismal graces are also attached to an outward sign.

Jesus compared Himself to a physician (cf. Mark 2.17). It was His mission to heal. While He healed bodily ailments, and His human compassion was real, He did not undertake to cure all the human sicknesses. Rather, He used such cures as signs of a more radical moral and spiritual therapy which He desired to extend to all. " 'But so that you may know that the Son of man has authority on earth to forgive sins' — He said to the paralytic — 'I say to you, stand up, take your mat and go to your home' " (Mark 2.10-11). In this incident the healing of the man's body was a visible sign of forgiveness, but it was not a sacramental sign through which Christ directly conferred grace.

The sign appropriate for the sacrament of forgiveness can be grasped by reflecting on the kind of sickness cured in the sacrament of penance. We are concerned now with spiritual illness; and such illness, afflicting an individual in the moral order, that is, in the sphere of his freedom and responsibility, also has social effects. The sign of the physician applying a physical remedy is in the context not altogether adequate. In penance two things happen. The sinner is restored with healing grace to share in the divine life, as signified by the young man raised to life at Naim (cf. Luke 7.14), and is welcomed back by the Father, like the prodigal son (cf. Luke 15.20-24). At the same time, the sinner is reinstated in the community, and again shares at the community Eucharistic table. God can forgive sins secretly, but it is appropriate for the sinner to be reconciled outwardly, visibly, with the Church community. The community itself is healed as the penitent is healed.

A Saving Tribunal

An analogy for this healing of sickness which affects both the individual and the community is found in the manner society deals with its offenders through a judicial process. The Council of Trent uses this image in developing the theology of penance and distinguishing this sacrament from baptism. It explains and justifies this approach by appealing to the power of the keys granted to St. Peter.[3] Moreover, the teaching of Trent, and of the Church today, is that "absolution is given by a priest, who acts as judge."[4] Indeed, in the manner of a judge the priest — except in the case of penitents in danger of death — ordinarily must have jurisdiction from the local bishop in order to absolve.[5] The *Rite of Penance* states: "Confession requires in the penitent the will to open his heart to the minister of God, and in the minister a spiritual judgment by which, acting in the person of Christ, he pronounces his decision of forgiveness or retention of sins in accord with the power of the keys."[6]

Jesus Himself was, of course, aware of judges like Pilate, Herod, Caiaphas. He nevertheless took the risk of making a human judicial process the sign of divine justice when He gave to Peter the power of the keys and authorized the apostles to bind and loose on earth (cf. Matt. 18.18), just as they would have judicial authority in the age to come (cf. Matt. 19.28). Clearly in His opinion the sign is not unworthy of a sacrament so necessary and so holy.

The words with which Christ instituted the sacrament ("If you forgive the sins of any. . .") also contain the authority to judge. It is fitting for the divine tribunal to include dialogue and spiritual counsel. Yet we do not need precisely a sacrament of dialogue or counsel; other available means are adequate for these purposes. As sinners, we need divine forgiveness. Jesus has indicated the sacramental tribunal as His way to forgiveness and reconciliation — a way that in healing the individual sinner also heals the injured community.

Judgment of Mercy

The sacrament of penance is an unusual tribunal. The guilty party, the penitent, accuses oneself and approaches the Lord in sorrow, ad-

---

[3]Cf. Council of Trent, Session 14, November 25, 1551, *Doctrine on Sacrament of Penance*, chs. 2 (DS 1671) and 5 (DS 1679).

[4]Congregation for the Doctrine of the Faith, *Sacramentum Paenitentiae* ("Pastoral Norms concerning the Administration of General Sacramental Absolution," June 16, 1972) (EV 4.1653). Cf. Council of Trent, Session 14, November 25, 1551, *Doctrine on the Sacrament of Penance*, ch. 6 (DS 1685) and canon 9 on the sacrament of penance (DS 1709).

[5]"Cf., e.g., *Rite of Penance*, Introduction, n. 9b (EV 4.2690); *Code of Canon Law*, canon 969.

[6]*Rite of Penance*, Introduction, n. 6b (EV 4.2683).

mitting guilt before His representative. The priest, who is Christ's minister in penance, listens to the confession in the name of the Lord, to discover in the penitent's openness, sorrow, and will to conversion the grounds for a judgment of forgiveness. It is for Christ that the priest hears the confession of guilt; the words spoken to him there are therefore guarded by the most solemn obligation of complete secrecy. It is in the name of Christ that the priest speaks the judgment of the Savior's mercy: "I absolve you from your sins, in the name of the Father, and of the Son, and of the Holy Spirit." Such a sacramental sign is fitting. For Christ, who acts through the sign is our Judge (cf. Matt. 25.31-46). "For we will all stand before the judgment seat of God" (Rom. 14.10).

This judicial form of penance reminds us also that God's word also provides a continuing judgment throughout our days of pilgrimage. The manner of this judgment is shown in the Epistle to the Hebrews: "Indeed the word of God is living and active, sharper than any two-edged sword, piercing until it divides soul from spirit, joints from marrow; it is able to judge the thoughts and intentions of the heart. And before Him no creature is hidden, but all are naked and laid bare to the eyes of the One to whom we must render an account" (Heb. 4.12-13). The continuation of this passage indicates that, for those who live by faith, the judgment is still redemptive, made by the "great high priest who has passed through the heavens" (Heb. 4.14).

Similarly, in the sacrament of penance, we have, as we move along our pilgrim way, a tribunal of mercy in which judgment is not punitive or final, but healing and redemptive.

Personal Repentance

Sins are not forgiven in any automatic way. In the sacraments, it is Christ who works by His mighty power. Still, as we have seen, the sacraments presuppose (under God's grace) one's quest for God, the core of all religion, expressing itself in a faith that leads to God. They also require, for fruitfulness, a personal response to the grace of God communicated through them. In no sacrament are these personal acts more necessary than in penance. Very personal inward dispositions are needed in one who comes to Christ for forgiveness.

For full and perfect forgiveness of sins, three acts are required from the penitent as parts of the sacrament. These are contrition, confession, and satisfaction.[7]

---

[7]Cf. *Rite of Penance*, Introduction, n. 6 (EV 4.2681-2684). Cf. Council of Trent, Session 14, Nov. 25, 1551, *Doctrine on the Sacrament of Penance*, ch. 3 (DS 1673) and canon 4 on the sacrament of penance (DS 1704); Congregation for the Doctrine of Faith, *Sacramentum Paenitentiae* ("Pastoral Norms concerning the Administration of General Sacramental Absolution," June 16, 1972) (EV 4.1653-1667).

Necessity of this Sacrament

For those who have committed mortal sin after baptism, it is necessary to receive this sacrament to recover grace and the friendship of God. A worthy reception of this sacrament is "the ordinary way of obtaining forgiveness and the remission of serious sins committed after baptism. . . . It would therefore be foolish as well as presumptuous . . . to claim to receive forgiveness while doing without the sacrament which was instituted by Christ precisely for forgiveness."[8]

One who repents of a mortal sin but is not able to receive the sacrament of penance immediately can receive forgiveness through an act of perfect contrition, that is, sorrow motivated by true love of God, if one is resolved to confess the sin as soon as possible. But those who reject this sacrament of mercy, knowing the gift and the will of Christ that we utilize it, cannot find forgiveness in other ways.

Contrition

Contrition, or sincere sorrow for having offended God, is the most important of the three acts required of the penitent. Contrition is indeed but the other face of love; it is love rejecting all that destroys or threatens it. Hence contrition is placed first, as love must always be given first place (cf. 1 Cor. 13.13).

The sinner must come to God by way of repentance. From the beginning of the Gospel penance is preached as the preparation and condition for entering the kingdom of God. John the Baptist appeared "preaching a baptism of repentance for the forgiveness of sins" (Mark 1.4). This repentance (in Greek, *metanoia*) signifies a complete change of mind, of thinking; it is a turning around, a turning away from sin and a turning toward God. In it we find ourselves again at the heart of the paschal mystery, dying in order to live. "For while we live we are always being given up to death for Jesus' sake, so that the life of Jesus may be made visible in our mortal flesh" (2 Cor. 4.11).

There can be no forgiveness of sin if we do not have sorrow, that is, if we do not regret our sin, resolve not to repeat it, and turn back to God. Sorrow must be interior, from the heart, not merely expressed on the lips. It must spring from motives of faith, and not be merely a human sorrow based on regret for some natural bad consequences of our deeds. Sorrow should be supreme: the conversion to God means putting Him in the first place and resolving that, aided by His grace, we shall prefer nothing else to Him. Our sorrow must be universal: we

---

[8]Pope John Paul II, Post-Synodal Apostolic Exhortation, *Reconciliatio et Paenitentia* (December 2, 1984) n. 31 (EV 9.1181).

must be sorry for all grave or mortal sins, sins that exclude one from the friendship of God.

Sorrow for all our sins, even the lesser ones, is urged. Indeed, it is largely to overcome our venial faults, and so to allow a more intense faith and charity to rule our lives, that frequent confession is commended. Certainly one must have sincere sorrow for whatever sins one hopes to have forgiven.

Contrition is called "perfect contrition" if the motive of sorrow is true love for God, if we are sorry because we have offended the God whom we choose to love above all things. It is called "perfect," not because the quality of the penitent's act of contrition is itself perfect, but because charity is the perfect motive for conversion. Contrition is called "imperfect" if it is based on some other motive of faith, if, for example, one is sorry because one believes God, knows God is just and faithful to His word, and knows one will be rightly punished by God if one does not turn away from sin to serve Him.

Because it is an act of love of God and fruit of God's grace calling one to repentance, an act of perfect contrition can at once restore to the friendship of God one who has fallen into serious sin. But, except in extraordinary circumstances, one who has separated from Christ and the family of faith by grave sin is seriously obliged to receive the sacrament of penance before receiving the Eucharist. One who has a grave need to communicate and has no chance to go to confession is obliged to make a perfect act of contrition, which includes a promise to confess as soon as possible.[9]

Sorrow for sin implies a resolve not to fall back into sin. While we cannot be certain that our frailty will not betray us again, our present resolve must be honest and realistic. We must will to change, to be faithful to our Lord, to take realistic steps to make faithfulness possible. Christ's forgiveness always called for this. "Go, and do not sin again" (John 8.11).

Confession

The words of Christ instituting the sacrament of penance suggest that the minister of his forgiveness is to discriminate wisely: "If you forgive the sins of any. . . ." The Church teaches[10] that it is necessary by divine law to confess to a priest each and every mortal sin — and

[9]Cf. *Code of Canon Law*, canon 916; Council of Trent, Session 13, October 11, 1551, *Decree on the Most Holy Eucharist*, ch. 7 (DS 1647).

[10]Cf. *Rite of Penance*, Introduction, n. 7a (EV 4.2687); Council of Trent, Session 14, Nov. 25, 1551, *Doctrine on the Sacrament of Penance*, canon 7 on the sacrament of penance (DS 1707); Congregation for the Doctrine of the Faith, *Sacramentum Paenitentiae* ("Pastoral Norms concerning the Administration of General Sacramental Absolution," June 16, 1972) (EV 4.1653-1667). Cf. also *Code of Canon Law*, canon 988.1.

also circumstances which make a sin a more serious kind of mortal sin — that one can remember after a careful examination of conscience. Sins committed before baptism do not have to be confessed, for in baptism all sins of the past are forgiven. Moreover, a mortal sin which has been once confessed and for which absolution has been received need not be confessed again.

Devout penitents frequently are guilty of no grave sins; but they may fruitfully bring before Christ with sorrow the venial sins that mar their lives and limit their charity, taking care to have true sorrow for the sins they do confess. It is not necessary to seek to remember and to confess all the imperfections in one's life. Confessions of devotion may profitably center on those faults for which one can and should have a more genuine sorrow, because of the harm they do to others, or because of the way in which they hinder one's progress in grace.

Satisfaction

The Church believes that there are "temporal punishments" for sin. This means that the just and merciful God requires that the penitent sinner atone for his sins; he will receive punishment for them either in this life or after death in purgatory, unless he has taken punishment upon himself by deeds of penance.

That there are temporal punishments for sin is evidenced throughout the long history of Israel in all that it suffered for its infidelities, especially in its captivity. The sins of individuals have similar consequences. Moses is forgiven his doubt, but because of it he is not permitted to enter the Promised Land. David is forgiven his adultery, but the desired child of the sinful union does not survive. Temporal punishment persists even in death. Thus we read in the Second Book of Maccabees of the value of praying for the dead (cf. 2 Macc. 12.43-46). St. Paul indicates there is purification beyond death (cf. 1 Cor. 3.10-15).

Penitents, then, must complete their penitential acts by making some satisfaction for their sins, by doing a "penance" imposed by the priest. The penance imposed in earlier days was often severe. Today the penance is usually the recitation of certain prayers assigned by the priest to the penitent. "The kind and extent of the satisfaction should be suited to the personal condition of each penitent so that each one may restore the order which he disturbed and through the corresponding remedy be cured of the sickness from which he suffered. Therefore, it is necessary that the act of penance really be a remedy for sin and a help to renewal of life."[11]

Our sins are more serious than we realize, and our deeds of

---

[11]*Rite of Penance*, Introduction, n. 6c (EV 4.2684).

penance are often slight. To assist us in our frailty, the Church also makes possible indulgences for the faithful. An indulgence is a remission before God of all (plenary indulgence) or part (partial indulgence) of the temporal punishment due to sins that have already been forgiven.[12]

The principle underlying indulgences is as old as the Church. It is based on the doctrine of the Mystical Body of Christ. All members of this Body, St. Paul wrote (cf. 1 Cor. 12.21-26), should contribute to the well-being of an ailing member. Fully aware of the infinite and decisive value of Christ's atoning death, Paul rejoiced that his own sufferings could benefit the Christians of Colossae, and he added: "In my flesh I complete what is lacking in Christ's afflictions for the sake of His body, that is, the Church" (Col. 1.24). The Church teaches that in virtue of the authority given it by Christ, it may grant to sinners who have already received forgiveness of their sins a share in the merits of Christ and the saints, so that the burden of temporal punishment due for sins may be removed or lightened.

To gain an indulgence, one must say the prayer or do the good deed to which the Church attaches the indulgence, be in the state of grace, and have the proper intention. By a kind of spiritual leverage as it were, a relatively slight act of piety on the part of the individual brings upon him a great mercy.[13]

The "Laborious Baptism"

The Council of Trent, citing St. Gregory of Nazianzus and St. John of Damascus, stated that the sacrament of penance "has rightly been called by the holy Fathers 'a laborious kind of baptism.' "[14] In the same place the Council of Trent also asserted, against certain teachings of the day, that it is a sacrament distinct from baptism. It is called a kind of baptism because it restores baptismal holiness, and "laborious" because it cannot do this "without many tears and labors on our part."

Penance does really restore or renew baptismal holiness. When this holiness has been lost, it can be recovered in the sacrament of penance. A Catholic who has committed grave sin is obliged to ask forgiveness for it in this sacrament. One should do so promptly. Church law requires confession of sins once a year, though, strictly

---

12Cf. Pope Paul VI, Apostolic Constitution, *Indulgentiarum Doctrina* (January 1, 1967) Norm 1 (EV 2.935). This document, also on pp. 85-118 in *Enchirdion Indulgentiarum* (Libreria Editrice Vaticana, 1986), explains the history and theology of indulgences fairly fully. Cf. also Council of Trent, Session 25, December 4, 1563, *Decree on Indulgences*(DS 1835).

13Cf. *Code of Canon Law*, canon 996.

14Council of Trent, Session 14, November 25, 1551, *Doctrine on the Sacrament of Penance*, ch. 2 (DS 1672). Cf. St. Gregory of Nazianzus, *Oratio* 39.17 (MG 36.356); St. John of Damascus, *De Fide Orthodoxa* 4.9 (MG 94.1124).

speaking, this particular law does not bind those who would have no grave sins to confess.[15]

But penance is also useful to renew baptismal innocence, that is, to return it to full splendor, even when there are only venial sins or faults committed amidst the moral struggles of everyday living. In fact, "frequent and careful celebration of this sacrament is also very useful as a remedy for venial sins. This is not a mere ritual repetition or psychological exercise, but a serious striving to perfect the grace of baptism so that, as we bear in our body the death of Jesus Christ, his life may be seen in us ever more clearly."[16]

Penance and Children

The idea of a "laborious baptism" for children suggests a practical program to prepare them for the sacrament of penance. When infants are baptized, parents and sponsors act for them. As the minds of children develop, however, they can learn the meaning of baptism and also prepare for the second "laborious baptism." They can act out and relive their own infant baptism as they prepare to receive the sacrament of penance.

A child's introduction to the sacrament of penance is not to be long delayed, for "while the capacity to reason is evolving gradually in a child, his moral conscience too is being trained, that is, the faculty of judging his acts in relation to a norm of morality." An early introduction to penance will help the child make personal the choice implicit in his baptism. That baptism was a conversion, a turning to Christ; the first confession can be an early help in making that basic conversion more personal and free. Church law requires that the practice of having children receive the sacrament of penance before first Communion be maintained.[17]

"The suitable age for the first reception of these sacraments (of penance and the Eucharist) is deemed to be that which in documents of the Church is called the age of reason or of discretion. This age 'both for Confession and for Communion is that at which the child begins to reason, that is, about the seventh year, more or less. From that time on the obligation of fulfilling the precepts of Confession and Communion begins.' "[18]

---

[15]Cf. *Code of Canon Law*, canon 989.

[16]*Rite of Penance*, Introduction, n. 7b (EV 4.2687).

[17]On this paragraph, cf. Congregation for the Clergy, *General Catechetical Directory* (April 11, 1971) Addendum, nn. 2 and 5 (EV 4.649, 653-654); Congregation for the Clergy and Congregation for the Discipline of the Sacraments, Declaration, *Sanctus Pontifex* (May 24, 1973); Congregation for the Clergy and Congregation for the Discipline of the Sacraments, Circular Letter, *In Quibusdam Ecclesiae Partibus* (March 31, 1977) (EV 6.166-175); *Code of Canon Law*, canon 914.

[18]Congregation for the Clergy, *General Catechetical Directory* (April 11, 1971) Addendum, n. 1 (EV 4.648), quoting from Congregation for the Sacraments, Decree, *Quam Singulari* (August 8, 1910) n. 1 (DS 3530).

The Community Dimension

Viewing the sacrament of penance as a second baptism enables us also to realize that it is indeed part of the public liturgy of the Church. As baptism in the first place incorporates a convert into the Body of Christ, so penance restores to life within that Body one who by grave sin had ceased to be a living member. A public ritual of reconciliation made this clear in the early Church. Today, in approaching penance anew as reconciliation with the community as well as with God, and perhaps within a communal service, the parallel with baptism offers a perspective for seeing penance as belonging to the liturgical celebration of the whole Church community.

Communal Penance

The Second Vatican Council decreed: "The rite and formulas for the sacrament of penance are to be revised so that they may more clearly express the nature and effect of the sacrament" (SC 72). Penance thus could not remain unaffected by the fundamental change of the whole modern liturgical reform, namely, the growing sense of community as God's covenanted people, every member of which is invited to enter fully into His worship. Moreover, since penance was a community celebration among the early Christians, there was already at hand a model for reforming this rite, which in modern times had become relatively isolated from community celebration. What was needed, therefore, and what gradually came about, was the restoration of penance as a communal celebration in the Church.

To show more clearly that penance is a genuine liturgical celebration, it may be celebrated as an act of community worship, which forms the context of private confession. This was the practice of the early Church. While certain classes of sins were confessed privately to the bishop, and in time to a priest, this was done within a public liturgy that was carried out during Lent. This paralleled and widened the liturgy of resurrection centered in the first place around the catechumens.

Something more is needed, however, if there is to be a genuinely communal penance liturgy. There must also be a sense of the communal and ecclesial dimension of sin. In the early Church sinners guilty of some grave sins were excommunicated, required to do public works of penance, and were reconciled to God through the Church on Holy Thursday by returning to the Eucharist. Even in private confession there is a residue of this public penance. Penitents publicly join the line of people waiting to confess. Meanwhile they must, if guilty of grave sin, exclude themselves from Communion until they return to the life of grace within the Church through the sacrament of penance.

Their reconciliation with God and community is completed when they return publicly to the Eucharistic table.

To acknowledge, even to become aware, that our sins have a community dimension is not always easy, and perhaps not very pleasant for many in an era marked by highly individualistic thinking. By public penance we do not escape personal responsibility; we in fact enlarge the area of our awareness of responsibility for the sins of the society of which we are a part.

Since we are all members of one body in Christ, the sickness of one member causes a malaise throughout the body. At the very least, the failures of individuals hinder the growth and restrict the vitality of the whole body. "If one member suffers, all suffer together with it; if one member is honored, all rejoice together with it" (1 Cor. 12.26). "By the hidden and loving mystery of God's design men are joined together in the bonds of supernatural solidarity, so much so that the sin of one harms the others just as the holiness of one benefits the others."[19]

Social Dimensions of Sin

Within this wider context, all particular sins except those directly against God, such as blasphemy, are offenses against God's law precisely because they injure one's neighbor or oneself. Even those which directly harm only oneself have a potential for disturbing community harmony. The last seven commandments of the Decalogue are concerned with our neighbor. If I steal, for example, I injure my neighbor and perhaps cause privation to my neighbor's family. I also lower the level of openness and mutual confidence in the whole community, and in a sense I diminish the pulse and flow of life in the Body of Christ. This is true even of "secret" sins against the ninth and tenth commandments, which also have reference to my neighbor. Even blasphemy and other sins against the first three commandments can cause scandal. In a word, my personal and even secret sins can have extensive consequences in the community.

Moreover, certain evils, while involving personal guilt, especially sins of omission, have a communal dimension. An example here is racism. As a web that enmeshes all, it involves us all in its consequences.

The same is true of all widespread social injustices. Although few of us may be involved in large and dramatic ways, a very great many of us are in some measure responsible. "Countless millions are starving, countless families are destitute, countless men are steeped in ignorance; countless people need schools, hospitals, and homes worthy

[19]*Rite of Penance*, Introduction, n. 5 (EV 4.2680).

of the name. In such circumstances, we cannot tolerate public and private expenditures of a wasteful nature; we cannot approve a debilitating arms race. . . . No one is permitted to disregard the plight of his brothers living in dire poverty, enmeshed in ignorance and tormented by insecurity. The Christian, moved by this sad state of affairs, should echo the words of Christ: 'I have compassion on the crowd' (Mark 8.2)."[20]

The Synod of Bishops in 1971 spoke of the "serious injustices which are building around the world of men a network of domination, oppression, and abuses which stifle freedom and which keep the greater part of humanity from sharing in the building up and enjoyment of a more just and fraternal world"; the world is marked by a "grave sin of injustice."[21]

The follower of Christ will consider his social responsibilities and the social dimensions of sin in his examination of conscience.[22]

Celebrating the Sacrament

The sacrament of penance may be administered in two ways, either within a communal ceremony or in an individual one. Even the communal ceremony guards important personal elements of the sacrament: the individual penitent confesses his sins in private and there is individual absolution. And even the individual form guards certain public elements, as an act of the Church's liturgy must. The sacrament is usually administered in a publicly recognized place; a penitent who has sinned gravely must refrain from sharing in the Eucharistic table until he has been absolved; the priest who administers the sacrament must, except in special cases of necessity, be one who has been given public authority to absolve by the bishop of the place.

The Ancient Practice

The early Christians also confessed their sins privately, although within a community celebration. The real difference between ancient and modern practice, however, is that some early Christians felt they could receive the sacrament of penance only once, and it was only with difficulty that they came to feel penance could be received more often. The early Christians had such an exalted idea of the holiness befitting the baptized that it was hard for them to entertain the idea of a Christian relapsing into serious sin, at least repeatedly. There

[20]Pope Paul VI, Encyclical, *Progressio Populorum* (March 26, 1967) nn. 53, 74 (EV 2.1098-1119).

[21]Second General Assembly of the Synod of Bishops, 1971, *Justice in the World*, Introduction and Part II (EV 4.1238-1243, 1264-1273).

[22]Cf. the outline examination of conscience in *Rite of Penance*, Appendix III.

developed a tendency to defer absolution until the approach of death.

The Celtic monks broke through this difficulty by making popular private and frequent confession, first in their monasteries, then outside, and finally in their missionary journeys to the Continent as Europe strove to recover from the barbarian invasions. For the tortured in conscience, penance became a sacrament not only of healing but of continuing mercy. For the devout, it became a means of deepening their conversion and promoting their growth in the Spirit. In this spirit the Church recommends regular and frequent confession. It summons those in grave sin to prompt repentance. It urges the devout through use of the sacraments to receive the healing and sanctifying gifts of Christ.

The New Rite

The *Rite of Penance* joins ancient and modern practice in a new ceremony of reconciliation. Private administration of the sacrament, while retaining its judicial character, continues also to offer its merciful healing. It may do this within the setting of a communal service. "Communal celebration shows more clearly the ecclesial nature of penance."[23] Such celebrations acknowledge the social dimension of sin and the need to be reconciled to the community as one returns to God. The faithful support one another in their participation in communal celebration of penance. The readings, hymns, and prayers of the ceremony bind them together as a family of God coming before Him in sorrow and assisting each penitent to deeper personal repentance and new resolve.

The individual ceremony also has certain advantages. That it retains certain features of public worship has been noted above. The ceremonies suggested for it, such as the reading of a scriptural passage by the priest or by the penitent and the priest's extension of his hands over the head of the penitent while saying the words of absolution, can add even more dignity to its celebration. The individual ceremony has considerable flexibility, and provides an opportunity for combining a spiritual direction and pastoral guidance with the administration of the sacrament. Yet it is also an ecclesial act, a reconciliation with the Christian community, as the introduction to the words of absolution make clear:

God, the Father of mercies,
through the death and resurrection of his Son
has reconciled the world to himself
and sent the Holy Spirit among us for the forgiveness of sins:

[23]*Rite of Penance*, Introduction, n. 22 (EV 4.2703).

through the ministry of the Church may God give you pardon and peace,
and I absolve you. . . .[24]

When for extraordinary reasons groups of people are not able to confess their sins individually, they may in some circumstances receive sacramental forgiveness by a communal absolution. Such communal absolution, however, may be given only when there is a "grave need," which is to be determined by the local bishop, "who is to consult with the other members of the episcopal conference."[25] Unless prevented by some good reason, those who receive communal absolution should go to confession before receiving communal absolution again.[26] Unless it is morally impossible for them to do so, they are obliged to go to confession within a year. "Individual, integral confession and absolution remain the only ordinary way for the faithful to reconcile themselves with God and the Church, unless physical or moral impossibility excuses from this kind of confession."[27]

Whether the sacrament of penance is administered in individual ceremony or within a communal celebration, the deepest joy of the guilty is in their deliverance from the sin in a new passover that frees them from the grossest kind of servitude. They come forth from the sacrament, their turning to God complete, in the gladness of a clear conscience and restored justice, with the exhilarating prospect of a fresh start. Once more they are a "new creation," once more for them "everything has become new!" (2 Cor. 5.17).

Anointing of the Sick

Christ and the Infirm

Our Lord had compassion on the infirm. He revealed Himself to John as the Messiah simply by saying: "The blind receive their sight, the lame walk, the lepers are cleansed, the deaf hear, the dead are raised, and the poor have good news brought to them" (Matt. 11.5). In the parable of the great dinner, the servants were commanded, "Go out at once into the streets and lanes of the town and bring in the poor, the crippled, the blind, and the lame" (Luke 14.21). Many of His works were cures of the sick; and we have seen in the preceding section how He Himself, as well as the evangelists, deliberately used these works as signs of a spiritual healing (cf. Mark 2.10-11).

[24]*Rite of Penance*, n. 46.
[25]Cf. *Rite of Penance*, Introduction, nn. 31-33 (EV 4.2712-2715). Cf. *Code of Canon Law*, canon 961.
[26]Cf. *Rite of Penance*, Introduction, n. 34 (EV 4.2716). Cf. also *Code of Canon Law*, canon 962.1.
[27]*Rite of Penance*, Introduction, n. 31 (EV 4.2712).

Anointing in Scripture

Jesus not only taught His disciples to be compassionate, but He also told them who should be the special objects of their compassion. The parable of the great dinner with its humble guests was preceded by an instruction that He gave at a banquet: "But when you give a banquet, invite the poor, the crippled, the lame, and the blind" (Luke 14.13). In His parable previewing the Last Judgment, those were punished to whom He said, "I was . . . sick and in prison and you did not visit Me" (Matt. 25.43). On the other hand, they were rewarded to whom He said, "I was sick and you took care of Me. . ." (Matt. 25.36).

Meanwhile, as the apostles assisted Him in His mission, "Jesus summoned His twelve disciples and gave them authority over unclean spirits, to cast them out, and to cure every disease and every sickness" (Matt. 10.1). A similar commission was given to them after the resurrection: ". . . they will lay their hands on the sick, and they will recover" (Mark 16.18). In an earlier passage in the Gospel of St. Mark we read: "They cast out many demons, and anointed with oil many who were sick and cured them" (Mark 6.13). This is the first allusion to the sacrament of the anointing of the sick.[28] Jesus here authorized a practice that may have already existed in exorcistic healings; but He gave it a new meaning. Like His own healings, those of His disciples were signs proclaiming the coming of the kingdom: "The Spirit of the Lord is upon me, because He has anointed me to bring good news to the poor. He has sent me to proclaim release to the captives and recovery of sight to the blind, to let the oppressed go free, to proclaim the year of the Lord's favor" (Luke 4.18-19; cf. Isa. 61.1-2).

In His Church Christ wished all to care for the sick. The ministry to the sick is an obligation of every Christian. In a special way, however, Christ charged His priests to anoint the sick while praying over them in a sacramental gesture that would be more properly a deed of His own personal care (cf. James 5.14).

As with the sacrament of confirmation, we first see the actual anointing of the sick in the early Church described in the Epistle of St. James. The letter is chiefly a moral exhortation, and it is only as part of such an exhortation that the sacrament is spoken of. Thus: "Are any among you suffering? They should pray. Are any cheerful? They should sing songs of praise" (James 5.13). Then: "Are any among you sick? They should call for the elders of the church and have them pray over them, anointing them with oil in the name of the Lord. The prayer of faith will save the sick, and the Lord will raise them up; and anyone who has committed sins will be forgiven" (5.14-15). This passage is cited by the Council of Trent when it declares that "this sacred

---

[28]Cf. Council of Trent, Session 14, November 25, 1551, *Doctrine on the Sacrament of Extreme Unction*, ch. 1 (DS 1695).

anointing of the sick was instituted by Christ our Lord as truly and properly a sacrament of the New Testament. . . ."[29]

Sacrament of the Sick

The sacrament of anointing of the sick is, as the words of St. James make clear, for the sick and infirm.

Accordingly, "there should be special care and concern that those who are dangerously ill due to sickness or old age receive this sacrament."[30] Relatives and friends of the sick have a responsibility in charity to assist them in calling the priest, or to help get them ready to receive the sacrament worthily, especially in the case of graver illnesses.

During some centuries there was a tendency to reserve this sacrament only for those quite near death, and the sacrament came to be called "extreme unction," that is, "last anointing." The Church has made it clear that it wishes this sacrament for the sick to be more generously available. " 'Extreme unction,' which may also be more fittingly be called 'anointing of the sick,' is not a sacrament for those only who are at the point of death. Hence, as soon as any one of the faithful begins to be in danger of death from sickness or old age, the appropriate time for him to receive this sacrament has certainly already arrived" (SC 73).

Thus there is no need to wait until a person is at the point of death. To determine whether there is a dangerous illness, a prudent judgment is all that is needed; there is no need for scrupulosity.[31] "The sacrament may be repeated if the sick person recovers after anointing or if, during the same illness, the danger becomes more serious."[32] Moreover, "a sick person should be anointed before surgery when a dangerous illness is the reason for the surgery."[33]

"Old people may be anointed if they are in weak condition even though no dangerous illness is present. Sick children may be anointed if they have sufficient use of reason to be comforted by this sacrament." The faithful "should be encouraged to ask for the anointing and, as soon as the time for the anointing comes, to receive it with faith and devotion, not misusing this sacrament by putting it off." Also, people who are unconscious or who have lost the use of reason may be anointed "if, as Christian believers, they would have asked for it were they in control of their faculties." A priest is not to anoint "a

[29]Council of Trent, Session 14, November 25, 1551, *Doctrine of the Sacrament of Extreme Unction*, ch. 1 (DS 1695).

[30]Congregation for Divine Worship, *Rite of Anointing and Pastoral Care of the Sick*, published by authority of Pope Paul VI, December 7, 1972, Introduction, n. 8 (EV 4.1867).

[31]Cf. *Rite of Anointing. . .* , Introduction, n. 8 (EV 4.1867).

[32]*Rite of Anointing. . .* , Introduction, n. 9 (EV 4.1868).

[33]*Rite of Anointing. . .* , Introduction, n. 10 (EV 4.1869).

person already dead." If there is a doubt as to death, the priest may administer the sacrament conditionally.[34]

In the sacrament of anointing of the sick the Church extends the healing hand of Christ to one who is dangerously ill or weakened by age. It is his encounter with Christ the Healer, Christ the divine Physician. The woman in the Gospel was eager to touch only the Lord's cloak: "If I touch even His garments," she thought, "I shall be made well" (Mark 5.28). The sick person today "touches" Him and experiences His power through the sacramental anointing.

The Community Dimension

Sickness is a crisis of life, both for the individuals who are ill and for the communities to which they belong. Even pagan societies have understood this and provided some socio-religious ritual to help resolve the crisis. St. James clearly sees the community dimension of sickness when he says that the sick person should "call for the elders of the church." These "elders," that is "presbyters," represent the community and the community's concern. Such concern is further shown in the "prayer of faith" that St. James says will reclaim the one who is ill; the prayer arises from the community of faith, the Church gathered around the sick person precisely to invoke "the name of the Lord."

The *Rite of Anointing and Pastoral Care of the Sick* provides a substantial and expressive liturgy. It begins with a greeting, introduction, and penitential rite (which may be replaced by sacramental penance). A Liturgy of the Word follows. Suitable readings are suggested. Friends and relatives can add a communal dimension; they may assist in the readings, as also in prayers and singing. There may be a homily, after which the sacrament is conferred. First, there is a laying on of hands — that characteristic scriptural gesture of blessing — by all the priests who are participating. Then the anointing by the minister of the sacrament of the recipient's forehead and hands, or, in case of necessity, of the forehead only or another part of the body. This anointing is also a laying on of hands, now with the blessed oil.

The sacramental sign is especially this anointing, together with the prayer that accompanies it:

Through this holy anointing
may the Lord in his love and mercy help you
with the grace of the Holy Spirit.
(Amen.)
May the Lord who frees you from sin
save you and raise you up.
(Amen.)[35]

---

[34]On the paragraph, cf. *Rite of Anointing.* . . , Introduction, nn. 11-15 (EV 4.1870-1875).
[35]*Rite of Anointing.* . . , n. 76.

This prayer speaks of salvation and resurrection with the wise ambiguity of St. James, and it treats the sacrament as the gift of the Holy Spirit, who is also God's first gift to the Church through the paschal mystery.

The oil used for the anointing is olive oil, although the use of another oil may be authorized if olive oil is not available. Ordinarily the oil is blessed by the bishop at the Chrism Mass on Holy Thursday, a custom that also recalls how this sacrament derives its power from the paschal mystery. Oil signifies strength and health. In the blessing, the bishop prays that "all anointed with this oil . . . may be freed from pain, illness, and disease and made well again in body, mind, and soul." By an invocation taken from the earliest known blessing for the oil of the sick, he further begs that God will "send the Holy Spirit, the Comforter, from heaven upon this oil which nature has provided." Even in sickness, therefore, the Holy Spirit, the gift of the paschal mystery, continues His care.

The ceremony of anointing of the sick concludes with a special prayer for the sick, followed by the Lord's Prayer, perhaps the reception of Communion, and a blessing.

The anointing may also be done within the Mass. This indicates the source of the sacrament, the mystery of the Lord's death and resurrection, continued in the Mass and the origin of all sacramental power. This mystery also gives meaning to human suffering, as we shall see, and draws it, with the passion of the Lord, into resurrection.

The Sacramental Grace

The fruit of this sacrament is indicated in these words of St. James: ". . .The prayer of faith will save the sick, and the Lord will raise them up" (James 5.15). The ambiguity here is simply the result of the way biblical people look at sickness, as distinct from our modern way. They see it, not merely as a physical reality, but as situated in actual condition of sin. Further, they do not distinguish clearly between body and soul, but see the individual as a unity; the healing is intended for the whole person.

Pope Paul VI, quoting the Council of Trent, explains and summarizes the effects of the sacrament: "This reality is in fact the grace of the Holy Spirit, whose anointing takes away sins, if any still remain to be taken away, and the remnants of sin; it also relieves and strengthens the soul of the sick person, arousing in him a great confidence in the divine mercy; thus sustained, he may easily bear the trials and hardships of his sickness, more easily resist the temptations of the devil 'lying in wait' (Gen. 3.15), and sometimes regain bodily health, if this is expedient for the health of the soul."[36]

The anointing of the sick is not intended to replace the sacrament of penance. The sacrament of penance should precede the anointing,[37] and it would be gravely wrong to receive the sacrament of anointing of the sick while one is knowingly guilty of grave sin. Still, in certain circumstances the anointing of the sick may replace penance. If the person to be anointed is unconscious and in grave sin, but is prepared by prior acts of faith and hope and right fear of God so that he is properly disposed to receive the gifts of a sacrament, the sacrament of anointing of the sick brings forgiveness of even serious sin.

The sacrament draws those who receive it into that interior penance, that *metanoia*, which leads into the mystery of Christ. That such a sacrament has been instituted shows also that suffering does not of itself bring salvation; if our suffering is to be a means of healing, the Lord Himself must associate it with His death and resurrection. As St. James indicates, that is the distinctive sacramental grace of the anointing of the sick.

This sacrament "prolongs the concern which the Lord himself showed in the bodily and spiritual welfare of the sick, as the gospels testify, and which he asked his followers to show also."[38] It "provides the sick person with the grace of the Holy Spirit, by which the whole man is brought to health, trust in God is encouraged, and strength is given to resist the temptations of the Evil One and anxiety about death."[39]

The sacramental action of Christ on the whole person, body and soul, while it may lead to physical healing, goes beyond this to mental and spiritual health and even to eternal salvation. "The sick man will be saved by his faith and the faith of the Church which looks back to the death and resurrection of Christ, the source of the sacrament's power, and looks ahead to the future kingdom which is pledged in the sacraments."[40] St. James says all this when he attributes the healing to the Lord in whose name the prayer of faith is uttered. In all their weakness and in all their trust, the sick encounter the healing power of the Lord's death and resurrection in this sacrament. The Lord "will save the sick" and "raise them up" (James 5.15).

Sickness and the Paschal Mystery

The Second Vatican Council, in speaking of the anointing of the sick, showed how sufferings caused by sickness may be drawn into

---

[36]Pope Paul VI, Apostolic Constitution, *Sacram Unctionem Infirmorum* (November 30, 1972) (EV 4.1838-1848). Cf. Council of Trent, Session 14, November 25, 1551 *Doctrine on the Sacrament of Extreme Unction*, ch. 2 (DS 1696).

[37]Cf. *Rite of Anointing. . .* , n. 65.

[38]*Rite of Anointing. . .* , n. 5.

[39]*Rite of Anointing. . .* , n. 6.

[40]*Rite of Anointing. . .* , n. 7.

the paschal mystery. The whole Church, said the council, exhorts the sick "to contribute to the welfare of the People of God by associating themselves freely with the passion and death of Christ" (LG 11). The council cited in illustration certain passages of the New Testament: "We are children of God, and if children, then heirs, heirs of God and joint heirs with Christ — if, in fact, we suffer with Him so that we may also be glorified with Him" (Rom. 8.16-17). "I am now rejoicing in my sufferings for your sake, and in my flesh I am completing what is lacking in Christ's afflictions for the sake of His body, that is, the church" (Col. 1.24). "The saying is sure: If we have died with Him, we will also live with Him; if we endure, we will also reign with Him" (2 Tim. 2.11-12). "But rejoice in so far as you are sharing Christ's sufferings, so that you may also be glad and shout for joy when His glory is revealed" (1 Peter 4.13).

Anointing of the sick, whether or not it heals the body, becomes a remedy for the spirit in which all events are drawn together in a hopeful and joyous experience of life even in its hardships. "So we do not lose heart. Though our outer nature is wasting away, our inner nature is being renewed day by day. For this slight momentary affliction is preparing for us an eternal weight of glory beyond all measure, because we look not at what can be seen but at what cannot be seen; for what can be seen is temporary, but what cannot be seen is eternal" (2 Cor. 4.16-18).

The Sacrament of the Dying

Eventually all physical remedies fail. In the cycle of life in a person's present condition, life begins, grows, matures, declines, and ends in death. Although anointing should be given at the onset of dangerous illness or in the weakness of old age, the Church allows the sacrament to be administered again if there has been a recovery and relapse or if the danger becomes more serious. If the sickness continues or deepens, the invalid may and should receive the Eucharist regularly.

Communion received by the dying is called Viaticum, "Food for the journey," here the spiritual food one takes for his last journey. "When the Christian, in his passage from this life, is strengthened by the body and blood of Christ, he has the pledge of the resurrection which the Lord promised: 'He who feeds on my flesh and drinks my blood has life eternal, and I will raise him up on the last day' (John 6.54). Viaticum should be received during Mass when possible so that the sick person may receive communion under both kinds. Communion received as viaticum should be considered a special sign of participation in the mystery of the death of the Lord and his passage to the Father, the mystery which is celebrated in the eucharist."[41]

---

[41]*Rite of Anointing. . .* , n. 26.

In death, sign gives way to Reality; but on the journey the Eucharistic sign containing Reality is the most appropriate provision, which is the very meaning of the word Viaticum. Soon, however, the bonds of the sign will burst and Reality will be seen "face to face" (1 Cor. 13.12).

Even "death has been swallowed up in victory" (1 Cor. 15.54), and only in death does the Christian retrieve all past losses and reap a hundredfold and receive everlasting life (cf. Matt. 19.29). The ordeal of sickness, losses and privations through various trials, and accumulating diminishments of aging, are so many little deaths, mystical deaths, as writers have called them, losses foreshadowing the final separation through death from all that is here loved. Yet in this final and complete loss, all is retrieved. "The one who sows bountifully will also reap bountifully" (2 Cor. 9.6). The funeral of the Christian is a celebration revolving around the words of Christ concerning the seed: "But if it dies, it bears much fruit" (John 12.24). In every Eucharist we say that "we wait in joyful hope for the coming of our Savior, Jesus Christ." The last, the complete healing, is the resurrection.

Christian Marriage:
Christ And Human Love

We have found that the sacramental signs whereby Jesus has chosen to act on us through His Church for the most part make use of material elements — water, bread, wine, and oil. Marriage has a more sublime sign, one taken from human love. The sacramental sign is expressed in a pledge of enduring commitment. The love of husband and wife for each other signifies God's eternal love for His people and the love that binds together Christ and His Church.

The Church honors the married vocation, and recognizes the supreme compliment Christ has paid to marriage in giving it sacramental status. The Church proclaims marriage a sacred sign, a sacrament, an act of worship, a reminder of Christ's love, an effective means by which He acts to make human love capable of being lasting, faithful, fruitful, like His own love of the Church.

In this chapter we discuss covenant love in marriage, the relation of virginity and marriage, and the threefold good of marriage: offspring, fidelity, and the sacrament. Also treated here are the problem of broken marriages, the actions taken by the Church to guard the married state, and the vocation of married persons to holiness.

Covenant Love in Marriage

In the Old Testament, marriage was not sacred in our sense, nor was it celebrated with a religious ceremony. Yet marriage was preordained by God, who established it at the climax of creation.

As there are two accounts of creation, so there are two accounts of the institution on marriage. Each indicates an element of the meaning of marriage, and both themes are joined throughout the history of marriage down to the present. In the first creation account, procreation is stressed: "So God created humankind in His own image, in the image of God He created them; male and female He created them. God blessed them, and God said to them, 'Be fruitful and multiply, and fill the earth and subdue it' " (Gen. 1.27-28). In the other account, the companionship of man and woman comes to the fore. All the animals were created, "but for the man there was not found a helper as his partner." But after the woman was created, the man said: "This at last is bone of my bones and flesh of my flesh." The sacred writer adds: "Therefore a man leaves his father and his mother and clings to his wife, and they become one flesh" (Gen. 2.20-24).

God's ancient design of faithful monogamy was not preserved — "because you were so hard-hearted," as Jesus was to say to the Pharisees (Matt. 19.8).

Nevertheless, exclusive attachment was prized in the Old Testament. While the wife was subject to her husband, she was no mere chattel, as with the pagans. The famous portrait of the ideal wife in the Book of Proverbs shows her as a partner with responsibilities and dignity (cf. Prov. 31.10-31). The Song of Songs reveals a passionate dialogue between two free partners whose love is obviously undivided. It thus presents a picture of marriage as a union of love in ancient Israel. The history of Tobit shows a deeply religious home from which his son Tobiah goes to marry Sarah and enter with her into a union at once truly loving and pleasing to the Lord.

The New Covenant

Both the Song of Songs and Tobit introduce us into Jewish households after the exile. At this time, too, the sages who wrote the Wisdom literature were praising monogamy and urging fidelity in marriage (cf. Prov. 5.1-23, 6.20-35). Malachi wrote: "So take heed to yourselves, and let none be faithless to the wife of his youth. For I hate divorce, says the LORD the God of Israel" (Mal. 2.15-16). He here also speaks of marriage as a covenant, comparing it to the covenant of God with Israel.

The climax of this long saga of love covenant and marriage, and the point at which marriage becomes a sacrament in the New Covenant, is noted in St. Paul's Epistle to the Ephesians: "Husbands, love your wives, just as Christ loved the church and gave Himself up for her, in order to make her holy with the washing of water by the word, so as to present the church to himself in splendor, without a spot or wrinkle or anything of the kind — yes, so, that she may be holy and without blemish. In the same way, husbands should love their wives as they do their own bodies. He who loves his wife loves himself. For no one ever hates his own body, but he nourishes and tenderly cares for it, as Christ does for the church, because we are members of His body. 'For this reason a man will leave his father and mother and be joined to his wife, and the two will become one flesh.' This is a great mystery, and I am applying it to Christ and the church" (5.25-32).

Perhaps we can best understand what the apostle is saying here by starting at the end. The word translated as "mystery" is *sacramentum* in Latin and *mysterion* in Greek. It is the very word St. Paul uses and enlarges on at the beginning of his letter, in describing the hidden plan of God whereby all are to be united in Christ: the mystery of God in Christ, the paschal mystery, which is at the center and heart of the New Covenant. What the apostle says about marriage, therefore, is related to or falls within this divine plan. The union of Christ with His Church is so intimate as to find no more apt comparison than the relation of husband and wife. Furthermore, since the union of Christ with His Church is sanctifying, making her holy, so the union of husband and wife is mutually sanctifying because it is situated within the mystery of Christ's union with His Church. This is especially so since Christ "gave Himself up" for the Church, purifying her. In this way the union of husband and wife is drawn into Christ's sacrificial love for His Church, and thus into the mystery of His death and resurrection.

Marriage, then, is a sacrament. It is a covenant between a man and a woman, committing them to live with one another in a bond of married love whose charter was established by God. This covenant is a symbol of the undying covenant love established by Christ with His Church in the paschal mystery. It is an encounter with Christ which makes effective the graces it signifies, the graces needed to make human love enduring, faithful, and fruitful, and so a suitable image of the love between Christ and His Church.

Marriage and Virginity

Although St. Paul is a striking witness to the sanctity of marriage, he also commends warmly another way of life, that of virginity or celibacy.

"I want you to be free from anxieties. The unmarried man is anxious about the affairs of the Lord, how to please the Lord; but the married man is anxious about the affairs of the world, how to please his wife, and his interests are divided. And the unmarried woman and the virgin are anxious about the affairs of the Lord, so that they may be holy in body and spirit; but the married woman is anxious about the affairs of the world, how to please her husband" (1 Cor. 7.32-34).

We have here indicated an alternate form of Christian life. The same faith which honors marriage honors also that form of life which forgoes the blessings of marriage precisely to further God's kingdom and to bear a striking witness to faith in eternal life. A life of Christian virginity may be lived in a religious community or in the midst of secular responsibilities. For those called to such a life, virginity offers a richer freedom to give themselves more exclusively to the Lord. Virginity is a forceful way of expressing faith in eternal life while "the present form of this world is passing away" (1 Cor. 7.31).

We can understand the apparent paradox of the teaching that describes marriage as a sacrament and yet recommends virginity if we see both these ways as ultimately leading to God's love. In the context of that love, the apostolic recommendations are not contradictory — and even the paradox disappears.

Those joined in sacramental marriage are a visible sign of God's love for the Church and of God's love for mankind. They remind us all of God's love, and of the fact that all love comes from God, for "God is love" (1 John 4.16), and should lead back to God. Celibates on their part, while renouncing marriage, do not renounce love: they are rather witnesses in a special way to that greater love of Christ, of which marriage itself is a sign. They are reminders to all that married love, sacred as it is, is transitory as a means to that perfect love of God and one another that we are to strive for and to have perfected in eternal life. Both married love and perfect chastity should direct the heart toward eternity and love fulfilled. The sacramental meaning of marriage points to this. So also does the life of those vowed to perfect chastity; their generous love should "recall to the minds of all the faithful that wondrous marriage decreed by God which is to be fully revealed in the future age in which the Church has Christ as its only Spouse" (PC 12). The married and celibate vocations, then, far from being opposed to each other, support each other within the basic Christian vocation to seek holiness in love.

The Threefold Good of Marriage

"In marriage, let the goods of marriage be loved: offspring fidelity, and the sacrament."[1] In these few words St. Augustine crystallized the teaching of faith on the purposes of matrimony, the goods for which God established and sanctified it. He takes the two goods of marriage already indicated in the creation accounts in Genesis, offspring and fidelity, and crowns them with the New Testament creation of sacrament. In so doing he provides a framework for the study of Christian marriage, a framework which has been used by the Church down to this day (cf. GS 48).

Conjugal Love

"The first natural tie of human society," says St. Augustine, "is man and wife."[2] The Second Vatican Council calls marriage "a community of love" (GS 47). Mutual fidelity, at its minimum and considered negatively, forbids intercourse with anyone other than one's married partner; thus it is a bulwark to protect conjugal love. "The intimate partnership of married live and love has been established by the

---

[1]St. Augustine, *De Nuptiis et Concupiscientia* 1.17.19 (ML 44.424).
[2]St. Augustine, *De Bono Coniugali* 1 (ML 40.373).

Creator and qualified by His laws and is rooted in the conjugal covenant of irrevocable personal consent. . . . As a mutual gift of two persons, this intimate union and the good of the children impose total fidelity on the spouses and argue for an unbreakable oneness between them" (GS 48).

Mutual and loving fidelity presupposes the fundamental equality of the partners in marriage. "Firmly established in the Lord, the unity of marriage will radiate from the equal personal dignity of wife and husband, a dignity acknowledged by equal and total love" (GS 48). Nor can this equality be taken for granted even today. One of the Church's first tasks, in order to make Christian marriage possible, was to secure this basic personal equality. The words of Jesus recorded in the Gospel laid the foundation for this by teaching what was then a revolutionary idea, namely, that the mutual duties of husband and wife are the same: "Whoever divorces his wife and marries another, commits adultery against her; and if she divorces her husband and marries another, she commits adultery" (Mark 10.11-12).

St. Paul carried this principle of equal rights into the home: "For the wife does not have authority over her own body, but the husband does; likewise the husband does not have authority over his own body, but the wife does. Do not deprive one another except perhaps by agreement for a set time, to devote yourselves to prayer" (1 Cor. 7.4-5).

The Fathers and theologians, and the Second Vatican Council, sometimes speaks of conjugal love as friendship. "Friendship" may seem to some a weak word for so close a union; but "friendship" is in fact a rich concept. Friendship is the most perfect form of love: Christ calls those bound most intensely to Him by divine love His friends (cf. John 15.15). For friendship, in its most authentic form, is an unselfish and mutual love persons have for each other, as each knows he or she is loved by the other. In sincere friendship the tie of love is enduring, for it is not based on the hope of gratification from personal traits that can fade with time, but on the free and firm commitment of each to pursue the good of the other, for the other's sake.[3] To speak of married friendship is to recognize the fundamental equality of the husband and wife, and, therefore, the possibility of intimate sharing of life not only on the physical level but also on the level of mind and spirit. Such married friendship must be the human component of Christian conjugal love, which is authentic human love made fruitful by divine grace, and thereby transformed into an expression of charity. Unlike mere eroticism, it does not exploit the sensate, nor, on the other hand,

---

[3]Cf. St. Thomas Aquinas, *Commentarium in Librum III Sententiarum*, q. 27, a. 2, c. See also Pope John Paul II, Apostolic Exhortation, *Familiaris Consortio* (November 22, 1981) nn. 18-19 (EV 7.1582-1585).

does it strain for an impossible angelism; it seeks to integrate sexuality into the "new self created according to the likeness of God in true righteousness and holiness" (Eph. 4.24).

Christian conjugal love "therefore far excels erotic inclination, which, selfishly pursued, soon enough fades wretchedly away" (GS 49). Yet this love "is eminently human since it is directed from one person to another through an affection of the will; it involves the good of the whole person, and can therefore enrich the expressions of body and mind with unique dignity, ennobling these expressions as special ingredients and signs of the friendship distinctive of marriage. This love the Lord has deigned to heal, perfect, and exalt with a special gift of grace and charity" (GS 49). With this special gift, a divine element has introduced into the human relationship between the spouses, assimilating it to the love of God and giving it the durability and power of this love. "Christian couples, therefore, nourish and develop their marriage by undivided affection, which wells up from the fountain of divine love, while in a merging of human and divine love, they remain faithful in body and mind, in good times as in bad."[4]

Offspring

It may seem a laboring of the obvious to mention offspring, children, as a blessing and purpose of marriage. Yet this could not be taken for granted in St. Augustine's time, nor can it now in our own. In that earlier age the Manichaeans attacked marriage itself as evil and hence the offspring of marriage as well. In the world today there is no doctrinaire Manichaeanism, but there is a widespread attitude hostile to the procreative good and intent on weakening the bond between marriage and concern for new life.

The Second Vatican Council has reaffirmed in our time that the procreation of children is a basic good of marriage. This good cannot be assailed without harming conjugal love. The distinctive traits of marriage are ordered to the good of offspring. Married love must be faithful and enduring precisely to unite husband and wife in a love of such strength and personal concern that they can suitably carry out the duties of parents. "Marriage and conjugal love are by their nature ordained toward the begetting and educating of children. Children are really the supreme gift of marriage..." (GS 50).[5] This in no way detracts from the other purposes of marriage. "Hence, while not making the other purposes of matrimony of less account, the true practice of conjugal love, and the whole meaning of family life which

[4]Congregation of Rites, *Rite of Marriage*, published by authority of Pope Paul VI, March 19, 1969, Introduction, n. 3 (EV 3.867).
[5]Cf. Pope John Paul II, Apostolic Exhortation, *Familiaris Consortio* (November 22, 1981) nn. 36-41 (EV 7.1638-1661).

results from it, have this aim: that the couple be ready with stout hearts to cooperate with the love of the Creator and the Savior who through them will enlarge and enrich His own family day by day" (GS 50).

This does not mean that parents should bring children into the world irresponsibly. As we have noted in an earlier chapter, Christian couples may indeed rightly reflect on the number of children they can wisely bring into this world, taking into account here all relevant factors. At the same time, however, they will rule out any and all forms of artificial birth control.

"God is love" (1 John 4.8). Because He is love, He has created us. There could be no other motive for this except to extend and diffuse and share His boundless goodness. His love is so vast, so limitless, that He pours it forth into creation. It is to be expected, then, that in willing to share His love with men, He would also will to share with them the creative power of His love. This he does in making them capable of conjugal love, which is procreative. "Parents should regard as their proper mission the task of transmitting human life and educating those to whom it has been transmitted. They should realize that they are cooperators with the love of God the Creator, and are, so to speak, the interpreters of that love" (GS 50). Their mutual love also bursts its bounds into creativity. For this, all the living can be grateful.

The Sacrament

The third good or blessing of marriage is sacramentality. Marriage is a covenant of indissoluble love. It is a sacred sign recalling and drawing upon the perpetual love between Christ and His Church. Like that covenant, a consummated sacramental marriage is entirely indissoluble. It endures until death.

The ministers of the sacrament of matrimony are the matrimonial partners themselves. The priest assisting at a marriage "must ask for and obtain the consent of the contracting parties" (SC 77). The consummation of the marriage seals it in a personal and mutual self-surrender of sexual union. "But the grace which would perfect the natural love and confirm the indissoluble unity, and sanctify the persons married, Christ Himself, the instructor and perfecter of the venerable sacraments, merited for us by His passion."[6]

Marriage in the sense of covenanted love — sacred, solemn, serious — of itself requires indissoluble union after the model of God's love. "The intimate partnership of married life and love has been established by the Creator and qualified by His laws, and is rooted in the conjugal covenant of irrevocable personal consent" (GS 48).

---

[6]Council of Trent, Session 24, November 11, 1563, *Doctrine on the Sacrament of Matrimony* (DS 1799).

"Marriage arises in the covenant of marriage, or irrevocable consent, which each partner freely bestows on and accepts from the other. This intimate union and the good of the children impose total fidelity on each of them and argue for an unbreakable oneness between them. Christ the Lord raised this union to the dignity of a sacrament so that it might more clearly recall and more easily reflect his own unbreakable union with his Church."[7]

Here marriage is seen as a lifelong companionship, reflecting Christ's self-sacrificing and redeeming love in His new covenant with the Church (cf. GS 48).

The Church teaches that marriage, even as a natural institution, cannot be dissolved by the will of the partners or by any human authority.[8] To teach this is certainly not to teach that it is easy to remain faithful until death in marriage, or to say that married partners can succeed in doing so without the grace of God. But the Church does teach that by divine law marriage demands such faithfulness, and that only special divine authority can legitimately dissolve such a bond. "So they are no longer two, but one flesh. Therefore what God has joined together, let no one separate" (Matt. 19.6).

In some cases God does permit the dissolution of a purely natural bond of marriage, that is, one not contracted by two baptized persons. In the case of married unbelievers, one of whom becomes a Christian, the Church may permit the Christian to remarry, if the unbelieving spouse refuses to live peacefully with him or her. The Church has so understood the words of St. Paul (cf. 1 Cor. 7.12-16), and has judged that in such cases God gives it the right to dissolve a non-sacramental marriage. This right is called the Pauline privilege. The Church, starting from this principle and recalling the "power of the keys" given to it, continues where conditions warrant to dissolve the natural, non-sacramental marriage in favor of the faith.

But the Church has firmly proclaimed and always taught that a sacramental marriage between Christians in which there has been true matrimonial consent and consummation is absolutely indissoluble except by death of one of the partners. A sacrament recalling Christ's undying love for the Church, it is expressed in a binding tie that endures for life, no matter what happens between the spouses.[9]

Special Marriage Questions

In no area of life with all its problems do people suffer grief and anxiety more than in broken marriages. Catholics are not exempt from

[7]*Rite of Marriage*, Introduction, n. 2 (EV 3.866).
[8]Cf. Council of Trent, Session 24, November 11, 1563, *Doctrine on the Sacrament of Matrimony* (DS 1797-1799, 1807); Pope Pius XI, Encyclical, *Casti Connubii* (December 31, 1930) (DS 3712, 3724); Pope John Paul II, Apostolic Exhortation, *Familiaris Consortio* (November 22, 1981) n. 20 (EV 7.1586-1588). Cf. also GS 48-49; AA 11.
[9]See note 8.

the pressures that make for such difficulties; the number of those divorced and perhaps remarried outside the Church presents a grave and urgent pastoral problem.

The Church, faithful to the word of Christ that excludes divorce (cf. Matt. 19.3-12; Mark 10.1-12), does not and cannot permit divorce and remarriage as a solution to these problems.[10] Such a solution, while it might seem kind to individuals in painful situations, is excluded by the divine command. Moreover, the good of husbands, wives, and children generally is that the enduring force of the marriage covenant be stoutly asserted. Precisely because it is not dissoluble, married couples are assisted in their efforts to overcome the grave obstacles that can threaten any married life.

Still the Church does, when there are grave reasons for this, permit the separation of married partners from common life together.[11]

In some extreme circumstances, it can be imprudent for a couple to try to continue to live together. Such cases, however, never justify any claim to a right to dissolve the sacramental marriage bond, or a right to enter on a new marriage.

Some apparent marriages that "fail" were in fact never true marriages. No real marriage covenant was established if one or both of the partners failed to give, or was incapable of giving, free consent; or if one or both did not intend a real marriage, a bond of faithful love at least in principle open to offspring. If for any reason an apparent marriage was not a genuine marriage from the start, it may be possible to obtain from the Church an official acknowledgment of that fact, that is, an annulment, or, more exactly, a decree of nullity. Each diocese is required to have a matrimonial tribunal or court to hear and judge matrimonial cases. Should it be determined that one had not been validly married, genuine marriage with another partner would not be excluded.

Since divorce is forbidden by Christ, the Church wishes to guard carefully entrance into the married state. Normally Catholics can be married validly only in the presence of a priest and witnesses.[12] The priest assisting at a marriage, who is to be the bishop or pastor of the place or his delegate, has the responsibility to see that the couple is in fact free to marry, that they receive sufficient instruction to realize the importance and dignity of the sacrament they are to receive, and that

---

[10]Cf. Council of Trent, Session 24, November 11, 1563, *Doctrine on the Sacrament of Matrimony*, especially canons 7 and 8 (DS 1807, 1808). Proper pastoral treatment for disordered marriage is discussed in Pope Paul II, Apostolic Exhortation, *Familiaris Consortio* (November 22, 1981) nn. 77-85 (EV 7.1768-1804).

[11]Cf. *Code of Canon Law*, canons 1152-1153; Council of Trent, Session 24, November 11, 1563, *Doctrine on the Sacrament of Matrimony*, canon 8 (DS 1808).

[12]Cf. *Code of Canon Law*, canon 1108.1.

they are aware of the purposes and meaning of marriage, and are entering into a genuine marriage covenant.

Impediments

To guard the married state, the Church has also the right to proclaim the existence of, and to establish, impediments to marriage. A diriment impediment is a circumstance which because of divine or ecclesiastical law causes a marriage to be invalid.

The Church teaches, for example, that impotence, when it precedes the marriage and is permanent, makes a marriage invalid by the very law of nature, and that the same natural law excludes the possibility of a valid marriage between certain very close relatives.[13] Other diriment impediments include lack of sufficient age, a preexisting and existing marriage, prior reception of holy orders, prior assumption of a solemn vow of chastity in a religious institute, and certain prior crimes.[14] The attempted marriage of a Catholic with an unbaptized person without a prior dispensation is also declared invalid.

Church law also declares marriage to be illicit in certain cases. For example, it forbids marriage between a Catholic and a baptized non-Catholic. Should a Catholic wish to marry a baptized non-Catholic, permission for such a marriage must first be obtained from the bishop. The bishop can grant permission for such a marriage if there is a reasonable cause. Before granting permission, the Church seeks to see to it that the threats to a successful marriage that often arise from differences in faith are countered by taking steps to guard the faith of the Catholic partner for which the Church has special responsibility, and to provide for the proper instruction to assist each of the partners.[15]

Invalid Marriages

A Catholic who is knowingly a partner in an invalid marriage is in reality and before God not married to his or her apparent spouse. Hence performance of the marriage act within that union is not a sacred and holy seal of married love, but really a wrongful use of sex. Those who have seriously disobeyed divine or ecclesiastical law by entering into an invalid marriage, and have perhaps committed many sins within that union, have a duty to return to the state of grace as quickly as possible, and certainly to abstain from Holy Communion until they do so. Some solution is always possible, even in the most difficult cases. At times one must accept a considerable amount of

---

[13]Cf. *Code of Canon Law*, canons 1084 and 1091.

[14]Cf. *Code of Canon Law*, canons 1083, 1085, 1087, 1088, 1089, and 1090.

[15]Cf. *Code of Canon Law*, canons 1124, 1125.

self-denial and bear the cross generously; but God's grace is able to make even difficult burdens bearable. Even if individuals feel that they do not now have the moral strength to do what the law of God demands of them, they ought not despair. In prayer, in faithful attendance at Mass, in doing the works of Christian love, they can with God's grace gradually acquire the courage needed to do with peace whatever is necessary. Pastors and diocesan marriage tribunals will try to be of assistance to those in invalid marriages. Those seeking a good conscience in these matters must remember that their consciences are to be formed in the light of Church teaching. Every solution that is reached must be entirely faithful to the command of Christ that consummated and sacramental marriages can in no way be dissolved or treated as though they can be.[16]

The Married Vocation

Although indissolubility undergirds conjugal love, it does not exhaust the meaning of the marriage covenant. The Church "is believed to be holy in a way which cannot fail. For Christ . . . loved the Church as His bride, delivering Himself up for her, so that He might sanctify her (cf. Eph. 5.25-26). . . . Therefore, in the Church all . . . are called to holiness" (LG 39).

The Second Vatican Council spoke of how that principle embraces those who enter the sacramental covenant: "Married couples and Christian parents should follow their own proper path to holiness by faithful love, sustaining one another in grace throughout the entire length of their lives. They should imbue their offspring, lovingly welcomed from God, with Christian truth and evangelical virtues. For thus can they offer all men an example of unwearying and generous love, build up the brotherhood of charity, and stand as the witnesses to and cooperators in the fruitfulness of Holy Mother Church. By such lives, they signify and share in that very love with which Christ loved His Bride and because of which He delivered Himself up on her behalf" (LG 41).

Pope Pius XI had stated this teaching for the married: "This outward expression of love in family life not only embraces mutual help, but should also extend to this, and indeed should have this as its primary purpose, that the married partners help each other in forming and perfecting themselves daily more fully in the interior life, so that through their partnership in life they may advance ever more and more in virtue, and especially that they may grow in true love towards God

---

16Cf. Pope John Paul II, Apostolic Exhortation, *Familiaris Consortio* (November 22, 1981) n. 84 (EV 7.1796-1802). Cf. also Congregation for the Doctrine of the Faith, *Letter* to all the bishops (April 11, 1973) (EV 4.2383).

and their neighbors, on which indeed 'depends the whole law and the prophets' (Matt. 22.40). For all men, of every condition, in whatever honorable walk of life they may be, can and ought to imitate the most perfect example of holiness placed before man by God, namely, Christ our Lord, and by God's grace to arrive at the summit of perfection, as is proved by the example set us of many saints."[17]

Marriage and the Paschal Mystery

Christ's love for the Church is the pattern for married love. Christ's love was a sacrificial love, and it included suffering where necessary. "No one has greater love than this, to lay down one's life for one's friends" (John 15.13). Such also is the love, for one another as well as for Himself, that He expects of His followers. "I give you a new commandment, that you love one another. Just as I have loved you, you also should love one another" (John 13.34). This is far more than loving one's neighbor as oneself; it goes beyond the Golden Rule, even to the limit: "We know love by this, that He laid down His life for us — and we ought to lay down our lives for one another" (1 John 3.16).

Now it is this sacrificial love which is the exemplar of Christian marriage and the sacrament, the mystery, the foreshadowing, through which Christ blesses the married couple. To love each other faithfully until death, they must learn to forgive each other and to bear crosses well. In raising a family, with all the joys and all the heartaches that implies, they will be required to give of self.

St. Paul exhorted: "Husbands, love your wives just as Christ loved the church and gave Himself up for her. . ." (Eph. 5.25). Thus the married couple are in a special way plunged into the mystery of the Lord's death and resurrection; through this sacrament their love shares in the saving mystery of Christ and signifies its final perfection in the Church fully realized. This is why Christian marriage must be indissoluble, literally unto death. It is why the perfection of Christian love is so necessary to the married couple, lest human selfishness separate what God has joined together; and why, therefore, a special sacrament is given to foster such love. The marriage covenant must partake of the quality and durability of the love of Him who said: "I have loved you with an everlasting love" (Jer. 31.3).

The celebration of marriage "normally should be within the Mass."[18] This also signifies its issuance from the paschal mystery. In the wedding Mass, the Liturgy of the Word "shows the importance of Christian marriage in the history of salvation and the duties and

---

[17]Pope Pius XI, Encyclical, *Casti Connubii* (December 31, 1930) (cf. DS 3707).
[18]*Rite of Marriage*, Introduction, n. 6 (EV 3.870).

responsibilities of the couple in caring for the holiness of their children."[19]

Then in the Liturgy of the Eucharist, in which salvation history rises to its climax, the now-married couple enter the sacramental source of the paschal mystery and "eat this bread and drink the cup" to "proclaim the Lord's death until He comes" (1 Cor. 11.26). Even in its ceremony, the Church seeks to enshrine and consecrate marriage by her most sublime possession, the mystery of the faith.

[19]*Rite of Marriage*, Introduction, n. 6 (EV 3.870).

Part Four

In Christ:
Fulfillment Of All

31

The Death Of A Christian

"And just as it is appointed for mortals to die once, and after that the judgment" (Heb. 9.27).

Earthly life can be made rich with Christ's presence. Through faith and sacraments and works of love our lives are penetrated by Christ's life. Still, though Christ is present to us, with the Father and the Holy Spirit, the divine presence remains veiled. For in this life "we walk by faith, not by sight" (2 Cor. 5.7). The gifts of grace give joy and energy, but also a thirst for fulfillment in ways not now possible.

At the end of time, when Christ will come to pass judgment on all, and when those who have died will rise again, our redemption will be brought to its total fullness. But this world, and our time of trial, ends for each of us with death. In this chapter we speak of death, of the judgment which follows it, and of purgatory, hell, and heaven.

Death

Death has many meanings for the Christian. In a sense death is entirely natural. But it is also seen in faith as a punishment for sin. Christian death is seen also as a sharing in the paschal mystery, a personal sharing in Christ's death so that one may share also in His resurrection.

Death Is Natural

There is "a time to be born, and a time to die" (Eccle. 3.2). Death is natural for us. Our lives are measured by time, in which we change; we grow old, and death seems even appropriate after a full life. "And the dust returns to the earth as it was, and the breath returns to God who gave it" (Eccle. 12.7).

The natural reality of death gives an urgency to our lives. Remembrance that we are mortal serves also to remind us that we have but a limited time in which to shape good and meaningful lives.

Result of Sin

But death is also a penalty for sin. "Just as sin came into the world through one man, and death came through sin, and so death spread to all because all have sinned" (Rom. 5.12; cf. Wisd. 1.13, 2.23-24; Rom. 5.21, 6.23; James 1.15). Because of sin the sinner suffers "bodily death, from which man would have been immune had he not sinned" (GS 18).

Death, then, appears to us not merely as a liberator from the burdens and limitations of earthly life, but as something fearful, the "last enemy" that will be destroyed by the all-embracing redemption of Christ (cf. 1 Cor. 15.26). For death is more than a passing on to another land and to another manner of living. We are not merely souls; we are beings of flesh and blood. To die is to lose the fullness of our being, which we love; it is to be dissolved (cf. 2 Cor. 5.1-4).

Transformed by Christ

Christian faith neither denies the profound reality of death nor yields to despair because of it. True, "in the face of death the riddle of human existence becomes more acute," and the very fact of death can arouse a "dread of perpetual extinction" (GS 18). But one "rightly follows the intuition of his heart when he abhors and repudiates the absolute ruin and total disappearance of his own person" (GS 18). Indeed, this natural intuition as well as the explicit message of the faith enables the Christian to accept death in all its reality and yet remain sure that death is neither total nor final.

Christ Himself shared the most bitter aspects of human death, and the Gospel accounts show in Him both anxiety and deep tranquility in the presence of death. Certainly death is not the evil which we should fear most. Even when we find death most mysterious and frightening, we are reassured by the firm testimonies of God.

"Do not fear those who kill the body but cannot kill the soul" (Matt. 10.28). Something of our very being, most proper to us, can yet live when the flesh that is part of our reality is dissolved in death. Our soul is not the whole of our being, the temporary occupant as it were of an alien body. Rather, the soul is the living principle of a human person, created to give life to the body. After bodily death, this living principle continues to exist.[1] Because of this, one can continue to love God, and come to share God's life in the beatific vision, even when one's mortal flesh is dissolved. Thus faith has understood the words Jesus spoke to the good thief on Calvary: "Truly I tell you, today you

---

[1]Cf. Congregation for the Doctrine of the Faith, *Letter on Certain Questions concerning Eschatology* (May 17, 1979) n. 3 (EV 6.1539).

will be with Me in Paradise" (Luke 23.43). For this reason too St. Paul could confess his longing to be "away from the body and at home with the Lord" (2 Cor. 5.8). Still, to be "away from the body" is to not be a full person.[2] The departed in Christ took forward to "the resurrection of the body."[3]

Revelation and the Meaning of Death

Over the long periods of salvation history revelation concerning the significance of death became progressively more complete. In the centuries since public revelation was completed there has been a progressively fuller understanding of this revelation.

Old Testament

In the Old Testament there is a definite awareness of the relationship between sin and death (cf. Gen 2.16-17; 3.3, 19). There is general assurance that life and death are in the hands of God. But in earlier times there was no clear recognition that significant personal life continued after bodily death. Death was considered to bring religious activity to a close. The place into which the dead descended was called Sheol, a place of obscurity over which God continued to reign, but for which God seemed not to have much concern (cf. Ps. 6.5; Isa. 38.17-19). Because death seemed to offer little or no comfort in terms of human fulfillment or of personal relationship with God, a long life on earth was viewed as a special divine favor.

Apocalyptic literature (e.g., Dan. 12.1-4) gave a new understanding of the meaning of death to the believer. God would rescue at least some from death. "Many of those who sleep in the dust of the earth shall awake, some to everlasting life, and some to shame and everlasting contempt" (Dan. 12.2). By the power of God a totally new existence will come to be; God will triumph over death for and in His chosen ones. Hope in the resurrection of the dead emerged.

Wisdom literature gave an even brighter picture of human immortality. "But the souls of the righteous are in the hands of God, and no torment will ever touch them. In the eyes of the foolish they seemed to have died . . . but they are at peace. For though in the sight of others they were punished, their hope is full of immortality" (Wisd. 3.1-4).

New Testament

In New Testament times Christ was seen as the Conqueror of death. The early Christian community did not focus its reflections so

---

[2]Cf. St. Thomas Aquinas, *Summa Theologica*, I, 29, 1 ad 5.
[3]Apostles' Creed.

much on death as on the awaited triumphal return of Christ, at which time "death shall be no more" (Rev. 21.4). The emphasis in its hope for salvation was communitarian: Christians looked for the coming of Christ that was to bring to fulfillment the lives of all His people. Hence in early New Testament times there was no great preoccupation with the death of the individual.

Faith in Christ's coming in glory remained, but as years passed and many believers died, it became clearer that the repeated warnings about the unpredictable hour of His coming were no guarantee that any particular person would certainly live to see it. Some would take this delay as an excuse for mockery. "Where is the promise of His coming? For ever since our ancestors died, all things continue as they were from the beginning of creation" (2 Peter 3.4). The response to this was that the time God provided was being given in mercy: "The Lord is not slow about His promise, as some think of slowness, but is patient with you, not wanting any to perish, but all to come to repentance" (2 Peter 3.9). What was awaited were "new heavens and a new earth" (2 Peter 3.13), and the time would come quickly, compared with the years of eternity. "With the Lord one day is like a thousand years, and a thousand years are like one day" (2 Peter 3.8; cf. Ps. 90.4).

Concern for those who had died, and for themselves, led the living faithful to reflect earnestly on the mystery of death. Remembrance of such words as those of Christ to the dying thief on the cross (cf. Luke 23.43) and those of Paul in his longing to be "away from the body and at home with the Lord" (2 Cor. 5.8; cf. Phil. 1.23) helped guide the Church as it reflected on death with the assistance of the Holy Spirit. The warning that Christ would come as unexpectedly as a thief (cf. Matt. 24.43-44; Luke 12.39-40; 2 Peter 3.10; Rev. 16.15) began to be understood as equally true of His coming to the individual at death. The individual life, like that of the community, had to be looking forward to Christ's coming, a life lived in constant preparedness for that event.

Only gradually, then, did a fuller understanding of faith's teaching on last things emerge. The sacramental life of the Church clarified its insight. Pastoral care fortified the sick and the dying with the sacrament of anointing and with Viaticum, the Eucharistic Food for the last journey of death. Reception in the sacramental signs of Him whom they looked forward to greeting as their Savior intensified the longing of the faithful to be with the Lord, and helped the community to realize more fully the personal dimensions of the mystery of salvation.

In later centuries the Church's teaching on the condition of the individual after his death and before the final resurrection at the end of time was solemnly defined.

Particular Judgment

Implicit in the defined teaching of the Church is the teaching that the death of an individual marks an end of the period of trial. For we are then no longer pilgrims, and no more will we sin or earn merit. God's judgment comes upon us. Explicitly defined are the teachings that those who die in grace and in need of no further purification enter heaven promptly after death, and that those who die in the state of grace but in need of some purification enter heaven after that purgation or cleansing is completed. Also explicitly defined is the teaching that those who die in actual mortal sin enter their unending punishment promptly after death.[4]

God made human persons free and responsible, "in the power of their own free choice" (Sir. 15.14). Neither in life nor in death does God force us to walk in the ways to which He calls us. But He "sees everything ... and He knows every human action" (Sir. 15.18-19). And when this life has ended, each of us must render an account to our Lord. "All of us must appear before the judgment seat of Christ, so that each may receive recompense for what has been done in the body, whether good or evil" (2 Cor. 5.10).

The Church has constantly taught that each individual will appear before God after death to receive judgment, and then begin either eternal happiness or eternal punishment, unless he died in grace but in need of further purgation.[5] The fact of this particular judgment, the judgment of each individual after death, is not explicitly defined. The teaching is, however, implicitly contained in the Church's definition concerning the fact that the reward or punishment of the individual begins promptly after the individual's death. It is suggested also in St. Paul's expression of a desire to die and to be with Christ (cf. Phil. 1.21-23; 2 Cor. 5.6-9). The teaching of the Second Vatican Council contains implicit references to the particular judgment when it says that already, before the final resurrection, some of Christ's disciples "have finished with this life and are being purified" and some "are in glory, beholding 'clearly God Himself triune and one, as He is' " (LG 49).[6]

God's judgment is not to be thought of as simply a judicial procedure. It is perhaps best understood as an activity by which He accomplishes His designs for this world. God's judgment is essentially related to divine government; it involves His knowledge of one's free

---

[4]Cf. Second Council of Lyons, Session 4, July 6, 1274, *Profession of Faith of Emperor Michael Palaeologus* (DS 856-858); Pope Benedict XII, Constitution, *Benedictus Deus* (January 29, 1336) (DS 1000-1002); Council of Florence, Bull, *Laetentur Caeli* ("Decree for the Greeks," July 6, 1439) (DS 1304-1306). Cf. also LG 48-49; 51; GS 17.

[5]See the references cited in note 4.

[6]The internal quotation is from the Council of Florence, Bull, *Laetentur Caeli* ("Decree for the Greeks," July 6, 1439) (DS 1305).

responses to His plan throughout one's earthly life, as well as His decision as to how to fit these responses into His design for the universe.

All of us are at the moment of our death everything that we have made ourselves to be by our free acceptance or free rejection of the divine call and gifts. Each one is thus related to God and to the whole of creation at that moment in a decisive way. God's judgment clearly indicates to each of us what we have made ourselves to be, and it gives each of us the place for which we have fitted ourselves. In the light of divine judgment the individual recognizes and affirms what he or she has merited and has become. Those who have been justified in Christ and have died in the Lord experience God's judgment after death as a completion, a fulfillment of all their human efforts during life.

Purgatory

Some die in grace and in the friendship of God, but burdened with venial sins and imperfections, or before they have done suitable penance for their sins. The Church teaches that the souls of these are cleansed in purgatory of these last hindrances to their entry into the vision of God.[7] Their communion with the faithful on earth is not thereby broken. The living can bring comfort and alleviation to those in purgatory by their intercessions, by "Masses, prayers, almsgiving, and other pious works which, in the manner of the Church, the faithful are accustomed to do for others of the faithful."[8]

The word "purgatory" is not in the Bible, nor is the doctrine of purgatory explicitly taught there. But the ancient belief in purgatory is deeply grounded in what Scripture explicitly teaches about divine judgment, on the need for holiness to enter the vision of God, and on the reality of divine temporal punishment for sins which have been forgiven. The teaching on purgatory seems to be implicit, for example, in a narrative in the Second Book of Maccabees. About the year 165 B.C. there was a battle for liberation which was won by the Jews. When the Jews went to bury their dead after the battle, they found on the slain charms or amulets which the law forbade Jews to wear. Judas Maccabeus, the commander of the troops, ordered his soldiers to pray for the dead that they might be released from their sins. The sacred

[7]Cf. Congregation for the Doctrine of the Faith, *Letter on Certain Questions concerning Eschatology* (May 17, 1979) n. 4 (EV 6.1540).

[8]Second Council of Lyons, Session 4, July 6, 1274, *Profession of Faith of Emperor Michael Palaeologus* (DS 856); Council of Florence, Bull, *Laetentur Caeli* ("Decree for the Greeks," July 6, 1439) (DS 1304). Cf. Council of Trent, Session 22, September 17, 1562, *Doctrine on the Most Holy Sacrifice of the Mass*, ch. 2 (DS 1743) and canon 3 (DS 1753), and Session 25, December 3, 1563, *Decree on Purgatory* (DS 1820); etc. Cf. also LG 51, which explicitly reaffirms these teachings.

writer who records this incident comments: "But if he was looking to the splendid reward that is laid up for those who fall asleep in godliness it was a holy and pious thought. Therefore he made atonement for the dead, so that they might be delivered from their sin" (2 Macc. 12.45).

What was the implicit in Scripture was much clearer in the teaching of the Fathers and the practices of the Church. For example, St. Clement of Alexandria taught that those who repent on their deathbeds, and so do not have time to do works of penance in this life, will yet be sanctified in the next by purifying fire.[9] St. Augustine, in his commentary on the Psalms, asks God to purify him in this life so that it will not be necessary for him after death to undergo the cleansing fire.[10]

The works of the Fathers have many references not only to the existence of purgatory, but also to the fact that the faithful departed can be helped by the prayers of the living, especially by the Sacrifice of the Mass.[11] Ancient inscriptions as well show that the Mass was offered for the departed in the earliest centuries of the Church. Very much aware of the bonds that link us with those who have died in Christ, the Church never ceases so to remember and pray for the departed (cf. LG 50).

The Pains of Purgatory

St. Augustine says the "fire" of purgatory will be "more severe than anything a person can suffer in this life."[12] The precise nature of the sufferings in purgatory, however, has never been defined by the Church. Certainly the greatest pain of purgatory is that of separation from God. The soul in purgatory now realizes far more than it ever could before the infinite goodness of God, and it suffers from knowing that it is for a while impeded from the beatific vision by obstacles of its own making.

Although the soul suffers, it is in peace, for it is now utterly certain of salvation, and it knows that God wills this "purgation" for it out of great love. St. Catherine of Genoa, a mystic of the fifteenth century, wrote that the fire of purgatory is God's love burning into the soul to the extent that it had not yet succeeded, and so that it might succeed, in inflaming the soul.[13]

[9]Cf. St. Clement of Alexandria, *Stromata* 6.7 (MG 9.281-282).

[10]Cf. St. Augustine, *Enarratio in Psalmum* 37(38).3 (ML 36.397 = ACW 30.330-331).

[11]Cf., e.g. St. Ephraem, *Testamentum* 72; St. Cyril of Jerusalem, *Catechesis* 23 (myst. 5). 9-10 (MG 33.1116); St. Epiphanius, *Adversus Haereses Panarium* 75.8 (MG 42.513); St. John Chrysostom, *In Epistulam ad Philippenses Homilia* 3.4 (MG 62.203); St. Augustine, *Enchiridion* 110 (ML 40.283 = ACW 3.103-104); etc.

[12]St. Augustine, *Enarratio in Psalmum* 37(38).3 (ML 36.397 = ACW 30.331).

[13]Cf. St. Catherine of Genoa, *Treatise on Purgatory*, chs. 11-13. Cardinal Newman's *The Dream of Gerontius* is a literary masterpiece on purgatory based on St. Catherine's teaching.

Beyond the soul's great sense of longing for God, the nature of the punishment in purgatory is not known to us. The ordinary teaching of the Church is that there is some positive punishment in addition to the pain of deprivation, but there is no definitive teaching on the exact nature of this punishment.

Unbaptized Infants

Infants who die without being baptized are guilty of no personal sin; neither, however, have they received saving grace in sacramental baptism, or, so it would seem, in free personal responses to grace offered in other ways. Most theologians, following St. Thomas, have taught that such infants will certainly not have any personal suffering after death, and that although they will be deprived of the blessed vision of God because they have died without grace, God will bless them with natural happiness.[14] Since the thirteenth century "limbo" (from the Latin *limbus*, meaning "border" or "hem") has been used to designate the abode or status which such unbaptized children could come to after death. The Church has never made any official pronouncement on the reality or nature of limbo; but it does teach that baptism in some form is required for salvation.

Many contemporary scholars have suggested that God will provide for the eternal salvation of these persons, enabling them in some way to obtain grace by a baptism of desire before death. Revelation does not give any certainty on this point. God remains infinitely merciful, but the gifts of grace are entirely gratuitous, and we are not certain that the mercy He shows them will include the gift of supernatural beatitude. For this reason the Church insists that the faithful take care so that their children are baptized promptly.[15] The vision of God is so precious a gift that we must take every reasonable step to obtain it for ourselves and for those entrusted to our care.

Hell

Following the example of Christ, the Church has in all centuries warned the faithful of the "sad and lamentable reality of eternal death."[16]

Scripture speaks of this eternal punishment and warns us against

[14]Cf. St. Thomas Aquinas, *De Malo*, q. 5, a. 2-3.

[15]Cf. *Code of Canon Law*, canon 867; Congregation of the Holy Office, Monitum (February 18, 1958), AAS 50 (1958) p. 114.

[16]Congregation for the Clergy, *General Catechetical Directory* (April 11, 1971) n. 69 (EV 4.561). For early credal recognitions of the everlasting reality of hell, cf. the affirmations commonly known as the "Faith of Damasus" (DS 72) and the so-called "Athanasian Creed" (DS 76).

the deliberate malice which destroys a person from within and leads to eternal death. There is an essential relationship between hell and the mystery of evil, and ultimately between hell and personal freedom. A refusal to believe in hell is a refusal to take God seriously, and also a refusal to take seriously our own humanity and our freedom and our responsibility to do good. For this reason some understanding of hell is necessary for a proper understanding of one's meaning and place in this world according to the plan of God.

Old Testament

In the earliest stages of salvation history there was no real perception of the reality of hell as it came to be understood in later revelation. "Sheol" was conceived of as the place where both the good and the bad reside after death, having there a shadowy, unsatisfactory form of existence. That God would severely punish the persistently wicked was understood, but it puzzled many that the evil seemed to fare as well as the good. The revelation that "Sheol" would be a place of punishment for the wicked came only gradually. With it came fuller understanding of the responsibility people have for what they do. Divine retribution for evil has nothing to do with revenge; rather, it is a matter of justice and mercy on the part of a loving and almighty God who maintains and restores a universal order, which every sin disturbs. We must take ourselves seriously because God does.

In time there was a growing understanding of the kind of punishment appropriate for sin. Early in the Old Testament period punishment was conceived in materialistic images, in terms of trials, illnesses, and brevity of life. Only gradually did it become clear that the deepest punishment is implicit in the very nature of sin: that to reject God is to separate oneself from the infinite Goodness for which the heart truly hungers (cf. Ps. 63.1).

In the Old Testament, images of physical fire were attached to the notion of hell with reference to "Gehenna," the "Valley of Ben-Hinnom." There in forbidden human sacrifices children had been consumed in fire (cf. 2 Kings 23.10; 2 Chron. 28.3, 33.6; Jer. 7.31, 19.5, 32.35). In later years the city refuse was burned there in fires that smoldered day and night. Isaiah refers to this valley, though not by name, as the place where the corpses of those who rebel against God shall lie (cf. Isa. 66.24). In rabbinic literature "Gehenna" became the pit of fire in which the wicked are punished after death.

New Testament

Christ spoke often of hell. When He spoke of "hell ... the unquenchable fire" (Mark 9.43; cf. Matt. 25.31; Luke 16.22), He spoke in compassion, to warn us away from this ultimate tragedy (cf. Mark 9.43-50), this "second death" (Rev. 21.8) with its permanent separation from the everlasting life in God for which we were made (cf. Matt. 25.31). Christ spoke forcefully in the images used in that time, of "hell, where their worm never dies, and the fire is never quenched" (Mark 9.47-48; cf. Isa. 66.24). In using these images Christ was not giving a literal description of hell, for the evil of separation from God cannot be adequately described. But Christ wished to call to conversion, and to warn that those who deliberately persist in malice will come to total ruin.

Frequently the New Testament refers to the punishments of hell as unending. "And these will go away into eternal punishment, but the righteous into eternal life" (Matt. 25.46; cf. Mark 9.43-48; 2 Thess. 1.9; Rev. 14.9-11). This entered into the ordinary teaching of the Church from the beginning. Some early theologians, notably Origen in the third century, took the position that all sinners, including even Satan, will eventually be brought to salvation. This and similar views, however, the Church has always decisively rejected, as incompatible with revealed truth, and the Church has solemnly confirmed the doctrine that punishment in hell is eternal.[17]

Nature of Punishment

There are two chief elements in the punishment of hell. Christ's words, "You that are accursed, depart from me" (Matt. 25.41), indicate what is by far the most bitter part of hell: eternal separation from the God in whom alone we can have the life we long for. The damned also suffer pains of sense, caused by "the eternal fire" (Matt. 25.41) of which Scripture speaks.

The Church does not define the nature of that fire, but it does teach that the punishment of the damned is not only that of loss (corresponding to their turning away from God), but also a suffering caused by created realities (corresponding to their turning toward finite things in evil ways). With these there is also the endless pain of remorse, of unredeeming self-hatred, for "their worm never dies" (Mark 9.48; cf. Isa. 66.24).

Justice and Mercy

The punishment of hell is great, but is in no way excessive. Faith teaches that God is just and merciful, that no one is punished more

[17]The Origenistic position was rejected by a Synod of Constantinople in 543 (DS 411); cf. also Second Council of Constantinople, Session 8, June 2, 553 (DS 433). The doctrine of eternity of hell was solemnly taught by the Fourth Lateran Council, November 1215, *The Catholic Faith* (DS 801).

harshly than he deserves. No one goes to hell as one predestined there by God,[18] but only by deliberately and knowingly doing grave evil and persisting in it to the end. Deeds done without real freedom, or without sufficient understanding of their malice, do not merit the eternal damnation given to those who die in actual mortal sin.

Those who deny God's right to demand of them faithful service in justice and mercy not only do evil deeds, but place themselves in a state and attitude hostile to God. Those who die in such a state, having rejected the friendship of God, fix their wills in an enduring hostility of God. They were made by God to enjoy God's very life, but they have fixed themselves in a firm will not to have divine life. God's judgment on them, then, is an affirmation of their own turning aside into self-frustrating malice, a malice which has been freely willed and which is hardened into permanence by death. Their punishment, then, their turning from God, is their own will. Thus human malice, not divine harshness, makes hell necessary.

The mystery of hell remains disturbing. We ought to dread the thought that persons created for eternal life could shape their wills to unending rejection of God. But it is our comfort that the Son of God chose to die on the cross to save from such punishment all who would be willing to come to everlasting life.

Eternal Life

The Christian who unites one's own dying with the death of Jesus sees death as coming to Him and as an entering into eternal life. When the Church has for the last time spoken the forgiving words of Christ's absolution over the dying Christian, and for the last time sealed one with strengthening anointing, and has given one Christ in Viaticum as food for the journey, it speaks with gentle assurance:
Go forth, faithful Christian.
May you live in peace this day,
may your home be with God in Zion,
with Mary the virgin Mother of God,
with Joseph, and all the angels and saints.
My brother (sister) in faith,
I entrust you to God who created you. . . .
May Mary, the angels, and all the saints
come to meet you as you go forth from this life.
May Christ who has crucified for you
bring you freedom and peace. . . .

---

[18]Cf. Second Council of Orange, 529 (DS 397); Council of Trent, Session 6, January 13, 1547, *Decree on Justification*, canon 17 on justification (DS 1567).

May you see your Redeemer face to face
and enjoy the sight of God for ever.[19]

The Church teaches that those who die in grace will enter into the presence of Jesus and the beatifying vision of the Blessed Trinity. Should they die in venial sin, or still have penance to do for forgiven sins, there may first be a time of purification. But those who die in faith and love may die with great peace. They are entering into life (cf. LG 48).

The Church, to be sure, makes a clear distinction between the events that occur when the individual Christian dies and those which will occur when Christ comes on the last day as Lord and Judge of all. But in each case there is a coming of Christ to His own, and an entrance into life. Already at the death of the individual what may be called the "relative fullness" of eternal life begins for those who are rightly disposed. For already they enter into companionship with Christ, His mother, and the blessed, and in glory behold God Himself as He is (cf. LG 49).

Communion of Saints

The death of the individual has ecclesial significance. For the Church is not only the family of those living in faith here on earth. It is a communion of saints. It reaches into eternity, embracing also all who are being purified to enter the blessed vision and all who are already rejoicing in beholding God's glory (cf. LG 49). Our union with those we love "who have gone to sleep in the peace of Christ is not in the least interrupted" (LG 49). Their entrance into life has not ended their relevance to us. Through their entrance into life we too are brought nearer to God (cf. LG 49).

Their blessedness is not yet totally fulfilled, for they await the final resurrection and the sharing of that flesh which is part of their being in the joy of eternal life. They await the glorification of Jesus which the events of the last day will mean, and the gathering into total newness of life of the full number of all the redeemed. But the essential core of beatitude is already and irrevocably theirs. They have come to see and to possess their God in the blessed vision.

Even now the life of the blessed is a dynamic reality. They not only enjoy the blessedness of God's immediate presence, the indescribable happiness of knowing and loving God as He knows and loves Himself, but they also contribute to the building of the kingdom by praying for their brothers and sisters in Christ who are still here on

---

[19]*Rite of Anointing and Pastoral Care of the Sick*, Rite for the Commendation of the Dying, nn. 146-147.

earth (cf. LG 49). Their happiness is intensified by the realization that they can influence the salvation of those whom they know and love. They perceive in glory the absolute goodness of God, and they share with the great "cloud of witnesses" (Heb. 12.1) the perfect peace of Christ as they await with joyful longing the final resurrection and final judgment when all will be made perfect in God.

32

The Fulfillment Of All

"Here we have no lasting city, but we are looking for the city that is to come" (Heb. 13.14). Salvation history aims at a final fulfillment. Even now the work of Christ goes on in the world. Already the kingdom of God has begun to appear; already it grows. But it awaits a decisive act of God, a deed of Christ, to bring to completion the work He has begun in us. Christian faith is not waiting for a final catastrophe to mark the end of time; rather, it looks forward with confidence to God's total deliverance of His people into perfect freedom and complete fullness of life.

In this chapter we discuss the elements that enter into this crowning of God's work in Christ: the end of history as it now is, and the transformation of the world by God; Christ's second coming, the resurrection of the body, the final judgment, and the life to come.

The End Is the Beginning

Everlasting life is not a joy or blessedness unrelated to the labors and love manifest in history. It is that for which this world was made, the fullness of life "prepared for you from the foundation of the world" (Matt. 25.34). Every blessing we receive in this present life is to lead toward that fulfillment which is the crown and meaning of all the things that are.

God's plan for creation began to be fulfilled in the very act of His creating. The final triumph of God's heavenly victory has its seeds in this world.

This is one reason why our work in this world has such importance and dignity. Human efforts to put intelligence and care into the service of divine love, and into the remaking of this world, are elements in the building up of God's kingdom. Here on earth God's kingdom "is already present in mystery" (GS 39); human labors can serve the growth of that kingdom, and then "when the Lord comes, it will be brought to full flower" (GS 39).

God did not create us to be a merely passive recipients of His mercies. He calls us to a greater glory. God made us in His image, that by His grace we might freely work with God in history, doing His deeds, and by His mercy ourselves assisting in building up fruits of our labor that will never perish.

Transformation of the World

To say that this world will end is not to say that it will be utterly annihilated. It is the world as we know it that is passing away (cf. 1 Cor. 7.31; 1 John 2.17). For the world itself is to be radically transformed.

"As deformed by sin, the shape of this world will pass away" (GS 39). All that is unworthy of the final glory of God's loved ones will be destroyed, but all that is precious and good will be brought to full flowering. "After we have obeyed the Lord, and in His spirit nurtured on earth the values of human dignity, brotherhood, and freedom, and indeed all the good fruits of nature and of our enterprise, we will find them again, but freed of stain, burnished, transfigured. . ." (GS 39).

Thus the material world itself will in a certain sense participate in the paschal mystery. It too will have a death or destruction that leads to rich renewal. Some passages of Scripture stress the dying aspect of this transition. "The elements will be dissolved with fire, and the earth and everything that is done on it will be disclosed" (2 Peter 3.10). But, as the sacred author of that passage goes on to say: "We wait for new heavens and a new earth" (2 Peter 3.13; cf. Isa. 65.17; 66.22). St. Jerome speaks with the voice of Catholic tradition when he says in his commentary on Isaiah: "He did not say that we shall see different heavens and a different earth, but the old and ancient ones transformed into something better."[1] St. Thomas Aquinas writes of the enduring gift of creation: " 'God has formed all things that they might have being' (Wisd. 1.14) and not that they might revert to nothingness."[2]

Some of the scriptural language on last things is written in a special literary style. It is apocalyptic language, language that is deliberately heavy with intensely vivid imagery. But the apocalyptic images must be balanced with other scriptural promises of renewal and restoration if one is to understand the balanced message of faith. St. Thomas Aquinas drew on a vast treasury of Christian tradition when he offered his interpretation of the signs which Scripture says will mark the last days and indicate the time of Christ's coming, that is, the wars, the terrors, the signs in the heavens and on earth. "But it is not easy to know what these signs may be. For the signs we read of in the Gospels, as Augustine says, . . . refer not only to Christ's coming in judgment, but also to the time of the sack of Jerusalem, and to the coming of Christ in ceaselessly visiting His Church. . . . These signs that are mentioned in the Gospel, such as wars, fears, and so

[1]St. Jerome, *In Isaiam* 18.65 (ML 24.644).
[2]St. Thomas Aquinas, *Quaestiones Quodlibetales* 4.4.

forth, have been from the beginning of the human race; unless perhaps we say that at that time they will be more prevalent."[3]

Equally to be remembered is the promise of positive fulfillment of material creation when, in the last days, God's own saving action will bring to glorious completion all His mercies, and all the works that the just have done in His name. "The creation itself will be set free from its bondage to decay and will obtain the freedom of the glory of the children of God" (Rom. 8.21).

Against this background we can see the goodness of created things and the fruitfulness of grace-inspired labor and their place in the world to come. "For all things are yours, whether . . . the world of life or death or the present or the future" (1 Cor. 3.21-22). Created realities are good, and they are to be transformed in Christ so as to be given eventually to the Father. "All belongs to you; and you belong to Christ; and Christ belongs to God" (1 Cor. 3.22-23). And all the labors by which we seek now to make the kingdom grow will become part of that harvest which is to be gathered into eternal life (cf. Matt. 13.30).

We do not know exactly how this world will be transformed, and we cannot adequately imagine the future shape of present realities. But we do know that there is a certain permanence to our temporal activity. The ultimate factor in this permanence is love, that which "never ends" (1 Cor. 13.8).

The Transforming Love of God

What is built on selfless, benevolent love will not pass away. It is our most important contribution to the transforming work of Christ. And like His love, it will remain. Selfless love is our contribution to the final reality, the "new creation." Toward that we labor by seeking to transform the world now by works of love.

The Book of Revelation deals with judgment and hope, with sin and deliverance. It speaks of the struggles in time of those who serve God's kingdom on earth, and it speaks also of the triumphant joy of the final realization of that kingdom.

"Listen! I am standing at the door and knocking; if you hear My voice and open the door, I will come in to you and eat with you, and you with Me. To the one who conquers I will give a place with Me on My throne, just as I Myself conquered and sat down with My Father on His throne" (Rev. 3.20-21).

It is Christ who speaks, and He calls Himself "the Amen, the faithful and true witness, the origin of God's creation" (Rev. 3.14). In Jesus the divine promises have been realized; in His humanity there

---

[3]St. Thomas Aquinas, *Summa Theologica*, Suppl. 73,1. Cf. St. Augustine, *Epistula* 199 (ML 33.904-925).

already shines the glory that God will give on the last day to those who are His adopted sons and daughters in Christ. The risen Christ is the culmination of the history of salvation. He is not only the goal of that history; He is also its starting point, for all things have been created in Him (cf. John 1.3). Anyone who responds to the personal call of Christ will participate with his Lord in the joys of the banquet in the life that is to come. The victor will not only live with Christ, but will also share in Christ's royalty and His power as judge.

But the new creation is described also in more social terms. "I heard a loud voice from the throne saying, 'See, the home of God is among mortals. He will dwell with them as their God; they shall be His people, and God Himself will be with them; He will wipe away every tear from their eyes. Death will be no more; mourning and crying and pain will be no more, for the first things have passed away. . . . It is done! I am the Alpha and the Omega, the beginning and the end. To the thirsty I will give water as a gift from the spring of the water of life' " (Rev. 21.3-4, 6).

Here we find the fulfillment of the Old Testament promises. All of humanity's ancient enemies, death, pain, sorrow, are removed. Their deepest longings, their thirst for an infinite good, will be satisfied. God, who is with His people even now, will be with them then in a far richer way. Then indeed we shall be made utterly different, for we shall see God as He is (cf. 1 John 3.2), not "in a mirror dimly," but "face to face" (1 Cor. 13.12).

The passages of Revelation quoted above proclaim the mystery of God's redeeming love. Final fulfillment and peace are depicted as the work of God and His benevolent gift. But they are also shown to be the fruit of active response to God. They are reserved for those who have been faithful, who have cared, who have thirsted.

What we shall be and have in eternal life is, however, already in its seed present in those who love Christ, who live in faith, hope, and love. Though we are but wayfarers, in a pilgrim Church, we have already within us the beginnings of eternal life. Already we have been set free from the despair and the blindness of not knowing God; already His life gives energy to us in the gifts of grace. Already we are signed with the Holy Spirit, the "pledge of our inheritance" (Eph. 1.14).

Hence our longing for eternal life is not just a dream; nor is it a turning aside from the tasks of this life. It is a thirst for that life which we have already begun to possess in drawing near to Christ. It is not a renouncement of this world, but a recognition that this world is only a beginning, and that within its depths already lie the beginnings of what is to be. It is because we love the world, and wish it to be fulfilled, to have its longings entirely satisfied and its life brought to perfection, that we look forward in hope to the life that is to come.

The Parousia

Catholic faith has always looked forward with confident hope to the final coming of Christ in glory. The early Christians' "Marana tha," Aramaic for "Our Lord, come!" (1 Cor. 16.22; cf. Rev. 22.20), was an expression of their eager desire to see the final triumph of Christ's saving work. Christ indeed comes to His people in many ways, but they looked for that definitive coming of His that would crown all His mercies, end all sorrows, and bring His people to the fulfillment of all their hopes.

Jesus Himself promised that He will come in glory as Lord and Judge (cf. Matt. 16.27; 26.64; cf. also Dan. 7.13). At His ascension, when He ceased to be visibly present to His disciples, the promise was renewed: "This Jesus, who has been was taken up from you into heaven, will come in the same way as you saw Him go into heaven" (Acts 1.11). Expectation of His coming shines throughout the New Testament, and in the Creed of the Mass the Church ever professes its faith in His promise: "He will come again in glory to judge the living and the dead."[4]

The awaited coming of Christ in glory is called the "Parousia." The word literally means presence or arrival; the ceremonial entry of a king or triumphant conqueror into a city was called a "parousia." The coming of Jesus, the Lord and Savior of all, will be the most joyful and triumphant of all. In His Parousia He will be universally recognized as Lord of all. On that day those who have believed in Him and served Him will be proved right; His glorification will be the beginning of the "life of the world to come."[5]

The Time of Parousia

We do not know when Jesus will come in glory. Some scriptural passages suggest it is imminent (cf., e.g., Matt. 10.33; Luke 21.32; 1 Thess. 4.13-18), while others caution against concluding that it is at hand (cf. 2 Thess. 2.1-6; 2 Peter 3.3-9). Some passages that seem to suggest imminence may more properly have reference to the fall of Jerusalem in the first century; some scriptural scholarship suggests that sayings of Jesus about the fall of Jerusalem may have been inter-mingled with His sayings about the last days by the evangelists, be-cause they viewed the fall of Jerusalem as a symbol and sign of the day of the Lord's final judgment. Moreover, the hopes and desires of the early Christians to see the Parousia may have led many to expect that it would occur soon. But equally prominent in the New Testament are passages that stress the complete uncertainty about the time of

[4]Roman Missal, The Order of Mass, Profession of Faith.
[5]Roman Missal, The Order of Mass, Profession of Faith.

Christ's second coming. "The Son of Man is coming at an unexpected hour" (Matt. 24.44; cf. Mark 13.30-32).

Even as the early Christians longed and hoped to see His coming, they planted the Church in many places and provided for the future years. For they knew that all time is short in comparison with eternity, that with the Lord a thousand years are "like one day" (2 Peter 3.8). The actual time of Parousia is known only to God, but it will come unexpectedly, "like a thief" (2 Peter 3.10).

The promises of Jesus' second coming are often framed in the colorful style of apocalyptic literature. The different images found in different parts of Scripture are not themselves elements of the message of faith, but they express in vivid ways that which the faith does proclaim. They express the Christian belief that history as it now is, with its ambiguous intermingling of faith and unbelief, of good and evil, will come to an end, that God will be vindicated and evil definitively overcome, and that in this saving deed of God Christ will be revealed clearly to all as the Redeemer and Lord of all.

The Catholic faith does not encourage naive literalism in the interpretation of the symbolic expressions used in Scripture to describe the end of history. Such literalism can lead to misreadings of revelation. Faulty interpretation of certain scriptural passages (e.g., 2 Peter 3.10; Rev. 20.4-5) has led some to describe what early Christians looked forward to with great joy as cruel destruction at the end of time. Similarly, some people have mistakenly come to expect a Messianic kingdom in which Christ together with the saints would rule a temporal kingdom on earth for a thousand years (hence the term "millenarianism") before the final entrance into heaven. But such millenarianism is alien to the message of faith.[6] The Church's teaching associates Christ's second coming proximately with the resurrection of the dead, with final judgment, and with the glory of His eternal kingdom.

The expectation of Christ's coming is indeed a longing for a fulfillment that is to come. But it is also a revelation of a kingdom present even now in those who share by grace in the saving work of Christ (cf. John 12.31; 2 Cor. 5.17;6.2). The Parousia will bring to completion what already is, for we are God's children now (cf. 1 John 3.2). The central event in history is not the last day, but the resurrection of Jesus. When He rose from the dead, the "end of the age" (Matt. 28.20) had already begun. In the Parousia the full glory of Christ's rising will shine forth. Its power will extend to His disciples, raising them from the dead. Its splendor will renew the whole universe, making "all things new" (Rev. 21.5).

---

[6]Cf. Decree of the Holy Office, July 19, 1944, confirmed by Pope Pius XII, July 20, 1944 (DS 3839).

The Resurrection of the Body

Intimately associated with Christ's Parousia is the resurrection of the dead. "For the Lord Himself, with a cry of command, with the archangel's call and with the sound of God's trumpet, will descend from heaven, and the dead in Christ will rise first" (1 Thess. 4.16).

Catholic teaching on what it is to be a human person, and on the breadth of our hope, and on the power of Christ's resurrection, demands faith in our bodily resurrection. All of us, both those who are saved and those who have rejected salvation (cf. John 5.29), will rise again with our own bodies. Those who have died will no longer be dead. The Church "firmly believes and steadfastly teaches" that "on the day of judgment all men will appear before the tribunal of Christ with their own bodies, to give an account of their deeds."[7]

Faith in our resurrection is inseparable from faith in Jesus' resurrection. For He is the new Adam; He rose not for His own sake, but as our Head, as the pattern of our rising and as the life-giving source of our new life. "Now if Christ is proclaimed as raised from the dead, how can some of you say that there is no resurrection of the dead? If there is no resurrection of the dead, then Christ has not been raised; and if Christ has not been raised, then our proclamation has been in vain and your faith has been in vain" (1 Cor. 15.12-14).

This is a constant theme in Pauline thought. "The One who raised the Lord Jesus will raise us also with Jesus and will bring us with you into His presence" (2 Cor. 4.14). "Therefore we have been buried with Him by baptism into death, so that just as Christ was raised from the dead by the glory of the Father, so we too might walk in newness of life. ... We know that Christ, being raised from the dead will never die again; death no longer has dominion over Him. ... So you also must consider yourselves dead to sin and alive to God in Christ Jesus" (Rom. 6.4, 9, 11). All Christian life, even now on earth, is a sharing in the resurrection; but our rising with Him will be fulfilled in the resurrection on the last day.

Then will be fulfilled the promise of Christ: "I am the resurrection and the life. Those who believe in Me, even though they die, will live" (John 11.25). For He is the Author of life (cf. John 1.4) and the living Bread come down from heaven so that those who eat of it might have everlasting life (cf. John 6.50).

Christian belief in this mystery was considered so essential that there is an abundance of writing in the Fathers defending this truth and seeking to explain its full significance. It is mentioned in most of the

---

[7]Second Council of Lyons, Session 4, July 6, 1274, *Profession of Faith of Emperor Michael Palaeologus* (DS 859). Cf. Fourth Council of the Lateran, November 1215, *The Catholic Faith* (DS 801); also LG 48; also Congregation for the Doctrine of the Faith, *Letter on Certain Questions concerning Eschatology* (May 17, 1979) (EV 6.1528-1549).

early professions of faith, and it received clear dogmatic affirmation in councils of the Church.[8] It will be a universal resurrection; all the dead, both the just and the unjust, will rise with the same bodies they had before death.

The doctrine of the final resurrection reminds us again of what we are, of the fact that a human person is not simply a spirit. It is the whole person, flesh enlivened by spirit, who accomplishes the tasks to which we have been called by God; it is the whole person who is called to life forever with God.

The Same Flesh Transformed

In the final resurrection our bodies will be transformed. We do not know precisely how. "But someone will ask, 'How are the dead raised? With what kind of body do they come?' Fool!" (1 Cor. 15.35-36). One who sees only a seed, a beginning of life, cannot grasp from that the splendor of what will be. "And as for what you sow, you do not sow the body that is to be, but a bare seed, perhaps of wheat or of some other grain. But God gives it a body as He has chosen, and to each kind of seed its own body" (1 Cor. 15.37-38). But of this we are certain: "For this perishable body must put on imperishability, and this mortal body must put on immortality" (1 Cor. 15.53). Then shall we rejoice in the fulfillment of the ancient promises, and the last enemy, death, will be definitively conquered, "swallowed up in victory" (1 Cor. 15.54; cf. Isa. 25.8).

Christ's resurrection from the dead is the pattern of our rising. The Gospels recognize the mystery and glory of His new life, but they emphasize two points. One is the element of identity. The risen body of Jesus is that very body in which He suffered and died on the cross. "Look at My hands and My feet, see that it is I Myself" (Luke 24.39). The other point is that His risen body is transformed. He "became a life-giving spirit" (1 Cor. 15.45).

So also, then, will all who rise to new life in Christ be transformed. Each will rise as the same person as before, in the same flesh made living by the same spirit. But the life of those who have risen will be richly enlarged and deepened.

St. Paul tells us that the Spirit dwelling in us will bring our mortal bodies to life (cf. Rom. 8.11). Because of His resurrection, Christ has become a life-giving Spirit, and He sends His Spirit to us as a pledge of our own future resurrection (cf. Rom. 8.23). All of us who have the Spirit dwelling in us are already being "transformed into the same image from one degree of glory to another" (2 Cor. 3.18); we are already being prepared for our bodily resurrection.

[8]See note 7.

The just will come forth "to the resurrection of life" (John 5.29). The life they will enter is a rich personal life in union with the risen Christ and with all the saved. Jesus is described as being in heaven (cf. 1 Thess. 1.10), and heaven is our homeland: "Our citizenship is in heaven" (Phil. 3.20). Our presence with the risen Lord will be permanent (cf. 1 Thess. 4.17). There will be a reunion of all those who believe in and love Christ (cf. 1 Thess. 4.17; 2 Cor. 4.14). Bodily resurrection, implying the transformation of the whole person, will be the beginning and in a real sense the source of the definitive happiness of the community of believers in Christ.

General Judgment

"When the Son of man comes in His glory . . . all the nations will gathered before Him, and He will separate people one from another as a shepherd separates the sheep from the goats. . . . Then the King will say to those at His right hand, 'Come, you that are blessed by My Father, inherit the kingdom prepared for you from the foundation of the world' " (Matt. 25.31-34).

The general judgment will not be simply a collective summing up of all the particular and individual judgments of men and women after their deaths. For this last judgment will be far more than a judicial passing of sentence upon the good and the evil. In and through this judgment God will establish the heavenly community, the ultimate stage of His kingdom. In judging, He will bring all to completion.

There we will be judged by our deeds of love. "I was hungry and you gave Me food, I was thirsty and you gave Me something to drink" (Matt. 25.35). We will be judged according to our relationship to Christ. Not only those who know Him explicitly in the light of clear faith, but all human persons, at least in obscure but real ways, are affected in this life by His saving power. He invites all to respond freely to His saving love, and He invites all to life. To love Him is to keep the great command of love, to love God with the whole heart and to love the neighbor in whom He dwells. At the last judgment, then, each of us will be judged by the love we have shown Christ in our midst.

Christ as Judge

It is God who judges. The final judgment of all will be shared in by the three Persons of the Trinity, each in a way befitting His role in redemption. Because it is through the incarnate Word that the Blessed Trinity has saved us, it is Christ as man who is presented as the supreme Judge of people. "He is the one ordained by God as judge of the living and the dead" (Acts 10.42). This will be the crowning act of Christ as Savior. Through it He will complete His work as Redeemer, because through it He will bring about His Father's will that all might be made one, that they might be gathered into the final kingdom.

Christ's goodness will shine even in the condemnation of those who have rejected God, and have said no to the love that is the center and crown of existence, who have refused to build up the kingdom of justice, mercy, and peace. Christ's just sentence will recognize and confirm their own deliberate and definitive rejection of God. His holiness will be exalted by the manifest fairness of His condemnation of those who have freely chosen not to respond to that Love which called them to a life to which they could come only freely. The condemned will be bitterly aware that it is they themselves who have freely rejected the saving mercy of their Lord.

The centrality and lordship of Christ will shine in the hour of judgment; so also will His boundless love for the Father and His will to draw us to that first Source of all that is good. "When all things are subjected to Him, then the Son Himself will also be subjected to the One who put all things in subjection under Him, so that God may be all in all" (1 Cor. 15.28). At that hour all who have died in Christ will fully realize that which cannot now be comprehended: "What no eye has seen, nor ear heard, nor the human heart conceived, what God has prepared for those who love Him" (1 Cor. 2.9).

Eternal Life

To enter heaven is not simply to go to a particular place. Heaven is more a way of being, a sharing in divine life and joy, than a place. Still, for human beatitude, place is not entirely irrelevant. Jesus has risen bodily, and where His living humanity is it is good for those who love Him to be. We do not know where heaven is, but we do know that God is able to provide for the bodily creatures He has made a splendor to adorn their glorious life in Him.

The scriptural expectation of "new heavens and a new earth" (2 Peter 3.13; cf. Isa. 65.17; 66.22; Rev. 21.1) seem to suggest that in the age to come the whole renewed universe will be heaven to those who have loved God and dwell in His light. The Church in its teaching on heaven, however, is not concerned with any particular theories of space and time. It does not teach, for example, that all places that are real are part of an indefinitely large space, and that heaven is some finite distance from here. It makes no effort to locate heaven. But it teaches that God is real, and life in Him is real, that the risen Christ is real, and that it is the joy of His people to be with Christ.

To enter heaven is to reach the fullness of life. Even here, in this present life, we share in divine life by faith, hope, and love. But our eternal life in time is only a seed, a promise; it imperfectly expresses and points us toward that fullness of life we shall have in heaven. Then, when faith is no more, because we shall see God as He is, and when we no longer hope, because the promises of God will be completely fulfilled, and when we love with a gladness no one will take from us (cf. John 16.22), then we shall live with the fullness of eternal life for which we were made.

Scripture speaks to us in many images of that life to come which we cannot now fully understand. But in its images it brings a message that is an essential teaching of faith, for there is much rich content in Catholic belief about everlasting life.

It will be a life of rich interpersonal love. Our being will not be dissolved from its personal autonomy and individuality into some vast divine substance. We shall remain persons, personally sharing the intense love of the personal God. Thus Scripture speaks often of eternal life under the image of the joyful personal celebration of a banquet and often as a wedding meal (cf. Matt. 22.1-4; 25.1-13; Rev. 21.2; 22.17), and Christ is present as the Bridegroom. Persons and personal love endure forever (cf. 1 Cor. 13.8).

While we will become like God in the splendor of His gifts in seeing Him and loving Him, God remains forever God and we will always be His creatures. No shadowy pantheism will dilute the joy of eternal thanks and gladness before God.

"The throne of God and of the Lamb will be in it, and His servants shall worship Him; they will see His face, and His name will be on their foreheads. And there will be no more night; they need no light of lamp or sun, for the Lord God will be their light, and they will reign forever and ever" (Rev. 22.3-5).

God Is Our Beatitude

Those who come to eternal life will enjoy every manner of blessing, but the heart of their joy will be the possession of God Himself. "Nevertheless I am continually with You; You hold my right hand. You guide me with Your counsel, and afterward You will receive me with honor. Whom have I in heaven but You? And there is nothing on earth that I desire other than You. ... But God is the strength of my heart and my portion forever" (Ps. 73.23-26).

Eternal life is possessing God perfectly. No longer shall we see Him merely by faith, but we shall see Him "face to face" (1 Cor. 13.12). "We will be like Him, for we will see Him as He is" (1 John 3.2). Those who enter eternal life "see the divine essence intuitively and face to face, with no creature acting as a medium of vision for what they see, but with the divine essence showing itself to them plainly, clearly, and openly," and by so grasping and rejoicing in the immediately present reality of God they are "truly happy and have life and eternal rest."[9]

To possess God in that way is far more than simply to "see" Him or to know Him. As His infinite life is His knowing and loving and His rejoicing in infinite goodness, so God brings those who come to eternal life to share intensely in His inner life. "Enter into the joy of your master" (Matt. 25.21).

Then we shall understand why we have been called to God to love, as we see in the Blessed Trinity the pattern of all love. Then we shall see what it is to be a person, and how being a person is being called to community and the giving of self. The inner life of the Trinity is personal self-giving. The Father communicates Himself totally to the Son, giving Him all that He has and is, while remaining the Father. The Father and the Son is boundless love communicate their whole being to the Spirit, giving Him all that He has and is, while remaining distinct from Him. In the glory of God's kingdom we shall not only see the eternally generous love of the Trinity; we shall be invited to be shaped by it as fully as possible. We shall taste Their joy in giving ourselves fully to the Father, Son, and Holy Spirit, and to one another, when God has strengthened and transformed our love.

Our Native Land

Then only shall we cease to be pilgrims and strangers (cf. Heb. 11, 13), and we shall know that we have come to the land where we are fully at home. Our period of exile (cf. 1 Peter 1.17) will be ended when we have come to the Life to which our whole heart can give itself in gladness. Then shall we begin to know one another fully, in the light of God, and love one another entirely. We shall remember and understand all the experiences and trials of this life without regret,[10] infinitely grateful that God has enabled us to serve Him freely and has crowned His first gifts with the second life that exceeds all our longing.

Nothing will be lost of all the precious things that were. In the resurrection the flesh of all whom we have loved will have been restored; the new heavens and new earth will guard all that has been holy and precious in time. God is our infinite treasure; but it is His glory to give superabundantly, and to enrich with added joys and human interpersonal love the deep central joy that is the life of each heart.

Each shall be perfectly happy in knowing and loving the Blessed Trinity and all the brothers and sisters in Christ. But though each will have all the understanding and joy one can bear, the gladness of the blessed will differ according to the measure of each one's love. "In-

[9]Pope Benedict XII, Constitution, *Benedictus Deus* (January 29, 1336) (DS 1000).
[10]Cf. St. Augustine, *De Civitate Dei* 22.30.1 (ML 41.801).

deed star differs from star in glory. So it is with the resurrection of the dead" (1 Cor. 15.41-42). Some are rewarded in clarity of vision "more perfectly than others according to their respective merits."[11] But this difference is known and rejoiced in without jealousy, for each is filled with all the gladness one is capable of. "They feast on the abundance of Your house, and You give them drink from the river of Your delights. For with You is the fountain of life; in Your light we see light" (Ps. 36.8-9).

To this life, which we now understand so poorly, Christ earnestly invites us. Now, in time, He calls out to us through the promptings of His Holy Spirit and the voice of His Bride, the Church. "The Spirit and the Bride say, 'Come.' And let everyone who hears say, 'Come.' And let everyone who is thirsty come. Let anyone who wishes take the water of life as a gift" (Rev. 22.17).

[11]Council of Florence, Bull, *Laetentur Caeli* (July 6, 1439) (DS 1305).

Appendixes

The Bible

Throughout this catechism we have referred to the Bible and to particular sections within it. Even though it is now commonly published as a single volume, the Bible actually consists of a collection of sacred writings, or scriptures, composed over the course of many centuries. They are entirely exceptional writings, which the Church recognizes in faith as God's special message to those whom He calls. All of the Church's teaching and preaching must be nourished and regulated by Holy Scripture. "For in the sacred books, the Father who is in heaven meets His children with great love and speaks with them; and the force and power in the word of God is so great that it stands as the support and energy of the Church, the strength of faith for her sons, the food of the soul, the pure and perennial source of spiritual life. Consequently, these words are perfectly applicable to Sacred Scripture: 'For the word of God is living and efficient' (Heb. 4.12) and it is 'able to build up and give the inheritance among all the sanctified" (Acts 20.32; cf. 1 Thess. 2.13)" (DV 21).

Inspiration and Inerrancy

Other groups besides Christians possess and revere collections of religious literature, but the distinguishing characteristic of the Bible in its divine inspiration. Acting as the principal Author, God moved ("inspired") the human authors of the Scriptures to understand and freely will to write precisely what He wished them to write. Being God's word in this unique fashion did not keep the Scriptures from being cast in a rich variety of literary forms ranging from intricate and mystical psalm prayers to highly interpretative and often poetically formulated styles of religious historical narratives. Though common in the Ancient Near East and as accurate as our contemporary equivalents, these literary forms can at times be very enigmatic to modern readers. Yet, because it is divine as well as human, the Bible achieves the varieties of communication peculiar to each of these forms free from any error regarding that which the divine Author wished specifically to express.

The Canon of Scripture

The dual traits of inspiration and inerrancy have been recognized and taught by the People of God Since even before the Bible was completed. Corresponding to these qualities of the text of Scripture, the Church possessed the ability in faith first to distinguish and then to preserve and use the various parts or "books" of what came to be called the Bible. These divinely inspired works were produced over a period of more than a thousand years.

The official or standard list of these inspired writings is still referred to by the Greek word "canon," a word used among the early Christians and meaning a measuring standard or rule. The Canon of Scripture is divided into two main sections, called the Old Testament and the New Testament, and these contain the books written before and after the life of Jesus respectively. This terminology derives from the testaments or contractual agreements dominating the relationship between God and His people ratified at Sinai (the Mosaic Covenant) and at the Last Supper (the New Covenant).

Content and Arrangement

There is no universally accepted sequence which the Old Testament canon follows, although the most frequent pattern places historical materials first (within this class the first five books of the Old Testament form a special set, often called the Pentateuch, or the Mosaic Books, or the *Torah*, the Law), followed by so-called wisdom or sapiential literature, and then prophetic or exhortational writings. When this division is used, the books of the Old Testament (some of which have alternative names) are typically listed in the following order:

> *The Pentateuch*
> > Genesis
> > Exodus
> > Leviticus
> > Numbers
> > Deuteronomy
>
> *The Historical Books*
> > Joshua (Josue)
> > Judges
> > Ruth
> > 1 Samuel (1 Kings)
> > 2 Samuel (2 Kings)
> > 1 Kings (3 Kings)
> > 2 Kings (4 Kings)

1 Chronicles (1 Paralipomenon)
2 Chronicles (2 Paralipomenon)
Ezra (1 Esdras)
 Nehemiah (2 Esdras)
Tobit (Tobias)
Judith
Esther
1 Maccabees (1 Machabees)
2 Maccabees (2 Machabees)
The Wisdom Books
Job
Psalms
Proverbs
Ecclesiastes (Qoheleth)
Song of Songs
Wisdom
Sirach (Ecclesiasticus)
The Prophets
Isaiah (Isaias)
Jeremiah (Jeremias)
Lamentations
Baruch
Ezekiel (Ezechiel)
Daniel
Hosea (Osee)
Joel
Amos
Obadiah (Abdias)
Jonah (Jonas)
Micah (Michaeas)
Nahum
Habakkuk (Habacuc)
Zephaniah (Sophonias)
Haggai (Aggeus)
Zechariah (Zecharias)
Malachi (Malachias)

A standardized order of the New Testament books is more commonly found. It begins with four accounts of events in the life of Jesus called Gospels. The word "gospel" means "good news," a term Christianity has applied from earliest times to its Founder's presence and deeds and their saving effects. All four canonical Gospels present the "good news" in this basic sense. Differences in the evangelists' choice of material and manner of retelling it (vocabulary, sequence, inclusion of details, and the like) evidence the different readerships for which the Gospels were originally designed as well as the theological emphases of their human composers. The fifth book in the New Testament canon is the Acts of the Apostles, in which we have an historical record of the first decades of the Church. Next are the Epistles, letters of instruction and correction written to the first Christian communities by their apostolic pastors. Varying in length from the sixteen chapters of the Epistle to the Romans down to the few sentences of the Second and Third Epistles of St. John, they preserve a treasure of details about the joys and problems of the first-century Church. The last book of the New Testament, and hence of the Bible, is Revelation, known also as the Apocalypse. This is a highly symbolic depiction of the final triumph of Christ, the punishment of His adversaries, and the establishment of the just in heaven to praise and share the divine glory. The New Testament canon, then, is as follows:

Gospels: Matthew
Mark
Luke
John
The Acts of the Apostles
Epistles: Romans
1 Corinthians
2 Corinthians
Galatians
Ephesians
Philippians
Colossians
1 Thessalonians
2 Thessalonians
1 Timothy
2 Timothy
Titus
Philemon
Hebrews
James
1 Peter
2 Peter
1 John
2 John
3 John
Jude
Revelation (Apocalypse)

For a period of time shortly before the rise of Protestantism in the sixteenth century certain critics questioned the canonical authenticity or divine inspiration of some parts of the Bible. To some extent at least this was a revival of questions raised in some quarters centuries earlier. The Council of Trent (Session 4, April 8, 1546) resolved any doubts in this area for Catholics by declaring that all the books of the Old and New Testaments (as listed above) were equally inspired in their entirety, a declaration reaffirmed by both the First and Second Vatican Councils. One surviving residue of the historical disagreement is reflected in Catholic authors' references to the sections that had been called into question as "deuterocanonical," while some or all of the same material is usually labeled "apocryphal" by other church groups which exclude some or all of it from their Bibles or include the parts they consider noncanonical in separate appendixes. The word "deuterocanonical" means literally "of or pertaining to a second canon." The Council of Trent did not establish a new list of the books of the Bible, but rather it formally confirmed the canonicity of all parts of the list fixed in tradition more than a thousand years earlier. The deuterocanonical parts of the Bible are Tobit, Judith, 1 Maccabees, 2 Maccabees, Wisdom, Sirach, Baruch, and parts of Esther and Daniel, and, in the New Testament, Hebrews, James, 2 Peter, 2 John, 3 John, Jude, and Revelation.

Interpretation and Use

Just as it has the exclusive ability to distinguish which writings constitute the Bible, the Church alone possesses the means to understand and interpret Scripture infallibly. Since God chose a literature and culture already separated from us by more than nineteen centuries, continual research into the world of the human authors and their contemporaries is the indispensable cost of further insight into the sacred text. To help those without special training to read this literature, the Catholic Church has long insisted on the tradition that editions of the Bible include notes explaining unusual or disputed passages.

Moreover, because God and His Self-revelation infinitely transcend and surpass us, His help is an absolute necessity if we are to expand our horizons, so limited by sin, apathy, and human nature itself. The use of the Bible by groups or individuals remains an occasion for God's continuous grace and enlightenment to those who avail themselves of its riches. This is why the Church so strongly urges that studying and praying from the Bible be the lifelong project of every Christian. The Catholic reads and studies the Scripture always within the family and Spirit of the Church. "Sacred tradition and Sacred Scripture form one sacred deposit of the word of God, which is committed to the Church. . . . The task of authentically interpreting the word of God, whether written or handed on, has been entrusted exclusively to the living teaching office (*Magisterium*) of the Church, whose authority is exercised in the name of Jesus Christ. This teaching office is not above the word of God, but serves it, teaching only what has been handed on, listening to it devoutly, guarding it scrupulously and explaining it faithfully in accord with a divine commission and with the help of the Holy Spirit; it draws from this one deposit of faith everything which it presents for belief as divinely revealed. It is clear, therefore, that sacred tradition, Sacred Scripture and the teaching authority (*Magisterium*) of the Church, in accord with God's most wise design, are so linked and joined together that one cannot stand without the others, and that all together and each in its own way under the action of the one Holy Spirit contribute effectively to the salvation of souls" (DV 10).

For those who wish further information on the Bible there is a vast amount of literature available, including Church documents, biblical commentaries and dictionaries, encyclopedias, and many individual works on parts and aspects of the Scriptures. The Bibliography in Appendix VI lists some of the many reference materials available. Of Church documents dealing with Scripture and various scriptural questions, special mention may be made here of Pope Pius XII's encyclical, *Divino Afflante Spiritu* (September 30, 1943), the Second Vatican Council's Dogmatic Constitution on Divine Revelation (*Dei Verbum*), and the Pontifical Biblical Commission's Instruction on the historical truth of the Gospels (*Sancta Mater Ecclesia*, April 21, 1964).

St. Peter And His Successors

St. Peter of Bethsaida in Galilee, Prince of the Apostles, who received from Jesus Christ the Supreme Pontifical Power to be transmitted to his Successors, resided first at Antioch, and then for twenty-five years at Rome, where he was martyred in the year 64 or 67.

Following is a listing of the successors of St. Peter, the Supreme Roman Pontiffs. The date in each instance, set off to the right, marks the end of each pontificate.

The General Councils Of The Church

A general or ecumenical council is an assembly of the bishops of the Church gathered together to consider and make decisions on ecclesiastical matters: on the doctrine, discipline, liturgy, and life of the Church. Decisions of a general council are binding on all members of the faithful. Church law, reflecting the teaching on the role of Peter in the Church, requires that a general council be called by and be approved by the Holy Father. No assembly of bishops can be a general council unless it is convoked by, or its convocation is approved by, the Roman Pontiff; no decrees or actions of a general council are effective and binding unless they are approved by the Roman Pontiff.

There have been twenty-one general councils. These are listed below with their dates and brief notes about them. The first eight general councils were held in the Greek-speaking East; all subsequent ones have been held in the West. The first general council was held in Nicaea in the year 325; the most recent was held at the Vatican in 1962-1965. The spacing of the general councils in the history of the Church has varied widely. There were two general councils in the fourth century, two in the fifth, one in the sixth, one in the seventh, one in the eighth, one in the ninth, none in the tenth or eleventh, three in the twelfth, three in the thirteenth, one in the fourteenth, two in the fifteenth, two in the sixteenth, and then none until the latter half of the nineteenth century. A mere sixteen years separated the ninth and tenth general councils; more than three centuries elapsed between the nineteenth and twentieth.

Considerable detail about the general councils is readily available in various histories of the Church, in encyclopedia and dictionary articles, and in separate works on individual councils or on certain periods of Church history. An excellent one-volume account in English of the first twenty general councils in historical perspective is *The Church in Crisis: A History of the General Councils, 325-1870*, by Philip Hughes (New York, Hanover House, 1961). The texts of the documents of all the general councils in their original languages and in English are published in *Decrees of the Ecumenical Councils*, ed. by N. P. Tanner (2 vols., Georgetown University Press, 1990). The documents of the Second Vatican Council are easily available in the original Latin and in translation in various editions. Some of these editions as well as other general reference works in English which include important selections from the documents of the earlier general councils are listed in the Bibliography given in Appendix VI.

1. First General Council of Nicaea, 325

The first general council, held in Nicaea in Asia Minor in 325, at a time when the Church faced the problem of Arianism, that is, the Christological heresy of Arius, defined that Christ is true God and true man, and is of the same substance (*homoousios*) as the Father. This council also promulgated twenty canons on disciplinary matters, especially the treatment of believers who had denied the faith during the persecutions.

2. First General Council of Constantinople, 381

This council ratified the teaching of Nicaea about Christ, and asserted that He had an integral human nature. The council defined that the three divine Persons of the Trinity are eternal and of the same divine nature. The creed attributed to this council is essentially the creed (Profession of Faith) of the Mass.

3. General Council of Ephesus, 431

Condemning the Christological heresy of Nestorius, this council defined again the doctrine of the true humanity of Christ, and taught that His mother, the blessed Virgin Mary, is, in virtue of the Incarnation, truly *Theotokos*, Mother of God.

4. General Council of Chalcedon, 451

This council taught that although Jesus Christ is God and man, He is but one Person, that is, one Person in two natures, one divine and one human.

5. Second General Council of Constantinople, 553

This council confirmed the teaching that Christ has two natures and condemned by name those who had taught differently concerning Him.

6. Third General Council of Constantinople, 680-681

This council upheld the truth that Christ, possessing two natures, also has two wills and two "operations," undivided, inseparable, and without confusion. The council taught that the human will of Christ is distinct from, but not opposed to, His divine will.

7. Second General Council of Nicaea, 787

This council proclaimed the efficacy of the intercession of saints and approved the veneration of icons and statues. This action assured the rightful place of sacred art in the religious life of the faithful.

8. Fourth General Council of Constantinople, 869-870

This council met to settle a quarrel over the legitimate patriarch of the see of Constantinople and to normalize relations of the Byzantine Church with the Holy See. The council's twenty-seven canons dealt with disciplinary matters. This was the last general council held in the East.

9. First General Council of the Lateran, 1123

This council, the first of the general councils held in the West, solemnly approved the texts of the Concordat of Worms, the agreement reached with Emperor Henry V in 1122 ending the old controversy over investiture. The council issued twenty-two canons dealing with disciplinary and moral matters.

10. Second General Council of the Lateran, 1139

This council as well was concerned largely with regulating the internal discipline of the Church. The council issued thirty canons.

11. Third General Council of the Lateran, 1179

This council also dealt with Church discipline and reform. Twenty-seven canons were issued. Among the acts of the council was change in the legislation on papal elections.

12. Fourth General Council of the Lateran, 1215

This council touched on almost every area of Catholic teaching about faith and morals. The first of its seventy canons is the famous profession of faith, *Firmiter*; the passage here on the sacrament of the Eucharist has the first use by a general council of the term "transubstantiated" (*transsubstantiatis pane in corpus, et vino in sanguinem*) to describe the mystery. The council condemned false notions about the nature and place of evil in the world and framed a number of general laws, including that concerning the Easter duty (confession at least once a year; reception of the Eucharist at least in Easter time).

13. First General Council of Lyons, 1245

This council concerned itself mainly with disciplinary legislation. Its principal achievement was the formal deposition of Emperor Frederick II.

14. Second General Council of Lyons, 1274

This council reunited the Greek Church and Rome. It defined that the Holy Spirit proceeds from both the Father and the Son (the Double Procession of the Holy Spirit), gave rulings about the election of the pope in conclave, and suppressed some of the minor religious orders.

15. General Council of Vienne, 1311-1312

This council issued a large number of disciplinary decrees. It defined that the rational or intellectual soul is *per se* and essentially the form of the human body.

16. General Council of Constance, 1414-1418

This council settled in Western Schism, a division in the Church that had resulted from the election of rival claimants to the papal throne. It was at this council that Pope Martin V was elected. The council provided for the holding of general councils more frequently, and enacted a number of decrees dealing with discipline and reform. Not all the degrees of this council received papal confirmation and approval.

17. General Council of Basel-Ferrara-Florence, 1431-1445

The sessions of this council were held at Basel were marked by conflict among the bishops and between them and Pope Eugene IV. Disciplinary decrees were enacted during this period. The Ferrara sessions dealt with the question of their legitimacy in opposition to schismatical sessions that continued at Basel; also at Ferrara, discussions were begun with representatives of the Greek Church over purgatory and the procession of the Holy Spirit from the Father and the Son. During the Florentine period of the council, the Greeks and Rome were again reunited, the reunion coming at the end of long debates on questions concerning Trinitarian theology, the primacy of the See of Peter, and other points. Reunions were also effected with the Armenians, Copts (Jacobites), and, after the site of the council had been moved to Rome, certain Syrian churches, Chaldeans, and the Maronites of Cyprus. The council's individual decrees touch on many doctrinal matters. The lengthy Decree for the Armenians repeats material from earlier councils and sets forth doctrine about the elements (matter and form) of the sacraments; the Decree for the Jacobites, also quite lengthy, includes an enumeration of the books of the Bible and presents a detailed teaching about Christ (Christology).

18. Fifth General Council of the Lateran, 1512-1517

This council taught, against an error of the day, the individuality and immortality of the human soul, and dealt with a number of disciplinary and reform matters.

19. General Council of Trent, 1545-1563

This Council reacted to the rise of Protestantism and reexamined and defined more fully the whole range of Christian teaching. It also enacted a comprehensive body of disciplinary legislation. The longest of the general councils in time elapsed from beginning to final closing, this council was interrupted for long periods by political and other circumstances and actually did its work during three relatively short periods: December 1545 to March 1547 (sessions 1-8); May 1551 to April 1552 (sessions 11-16); January 1962 to December 1963 (sessions 17-25). (Sessions 9 and 10 were at Bologna, to which the council was transferred in 1547; the council was suspended provisionally in February 1548 and formally in September 1549, and when the council reconvened in 1551 the site was again Trent.)

From the first Tridentine period we have dogmatic decrees on Scripture and tradition (session 4; this decree lists the books of the Bible and says that apostolic traditions are accepted with same piety and reverence as Scripture), on original sin (session 5), on justification (with 33 canons; session 6), and on the sacraments (with 13 canons on the sacraments in general, 14 on baptism, and 3 on confirmation; session 7).

Dogmatic decrees on the second Tridentine period are on the Eucharist (with 11 canons; session 13), on the sacrament of penance (with 15 canons; session 14), and on the sacrament of extreme unction (with 4 canons; session 14).

The third and final period at Trent issued dogmatic decrees on Communion under both species and the Communion of children (with

4 canons; the decree affirms earlier teaching on the Eucharistic presence of Christ, whole and entire, under each species; session 21), on the Sacrifice of the Mass (with 9 canons; session 22), on the sacrament of orders (with 8 canons; session 23), on the sacrament of matrimony (with 12 canons; session 24), on purgatory (session 25), on the invocation, veneration, and relics of saints and on sacred images (session 25), and on indulgences (session 25).

20. First General Council of the Vatican, 1869-1870

This council produced two dogmatic constitutions. The first of these, on the Catholic faith (*Dei Filius*), defined that God the Creator reveals Himself even though His existence can be known by reason, expounded the nature and gratuity of faith, explained the relationship between faith and reason, and declared that only the interpretation of the Sacred Scripture which the Church has held and holds can be accepted as true. The second, on the Church of Christ (*Pastor Aeternus*), affirmed the universal primacy of the Roman Pontiff over the whole Church and defined his infallible teaching authority.

21. Second General Council of the Vatican, 1962-1965

This council, the largest of the general councils in numbers of Council Fathers attending, opened October 11, 1962. The first period of deliberations ended December 8, 1962. The succeeding periods of the council were September 29 to December 4, 1963, September 14 to November 21, 1964, and September 14 to December 8, 1965. In a series of documents the council treated a wide range of doctrinal and moral matters and provided norms and guidance in its treatment of questions, issues, concerns, and interests of the Church and of humankind in the present-day world. The council produced four constitutions, nine decrees, and three declarations.

The constitutions produced at this council are the Dogmatic Constitution on the Church (*Lumen Gentium*), the Dogmatic Constitution on Revelation (*Dei Verbum*), the Constitution on the Liturgy (*Sacrosanctum Concilium*), and the Pastoral Constitution on the Church in the Modern World (*Gaudium et Spes*).

The decrees are the Decree on the Instruments of Social Communication (*Inter Mirifica*), the Decree on Ecumenism (*Unitatis Redintegratio*), the Decree on the Eastern Catholic Churches (*Orientalium Ecclesiarum*), the Decree on the Bishops' Pastoral Office in the Church (*Christus Dominus*), the Decree on Priestly Formation (*Optatum Totius*), the Decree on the Appropriate Renewal of the Religious Life (*Perfectae Caritatis*), the Decree on the Apostolate of the Laity (*Apostolicam Actuositatem*), the Decree on the Ministry and Life of

Priests (*Presbyterorum Ordinis*), and the Decree on the Missionary Activity of the Church (*Ad Gentes*).

The declarations are the Declaration on Christian Education (*Gravissimum Educationis*, the Declaration on the Relationship of the Church to Non-Christian Religions (*Nostra Aetate*), and the Declaration on Religious Freedom (*Dignitatis Humanae*).

Fathers And Doctors Of The Church

Christian writings contain frequent references to "Fathers of the Church" and "Doctors of the Church." The two terms are not synonymous, but to some extent they overlap in meaning. Both are titles applied to certain ecclesiastical writers. Both refer to teachers, witnesses of authentic Christian tradition.

From a very early date the title "father" was applied to bishops as witnesses of the Christian tradition. Bishops were teachers, and this was in accord with the concept of teachers as father of their students. We find this in St. Paul, who wrote to the Corinthians: "For though you might have ten thousand guardians in Christ, you do not have many fathers. Indeed, in Christ Jesus I became your father through the gospel" (1 Cor. 4.15). In time the term came to be used in a more comprehensive sense, being extended to ecclesiastical writers who were not bishops but who were accepted as representative of the tradition of the Church. St. Jerome, for example, was not a bishop, but was numbered by St. Augustine among the Fathers. Already in the early centuries of the Church, the teaching of the earlier Fathers was being cited by later Fathers as proof of the authentic faith.

Today the title "Fathers of the Church" is applied only to those writers who combine four necessary qualifications: orthodoxy of doctrine, holiness of life, ecclesiastical approval, and antiquity. Each of these qualifications is to be considered in a broad sense. The ecclesiastical approval required may be either explicit, formally expressed by the Church magisterium, or implicit, that is, evident in the practice and custom of the Church.

The patristic era, the time of the Fathers, is not an age precisely determined by fixed dates. While in one sense the apostles themselves were "Fathers of the Church," the patristic era as a literary period is held to begin with the first noncanonical (that is, nonscriptural) Christian writings. The authors of these writings which have survived from the first and early second centuries are sometimes called the "Apostolic Fathers," indicating that they had personal contact with apostles or were instructed by disciples of the apostles. The term "Apostolic Fathers" was not known in the early Church. It is a term introduced by scholars in the seventeenth century and has been used for St. Clement of Rome, St. Ignatius of Antioch, St. Polycarp of Smyrna, Hermas, Papias of Hieropolis, and the unknown authors of the *Epistle of Barnabas*, the *Epistle to Diognetus*, and the *Didache*.

The patristic age is generally considered to end with St. John of Damascus (d. 749) in the East, and, in the West, with St. Gregory the Great (d. 604) or St. Isidore of Seville (d. 636), though some would extend the period to include St. Bede the Venerable (d. 735).

Near the end of the thirteenth century, Pope Boniface VIII declared that he wished St. Ambrose, St. Jerome, St. Augustine, and St. Gregory the Great to be known as "outstanding teachers (doctors) of the Church" (*egregii doctores ecclesiae*). These four saints are also called "the great Fathers of the Church." The four "great Fathers of the East," all also designated Doctors of the Church, are St. Basil the Great, St. Gregory of Nazianzus, St. John Chrysostom, and St. Athanasius.

Although some Fathers of the Church are also Doctors of the Church, "antiquity" is not required for one to be declared a Doctor of the Church. In addition to orthodoxy of doctrine and holiness of life, Doctors of the Church are recognized for the eminence of their learning and the excellence of their teaching. A further requirement is explicit proclamation as a Doctor of the Church by a pope or general council.

The number of Doctors of the Church now (1990) stands at 32. The first saints to be so designated were those noted above as declared such by Pope Boniface VIII, in 1295. The latest to be declared Doctors of the Church, in 1970 by Pope Paul VI, and the first female saints to be so designated, are St. Teresa of Jesus and St. Catherine of Siena. Following is an alphabetical list of the Doctors of the Church (with the dates of such designation and by whom):

St. Albert the Great (1932, by Pope Pius XI)
St. Alphonsus Liguori (1871, by Pope Pius IX)
St. Ambrose (1295, by Pope Boniface VIII)
St. Anselm (1720, by Pope Clement XI)
St. Anthony of Padua (1946, by Pope Pius XII)
St. Athanasius (1568, by Pope Pius V)
St. Augustine (1295, by Pope Boniface VIII)
St. Basil the Great (1568, by Pope Pius V)
St. Bede the Venerable (1899, by Pope Leo XIII)
St. Bernard of Clairvaux (1830, by Pope Pius VIII)
St. Bonaventure (1588, by Pope Sixtus V)
St. Catherine of Siena (1970, by Pope Paul VI)
St. Cyril of Alexandria (1882, by Pope Leo XIII)
St. Cyril of Jerusalem (1882, by Pope Leo XIII)
St. Ephraem the Syrian (1920, by Pope Benedict XV)
St. Francis de Sales (1877, by Pope Pius IX)

St. Gregory the Great (1295, by Pope Boniface VIII)
St. Gregory of Nazianzus (1568, by Pope Pius V)
St. Hilary of Poitiers (1851, by Pope Pius IX)
St. Isidore of Seville (1722, by Pope Innocent XIII)
St. Jerome (1295, by Pope Boniface VIII)
St. John Chrysostom (1568, by Pope Pius V)
St. John of Damascus (1890, by Pope Leo XIII)
St. John of the Cross (1926, by Pope Pius XI)
St. Lawrence of Brindisi (1959, by Pope John XXIII)
St. Leo the Great (1754, by Pope Benedict XIV)
St. Peter Canisius (1925, by Pope Pius XI)
St. Peter Chrysologus (1729, by Pope Benedict XIII)
St. Peter Damian (1828, by Pope Leo XII)
St. Robert Bellarmine (1931, by Pope Pius XI)
St. Teresa of Jesus (1970, by Pope Paul VI)
St. Thomas Aquinas (1567, by Pope Pius V)

Appendix V

Catholic Prayers

The most sacred prayers of the Church are its liturgical prayers. In them we share in the perfect prayer and worship of Christ. But private prayer also is important in the life of faith.

At times, as families and in other groups, Christians should offer prayers together. At times, however, the Christian should pray alone to God. "The Christian is assuredly called to pray with his brethren, but he must also enter into his chamber to pray to the Father in secret (cf. Matt. 6.6); indeed, according to the teaching of the Apostle Paul, he should pray without ceasing (cf. 1 Thess. 5.17)" (SC 12).

In this appendix we include some of the most cherished prayers of the Church that are found often on the lips of Catholics.

Our Father

The Our Father, or Lord's prayer, is the prayer that Jesus taught His disciples (cf. Matt. 6.9-13; Luke 11.2-4). It is probably the best known of all Christian prayers.

Our Father, who art in heaven,
hallowed be Thy name;
Thy kingdom come;
Thy will be done on earth as it is in heaven.
Give us this day our daily bread;
and forgive us our trespasses
as we forgive those who trespass against us;
and lead us not into temptation,
but deliver us from evil. Amen.

Amen

The word "Amen" is added at the end of prayers. It is a Hebrew word meaning "truly" or "verily." It is also translated "So be it!" Its use in prayer, to express personal assent and agreement of heart and mind, is noted both in the Old Testament and in the New (cf., e.g., 1 Kings 1.36; 1 Cor. 14.16).

Sign of the Cross

The Sign of the Cross is a simple and profound prayer. In part it is an action or gesture. One marks oneself with the cross to show faith in Christ's redeeming work. A cross is described on the body by the right hand moving from the forehead to the breast, and then from shoulder to shoulder. In the Western Church the cross stroke is made from left to right; in the Eastern Church, from right to left. While tracing the sign of the cross, one says: "In the name of the Father, and of the Son, and of the Holy Spirit." This formula, which recalls the words of Christ sending His apostles to teach and baptize (cf. Matt. 28.19), expresses here an act of faith in the Blessed Trinity.

Glory to the Father

This is a simple and much loved prayer in praise of the Blessed Trinity. In the Liturgy of the Hours it is prayed after each Psalm.

Glory be to the Father,
and to the Son, and to the Holy Spirit.
As it was in the beginning,
is now, and ever shall be,
world without end. Amen.

Hail Mary

The Hail Mary is known also as the Angelic Salutation and as the Ave Maria (from its first words in Latin). It consists of three parts: the words of the Archangel Gabriel to Mary at the Annunciation (cf. Luke 1.28); the words of Elizabeth to Mary at the time of Mary's Visitation (cf. Luke 1.42); and a formula of petition to Mary. The first two parts are found together in liturgical prayers as early as the sixth century. This prayer has an important place in the devotional life of Catholics.

Hail Mary, full of grace,
the Lord is with thee;
blessed art thou among women,
and blessed is the fruit of thy womb, Jesus.
Holy Mary, Mother of God,
pray for us sinners,
now and at the hour of our death. Amen.

The Rosary

The rosary is a popular form of prayer that combines meditation on the mysteries of faith with the recitation of vocal prayers. A "decade" of the rosary corresponds to each of the fifteen mysteries commemorated in the rosary. Ten, Hail Marys are said for each decade; they are preceded by an Our Father and followed by a Glory to the Father. While reciting a decade of the rosary, one is to meditate on the particular mystery for that decade and on its meaning for our life. The entire rosary is divided into three chaplets: the joyful, the sorrowful, and the glorious mysteries. To "say a rosary" commonly means to pray one such chaplet of five mysteries. Commonly a chaplet is preceded by the recitation of the Apostles' Creed and of an Our Father and three Hail Marys, offered as a petition for an increase of faith, hope, and love. The Church has long recommended this form of prayer as a convenient and effective way of meditating on the great mysteries of our salvation.

The Joyful Mysteries
1. The Annunciation.
2. The Visitation of Mary to Elizabeth.
3. The Nativity.
4. The Presentation of Jesus in the Temple.
5. The Finding of Jesus in the Temple.

The Sorrowful Mysteries
1. The Agony of Jesus in the Garden.
2. The Scourging at the Pillar.
3. The Crowning with Thorns.
4. The Carrying of the Cross.
5. The Crucifixion.

The Glorious Mysteries
1. The Resurrection of Jesus.
2. The Ascension of Jesus into Heaven.
3. The Descent of the Holy Spirit upon the Apostles.
4. The Assumption of Mary into Heaven.
5. The Coronation of Mary as Queen of Heaven.

Hail, Holy Queen

Another Marian prayer (originally a hymn) very popular among Catholics because of its tender devotional language is the "Hail, Holy Queen." It dates from the eleventh century. It is one of the antiphons at the end of Compline, or Night Prayer, in the Liturgy of the Hours, and it is also used at times to conclude the recitation of the Rosary.

Hail, Holy Queen, Mother of Mercy, our life, our sweetness, and our hope! To you we cry, poor banished children of Eve;

to you we send up our sighs, mourning and weeping in this valley of tears. Turn then, O most gracious advocate, your eyes of mercy toward us, and after this our exile, show unto us the blessed fruit of your womb, Jesus. O clement, O loving, O sweet Virgin Mary.

V. Pray for us, O holy Mother of God.

R. That we may be made worthy of the promises of Christ.

The Apostles' Creed

This Apostles' Creed is a profession of faith used in the Western Church since the time of the Fathers. Though not written by the apostles, it is a faithful summary of the truths taught from the earliest days of the Church.

I believe in God, the Father almighty, Creator of heaven and earth.

And in Jesus Christ, His only Son, our Lord; who was conceived by the Holy Spirit, born of the Virgin Mary, suffered under Pontius Pilate, was crucified, died, and was buried. He descended into hell; the third day He arose again from the dead; He ascended into heaven, sits at the right hand of God the Father almighty; from thence He shall come to judge the living and the dead.

I believe in the Holy Spirit, the Holy Catholic Church, the communion of saints, the forgiveness of sins, the resurrection of the body, and life everlasting. Amen.

Acts of Faith, Hope, and Love

The living faith of the believer ought to be expressed in prayer as well as in words and deeds. Some of the traditional prayers used to express the faith, hope, and love of the Christian are the following:

Faith

O my God, I firmly believe that You are one God in three Divine Persons, the Father, the Son, and the Holy Spirit. I believe in Jesus Christ, Your Son, who became man and died for our sins, and who will come to judge the living and the dead. I believe these and all the truths which the Holy Catholic Church teaches, because You have revealed them, who can neither deceive nor be deceived. Amen.

Hope

O my God, trusting in Your infinite goodness and promises, I hope to obtain pardon of my sins, the help of Your grace, and life everlasting, through the merits of Jesus Christ, my Lord and Redeemer. Amen.

Love
O my God, I love You above all things, with my whole heart and soul, because You are all-good and worthy of all my love. I love my neighbor as myself for love of You. I forgive all who have injured me, and I ask pardon of all whom I have injured. Amen.

Act of Contrition

Sorrow for having offended God by sin is expressed in prayer in an act of contrition. Such a prayer is recited often, but particularly in preparation for confession and before retiring for the night.

O my God, I am heartily sorry for having offended You, and I detest all my sins, because I dread the loss of heaven and the pains of hell, but most of all because they offend You, my God, who are all-good and deserving of all my love. I firmly resolve, with the help of Your grace, to confess my sins, to do penance, and to amend my life. Amen.

Miserere: Prayer of Repentance

Psalm 51, which is commonly known as the Miserere (the first word of the Latin version), is a moving and inspired prayer of repentance for sin. This prayer begins:

Have mercy on me, O God,
    according to Your steadfast love;
    according to Your abundant mercy blot out my transgressions.
Wash me thoroughly from my iniquity,
    and cleanse me from my sin.

For I know my transgressions,
    and my sin is ever before me.
Against You, You alone, have I sinned,
    and done what is evil in Your sight. . . .

Morning and Evening Prayers

The most unusual and convenient times for private prayer in the lives of many believers is in the morning on arising and in the evening before going to bed. Traditionally the Church has recommended these times for prayer "to the Father in secret."

Morning Offering
O my God, I adore you, and I love You with all my heart. I thank you for having created me and saved me by Your grace, and for having preserved me during this night. I offer you all my prayers, works, joys, and sufferings of this day. Grant that they may be all according to Your will and for Your greater glory. Keep me from all sin and evil, and may Your grace be with me always. Amen.

Evening Prayer
O my God, I adore You, and I love you with all my heart. I thank You for having created me and saved me by Your grace, and for having preserved me during this day. I pray that You will take for Yourself whatever good I might have done this day, and that You will forgive me whatever evil I have done. Protect me this night, and may Your grace be with me always. Amen.

Grace at Meals

The custom of giving thanks at meals was followed by Christ (cf. John 6.11) and the apostles (cf. Acts 27.35). A meal can have sacred significance; it can nourish not only the body, but also community love. Grace at meals can be expressed in many forms of prayer; the ones given here are among the traditional forms of saying grace.

Before Meals
Bless us, O Lord, and these Your gifts, which we are about to receive from Your bounty. Through Christ our Lord. Amen.

After Meals
We give You thanks, almighty God, for these and all the gifts which we have received from Your bounty. Through Christ our Lord. Amen.

Prayers for the Dead

Sacred Scripture reminds us that it is good to pray for the dead (cf. 2 Macc. 12.39-45). We have a special obligation to ask God's mercy on the souls of our parents, family members, relatives, friends, and benefactors who have gone from this world and await the final judgment of God. The Book of Psalms has a beautiful prayer that the Church has long used in prayers for the departed. Christian prayers for the dead usually end with the Eternal Rest, a plea for God's mercy.

Psalm 130
Out of the depths I cry to You, O LORD!
Lord, hear my voice!
Let Your ears be attentive
to the voice of my supplications!

If You, O LORD, should mark iniquities,
Lord, who could stand?
But there is forgiveness with You,
so that You may be revered.

I wait for the LORD, my soul waits,
and in His word I hope;
my soul waits for the LORD
more than those who watch for the morning,
more than those who watch for the morning.

O Israel, hope in the LORD!
For with the LORD there is steadfast love,
and with Him is great power to redeem.
It is He who will redeem Israel
from all its iniquities.

Eternal Rest
Eternal rest grant unto them, O Lord,
and let perpetual light shine upon them.
May they rest in peace. Amen.

Magnificat

Over the centuries of Christian devotion to Mary, the Mother of God, many prayers have come to be cherished. Among these is the Magnificat. This prayer of praise was first the prayer of Mary (cf. Luke 1.46-55). The prayer takes its name from the initial word of the Latin version.

My soul magnifies the Lord,
and my spirit rejoices in God my Savior,
for He has looked with favor on the lowliness of His servant.
Surely, from now on all generations will call me blessed;
for the Mighty One has done great things for me,
and holy is His name.
His mercy is for those who fear Him
from generation to generation.
He has shown strength with His arm,

He has scattered the proud in the thoughts of their hearts,
He has brought down the powerful from their thrones,
and lifted up the lowly;
He has filled the hungry with good things,
and sent the rich away empty.
He has helped His servant Israel,
in remembrance of His mercy,
according to the promise He made to our ancestors,
to Abraham and to his descendants forever.

The Angelus

The tradition of taking time to pray at dawn, at noon, and in the evening is reflected in the Angelus. This prayer dates from about the thirteenth century and celebrates the coming of the Lord as man.

V. The angel of the Lord declared unto Mary,
R. And she conceived by the Holy Spirit.
  Hail Mary, etc.
V. Behold the handmaid of the Lord.
R. Be it done unto me according to your word.
  Hail Mary, etc.
V. And the Word was made flesh
R. And dwelt among us.
  Hail Mary, etc.
V. Pray for us, O holy Mother of God.
R. That we may be made worthy of the promises of Christ.

Let us pray.

Pour forth, we beseech You, O Lord, Your grace into our hearts, that as we have known the incarnation of Christ, Your Son, by the message of an angel, so by His passion and cross we may be brought to the glory of His resurrection. Through the same Christ our Lord. Amen.

Regina Caeli

The Regina Caeli ("Queen of Heaven") is recited in place of the Angelus during the Easter season. This prayer reflects the joy of the Church at Christ's resurrection.

O Queen of heaven, rejoice! Alleluia.
For He whom you merited to bear, Alleluia,
Has arisen, as He said. Alleluia.
Pray for us to God. Alleluia.
  V. Rejoice and be glad, O Virgin Mary, Alleluia.

R. For the Lord has risen indeed. Alleluia.

Let us pray.

O God, who through the resurrection of Your Son, our Lord Jesus Christ, willed to fill the world with joy, grant, we beseech You, that through His Virgin Mother, Mary, we may come to the joys of everlasting life. Through the same Christ our Lord. Amen.

Benedictus

The Benedictus ("Blessed") is the prayer of Zechariah at the birth of St. John the Baptist (cf. Luke 1.68-79). This prayer, or hymn, thanks God for the fulfillment of the Messianic prophecies and addresses the child who is to be the Lord's forerunner.

Blessed be the Lord God of Israel,
for He has looked favorably on His people and redeemed them.
He has raised up a mighty savior for us
in the house of His servant David,
as He spoke through the mouth of His holy prophets from of old,
that we would be saved from our enemies and from the hand of all
    who hate us.
Thus He has shown the mercy promised to our ancestors,
and has remembered His holy covenant,
the oath which He swore to our ancestor Abraham,
to grant us that we, being rescued from the hand of our enemies,
might serve Him without fear, in holiness and righteousness be-
    fore Him all our days.
And you, child, will be called the prophet of the Most High;
for you will go before the Lord to prepare His ways,
to give knowledge of salvation to His people
by the forgiveness of their sins.
By the tender mercy of our God,
the dawn from on high will break upon us,
to give light to those who sit in darkness and in the shadow of
    death,
to guide our feet into the way of peace.

Prayer to the Holy Spirit

Come, Holy Spirit, fill the hearts of Your faithful, and kindle in them the fire of Your love.

V. Send forth Your Spirit and they shall be created.

R. And You shall renew the face of the earth.

Let us pray.

O God, You have taught the hearts of the faithful by the light of the Holy Spirit; grant us, in the same Spirit; to have a taste for what is right, and to rejoice always in His consolation. Through Christ our Lord. Amen.

Prayer for the Pope

The Church urges us to pray for all whom Christ has called to positions of responsibility in the Church, that God may guard them in truth and in love, and reward them for their service to us. We should pray for our parish priests, for our bishops, and in a special way for the Holy Father, the Vicar of Christ.

Father of providence,
look with love on N., our Pope,
your appointed successor to St. Peter
on whom you built your Church.
May he be the visible center and foundation
of our unity in faith and love.[1]

[1]Roman Missal, Sacramentary, Prayer from the Votive Mass for the Holy Father.

Appendix VI

Bibliography

This bibliography is intended as an aid for those who study and teach the Catholic faith. It is of necessity selective; a detailed bibliography on any of the major areas covered would in itself be a book. Special emphasis is given to official documents of the Church; for one who studies and teaches the Catholic faith studies and teaches what the Church believes and teaches, and this message is found most authentically in documents of the Church itself.

Both scholarly and popular works are listed. Brief annotations are given to assist the user. For the most part the bibliography is limited to books in English (many of them available in paperback), through a number of standard sources are cited for those who wish to seek out basic texts in their original languages.

The plan of the bibliography is as follows: First, there is a general bibliography, with sections on (a) Church documents, (b) Scripture, (c) patristics, and (d) theology, history, and general reference. Next, there are specialized bibliographies for the individual chapters (some of them grouped) of the catechism; in these, Church documents are listed before other works.

General

(a) Church documents

Official texts of documents issued by the Holy Father and by the Congregations of the Holy See are published in *Acta Apostolicae Sedis* (Rome, 1909-), the predecessor of which was the *Acta Sanctae Sedis* (Rome, 1865-1908), and *L'Osservatore Romano*.

English translations of papal encyclicals and other Church documents are often available from a number of sources and in various editions. Periodicals which regularly publish in English the texts of important statements of the Church Magisterium include *L'Osservatore Romano*, Weekly English edition (Rome, 1968-), *The Pope Speaks* (Washington, D.C., 1954-1974; Huntington, Ind., Our Sunday Visitor, Inc., 1975-), and *Catholic Mind* (New York, America Press, 1902-). A useful guide to texts and translations of papal statements can be found, under the names of the popes, in various issues of *The Catholic Periodical and Literature Index* (Haverford, Pa., The Catholic Library Association).

Listed below are several of the editions published of the documents of the Second Vatican Council in English translations, some standard references for other Church documents, and a few specific documents having special catechetical significance:

The Documents of Vatican II, ed. W. M. Abbott (copyright 1966 by America Press, New York). This is the basic edition used in the preparation of this catechism for citing and quoting from the documents of the Second Vatican Council.

Vatican Council II: The Conciliar and Post Conciliar Documents, ed. A. Flannery (Northport, N.Y., Costello Publishing Company, 1975).

The Teachings of the Second Vatican Council: Complete Texts of the Constitutions, Decrees, and Declarations (Westminster, Md., The Newman Press, 1966).

Vatican II Documents (Glen Rock, N.J., Paulist Press, 1965).

The Sixteen Documents of Vatican II and the Instruction on the Liturgy (Boston, Daughters of St. Paul, 1966).

Decrees of the Ecumenical Councils, ed. N. P. Tanner, (Georgetown University Press, 1990). This two-volume work presents in the original languages and in a new English translation all the decrees of all general councils from Nicaea I to Vatican II. Well indexed.

H. Denzinger-A. Schönmetzer, *Enchiridion Symbolorum Definitionum et Declarationum de Rebus Fidei et Morum* (34th ed., Frieburg i. Br., Herder, 1967). A standard source book, that is, as the title indicates, a "handbook of creeds, definitions, and declarations on matters of faith and morals." Texts are in their original languages and are given in chronological order. Thoroughly indexed.

Enchiridion Vaticanum (Bologna, Edizioni Dehoniane, 10 vols. thus far). Starting with the documents of Vatican II in vol. 1, this series prints the official documents of the Holy See, with complete texts in the original language and also in Italian translation. Well indexed.

The Church Teaches: Documents of the Church in English Translation (St. Louis, Mo., B. Herder Book Co., 1955). Includes a large percentage of the texts found in Denzinger-Schönmetzer, but topically ordered. Several indexes.

The Teaching of the Catholic Church, originally prepared by J. Neuner and H. Roos, ed. by K. Rahner, trans. by G. Stevens from the original German (Staten Island, N.Y., Alba House, 1967). This also includes a large percentage of the texts found in Denzinger-Schönmetzer. Topically ordered. Indexed.

The Christian Faith in the Doctrinal Documents of the Catholic Church, ed. J. Neuner and J. Dupuis (rev. ed., Staten Island, N.Y.,

Alba House, 1983). Later and larger than the two works cited immediately above. Incorporates excerpts from Vatican II and post-
Vatican II documents. Topically ordered. Several indexes.

Official Catholic Teaching (Wilmington, N.C., McGrath, 1978). These
six volumes, collections of official Church documents, are: *Bible Interpretation; Christ Our Lord; Worship and Liturgy; Clergy and
Laity; Love and Sexuality*; and *Social Justice*.

The Papal Encyclicals, ed. C. Carlen (Wilmington, N.C., Consortium
Books, 1981). This 5-volume set contains the first full edition of en-
cyclicals ever published in English, from *Ubi Primum* to 1740 to
Laborem Exercens in 1981. Indexed.

Pope John Paul II, Apostolic Exhortation, *Catechesi Tradendae* (October 16, 1979). On catechesis in our time.

Pope Paul VI, Apostolic Exhortation, *Evangelii Nuntiandi* (December
8, 1975). On evangelization in the modern world.

Congregation for the Clergy, *General Catechetical Directory* (April
11, 1971). Prepared in accord with a directive of the Second Vatican
Council and confirmed and ordered published by Pope Paul VI, this
Directory sets norms and guidelines for Catholic catechetical work
throughout the world.

United States Catholic Conference, *Sharing the Light of Faith — National Catechetical Directory for Catholics of the United States*
(1979). Text approved by the United States National Conference of
Catholic Bishops in November 1977 and approved by the Congregation for the Clergy in October 1978.

United States National Conference of Catholic Bishops, *To Live in
Christ Jesus* (Washington, D.C., 1976). A pastoral reflection on the
moral life.

(b) Scripture

The Bible is available in many translations and editions. Some of
these translations are published by more than one publisher. Among
the best are the three listed below. Also listed here are the *Enchiridion
Biblicum*, several biblical commentaries, and a number of other works
useful for reference or study.

The Holy Bible, New Revised Standard Version (copyright 1989 by the
Division of Christian Education of the National Council of the Churches of Christ in the United States of America). This is the version
used in the preparation of this catechism for citing and quoting Scripture.

The Jerusalem Bible (copyright 1966 by Darton, Longman & Todd,
Ltd. and Doubleday & Company, Inc.). Particularly valuable for its
generous notes and introductions, which are "with minor variations

and revisions a translation of those which appear in *La Bible de Jerusalem* published by Les Editions du Cerf Paris. . . ."

The New American Bible (copyright by Confraternity of Christian Doctrine, Washington, D.C.). Translation by members of the Catholic Biblical Association of America. Sponsored by the Bishops' Committee of the Confraternity of Christian Doctrine.

Nova Vulgata Bibliorum Sacrorum Editio (Vatican City, Libreria Editrice Vaticana, 1979).

Enchiridion Biblicum. Documenta ecclesiastica Sacram Scripturam spectantia auctoritate Pontificiae Commissionis de Re Biblica edita (4th ed. enlarged and revised, Rome, repr. 1965). Collects in one volume in their original languages texts of important Church documents on such matters as the canon of Scripture and scriptural interpretation.

The Jerome Biblical Commentary, ed. R. Brown *et al.* (Englewood Cliffs, N.J., Prentice-Hall, 1990).

A New Catholic Commentary on Holy Scriptures, ed. R. Fuller *et al.* (London, Nelson, revised 1975).

Bauer, J. B., ed., *Sacramentum Verbi*, 3 vols. (New York, Herder and Herder, 1970). An encyclopedia of biblical theology.

Daniel-Rops, H., *What is the Bible?* (vol. 60 of The Twentieth Century Encyclopedia of Catholicism; New York, Hawthorn Books, 1958). A small book, but readable and useful.

Fuentes, A., *A Guide to the Bible* (Dublin, Four Courts Press, 1987). A brief yet clear account of all the books of the Bible.

Hartman, L., ed., *Encyclopedic Dictionary of the Bible* (New York, McGraw-Hill, 1963). A reference handbook on the themes and names in the books of the Bible.

Leon-Dufour, X., *Dictionary of Biblical Theology* (2nd rev. ed., New York, Seabury, 1973). A reference tool that makes readily accessible the latest developments in biblical theology.

McKenzie, J., *Dictionary of the Bible* (Milwaukee, Bruce, 1965). A reference tool on the names, concepts, and themes in Sacred Scripture.

(c) Patristics

Listed here are some major sets or series offering the works of the early Christian writers in their original languages, then some major sets or series of English translations, and finally several additional works, including two patrologies.

Patrologiae cursus completus, series latina, ed. J. P. Migne, 221 vols. (Paris, 1844-1855).

Patrologiae cursus completus, series graeca, ed. J. P. Migne, 161 vols. (Paris, 1857-1866).

Die griechischen christlichen Schriftsteller der ersten drei Jahrhunderte (Leipzig, 1897-   ).

Corpus scriptorum ecclesiasticorum latinorum (Vienna, 1866-   ).

Corpus scriptorum christianorum orientalium (Paris, 1903-   ).

Patrologia orientalis (Paris, 1907-   ).

Patrologia syriaca, 3 vols. (Paris, 1894-1926).

Sources chrétiennes (Paris, 1941-   ).

Corpus Christianorum, series latina (Turnhout-Paris, 1953-   ).

Corpus Christianorum, series graeca (Turnhout-Paris, 1974-   ).

Library of the Fathers, 45 vols. (Oxford, 1838-1888).

The Ante-Nicene Christian Library, 24 vols. (Edinburgh, 1866-1872), with a supplementary vol. (Edinburgh, 1897).

The Ante-Nicene Fathers, 8 vols. (Buffalo, 1884-1886). American rev. reprint of the Edinburgh edition, with two supplementary volumes (9 and 10). Repr. Grand Rapids, 1950 ff.

A Select Library of Nicene and Post-Nicene Fathers of the Christian Church, 28 vols. (Buffalo and New York, 1886-1900). Repr. Grand Rapids, 1951 ff.

Translations of Christian Literature (London, Society for Promoting Christian Knowledge, 1914-   ).

Ancient Christian Writers, now ed. W. J. Burghardt and T. C. Lawler (Westminster, Md.-London-New York-Paramus, N.J.-Mahwah, N.J., 1946-   ).

The Fathers of the Church, ed. R. J. Deferrari *et al.* (New York-Washington, D.C., 1947-   ).

The Library of Christian Classics, ed. J. Baillie *et al.* (London and Philadelphia, 1953-   ).

Oxford Early Christian Texts (New York, 1971-   ).

Jurgens, W. A., *The Faith of the Early Fathers* (Collegeville, Liturgical Press, 3 vols.: 1, 1970; 2 and 3, 1979). A florilegium.

Rouët de Journel, M. J., *Enchiridion Patristicum* (24th ed., Barcinone-Freiburg i. Br.-Rome-New York, Herder, 1969). A standard reference, this is a one-volume collection of important texts, in their original languages, from the early Christian writers. Thoroughly indexed.

Beatrice, P. F., *Introduction to the Fathers of the Church* (Vicenza, Edizioni Istituto San Gaetano, 1987). An attractive and well-illustrated work.

Wuerl, D. W., *Fathers of the Church* (Boston, St. Paul Editions, revised 1982). A popular study of the life, times, and doctrine of some of the great Fathers of the Church.

Altaner, B., *Patrology* (trans. by H. C. Graef; 2nd ed., New York, Herder and Herder, 1961).

Quasten, J., *Patrology*, 4 vols. (Westminster, Md.-Utrecht-Antwerp); Christian Classics): 1 (1950) *The Beginnings of Patristic Literature*;

2 (1953) *The Ante-Nicene Literature after Irenaeus*; 3 (1960) *The Golden Age of Greek Patristic Literature from the Council of Nicaea to the Council of Chalcedon;* and 4 (1986, introduced by J. Quasten, edited by A. Di Bergardino) *The Golden Age of Latin Patristic Literature from the Council of Nicea to the Council of Chalcedon.* This is the finest work of its kind. Several indexes.

(d) Theology, history, and general reference

Here are listed some histories of the Church, and then a number of reference works which the catechist or student of the faith will find useful. Because of the special place St. Thomas Aquinas holds among Catholic theologians, also listed are some editions of his major works translated in English.

Enchiridion Fontium Historiae Ecclesiasticae Antiquae, quod collegit C. Kirch (8th ed., Barcinone, Herder, 1960). A standard source book, this gives selections in their original languages from a large number of writers, including some non-Christian, of the life and times of the early Church.
Daniel-Rops, H., History of the Church of Christ, 10 vols. (New York, 1957-1967). Vol. 1: *The Church of the Apostles and Martyrs* (1960); vol. 2: *The Church in the Dark Ages* (1959); vol. 3: *Cathedral and Crusade: Studies of the Medieval Church* (1957); vol. 4: *The Protestant Reformation* (1961); vol. 5: *The Catholic Reformation* (1962); vol. 6: *The Church in the Seventeenth Century* (1963); vol. 7: *The Church in the Eighteenth Century* (1964); vol. 8: *The Church in an Age of Revolution*, 1789-1870 (1965); vol. 9: *A Fight for God* (1966); vol. 10: *Our Brothers in Christ* (1967). A splendid popular history of the Church.
Hughes, P., *A History of the Church*, 3 vols. (London, Sheed & Ward, Ltd., 1934-1947). A standard history of the Church to the early sixteenth century.
Hughes, P., *A Popular History of the Catholic Church* (New York, Macmillan, 1947; Image Books, 1954). A fine, brief survey of the history of the Church. Eminently readable.
Hughes, P., *The Church in Crisis: A History of the General Councils, 325-1870* (New York, Hanover House, 1961). An excellent one-volume account of the first twenty general councils in historical perspective.
Mourret, F., *History of the Catholic Church*, 8 vols. (trans. by N. Thompson; St. Louis, B. Herder, 1931-1957). A standard, scholarly history of the Church.
Newman, J. H., *The Church of the Fathers* (London, Burns & Oates, 1868). This was reprinted as vol. 2 of Historical Sketches (New

York, Longmans, Green and Co., 1917). An historical and theological study of several of the great Fathers.

Orlandis, J., *A Short History of the Catholic Church* (Dublin, Four Courts Press, 1985). Short, but good.

Schreck, A., *The Compact History of the Catholic Church* (Ann Arbor, Servant Books, 1987). A readable guide to the history of the Church.

Bouyer, L., *Dictionary of Theology* (trans. by C. Quinn; New York, Desclée, 1966). An excellent general dictionary of theological concepts.

Cross, F. L., and Livingstone, E. A., eds., *The Oxford Dictionary of the Christian Church* (2nd ed., New York, Oxford University Press, 1974). An excellent reference work, edited by Anglican scholars, on Christian history, biography, doctrine, and practice. Individual articles include bibliographies.

Kelly, J. N. D., *The Oxford Dictionary of Popes* (Oxford, Oxford University Press, 1986). An Anglican scholar prepared here an excellent history except for the first 150 years of the papacy.

New Catholic Encyclopedia. 15 vols. (New York, McGraw-Hill, 1967). Vol. 16, Supplement 1967-1974 (1974). Vol. 17, Supplement 1975-1978 (1979). Supplement 1978-1988 (1989). Articles on all facets of Catholic faith.

Rahner, K., and Vorgrimler, H., *Theological Dictionary* (New York, Herder and Herder, 1965). A dictionary of theological concepts.

Vorgrimler, H., ed., *Commentary on the Documents of Vatican II*, 5 vols. (New York, Herder and Herder, 1967). Offers an extensive commentary on the constitutions, decrees, and declarations of the Second Vatican Council.

St. Thomas Aquinas, *Summa Theologica*, 5 vols., trans. by the Fathers of the English Dominican Province (Westminster, Md., Christian Classics, 1981). English translation of the *Summa Theologica*.

St. Thomas Aquinas, *Summa Theologica*, ed. T. Gilby and T. C. O'-Brien (New York, McGraw-Hill, 1964-   ). Original text, translation, and extensive notes.

St Thomas Aquinas, *Summa contra gentiles*, 5 vols., trans. by A. C. Pegis (London, U. of Notre Dame Press, 1975). English translation.

Farrell, W., *A Companion to the Summa*, 4 vols. (New York, Sheed & Ward, 1938-1942). A popular presentation of the theology of the *Summa Theologica*.

Chapter 1

Second Vatican Council, *Pastoral Constitution on the Church in the Modern World* (December 7, 1965), esp. nn. 11-22.

Pope Paul VI, Apostolic Exhortation, *Gaudete in Domino* (May 9,

1975), on Christian joy; Apostolic Exhortation, *Evangelii Nuntiandi* (December 8, 1975), on evangelization in the modern world.

St. Augustine, *Confessions*. An ever-popular work, available in many translations and editions, in which St. Augustine records the dramatic story of his own journey to God and his decisive coming to the faith.

Chesterton, G. K., *Orthodoxy* (London, 1908). Republished a number of times, this short work in a classic defense of Christian belief by a celebrated convert. A book rich also in imagination and joy.

Congar, Y., *Revelation of God* (New York, Herder & Herder, 1968). A study of revelation by a modern theologian.

Jaki, S., *Miracles and Physics* (Front Royal, Va. Christendom College Press, 1989). An unusual defense of the reality of Miracles.

Kasper, W., *Transcending All Understanding* (San Francisco, Ignatius Press, 1985). A study of the meaning of faith and an examination of contemporary challenges to it.

Latourelle, R., *Theology of Revelation* (Staten Island, N.Y., Alba House, 1967). A thorough study on the meaning of revelation in Scripture, in the Fathers, in the councils, and in the great theologians of all centuries.

Lewis, C. S., *Mere Christianity* (London, Bles, 1952). A popular presentation of a defense of Christian faith by a well-known Anglican.

Mascall, E. L., *Theology and the Gospel of Christ* (London, S.P.C.K., 1977). A guide to the intelligent use of new theologies, and a critique of accepting philosophical assumptions hostile to the faith.

Mirus, J. A., ed., *Reasons for Hope* (Triangle, Va., Christendom College Press, 1978). Essays in Christian apologetics.

Monden, L., *Signs and Wanders: A Study of the Miraculous Element in Religion* (New York, Desclée, 1966). A careful study on the theology of miracles.

Most, W., *Catholic Apologetics Today* (Rockford, Ill., Tan Books, 1987). A reasoned defense of the credibility of Catholic faith.

Newman, J. H., *Essay on the Development of Christian Doctrine* (Garden City, N.Y., Image Books, 1960). Originally published in 1845, this work is very timely today. A classic on the meaning and nature of the development of doctrine.

Newman, J. H., *An Essay on the Grammar of Assent* (Garden City, N.Y., Image Books, 1955). First published in 1870, this treats of how one comes to personal and real assent in religious matters.

Ratzinger, J., *Introduction to Christianity* (New York, Herder & Herder, 1970). On the meaning of faith and of its central mysteries.

Schmaus, M., *God in Revelation* (New York, Sheed & Ward, 1968). A fresh approach to classic problems concerning revelation.

Trigg, R., *Reason and Commitment* (New York, Cambridge University Press, 1973). A book, effectively written, against radical relativism.

Chapter 2

Second Vatican Council, *Dogmatic Constitution on Divine Revelation* (November 18, 1965).

First Vatican Council, *Dogmatic Constitution on the Catholic Faith* (April 24, 1870). Treats of the power of reason to know God and of the necessity of revelation. The roles of faith and reason.

Pope John Paul II, Encyclical, *Dives in Misericordia* (November 30, 1980). On divine mercy.

Pope Pius XII, Encyclical, *Humani Generis* (August 12, 1950). Touches many questions on the nature of revelation and related matters.

Pope Pius IX, Encyclical, *Qui Pluribus* (November 8, 1848). Has much on the relation of faith and reason.

Daniélou, J., *God and the Ways of Knowing* (New York, Meridian Books, 1957). Discusses the varieties of ways in which men have come to know God.

D'Arcy, M., *No Absent God: The Relations Between God and the Self* (London, Routledge & Kegan Paul, 1962). A thoughtful essay on the profound relevance of God's reality to man.

Fabro, C., *God in Exile: Modern Atheism* (Westminster, Md., Newman Press, 1968). A masterwork on the development of modern atheism.

Fortman, E. J., ed., *The Theology of God: Commentary* (Milwaukee, Bruce, 1968). A collection of excerpts from various works.

Grisez, G., *Beyond the New Theism: A Philosophy of Religion* (Notre Dame, Ind., Notre Dame University Press, 1975). A new approach to a Christian theism.

Guardini, R., *The Living God* (trans. by S. Godman; New York, Pantheon Books; Chicago, Regnery, 1957). A popular presentation of profound reflections on God and His attributes.

Jaki, S., *The Road of Science and the Ways of God* (Chicago, University of Chicago Press, 1978). The Gifford Lectures of 1974-1976, by a physicist and theologian.

Kehoe, K., *The Theology of God: Sources* (New York, Bruce, 1971). A book of readings in the theology of God from the earliest Fathers to contemporary theologians.

Lubac, H. de, *The Discovery of God* (London, Darton, Longman & Todd, 1960). Reflection on the profound roots of man's convictions concerning the reality of God.

Lubac, H. de, *The Drama of Atheistic Humanism* (London, Sheed & Ward, 1949). An account of the special characteristics of contemporary atheism and of the failures of every humanism without Christ.

Maritain, J., *Approaches to God* (New York, Harper, 1954). A popular study of the methods by which man comes to know his Creator.

Miceli, V., *The Gods of Atheism* (New Rochelle, N.Y., Arlington House, 1971). A popular account of the origins, forms, and presuppositions of contemporary atheism.

Murray, J. C., *The Problem of God* (New Haven and London, Yale University Press, 1964). A small, scholarly volume with historical and theological treatment of key questions about God.

Weinandy, T. G., *Does God Change?* (Still River, Mass., St. Bede's Publications, 1985). A serious and rewarding study.

Chapter 3

Pope John Paul II, Apostolic Exhortation, *Familiaris Consortio* (November 22, 1981), on the role of the Christian family in the modern world.

Pope Pius XII, Encyclical, *Humani Generis* (August 12, 1950), on questions regarding the first eleven chapters of Genesis; Encyclical, *Divino Afflante Spiritu* (September 30, 1943), providing guidelines for the study and interpretation of Sacred Scripture.

Boadt, L., *Reading the Old Testament* (Mahwah, N.J., Paulist Press, 1989). A comprehensive, clearly written introduction to the Old Testament.

Daniélou, J., *The Angels and Their Mission* (Westminster, Md., Christian Classics, repr. 1987). An excellent study on the role of angels in salvation history, drawn chiefly from the works of the Fathers.

Hauret, C., *Beginnings: Genesis and Modern Science* (2nd ed., Dubuque, Iowa, Priory Press, 1964). An excellent popular study of the creation account in Genesis, together with some observations from the world of science.

Moriarity, F., *Introducing the Old Testament* (Milwaukee, Bruce, 1959). This introduction is built around the personalities of leading Old Testament personages.

Murphy, C., *At Home on Earth* (New York: Crossroad, 1989). A Catholic ethic of the environment.

Ratzinger, J., *"In the Beginning" — A Catholic Understanding of the Story of Creation and the Fall* (Huntington, Ind., Our Sunday Visitor, 1989). A brief and theologically sound account.

Sheed, F., *Genesis Regained* (London, Sheed & Ward, 1969). A good popular presentation of the meaning of the Genesis account of creation and of the problems that surround it.

Wright, J., "Some Reflections on the Angels," in *Homiletic and Pastoral Review*, June, 1973, pp. 10-21.

Chapters 4 and 5

Second Vatican Council, *Dogmatic Constitution on the Church* (November 21, 1964), ch. 1, which tells of God's plan for His people as it is worked out in history; *Pastoral Constitution on the Church in the Modern World* (December 7, 1965), nn. 4-10, a discussion of the situation of men in the modern world; *Decree on the Missionary Activity of the Church* (December 7, 1965), ch. 1, on doctrinal principles.

Council of Trent, *Decree on Original Sin* (June 17, 1546); *Decree on Justification* (January 13, 1547).

Pope John Paul II, Encyclical, *Laborem Exercens* (September 14, 1981), on human work, Post-Synodal Apostolic Exhortation, *Christifideles Laici* (December 30, 1988), on the vocation and the mission of the lay faithful in the Church and in the world.

Pope Paul VI, *Professio Fidei* ("The Credo of the People of God," June 30, 1968). A beautiful expression of Catholic faith for modern man.

Azar, L., *Man: Computer, Ape, or Angel?* (Hanover, The Christopher Publishing House, 1988). A philosphically sound presentation of the meaning of human personhood.

Dubarle, A. M., *The Biblical Doctrine of Original Sin* (trans. by E. M. Steward; New York, Herder & Herder, 1967). A scholarly inquiry.

Guardini, R., *The World and the Person* (Chicago, Regnery, 1965). Thoughtful essays on the Christian meaning of man and of his present existence in the world.

Journet, C., *The Meaning of Evil* (New York, Kennedy, 1963). A profound theological study of the mystery of evil.

Lewis, C. S., *The Problem of Pain* (New York, Macmillan, 1944). A popular treatment of the question by an Anglican scholar.

Mork, W., *The Biblical Meaning of Man* (Milwaukee, Bruce, 1967). A presentation of recent biblical studies on the nature of man.

Mouroux, J., *The Meaning of Man* (New York, Sheed & Ward, 1948). A joyful, enthusiastic presentation of the authentic Christian teaching on the sublime dignity of man.

Staab, G., *The Dignity of Man in Modern Papal Teaching* (Washington, D.C., The Catholic University of American Press, 1957). A study of the Church's teaching about the meaning of human dignity, drawn from papal documents between 1878 and 1955.

Chapters 6, 8, 9, and 10

Second Vatican Council, *Dogmatic Constitution on the Church* (November 21, 1964); *Dogmatic Constitution on Divine Revelation* (November 18, 1965); *Decree on the Ministry and Life of Priests*

(December 7, 1965), esp. chs. 1 and 2 on priests' relation to Christ.

Pope John Paul II, Encyclical, *Redemptor Hominis* (March 4, 1979); Encyclical, *Dives in Misericordia* (November 30, 1980), on divine mercy.

Pope Pius XII, Encyclical, *Sempiternus Rex* (September 8, 1951), on the natures and person of Christ; Encyclical, *Haurietis Aquas* (May 15, 1956), on the Sacred Heart, with much doctrinal content on Jesus and His work.

Pope Pius XI, Encyclical, *Miserentissimus Redemptor* (May 7, 1928). On the Sacred Heart, with much doctrinal content on the incarnation and man's relation to Christ the Redeemer.

Congregation for the Doctrine of the Faith, *Declaration for the Protection of Faith in the Mysteries of the Incarnation and the Most Holy Trinity* (February 21, 1972).

Benoit, P., *The Passion and Resurrection of Jesus Christ* (New York, Herder & Herder, 1969). Shows the historical value of the scriptural accounts of Christ's passion and resurrection.

Bouyer, L., *The Eternal Son* (trans. by S. Inkel and J. F. Laughlin; Huntington, Our Sunday Visitor, 1978).

Carmody, J., and Clarke, Th. E., *Word and Redeemer* (New York, Paulist Press, 1965). A fine short collection of patristic texts, with brief commentaries, on Christ and His saving work.

Cerfaux, L., *Christ in the Theology of St. Paul* (New York, McGraw-Hill, 1959). On Christ and His centrality in Pauline theology.

Congar, Y., *Jesus Christ* (New York, Herder & Herder, 1966). Christological essays on aspects of Christ's life.

Daniel-Rops, H., *Jesus and His Times* (New York, E. P. Dutton & Co., 1954). An excellent account of Jesus Christ and His work in historical context.

Daniel-Rops, H., *Daily Life in the Time of Jesus* (New York, Hawthorn Books, 1962). A companion volume to the same author's work cited immediately above.

De Margerie, B., *The Human Knowledge of Christ* (Boston, St. Paul Editions, 1977). Traditional positions.

Dulles, A., *Apologetics and the Biblical Christ* (Westminster, Md., Newman Press, 1964). A treatment of the nature and credibility of Gospel witness and the basis for the credibility of the resurrection.

Durrell, F. X., *The Resurrection: A Biblical Study* (New York, Sheed & Ward, 1960). An excellent work that shows how central the resurrection of Jesus is for the New Testament revelation and for the Christian life.

Galot, J., *A Theology of Incarnation* (Chicago, Franciscan Herald Press, 1981). A major theologian studies the mystery of the Incarnation and the human knowledge of Jesus.

Gelin, A., ed., *Son and Savior* (Baltimore, Helicon Press, 1962). A valuable collection of essays, by five biblical experts, on the divinity of Jesus as witnessed in the New Testament.

Grillmeier, A., *Christ in Christian Tradition* (London, Mowbray, revised 1975). An excellent, thorough treatment of Christological development from New Testament times to the Council of Chalcedon.

Guillet, J., *The Consciousness of Jesus* (trans. by E. Bonin; New York, Newman Press, 1972). A careful evaluation of the scriptural evidence of Jesus' own awareness of His identity.

Kasper, W., *Jesus the Christ* (Paulist Press, 1976). A balanced treatment of Christology.

Laurentin, R., *The Truth of Christmas Beyond the Myths* (Petersham, Mass., St. Bede's Publications, (1986). A major contribution on the Infancy Narratives.

Lyonnet, S., *Sin, Redemption and Sacrifice* (Rome, Biblical Institute, 1970). A biblical-patristic study of redemption from sin by the sacrificial death of Christ.

Messori, V., *Faith's Answer: The Mystery of Jesus* (New Rochelle, Don Bosco Publications, 1986). An accurate and readable account of Church teaching on Jesus.

Most, W. G., *The Consciousness of Christ* (Front Royal, Va., Christendom College Press, 1980). It answers questions clearly and boldly.

Mussner, F., *The Miracles of Jesus* (Shannon, Ireland, Ecclesia Press, 1968). On the reliability of the Gospel witness to the miracles of Jesus.

O'Collins, G., *Interpreting Jesus* (Ramsey, N.J., Paulist Press, 1983). This explores and clarifies what Christian belief in the risen Jesus originally meant and now continues to mean.

O'Connor, J., *The Father's Son* (Boston, St. Paul Editions, 1984). A clearly written comprehensive Christology.

Sabourin, L., *Christology: Basic Texts in Focus* (New York, Alba House, 1984). Studies Christ's identity in Scripture and the Church's tradition.

Sabourin, L., *The Names and Titles of Jesus* (New York, Macmillan, 1967). Investigates the theological significance of the names and titles given Jesus in the New Testament.

Schmaus, M., *God and His Christ* in *Modern Theology Library* (New York, Sheed & Ward, 1971). Rich insights into the mystery of Christ, with sound bases in Scripture and patristic tradition.

Sheed, F. J., *What Difference Does Jesus Make?* (London, Sheed & Ward, 1971). Very readable work intended to show how relevant Jesus, and a deep knowledge of Him, is for our living.

Wainwright, A. W., *The Trinity in the New Testament* (London, S.P.C.K., 1962). An excellent expression, by an Anglican scholar, of the biblical teaching on the divinity of Jesus and of the Holy Spirit.

Wright, J., *Words in Pain* (Notre Dame, Ind., Fides, 1961). Thoughtful meditations on the Last Words of the Savior.

Chapter 7 and 15

Second Vatican Council, *Dogmatic Constitution on the Church* (November 21, 1964), ch. 8, on the role of Mary in the mystery of Christ and the Church.

Pope John Paul II, Encyclical, *Redemptoris Mater* (March 25, 1987), on the Blessed Virgin Mary in the life of the Church.

Pope Paul VI, Apostolic Exhortation, *Marialis Cultus* (February 2, 1974). On devotion to the Blessed Virgin Mary in the liturgy and in private prayer. Treats the basis for and value of such devotion.

Pope Pius XII, Apostolic Constitution, *Munificentissimus Deus* (November 1, 1950). Includes the solemn definition of the Blessed Virgin Mary's assumption into heaven.

Pope Pius IX, Bull, *Ineffabilis Deus* (December 8, 1854). Here is defined the dogma of the immaculate conception of the Blessed Virgin Mary.

United States National Conference of Catholic Bishops, *Behold Your Mother* (November 21, 1973). A pastoral letter on correct doctrine about and devotion to Mary.

Braun, F. M., *Mother of God's People* (New York, Alba House, 1967). Johannine teaching on Mary by a biblical scholar.

Carol, J., ed., *Mariology*, 3 vols. (Milwaukee, Bruce, 1955-1961). A standard reference work for all topics on Marian doctrine and devotions.

Carroll, E., *Understanding the Mother of Jesus* (Wilmington, Del., Glazier, 1979). A popular study of Mary by a renowned Marian scholar.

Congar, Y., *Christ, Our Lord, and the Church; a Study of Eirenic Theology* (Westminster, Md., Newman Press, 1957). A study of Our Lady in her relation to Christ and the Church.

Feuillet, A., *Jesus and His Mother* (St. Bede's Publications, 1985). An excellent study in biblical theology of Mary.

Galot, J., *Mary in the Gospel* (Westminster, Md., Newman Press, 1965). Develops the biblical basis for Marian doctrine and devotion.

Jelly, F.M., *Madonna: Mary in the Catholic Tradition* (Huntington, Ind., Our Sunday Visitor, 1986). Dwells on the authentic Mary of Scripture, tradition, and infallible Church teaching.

McHugh, J., *The Mother of Jesus in the New Testament* (London, Darton, Longman & Todd, 1975). A scholarly treatment of the Virgin Mary.

Miguens, M., *Mary, The Servant of the Lord* (Boston, St. Paul Editions, 1978). A biblical mariology.

Miguens, M., *The Virgin Birth* (2nd ed., St. Paul Editions, 1981). Shows that the New Testament is not so silent as some would believe.

O'Carroll, M., *Theotokos* (Wilmington, Del., Michael Glazier, 1982). An encyclopedia of Marian theology and literature.

Scheeben, M. J., *Mariology*, 2 vols. (trans. by T.L.M.J. Geukers; St. Louis, Herder, 1946-1947). A classic study by a master theologian of the nineteenth century.

Vollert, C., *A Theology of Mary* (New York, Herder & Herder, 1965). An excellent treatment.

Wright, J., *Mary Our Hope* (San Francisco, Ignatius Press, 1984). A selection from the sermons, addresses, and papers of the late cardinal.

Chapter 11

Second Vatican Council, *Dogmatic Constitution on the Church* (November 21, 1964), nn. 4, 7, 12, 13, 20, 22, 25-27, 32; *Dogmatic Constitution on Divine Revelation* (November 18, 1965), nn. 7-12; *Decree on the Missionary Activity of the Church* (December 7, 1965), nn. 2, 4, 15; *Decree on the Apostolate of the Laity* (November 18, 1965), nn. 3, 23; *Decree on Ecumenism* (November 21, 1964), nn. 2, 3, 4, 24. — The documents of the Second Vatican Council speak frequently of the Holy Spirit; the references given here are to some key passages.

Pope John Paul II, Encyclical, Dominum et Vivificantem (May 18, 1986), on the Holy Spirit in the life of the Church and the world.

Pope Paul VI, Address to Congress of Catholic Charismatic Renewal, May 19, 1975; Address at General Audience, May 26, 1971; Homily on the Feast of Pentecost, May 25, 1969.

Pope Leo XIII, Encyclical, *Divinum Illud Munus* (May 9, 1897). On the Holy Spirit.

United States National Conference of Catholic Bishops, *A Pastoral Statement on the Catholic Charismatic Renewal* (1984). A discussion of the meaning and implication of the Catholic charismatic renewal.

Congar, Y., *I Believe in the Holy Spirit* (Philadelphia, Seabury, 1983). Vol. 1: *The Experience of the Spirit*; vol. 2; *The Lord and Giver of Life*; vol. 3; *The River of Life Flows in the East and the West*. A major study by a leading theologian.

Froget, G., *The Indwelling of the Holy Spirit in the Souls of the Just*, Baltimore, Carroll Press, 1950). A classic study of the doctrine according to St. Thomas Aquinas.

Gardeil, A., *The Holy Spirit in Christian Life* (St. Louis, Herder,

1954). A modern classic on the Holy Spirit, and on His gifts in the life of the Christian.

Haughey, J. C., *The Conspiracy of God: The Holy Spirit in Men* (Garden City, N.Y., Doubleday, 1973). Presents a series of thoughtful and provocative reflections on the meaning of being led by the Spirit.

Henry, A. M., *The Holy Spirit* (vol. 18 of The Twentieth Century Encyclopedia of Catholicism; New York, Hawthorn Books, 1960). A readable summary of the Church's teaching on the Spirit.

Hocken, P., *One Lord, One Spirit, One Body* (Gaithersburg, Md., Word Among Us Press, 1989). A discussion of the outpourings of the Holy Spirit in all Christians in this century.

Martinez, L. M., *The Sanctifier* (Paterson, N.J., St. Anthony Guild Press, 1961). A popular presentation.

Potterie, I. de la, *The Christian Lives by the Spirit* (New York, Alba House, 1971). A well-written study, with solid basis in Scripture, of grace, of divine sonship, and of the Spirit's part in this.

Sheed, Frank J., *The Holy Spirit in Action* (Ann Arbor, Servant Publications, 1981). A clear and pastoral presentation by a master teacher of the faith.

Weinandy, T., *Receiving the Promise: The Spirit's Work of Conversion* (Gaithersburg, Md., Word Among Us Press, 1985). A theological study of the Holy Spirit's work.

Chapter 12

Congregation for the Doctrine of the Faith, *Declaration for the Protection of Faith in the Mysteries of the Incarnation and the Most Holy Trinity* (February 21, 1972).

De Margerie, B., *The Christian Trinity in History* (Still River, St. Bede's Publications, 1982). Meaning and truth of the doctrine of the Trinity and its centrality in Christian faith.

Fortman, E., *The Triune God* (Philadelphia, Westminster, 1972). An historical, theological study reaffirming faith in the Trinity, with a forceful critique of unorthodox views.

Hill, W., *The Three-Personed God* (Washington, D.C., The Catholic University of America Press, 1985). A scholarly study.

O'Carroll, M., *Trinitas* (Wilmington, Michael Glazier, 1987). A comprehensive study.

O'Donnell, J. J., *The Mystery of the Triune God* (Paulist Press, 1988). A popular, accurate account.

Piault, B., *What is the Trinity?* (vol. 17 of The Twentieth Century Encyclopedia of Catholicism; New York, Hawthorn Books, 1959). A presentation of the scriptural, patristic, and credal witness to the teaching on the Trinity, with an account of the relation of the Trinity to the Christian life.

Rondet, H., *The Grace of Christ* (New York, Newman Press, 1966). A useful study on the living presence of the Trinity in the believer.

Sheed, F. J., *God and the Human Condition* (New York, Sheed & Ward, 1966). A simple but excellent presentation of the Christian faith in one God and the Trinity of Persons.

Spicq., C., *The Trinity and Our Moral Life* (Westminster, Md., Newman Press, 1963). The subject is examined according to the teaching of St. Paul.

Chapters 13 and 14

Second Vatican Council, *Dogmatic Constitution on the Church* (November 21, 1964); *Decree on the Bishops' Pastoral Office in the Church* (October 28, 1965).

First Vatican Council, *First Dogmatic Constitution on the Church of Christ* (July 18, 1870).

Pope Paul VI, Encyclical, *Ecclesiam Suam* (August 6, 1964). On the paths of the Church.

Pope Pius XII, Encyclical, *Mystici Corporis* (June 29, 1943). On the Mystical Body of Christ.

Congregation for the Doctrine of the Faith, *Mysterium Ecclesiae* ("Declaration in Defense of the Catholic Doctrine on the Church against Certain Errors of the Present Day," June 24, 1973).

Balthasar, H. Urs von, *Church and Word* (New York, Herder & Herder, 1967). Good on the Church itself and on the concept of sacred office in the Church.

Bouyer, L., *The Church of God* (trans. by C. Quinn; Chicago, Franciscan Herald Press, 1982). A creative presentation of received teaching.

Burke, C., *Authority and Freedom in the Church* (San Francisco, Ignatius Press, 1989). A clear presentation of Church teaching authority and the meaning of Christian freedom.

Butler, B. C., *The Idea of the Church* (Aberdeen, University Press, 1962; Baltimore, Helicon Press, 1962). A study of the Church's nature, based on a scholarly analysis of both Scripture and tradition.

Butler, B. C., *The Church and Infallibility* (New York, Sheed & Ward, 1954). Analysis and defense of the historical credentials of the Church's teaching on infallibility.

Cerfaux, L., *The Church in the Theology of St. Paul* (New York, Herder & Herder, 1959). A study of St. Paul's teaching on the Church.

Congar, Y., *Tradition and Traditions: An Historical and Theological Essay* (New York, Macmillan, 1967). A scholarly work on a difficult and important doctrine.

Duggan, G. H., *Beyond Reasonable Doubt* (Boston, St. Paul Books and Media, 1987). A work of apologetics: the immortality of the soul, the existence of God, the divinity of Christ, and the divine origin of the Church.

Hamer, J., *The Church Is a Communion* (London, Chapman, 1964). Emphasizes the theme of *koinonia*, that is, of communion or fellowship.

Long, V., *Upon This Rock* (Chicago, Franciscan Herald Press, 1982). Beautifully geared to offer an unequivocal stand concerning the dogmatic teachings of the Church.

Lubac, H. de, *The Splendor of the Church* (New York, Sheed & Ward, 1956; Newman Press, 1963).

Lubac, H. de, *Church, Paradox and Mystery* (New York, Alba House, 1970). A fine study of the Church as mystery, in the light the Second Vatican Council's *Dogmatic Constitution on the Church*.

Mersch, E., *The Whole Christ* (trans. by J. Kelly; Milwaukee, Bruce, 1938). An historical survey of the teaching, especially patristic, on the Church as Mystical Body.

Rahner, K., and Ratzinger, J., *The Episcopate and the Primacy* (New York, Herder & Herder; London, Nelson, 1962). On the bishop's function in the Church, as a member of a "college" of bishops.

Richards, M., *The Nature and Necessity of Christ's Church* (New York, Alba House, 1987). Affirms the Catholic Church as the only true and universal Church, historically and necessarily.

Schnackenburg, R., *The Church in the New Testament* (London, Burns & Oates, 1967). On the Church as it was in the days of the apostles and their immediate successors.

Walgrave, J., *Unfolding Revelation: The Nature of Doctrinal Development* (Philadelphia, Westminster, 1972). A scholarly study.

Wright, J., *The Church: Hope of the World* (Kenosha, Wisc., Prow Books, 1972). This volume, edited by D. W. Wuerl, presents a collection of talks by John Cardinal Wright.

Chapter 16

Second Vatican Council, *Decree on the Missionary Activity of the Church* (December 7, 1965); *Decree on the Eastern Catholic Churches* (November 21, 1964); *Decree on Ecumenism* (November 21, 1964); *Declaration on the Relationship of the Church to Non-Christian Religions* (October 28, 1965); *Declaration on Religious Freedom* (December 7, 1965).

Secretariat for Promoting Christian Unity, *Directory for the Application of the Decisions of the Second Vatican Council Concerning Ecumenical Matters* I (May 14, 1967) and II (January 22, 1970); *Reflexions and Suggestions Concerning Ecumenical Dialogue* (August 15, 1970); *Ecumenical Collaboration at the Regional, National and Local Levels* (February 22, 1975).

Commission for Religious Relations with Jews, *Guidelines and Suggestions for Implementing the Conciliar Declaration "Nostra Aetate" (n.4)* (December 1, 1974).

Bea, A., *Ecumenical Movement, Unity in Freedom* (New York, Harper & Row, 1964). Quite informative. By Cardinal Bea, first head of the Secretariat for Christian Unity.

Boyer, C., *Christian Unity* (vol. 138 of The Twentieth Century Encyclopedia of Catholicism; New York, Hawthorn Books, 1962). A useful study on the nature and purpose of ecumenism.

Congar, Y., *Ecumenism and the Future of the Church* (Chicago, Priory Press, 1967). On various aspects of ecumenism and its future impact on the Church.

Hardon, J. A., *The Protestant Churches of America* (Westminster, Md., Newman Press, 1956; rev. ed., Garden City, N.Y., Image Books, 1969). An informative description of the various Protestant denominations in the United States of America, particularly of their theological positions.

Hardon, J. A., *Religions of the World* (Westminster, Md., Newman Press, 1963). A helpful reference.

Nevins, A., *Strangers at Your Door* (Huntington, Ind., Our Sunday Visitor, 1988). A practical guide to recognizing, understanding proselytizing sects and cults and ways to deal with them.

Ratzinger, J., *Church, Ecumenism, and Politics: New Essays in Ecclesiology* (New York, Crossroads, 1988). A thoughtful, clear, and authoritative discussion.

Stravinskas, P., *The Catholic Response* (Huntington, Ind., Our Sunday Visitor, 1988). A reasoned answer to fundamentalist criticism of the Church.

Chapters 17 and 23

Second Vatican Council, *Dogmatic Constitution on the Church* (November 21, 1964), esp. ch. 6, on the universal call to holiness; *Pastoral Constitution on the Church in the Modern World* (December 7, 1965), ch. 3, on human activity and its transformation in the mystery of Christ.

Council of Trent, *Decree on Justification* (January 13, 1547).

Pope Pius XII, Encyclical, *Mystici Corporis* (June 29, 1943). On the Mystical Body of Christ.

Aumann, J., *Spiritual Theology* (Huntington, Our Sunday Visitor, 1980). An exposition of Catholic spiritual life.

Balthasar, H. Urs von, *In the fullness of Faith* (San Francisco, Ignatius Press, 1988). Reflection on our union with Christ through faith and charity.

Daujat, J., *The Theology of Grace* (vol. 23 of The Twentieth Century

Encyclopedia of Catholicism; New York, Hawthorn Books, 1959). A basic presentation of the theology of sanctifying grace.

Fransen, P., *The New Life of Grace* (New York, Herder & Herder, 1972). An up-to-date guide on the Church's teaching on grace and on various theologies about grace and justification.

Journet, C., *The Meaning of Grace* (New York, Kenedy, 1960). A study by a master theologian.

Leen, E., *In the Likeness of Christ* (London, Sheed & Ward, 1936). A readable book that makes the theme attractive as well as intelligible.

Lonergan, B., *Grace and Freedom* (New York, Herder & Herder, 1971). For those interested in going more deeply into the theology of grace according to St. Thomas Aquinas.

Lubac, H. de, *Brief Catechism on Nature and Grace* (San Francisco, Ignatius Press, 1985). Scholarly, historical, theological in scope.

Marmion, Dom, *Christ the Life of the Soul* (St. Louis, Herder, 1925). A classic by a master of the priesthood life.

Phan, P., *Grace and the Human Condition* (Wilmington, Michael Glazier, 1989). He is scholarly and is particularly good on patristic thought.

Rondet, H., *The Grace of Christ* (New York, Newman Press, 1966). A summary of Catholic teaching on justification and grace.

Scheeben, M. J., *Nature and Grace* (trans. by C. Vollert; St. Louis, Herder, 1954). An outstanding theologian's theology on grace.

Wrobleski, S., *Christ-centered Spirituality* (Staten Island, N.Y., Alba House, 1967). This orients Christian spirituality towards its only true center, Jesus Christ.

Chapters 18, 19, 20, and 21

Second Vatican Council, *Pastoral Constitution on the Church in the Modern World* (December 7, 1965), esp. Part II on spiritual and moral problems.

Pope John Paul II, Encyclical, *Laborem Exercens*, (September 14, 1981), on human work; Apostolic Exhortation, *Familiaris Consortio* (November 22, 1981), on the duties of a Christian family in the modern world; Encyclical, *Sollicitudo Rei Socialis* (December 30, 1987), on the twentieth anniversary of *Populorum Progressio*; Apostolic Letter, *Mulieris Dignitateum* (October 2, 1988).

Pope Paul VI, Encyclical, *Humanae Vitae* (July 25, 1968), on the regulation of birth; Encyclical, *Populorum Progressio* (March 26, 1967), on the development of peoples: Apostolic Exhortation, *Octogesima Adveniens* (May 14, 1971), a call to action on the eightieth anniversary of *Rerum Novarum*, the great social encyclical of Pope Leo XIII; Allocution on the moral conscience, February 12, 1969;

Allocution on the demands of the moral law in law in contemporary life, July 14, 1971.

Pope John XXIII, Encyclical, *Pacem in Terris* (April 11, 1963), on peace for all nations to be achieved through truth, justice, love, and freedom; Encyclical, *Mater et Magistra* (May 15, 1961), on the social order, on the seventieth anniversary of *Rerum Novarum.*

Pope Pius XII, Allocution on moral law and the new morality, April 18, 1952; Radio Message on the Christian conscience as the object of education, March 23, 1952; Address to the Italian society of obstetrical nurses, October 29, 1951.

Pope Pius XI, Encyclical, *Quadragesimo Anno* (May 15, 1931). On the social order and Christian principles. Issued on the fortieth anniversary of *Rerum Novarum.*

Pope Leo XIII, Encyclical, *Rerum Novarum* (May 15, 1891). On the condition of labor, and the principles by which economic justice may be obtained.

Second General Assembly of the Synod of Bishops, *Justice in the World* (November, 1971).

Congregation for the Doctrine of the Faith, *Declaration on Abortion* (November 18, 1974); *Declaration on Certain Questions concerning Sexual Ethics* (December 29, 1975); *Declaration on Euthanasia* (May 5, 1980); *Instruction on Certain Aspects of The "Theology of Liberation"* (August 6, 1984); *Instruction on Christian Freedom and Liberation* (March 22, 1986); *Letter to the Bishops of the Catholic Church on the Pastoral Care of Homosexual Persons* (October 1, 1986); *Instruction on Respect for Human Life in Its Origins and on the Dignity of Procreation* (February 22, 1987).

Bishops of the United States, *Human Life in our Day* (November 15, 1968). A collective pastoral on the doctrine and defense of life, including the teaching of *Humanae Vitae.*

United States National Conference of Catholic Bishops, *To Live in Christ Jesus* (Washington, D.C., 1976). A pastoral reflection on the moral life; *Economic Justice for All* (Washington, D.C., 1986), a pastoral letter on Catholic social teaching and the United States economy.

Canadian Catholic Conference, *Statement on the Formation of Conscience* (Crux Special, January 4, 1974).

Ashly, B. M., and O'Rourke, K. D., *Health Care Ethics* (St. Louis, Catholic Health Association, 1978).

Benestad, B., *The Pursuit of a Just Social Order* (Washington, D.C., Ethics, and Public Policy Center, 1982). Major themes in Catholic social policy and ways of teaching them.

Cafarra, C., *Living in Christ* (San Francisco: Ignatius Press, 1987). A fine presentation of Catholic moral life.

Calvez, J. Y., *The Social Thought of John XXIII* (Chicago, Regnery; London, Burns & Oates, 1964). An explanation of the encyclical *Mater et Magistra*.

Calvez, J. Y., and Perrin, J., *The Church and Social Justice* (London, Burns and Oates, 1961). Concentrates on the teaching of the popes up to, but exclusive of, John XXIII.

Charles, R., *The Social Teaching of Vatican II* (San Francisco: Ignatius Press, 1982). A comprehensive study.

Delhaye, P., *The Christian Conscience* (New York, Desclée, 1968). An important study on science.

Finnis, J., *Fundamentals of Ethics* (Washington, D.C.: Georgetown University Press, 1986). A cogently argued work clarifying the inner logic of Christian moral thought.

Finnis, J., *Natural Law and Natural Rights* (Oxford, Clarendon Press, 1980). A presentation of Catholic teaching on natural law.

Ford, J. C., and Kelly, G., *Contemporary Moral Problems*, 2 vols. (Westminster, Md., Newman Press, 1958-1963). Treats of general principles (vol. 1) and marriage problems (vol. 2).

Gileman, G., *The Primacy of Charity in Moral Theology* (trans. by W. F. Ryan and A. Vachon; Westminster, Md., Newman Press, 1959). Inspired principally by St. Thomas Aquinas, this book makes Christian love the orientation of moral theology.

Grisez, G. G., *The Way of the Lord Jesus*, vol. 1, *Christian Moral Principles* (Chicago: Franciscan Herald Press, 1981). A comprehensive study of Christian moral foundations; the best study available in English.

Grisez, G.G., *The Teaching of "Humanae Vitae": A Defense* (San Francisco: Ignatius Press, 1988). A cogently argued defense of the teaching of the encyclical.

Grisez, G. G., and Shaw, R., *Beyond the New Morality: The Responsibilities of Freedom* (Notre Dame-London, Notre Dame University Press, 1974). A sound Christian philosophy of moral life attractively presented.

Joyce, M. R., *Love Responds to Life: The Challenge of "Humanae Vitae"* (Kenosha, Wisc., Prow Books, 1971). A readable presentation of a Christian philosophy on sex and contraception.

Kippley, J. F., *Birth Control and The Marriage Covenant* (Collegeville, Minn.: Liturgical Press, 1976). A sound treatise on the Church's teaching on contraception.

Lawler, R., Boyle, J., and May, W.E., *Catholic Sexual Ethics* (Huntington, Ind.: Our Sunday Visitor, 1985). A clear presentation of Catholic teaching in sexual morality.

May, W. E., ed., *Principles of Catholic Moral Life* (Chicago, Franciscan Herald Press, 1980). Basic principles of Catholic moral thought by a group of moralists.

May, W. E., *Sex, Marriage, and Chastity* (Chicago, Franciscan Herald Press, 1981). A look at the fundamental Christian vision of marriage and of sexual morality.

May, W.E., *Moral Absolutes: Catholic Tradition, Current Trends, and The Truth* (Milwaukee: Marquette University Press, 1989). An important defense of a basic Catholic position in morality.

Mersch, E., *Morality and the Mystical Body* (New York, Kenedy, 1939). Anticipated the sort of moral theology called for by the Second Vatican Council. Fundamental moral theology is securely founded on Catholic dogma, not divorced from it.

Noonan, J., *A Private Choice: Abortion in America* (New York: Macmillan, 1980). A defense of the unborn and a brilliant critique of pro-abortion arguments.

Schnackenburg, R., *The Moral Teaching of the New Testament* (New York, Herder & Herder, 1965). A masterful investigation into the roots of Christian moral practices.

Shaw, R., *Choosing Well* (Notre Dame, Ind., University of Notre Dame Press, 1982). A practical guide to the way of making moral choices well.

Von Hildebrand, D., *Christian Ethics* (Chicago, Franciscan Herald Press, 1973). Has a personalistic orientation, and is in the tradition of St. Augustine.

Chapter 22

Second Vatican Council, *Dogmatic Constitution on the Church* (November 21, 1964), chs. 3-6; *Decree on the Appropriate Renewal of the Religious Life* (October 28, 1965); *Decree on the Apostolate of the Laity* (November 18, 1965).

Pope John Paul II, Apostolic Exhortation, *Christifideles Laici:* (December 30, 1988). On the vocation and mission of the faithful in the Church and in the world.

Pope John Paul II, *Letter* to Bishops in the United States (April 3, 1983). On religious life in the United States. The following document accompanied the Pope's letter: Congregation for Religious and Secular Institutes, *Document*, Essential Elements in the Church's Teaching as applied to Institutes Dedicated to Works of the Apostolate (May 31, 1983).

Pope Paul VI, Apostolic Exhortation, *Evangelica Testificatio* (June 29, 1971). On the renewal of the religious life according to the teaching of the Second Vatican Council.

Pope Pius XII, Apostolic Constitution, *Provida Mater Ecclesia* (February 11, 1947). On Secular Institutes.

Congregation for Religious and for Secular Institutes, *Life and Mission of Religious in the Church* (August 12, 1980), *I. Religious and*

Human Promotion, and *II. The Contemplative Dimension of Religious Life*.

Aumann, J., *Christian Spirituality in the Catholic Tradition* (San Francisco: Ignatius Press, 1985). An excellent history.

Balthasar, H. Urs von, *Christian States of Life* (San Francisco: Ignatius Press, 1988). A scholarly study of the various ways of living a life of Christian perfection.

Congar, Y., *Lay People in the Church* (trans. by D. Attwater; Westminster, Md., Newman Press, 1957). On the roles and functions of the laity in the Church.

Dubay, T., *Ecclesial Women: Towards a Theology of the Religious State* (New York, Alba House, 1970). Shows there are valid and valued reasons for the religious life that are based on changeless foundations within the Church.

Gambari, E., *The Global Mystery of Religious Life* (Boston, St. Paul Editions, 1973). An up-to-date treatment of the various apostolates in the Church for members of religious and lay institutes. Explains the nature of religious life and its place in the Church.

Illanes, J. L., *On the Theology of Work* (New Rochelle, N.Y.: Scepter Press, 1989). An excellent study of lay spirituality.

Martin, F., *The Life-Changer* (Ann Arbor, Mich.: Servant Publications, 1980). How the Christian can live a life led by the Spirit.

Merton, T., *The Silent Life* (New York, Farrar-Straus & Cudahy, 1957). On the meaning and value of religious life, especially the contemplative form.

Philips, G., *Achieving Christian Maturity* (trans. by E. Kane; Chicago, Franciscan Herald Press, 1966). On the role of the laity in the Church.

Regamey, P. R., *Renewal in the Spirit: Rediscovering the Religious Life* (Boston, St. Paul Editions, 1980). An important study of religious life.

Unger, D. J., *The Mystery of Love for the Single* (Chicago, Franciscan Herald Press, 1958). Explains the value of the single life lived by men and women in the world for the sake of Christ's kingdom.

Van Kaam, A., *Fundamental Formation: Formative Spirituality* (New York: Crossroad, 1983). A five volume introduction to human Christian life formation.

Vermeersch, A., *Religious and Ecclesiastical Vocation* (St. Louis, Herder, 1925). A standard work on the meaning in the Church of a call from God.

Chapters 24 and 25

Liturgy of the Hours, promulgated by Pope Paul VI, Apostolic Constitution, *Laudis Canticum* (November 1, 1970). The "General Instruction," nn. 3-9, gives an excellent compact view of Christ's prayer and the prayer of Church in general.

Congregation for the Doctrine of the Faith, *Letter to the Bishops of the Catholic Church on Some Aspects of Christian Meditation* (December 14, 1989).

St. Alphonsus Liguori, *Prayer* (trans. by E. Grimm; St. Louis, Redemptorist Press, 1972). A readable version of this saint's classic work on prayer.

St. Francis de Sales, *Introduction to the Devout Life* (trans. and intro, by J. K. Ryan; Garden City, N.Y., Image Books, 1966). This classic was written for the laity.

St. Teresa of Avila, *The Way of Perfection* (Garden City, N.Y., Image Books, 1964). A masterpiece by a great mystic and teacher of prayer.

Aumann, J., *Spiritual Theology* (Huntington, Ind.: Our Sunday Visitor, 1979). A basic introduction to the life of grace and prayer.

Balthasar, H. Urs von, *Prayer* (trans. by A. V. Littledale; New York, Sheed & Ward, 1961). An excellent book. Difficult to read, but well worth the effort.

Bloom, A., *Beginning to Pray* (New York, Paulist Press, 1970). A short but direct work on the meaning and practice of prayer, by an Orthodox bishop.

Breton, V., *Life and Prayer* (Chicago, Scepter, 1960). A practical guide for prayer.

Gabriel of St. Mary Magdalen, *Divine Intimacy* (San Francisco: Ignatius Press, 1986). 4 vol. Provides excellent assistance for those seriously concerned with the practice of meditation.

Guardini, R., *Prayer in Practice* (New York, Pantheon Books, 1957). A good guide in the ways of prayer.

Jeremias, J., *The Prayer of Jesus* (Naperville, Ill., Allenson, 1967). This book, by a Lutheran Scripture scholar, shows us Jesus living prayer and teaching it.

Leheux, M., *The Art of Prayer* (trans. by P. J. Oligny; Chicago, Franciscan Herald Press, 1961). A practical guide.

Merton, T., *Contemplative Prayer* (New York, Herder & Herder, 1969). Draws heavily on the wisdom of Christian tradition.

Ratzinger, J., *Feast of Faith* (San Francisco: Ignatius Press, 1986). A theology of prayer with reflections on the liturgy, especially on the Eucharist.

Sheets, J., *The Spirit Speaks in Us: Personal Prayer in the New Testament* (Wilkes-Barre, Pa., Dimension Books, 1968). The theology on prayer in the New Testament.

Stanley, D., *Boasting in the Lord: The Phenomenon of Prayer in St. Paul* (New York, Paulist Press, 1973).

Chapter 26

Second Vatican Council, *Constitution on the Sacred Liturgy* (December 4, 1963).

Pope Pius XII, Encyclical, *Mediator Dei* (November 20, 1947). On the sacred liturgy, the place of liturgical prayer in the Church, in particular the worship of the Eucharistic Sacrifice.

Bouyer, L., *Liturgical Piety* (Notre Dame, Ind., Notre Dame University Press, 1955). A balanced, scholarly, popular study.

Casel, O., *The Mystery of Christian Worship* (Westminster, Md., Newman Press, 1962). A sacramental theology based on the mystery celebrated in the liturgy.

Davies, J. G., ed., *A Dictionary of Liturgy and Worship* (New York, Macmillan, 1972). Liturgical theology, practice, art, and history. Articles by both Catholic and non-Catholic contributors.

Guardini, R., *The Spirit of the Liturgy* (New York, Sheed & Ward, 1935). A brief work, profound but readable.

Jungmann, J., *The Early Liturgy* (Notre Dame, Ind., Notre Dame University Press, 1959). Gives a broad treatment of Church worship up to the time of St. Gregory the Great.

Leeming, B., *Principles of Sacramental Theology* (Westminster, Md., Newman Press, 1960). An excellent general study.

Loret, P., *The Story of the Mass* (Ligouri, Missouri: Ligouri Publications, 1982). Traces the development of the Mass from the Last Supper until today.

Mitchell, L., *The Meaning of Ritual* (New York: Paulist Press, 1977). An exploration of the power of symbol in worship and liturgy.

Oster, H., *The Paschal Mystery in the Parish Life* (New York, Herder & Herder, 1967). Has a practical pastoral orientation.

Palmer, P. F., *Sacraments and Worship* (Sources of Christian Theology, 1; Westminster, Md., Newman Press, 1955). An excellent collection of authentic source materials for the study of the sacraments from early liturgies, the Church Fathers, Church documents, and so on.

Rahner, K., *The Church and the Sacraments* (New York, Herder & Herder, 1963). The Church is presented as the enduring presence of Christ, the fundamental Sacrament, and the sacraments are related to her.

Semmelroth, O., *Church and Sacrament* (Notre Dame, Ind., Fides, 1965). On sacramentality in the Church.

Sullivan, C. S., ed., *Readings in Sacramental Theology* (Englewood Cliffs, N.J., Prentice-Hall, 1964). Selections from a variety of contemporary scholars.

Worden, T., ed., *Sacraments in Scripture* (Springfield, Ill, Templegate, 1966). A useful collection of articles on the sacraments by nine ex-

perts, giving the scriptural foundations of the sacramental economy.

Wuerl, D., *The Church and Her Sacraments* (Huntington, Ind.: Our
Sunday Visitor, 1990). A pastoral and theological explanation of the
meaning of each of the sacraments.

Chapter 27 (Eucharist)

Second Vatican Council, *Constitution on the Sacred Liturgy* (December 4, 1963), esp. ch. 2, on the Eucharist.

Council of Trent, *Decree on the Most Holy Eucharist* (October 11,
1551); *Doctrine on the Most Holy Sacrifice of the Mass* (September
17, 1562).

Pope John Paul II, Letter to all bishops of the Church (April 8, 1979);
Letter to all priests of the Church (April 8, 1979) as Holy Thursday
approached; Letter to all bishops of the Church, *Dominicae Cenae*
(February 24, 1980), on the mystery and worship of the Eucharist.

Pope Paul VI, Encyclical, *Mysterium Fidei* (September 3, 1965). On
the Holy Eucharist. Explains the supreme importance of the
Eucharist in the life of the Christian and the need for a correct understanding of the Real Presence, and of the Eucharist as sacrifice and
sacrament.

The Roman Missal: The Sacramentary, promulgated by Pope Paul VI,
Apostolic Constitution, *Missale Romanum* (April 3, 1969).

The Roman Missal: Lectionary for Mass, issued by decree of the
Sacred Congregation for Divine Worship by authority of Pope Paul
VI (May 25, 1969).

Congregation for the Sacraments and Divine Worship, Instruction, *Inaestimabile Donum* (April 3, 1980), on certain norms concerning the
worship of the Eucharist.

Congregation for the Discipline of the Sacraments, Instruction, *Im-
mensae Caritatis* (January 29, 1973). On sacramental Communion in
particular circumstances.

Biffi, I., *Story of the Eucharist* (San Francisco: Ignatius Press, 1986).
An excellent historical and theological account.

Bouyer, L., *Eucharist: Theology and Spirituality of the Eucharistic
Prayer* (trans. by C. U. Quinn; Notre Dame, Ind., Fides, 1968). An
excellent study.

Delorme, J., Benoit, P., *et al.*, *The Eucharist in the New Testament: A
Symposium* (London, Chapman, 1965). A good introduction on what
the New Testament offers on the Eucharist.

Hedley, C., *The Holy Eucharist* (London, Longmans, 1907). A standard work on traditional theology of the Eucharist as sacrifice and
sacrament.

Jungmann, J. A., *The Mass of the Roman Rite: Its Origins and*

Development (Missarum Sollemnia), 2 vols. (trans. by F. A. Brunner; New York, Benziger, 1951-1955). A thorough history of the liturgy of the Mass.

Martimort, A. G., *The Eucharist* (vol. 2 of *The Church at Prayer*; New York, Seabury, 1971). A thorough, up-to-date study.

O'Carroll, M., *Corpus Christi* (Wilmington, Del.: Michael Glazier, 1988). An encyclopedia of the Eucharist.

O'Connor, J., *The Hidden Manna* (Boston: St. Paul Editions, 1988). A theology of the Eucharist.

Taille, M. de la, *The Mystery of Faith*, 2 vols. (New York, Sheed & Ward, 1940-1947). An important standard work on the Eucharist.

Vonier, A., *A Key to the Doctrine of the Eucharist* (Westminster, Md., Newman Press, 1946). A still valuable work.

Chapter 27 (Holy Orders)

Second Vatican Council, *Dogmatic Constitution on the Church* (November 21, 1964), sp. ch. 3; *Decree on the Bishops's Pastoral Office in the Church* (October 28, 1965); *Decree on the Ministry and Life of Priests* (December 7, 1965).

Council of Trent, *Doctrine on the Sacrament of Order* (July 15, 1563).

Pope Paul VI, Encyclical, *Sacerdotalis Caelibatus* (June 24, 1967), on priestly celibacy and on continuation of the rule of celibacy in the Latin rite; Apostolic Letter, *Sacrum Diaconatus Ordinem* (June 18, 1967), establishing canonical norms for the permanent diaconate.

The Roman Pontifical: The Ordination of Deacons, Priests, and Bishops, promulgated by Pope Paul VI, Apostolic Constitution, *Pontificalis Romani Recognitio* (June 17, 1968).

Second General Assembly of the Synod of Bishops, *The Ministerial Priesthood* (November, 1971). Gives doctrinal principles and then guidelines for the priestly life and ministry.

Congregation for the Doctrine of the Faith, *Declaration on the Question of the Admission of Women to the Ministerial Priesthood* (October 15, 1976); *Letter on Certain Questions Concerning the Minister of the Eucharist* (August 6, 1983).

United States National Conference of Catholic Bishops, *Norms for Priestly Formation* (Washington, D.C., 1982). A compendium of official documents from the Vatican on training candidates for the priesthood.

St. John Chrysostom, *On the Priesthood*. Among all the treatises of the Fathers, this work, available in a number of English translations, remains the classic on the priesthood.

Blight, J., *Ordination to the Priesthood* (New York, Sheed & Ward, 1956). A liturgical and theological study of priestly ordination.

Bouyer, L., *Women in the Church* (San Francisco, Ignatius Press,

1979). A study of the role of women in the Church, with reflections on the question of ministerial priesthood.

Daughters of St. Paul, compilers, *Dimensions of the Priesthood* (Boston, St. Paul Editions, 1973). Provides a useful collection of papal documents on the priesthood.

Feuillet, A., *The Priesthood of Christ and His Ministers* (Garden City, N.Y., Doubleday, 1975). A scholarly study of Christ's priesthood in the New Testament, especially in John.

Galot, J., *Theology of the Priesthood* (San Francisco: Ignatius Press, 1984). A thorough theological and historical presentation of the priesthood.

Gibbons, J., *The Ambassador of Christ* (Baltimore-New York, Murphy, 1896). A classic work on the priesthood.

Hauck, M., *Women in the Priesthood?* (San Francisco: Ignatius Press, 1986). A detailed analysis of the question.

Kloppenburg, B., *The Priest: Living Instrument and Minister of Christ the Eternal Priest* (trans. by M. O'Connell; Chicago, Franciscan Herald Press, 1974).

Palmer, P. F., *Sacraments of Healing and of Vocation* (Englewood Cliffs, N.J., Prentice-Hall, 1963). A good, short theological analysis.

Stockums, W., *The Priesthood* (trans. by J. W. Grundner; St. Louis, Herder, 1938). Traditional Catholic theology on the priesthood.

Veuillet, P., ed., *The Catholic Priesthood According to the Teaching of the Church*, 2 vols. (Westminster, Md., Newman Press, 1958-1961). Provides a number of papal statements on the priesthood.

Wuerl, D. W., *The Priesthood the Doctrine of the Third Synod of Bishops and Recent Theological Conclusions* (Rome, Angelicum, 1974).

Wuerl, D. W., *The Priesthood: The Catholic Concept Today* (Chicago, Franciscan Herald Press, 1976).

Chapter 28

Second Vatican Council, *Constitution on the Sacred Liturgy* (December 4, 1963), esp. nn. 59-71.

Council of Trent, *Canons on the Sacraments in General, Canons on the Sacrament of Baptism, Canons on the Sacrament of Confirmation* (March 3, 1547).

The Roman Ritual: Rite of Baptism for Children, issued with decree of the Congregation for Divine Worship by authority of Pope Paul VI (May 15, 1969).

The Roman Ritual: Rite of Christian Initiation of Adults, issued with decree of the Congregation for Divine Worship by authority of Pope Paul VI (January 6, 1972). A new edition of the *Rite of Christian Initiation for Adults*, approved by the National Conference of Catholic

Bishops and confirmed by The Congregation for Divine Worship, was published in 1988.

The Roman Pontifical: Rite of Confirmation, approved by Pope Paul VI, Apostolic Constitution, *Divine Consortium Naturae* (August 15, 1971), and issued with decree of the Congregation for Divine Worship (August 22, 1971).

Congregation for the Doctrine of the Faith, *Instruction on Infant Baptism* (October 20, 1980).

Halligan, F. N., *Sacraments of Initiation and Union: Baptism, Confirmation, and Eucharist* (New York, Alba House, 1973). Pastoral study on the celebration of the sacraments.

Hamman, A., *Baptism: Ancient Liturgies and Patristic Texts* (New York, Alba House, 1967). A collection of patristic and liturgical source materials.

Jeremias, J., *The Origin of Infant Baptism* (Naperville, Ill., Alenson, 1963). This work, by a Lutheran scholar, shows historical evidences for the practice of infant baptism in the first four centuries.

McCormack, A., *Christian Initiation* (New York, Hawthorn Books, 1969). Theological study of baptism, confirmation, and the Eucharist, with reference to contemporary issues.

Neunhauser, B., *Baptism and Confirmation* (New York, Herder & Herder, 1964). An historical treatment of the theology of these sacraments.

Schnackenburg, R., *Baptism in the Thought of St. Paul* (New York, Herder & Herder, 1964). A profound study in biblical theology.

Chapter 29

Second Vatican Council, *Constitution on the Sacred Liturgy* (December 4, 1963), esp. nn. 72-75.

Council of Trent, *Doctrine on the Sacrament of Penance* and *Doctrine on the Sacrament of Extreme Unction* (November 25, 1551).

Pope John Paul II, Apostolic Exhortation, *Reconciliation et Paenitentia* (December 2, 1984). On reconciliation and penance in the mission of the Church today.

Pope Paul VI, Apostolic Constitution, *Paenitemini* (February 17, 1969), on fast and abstinence, with explanation of the basic Catholic principles on doing penance and their practical expressions; Apostolic Constitution, *Indulgentiarum Doctrina* (January 1, 1967), an important document on indulgences, with valuable notes also on penance and the Communion of Saints.

The Roman Ritual: Rite of Penance, issued with decree of the Congregation for Divine Worship by authority of Pope Paul VI (December 2, 1973).

The Roman Ritual: Rite of Anointing and Pastoral Care of the Sick, approved by Pope Paul VI, Apostolic Constitution, *Sacram Unctionem Infirmorum* (November 30, 1972), and issued with decree of the Congregation for Divine Worship (December 7, 1972).

Sacred Paenitentiary, *Enchiridion Indulgentiarum* (May 18, 1986), 3rd edition. A handbook on indulgences and their use in Catholic life.

Anciaux, P., *The Sacrament of Penance* (New York: Sheed and Ward, 1964). A classic study, especially good for historical development.

Palmer, P. F., *Sacraments of Forgiveness* (Westminster, Md., Newman Press, 1960). A short, sound study of the sacraments of penance and anointing of the sick.

Poschmann, B., *Penance and the Anointing of the Sick* (London, Burns & Oates, 1963). An excellent study of the history, theology, and practice of the two sacraments.

Richter, G., *Metanoia, Christian Penance and Confession* (trans. by R. T. Kelly; New York, Sheed & Ward, 1966). A popular presentation of conversion and confession.

Shaw, R., *Why We Need Confession* (Huntington, Ind.: Our Sunday Visitor, 1985). An account of the nature and purpose of this sacrament and of the importance of restoring it to frequent use.

Weinandy, T., *Be Reconciled to God: A Family Guide to Confession* (Gaithersburg, Md.: Word Among Us Press, 1988). An excellent practical work.

Wilson, A., *Pardon and Peace* (New York, Sheed & Ward, 1947; repr. 1973). An encouraging and helpful study of the practice of frequent confession.

Chapter 30

Second Vatican Council, *Pastoral Constitution on the Church in the Modern World* (December 7, 1965), esp. nn. 25, 42, 47-52, 87.

Council of Trent, *Doctrine on the Sacrament of Matrimony* (November 11, 1563).

Pope John Paul II, Apostolic Exhortation, *Familiaris Consortio* (November 22, 1981), on the duties of a Christian family in the modern world.

Pope Paul VI, Encyclical, *Humanae Vitae* (July 25, 1968). On the transmission of life and the regulation of birth.

Pope Pius XI, Encyclical, *Casti Connubii* (December 31, 1930). On Christian marriage.

The Roman Ritual: Rite of Marriage, issued with decree of the Congregation of Rites by authority of Pope Paul VI (March 19, 1969).

United States Bishops Committee for Pastoral Research and Practices, *Faithful to Each Other Forever* (Washington, D.C.: United States Catholic Conference, 1989).

Ashly, B., *Theologies of the Body* (Braintree, Mass.: Pope John XXIII

Center, 1985). A masterful work on theological anthropology, providing important insights into human sexuality and marriage.

Groeschel, B., *The Courage to Be Chaste* (New York: Paulist Press, 1985). A practical guide for Christians seeking to lead a chaste life.

Hogan, R., and LeVoir, J., *Covenant of Love* (New York: Doubleday, 1984). A careful summary of Pope John Paul II's thought on marriage and family.

Hugo, J., *St. Augustine on Nature, Sex and Marriage* (Chicago, Scepter, 1969). Treats the great theological contribution of St. Augustine in the area of Christian marriage.

Joyce, G. H., *Christian Marriage: An Historical and Doctrinal Study* (2nd ed., London, 1948). A thorough study of the theology of marriage.

Werth, A., and Milanovich, C., eds., *Papal Pronouncements on Marriage and Family from Leo XIII to Pius XII* (Milwaukee, Bruce, 1955). A useful collection.

Wojtyla, K. (Pope John Paul II), *Love and Responsibility* (New York: Farrar, Straus, Gitoux, 1981). A profound study of the Christian vision of Love, sexuality, and marriage.

Wrenn, M., ed., *Pope John Paul II and the Family* (Chicago, Franciscan Herald Press, 1983). A pastoral commentary and study guide by several theologians on *Familiaris Consortio*.

Chapters 31 and 32

Second Vatican Council, *Dogmatic Constitution on the Church* (November 21, 1964), ch. 7.

Pope Benedict XII, Constitution, *Benedictus Deus* (January 29, 1336). On the beatific vision and on the last things.

The Roman Ritual: Rite of Funerals, issued by the Sacred Congregation for Divine Worship by authority of Pope Paul VI) August 15, 1969). The National Conference of Catholic Bishops approved a new edition on November 14, 1985; their approval was confirmed by the Congregation for Divine Worship on April 29, 1987; and the Conference authorized its publication as the *Order of Christian Funerals* on November 2, 1989.

Congregation for the Doctrine of the Faith, *Letter on Certain Questions concerning Eschatology* (May 17, 1979).

St. Thomas More, *The Supplication of Souls* (ed. by S. M. Thecla; Westminster, Md., Newman Press, 1950). On purgatory and the value of Masses for the departed.

Benoit, P., and Murphy, R., eds., *Immortality and Resurrection* (New York, Herder & Herder, 1970). A study on death and the resurrection.

Cornelis, H., and Guillet, J., *The Resurrection of the Body* (Notre

Dame, Ind., Fides, 1964). On the meaning of the resurrection for us.

Gleason, R. W., *The World to Come* (New York, Sheed & Ward, 1958). A popular but solidly theological treatment of the last things.

Guardini, R., *The Last Things* (New York, Pantheon Books, 1954). An excellent theological study.

Hayes, Z., *Visions of the Future* (Wilmington, Del.: Michael Glazier, 1989). A study of the last things.

Kreeft, P., *Heaven* (San Francisco: Ignatius Press, 1988). A popular study.

Pieper, J., *Death* (New York, Herder & Herder, 1969). On the meaning of death for a believer in Christ.

Ratzinger, J., *Escatology: Death and Eternal Life* (Washington D.C.: The Catholic University of America Press, 1988). A stimulating and scholarly study.

Schnackenburg, R., *God's Rule and Kingdom* (trans. by J. Murray; New York, Herder & Herder, 1963). On the concept of the kingdom of God in Scripture and its eschatological significance.

Taylor, M., ed., *The Mystery of Suffering and Death* (New York, Alba House, 1973). Various authors study God's providence and the world's anguish; the meaning of man's suffering in the light of Christ's coming; and recent views on death.

Indexes

I. Scripture

II. General

Aaron, 332, 364, 408
Abba, 331, 378
Abbot, W. M., 513
Abelites, 211
abortion, 260, 268, 269, 274-275
Abraham, 33, 67, 104, 127, 206, 216, 364, 375, 395
absolution, 137, 461; form of, 417, 418; individual, 426; conditions for communal, 427-428; *see* penance
abstinence, days of, 399
Acta Apostolicae Sedis, 12, 512
Acta Sanctae Sedis, 12, 512
Adam, 52, 63, 96; sin of, 63, 118, 195; result of his sin, 65, 66; type and image of Christ, 54; Christ the new, 90, 110, 117, 128, 129, 151, 470; the second, 195; the final, 54
Adeodatus I or Deusdedit, pope, St., 486
Adeodatus II, pope, St., 487
Adonai, 145
adultery, 105, 279, 440; embracing of false doctrine likened to, 210
Agapitus I, pope, St., 486
Agapitus II, pope, 488
Agatho, pope, St., 487
Agatho, Abba, 338
agnosticism, 44
Albert the Great, St., 500
ʾxander I, pope, St., 485

Alexander II, pope, 488
Alexander III, pope, 489
Alexander IV, pope, 489
Alexander VI, pope, 490
Alexander VII, pope, 490
Alexander VIII, pope, 490
almsgiving, 389, 456
Alphaeus, 165
Altaner, B., 516
Ambrose, St., 94, 169, 201, 500
amen, 502; Christ the, 466
Anacletus or Cletus, pope, St., 485
Anastasius I, pope, St., 486
Anastasius II, pope, 486
Anastasius III, pope, 488
Anastasius IV, pope, 489
anawim, 89, 95
Anciaux, P., 542
Andrew, St., apostle, 165
angel, angels, 37, 47-48, 133, 266, 407, 461, 470; roles in salvation history, 47; Gabriel, 47, 88, 95; Raphael, 47; Michael, 47; fallen, 58
Angelus, the, 231, 340, 509
anger, capital sin, 327
Anicetus, pope, St., 485
annulment, 444
Annunciation, 88, 95, 133, 195, 196, 504
anointing of the sick, 138, 357, 408, 428-435; instituted by Christ, 429-430; sacrament of the sick and infirm, 430-431;

God, 376; Mediator, 111, 133, 198, 199, 336; the New Adam, 90, 110, 117, 128, 129, 158, 470; second Adam, 195; final Adam, 54; Prophet, 174; King, 88, 174; Priest, High Priest, 116, 117, 130, 199, 356, 368, 380, 390, 404; Servant, 127, 196, 356; Shepherd, 180; the Good Shepherd, 157, 166; Prince of Shepherds, 168; Prince of Peace, 132, 207; Physician, 415, 416, 431; Founder of The Church, 21, 152, 154, 156; Teacher, 15, 22, 167, 174, 257, 330, 382; the Way, 107; the Way, Truth, and Life, 22, 80, 174; Model and Teacher of prayer, 330-331; Model for every human life, 54; Exemplar of life, 226

Jews, bible of, 207; Messianic hopes of, 157; Christian relations with, 207-209; see Israel, Judaism

Job, 57-61

John I, pope, St., 486

John II, pope, 486

John III, pope, 486

John IV, pope, 486

John V, pope, 487

John VI, pope, 487

John VII, pope, 487

John VIII, pope, 487

John IX, pope, 487

John X, pope, 488

John XI, pope, 488

John XII, pope, 488

John XIII, pope, 488

John XIV, pope, 488

John XV, pope, 488

John XVII, pope, 488

John XVIII, pope, 488

John XIX, pope, 488

John XXI, pope, 489

John XXII, pope, 489

John XXIII, pope, 159, 187, 237, 240, 285, 288, 290, 291, 296, 297, 298, 299, 300, 302, 303, 491, 532

John, St., apostle, 114, 165

John Chrysostom, St., 209, 376, 381, 394, 457, 500, 501, 539

John of Damascus, St., 203, 333, 422, 500, 501

John of the Cross, St., 501

John Paul I, pope, 182, 491

John Paul II, pope, 16, 18, 22, 33, 57, 84, 97, 112, 127, 128, 129, 138, 139, 171, 184, 194, 197, 215, 218, 246, 251, 273, 282, 283, 284, 291, 292, 293, 296, 302, 310, 312, 353, 372, 374, 379, 380, 381, 419, 440, 441, 443, 446, 491, 514, 520, 521, 522, 523, 525, 526, 531, 534, 538, 541, 542

Jordan, 99

Joseph, St., 87, 89, 92, 133, 202, 204-205, 461; patron of universal Church, 205

Joshua, 67

Journet, C., 522, 531

joy, Christian, 307

Joyce, G. H., 543

Joyce, M. R., 533

Body of Christ, 266; love of the Trinity is model of, 256; conjugal, 276, 439-443.

Lubac, H. de, 520, 529, 531

Lucius I, pope, St., 485

Lucius II, pope, 489

Lucius III, pope, 489

lust, 260, 264, 276; capital sin, 327

lying, 286-287; *see* truth

Lyonnet, S., 524

Macedonianism, 149

magisterium, Church, 182, 185-193; ordinary, 185-186; extraordinary, 183-187; papal, 188-190; task of authentically interpreting Scripture and tradition entrusted exclusively to, 184, 483-484

Magnificat, 89, 95, 508-509

man and woman, creation of, 40; crown and glory of creation, 49; image of God, 37-38, 49-52; body and soul, 50; created in full friendship of God, 41; in holiness, freedom, and peace, 62; sin of, 62-65; after Adam, born in sinful state, 63; sins only by free choice, 64-65; freedom of choice of, 50-51, 246-247; determines own fate, 64-65; eternal significance of free choices of, 47; tasks of, 56-57; called to share divine life, 55-56; social nature of, 52-56, 288-289; dignity and worth of

each person, 53; basic equality of all, 53, 288-289, 293; death and immortality of, 51-52; eternal life with God is proper destiny of, 46

Manoah, wife of, 88

Manresa, 318

Marana tha, 468

Marcellinus, pope, St., 486

Marcellus I, pope, St., 486

Marcellus II, pope, 490

Marinus I, pope, 487

Marinus II, pope, 488

Maritain, J., 521

Mark, pope, St., 486

Marmion, Dom, 531

marriage, Christian, 436-488; institution of, 436; threefold good of, 436; 439-443, fidelity in, 439-441; offspring, 441-442; children are supreme gift of, 278, 441; sacrament, 436, 442-443; ministers of, 442; indissoluble, lifelong, 442-443; basic equality of partners in, 293-295, 439-441; sex in, 275-284; and virginity, 438-439; and the paschal mystery, 447-448; symbolizes union of Christ and the Church, 363, 437-439; the married vocation, 446-447; impediments to, 445; invalid, 445-446; annulment, decree of nullity, 444; sins against marital values, 279-282; no marriage in heaven, 95

Martha, 61

mystery of faith, 142, 144, 151; in Old Testament, 145; in New Testament, 145-146; revealed by Christ, 145-146; relation of Persons in, 146-148; inadequacy of analogies, 148; model and goal of every personal society, 147; model of all perfect love, 149; indwelling of, 151; and Christian life, 150-151, 321-322; and eternal life, 474-475

truth, value of, 284-287; duty to pursue religious, 284-285; duty to seek and to speak, 286-287; hierarchy of truths, 142

unbelief, mystery of, 27-28

Unger, D. J., 11, 535

United States Bishops, 164, 270, 532

United States Catholic Conference, 29, 201, 240, 242, 258, 340

United States National Conference of Catholic Bishops, 90, 201, 242, 275, 280, 397, 399, 514, 525, 526, 532, 539

Urban I, pope, St., 485

Urban II, pope, Bl., 488

Urban III, pope, 489

Urban IV, pope, 489

Urban V, pope, Bl., 489

Urban VI, pope, 489

Urban VII, pope, 490

Urban VIII, pope, 490

Valentine, pope, 487

values, basic human, 232-233, 268-269, 279-281

Van Kaam, A., 535

Vermeersch, A., 535

vespers, 351

Veuillet, P., 540

Viaticum, 434, 435, 454

Victor I, pope, St., 485

Victor II, pope, 488

Victor III, pope, Bl., 488

Vigilius, pope, 486

Vincent de Paul, St., 19

Vincent of Lerins, 180

virginity, Mary's, 85, 87, 92-95; life of Christian, 438-439; and marriage, 436, 438-439; for Christ is vocation of "surpassing excellence," 316

virtue, virtues, 232, 245-246, 264-265; natural, 264, 324; love and the moral, 264-265; cardinal, 324; infused, 246; the theological, 246, 249, 261, 324; natural virtue of religion, 261

Vitalian, pope, St., 487

vocation, of man or woman, 57; greatness of human, 54; Christian, 306-319; the lay, 308-312; the married, 438-439, 446-447; married and celibate, 438-439; to priesthood, 309, 390-394; religious, 306, 309, 314-318

Vollert, C., 526

Von Hildebrand, D., 534

Vonier, A., 539

List Of Abbreviations

Documents of the Second Vatican Council

AA   Decree on the Apostolate of the Laity (*Apostolicam Actuositatem*)

AG   Decree on the Missionary Activity of the Church (*Ad Gentes*)

CD   Decree on the Bishops' Pastoral Office in the Church (*Christus Dominus*)

DH   Declaration on Religious Freedom (*Dignitatis Humanae*)

DV   Dogmatic Constitution on Divine Revelation (*Dei Verbum*)

GE   Declaration on Christian Education (*Gravissimum Educationis*)

GS   Pastoral Constitution on the Church in the Modern World (*Gaudium et Spes*)

IM   Decree on the Instruments of Social Communication (*Inter Mirifica*)

LG   Dogmatic Constitution on the Church (*Lumen Gentium*)

NA   Declaration on the Relationship of the Church to Non-Christian Religions (*Nostra Aetate*)

OE   Decree on Eastern Catholic Churches (*Orientalium Ecclesiarum*)

OT   Decree on Priestly Formation (*Optatam Totius*)

PC   Decree on the Appropriate Renewal of Religious Life (*Perfectae Caritatis*)

PO   Decree on the Ministry and Life of Priests (*Presbyterorum Ordinis*)

SC   Constitution on the Sacred Liturgy (*Sacrosanctum Concilium*)

UR   Decree on Ecumenism (*Unitatis Redintegratio*)

Other abbreviations

AAS   Acta Apostolicae Sedis

ACW   Ancient Christian Writers

ASS   Acta Sanctae Sedis

DS   H. Denzinger-A. Schönmetzer, Enchiridion Symbolorum Definitionum et Declarationum de Rebus Fidei et Morum

EV   Enchiridion Vaticanum

MG   J. P. Migne, ed., Patrologiae cursus completus, series graeca

ML   J. P. Migne, ed., Patrologiae cursus completus, series latina